Get the eBook FREE!

(PDF, ePub, Kindle, and liveBook all included)

We believe that once you buy a book from us, you should be able to read it in any format we have available. To get electronic versions of this book at no additional cost to you, purchase and then register this book at the Manning website.

Go to https://www.manning.com/freebook and follow the instructions to complete your pBook registration.

That's it!
Thanks from Manning!

TensorFlow in Action

THUSHAN GANEGEDARA

MANNING
SHELTER ISLAND

Manning Publications Co.
20 Baldwin Road
PO Box 761
Shelter Island, NY 11964

Development editor: Patrick Barb
Technical development editor: Joel Kotarski
Review editor: Aleksandar Dragosavljević
Production editor: Andy Marinkovich
Copy editor: Michele Mitchell
Proofreader: Melody Dolab
Technical proofreader: Ninoslav Cerkez
Typesetter: Dennis Dalinnik
Cover designer: Marija Tudor

ISBN: 9781617298349
Printed in the United States of America

To my wife, Thushani

brief contents

contents

PART 2   LOOK MA, NO HANDS! DEEP NETWORKS
         IN THE REAL WORLD 147

preface

These days it is hard to find a real-world system or a product that is not driven or at least impacted by machine learning. Machine learning plays a paramount role in terms of boosting user experience as well as cutting costs and increasing savings for a company. TensorFlow is a machine learning framework that enables developers to develop machine learning solutions quickly for various bespoke use cases that can benefit from machine learning. If you are a machine learning practitioner or even a software engineer who touches on machine learning systems, it pays to have a well-grounded understanding of TensorFlow, as it's used by millions of developers to build ML solutions.

This book takes you through an informative journey covering most popular machine learning tasks as well as state-of-the-art models. You will learn about image classification and segmentation, and various natural language processing tasks, such as language modeling and sentiment analysis. While doing so, we will try to maintain our code production quality. This means we will explore ways in which we can standardize our code and models, such as building robust end-to-end data pipelines that can wrangle common data types such as images and text. We will also pay attention to other important dimensions, such as model explainability, current state-of-the-art performance on similar tasks, and so forth. We conclude the book with how TensorFlow can be used to build production-level machine learning pipelines to deliver a smooth operational experience for developers.

TensorFlow has good documentation coverage (although certain topics can be better documented) that is available for free. You might be wondering why, then, you need this book. TensorFlow has evolved to become a complex ecosystem with many moving parts. For someone initially learning the technology, it is quite easy to get lost in the documentation and waste hours (if not days). The rapid pace at which new features and new releases come out exacerbates this problem. Therefore, it helps to have a resource that collates all the most up-to-date and important information and best practices of TensorFlow into a digestible, well-explained text.

After reading this book, you will know how to build most of the common machine learning models, such as convolutional neural networks, recurrent neural networks, and Transformers. You will learn about the general machine learning life cycle and how it can be applied across many different tasks. Furthermore, you will become familiar with building data pipelines that can perform complex transformations in just a few lines of code.

I wish readers all the success in their machine learning careers and sincerely hope they will immensely benefit from the wide variety of topics covered in this book.

acknowledgments

First and foremost, I would like to thank my parents and my wife, Thushani, for supporting me throughout the journey and always standing by my side. I would also like to thank my editors at Manning for all the support and encouragement. Thanks also to the Manning production staff for the valuable guidance they provided.

To all the reviewers who took the time to read my manuscript and provide feedback: Alessandro Buggin, Amaresh Rajasekharan, Biswanath Chowdhury, Brian Griner, David Cronkite, Dhinakaran Venkat, Eduardo Paluzo Hidalgo, Francisco Rivas, Ganesh Swaminathan, Geoff Clark, Gherghe Georgios, Giri S, Jason Hales, José Antonio Quiles, Joshua A McAdams, Kaniskha Tyagi, Kelvin D. Meeks, Kim Falk Jørgensen, Krzysztof Jędrzejewski, Lawrence Nderu, Levi McClenny, Nguyen Cao, Nikos Kanakaris, Peter Morgan, Ryan Markoff, Sergio Govoni, Sriram Macharla, Tiklu Ganguly, Todd Cook, Tony Holdroyd, Vidhya Vinay, Vincent Ngo, Vipul Gupta, Vishwesh Ravi Shrimali, and Wei Luo, your suggestions are appreciated and helped make this a better book.

about this book

In this section, we will discuss who this book is for, the different chapters and their contents, and where you can find the code.

Who should read this book?

It is imperative that you are certain this book is for you. This book is written for a broad audience in the machine learning community to provide a low barrier for entry, so novices as well as machine learning practitioners with basic to medium knowledge and experience can push their TensorFlow skills further. To get the most out of this book, you need the following:

- Experience in the model development life cycle (through a research/industry project)
- Moderate knowledge in Python and object-oriented programming (OOP) (e.g., classes, generators, list comprehension)
- Basic knowledge of NumPy/pandas libraries (e.g., computing summary statistics, what pandas series DataFrame objects are)
- Basic knowledge of linear algebra (e.g., basic mathematics, vectors, matrices, n-dimensional tensors, tensor operations, etc.)
- Basic familiarity with the different deep neural networks available

However, if you have any of the following experience, you should also benefit greatly from this book:

- At least several months of experience as a machine learning researcher, data scientist, or machine learning engineer, or even a student who used ML for a university or school project
- Experience working closely with other machine learning libraries (e.g., scikit-learn), having heard of amazing feats of deep learning, and being keen to learn more about how to implement them
- Experience with basic TensorFlow functionality but wanting to improve yourself to write better TensorFlow code

How this book is organized: A roadmap

TensorFlow in Action is organized into three parts and 15 chapters that start with the basics in part 1, then move into moderately complex topics that ML practitioners should be comfortable with in part 2, and finish with coverage of advanced ML models, libraries, and tools in part 3.

Part 1 focuses on the basics, such as how TensorFlow works and how to implement simple, stripped-down machine learning models such as convolutional neural networks, recurrent neural networks, and Transformers:

- Chapter 1 introduces TensorFlow, the different types of hardware used in ML and their trade-offs, and when and when *not* to use TensorFlow.
- Chapter 2 goes into detail about how TensorFlow works under the hood, the different building blocks found in TensorFlow, and how to implement some of the common operations, such as convolution, used in TensorFlow.
- Chapter 3 discusses Keras, a sub-library in TensorFlow for building ML models easily, and how to load data into TensorFlow.
- Chapter 4 takes a first look at building models. In this chapter, we build a fully connected network, a convolutional neural network, and a recurrent neural network.
- Chapter 5 moves us on to the crown jewel of deep learning: Transformer models and what makes them tick.

Part 2 goes through several popular machine learning tasks and some of the best performing models on those tasks:

- Chapter 6 looks at the first use case: image classification. In this chapter, we work with a complex CNN model and train it on an image classification data set.
- In chapter 7, we dive into more advanced topics such as regularization, even more complex models, and model interpretation techniques.
- Chapter 8 introduces us to image segmentation, an important technique that empowers self-driving cars. We will train a model to segment image pixels according to the object class to which they belong.

- Chapter 9 is our first look at an NLP task in depth. Here, we will train a model to classify the sentiments expressed in movie reviews.
- In chapter 10, we take a closer look at the language modeling task, which is at the heart of the successful Transformer models we see today. Here, we leverage the language modeling task to build a model that can generate stories.

Part 3 delves into more advanced topics such as using Transformer models and Tensor-Board for monitoring and productionizing ML workflows in TensorFlow:

- Chapter 11 discusses the sequence-to-sequence model, a predecessor of Transformer models that enjoyed success in tasks like machine translation. Here we train a sequence-to-sequence model to translate English to German.
- In chapter 12, we continue our discussion of sequence-to-sequence models and introduce the reader to a very important concept: the attention mechanism. We learn how we can incorporate attention into our model, which will help boost performance as well as produce insightful visualizations.
- Chapter 13 extends our discussion from chapter 5 on Transformers. In this chapter, we use the Transformer model to solve two NLP tasks: spam classification and question answering. You will be also introduced to the Hugging Face's Transformers library.
- Chapter 14 focuses on a handy tool shipped with TensorFlow: the TensorBoard. The TensorBoard is vital for monitoring and tracking model performance. It can also be used to visualize data and for performance profiling.
- Chapter 15, the final chapter, focuses on building production-quality machine learning pipelines. TensorFlow provides a library called TFX that provides an API to standardize complex machine learning workflows as a series of steps.

You can take different approaches to getting the most out of this book depending on your skill level. For example, if you're a practitioner who has been in the field using TensorFlow for several years (e.g., 1–3 years), you will probably find part 3 more useful than the earlier sections. If you are a beginner, it makes the most sense to go through all of the chapters in chronological order.

About the code

This book contains many examples of source code, both in numbered listings and in line with normal text. In both cases, source code is formatted in a `fixed-width font` `like this` to separate it from ordinary text. Sometimes code is also **in bold** to highlight code that has changed from previous steps in the chapter, such as when a new feature adds to an existing line of code.

In many cases, the original source code has been reformatted; we've added line breaks and reworked indentation to accommodate the available page space in the book. In rare cases, even this was not enough, and listings include line-continuation markers (➥). Additionally, comments in the source code have often been removed from the listings when the code is described in the text. Code annotations accompany many of the listings, highlighting important concepts.

You can get executable snippets of code from the liveBook (online) version of this book at https://livebook.manning.com/book/tensorflow-in-action/. All chapters in this book, except chapter 1, are accompanied by code. The full code is available on the Manning website (www.manning.com) and on GitHub at https://github.com/thushv89/manning_tf2_in_action.

liveBook discussion forum

Purchase of *TensorFlow in Action* includes free access to liveBook, Manning's online reading platform. Using liveBook's exclusive discussion features, you can attach comments to the book globally or to specific sections or paragraphs. It's a snap to make notes for yourself, ask and answer technical questions, and receive help from the author and other users. To access the forum, go to https://livebook.manning.com/book/tensorflow-in-action/discussion. You can also learn more about Manning's forums and the rules of conduct at https://livebook.manning.com/discussion.

Manning's commitment to our readers is to provide a venue where a meaningful dialogue between individual readers and between readers and the author can take place. It is not a commitment to any specific amount of participation on the part of the author, whose contribution to the forum remains voluntary (and unpaid). We suggest you try asking the author some challenging questions lest his interest stray! The forum and the archives of previous discussions will be accessible from the publisher's website for as long as the book is in print.

about the author

THUSHAN GANEGEDARA is a seasoned ML practitioner with more than four years of experience in the industry. Currently, he is a senior machine learning engineer at Canva, an Australian start-up that founded the online visual design software Canva, serving millions of customers. His efforts are particularly concentrated in the search and recommendations group. Prior to Canva, Thushan was a senior data scientist at QBE Insurance, an Australian insurance company, where he developed ML solutions for use cases related to insurance claims. He also led efforts to develop a Speech2Text pipeline. Thushan obtained his PhD with a specialization in machine learning from the University of Sydney.

about the cover illustration

The figure on the cover of *TensorFlow in Action* is captioned "Laitiere des Environs de Berne," or "Milkmaid from the surroundings of Berne," taken from a collection by Jacques Grasset de Saint-Sauveur, published in 1797. Each illustration is finely drawn and colored by hand.

In those days, it was easy to identify where people lived and what their trade or station in life was just by their dress. Manning celebrates the inventiveness and initiative of the computer business with book covers based on the rich diversity of regional culture centuries ago, brought back to life by pictures from collections such as this one.

Part 1

Foundations of TensorFlow 2 and deep learning

It is difficult to name a company that has not adopted machine learning into its workflow. Tech giants like Google, Airbnb, and Twitter and even small start-ups are using machine learning to fuel their systems and products in both subtle and obvious ways. If you see an advertisement on Google or see an eye-catching listing on Airbnb, ML is at the heart of driving those decisions. And TensorFlow is an enabler for developing solutions for these machine learning use cases. In other words, TensorFlow is a deep learning framework that manages almost all the stages of a model's life cycle, from development and deployment to monitoring performance.

In part 1, you will be introduced to the TensorFlow framework. We will provide a gentle introduction to this versatile framework. We will first go through some high-level topics such as what machine learning is, how TensorFlow works, the Keras library, and how to handle data in TensorFlow. We will walk through simple scenarios to contextualize the knowledge gained during the discussions. We will look at basic versions of popular deep learning models such as fully connected networks, convolutional neural networks, recurrent neural networks, and Transformer models.

The amazing world of TensorFlow

This chapter covers

- What TensorFlow is
- Hardware in machine learning: GPUs and CPUs
- When and when not to use TensorFlow
- What this book teaches
- Who this book is for
- Why we should care about TensorFlow

More than 5 million gigabytes—that's how much data is predicted to be generated a second by 2025 (https://www.weforum.org). Those tiny contributions we make using Google search queries, tweets, Facebook photos, and voice commands to Alexa will add up to unprecedented amounts of data. Therefore, there's no better time than the present to fight on the frontier of artificial intelligence, to make sense of and most importantly leverage the ever-growing universe of digital data. It is a no-brainer that data itself is not very useful until we elicit information from it. For example, an image is more useful if the machine knows what's in that image; a voice command is more useful if the machine can articulate/transcribe what was said. Machine learning is the gatekeeper that lets you cross from the world of data into the realm of information (e.g., actionable insights, useful patterns) by allowing machines to learn from data. Machine learning, particularly deep learning methods, deliver unparalleled performance in the presence of abundant data. With the explosive growth of data, more and more use cases will emerge for deep learning to be applied in. Of course, we cannot ignore the possibility of a better technique drowning the popular deep learning methods. However, it is an irrefutable reality that, to date, deep learning has been constantly outperforming other algorithms, particularly when ample data is present.

What is machine learning?

Machine learning is a process where we train and deploy a computational model to predict some output given the data as input. A machine learning problem typically consists of the following steps:

1 *Understanding/exploratory analysis of data*—This is where you will explore the data provided to you (e.g., understand the dependent/independent variables).
2 *Cleaning data*—Real-world data is usually messy, so data cleaning is of the utmost importance to make sure the model sees high-quality data.
3 *Feature engineering*—New features need to be engineered from the existing features or raw data.
4 *Modeling*—In this stage, you train a model using the selected features and corresponding targets.
5 *Evaluation*—After training the model, you must ensure it is reliable and can perform well on unseen data (e.g., test data).
6 *Creating a user interface for stakeholders to use the model*—In most cases, you will need to provide a dashboard/user interface for users to interact with the model.

Though it looks like a well-defined set of steps, a typical machine learning problem does not involve a straight path from A to B, but a rather convoluted path consisting of repetitive cycles or iterations. For example, during the feature engineering phase, you might realize that you haven't explored a certain aspect of the data, which warrants more data exploration.

Deep learning models can easily exceed millions (and recently billions) of parameters (i.e., weights and biases), and they have a large appetite for data. This signifies the need for frameworks that allow us to train and infer from deep learning models efficiently while utilizing optimized hardware such as graphical processing units (GPUs) or tensor processing units (TPUs) (http://mng.bz/4j0g). One aspect of achieving this is to develop highly scalable data pipelines that can read and process data efficiently.

1.1 *What is TensorFlow?*

TensorFlow is a machine learning framework and has been making its mark in the community of machine learning for almost five years. It is an end-to-end machine learning framework that is designed to run faster on optimized hardware (e.g., GPUs and TPUs). A machine learning framework provides the tools and operations needed to implement machine learning solutions easily. Though TensorFlow is not limited to implementing deep neural networks, that has been its main use. TensorFlow also supports the following:

- Implementing probabilistic machine learning models (https://www.tensorflow.org/probability)
- Computer graphics–related computations (https://www.tensorflow.org/graphics)
- Reusing (pretrained) models (https://www.tensorflow.org/hub)
- Visualizing/debugging TensorFlow models (https://www.tensorflow.org/tensorboard)

TensorFlow was one of the earliest frameworks to enter the bustling market of machine learning. Developed and maintained by Google, TensorFlow has released more than 100 versions with around 2,500 contributors, making the product bigger and better every day. It has evolved to become a holistic ecosystem that moves from the early prototyping stage to productionizing the model. Between these stages, Tensor-Flow supports a range of functionalities:

- *Model development*—Building deep learning models easily by stacking predefined layers or creating custom layers
- *Performance monitoring*—Monitoring performance of the model as it is trained
- *Model debugging*—Debugging any issues, such as numerical errors, that occur during model training/prediction
- *Model serving*—Once the model is trained, deploying the model to the wider public so that it can be used in the real world

As you can see, TensorFlow supports almost all the stages of building your machine learning solutions and eventually serving it to users in the real world. All these services are made into and shipped in a single convenient package, which will be at your disposal with a single line of installation instructions.

> ### Other deep learning frameworks
>
> There are several competing deep learning frameworks on the market that enable you to implement and productionize deep learning models quite easily:
>
> - *PyTorch* (https://pytorch.org)—PyTorch is a framework that is predominantly implemented using a machine library called Torch that is built on the programming language Lua. PyTorch and TensorFlow have similar functionality.
> - *MXNet* (https://mxnet.apache.org)—MXNet is another machine learning framework maintained by the Apache Software Foundation.
> - *DeepLearning4J* (https://deeplearning4j.konduit.ai/)—DeepLearning4J is a Java-based deep learning framework.

The various components that come together to solve an ML problem will be discussed in detail in the coming sections.

Next, we will discuss different components of TensorFlow. These components will go from raw data all the way to deploying models to be accessed by customers.

1.1.1 *An overview of popular components of TensorFlow*

As previously mentioned, TensorFlow is an end-to-end machine learning framework. This means TensorFlow needs to support many different capabilities and stages of a machine learning project. After a business problem is identified, any machine learning project starts with data. An important step is to perform exploratory data analysis. Typically, this is done using a mix of TensorFlow and other data manipulating libraries (e.g., pandas, NumPy). In this step, we try to understand our data because that will determine how well we can use it to solve the problem. With a solid understanding of the data (e.g., data types, data-specific attributes, various cleaning/processing that needs to be done before feeding data to the model), the next step is to find an efficient way to consume data. TensorFlow provides a comprehensive API (application programming interface), known as the `tf.data` API (or `tensorflow.data` API) (https://www .tensorflow.org/ guide/data), that enables you to harness the data found in the wild. Specifically, this API provides various objects and functions to develop highly flexible custom-input data pipelines. Depending on your needs, you have several other options for retrieving data in TensorFlow:

- `tensorflow-datasets`—Provides access to a collection of popular machine learning data sets that can be downloaded with a single line of code.
- Keras data generators—Keras is a submodule in TensorFlow and provides various high-level functionality built on top of the TensorFlow's low-level API. The data generators provide ways to load specific types of data (e.g., images or time series data) from various sources (e.g., disk).

A brief history of Keras

Keras was initially founded by François Chollet as a platform-agnostic, high-level API that can use one of two popular low-level symbolic math libraries at a time: TensorFlow or Theano. Specifically, Keras provides layers (e.g., fully connected layers, convolution layers, etc.), which encapsulate core computations of neural networks.

Furthermore, Keras provides pretrained models that can be downloaded and used conveniently. As Theano retired in 2017, TensorFlow became the go-to backend for Keras. In 2017 (TensorFlow v1.4 upward), Keras was integrated into TensorFlow and is now a submodule in TensorFlow that provides a wide variety of reusable layers that can be used to build deep learning models as well as pretrained models.

Using any of these elements (or a combination of them), you can write a data-processing pipeline (e.g., a Python script). Data would vary depending on the problem you are trying to solve. For example, in an image recognition task, data would be images and their respective classes (e.g., dog/cat). For a sentiment analysis task, the data would be movie reviews and their respective sentiments (e.g., positive/negative/neutral). The purpose of this pipeline is to produce a batch of data from these data sets. The data sets typically fed to deep learning models can have tens of thousands (if not more) data points and would never fit fully in limited computer memory, so we feed a small batch of data (e.g., few hundred data points) at a time and iterate through the full data set in batches.

Next up is the model-building phase. Deep learning models come in many flavors and sizes. There are four main types of deep networks: fully connected, convolutional neural, recurrent neural, and Transformer. These models have different capabilities, strengths, and weaknesses, as you will see in later chapters. TensorFlow also offers different APIs that have varying degrees of control for building models. First, in its most raw form, TensorFlow provides various primitive operations (e.g., matrix multiplication) and data structures to store inputs and outputs of the models (e.g., n-dimensional tensors). These can be used as building blocks to implement any deep learning models from the ground up.

However, it can be quite cumbersome to build models using the low-level TensorFlow API, as you need to repetitively use various low-level operations in TensorFlow and ensure the correctness of the computations happening in the model. This is where Keras comes in. Keras (now a submodule in TensorFlow) offers several advantages over the TensorFlow API:

- It provides `Layer` objects that encapsulate various common functionality that repeatedly happens in neural networks. We will learn what layers are available to us in more detail in the coming chapters.
- It provides several high-level model-building APIs (e.g., Sequential, functional, and subclassing). For example, the Sequential API is great for building simple models that go from an input to an output through a series of layers, whereas the functional API is better if you are working with more complex models. We will discuss these APIs in more detail in chapter 3.

As you can imagine, these features drastically lower the barriers for using TensorFlow. For example, if you need to implement a standard neural network, all you need to do is stack a few standard Keras layers, which, if you were to do the same with the low-level TensorFlow API, would cost you hundreds of lines of code. But, if you need the flexibility to go wild and implement complicated models, you still have the freedom to do so.

Finally, TensorFlow offers its most abstract API known as the Estimator API (https://www.tensorflow.org/guide/estimator). This API is designed to be very robust against any user-induced errors. The robustness is guaranteed by a very restricted API, exposing the user to the bare minimum functionality to train, predict from, and evaluate models.

When you build the model, TensorFlow creates what's known as a data-flow graph. This graph is a representation of what your model looks like and the operations it executes. Then, if you have optimized hardware (e.g., a GPU), TensorFlow will identify those devices and place parts of this graph on that special hardware so that any operations you run on the model are executed as quickly as possible. Appendix A provides detailed instructions for setting up TensorFlow and other required dependencies to run the code.

1.1.2 *Building and deploying a machine learning model*

After you build the model, you can train it with the data you prepared using the `tf.data` API. The model's training process is critical, as for deep learning models, it is quite time-consuming, so you need a way to periodically monitor the progress of the model and make sure the performance stays at a reasonable level during the course of training. For that we write the loss value, the evaluation metric for performance on both training and validation data, so if something goes wrong, you can intervene as soon as possible. There are more advanced tools in TensorFlow that will allow you to monitor the performance and health of your model with more options and convenience. TensorBoard (https://www.tensorflow.org/tensorboard) is a visualization tool that comes with TensorFlow and can be used to visualize various model metrics (e.g., accuracy, precision, etc.) while the model is trained. All you need to do is log the metrics you'd like to visualize to a directory and then start the TensorBoard server, providing the directory as an argument. TensorBoard will automatically visualize the logged metrics on a dashboard. This way, if something goes wrong, you'll quickly notice it, and the logged metrics will help pinpoint any issues with the model.

After (or even during) the training process, you need to save the model; otherwise, it will be destroyed right after you exit the Python program. Also, if your training process gets interrupted during training, you can restore the model and continue training (if you saved it). In TensorFlow you can save models in several ways. You can simply save a model in HDF5 format (i.e., a format for large file storage). Another recommended method is saving it as a `SavedModel` (https://www.tensorflow.org/guide/saved_model), the standard way to save models adopted by TensorFlow. We will see how to save different formats in the coming chapters.

All the great work you've done has paid off. Now you want to joyfully tell the world about the very smart machine learning model you built. You want users to use the model and be amazed by it and for it to find its way into a news headline on artificial intelligence. To take the model to users, you need to provide an API. For this, TensorFlow has what is known as TensorFlow serving (https://www.tensorflow.org/tfx/guide/serving). TensorFlow serving helps you to deploy the trained models and implement an API for users and customers to use. It is a complex topic and involves many different subtopics, and we'll discuss it in a separate chapter.

We have gone on a long journey from mere data to deploying and serving models to customers. Next, let's compare several popular hardware choices used in machine learning.

1.2   GPU vs. CPU

If you have implemented simple computer programs (e.g., a commercial website) or worked with standard data science tools like NumPy, pandas, or scikit-learn, you would have heard the term *GPU*. To reap real benefits, TensorFlow relies on special hardware, such as GPUs. In fact, the progress we have achieved so far in deep neural networks can be heavily attributed to the advancement of GPUs in the last few years. What is so special about GPUs? How are they different from the brains of the computer, the *central processing unit* (CPU)?

Let's understand this with an analogy. Remind yourself of how you commute to work. If you get ready early and have some time to spare, you might take the bus. However, if you only have 10 minutes to spare for the important meeting happening at 9:00 a.m., you might decide to take your car. What is the difference between these two types of transportation? What different purposes do they serve? A car is designed to get a few people (e.g., four) quickly to a destination (i.e., low latency). On the other hand, a bus is slow but carries more people (e.g., 60) in a single trip (i.e., high throughput). Additionally, a car is fitted with various sensors and equipment that will make your drive/ride comfortable (e.g., parking sensors, lane detection, seat heaters, etc.). But the design of a bus would focus more on providing basic needs (e.g., seats, stop buttons, etc.) for a lot of people with limited options to make your ride joyful (figure 1.1).

A CPU is like a car, designed to run complex instruction sequences faster (i.e., low latency).

A GPU is like a bus, designed to run simple instructions at a bigger scale (i.e., high throughput).

A TPU is like an economical bus used in remote areas; it's not as versatile or comfortable, like a normal bus, but is suited for the specific purpose it's designed for.

Figure 1.1   Comparing a CPU, a GPU, and a TPU. A CPU is like a car, which is designed to transport a few people quickly. A GPU is like a bus, which transports many people slowly. A TPU is also like a bus, but it operates well in only specific scenarios.

A CPU is like a car, and a GPU is like a bus. A typical CPU has a handful of cores (e.g., eight). A CPU core does many things (I/O operations, coordinating communications between different devices, etc.) fast, but at a small scale. To support a variety of operations, CPUs need to support a large set of instructions. And to make these run fast, a CPU relies on expensive infrastructure (e.g., more transistors, different levels of caches, etc.). To summarize, CPUs execute a large set of instructions very fast at a small scale. In contrast, a typical GPU has many cores (e.g., more than a thousand). But a GPU core supports a limited set of instructions and focuses less on running them fast.

In the context of machine learning, particularly in deep learning, we mostly need to perform lots of matrix multiplications repeatedly to train and infer from models. Matrix multiplication is a functionality GPUs are highly optimized for, which makes GPUs desirable.

We shouldn't forget our friends, TPUs, which are the latest well-known addition to an optimized hardware list. TPUs were invented by Google and can be thought of as stripped-down GPUs. They are application-specific integrated circuits (ASICs) targeted for machine learning and AI applications. They were designed for low-precision high-volume operations. For example, a GPU typically uses 32-bit precision, whereas a TPU uses a special data type known as *bfloat16* (which uses 16 bits) (http://mng.bz/ QWAe). Furthermore, TPUs lack graphic-processing capabilities such as rasterizing/ texture mapping. Another differentiating characteristic of TPUs is that they are much smaller compared to GPUs, meaning more TPUs can be fit in a smaller physical space.

To extend our car–bus analogy to TPUs, you can think of a TPU as an economical bus that is designed to travel short distances in remote areas. It cannot be used as a normal bus to travel long distances comfortably or to suit a variety of road/weather conditions, but it gets you from point A to point B, so it gets the job done.

1.3 When and when not to use TensorFlow

A key component in knowing or learning TensorFlow is knowing what and what not to use TensorFlow for. Let's look at this through a deep learning lens.

1.3.1 When to use TensorFlow

TensorFlow is not a silver bullet for any machine learning problem by any means. You will get the maximum output by knowing what TensorFlow is good for.

PROTOTYPING DEEP LEARNING MODELS

TensorFlow is a great tool for prototyping models (e.g., fully connected networks, convolutional neural networks, long short-term memory networks), as it provides layer objects (in Keras), such as the following:

- Dense layers for fully connected networks
- Convolution layers for convolutional neural networks
- RNN (recurrent neural network)/LSTM (long short-term memory)/GRU (gated recurrent unit) layers for sequential models

(You do not need to know the underlying mechanics of these layers, as they will be discussed in depth in the chapters ahead.) TensorFlow even offers a suite of pretrained models, so you can develop a simple model with a few layers or a complex ensemble model that consists of many models with fewer lines of code.

IMPLEMENTING MODELS THAT CAN RUN FASTER ON OPTIMIZED HARDWARE

TensorFlow contains kernels (implementations of various low-level operations; e.g., matrix multiplication) that are optimized to run faster on GPUs and TPUs. Therefore, if your model can take advantage of such optimized operations (e.g., linear regression), and you need to run the model on large amounts of data repetitively, TensorFlow will help to run your model faster.

> ### Controlling TensorFlow code on hardware
>
> As much as it's important to leverage the power of GPUs/TPUs to run TensorFlow code, it's also important to know that we can control resource utilization (e.g., memory) when running the code. The following are the main aspects you can control when running TensorFlow code:
>
> - *Where specific TensorFlow operations should run*—Normally you wouldn't need to do this, but you can specify whether a certain operation should run on the CPU/GPU/TPU or which GPU/TPU to use, should you have multiple.
> - *The amount of memory to be used on the GPU*—You can tell TensorFlow to allocate only a certain percentage of the total GPU memory. This is quite handy for making sure that there will be some portion of GPU memory available for any graphics-related processes (e.g., used by the operating system).

PRODUCTIONIZE MODELS/SERVING ON CLOUD

The most common goal of a machine learning model is to serve in solving a real-world problem; thus the model needs to be exposed for predictions to interested stakeholders via a dashboard or an API. A unique advantage of TensorFlow is that you do not need to leave it when your model reaches this stage. In other words, you can develop your model-serving API via TensorFlow. Additionally, if you have lavish hardware (e.g., GPUs/TPUs), TensorFlow will make use of that when making predictions.

MONITORING MODELS DURING MODEL TRAINING

During the training of the model, it is crucial that you keep tabs on model performance to prevent overfitting or underfitting. Training deep learning models can be tedious, even with access to GPUs, due to their high computational demand. This makes it more difficult to monitor these models than simpler ones that run in minutes. If you want to monitor a model that runs in a few minutes, you can print the metrics to the console and log to a file for reference.

However, due to the high number of training iterations deep learning models go through, it is easier to absorb information when these metrics are visualized in graphs. TensorBoard provides exactly this functionality. All you need to do is log and persist your performance metrics in TensorFlow and point TensorBoard to the log directory. TensorBoard will take care of the rest by automatically converting this information in the log directory to graphs, which we can use to analyze the quality of our model.

CREATING HEAVY-DUTY DATA PIPELINES

We have stated several times that deep learning models have a big appetite for data. Typically, data sets that deep learning models sit on do not fit in memory. This means that we need to feed large amounts of data with low latency in smaller, more manageable batches of data. As we have already seen, TensorFlow provides rich APIs for streaming data to deep learning models. Most of the heavy lifting has been done for us. All we need to do is understand the syntax of the functions provided and use them appropriately. Some example scenarios of such data pipelines include the following:

- A pipeline that consumes large amounts of images and preprocesses them
- A pipeline that consumes large amounts of structured data in a standard format (e.g., CSV [comma separated value]) and performs standard preprocessing (e.g., normalization)
- A pipeline that consumes large amounts of text data and performs only simple preprocessing (e.g., text lowering, removing punctuation)

1.3.2   *When not to use TensorFlow*

It's important to know the don'ts as well as the do's when it comes to mastering a tool or a framework. In this section, we will discuss some of the areas where other tools might make you more efficient than TensorFlow.

IMPLEMENTING TRADITIONAL MACHINE LEARNING MODELS

Machine learning has a large portfolio of models (e.g., linear/logistic regression, supporting vector machines, decision trees, k-means) that fall under various categories (e.g., supervised versus unsupervised learning) and have different motivations, approaches, strengths, and weaknesses. There are many models used where you will not see much performance improvement using optimized hardware (e.g., decision trees, k-means, etc.) because these models aren't inherently parallelizable. Sometimes you'll need to run these algorithms as a benchmark for a new algorithm you developed or to get a quick ballpark figure as to how easy a machine learning problem is.

Using TensorFlow to implement such methods would cost you more time than it should. In such situations, scikit-learn (https://scikit-learn.org/stable/) is a better alternative, as the library provides a vast number of models readily implemented. TensorFlow does support some algorithms, such as boosted-tree-based models (http://mng .bz/KxPn). But from my experience, using XGBoost (extreme gradient boosting) (https://xgboost.readthedocs.io/en/latest/) to implement boosted trees has been more convenient, as it is more widely supported by other libraries than the TensorFlow alternative. Furthermore, should you need GPU-optimized versions of scikit-learn algorithms, NVIDIA also provides some of these algorithms that are adapted and optimized for GPUs (https://rapids.ai/).

MANIPULATING AND ANALYZING SMALL-SCALE STRUCTURED DATA

Sometimes we will work with relatively small-structure data sets (e.g., 10,000 samples) that can easily fit in memory. If the data can be loaded into memory fully, pandas and NumPy are much better alternatives for exploring and analyzing data. These are libraries that are equipped with highly optimized C/C++ implementations of various data manipulation (e.g., indexing, filtering, grouping) and statistics-related operations (e.g., mean, sum). For a small data set, TensorFlow can cause significant overhead (transferring data between the CPU and the GPU, launching computational kernels on the GPU), especially if a high volume of smaller, less expensive operations is run. Additionally, pandas/NumPy would be much more expressive in terms of how you can manipulate the data, as it's their primary focus.

CREATING COMPLEX NATURAL LANGUAGE PROCESSING PIPELINES

If you are developing a natural language processing (NLP) model, you would rarely pass data to the model without doing at least simple preprocessing on the data (e.g., text lowering, removing punctuation). But the actual steps that dictate your preprocessing pipeline will depend on your use case and your model. For example, there will be instances where you will have a handful of simple steps (e.g., case lowering, removing punctuation), or you might have a fully blown preprocessing pipeline that requires complex tasks (e.g., stemming, lemmatizing, correcting spelling). In the former case, TensorFlow is a good choice as it provides some simple text preprocessing functionality (e.g., case lowering, replacing text, string splitting, etc.). However, in the latter case, where costly steps such as lemmatization, stemming, spelling correction, and so on dominate the preprocessing pipeline, TensorFlow will hinder your progress. For this, spaCy (https://spacy.io/) is a much stronger candidate, as it provides an intuitive interface and readily available models to perform standard NLP processing tasks.

spaCy does support including TensorFlow models (through a special wrapper) when defining pipelines. But as a rule of thumb, try to avoid this when possible. Integrations between different libraries are generally time-consuming and can even be error prone in complex setups.

Table 1.1 summarizes various strengths and weaknesses of TensorFlow.

Table 1.1 Summary of TensorFlow benefits and drawbacks

Task	Yes	No
Prototyping deep learning models	X	
Implementing models (including non-deep learning) that can run faster on optimized hardware	X	
Productionizing models/serving on cloud	X	
Monitoring models during model training	X	
Creating heavy-duty data pipelines	X	
Implementing traditional machine learning models		X
Manipulating and analyzing small-scale structured data		X
Creating complex NLP pipelines		X

1.4   What will this book teach you?

In the coming chapters, this book will teach you some vital skills that will help you use TensorFlow principally and effectively for research problems.

1.4.1   TensorFlow fundamentals

First, we will learn the basics of TensorFlow. We will learn the different execution styles it provides, primary building blocks that are used to implement any TensorFlow solution (e.g., tf.Variable, tf.Operation), and various functionalities as low-level operations. Then we will explore various model-building APIs exposed by Keras (a submodule in TensorFlow) to users and their benefits and limitations, which will help with making decisions such as when to use a certain model-building API. We will also study various ways we can retrieve data for TensorFlow models. Unlike traditional methods, deep learning models consume large amounts of data, so having an efficient and scalable data ingestion pipeline (i.e., input pipeline) is of paramount importance.

1.4.2   Deep learning algorithms

Implementing efficient deep learning models is one of the primary purposes of TensorFlow. Therefore, we will be discussing the architectural details of various deep learning algorithms such as full connected neural networks, convolutional neural networks (CNNs), and recurrent neural networks (RNNs). Note that investigating theories of these models is not an objective of this book. We will only be discussing these models at a level that helps us understand how to implement them comfortably with TensorFlow/Keras.

We will further hone our understanding of these models by implementing and applying these models to popular computer vision and NLP applications such as image classification, image segmentation, sentiment analysis, and machine translation. It will be interesting to see how well these models do when it comes to such tasks, with no human-engineered features.

Then, we will discuss a new family of models that have emerged, known as Transformers. Transformers are very different from both convolutional and recurrent neural networks. Unlike CNNs and RNNs, which can only see part of a time-series sequence at a time, Transformers can see the full sequence of data, leading to better performance. In fact, Transformers have been surpassing the previously recorded state-of-the-art models in many NLP tasks. We will learn how we can incorporate such models in TensorFlow to improve the performance of various downstream tasks.

1.4.3   Monitoring and optimization

It is not enough to know how to implement a model in TensorFlow. Close inspection and monitoring of model performance are vital steps in creating a reliable machine learning model. Using visualization tools such as TensorBoard to visualize performance metrics and feature representations is an important skill to have. Model explainability has also emerged as an important topic, as black-box models like neural networks are becoming commodities in machine learning. TensorBoard has certain tools for interpreting models or explaining why a model made a certain decision.

Next, we will investigate ways we can make models train faster. The training time is one of the most prominent bottlenecks in using deep learning models, so we will discuss some techniques to make the models train faster!

1.5 Who is this book for?

This book is written for a broader audience in the machine learning community to provide a somewhat easy entry for novices, as well as machine learning practitioners with basic to medium knowledge/experience, to push their TensorFlow skills further. In order to get the most out of this book, you need the following:

- Experience in the model development life cycle (through a research/industry project)
- Moderate knowledge of Python and object-oriented programming (OOP) (e.g., classes/generators/list comprehension)
- Basic knowledge of NumPy/pandas libraries (e.g., computing summary statistics, what pandas series DataFrame objects are)
- Basic knowledge of linear algebra (e.g., basic mathematics, vectors, matrices, n-dimensional tensors, tensor operations, etc.)
- Basic familiarity with the different deep neural networks available

You will greatly benefit from this book if you are someone who has

- At least several months of experience as a machine learning researcher, data scientist, machine learning engineer, or even as a student during a university/school project in which you used machine learning
- Worked closely with other machine learning libraries (e.g., scikit-learn) and has heard of amazing feats of deep learning and is keen to learn more about how to implement them
- Experience with basic TensorFlow functionality but wants to write better TensorFlow code

You might be thinking, with the plethora of resources available (e.g., TensorFlow documentation, StackOverFlow.com, etc.), isn't it easy (and free) to learn TensorFlow? Yes and no. If you just need "some" solution to a problem you're working on, you might be able to hack one using the resources out there. But chances are that it will be a suboptimal solution, because to come up with an effective one, you need to build a strong mental image of how TensorFlow executes code, understand the functionality provided in the API, understand limitations, and so on. It is also important to understand TensorFlow and gain knowledge in an incremental and structured manner, which is very difficult to do by simply reading freely available resources at random. A strong mental image and solid knowledge come with many years of experience (while keeping a close eye on new features available, GitHub issues, and stackoverflow.com questions) or from a book written by a person with many years of experience. The million-dollar question here is not "How do I use TensorFlow to solve my problem?" but "How do I use TensorFlow *effectively* to solve my problem?" Coming up with an effective solution requires a solid grokking of TensorFlow. An effective solution, in my mind, can be one that does (but is not limited to) the following:

- Keeps the code relatively concise without sacrificing readability too much (e.g., avoiding redundant operations, aggregating operations when possible)
- Uses the latest and greatest features available in the API to avoid reinventing the wheel and to save time
- Utilizes optimizations whenever possible (e.g., avoiding loops and using vectorized operations)

If you asked me to summarize this book into a few words, I would say "enabling the reader to write effective TensorFlow solutions."

1.6   *Should we really care about Python and TensorFlow 2?*

Here we will get to know about the two most important technologies you'll be studying heavily: Python and TensorFlow. Python is the foundational programming language we will be using to implement various TensorFlow solutions. But it is important to know that TensorFlow supports many different languages, such as C++, Go, JavaScript, and so on.

The first question we should try to answer is "Why are we picking Python as our choice of programming language?" Python's popularity has recently increased, especially in the scientific community, due to the vast number of libraries that have fortified Python (e.g., pandas, NumPy, scikit-learn), which has made conducting a scientific experiment/simulation and logging/visualizing/reporting the results much easier. In figure 1.2, you can

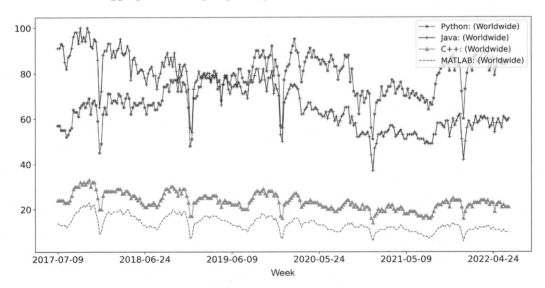

Figure 1.2   Popularity of different programming languages (2015–2020)

see how Python has become the most popular search term (at least in the Google search engine). If you narrow the results to just the machine learning community, you will see an even higher margin.

The next question to answer is "Why did we pick TensorFlow?" TensorFlow has been there almost since deep learning became popular (http://mng.bz/95P8). TensorFlow has been refined and revised over roughly five years, becoming more and more stable over time. Furthermore, unlike other counterpart libraries, TensorFlow provides an ecosystem of tools to satisfy your machine learning needs, from prototyping to model training to models. In figure 1.3, you can see how TensorFlow compares to one of its popular competitors, PyTorch.

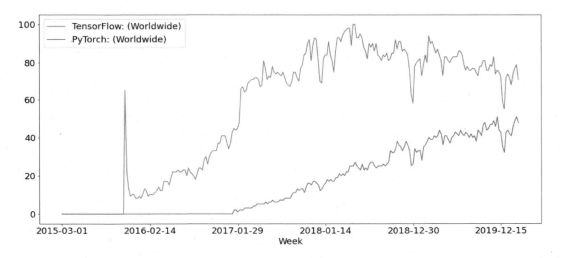

Figure 1.3   Popularity of TensorFlow and PyTorch (2015–2020)

It's also worth inspecting how much of a performance increase we gain as the size of the data grows. Figure 1.4 compares a popular scientific computation library (NumPy) to TensorFlow in a matrix multiplication task. This was tested on an Intel i5 ninth-generation processor and an NVIDIA 2070 RTX 8 GB GPU. Here, we are multiplying two randomly initialized matrices (each having size n × n). We have recorded the time taken for n = 100, 1000, 5000, 7500, 1000. On the left side of the graph, you can see the difference in time growth. NumPy shows an exponential growth of time taken as the size of the matrix grows. However, TensorFlow shows approximately linear growth. On the right side you can see how many seconds it takes if a TensorFlow operation takes one second. The message is clear: TensorFlow does much better than NumPy as the amount of data grows.

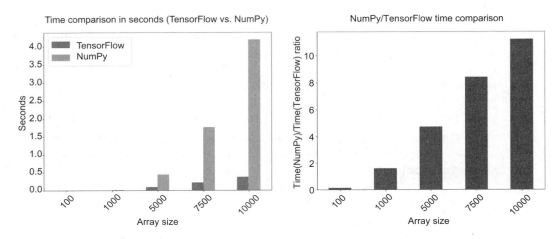

Figure 1.4   Comparing NumPy and TensorFlow computing libraries in a matrix multiplication task

Summary

- Deep learning has become a hot topic due to the unprecedented performance it delivers when provided ample amounts of data.
- TensorFlow is an end-to-end machine learning framework that provides ecosystem-facilitating model prototyping, model building, model monitoring, model serving, and more.
- TensorFlow, just like any other tool, has strengths and weaknesses. Therefore, it is up to the user to weigh these against the problem they are trying to solve.
- TensorFlow is a great tool to quickly prototype deep learning models with a vast range of complexities.
- TensorFlow is not suited to analyzing/manipulating a small-structure data set or developing complex text-processing data pipelines.
- This book goes beyond teaching the reader to implement some TensorFlow solution and teaches the reader to implement *effective* solutions with minimal effort while reducing the chance of errors.

TensorFlow 2

This chapter covers

- What TensorFlow 2 is
- Important data structures and operations in TensorFlow
- Common neural network related operations in TensorFlow

In the previous chapter, we learned that TensorFlow is an end-to-end machine learning framework predominantly used for implementing deep neural networks. TensorFlow is skillful at converting these deep neural networks to computational graphs that run faster on optimized hardware (e.g., GPUs and TPUs). But keep in mind that this is not the only use for TensorFlow. Table 2.1 delineates other areas TensorFlow supports.

Table 2.1 Various features offered in TensorFlow

Probabilistic machine learning	TensorFlow supports implementing probabilistic machine learning models. For example, models like Bayesian neural networks can be implemented with a TensorFlow API (https://www.tensorflow.org/probability).
Computer graphics– related computations	Computer graphic computations can be mostly achieved on GPUs (e.g., simulating various lighting effects, raytracing; https://www.tensorflow.org/graphics).

Table 2.1 Various features offered in TensorFlow *(continued)*

TensorFlow Hub: Reusable (pre-trained) models	In deep learning we usually try to leverage models that have already been trained on large amounts of data for the downstream tasks we're interested in solving. TensorFlow Hub is a repository in which such models implemented in TensorFlow are stored (https://www.tensorflow.org/hub).
Visualize/debug TensorFlow models	TensorFlow provides a dashboard for visualizing and monitoring model performance and even visualizing data (https://www.tensorflow.org/tensorboard).

In the coming chapters, we will go on an exciting journey exploring the bells and whistles in TensorFlow and learning how to excel at things TensorFlow is good at. In other words, we will look at how to solve real-world problems with TensorFlow, such as image classification (i.e., recognizing objects in images), sentiment analysis (i.e., recognizing positive/negative tones in reviews/opinions), and so on. While solving these tasks, you will learn how to overcome real-world challenges such as overfitting and class imbalance that can easily throw a spanner in the works. This chapter specifically focuses on providing a strong foundational knowledge of TensorFlow before we head toward complex problems that can be solved with deep networks.

First, we will implement a neural network in both TensorFlow 2 and TensorFlow 1 and see how much TensorFlow has evolved in terms of user friendliness. Then we will learn about basic units (e.g., variables, tensors, and operations) provided in TensorFlow, which we must have a good understanding of in order to develop solutions. Finally, we will understand the details of several complex mathematical operations through a series of fun computer vision exercises.

2.1   *First steps with TensorFlow 2*

Let's imagine you are taking a machine learning course and have been given an assignment to implement a *multilayer perceptron* (MLP) (i.e., a type of neural network) and compute the final output for a given datapoint using TensorFlow. You are new to TensorFlow, so you go to the library and start studying what TensorFlow is. While you research, you realize that TensorFlow has two major versions (1 and 2) and decide to use the latest and greatest: TensorFlow 2. You've already installed the required libraries, as outlined in appendix A.

Before moving on, let's learn about MLPs. An MLP (figure 2.1) is a simple neural network that has an input layer, one or more hidden layers, and an output layer. These networks are also called *fully connected networks.*

> **NOTE** Some research only uses the term MLP to refer to a network made of multiple perceptrons (http://mng.bz/y4lE) organized in a hierarchical structure. However, in this book, we will use the terms MLP and fully connected network interchangeably.

In each layer, we have weights and biases, which are used to compute the output of that layer. In our example, we have an input of size 4, a hidden layer with three nodes, and an output layer of size 2.

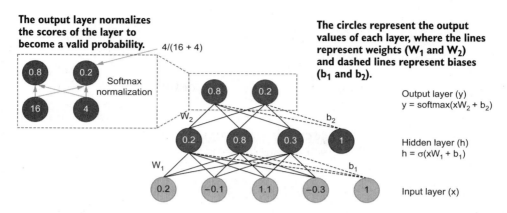

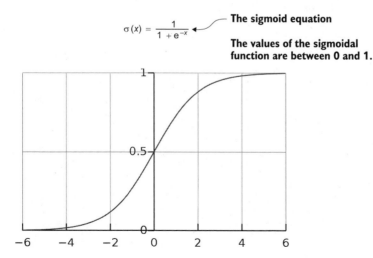

Figure 2.1   Depiction of a multilayer perceptron (MLP) or a fully connected network. There are three layers: an input layer, a hidden layer (that has weights and biases), and an output layer. The output layer produces normalized probabilities as the output using softmax activation.

The input values (x) are transformed to hidden values (h) using the following computation

$$h = \sigma(x\ W_1 + b_1)$$

where σ is the sigmoid function. The sigmoid function is a simple nonlinear element-wise transformation, as shown as in figure 2.2.

Figure 2.2   A visualization of the sigmoidal activation function for different inputs

x is a matrix of size 1×4 (i.e., one row and four columns), W_1 is a matrix of size 4×3 (i.e., four rows and three columns), and b_1 is 1×4 (i.e., one row and four columns). This gives an h of size 1×3. Finally, the output is computed as

$$y = softmax(h \ W_2 + b_2)$$

Here, W_2 is a 3×2 matrix, and b_2 is a 1×2 matrix. Softmax activation normalizes the linear scores of the last layer (i.e., $h \ W_2 + b_2$) to actual probabilities (i.e., values sum up to 1 along columns). Assuming an input vector x of length K, the softmax activation produces a K-long vector y. The ith element of y is computed as

$$y_i = \frac{x_i}{\sum_{j=1}^{K} x_j}$$

where y_i is the ith output element and x_i is the ith input element. As a concrete example, assume the final layer without the softmax activation produced,

```
[16, 4]
```

Applying the softmax normalization converts these values to

```
[16/(16+4), 4/(16+4)] = [0.8, 0.2]
```

Let's see how this can be implemented in TensorFlow 2. You can find the code in the Jupyter notebook (Ch02-Fundamentals-of-TensorFlow-2/2.1.Tensorflow_Fundamentals.ipynb). How to install the necessary libraries and set up the development environment is delineated in appendix A. Initially, we need to import the required libraries using import statements:

```
import numpy as np
import tensorflow as tf
```

Then we define the input to the network (x) and the variables (or parameters) (i.e., w_1, b_1, w_2, and b_2) of the network:

```
x = np.random.normal(size=[1,4]).astype('float32')

init = tf.keras.initializers.RandomNormal()

w1 = tf.Variable(init(shape=[4,3]))
b1 = tf.Variable(init(shape=[1,3]))

w2 = tf.Variable(init(shape=[3,2]))
b2 = tf.Variable(init(shape=[1,2]))
```

Here, x is a simple NumPy array of size 1×4 (i.e., one row and four columns) that is filled with values from a normal distribution. Then we define the parameters of the network (i.e., weights and biases) as TensorFlow variables. A tf.Variable behaves similar to a typical Python variable. It has some value attached at the time of the definition and can change over time. `tf.Variable` is used to represent weights and biases of a neural network, which are changed during the optimization or the training procedure. When defining TensorFlow variables, we need to provide an initializer and a shape for the variables. Here we are using an initializer that randomly sample values from a normal distribution. Remember that W_1 is 4×3 sized, b_1 is 1×3 sized, W_2 is 3×2 sized, and b2 is 1×2 sized, and that the `shape` argument for each of these is set accordingly. Next, we define the core computations of the MLP as a nice modular function. This way, we can easily reuse the function to compute hidden layer outputs of multiple layers:

```
@tf.function
def forward(x, W, b, act):
    return act(tf.matmul(x,W)+b)
```

Here, `act` is any nonlinear activation function of your choice (e.g., `tf.nn.sigmoid`). (You can look at various activation functions here: https://www.tensorflow.org/api_docs/python/tf/nn. Be mindful that not all of them are activation functions. The expression `tf.matmul(x,W)+b` elegantly wraps the core computations we saw earlier (i.e., $x\,W_1 + b_1$ and $h\,W_2 + b_2$) to a reusable expression. Here, `tf.matmul` performs the matrix multiplication operation. This computation is illustrated in figure 2.3.

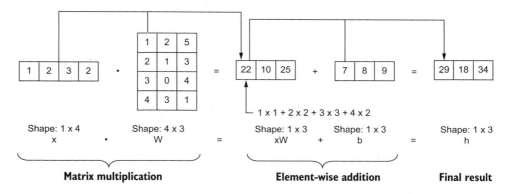

Figure 2.3   The matrix multiplication and bias addition illustrated for example input, weights, and bias

Having `@tf.function` on top of the function is a way for TensorFlow to know that this function contains TensorFlow code. We will discuss the purpose of `@tf.function` in more detail in the next section. This brings us to the final part of the code. As we have the inputs, all the parameters, and core computations defined, we can compute the final output of the network

```
# Computing h
h = forward(x, w1, b1, tf.nn.sigmoid)
```

```
# Computing y
y = forward(h, w2, b2, tf.nn.softmax)

print(y)
```

which will output

```
tf.Tensor([[0.4912673 0.5087327]], shape=(1, 2), dtype=float32)
```

Here, h and y are the resulting tensors (of type tf.Tensor) of various TensorFlow operations (e.g., tf.matmul). The exact values in the output might differ slightly (see the following listing).

Listing 2.1   Multilayer perceptron network with TensorFlow 2

```
import numpy as np                                      Importing NumPy and
import tensorflow as tf                                 TensorFlow libraries

x = np.random.normal(size=[1,4]).astype('float32')      The input to
                                                        the MLP (a
                                                        NumPy array)
init = tf.keras.initializers.RandomNormal()             The initializer used to
                                                        initialize variables
w1 = tf.Variable(init(shape=[4,3]))
b1 = tf.Variable(init(shape=[1,3]))                     The parameters of
                                                        layer 1 (w1 and b2)
w2 = tf.Variable(init(shape=[3,2]))                     and layer 2 (w2 and b2)
b2 = tf.Variable(init(shape=[1,2]))

@tf.function
def forward(x, W, b, act):                              MLP layer computation, which takes in an input,
    return act(tf.matmul(x,W)+b)                        weights, bias, and a nonlinear activation

h = forward(x, w1, b1, tf.nn.sigmoid)                   Computing the first
                                                        hidden layer output, h
y = forward(h, w2, b2, tf.nn.softmax)
                                                        Computing the
print(y)                                                final output, y
```

This line tells TensorFlow's
AutoGraph to build the graph.

Next, we will look at what happens behind the scenes when TensorFlow runs the code.

2.1.1   How does TensorFlow operate under the hood?

In a typical TensorFlow program, there are two main steps:

1 Define a data-flow graph encompassing the inputs, operations, and the outputs. In our exercise, the data-flow graph will represent how x, w1, b1, w2, b2, h, and y are related to each other.

2 Execute the graph by feeding values to the inputs and computing outputs. For example, if we need to compute h, we will feed a value (e.g., a NumPy array) to x and get the value of h.

TensorFlow 2 uses an execution style known as *imperative style execution*. In imperative style execution, declaration (defining the graph) and execution happen simultaneously. This is also known as *eagerly executing* code.

You might be wondering what a data-flow graph looks like. It is a term TensorFlow uses to describe the flow of computations you defined and is represented as a *directed acyclic graph* (DAG): a graph structure where arrows represent the data and nodes represent the operations. In other words, tf.Variable and tf.Tensor objects represent the edges in the graph, whereas operations (e.g., tf.matmul) represent the nodes. For example, the data-flow graph for

$$h = x\ W_1 + b_1$$

would look like figure 2.4. Then, at runtime, you could get the value of y by feeding values to x, as y is dependent on the input x.

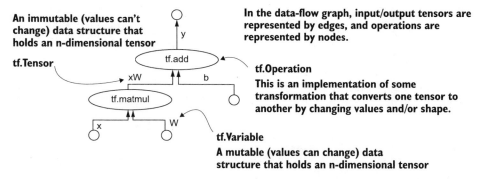

Equation h = Wx + b represented as a data-flow graph

An immutable (values can't change) data structure that holds an n-dimensional tensor

tf.Tensor

In the data-flow graph, input/output tensors are represented by edges, and operations are represented by nodes.

tf.Operation

This is an implementation of some transformation that converts one tensor to another by changing values and/or shape.

tf.Variable

A mutable (values can change) data structure that holds an n-dimensional tensor

Figure 2.4   An example computational graph. The various elements here are covered in more detail in section 2.2.

How does TensorFlow know to create the data-flow graph? You might have noticed the line starting with the symbol @ hanging on top of the forward(...) function. This is known as a *decorator* in Python language. The @tf.function decorator takes in a function that performs various TensorFlow operations, traces all the steps, and turns that into a data-flow graph. How cool is that? This encourages the user to write modular code while enabling the computational advantages of a data-flow graph. This feature in TensorFlow 2 is known appropriately as AutoGraph (https://www.tensorflow.org/guide/function).

What is a decorator?

A decorator modifies the behavior of a function by wrapping it, which happens before/after the function is invoked. A good example of a decorator is logging the inputs and outputs of a function whenever it is invoked. Here's how you would use decorators for this:

```
def log_io(func):
    def wrapper(*args, **kwargs):
        print("args: ", args)
        print("kwargs: ", kwargs)
        out = func(*args, **kwargs)
        print("return: ", out)
    return wrapper

@log_io
def easy_math(x, y):
    return x + y + ( x * y)

res = easy_math(2,3)
```

This will output

```
args:   (2, 3)
kwargs:  {}
return:  11
```

as expected. Therefore, when you add the `@tf.function` decorator, it essentially modifies the behavior of the invoked function by building a computational graph of the computations happening within the given function.

The diagram in figure 2.5 depicts the execution path of a TensorFlow 2 program. The first time the functions a(…) and b(…) are invoked, the data-flow graph is created.

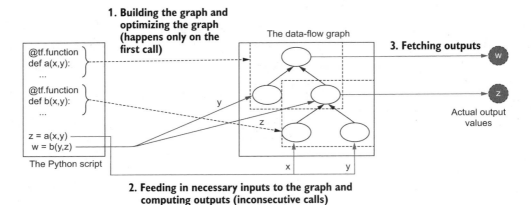

Figure 2.5 Typical execution of a TensorFlow 2 program. In the first run, TensorFlow traces all functions annotated with `@tf.function` and builds the data-flow graph. In the subsequent runs, corresponding values are fed to the graph (according to the function call) and the results are retrieved.

Then, inputs passed to the functions will be fed to the graph and obtain the outputs you are interested in.

> ### AutoGraph
>
> AutoGraph is a great feature in TensorFlow that reduces the developer's workload by working hard behind the scene. To build true appreciation for the feature, read more at https://www.tensorflow.org/guide/function. Though it is quite amazing, AutoGraph is not a silver bullet. Therefore, it is important to understand its advantages as well as its limitations and caveats:
>
> - AutoGraph will provide a performance boost if your code consists of lots of repetitive operations (e.g., training a neural network for many iterations).
> - AutoGraph might slow you down if you run many different operations that only run once; because you run the operation only once, building the graph is just an overhead.
> - Be careful of what you include inside the function you are exposing to Auto-Graph. For example
>   - NumPy arrays and Python lists will be converted to `tf.constant` objects.
>   - `for` loops will be unwrapped during function tracing, which might result in large graphs that eventually run out of memory.

TensorFlow 1, the predecessor of TensorFlow 2, used an execution style known as *declarative graph–based execution*, which consists of two steps:

1. Explicitly define a data-flow graph using various symbolic elements (e.g., placeholder inputs, variables, and operations) of what you need to achieve. Unlike in TensorFlow 2, these do not hold values at declaration.
2. Explicitly write code to run the defined graph and obtain or evaluate results. You can feed actual values to the previously defined symbolic elements at runtime and execute the graph.

This is very different from TensorFlow 2, which hides all the intricacies of the dataflow graph by automatically building it in the background. In TensorFlow 1, you have to explicitly build the graph and then execute it, leading to code that's more complex and difficult to read. Table 2.2 summarizes the differences between TensorFlow 1 and TensorFlow 2.

Table 2.2   Differences between TensorFlow 1 and TensorFlow 2

TensorFlow 1	TensorFlow 2
Does not use eager execution by default	Uses eager execution by default
Uses symbolic placeholders to represent inputs to the graph	Directly feeds actual data (e.g., NumPy arrays) to the data-flow graph
Difficult to debug as results are not evaluated imperatively	Easy to debug as operations are evaluated imperatively

Table 2.2   Differences between TensorFlow 1 and TensorFlow 2 *(continued)*

TensorFlow 1	TensorFlow 2
Needs to explicitly and manually create the data-flow graph	Has AutoGraph functionality, which traces TensorFlow operations and creates the graph automatically
Does not encourage object-oriented programming, as it forces you to define the computational graph in advance	Encourages object-oriented programming
Results in poor readability of code due to having separate graph definition and runtime code	Has better readability of code

In the next section, we discuss the basic building blocks of TensorFlow that set the foundation for writing TensorFlow programs.

EXERCISE 1

Given the following code,

```
# A
import tensorflow as tf
# B
def f1(x, y, z):
    return tf.math.add(tf.matmul(x, y) , z)
#C
w = f1(x, y, z)
```

where should the `tf.function` decorator go?

1 A
2 B
3 C
4 Any of above

2.2   *TensorFlow building blocks*

We have seen the core differences between TensorFlow 1 and TensorFlow 2. While doing this, you were exposed to various data structures (e.g., `tf.Variable`) and operations (e.g., `tf.matmul`) exposed by the TensorFlow API. Let's now see where and how you might use these data structures and operations.

In TensorFlow 2, there are three major basic elements we need to learn about:

- `tf.Variable`
- `tf.Tensor`
- `tf.Operation`

You have already seen all of these being used. For example, from the previous MLP example, we have these elements, as shown in table 2.3. Having knowledge of these primitive components is helpful in understanding more abstract components, such as a Keras layer and model objects, and will be discussed later.

Table 2.3 `tf.Variable`, `tf.Tensor`, and `tf.Operation`
entities from the MLP example

Element	Example
`tf.Variable`	`w1, b1, w2` and `b2`
`tf.Tensor`	`h` and `y`
`tf.Operation`	`tf.matmul`

It is important to firmly grok these basic elements of TensorFlow for several reasons. The main reason is that everything you see in this book, from this point on, is built on top of these elements. For example, if you are using a high-level API like Keras to build a model, it still uses `tf.Variable`, `tf.Tensor`, and `tf.Operation` entities to do the computations. Therefore, it is important to know how to use these elements and what you can and cannot achieve with them. The other benefit is that the errors returned by TensorFlow are usually presented to you using these elements. So, this knowledge will also help us understand errors and resolve them quickly as we develop more complex models.

2.2.1 Understanding tf.Variable

When building a typical machine learning model, you have two types of data:

- Model parameters that change over time (mutable) as the model is optimized with regard to a chosen loss function
- Outputs of the model that are static given data and model parameters (immutable)

`tf.Variable` is ideal for defining model parameters, as they are initialized with some value and can change the value over time. A TensorFlow variable must have the following:

- A shape (size of each dimension of the variable)
- An initial value (e.g., randomly initialized from values sampled from a normal distribution)
- A data type (e.g., int32, float32)

You can define a TensorFlow variable as follows

```
tf.Variable(initial_value=None, trainable=None, dtype=None)
```

where

- `initial_value` contains the initial value provided to the model. This is typically provided using a variable initializer provided in the `tf.keras.initializers` submodule (the full list of initializers can be found at http://mng.bz/M2Nm). For example, if you want to initialize the variable randomly with a 2D matrix

having four rows and three columns using a uniform distribution, you can pass
`tf.keras.initializers.RandomUniform()([4,3])`. You must provide a value
to the `initial_value` argument.

- `trainable` parameter accepts a Boolean value (i.e., `True` or `False`) as the input.
  Setting the trainable parameter to `True` allows the model parameters to be
  changed by means of gradient descent. Setting the trainable parameter to
  `False` will freeze the layer so that the values cannot be changed using gradient descent.

- `dtype` specifies the data type of the data contained in the variable. If unspecified, this defaults to the data type provided to the `initial_value` argument
  (typically `float32`).

Let's see how we can define TensorFlow variables. First, make sure you have imported
the following libraries:

```
import tensorflow as tf
import numpy as np
```

You can define a TensorFlow variable with one dimension of size 4 with a constant
value of 2 as follows:

```
v1 = tf.Variable(tf.constant(2.0, shape=[4]), dtype='float32')
print(v1)

>>> <tf.Variable 'Variable:0' shape=(4,) dtype=float32, numpy=array([2., 2.,
    2., 2.], dtype=float32)>
```

Here, `tf.constant(2.0, shape=[4])` produces a vector of four elements having a
value 2.0, which then is used as the initial value of `tf.Variable`. You can also define
a TensorFlow variable with a NumPy array:

```
v2 = tf.Variable(np.ones(shape=[4,3]), dtype='float32')
print(v2)

>>> <tf.Variable 'Variable:0' shape=(4, 3) dtype=float32, numpy=
array([[1., 1., 1.],
       [1., 1., 1.],
       [1., 1., 1.],
       [1., 1., 1.]], dtype=float32)>
```

Here, `np.ones(shape=[4,3])` generates a matrix of shape `[4,3]`, and all the elements
have a value of 1. The next code snippet defines a TensorFlow variable with three
dimensions (3×4×5) with random normal initialization:

```
v3 = tf.Variable(tf.keras.initializers.RandomNormal()(shape=[3,4,5]),
    dtype='float32')
print(v3)
```

```
>>> <tf.Variable 'Variable:0' shape=(3, 4, 5) dtype=float32, numpy=
array([[[-0.00599647, -0.04389469, -0.03364765, -0.0044175 ,
          0.01199682],
        [ 0.05423453, -0.02812728, -0.00572744, -0.08236874,
         -0.07564012],
        [ 0.0283042 , -0.05198685,  0.04385028,  0.02636188,
          0.02409425],
        [-0.04051876,  0.03284673, -0.00593955,  0.04204708,
         -0.05000611]],


        ...


        [[-0.00781542, -0.03068716,  0.04313354, -0.08717368,
          0.07951441],
        [ 0.00467467,  0.00154883, -0.03209472, -0.00158945,
          0.03176221],
        [ 0.0317267 ,  0.00167555,  0.02544901, -0.06183815,
          0.01649506],
        [ 0.06924769,  0.02057942,  0.01060928, -0.00929202,
          0.04461157]]], dtype=float32)>
```

Here, you can see that if we print a `tf.Variable` it is possible to see its attributes such as the following:

- The name of the variable
- The shape of the variable
- The data type of the variable
- The initial value of the variable

You can also convert your `tf.Variable` to a NumPy array with a single line using

```
arr = v1.numpy()
```

You can then validate the result yourself by printing the Python variable `arr` using

```
print(arr)
```

which will return

```
>>> [2. 2. 2. 2.]
```

A key characteristic of a `tf.Variable` is that you can change the value of its elements as required even after it is initialized. For example, to manipulate individual elements or slices of a `tf.Variable`, you can use the `assign()` operation as follows.

For the purpose of this exercise, let us assume the following TensorFlow variable, which is a matrix initialized with zeros that has four rows and three columns:

```
v = tf.Variable(np.zeros(shape=[4,3]), dtype='float32')
```

You can change the element in the first (i.e., index 0) row and third (i.e., index 2) column as follows:

```
v = v[0,2].assign(1)
```

This will produce the following array:

```
>>> [[0. 0. 1.]
     [0. 0. 0.]
     [0. 0. 0.]
     [0. 0. 0.]]
```

> **NOTE**   Remember that Python uses zero-based indexing. This means that indexing starts from zero (not one). For example, if you want to get the second element of a vector vec, you would use `vec[1]`.

You can also change values using slicing as follows. Here, we are changing the values that lie in the last two rows and first two columns:

```
v = v[2:, :2].assign([[3,3],[3,3]])
```

This results in

```
>>> [[0. 0. 1.]
     [0. 0. 0.]
     [3. 3. 0.]
     [3. 3. 0.]]
```

EXERCISE 2
Can you write the code to create a `tf.Variable` that has the following values and has type `int16`? You can use `np.array()` for this purpose.

```
1 2 3
4 3 2
```

2.2.2 *Understanding tf.Tensor*

As we have seen, `tf.Tensor` is the output of performing a TensorFlow operation on some data (e.g., on a `tf.Variable` or a `tf.Tensor`). `tf.Tensor` objects are heavily used when defining machine learning models, as they are used to store inputs, interim outputs of layers, and final outputs of the model. So far, we have looked mostly at vectors (one dimension) and matrices (two dimension). However, there's nothing stopping us from creating n-dimensional data structures. Such an n-dimensional data structure is known as a *tensor*. Table 2.4 shows a few examples of tensors.

Tensors also have axes. Each dimension of the tensor is considered an axis. Figure 2.6 depicts the axes of a 3D tensor.

Table 2.4   Examples of tensors

Description	Example

A 2D tensor with two rows and four columns	`[`
	`  [1,3,5,7],`
	`  [2,4,6,8]`
	`]`

A 4D tensor of size 2 × 3 × 2 × 1	`[`
	`  [`
	`    [[1],[2]],`
	`    [[2],[3]],`
	`    [[3],[4]]`
	`  ],`
	`  [`
	`    [[1],[2]],`
	`    [[2],[3]],`
	`    [[3],[4]]`
	`  ]`
	`]`

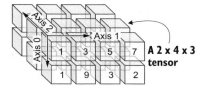

Figure 2.6   A 2 × 4 × 3 tensor with the three axes. The first axis (axis 0) is the row dimension, the second axis (axis 1) is the column axis, and the final axis (axis 2) is the depth axis.

Technically, a tensor can also have just a single dimension (i.e., vector) or be a scalar. An important distinction to make is how the terms *tensor* and `tf.Tensor` are used. We will use *tensor/vector/scalar* to refer to a tensor when we are discussing mathematical aspects of our models. We will refer to any data-related output produced by our Tensor-Flow code as a `tf.Tensor`.

Next we will discuss a few instances where you will end up with a `tf.Tensor`. For example, you can produce a `tf.Tensor` by multiplying a `tf.Variable` with a constant:

```
v = tf.Variable(np.ones(shape=[4,3]), dtype='float32')
b = v * 3.0
```

If you analyze the type of the object produced after the previous operation using `print(type(b).__name__)`, you will see the following output:

```
>>> EagerTensor
```

EagerTensor is a class inherited from `tf.Tensor`. It is a special type of `tf.Tensor`, the value of which is evaluated eagerly (i.e., immediately after defined). You can verify that EagerTensor is, in fact, a `tf.Tensor` by executing the following command:

```
assert isinstance(b, tf.Tensor)
```

You can also produce a tf.Tensor by adding a tf.Tensor to another tf.Tensor

```
a = tf.constant(2, shape=[4], dtype='float32')
b = tf.constant(3, shape=[4], dtype='float32')
c = tf.add(a,b)
```

where print(c) will yield

```
>>> [5. 5. 5. 5]
```

Here, tf.constant() is used to produce tf.Tensor objects a and b. By adding a and b, you will get a tensor c of type tf.Tensor. As before, you can validate this claim by running

```
assert isinstance(c, tf.Tensor)
```

The key difference between a tf.Variable and a tf.Tensor is that tf.Variable allows its values to change even after the variable is initialized (known as a mutable structure). However, once you initialize a tf.Tensor, you cannot change it during the lifetime of the execution (known as an *immutable data structure*). tf.Variable is a mutable data structure, whereas tf.Tensor is an immutable data structure.

Let's see what happens if you try to change the value of a tf.Tensor after it's initialized:

```
a = tf.constant(2, shape=[4], dtype='float32')
a = a[0].assign(2.0)
```

You will get the following error:

```
-------------------------------------------------------------------------
AttributeError                          Traceback (most recent call last)
<ipython-input-19-6e4e6e519741> in <module>()
      1 a = tf.constant(2, shape=[4], dtype='float32')
----> 2 a = a[0].assign(2.0)

AttributeError: 'tensorflow.python.framework.ops.EagerTensor' object has no
    attribute 'assign'
```

Clearly, TensorFlow isn't amused by our rebellious act of trying to modify tf.Tensor objects.

Tensor Zoo

TensorFlow has an arsenal of different Tensor types for attacking various problems. Here are a few different Tensor types available in TensorFlow:

RaggedTensor—A type of data used for variable sequence-length data sets that cannot be represented as a matrix efficiently

> `TensorArray`—A dynamic-sized data structure that can start small and stretch as more data is added (similar to a Python list)
>
> `SparseTensor`—A type of data used to represent sparse data (e.g., a user-by-movie rating matrix)

In the next subsection, we will discuss some of the popular TensorFlow operations.

EXERCISE 3

Can you write the code to create a `tf.Tensor` that is initialized with values sampled from a normal distribution and that has the shape $4 \times 1 \times 5$? You can use `np.random.normal()` for this purpose.

2.2.3   *Understanding tf.Operation*

The backbone of TensorFlow that allows you to do useful things with the data are the operations available. For example, one of the core operations in a deep network is matrix multiplication, which makes TensorFlow a great tool for implementing core operations. Like matrix multiplication, TensorFlow offers a wide range of low-level operations that can be used in TensorFlow. A full list of operations available via the TensorFlow API can be found at http://mng.bz/aDWY.

Let's discuss some popular arithmetic operations you have at your disposal. First, you have basic arithmetic operations such as addition, subtraction, multiplication, and division. You can perform these just like you would with normal Python variables. To demonstrate this, let's assume the following vectors:

```
import tensorflow as tf
import numpy as np

a = tf.constant(4, shape=[4], dtype='float32')
b = tf.constant(2, shape=[4], dtype='float32')
```

We can look at what a and b look like by executing the following

```
print(a)
print(b)
```

which gives

```
>>> tf.Tensor([4. 4. 4. 4.], shape=(4,), dtype=float32)
>>> tf.Tensor([2. 2. 2. 2.], shape=(4,), dtype=float32)
```

Performing addition on a and b

```
c = a+b
print(c)
```

gives

```
>>> tf.Tensor([6. 6. 6. 6.], shape=(4,), dtype=float32)
```

Performing multiplication on a and b

```
e = a*b
print(e)
```

gives

```
>>> tf.Tensor([8. 8. 8. 8.], shape=(4,), dtype=float32)
```

You can also do logical comparisons between tensors. Assuming

```
a = tf.constant([[1,2,3],[4,5,6]])
b = tf.constant([[5,4,3],[3,2,1]])
```

and checking for element-wise equality

```
equal_check = (a==b)
print(equal_check)
```

gives

```
>>> tf.Tensor(
    [[False False  True]
     [False False False]], shape=(2, 3), dtype=bool)
```

Checking less than or equal elements

```
leq_check = (a<=b)
print(leq_check)
```

gives

```
>>> tf.Tensor(
    [[ True  True  True]
     [False False False]], shape=(2, 3), dtype=bool)
```

Next, you have reduction operators that allow you to reduce a tensor (e.g., minimum/maximum/sum/product) on a specific axis or all axes:

```
a = tf.constant(np.random.normal(size=[5,4,3]), dtype='float32')
```

Here, a is a tf.Tensor that looks like this:

```
>>> tf.Tensor(
    [[[-0.7665215   0.9611947   1.456347  ]
      [-0.52979267 -0.2647674  -0.57217133]
      [-0.7511135   2.2282166   0.6573406 ]
      [-1.1323775   0.3301812   0.1310132 ]]
```

```
...
[[ 0.42760614   0.17308706  -0.90879506]
 [ 0.5347165    2.569637     1.3013649 ]
 [ 0.95198756  -0.74183583  -1.2316796 ]
 [-0.03830088   1.1367576   -1.2704859 ]]], shape=(5, 4, 3), dtype=float32)
```

Let's first get the sum of all elements of this tensor. In other words, reduce the tensor on all axes:

```
red_a1 = tf.reduce_sum(a)
```

This produces

```
>>> -4.504758
```

Next, let's get the product on axis 0 (i.e., element-wise product of each row of a):

```
red_a2 = tf.reduce_prod(a, axis=0)
```

This produces

```
>>> [[-0.04612858   0.45068324   0.02033644]
     [-0.27674386  -0.03757533  -0.33719817]
     [-1.4913832   -2.1016302   -0.39335614]
     [-0.00213956   0.14960718   0.01671476]]
```

We will now get the minimum over multiple axes (i.e., 0 and 1):

```
red_a3 = tf.reduce_min(a, axis=[0,1])
```

This produces

```
>>> [-1.6531237 -1.6245098 -1.4723392]
```

You can see that whenever you perform a reduction operation on a certain dimension, you are losing that dimension. For example, if you have a tensor of size [6,4,2] and reduce that tensor on axis 1 (i.e., second axis), you will have a tensor of size [6,2]. In certain instances, you need to keep this dimension there while reducing the tensor (resulting in a [6,1,2]–shaped tensor). One such instance is to make your tensor broadcast compatible with another tensor (http://mng.bz/g4Zn). *Broadcasting* is a term used to describe how scientific computation tools (e.g., NumPy/TensorFlow) treat tensors during arithmetic operations. In such situations, you can set the keepdims parameter to True (which defaults to False). You can see the difference in the shape of the final output

```
# Reducing with keepdims=False
red_a1 = tf.reduce_min(a, axis=1)
print(red_a1.shape)
```

which produces

```
>>> [5,3]

# Reducing with keepdims=True
red_a2 = tf.reduce_min(a, axis=1, keepdims=True)
print(red_a2.shape)
```

This produces

```
>>> red_a2.shape = [5,1,3]
```

Several other important functions are outlined in table 2.5.

Table 2.5   Mathematical functions offered in TensorFlow

tf.argmax	Description	Computes the index of a maximum value on a given axis. For example, the following example shows how to compute tf.argmax on axis 0.
	Usage	`d = tf.constant([[1,2,3],[3,4,5],[6,5,4]])` `d_max1 = tf.argmax(d, axis=0)`
	Result	`tf.Tensor ([2,2,0])`
tf.argmin	Description	Computes the index of a minimum value on a given axis. For example, the following example shows how to compute tf.argmin on axis 1.
	Usage	`d = tf.constant([[1,2,3],[3,4,5],[6,5,4]])` `d_min1 = tf.argmin(d, axis=1)`
	Result	`tf.Tensor([[0],[0],[0]])`
tf.cumsum	Description	Computes the cumulative sum of a vector or a tensor on a given axis
	Usage	`e = tf.constant([1,2,3,4,5])` `e_cumsum = tf.cumsum(e)`
	Result	`tf.Tensor([1,3,6,10,15])`

We conclude our discussion about basic primitives of TensorFlow here. Next we will discuss some of the computations that are commonly used in neural network models.

EXERCISE 4

There is another function for computing mean called tf.reduce_mean(). Given the tf.Tensor object a, which contains the following values, can you compute the mean for each column?

```
0.5 0.2 0.7
0.2 0.3 0.4
0.9 0.1 0.1
```

2.3   *Neural network–related computations in TensorFlow*

Here we will talk about some key low-level operations that underpin deep neural networks. Let's
say you are taking a computer vision class at
school. For your assignment, you have to manipulate an image using various mathematical operations to achieve various effects. We will be using
the famous image of a baboon (figure 2.7), which
is a popular choice for computer vision problems.

2.3.1   *Matrix multiplication*

Your first task is to convert the image from RGB to
grayscale. For this, you must employ matrix multiplication. Let's first understand what matrix multiplication is.

Figure 2.7   Image of a baboon

> ### Story of Lena
> Though we are using an image of a baboon for the exercises, there's a long-standing
> tradition of using Lena's (a Swedish model) photo to demonstrate various computer
> vision algorithms. There is a very interesting backstory behind how this became a
> norm for computer vision problems, which you can read at http://mng.bz/enrZ.

You perform matrix multiplication between two tensors using the `tf.matmul()` function. For two matrices, `tf.matmul()` performs matrix multiplication (e.g., if you have
a of size `[4,3]` and b of size `[3,2]`, matrix multiplication results in a `[4,2]` tensor. Figure 2.8 illustrates the matrix multiplication operation.

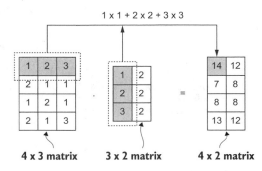

Matrix multiplication

4 x 3 matrix   **3 x 2 matrix**   **4 x 2 matrix**

**Figure 2.8   Matrix multiplication
between a 4 × 3 matrix and 3 × 2
matrix, resulting in a 4 × 2 matrix**

More generally, if you have an n x m matrix (a) and a m x p matrix (b), the result of matrix multiplication c is given by

$$c_{ij} = \sum_{k=1}^{m} a_{ik} b_{kj}$$

However, if you have high-dimensional tensors a and b, the sum product over the last axis of a and second-to-last axis of b will be performed. Both a and b tensors need to have identical dimensionality except for the last two axes. For example, if you have a tensor a of size [3,5,7] and b of size [3,7,8], the result would be a [3,5,8]—sized tensor.

Coming back to our problem, given three RGB pixels, you can convert it to a grayscale pixel using

$$0.3 * R + 0.59 * G + 0.11 * B$$

This is a common operation for converting any RGB image to grayscale (http://mng .bz/p2M0), which can be important depending on the problem at hand. For example, to recognize digits from images, color is not so important. By converting images to grayscale, you are essentially helping the model by reducing the size of the input (one channel instead of three) and by removing noisy features (i.e., color information).

Given a $512 \times 512 \times 3$ image, if you multiply that with a 3×1 array representing the weights provided, you will get the grayscale image of size $512 \times 512 \times 1$. Then we need to remove the last dimension of the grayscale image (as it is one), and we end up with a matrix of size 512×512. For this you can use the tf.squeeze() function, which removes any dimensions that are of size one (see the next listing).

Listing 2.2 Converting an RGB image to grayscale using matrix multiplication

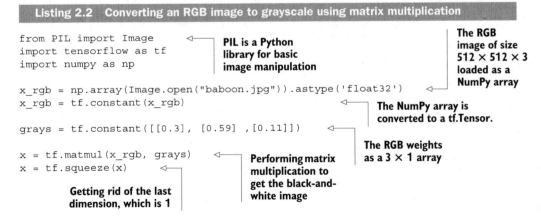

```
from PIL import Image
import tensorflow as tf
import numpy as np

x_rgb = np.array(Image.open("baboon.jpg")).astype('float32')
x_rgb = tf.constant(x_rgb)

grays = tf.constant([[0.3], [0.59] ,[0.11]])

x = tf.matmul(x_rgb, grays)
x = tf.squeeze(x)
```

PIL is a Python library for basic image manipulation

The RGB image of size 512 × 512 × 3 loaded as a NumPy array

The NumPy array is converted to a tf.Tensor.

The RGB weights as a 3 × 1 array

Performing matrix multiplication to get the black-and-white image

Getting rid of the last dimension, which is 1

Matrix multiplication is an important operation in fully connected networks as well. To go from an input layer to a hidden layer, we employ matrix multiplication and add operation. For the moment, we will ignore the nonlinear activation, as it is just an element-wise transformation. Figure 2.9 visualizes the hidden layer computation of the MLP you built earlier.

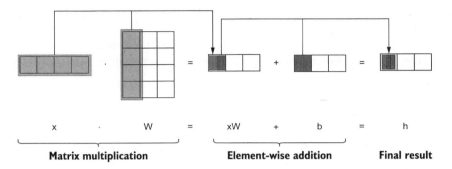

$$x \cdot W = xW + b = h$$

Matrix multiplication　　　　**Element-wise addition**　　**Final result**

Figure 2.9 An illustration of the computations taking place in a hidden layer. x is the input (1 × 4), W is the weight matrix (4 × 3), b is the bias (1 × 3), and finally, h is the output (1 × 3).

2.3.2 Convolution operation

The next task is to implement an edge-detection algorithm. Knowing that you can detect edges using the convolution operation, you also want to show your skills off by achieving this with TensorFlow. The good news is, you can!

The convolution operation is essential in convolutional neural networks, which are deep networks heavily utilized for image-related machine learning tasks (e.g., image classification, object detection). A convolution operation shifts a *window* (also known as a *filter* or a *kernel*) over the data while producing a single value at every position. The convolution window will have some value at each location. And at a given position, the values in the convolution window are element-wise multiplied and summed over with what's overlapping with that window in the data to produce the final value for that location. The convolution operation is shown in figure 2.10.

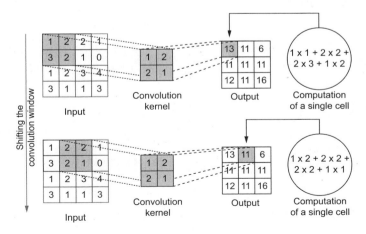

Figure 2.10 Computational steps of the convolution operation

Depending on the values you choose for the convolution window, you can produce some unique effects. You can try out some popular kernels at https://setosa.io/ev/image-kernels/. Edge detection is also a popular computer vision technique that can be achieved using the convolution operation. TensorFlow provides the `tf.nn` `.convolution()` function to perform convolution.

Initially, we have our black-and-white image of the baboon stored as a `tf.Tensor` in the variable x. x is a matrix of size 512×512. Let's create a new variable y from this:

```
y = tf.constant(x)
```

Next, let's define our edge detection filter. We will use an edge detection filter known as an *approximate Laplacian filter*, which is a 3×3 matrix filled with value −1 except for the middle-most value, which is 8. Note how the sum of the kernel is zero:

```
filter = tf.Variable(np.array([[-1,-1,-1],[-1,8,-1],[-1,-1,-1]]).astype('float32'))
```

Next, we need to reshape y and `filter`, because the `tf.nn.convolution()` function accepts a very specifically shaped input and a filter. The first constraint is that your y and `filter` should have the same rank. Rank here refers to the number of dimensionalities in the data. Here we have rank 2 tensors and will perform 2D convolution. To perform 2D convolution, both the input and the kernel need to be of rank 4. Therefore, we need to reshape the input and the kernel in a few steps:

1   Add two more dimensions at the beginning and end of the input. The dimension at the beginning represents the batch dimension, and the last dimension represents the channel dimension (e.g., RGB channels of an image). Though the values will be 1 in our example, we still need those dimensions to be present (e.g., an image of size `[512,512]` will be reshaped to `[1,512,512,1]`).

2   Add two more dimensions of size 1 at the end of the filter. These new dimensions represent the incoming and outgoing channels. We have a single channel (i.e., grayscale) coming in, and we want to produce a single channel (i.e., grayscale) as well (e.g., a kernel of size `[3,3]` will be reshaped to `[3,3,1,1]`).

NOTE   Rank of a tensor refers to the number of dimensions of that tensor. This is different from the rank of a matrix.

Don't worry if you don't fully understand why we added these additional dimensions. This will make more sense when we discuss the convolution operation in the context of convolutional neural networks in a later chapter. For now, you only need to understand the high-level behavior of the convolution operation. In TensorFlow, you can reshape y and `filter` as follows:

```
y_reshaped = tf.reshape(y, [1,512,512,1])
filter_reshaped = tf.reshape(filter, [3,3,1,1])
```

Here, y is a 512×512 tensor. The expression `tf.reshape(y, [1,512,512,1])` converts y (i.e., a 2D tenor) to a 4D tensor of size $1 \times 512 \times 512 \times 1$. Similarly, the `filter` (i.e., a 2D tensor of size 3×3) is reshaped to a 4D tensor of size $3 \times 3 \times 1 \times 1$. Note that the total number of elements is unchanged during the reshaping. Now you can compute the convolution output as follows:

```
y_conv = tf.nn.convolution(y_reshaped, filter_reshaped)
```

You can visualize the result of edge detection and compare that to the original image, as shown in figure 2.11.

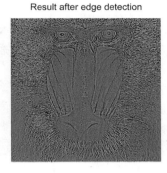

Original image   Result after edge detection

Figure 2.11   Original black-and-white image versus result of edge detection

In the next section, we will discuss another operation known as the pooling operation.

2.3.3   *Pooling operation*

We are off to the next task, which is to resize the image resultant after edge detection by halving the width and height of the image. For example, if we have a 512×512 image and need to rescale it to 256×256, the *pooling operation* is the best way to achieve this easily. The pooling (or sub-sampling) operation is commonly used in convolutional neural networks for this reason: to reduce the size of the output so fewer parameters can be used to learn from data.

Why is it called the pooling operation?

The reason why the sub-sampling operation is also called "pooling" probably has its roots in the word's meaning, as well as in statistics. The word *pooling* is used to describe combining things into a single entity, which is exactly what is done in this operation (e.g., by means of averaging or taking maximum). In statistics, you will find the term *pooled variance*, which is a weighted average of the variance between two populations (http://mng.bz/OGdO), essentially combining two variances into a single variance.

In TensorFlow, you can call the `tf.nn.max_pool()` function to perform max pooling and `tf.nn.avg_pool()` for average pooling:

```
z_avg = tf.nn.avg_pool(y_conv, (1,2,2,1), strides=(1,2,2,1), padding='VALID')
z_max = tf.nn.max_pool(y_conv, (1,2,2,1), strides=(1,2,2,1), padding='VALID')
```

The pooling operation is another commonly found operation in convolutional neural networks and works similarly to the convolution operation. But unlike the convolution operation, the pooling operation does not have values in the kernel. At a given location, it takes either the average or maximum value of what's overlapping the kernel in the data. The operation that produces the average at a given location is known as average pooling, whereas the operation that produces the maximum is known as max pooling. Figure 2.12 illustrates the max pooling operation.

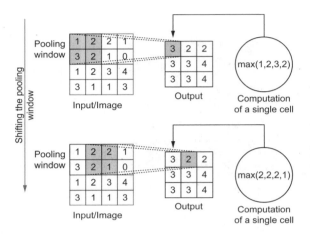

Figure 2.12   Max-pooling operation. The pooling window goes from one position to another on the image, while producing a single value (i.e., maximum value in the image overlapping the pooling window) at a time.

We have `y_conv`, which is a 4D tensor having the shape `[1,510,510,1]`. You might notice that the dimensions are slightly smaller than the original image size (i.e., 512). This is because, when doing convolution with a window of size `c x c` (without extra padding) on an image having `h` height and `w` width, the resulting image has the dimensions `h-c+1` and `w-c+1`. We can perform pooling as shown. You can perform either average pooling or max pooling with the following functions:

```
z_avg = tf.nn.avg_pool(y_conv, (1,2,2,1), strides=(1,2,2,1), padding='VALID')
z_max = tf.nn.max_pool(y_conv, (1,2,2,1), strides=(1,2,2,1), padding='VALID')
```

This will result in two images, z_avg and z_max; both have the shape `[1,255,255,1]`. In order to keep just the height and width dimensions and remove redundant dimensions of size 1, we use the `tf.squeeze()` function:

```
z_avg = np.squeeze(z_avg.numpy())
z_max = np.squeeze(z_max.numpy())
```

You can plot z_avg and z_max using `matplotlib` (a plotting library in Python) and get the result shown in figure 2.13. The code is provided in the notebook.

Figure 2.13 shows the different effects we get with different types of pooling. If you look closely, you will see that average pooling results in more consistent and continuous lines, whereas max pooling results in a noisier image.

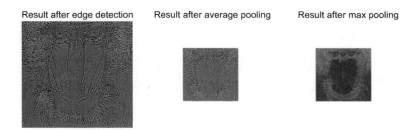

Result after edge detection   Result after average pooling   Result after max pooling

Figure 2.13   Result after edge detection versus result after average or max pooling

Note that, unlike in the convolution operation, we are not providing a filter (or a kernel), as the pooling operation doesn't have a kernel. But we need to pass in the dimensions of the window. These dimensions represent the corresponding dimensions of the input (i.e., it is a [batch dimension, height, width, channels] window). In addition to that, we are also passing two arguments, stride and padding. We will discuss these in detail in a later chapter.

EXERCISE 5
You are given a grayscale image `img` of size 256×256 and a convolution filter `f` of size 5×5. Can you write the `tf.reshape()` function calls and the `tf.nn.convolution()` operation? What would be the size of the output?

Great work! Now you know most common operations used in deep learning networks. We will end our discussion about TensorFlow basics here. In the next chapter, we will discuss a high-level API available in TensorFlow called Keras, which is particularly useful for model building.

Summary

- TensorFlow is an end-to-end machine learning framework.
- TensorFlow provides an ecosystem facilitating model prototyping, model building, model monitoring, and model serving.
- TensorFlow 1 uses declarative graph execution style (define then run), whereas TensorFlow 2 uses imperative graph execution style (define by run).
- TensorFlow provides three main building blocks: `tf.Variable` (for values that change over time), `tf.Tensor` (values that are fixed over time), and `tf.Operation` (transformations performed on `tf.Variable` and `tf.Tensor` objects).
- TensorFlow provides several operations that are used to build neural networks such as `tf.matmul`, `tf.nn.convolution`, and `tf.nn.max_pool`.
- You can use `tf.matmul` to convert an RGB image to grayscale.
- You can use `tf.nn.convolution` to detect edges in an image.
- You can use `tf.nn.max_pool` to resize an image.

Answers to exercises

Exercise 1: 2

Exercise 2: tf.Variable(np.array([[1,2,3],[4,3,2]], dtype="int16")

Exercise 3: tf.constant(np.random.normal(size=[4,1,5]))

Exercise 4: tf.reduce_mean(a, axis=1)

Exercise 5:

```
img_reshaped = tf.reshape(img, [1,256,256,1])
f_reshaped = tf.reshape(f, [5,5,1,1])
y = tf.nn.convolution(img_reshaped, f_reshaped)
```

The shape of the final output would be [1,252,252,1]. The resulting size of the convolution operation is image size − convolution window size + 1.

Keras and data retrieval in TensorFlow 2

This chapter covers

- Different APIs for building models in Keras
- Retrieving and manipulating persisted data

We have explored the details of the low-level TensorFlow API, such as defining `tf.Variable` objects and `tf.Tensor` objects, which can be used to store things like numbers and strings. We also looked at some of the commonly used functionality provided in TensorFlow in the form of `tf.Operation`. Finally, we looked at some complex operations, such as matrix multiplication and convolution, in detail. If you analyze any standard deep neural network, you will see that it is made from standard mathematical operations such as matrix multiplication and convolution.

However, if you were to implement these networks using the low-level TensorFlow API, you'd find yourself replicating these operations in code many times, costing you valuable hours and making the code unmaintainable. But the good news is that you don't have to. TensorFlow provides a submodule called Keras that takes care of this problem, and this is the focus of this chapter. Keras is a sub-library in TensorFlow that hides building blocks and provides a high-level API for developing machine learning models. In this chapter, we will see that Keras has several different APIs to choose from, depending on the complexity of your solution.

We will conclude this chapter by discussing another important aspect of machine learning: feeding data to models. Typically, we need to retrieve data from the disk (or web) and clean and process the data before feeding it to the model. We will discuss several different data retrieval facilities in TensorFlow such as the `tf.data` and `tensorflow-datasets` APIs and how they simplify reading and manipulating data that eventually feeds into models.

3.1 *Keras model-building APIs*

You are developing a flower species classifier as part of a hackathon. Your team is going to create several different variations of multilayer perceptron to compare their performance against a flower species identification data set. The goal is to train the models that can output the flower species given several measurements of the flowers. The models you have to develop are as follows:

- *Model A*—A model that learns only from the provided features (baseline)
- *Model B*—A model that uses the principal components of the features in addition to the features themselves (details discussed in section 3.1.3)
- *Model C*—A model that uses an unorthodox hidden layer computation, which uses a multiplicative bias, in addition to the additive bias, not typically found in neural networks (details discussed in section 3.1.4)

You are planning to use Keras, and you know it offers multiple model-building APIs. In order to provide the results quickly, you need to know which Keras API to use for which model.

Keras (https://keras.io/) initially started as a high-level API that can use multiple low-level backends (e.g., TensorFlow, Theano) and allow developers to build machine learning models easily. In other words, Keras hides the gory details of low-level operations and provides an intuitive API with which you can build models with a few lines of code. Since TensorFlow 1.4, Keras has been integrated into TensorFlow (https://www.tensorflow.org/guide/keras/overview). You can import Keras using `import tensorflow.keras`. Keras has three main APIs:

- Sequential
- Functional
- Sub-classing

The Sequential API is the easiest to use. However, it is a very constrictive API that only allows you to create a network that starts with one input, go through a sequence of layers, and end with one input. Next, the functional API requires more work to use. But it also provides more flexibility, such as having multiple inputs, parallel layers, and multiple outputs. Finally, the sub-classing API can be identified as the most difficult to wield. The idea is to create a Python object that represents your model or a layer in your model while using the low-level functionality provided by TensorFlow to achieve what's needed. Let's briefly go over how you can use these APIs. But we won't stop there; we will look at these APIs in more detail in the coming chapters. Figure 3.1 highlights the main differences between the APIs.

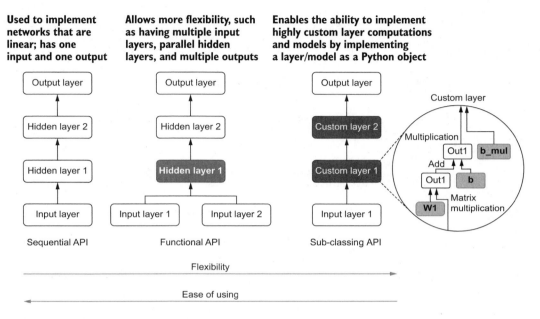

Figure 3.1 Sequential, functional, and sub-classing APIs in comparison.

Here, for model A we will use the Sequential API, as it is the simplest. To implement model B, which will have two input layers, we will use the functional API. Finally, to implement model C, for which we will need to implement a custom layer, we will use the sub-classing API.

3.1.1 Introducing the data set

Say you decided to use a popular machine learning data set known as the Iris data set (https://archive.ics.uci.edu/ml/datasets/Iris). This data set records sepal length, sepal width, petal length, and petal width for several different species of Iris flowers: `Iris-setosa`, `Iris-versicolor`, and `Iris-virginica`. For each flower, we have the sepal length/width and the petal length/width. As you can see, each input has four features, and each input can belong to one of three classes. To start, let's download the data, do some quick analysis on it, and put it in a format that we can readily use for model training.

Initially, you need to make sure the environment is set up and the libraries are installed, as outlined in appendix A. Next, open the Jupyter notebook found at `Ch03-Keras-and-Data-Retrieval/3.1.Keras_APIs.ipynb`. Now, as shown in the code found in the notebook, we need to import the requests library for downloading data, pandas for manipulating that data, and, of course, TensorFlow:

```
import requests
import pandas as pd
import tensorflow as tf
```

Now we will download the data and save the data to a file:

```
url = "https:/ /archive.ics.uci.edu/ml/machine-learning-databases/iris/iris.data"
r = requests.get(url)

# Writing data to a file
with open('iris.data', 'wb') as f:
  f.write(r.content)
```

We then read the data using pandas library's read_csv() function (http://mng.bz/j2Op):

```
iris_df = pd.read_csv('iris.data', header=None)
```

Here, iris_df is a pandas DataFrame (http://mng.bz/Wxaw). In its simplest form, a data frame can be thought as an informative matrix organized into rows and columns. You can inspect the first few rows of the data using the iris_df.head() command, which produces the following result:

```
0     1     2     3     4
0     5.1   3.5   1.4   0.2   Iris-setosa
1     4.9   3.0   1.4   0.2   Iris-setosa
2     4.7   3.2   1.3   0.2   Iris-setosa
```

Then, we will make some cosmetic changes to the data to make it look better. We will provide appropriate column names (available from the data set's webpage)

```
iris_df.columns = ['sepal_length', 'sepal_width', 'petal_width',
    'petal_length', 'label']
```

and mapping the string label to an integer:

```
iris_df["label"] = iris_df["label"].map({'Iris-setosa':0, 'Iris-versicolor':1,
    'Iris-virginica':2})
```

We end up with the following improved pandas DataFrame in our possession:

```
   sepal_length   sepal_width   petal_width   petal_length   label
0     5.1            3.5           1.4           0.2           0
1     4.9            3.0           1.4           0.2           0
2     4.7            3.2           1.3           0.2           0
```

As the last step, we will shuffle the data by and separate the data features as x and data labels as y. We will also center the data by subtracting the mean from each column, as this usually leads to better performance:

```
iris_df = iris_df.sample(frac=1.0, random_state=4321)
x = iris_df[["sepal_length", "sepal_width", "petal_width", "petal_length"]]
x = x - x.mean(axis=0)
y = tf.one_hot(iris_df["label"], depth=3)
```

Here, print(x) will print out

```
       sepal_length   sepal_width   petal_width   petal_length
31       -0.443333        0.346      -2.258667      -0.798667
23       -0.743333        0.246      -2.058667      -0.698667
70        0.056667        0.146       1.041333       0.601333
100       0.456667        0.246       2.241333       1.301333
44       -0.743333        0.746      -1.858667      -0.798667
..          ...            ...          ...            ...
```

Note how the indices are not in order after shuffling the data. print(y) will output

```
tf.Tensor(
    [[1. 0. 0.]
     [1. 0. 0.]
     [0. 1. 0.]
     ...
     [0. 0. 1.]
     [0. 0. 1.]
     [0. 1. 0.]],
shape=(150, 3), dtype=float32)
```

Shuffling the data is an important step: the data is in a very specific order, with each class appearing one after another. But you achieve the best results when data has been shuffled so that each batch presented to the network has a good mix of all classes found in the full data set. You can also see that we used a transformation on y (or labels), known as *one-hot encoding*. One-hot encoding converts each label to a unique vector of zeros, where a single element is one. For example, the labels 0, 1, and 2 are converted to the following one-hot encoded vectors:

$$0 \rightarrow [1, 0, 0]$$

$$1 \rightarrow [0, 1, 0]$$

$$2 \rightarrow [0, 0, 1]$$

3.1.2   The Sequential API

With the data ready to be fed in, it's time to implement model A, the first neural network. The first model is quite straightforward and only needs to take the provided features and predict the flower species. You can use the Keras Sequential API, as it is the simplest, and all we need to do is stack several layers on top of each other sequentially. Figure 3.2 depicts the Sequential API compared to other APIs.

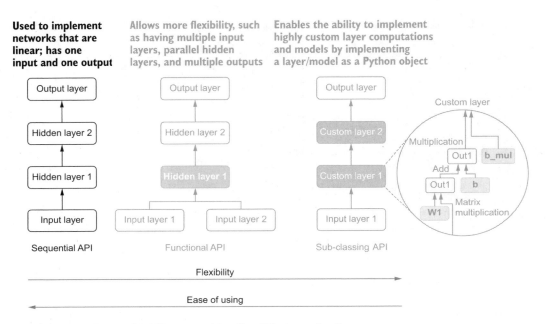

Figure 3.2   The Sequential API compared to other APIs (grayed out)

Let's create a network that has the following:

- An input layer of 4 nodes
- A 32-node hidden layer
- A 16-node hidden layer
- A 3-node output layer

NOTE   The number of nodes for each layer is a hyperparameter of the model. In this case, we chose these values arbitrarily. But to obtain the best results, we should use a hyperparameter optimization algorithm (http://mng.bz/8MJB) to find the best hyperparameters for a given problem.

Before we define the model, we need to import certain layers and the sequential model from TensorFlow. Then you can implement this model using just a single line of code (see the next listing).

Listing 3.1   Model A implemented with the Sequential API

```
from tensorflow.keras.layers import Dense          Import necessary
from tensorflow.keras.models import Sequential     modules and
import tensorflow.keras.backend as K               classes.

K.clear_session()
model = Sequential([
    Dense(32, activation='relu', input_shape=(4,)),    Define the
    Dense(16, activation='relu'),                      model with the
    Dense(3, activation='softmax')                     Sequential API.
])
```

**Clear the TensorFlow computational
graph before creating the model.**

Let's analyze what we just did. You can create a sequential model using the `Sequential` object and then pass a sequence of layers, such as the `Dense` layer. A layer encapsulates typical reusable computations you can find in a neural network (e.g., hidden layer computation, convolution operations).

The `Dense` layer offers the core computation that happens in a fully connected network (i.e., going from an input (x) to a hidden output (h) using $h = activation(xW + b)$). The `Dense` layer has two important parameters: the number of hidden units and the nonlinear activation. By stacking a set of `Dense` layers, you have a multilayer, fully connected network. We are building the network using the following layers:

- `Dense(32, activation='relu', input_shape=(4,))`
- `Dense(16, activation='relu')`
- `Dense(3, activation='softmax')`

In the first `Dense` layer you can see that an additional parameter called `input_shape` has been passed. `input_shape` is a key attribute in any model you create with Tensor-Flow. It is imperative that you know the exact shape of the input you want to pass to a model because the output of all the layers that follow depends on the shape of the input. In fact, certain layers can only process certain input shapes.

In this example, we are saying the input will be of shape `[None, 4]`. Though we have only specified 4 in the shape, Keras automatically adds an unspecified (i.e., `None`) dimension to the `input_shape`, which represents the batch dimension of the input. As you probably already know, deep neural networks process data in batches (i.e., more than a single example at once). The other dimension (of size 4) is the feature dimension, meaning that the network can accept an input that has four features in it. Having the batch dimension as `None` leaves the batch dimension unspecified, allowing you to pass any arbitrary number of examples at model training/inference time.

Another important aspect of a layer is the nonlinear activation used in the layer. Here, we can see that the first two layers use ReLU (rectified linear units) activation. It is a very simple yet powerful activation that's prevalent in feed-forward models. ReLU does the following:

$$y = \max\ (0, x)$$

The final layer has a softmax activation. As previously discussed, softmax activation normalizes the final scores of the last layer (i.e., logits) to a valid probability distribution. Specifically,

$$y_i = \frac{x_i}{\sum_{j=1}^{K} x_j}$$

As an example, assume the final layer without the softmax activation produced

```
[15, 30, 5]
```

Applying the softmax normalization converts these values to

```
[15/(15+30+5), 30/(15+30+5), 5/(15+30+5)]
= [0.3, 0.6, 0.1]
```

Now that the model is defined, we need to perform a crucial step, known as *model compilation*, if we are to successfully use it. For our model we will use

```
model.compile(loss='categorical_crossentropy', optimizer='adam', metrics=['acc'])
```

Here, we are setting the model up with a loss function, optimizer, and metric. The loss function says how good or bad the model is doing on the given data (e.g., categorical cross-entropy). The lower the loss, the better. Along with that loss function, we use an optimizer, which knows how to change the weights and biases of the model in such a way that the loss is reduced. Here, we chose the loss categorical_crossentropy (http://mng.bz/EWej), which typically works well for multiclass classification problems and the optimizer adam (https://arxiv.org/pdf/1412.6980.pdf), which is a common choice due to its remarkable performance in a variety of problems. We can also optionally define metrics to keep an eye on the model (e.g., model accuracy). Finally, we can inspect the model you just created using

```
model.summary()
```

which outputs

```
Model: "sequential"
```

Layer (type)	Output Shape	Param #
dense_3 (Dense)	(None, 32)	160

```
dense_4 (Dense)                 (None, 16)                  528

dense_5 (Dense)                 (None, 3)                   51
=================================================================
Total params: 739
Trainable params: 739
Non-trainable params: 0
```

The model summary clearly shows the number of layers, type of layers, output shape of each layer, and number of parameters in each layer. Let's train this model to classify various iris flowers using the data set we prepared earlier. We train a Keras model using the convenient `fit()` function:

```
model.fit(x, y, batch_size=64, epochs=25)
```

The `fit()` function accepts many different arguments:

- `x`—Data features
- `y`—Data labels (one-hot encoded)
- `batch size` (optional)—Number of data points in a single batch
- `epochs` (optional)—Number of times repeating the data set during model training

The values, such as `batch_size` and `epochs`, have been chosen empirically. If you run the previous code, you will get the following result:

```
Train on 150 samples
Epoch 1/25
150/150 [==============================] - 0s 2ms/sample - loss: 1.1773 - acc: 0.2667
Epoch 2/25
150/150 [==============================] - 0s 148us/sample - loss: 1.1388 - acc: 0.2933
...
Epoch 24/25
150/150 [==============================] - 0s 104us/sample - loss: 0.6254 - acc: 0.7400
Epoch 25/25
150/150 [==============================] - 0s 208us/sample - loss: 0.6078 - acc: 0.7400
```

It looks like our mini project was reasonably successful, as we observe a steady increase of the training accuracy ("acc") up to 74% in just 25 epochs. However, it is not advisable to rely only on the training accuracy to decide if a model has performed better. There are various techniques to do so, which we will review in the coming chapters.

Reproducibility in machine learning

Reproducibility is an important concept in machine learning. Reproducibility means that you can run an experiment, publish the results, and ensure that someone interested in your research can reproduce the results. It also means that you will get the

(continued)

same result across multiple trials. If you look at the notebook ch02/1.Tensorflow_
Fundamentals.ipynb, you will see one such measure we have taken to make sure
the results are consistent across multiple trials. You will see the following code in
the "Library imports and some setups" section:

```
def fix_random_seed(seed):
    try:
        np.random.seed(seed)
    except NameError:
        print("Warning: Numpy is not imported. Setting the seed for
            Numpy failed.")
    try:
        tf.random.set_seed(seed)
    except NameError:
        print("Warning: TensorFlow is not imported. Setting the seed for
            TensorFlow failed.")
    try:
        random.seed(seed)
    except NameError:
        print("Warning: random module is not imported. Setting the seed
            for random failed.")

# Fixing the random seed
fix_random_seed(4321)
```

The random seed is a common element that affects the reproducibility of the research
as neural networks ubiquitously use random initializations. By fixing the seed, you
make sure you will get the same random number sequence every time you run your
code. This means that the weight and bias initializations of your model will be the
same across multiple trials. This results in the same accuracy values given the other
conditions are not changed.

To make sure that your code is producing consistent results, make sure you call the
fix_random_seed function (by running the first code cell) when you are trying out
the code exercises.

3.1.3   *The functional API*

Now it's time to implement the second model (i.e., Model B) that uses principal components as an extra set of inputs. The hope is that this additional input (the principal
components) will provide additional features to the model, which will improve model
performance. Principal components are extracted using an algorithm known as *principal component analysis* (PCA). PCA is a dimensionality reduction technique that will
project high-dimensional data to a lower-dimensional space while trying to preserve
the variance present in the data. Now you need to create a model that takes two different input feature sets.

You no longer can use the Sequential API as it is only designed to handle sequential models (i.e., single input layer going through a sequence of layers to produce a

single output). Here, we have two different inputs: the raw features of flowers and the PCA features. That means two layers work in parallel to produce two different hidden representations, concatenate that, and finally produce the class probabilities for the inputs, as highlighted in figure 3.3. The functional API is a great choice for these kind of models, as it can be used to define models with multiple inputs or multiple outputs.

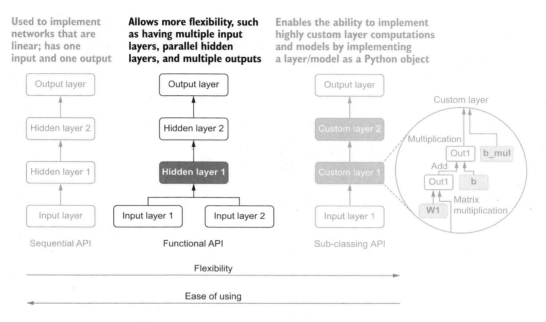

Figure 3.3 The functional API compared to other APIs (grayed out)

Let's get started. First, we need to import the following `layer` and `model` objects, as these will make the core of our model:

```
from tensorflow.keras.layers import Input, Dense, Concatenate
from tensorflow.keras.models import Model
```

Next, we need to create two `Input` layers (for the raw input features and the PCA features):

```
inp1 = Input(shape=(4,))
inp2 = Input(shape=(2,))
```

The `Input` layer for the raw input features will have four feature columns, whereas the `Input` layer for the PCA features will have two feature columns (as we are only keeping the first two principal components). If you look back at how we defined the model using the Sequential API, you will notice we didn't use an `Input` layer.

This is automatically added when using the Sequential API. However, when using the functional API, we need to explicitly specify the Input layers we need to include in our model.

With the two Input layers defined, we can now compute individual hidden representations for those layers:

```
out1 = Dense(16, activation='relu')(inp1)
out2 = Dense(16, activation='relu')(inp2)
```

Here, out1 represents the hidden representation of inp1 (i.e., raw features) and out2 is the hidden representation of inp2 (i.e., PCA features). We then concatenate the two hidden representations:

```
out = Concatenate(axis=1)([out1,out2])
```

Let's delve into what happens when you use the Concatenate layer in more detail. The Concatenate layer simply concatenates two or more inputs along a given axis. In this example, we have two inputs to the Concatenate layer (i.e., [None, 16] and [None, 16]) and want to concatenate them along the second axis (i.e., axis=1). Remember that Keras adds an additional batch dimension to the input/output tensors when you specify the shape argument. This operation results in a [None, 32]–sized tensor. From this point on, you only have a single sequence of layers. We will define a 16-node Dense layer with relu activation and finally an output layer that has three nodes with softmax normalization:

```
out = Dense(16, activation='relu')(out)
out = Dense(3, activation='softmax')(out)
```

We need to do one extra step: create a Model object that says what the inputs and outputs are. As of now, we have a bunch of layers and no Model object. Finally, we compile the model as we did before. We will choose categorical_crossentropy as the loss and adam as the optimizer, as we did before. We will also monitor the training accuracy:

```
model = Model(inputs=[inp1, inp2], outputs=out)
model.compile(loss='categorical_crossentropy', optimizer='adam',
    metrics=['acc'])
```

The full code for this model is provided in the following listing.

Listing 3.2   Model B implemented with the Keras functional API

```
from tensorflow.keras.layers import Input, Dense, Concatenate
from tensorflow.keras.models import Model
import tensorflow.keras.backend as K

K.clear_session()          ◁——  Making sure we are clearing
                                 out the TensorFlow graph
```

```
inp1 = Input(shape=(4,))          The two input layers. One input layer
inp2 = Input(shape=(2,))          has four features; the other has two.

out1 = Dense(16, activation='relu')(inp1)     The two parallel
out2 = Dense(16, activation='relu')(inp2)     hidden layers

out = Concatenate(axis=1)([out1,out2])    ◁──  The concatenation layer
                                               that combines two parallel
out = Dense(16, activation='relu')(out)        outputs: out1 and out2
out = Dense(3, activation='softmax')(out)

                                                    The model definition
model = Model(inputs=[inp1, inp2], outputs=out)  ◁──┘
model.compile(loss='categorical_crossentropy', optimizer='adam', metrics=['acc'])
```
Compiling the model with a loss, an optimizer, and a metric

Now you can print the model summary

```
model.summary()
```

which gives

```
Model: "model"
```

Layer (type)	Output Shape	Param #	Connected to
input_1 (InputLayer)	[(None, 4)]	0	
input_2 (InputLayer)	[(None, 2)]	0	
dense (Dense)	(None, 16)	80	input_1[0][0]
dense_1 (Dense)	(None, 16)	48	input_2[0][0]
concatenate (Concatenate)	(None, 32)	0	dense[0][0] dense_1[0][0]
dense_2 (Dense)	(None, 16)	528	concatenate[0][0]
dense_3 (Dense)	(None, 3)	51	dense_2[0][0]

```
Total params: 707
Trainable params: 707
Non-trainable params: 0
```

What do you think about this summary representation? Can you tell what kind of a model it is by looking at it? Unfortunately, no. Though we have parallel layers in our model, the summary looks like we have a sequence of layer-processing inputs and outputs one after another. Can we obtain a better representation than this? Yes, we can!

Keras also offers the ability to visualize the model as a network diagram. You can easily do this with

```
tf.keras.utils.plot_model(model)
```

If you run this command on a Jupyter notebook, you will have the inline output of the following graph (figure 3.4). It is now much clearer to see what's going on in our model.

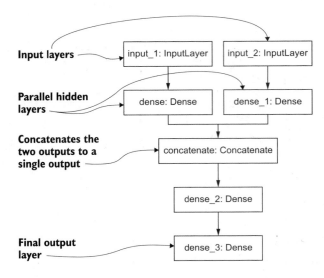

Figure 3.4   **An illustration of the model we created with the functional API. You can see the parallel input layers and hidden layers at the top. The final output layer is at the bottom.**

If you need to save this diagram to a file, simply do

```
tf.keras.utils.plot_model(model, to_file='model.png')
```

If you need to see input/output sizes in addition to the layer names and types, you can do that by setting the show_shapes parameter to True

```
tf.keras.utils.plot_model(model, show_shapes=True)
```

which will return figure 3.5.

Remember that we have two inputs, original features (x) and the first two principal components of x (let's call it x_pca). You can compute the first two principal components as follows (using the scikit-learn library):

```
from sklearn.decomposition import PCA

pca_model = PCA(n_components=2, random_state=4321)

x_pca = pca_model.fit_transform(x)
```

PCA is already implemented in scikit-learn. You define a PCA object and pass the value 2 to the n_components argument. You also fix the random seed to ensure consistency across trials. Then you can call the method fit_transform(x) to get the final PCA features. You can train this model as you did before by calling

```
model.fit([x, x_pca], y, batch_size=64, epochs=10)
```

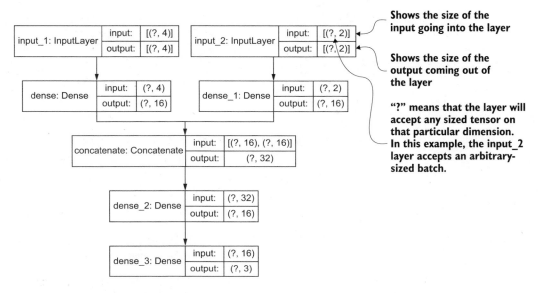

Figure 3.5 Keras model plot with `show_shapes=True`

Sadly, you will not see much of an accuracy improvement. The results will be on par with what you achieved earlier. In the given code example, you would have around 6% accuracy improvement when using this model. However, you will see that this gap will become smaller and smaller if you increase the number of epochs. This is mostly because adding PCA features doesn't really add much value. We are reducing four dimensions to two, which is unlikely to result in better features than what we already have. Let's try our luck in the next exercise.

3.1.4 The sub-classing API

Back in the research lab, it is a bit disheartening to see that adding principal components did not improve the results. However, the team is impressed with your knowledge of exactly which API to use for a given model. A team member suggested a final model. Currently a dense layer computes its output using

$$h = \alpha(xW + b)$$

where α is some nonlinearity. You want to see if results can be improved by adding another bias (i.e., in addition to the additive bias, we add a multiplicative bias) so that the equation becomes

$$h = \alpha([xW + b] \times b_{mul})$$

This is where layer sub-classing will save the day, as there is no prebuilt layer in Keras that readily offers this functionality. The final API offered by Keras is the sub-classing

API (figure 3.6), which will allow us to define the required computations as a unit of computation (i.e., a layer) and reuse it with ease when defining a model. Sub-classing comes from the software engineering concept of *inheritance*. The idea is that you have a super class that provides general functionality for a type of object (e.g., a Layer class), and you sub-class (or inherit) from that layer to create a more specific layer that achieves a specific functionality.

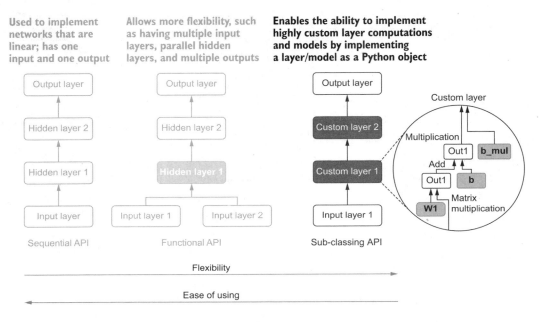

Figure 3.6   Sub-classing API compared to other APIs (grayed out)

The sub-classing API is drastically different from the sequential and functional APIs. Here, you are creating a Python class that defines the underlying operations of a layer or a model. In this book we will focus on sub-classing layers (i.e., not models). In my opinion, there will be more instances where you subclass a layer than a model because layer sub-classing is more commodious and can be needed in cases where you have a single model or multiple models. However, model sub-classing is only required if you are creating larger composite models that consist of many smaller models. It is also worthwhile to note that once you learn layer sub-classing, it's relatively easy to extend to model sub-classing.

When sub-classing a layer, there are three important functions that you need to override from the Layer base class you inherit from:

- __init__()—Initializes the layer with any parameters it accepts
- build()—Where the parameters of the model will be created
- call()—Defines the computations that need to happen during the forward pass

Here's how you would write our new layer. We will call our custom layer `MulBiasDense` appropriately. Notice how this layer inherits from the base layer `Layer` found in the `tensorflow.keras.layers` submodule.

Listing 3.3 Sub-classing a new layer with Keras

```
from tensorflow.keras import layers

class MulBiasDense(layers.Layer):

    def __init__(self, units=32, input_dim=32, activation=None):      Defines various
        super(MulBiasDense, self).__init__()                          hyperparameters
        self.units = units                                           required to
        self.activation = activation                                 define the layer

    def build(self, input_shape):
        self.w = self.add_weight(shape=(input_shape[-1], self.units),
                                 initializer='glorot_uniform', trainable=True)
        self.b = self.add_weight(shape=(self.units,),
                                 initializer='glorot_uniform', trainable=True)
        self.b_mul = self.add_weight(shape=(self.units,),
                                     initializer='glorot_uniform', trainable=True)

    def call(self, inputs):
        out = (tf.matmul(inputs, self.w) + self.b) * self.b_mul
        return layers.Activation(self.activation)(out)
```

Defines all the parameters in the layer as tf.Variable objects. self.b_mul represents the multiplicative bias.

Defines the computation that needs to happen when data is fed to the layer

First, we have the `__init__()` function. There are two parameters for the layer: the number of hidden units and the type of activation. The activation defaults to `None`, meaning that if unspecified, there will be no nonlinear activation (i.e., only a linear transformation):

```
def __init__(self, units=32, activation=None):
    super(MulBiasDense, self).__init__()
    self.units = units
    self.activation = activation
```

Next, we implement the `build()` function, a significant puzzle piece of sub-classing. All the parameters (e.g., weights and biases) are created within this function:

```
def build(self, input_shape):
    self.w = self.add_weight(shape=(input_shape[-1], self.units),
                             initializer='glorot_uniform', trainable=True)
    self.b = self.add_weight(shape=(self.units,),
                             initializer='glorot_uniform', trainable=True)
    self.b_mul = self.add_weight(shape=(self.units,),
                                 initializer='glorot_uniform', trainable=True)
```

Here, the parameters w, b, and b_mul refer to W, b, and b_{mul} in the equation. For each parameter, we provide the shape, an initializer, and a Boolean to indicate trainability.

The initializer `'glorot_uniform'` (http://mng.bz/N6A7) used here is a popular neural network initializer. Finally, we need to write the `call()` function, which defines how the inputs are going to be transformed to produce an output:

```
def call(self, inputs):
    out = (tf.matmul(inputs, self.w) + self.b) * self.b_mul
    return layers.Activation(self.activation)(out)
```

There it is: our first subclassed layer. It is worth noting that there are several other functions you need to be aware of when it comes to subclassing layers:

- `compute_output_shape()`—Typically, Keras will automatically infer the shape of the output of the layer. But, if you do too many complex transformations, Keras might lose track, and you will need to explicitly define what the output shape is using this function.
- `get_config()`—If you plan to save your model to disk after training, you need to implement this function, which returns a dictionary of the parameters taken in by the layer.

With the new layer defined, you can use the functional API as before to create a model, as the following listing shows.

Listing 3.4   Model C implemented with the Keras sub-classed API

```
from tensorflow.keras.layers import Input, Dense, Concatenate    ⟵ Importing
from tensorflow.keras.models import Model                             necessary
import tensorflow.keras.backend as K                                  modules and
import tensorflow as tf                                               classes

K.clear_session()    ⟵— Making sure we are clearing
                          out the TensorFlow graph
inp = Input(shape=(4,))
out = MulBiasDense(units=32, activation='relu')(inp)       Defining two layers with the new
out = MulBiasDense(units=16, activation='relu')(out)       sub-classed layer MulBiasDense
out = Dense(3, activation='softmax')(out)    ⟵
                                                 Defining the softmax
                                                 output layer
model = Model(inputs=inp, outputs=out)
model.compile(loss='categorical_crossentropy', optimizer='adam', metrics=['acc'])
```

Defining the input layer • *Defining the final model*

Compiling the model with a loss function, an optimizer, and accuracy as metrics

Unfortunately, in our experiments, none of the architectural improvements we tried delivered a significantly better result. But you have managed to impress your colleagues by knowing which API to use for which model, enabling the group to have the results ready for the paper deadline. Table 3.1 further summarizes main advantages and disadvantages of the APIs we discussed.

In the next section, we will discuss different ways you can import and ingest data in TensorFlow.

Table 3.1 Pros and cons of using various Keras APIs

Sequential API	Pros	Models implemented with the Sequential API are easy to understand and are concise.
	Cons	Cannot implement models having complex architectural characteristics such as multiple inputs/outputs.
Functional API	Pros	Can be used to implement models with complex architectural elements such as multiple inputs/outputs.
	Cons	The developer needs to manually connect various layers correctly and create a model.
Sub-classing API	Pros	Can create custom layers and models that are not provided as standard layers.
	Cons	Requires thorough understanding of low-level functionality provided by TensorFlow.
		Due to the user-defined nature, it can lead to instabilities and difficulties in debugging.

EXERCISE 1

Say you need to create a fully connected neural network that has a single input layer and two output layers. Which API you think is the most suitable for this task?

3.2 Retrieving data for TensorFlow/Keras models

So far, we have looked at how to implement various models with different Keras APIs. At this point, you should be comfortable with knowing which API to use (or sometimes which API *not* to use) when you see the architecture of a model. Moving forward, we will learn about reading data to train these models using TensorFlow/Keras.

Let's assume that you recently joined a startup as a data scientist who is experimenting with software encompassing a machine learning model to identify flower species (using images). They already have a custom-written data pipeline that can take a batch of images and a batch of labels and train a model. However, this data pipeline is quite obscure and difficult to maintain. You're tasked with implementing a replacement data pipeline that is easy to understand and maintain. This is a golden opportunity to impress your boss by quickly prototyping a data pipeline using TensorFlow.

A model doesn't have any value unless it has been trained with data. As more (quality) data means better performance, it is important to feed data to the model in a scalable and efficient manner. It's time to explore features of TensorFlow that allow you to create input pipelines that achieve this. There are two popular alternatives to retrieving data:

- The `tf.data` API
- Keras data generators

The data set you'll be working with (downloaded from http://mng.bz/DgVa) contains a collection of 210 flower images (in .png format) and a CSV (comma-separated value) file that contains the filename and label.

> **NOTE**   There is also a third method, which is to use a Python package to access popular machine learning data sets. This package is known as the `tensorflow-datasets`. This means that this method works only if you want to use a data set that is already supported by the package.

It's time to crack some knuckles and get to implementing the data pipeline.

3.2.1   *tf.data API*

Let's see what an input pipeline might look like. For example, an input pipeline for your image classification task might look like figure 3.7. Initially, the integer labels are read from a text file (stored as [filename, label] records). Next, the images corresponding to the filenames are read and resized to a constant height and width. The labels are

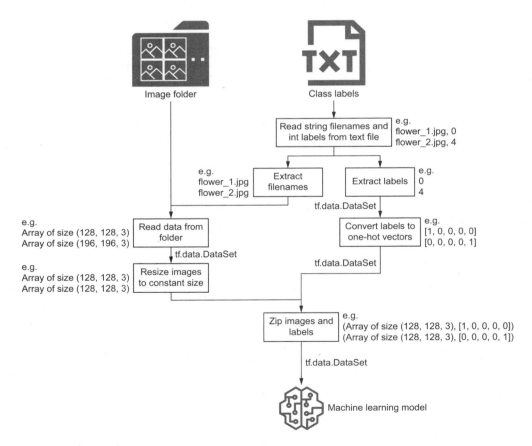

Figure 3.7   The input pipeline that you'll be developing using the `tf.data` API

then converted to a one-hot encoded representation. One-hot encoded representation converts an integer to a vector of zeros and ones. Then the images and one-hot encoded labels are zipped together to keep the correct correspondence between images and their respective labels. This data now can be fed directly to a Keras model.

In our data set, we have a collection of flower images and a CSV file that contains the filename and the corresponding label. We will perform the following steps in order to create the data pipeline:

- Read CSV file as a `tf.data.Dataset`.
- Extract filenames and labels as separate data sets.
- Read the image files corresponding to the filenames in the filename data set.
- Decode the image data and convert it to a float32 tensor.
- Resize the images to 64 × 64 pixels.
- Convert labels to one-hot encoded vectors.
- Zip the image data set and the one-hot vector data sets.
- Batch the data set in batches of five samples.

In order to read the CSV file as a data set entity, we will use the convenient `tf.data.experimental.CsvDataset` object. You might see that this is, in fact, an experimental object. This means it has not been tested as extensively as other functionality in the `tf.data` API and might break in certain instances. But for our small and simple example there won't be any issues:

```
import os # Provides various os related functions

data_dir = os.path.join('data','flower_images') + os.path.sep
csv_ds = tf.data.experimental.CsvDataset(
    os.path.join(data_dir,'flower_labels.csv') , record_defaults=("",-1),
    header=True
)
```

The `tf.data.experimental.CsvDataset` object expects two mandatory arguments: one or more filenames and a default record, which will be used as the default if a record is corrupted or unreadable. In our case, the default record is an empty filename ("") and the label -1. You can print some of the records from `tf.data.Dataset` by calling

```
for item in csv_ds.take(5):
    print(item)
```

Here, `take()` is a function that takes a number as the argument and returns that many records from the data set. This will output the following:

```
(<tf.Tensor: shape=(), dtype=string, numpy=b'0001.png'>, <tf.Tensor: shape=(),
    dtype=int32, numpy=0>)
(<tf.Tensor: shape=(), dtype=string, numpy=b'0002.png'>, <tf.Tensor: shape=(),
    dtype=int32, numpy=0>)
```

```
(<tf.Tensor: shape=(), dtype=string, numpy=b'0003.png'>, <tf.Tensor: shape=(),
    dtype=int32, numpy=2>)
(<tf.Tensor: shape=(), dtype=string, numpy=b'0004.png'>, <tf.Tensor: shape=(),
    dtype=int32, numpy=0>)
(<tf.Tensor: shape=(), dtype=string, numpy=b'0005.png'>, <tf.Tensor: shape=(),
    dtype=int32, numpy=0>)
```

If you remember, the `flower_labels.csv` file contains two columns: filenames and the corresponding labels. You can see in the data set output that each tuple carries two elements: the filename and the label. Next, we will split these two columns as two separate data sets. This can easily be done using the `map()` function, which applies a given function across all the records in a data set:

```
fname_ds = csv_ds.map(lambda a,b: a)
label_ds = csv_ds.map(lambda a,b: b)
```

Lambda expressions

Lambda expressions are a great tool that enables you to have anonymous functions in the code. Just like normal functions, they take in arguments and return some output. For example, the following function will add two given values (x and y):

```
lambda x, y : x + y
```

Lambda expressions are a great way to write functions if they are used only once and thus require no name. Learning to use lambda expressions effectively will keep your code clean and succinct.

Here, we use a succinct lambda expression to tell the `map()` function what we want to achieve. We can now focus on fetching the image data. In order to do that, we will again use the `map()` function. But this time, we will write a separate function defining what needs to happen:

```
import tensorflow as tf

def get_image(file_path):

    # loading the image from disk as a byte string
    img = tf.io.read_file(data_dir + file_path)
    # convert the compressed string to a 3D uint8 tensor
    img = tf.image.decode_png(img, channels=3)
    # Use `convert_image_dtype` to convert to floats in the [0,1] range.
    img = tf.image.convert_image_dtype(img, tf.float32)
    # resize the image to the desired size.
    return tf.image.resize(img, [64, 64])
```

To get the image tensors from the filename, all we need to do is apply this function to all filenames in the `fname_ds`:

```
image_ds = fname_ds.map(get_image)
```

With the image data set read, let's convert the label data to one-hot encoded vectors:

```
label_ds = label_ds.map(lambda x: tf.one_hot(x, depth=10))
```

In order to train an image classifier, we need two items: an image and a label. We do have both of these as two separate data sets. However, we need to combine them into one data set in order to ensure consistency. For example, if we need to shuffle data, it is immensely important to have the data sets combined into one to avoid different randomly shuffled states, which will destroy the image-to-label correspondence in the data. The tf.data.Dataset.zip() function lets you do this easily:

```
data_ds = tf.data.Dataset.zip((image_ds, label_ds))
```

We've done lots of work. Let's recap:

- Read a CSV file as a tf.data.Dataset, which contains filenames and labels
- Separated file names (fname_ds) and labels (label_ds) into two separate data sets
- Loaded images from file names as a data set (images_ds) while doing some preprocessing
- Converted labels to one-hot encoded vectors
- Created a combined data set using the zip() function

Let's take a moment to see what we have created. A tf.data.Dataset behaves like a normal python iterator. This means that you can iterate through items easily using a loop (e.g., for/while) and also use functions such as next() to get items. Let's see how we can iterate data in a for loop:

```
for item in data_ds:
    print(item)
```

This will return the following:

```
>>> (<tf.Tensor: shape=(64, 64, 3), dtype=float32, numpy=
array([[[0.05490196, 0.0872549 , 0.0372549 ],
        [0.06764706, 0.09705883, 0.04411765],
        [0.06862745, 0.09901962, 0.04509804],
        ...,
        [0.3362745 , 0.25686276, 0.21274512],
        [0.26568627, 0.18823531, 0.16176471],
        [0.2627451 , 0.18627453, 0.16960786]]], dtype=float32)>, <tf.Tensor:
    shape=(10,), dtype=float32, numpy=array([1., 0., 0., 0., 0., 0., 0., 0.,
    0., 0.], dtype=float32)>)
```

As you can see, item is a tuple, the first element being the image tensor (of size $64 \times 64 \times 3$) and the second being a one-hot encoded vector (of size 10). There's some more work to be done. First, let's shuffle the data set to make sure we are not introducing any consistent ordering of data when feeding to the model:

```
data_ds = data_ds.shuffle(buffer_size= 20)
```

The `buffer_size` argument serves an important purpose. It specifies, at run time, how many elements are loaded to memory for the shuffling. In this case, the input pipeline will load 20 records to memory and randomly sample from that when you iterate the data. A larger `buffer_size` will provide better randomization but will increase the memory requirement. Next, we will look at how to create a batch of data from the data set.

Remember that we said Keras adds a batch dimension automatically when you specify either `input_shape` (Sequential API) or the `shape` (functional API) when creating a model. That's how deep networks process data: as batches of data (i.e., not individual samples). Therefore, it is important to batch data before you feed it to the model. For example, if you use a batch size of 5, you will get a 5 × 64 × 64 × 3 image tensor and a 5 × 10 labels tensor if you iterate the previous data set. With `tf.data.Dataset`, API batching data is quite straightforward:

```
data_ds = data_ds.batch(5)
```

You can print one element of this using

```
for item in data_ds:
    print(item)
    break
```

which will show

```
(
    <tf.Tensor: shape=(5, 64, 64, 3), dtype=float32, numpy=
    array(
        [
            [
                [
                    [0.5852941 , 0.5088236 , 0.39411768],
                    [0.5852941 , 0.50980395, 0.4009804 ],
                    [0.5862745 , 0.51176476, 0.40490198],
                    ...,
                    [0.82156867, 0.7294118 , 0.62352943],
                    [0.82745105, 0.74509805, 0.6392157 ],
                    [0.8284314 , 0.75098044, 0.64509803]
                ],

                [
                    [0.07647059, 0.10784315, 0.05882353],
                    [0.07843138, 0.11078432, 0.05882353],
                    [0.11862746, 0.16078432, 0.0892157 ],
                    ...,
                    [0.17745098, 0.23529413, 0.12450981],
                    [0.2019608 , 0.27549022, 0.14509805],
                    [0.22450982, 0.28921568, 0.16470589]
                ]
            ]
        ],
```

```
            dtype=float32
    )>,
    <tf.Tensor: shape=(5, 10), dtype=float32, numpy=
    array(
        [
            [0., 1., 0., 0., 0., 0., 0., 0., 0., 0.],
            [1., 0., 0., 0., 0., 0., 0., 0., 0., 0.],
            [1., 0., 0., 0., 0., 0., 0., 0., 0., 0.],
            [0., 0., 1., 0., 0., 0., 0., 0., 0., 0.],
            [0., 0., 1., 0., 0., 0., 0., 0., 0., 0.]
        ],
        dtype=float32
    )>
)
```

That's the end of this exercise. The next listing shows what the final code looks like.

Listing 3.5   `tf.data` Input pipeline for the flower images data set

```
import tensorflow as tf                          Reading the data from the CSV
import os                                         file using TensorFlow

data_dir = os.path.join('data','flower_images', 'flower_images') +
    os.path.sep
csv_ds = tf.data.experimental.CsvDataset(
    os.path.join(data_dir,'flower_labels.csv') , ("",-1), header=True
)
fname_ds = csv_ds.map(lambda a,b: a)        Separating out the filenames and
label_ds = csv_ds.map(lambda a,b: b)        integer labels to two data set objects


def get_image(file_path):

    img = tf.io.read_file(data_dir + file_path)
    # convert the compressed string to a 3D uint8 tensor
    img = tf.image.decode_png(img, channels=3)
    # Use `convert_image_dtype` to convert to floats in the [0,1] range.
    img = tf.image.convert_image_dtype(img, tf.float32)
    # resize the image to the desired size.
    return tf.image.resize(img, [64, 64])           Reading in the       Converting the
                                                     images from         integer labels
                                                     filenames           to one-hot
    image_ds = fname_ds.map(get_image)        ◄┘                         encoded labels
    label_ds = label_ds.map(lambda x: tf.one_hot(x, depth=10))   ◄┘
    data_ds = tf.data.Dataset.zip((image_ds, label_ds))

    data_ds = data_ds.shuffle(buffer_size= 20)     Shuffling and batching data,
    data_ds = data_ds.batch(5)                     preparing it for the model
```

Combining the images and labels into a single data set

Note that you won't be able to use the models we created during the Iris data set exercise, as those are fully connected networks. We need convolutional neural networks for processing image data. To get your hands dirty, there is a very simple convolutional neural network model provided in the exercise notebook 3.2.Creating_Input_Pipelines.ipynb in the Ch03-Keras-and-Data-Retrieval folder. Don't worry about the various layers and their parameters used here. We will discuss convolutional neural networks in detail in the next chapter.

```
model = Sequential([
    Conv2D(64,(5,5), activation='relu', input_shape=(64,64,3)),
    Flatten(),
    Dense(10, activation='softmax')
])

model.compile(loss='categorical_crossentropy', optimizer='adam', metrics=['acc'])
```

Using this input pipeline, you can conveniently feed data to an appropriate model using

```
model.fit(data_ds, epochs=10)
```

Once you run this command, you'll get the following:

```
Epoch 1/10
42/42 [==============================] - 1s 24ms/step - loss: 3.1604 - acc: 0.2571
Epoch 2/10
42/42 [==============================] - 1s 14ms/step - loss: 1.4359 - acc: 0.5190
...
Epoch 9/10
42/42 [==============================] - 1s 14ms/step - loss: 0.0126 - acc: 1.0000
Epoch 10/10
42/42 [==============================] - 1s 15ms/step - loss: 0.0019 - acc: 1.0000
```

With some great results achieved quickly in your very first week on the job, you walk proudly up to your boss and demonstrate the work you have done. He is quite impressed with the clarity and efficiency of the pipeline you have built. However, you begin to wonder, can I do a better job with Keras data generators?

EXERCISE 2

Imagine you have a labels data set called labels_ds (i.e., a sequence of integer labels), and there are corrupted labels with the value −1. Can you write a lambda function and use that with the tf.Dataset.map() function to remove these labels?

3.2.2   *Keras DataGenerators*

Another avenue for fetching image data is to use a data generator provided in Keras. Currently, Keras provides two data generators:

```
tf.keras.preprocessing.image.ImageDataGenerator
tf.keras.preprocessing.sequence.TimeSeriesDataGenerator
```

Though not as customizable as the tf.data API, these generators still provide a quick and easy way to feed data into a model. Let's see how we can use the ImageData-Generator to feed this data to the model. The ImageDataGenerator (http://mng .bz/lxpB) has a very long list of allowed parameters. Here, we will only focus on how we can adapt ImageDataGenerator to read the data we have.

Then, to fetch data, Keras `ImageDataGenerator` offers the `flow_from_dataframe()` function. This function is ideal for us, as we have a CSV file that contains filenames and their associated labels, which can be represented as a pandas DataFrame. Let's start with some variable definitions:

```
data_dir = os.path.join('data','flower_images', 'flower_images')
```

Next, we'll define an `ImageDataGenerator` with default parameters:

```
img_gen = ImageDataGenerator()
```

Now we can use the `flow_from_dataframe()` function:

```
labels_df = pd.read_csv(os.path.join(data_dir, 'flower_labels.csv'), header=0)
gen_iter = img_gen.flow_from_dataframe(
    dataframe=labels_df,
    directory=data_dir,
    x_col='file',
    y_col='label',
    class_mode='raw',
    batch_size=5,
    target_size=(64,64)
)
```

We first load the CSV file, which contains two columns: file (filenames) and label (integer label). With that, we call the `flow_from_dataframe()` function, along with the following important parameters:

- `dataframe`—The data frame that contains label information
- `directory`—The directory to locate images
- `x_col`—The name of the column in the data frame that contains filenames
- `y_col`—The name of the column containing the labels
- `class_mode`—The nature of the labels (since we have the raw label, `class_mode` is set to raw)

You can see what the first sample looks like by running

```
for item in gen_iter:
    print(item)
    break
```

which will output

```
(
    array([[[[ 10.,   11.,   11.],
            [ 51.,   74.,   46.],
            [ 36.,   56.,   32.],
            ...,
            [  4.,    4.,    3.],
            [ 16.,   25.,   11.],
            [ 17.,   18.,   13.]],
```

```
      ...

      [[197., 199., 174.],
       [162., 160., 137.],
       [227., 222., 207.],
       ...,
       [ 57.,  58.,  50.],
       [ 33.,  34.,  27.],
       [ 55.,  54.,  43.]]]], dtype=float32
  ),
  array([5, 6], dtype=int64)
)
```

Again, with a batch size of 5, you see a batch of images (i.e., of size 5 × 64 × 64 × 3) and a one-hot encoded batch of labels (of size 5 × 6) generated as a tuple. The full code looks like the following listing.

Listing 3.6   Keras `ImageDataGenerator` for the flower image data set

```
from tensorflow.keras.preprocessing.image import ImageDataGenerator      Importing
import os                                                                necessary
import pandas as pd                                                      modules

data_dir = os.path.join('data','flower_images', 'flower_images')

img_gen = ImageDataGenerator()        ◁    Defining the ImageDataGenerator
                                           to process the images and labels

print(os.path.join(data_dir, 'flower_labels.csv'))
labels_df = pd.read_csv(os.path.join(data_dir, 'flower_labels.csv'), header=0)

gen_iter = img_gen.flow_from_dataframe(
    dataframe=labels_df, directory=data_dir, x_col='file', y_col='label',
    class_mode='raw', batch_size=2, target_size=(64,64))
```

Defining the data directory (points to `data_dir` line)

Defining the labels by reading the CSV as a data frame

Reading the images and labels from the filenames and labels in the data frame

---

This looks even better than the previous pipeline. In just three lines of code, you have created a data pipeline. You have definitely impressed your boss with your knowledge, and you are on track for a quick promotion.

We will discuss the parameters of the `ImageDataGenerator`, as well as some of the other data retrieval functions this supports, in detail in a later chapter.

However, it is important to keep in mind that concise is not always better. Usually, concise means that what you can achieve with that method is limited. And that is true for the `tf.data` API and Keras data generators. The `tf.data` API, despite requiring a bit more work than the Keras data generator, is much more flexible (and can be made efficient) than Keras data generators.

3.2.3 *tensorflow-datasets package*

The easiest way to retrieve data in TensorFlow is to use the `tensorflow-datasets` (https://www.tensorflow.org/datasets/overview) package. However, a key limitation is that `tensorflow-datasets` only supports a set of defined data sets, unlike the `tf.data` API or Keras data generators, which can be used to feed data from a custom data set. This is a separate package and is not a part of the official TensorFlow package. And if you have set up the Python environment as instructed, you already have this package installed in your environment. If not, you can easily install this by executing

```
pip install tensorflow-datasets
```

in your virtual Python environment's terminal (e.g., Anaconda command prompt). To make sure the package is installed correctly, run the following line in your Jupyter notebook and make sure you don't get any errors:

```
import tensorflow_datasets as tfds
```

`tensorflow-datasets` provides a plethora of data sets under many different categories. You can find a comprehensive list of what's available at https://www.tensorflow.org/datasets/catalog. Table 3.2 also outlines some popular data sets available in `tensorflow-datasets`.

Table 3.2 Several data sets available in `tensorflow-datasets`

Data type	Dataset name	Task
Audio	librispeech	Speech recognition
	ljspeech	Speech recognition
Images	caltech101	Image classification
	cifar10 and cifar100	Image classification
	imagenet2012	Image classification
Text	imdb_reviews	Sentiment analysis
	tiny_shakespeare	Language modelling
	wmt14_translate	Machine translation

Let's use `tensorflow-datasets` to retrieve the cifar10 data set, a widely used image classification data set that has images (RGB images of size 32×32) belonging to 10 categories (e.g., automobile, ship, cat, horse, etc.). First, let's make sure it's available as a data set. Execute the following on your Jupyter notebook:

```
tfds.list_builders()
```

We can see that cifar10 is one of those data sets, as expected. Let's load the data set using the `tfds.load()` function. When you initially call this method, TensorFlow will first download the data set and then load it for you:

```
data, info = tfds.load("cifar10", with_info=True)
```

When it is successfully downloaded, look at what information is available in the (info) variable:

```
print(info)

>>> tfds.core.DatasetInfo(
    name='cifar10',
    version=3.0.0,
    description='The CIFAR-10 dataset consists of 60000 32x32 colour images
     in 10 classes, with 6000 images per class. There are 50000 training
     images and 10000 test images.',
    homepage='https://www.cs.toronto.edu/~kriz/cifar.html',
    features=FeaturesDict({
        'image': Image(shape=(32, 32, 3), dtype=tf.uint8),
        'label': ClassLabel(shape=(), dtype=tf.int64, num_classes=10),
    }),
    total_num_examples=60000,
    splits={
        'test': 10000,
        'train': 50000,
    },
    supervised_keys=('image', 'label'),
    citation="""@TECHREPORT{Krizhevsky09learningmultiple,
        author = {Alex Krizhevsky},
        title = {Learning multiple layers of features from tiny images},
        institution = {},
        year = {2009}
    }""",
    redistribution_info=,
)
```

It's quite informative. We now know that there are 60,000 32 × 32 color images that belong to 10 classes. The data set is split into 50,000 (training) and 10,000 (testing). Let's now look at the data variable:

```
print(data)

>>> {'test': <DatasetV1Adapter
        shapes: {image: (32, 32, 3), label: ()},
        types: {image: tf.uint8, label: tf.int64}>,
      'train': <DatasetV1Adapter
        shapes: {image: (32, 32, 3), label: ()},
        types: {image: tf.uint8, label: tf.int64}>
    }
```

We can see that it is a dictionary with keys `'train'` and `'test'`, and each key has a `tf.data.Dataset`. Luckily, we have studied how `tf.data.Dataset` works, so we can race forward to understand how to prepare data. Let's look at the training data. You can access this training data set using

```
train_ds = data["train"]
```

However, if you try to iterate this data set, you will notice that the data has not been batched. In other words, data is retrieved a single sample at a time. But, as we have said many times, we need data in batches. And the fix is simple:

```
train_ds = data["train"].batch(16)
```

Now, to see what a batch of data looks like in `train_ds`, you can execute the following:

```
for item in train_ds:
    print(item)
    break
```

This will output

```
{
    'id': <tf.Tensor: shape=(16,), dtype=string, numpy=
        array(
            [
                b'train_16399', b'train_01680', b'train_47917', b'train_17307',
                b'train_27051', b'train_48736', b'train_26263', b'train_01456',
                b'train_19135', b'train_31598', b'train_12970', b'train_04223',
                b'train_27152', b'train_49635', b'train_04093', b'train_17537'
            ],
            dtype=object
        )>,
    'image': <tf.Tensor: shape=(16, 32, 32, 3), dtype=uint8, numpy=
        array(
            [
                [
                    [
                        [143,  96,  70],
                        [141,  96,  72],
                        [135,  93,  72],
                        ...,
                        [128,  93,  60],
                        [129,  94,  61],
                        [123,  91,  58]
                    ]
                ]
            ],
            dtype=uint8
        )>,
    'label': <tf.Tensor: shape=(16,), dtype=int64, numpy=
        array(
            [7, 8, 4, 4, 6, 5, 2, 9, 6, 6, 9, 9, 3, 0, 8, 7],
```

```
                dtype=int64
        ) >
}
```

It will be a dictionary with three keys: id, image, and label. id is a unique ID for each training record. image will have a tensor of size 16 × 32 × 32 × 3, whereas label will have a tensor of size 16 (i.e., integer labels). When passing a tf.data.Dataset to a Keras model, the model expects the data set object to produce a tuple (x,y), where x would be a batch of images and y would be the labels (e.g., one-hot encoded). Therefore, we need to write one additional function that will put data into the correct format:

```
def format_data(x):
    return (x["image"], tf.one_hot(x["label"], depth=10))

train_ds = train_ds.map(format_data)
```

With that simple transformation, you can feed this data set to a model as follows:

```
model.fit(train_ds, epochs=25)
```

This is amazing work. Now you know three different ways to retrieve data for your models: the tf.data API, Keras data generators, and the tensorflow-datasets package. We will conclude our discussion about Keras APIs and different data import APIs here.

EXERCISE 3
Can you write a line of code to import the caltech101 data set? After you do that, explore this data set.

Summary

- Keras, now integrated into TensorFlow, provides several high-level model-building APIs: the Sequential API, functional API and sub-classing API. These APIs have different pros and cons.
- The Sequential API is the easiest to use but can only be used to implement simple models.
- The functional and sub-classing APIs can be difficult to use but enable developers to implement complex models.
- TensorFlow encompasses several methods for retrieving data: the tf.data API, Keras data generators, and tensorflow-datasets. tf.data.
- An API provides the most customizable way to feed data to a model but requires more work to fetch data.
- tensorflow-datasets is the easiest to use but is limited as it only supports a limited set of data sets.

Answers to exercises

Exercise 1: The functional API. As there are two output layers, we cannot use the Sequential API. There is no need to use the sub-classing API, as everything we need can be done using Keras layers.

Exercise 2: `labels_ds.map(lambda x: x if x != -1)`. You can also use the `tf.Dataset.filter()` method (i.e., `labels_ds.filter(lambda x: x != -1)`).

Exercise 3: `tfds.load("caltech101", with_info=True)`

Dipping toes in deep learning

4

This chapter covers

- Implementing and training fully connected neural networks using Keras
- Implementing and training convolutional neural networks to classify images
- Implementing and training a recurrent neural network to solve a time-series problem

In chapter 3, you learned about the different model-building APIs provided by TensorFlow and their advantages and disadvantages. You also learned about some of the options in TensorFlow to retrieve and manipulate data. In this chapter, you will learn how to leverage some of that to build deep neural networks and use them to solve problems.

Deep learning is a broad term that has many different algorithms under its wings. Deep learning algorithms come in many different flavors and colors and can be classified by many criteria: the type of data they consume (e.g., structured data, images, time-series data), depth (shallow, deep, and very deep), and so on. The main types of deep networks we are going to discuss and implement are as follows:

- Fully connected networks (FCNs)
- Convolutional neural networks (CNNs)
- Recurrent neural networks (RNNs)

Being able to comfortably implement these neural networks is a key skill to be successful in the field, whether you are a graduate student, a data scientist, or a research scientist. This knowledge directly extends to becoming skillful in implementing more complex deep neural networks that deliver state-of-the-art performance in various problem domains.

In chapter 2, we discussed FCN and various operations in CNNs, such as convolution and pooling operations. In this chapter, you will see the FCNs again, as well as a holistic implementation of CNNs showing how convolution and pooling operations coalesce to form a CNN. Finally, you will learn about a new type of model: RNNs. RNNs are typically used to solve time-series problems, where the task is to learn patterns in data over time so that, by looking at the past patterns, we can leverage them to forecast the future. We will also see how RNNs are used to solve an exciting real-world time-series problem.

4.1 Fully connected networks

You have found some precious photos of your grandmother while going through some storage boxes you found in the attic. Unfortunately, they have seen better days. Most of the photos are scratched, smudged, and even torn. You know that recently deep networks have been used to restore old photos and videos. In the hope of restoring these photos, you decide to implement an image restoration model using TensorFlow. You will first develop a model that can restore corrupted images of handwritten digits, as this data set is readily available, in order to understand the model and the training process. You believe an autoencoder model (a type of FCN) would be a great starting point. This autoencoder will have the following specifications:

- Input layer with 784 nodes
- A hidden layer with 64 nodes, having ReLU activation
- A hidden layer with 32 nodes, having ReLU activation
- A hidden layer with 64 nodes, having ReLU activation
- An output layer with 784 nodes with tanh activation

Hyperparameter optimization for deep learning

You might have noticed that when defining neural networks, we are choosing structural hyperparameters (e.g., number of units in hidden layers) somewhat arbitrarily. These values have, in fact, been chosen empirically through a few rounds of trial and error.

Typically, in machine learning, these hyperparameters are chosen using a principled approach, such as hyperparameter optimization. But hyperparameter optimization is

(continued)

an expensive process that needs to evaluate hundreds of models with different hyper-parameter choices to choose the best set of hyperparameters. This makes it very difficult to use for deep learning methods, as these methods usually deal with large, complex models and large amounts of data.

Therefore, in deep learning, you will commonly see the following trends, in order to limit the time spent on hyperparameter optimization:

- Optimizing a subset of hyperparameters to limit the exploration space (e.g., type of activation instead of number of hidden units, regularization parameters, etc.)
- Using robust optimizers, early stopping, learning rate decay, and so on, which are designed to reduce or prevent overfitting
- Using model specifications from published models that have delivered state-of-the-art performance
- Following rules of thumb such as reducing the output size as you go deeper into the network

In this chapter, we will use model architectures chosen empirically. The focus of this chapter is to show how a given architecture can be implemented using TensorFlow 2 and not to find the architectures themselves.

Let's examine the data we'll use to implement the FCN.

4.1.1   *Understanding the data*

For this scenario, we will use the MNIST digit data set, a simple data set that contains the black-and-white images of hand-written digits and the corresponding labels representing the digits. Each image has a single digit and goes from 0–9. Therefore, the data set has 10 different classes. Figure 4.1 shows several samples from the data set along with the digit it represents.

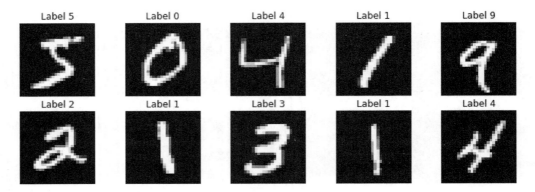

Figure 4.1   Sample digit images. Each image contains a number from 0 to 9.

In TensorFlow, you can load the MNIST data set with a single line. Loading this data set has become an integral part of various machine learning libraries (including TensorFlow) due to its extremely common usage:

```
from tensorflow.keras.datasets.mnist import load_data
(x_train, y_train), (x_test, y_test) = load_data()
```

The `load_data()` method returns two tuples: training data and testing data. Here, we will only use the training images (i.e., `x_train`) data set. As we covered earlier, this is an unsupervised task. Because of that, we will not need the labels (i.e., `y_train`) of the images to complete this task.

Better than MNIST?

It should be noted that, due to advancements in the field of computer vision over the last decade, MNIST is considered too easy, where a test accuracy of more than 92% can be achieved with a simple logistic regression model (http://mng.bz/j2l9) and a 99.84% accuracy with a state-of-the-art model (http://mng.bz/d2Pv). Furthermore, it's being overused in the computer vision community. Because of this, a new data set known as Fashion-MNIST (https://github.com/zalandoresearch/fashion-mnist) has emerged. This is a black-and-white data set containing images belonging to 10 classes. Instead of digits, it contains images of various fashion categories (e.g., T-shirt, sandal, bag, etc.), which poses a much harder problem than recognizing digits.

You can print `x_train` and `y_train` to understand those arrays a bit better using

```
print(x_train)
print('x_train has shape: {}'.format(x_train.shape))
```

This will produce

```
[[[0 0 0 ... 0 0 0]
  [0 0 0 ... 0 0 0]
  [0 0 0 ... 0 0 0]
  ...
  [0 0 0 ... 0 0 0]
  [0 0 0 ... 0 0 0]
  [0 0 0 ... 0 0 0]]

 ...

 [[0 0 0 ... 0 0 0]
  [0 0 0 ... 0 0 0]
  [0 0 0 ... 0 0 0]
  ...
  [0 0 0 ... 0 0 0]
  [0 0 0 ... 0 0 0]
  [0 0 0 ... 0 0 0]]]

x_train has shape: (60000, 28, 28)
```

And do the same for y_train:

```
print(y_train)
print('y_train has shape: {}'.format(y_train.shape))
```

This will give

```
[5 0 4 ... 5 6 8]

y_train has shape: (60000,)
```

Then we will do some basic data preprocessing. We will normalize all samples in the data set by bringing their pixel values from [0, 255] to [−1, 1]. This is done by subtracting 128 and dividing the result by 128 element-wise for all pixels. This is important because the final layer of the autoencoder has a tanh activation, which ranges between (−1, 1). Tanh is a nonlinear activation function like the sigmoid function, and for a given input, *x* is computed as follows:

$$tanh(x) = \frac{e^x - e^{-x}}{e^x + e^{-x}}$$

Therefore, we need to make sure we feed something to the model that is within the range of values that can be produced by the final layer. Also, if you look at the shape of x_train, you will see that it has a shape of (60000, 28, 28). The autoencoder takes a one-dimensional input, so we need to reshape the image to a one-dimensional vector of size 784. Both these transformations can be achieved by the following line:

```
norm_x_train = ((x_train - 128.0)/128.0).reshape([-1,784])
```

Here, reshape([-1, 784]) will unwrap the two-dimensional images (size 28 × 28) in the data set to a single dimensional vector (size 784). When reshaping, you do not need to provide all the dimensions of the reshaped tensor. If you provide the sizes of all dimensions except one, NumPy can still infer the size of the missing dimension as it knows the dimensions of the original tensor. The dimension that you want NumPy to infer is denoted by -1.

You might be wondering, "These images look crisp and clean. How on earth can we train our model to restore corrupted images?" That's a very easy fix. All we need to do is synthesize a corresponding corrupted set of images from the original set of images. For that, we will define the generate_masked_inputs(…) function:

```
import numpy as np

def generate_masked_inputs(x, p, seed=None):
    if seed:
        np.random.seed(seed)
    mask = np.random.binomial(n=1, p=p, size=x.shape).astype('float32')
    return x * mask

masked_x_train = generate_masked_inputs(norm_x_train, 0.5)
```

This function will set pixels randomly (with 50% probability) to zero. But let's inspect what we are doing in more detail. First, we will give the option to set a random seed so that we can deterministically change the generated random masks. We are creating a mask of 1s and 0s using the binomial distribution, which is the same size as norm_x_train. In simple words, the binomial distribution represents the probability of heads (1) or tails (0) if you flip a coin several times. The binomial distribution has several important parameters:

- N—Number of trials
- P—Probability of a success (1)
- Size—The number of tests (i.e., trial sets)

Here, we have x.shape tests and one trial in each with a 50% success probability. Then this mask is multiplied element-wise with the original tensor. This will result in black pixels randomly distributed over the image (figure 4.2).

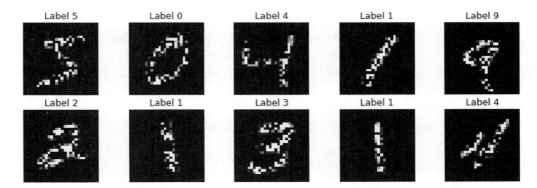

Figure 4.2 **Some of the synthetically corrupted images**

Next, let's discuss the fully connected network we'll be implementing. It's called an autoencoder model.

4.1.2 *Autoencoder model*

Both the autoencoder model and the multilayer perceptron (MLP) model (from chapter 1) are FCNs. These are called FCNs because all the input nodes are connected to all the output nodes, in every layer of the network. Autoencoders operate in a similar way to the multilayer perceptron. In other words, the computations (e.g., forward pass) you see in an autoencoder are exactly the same as in an MLP. However, the final objectives of the two are different. An MLP is trained to solve a supervised task (e.g., classifying flower species), whereas an autoencoder is trained to solve an unsupervised task (e.g., reconstructing the original image, given a corrupted/noisy image). Let's now delve into what an autoencoder actually does.

Supervised versus unsupervised learning

In supervised learning, a model is trained using a labeled data set. Each input (e.g., image/audio/movie review) has a corresponding label (e.g., object class for images, sentiment of the review) or continuous value(s) (e.g., bounding boxes of an object for images). Some examples of supervised tasks are image classification, object detection, speech recognition, and sentiment analysis.

In unsupervised learning, the models are trained using unlabeled data (e.g., images/audio/text extracted from websites without any labeling). The training process varies significantly depending on the final expected outcome. For example, autoencoders are trained to reconstruct images as a pretraining step for an image-based supervised learning task. Some examples of unsupervised tasks are image reconstruction, image generation using generative adversarial networks, text clustering, and language modeling.

Figure 4.3 depicts a simple autoencoder with two layers. An autoencoder has two phases in its functionality:

- *Compression phase*—Compresses a given image (i.e., the corrupted image) to a compressed hidden (i.e., latent) representation
- *Reconstruction phase*—Reconstructs the original image from the hidden representation

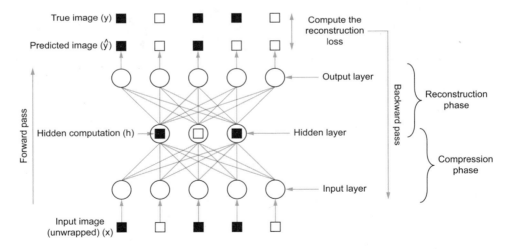

Figure 4.3   A simple autoencoder with one layer for compression and another layer for reconstruction. The black and white rectangles in the input image are the pixels present in the image.

In the compression phase, a compressed hidden representation is computed as follows

$$h_1 = ReLU(xW_1 + b_1)$$

where W_1, b_1 are the weights and biases of the first compression layer and h_1 is the final hidden representation of the layer.

Similarly, we compute the output of the reconstruction layers:

$$\hat{y} = ReLU(h_1 \ W_2 + b_2)$$

This is known as the forward pass, as you are going from the input to the output. Then you compute a loss (e.g., mean squared error [MSE]) between the expected output (i.e., target) and the prediction. For example, mean squared error for a single image is computed as

$$MSE = \sum_{j=1}^{D} (y_j - \hat{y}_j)^2$$

where D is the dimensionality of the data (784 in our example), y_j is the jth pixel in our image, and $(\hat{y}_j)$ is the jth pixel of the predicted image. We compute this loss for each batch of images and optimize the model parameters to minimize the computed loss. This is known as the backward pass.

You can have an arbitrary number of compression and reconstruction layers. In our assignment, we need to have two compression layers and two reconstruction layers (see the next listing).

Listing 4.1 The denoising autoencoder model

```
from tensorflow.keras import layers, models

autoencoder = models.Sequential(
    [layers.Dense(64, activation='relu', input_shape=(784,)),
    layers.Dense(32, activation='relu'),
    layers.Dense(64, activation='relu'),
    layers.Dense(784, activation='tanh')]
)
autoencoder.compile(loss='mse', optimizer='adam')
autoencoder.summary()
```

Defining four Dense layers, three with ReLU activation and one with tanh activation

Compiling the model with a loss function and an optimizer

Printing the summary

Let's go over what we did in more detail. The first thing you should notice is that we used the Keras Sequential API for this task. This makes sense as this is a very simple deep learning model. Next, we added four Dense layers. The first Dense layer takes an input with 784 features and produces a 64-elements-long vector. Then the second layer takes the 64-elements-long vector and produces a 32-elements-long vector. The third dense layer takes the 32-elements-long vector and produces a 64-elements-long vector, passing it on to the final layer, which produces a 784-elements-long vector (i.e., size of the input). The first three layers have ReLU activation, and the last layer has a tanh activation, as the last layer needs to produce values between (–1, 1). Let's remind ourselves how the ReLU and tanh activations are computed:

$$ReLU(x) = \max(0, x)$$

$$tanh(x) = \frac{e^x - e^{-x}}{e^x + e^{-x}}$$

Finally, we compile the model using the mean squared error as the `loss` function and `adam` as the optimizer. The model we just described has the specifications we defined at the beginning of the section. With the model defined, you can now train the model. You will train the model for 10 epochs with batches of size 64:

```
history = autoencoder.fit(masked_x_train, norm_x_train, batch_size=64, epochs=10)
```

The masked inputs we generated become the input, and the original images will be the ground truth. When you train the model, you will see a loss that goes down over time:

```
Train on 60000 samples
Epoch 1/10
60000/60000 [==============================] - 4s 72us/sample - loss: 0.1496
Epoch 2/10
60000/60000 [==============================] - 4s 67us/sample - loss: 0.0992
Epoch 3/10
...
60000/60000 [==============================] - 4s 66us/sample - loss: 0.0821
Epoch 8/10
60000/60000 [==============================] - 4s 66us/sample - loss: 0.0801
Epoch 9/10
60000/60000 [==============================] - 4s 67us/sample - loss: 0.0787
Epoch 10/10
60000/60000 [==============================] - 4s 67us/sample - loss: 0.0777
```

It seems the error (i.e., `loss` value) has gone down from approximately 0.15 to roughly 0.078. This is a strong indication that the model is learning to reconstruct images. You can get similar results by setting the seed using the `fix_random_seed(...)` function we used in chapter 2 (provided in the notebook). Note that for this task we cannot define a metric like accuracy, as it is an unsupervised task.

Denoising autoencoders

Normally an autoencoder maps a given input to a small latent space and then back to the original input space to reconstruct the original images. However, here we use the autoencoder for a special purpose: to restore original images or denoise original images. Such autoencoders are known as *denoising*. Read more about denoising auto-encoders at http://mng.bz/WxyX.

Let's now see what the trained model can do! It should now be able to decently restore an image of a corrupted digit. And to make things interesting, let's make sure we generate a mask that the training data has not seen:

```
x_train_sample = x_train[:10]
y_train_sample = y_train[:10]

masked_x_train_sample = generate_masked_inputs(x_train_sample, 0.5, seed=2048)
norm_masked_x = ((x_train - 128.0)/128.0).reshape(-1, 784)

y_pred = autoencoder.predict(norm_masked_x)
```

Here, we will be using the first 10 images in the data set to test out the model we just trained. However, we are making sure that the random mask is different by changing the seed. You can display some information about y_pred using

```
print(y_pred)
print('y_pred has shape: {}'.format(y_pred.shape))
```

which will give

```
[[-0.99999976 -0.99999976 -0.99999976 ... -0.99999976 -0.99999976
  -0.99999976]
 [-0.99999976 -0.99999976 -0.99999976 ... -0.99999976 -0.99999976
  -0.99999976]
 [-0.99999976 -0.99999976 -0.99999976 ... -0.99999976 -0.99999976
  -0.99999976]
 ...
 [-0.99999976 -0.99999976 -0.9999996  ... -0.99999946 -0.99999976
  -0.99999976]
 [-0.99999976 -0.99999976 -0.99999976 ... -0.99999976 -0.99999976
  -0.99999976]
 [-0.99999976 -0.99999976 -0.99999976 ... -0.99999976 -0.99999976
  -0.99999976]]

y_pred has shape: (60000, 784)
```

Finally, you can visualize what the model does by plotting the images (the code provided in the notebook). Figure 4.4 illustrates the corrupted images (top row) and the outputs of the model (bottom row). Though you are not yet restoring real-world photos of your grandmother, this a great start, as you now know the approach to follow.

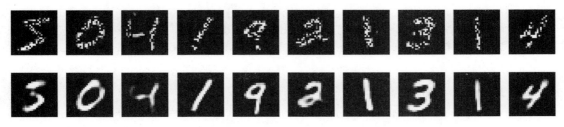

Figure 4.4 Images restored by the model. It seems our model is doing a good job.

You might be wondering, "What do autoencoders help you to achieve in general?" Autoencoders are a great tool for learning unsupervised features from unlabeled data, which is handy when solving more interesting downstream tasks like image classification. When autoencoders are trained on an unsupervised task, they learn useful features for other tasks (e.g., image classification). Therefore, training an autoencoder model to classify images will get you to a well-performing model faster and with less labeled data than training a model from scratch. As you are probably aware, there's much more unlabeled data in the world than labeled data, as labeling usually requires human intervention, which is time-consuming and expensive. Another use of autoencoders is that the hidden representation it produces can be used as a low-dimensional proxy to cluster the images.

In this section, you learned about the autoencoder model, which is a type of FCN and is used to reconstruct/restore damaged images in an unsupervised manner. This is a great way to leverage copious amounts of unlabeled data to pretrain models, which becomes useful in more downstream interesting tasks (e.g., image classification). You first learned the architecture and then how to implement an autoencoder model with the Keras Sequential API. Finally, you trained the model on a hand-written image data set (MNIST) to reconstruct the images in the data set. During the training process, to ensure the model was learning, you monitored the loss to make sure it decreased over time. Finally, you used the model to predict restorations of corrupted images and ensured the model was performing well.

In the next section, we will discuss a different type of deep learning network that has revolutionized the field of computer vision: CNNs.

EXERCISE 1

Implement an autoencoder model that takes in a 512-elements-long vector. The network has a 32-node layer, a 16-node layer, and finally an output layer. In total, there are three layers. All these layers have the sigmoid activation.

4.2   *Convolutional neural networks*

You have been working at a startup as a data scientist trying to model traffic congestion on the road. One important model in the company's solution is building a model to predict whether a vehicle is present, given a patch or image, as a part of a larger plan. You plan to develop a model first on the cifar-10 data set and see how well it classifies vehicles. This is a great idea, as it will give a rough approximation of the feasibility of the idea while spending minimal time and money on labeling custom data. If we can achieve good accuracy on this data set, that is a very positive sign. You have learned that CNNs are great for computer vision tasks. So, you are planning to implement a CNN.

4.2.1   *Understanding the data*

We will use is the cifar-10 data set. We briefly looked at this data set in the previous chapter, and it is a great cornerstone for this task. It has various vehicles (e.g., automobile, truck) and other objects (e.g., dog, cat) as classes. Figure 4.5 illustrates some of the classes and corresponding samples for them.

Figure 4.5   Sample images from cifar-10 data set along with their labels

The data set consists of 50,000 training instances and 10,000 testing instances. Each instance is a 32×32 RGB image. There are 10 different classes of objects in this data set.

Let's first load the data by executing the following line:

```
import tensorflow_datasets as tfds
data = tfds.load('cifar10')
```

`print(data)` will yield

```
{'test': <PrefetchDataset
   shapes: {id: (), image: (32, 32, 3), label: ()},
   types: {id: tf.string, image: tf.uint8, label: tf.int64}>, 'train':
      <PrefetchDataset
   shapes: {id: (), image: (32, 32, 3), label: ()},
   types: {id: tf.string, image: tf.uint8, label: tf.int64}>}
```

If you explore the data a bit, you will realize that

- Images are provided with the data type as unsigned eight-bit integers.
- Labels are provided as integer labels (i.e., not one-hot encoded).

Therefore, we will write a very simple function to convert the images to data type `float32` (to make the data type consistent with the model parameters) and labels to one-hot encoded vectors:

```
import tensorflow as tf

def format_data(x, depth):
    return (tf.cast(x["image"], 'float32'), tf.one_hot(x["label"], depth=depth))
```

Finally, we will create a batched data set by applying this function to all the training data:

```
tr_data = data["train"].map(lambda x: format_data(x, depth=10)).batch(32)
```

We can again look at the data with

```
for d in tr_data.take(1):
    print(d)
```

which will produce

```
(
    <tf.Tensor: shape=(32, 32, 32, 3), dtype=float32, numpy=
    array(
        [[[[143.,   96.,   70.],
           [141.,   96.,   72.],
           [135.,   93.,   72.],
           ...,
           [ 52.,   34.,   31.],
           [ 91.,   74.,   59.],
           [126.,  110.,   88.]]]],
        dtype=float32)
    >,
    <tf.Tensor: shape=(32, 10), dtype=float32, numpy=
    array(
        [[0., 0., 0., 0., 0., 0., 0., 1., 0., 0.],
         [0., 0., 0., 0., 0., 0., 0., 0., 1., 0.],
         [0., 0., 0., 0., 1., 0., 0., 0., 0., 0.],
         ...
         [0., 0., 0., 0., 1., 0., 0., 0., 0., 0.],
         [0., 0., 1., 0., 0., 0., 0., 0., 0., 0.]],
        dtype=float32)
    >
)
```

Now our data is ready to be fed to a model.

4.2.2 *Implementing the network*

To classify these images, we will employ a CNN. CNNs have gained a stellar reputation for solving computer vision tasks and are a popular choice for image-related tasks for two main reasons:

- CNNs process the images while preserving their spatial information (i.e., while keeping the height and width dimensions as is), while a fully connected layer will need to unwrap the height and width dimensions to a single dimension, losing precious locality information.
- Unlike a fully connected layer where every input is connected to every output, the convolution operation shifts a smaller kernel over the entire image, demanding only a handful of parameters in a layer, making CNNs very parameter efficient.

A CNN consists of a set of interleaved convolution and pooling layers followed by several fully connected layers. This means there are three main types of layers in a CNN:

- Convolution layers
- Pooling layers
- Fully connected layers

A convolution layer consists of several filters (i.e., convolution kernels) that are convolved over the image to produce a *feature map*. The feature map is a representation of how strongly a given filter is present in the image. For example, if the filter represents a vertical edge, the feature map represents where (and how strongly) in the image vertical edges are present. As another example, think of a neural network that is trained to identify faces. A filter might represent the shape of an eye and activate the corresponding area of the output highly when an eye is present in a given image (figure 4.6). We will discuss the convolution operation in more detail later in the chapter.

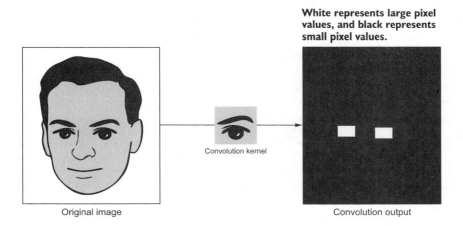

Figure 4.6 **The result of a convolution operation at a very abstract level. If we have an image of a human face and a convolution kernel that represents the shape/color of an eye, then the convolution result can be roughly thought of as a heatmap of where that feature (i.e., the eyes) are present in the image.**

Another important characteristic of the convolution layers is that the deeper you go in the network (i.e., further away from the input), the more high-level features the layers learn. Going back to our face recognition example, the lower layers might learn various edges present; the next layer, the shape of an eye, ear, and a nose; the next layer, how two eyes are positioned, the alignment of the nose and mouth; and so on (figure 4.7).

Next, the pooling layer takes in feature maps generated by a convolution layer and reduces their height and width dimensions. Why is it useful to reduce the height and width of the feature maps? It helps the model be translation invariant during the

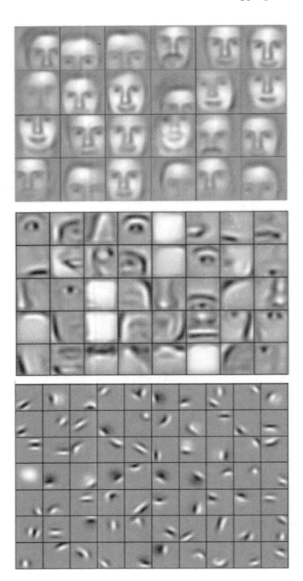

Figure 4.7   Features learned by a convolutional neural network. The lower layers (closest to the input) are learning edges/lines, whereas the upper layers (furthest from input) are learning higher-level features. (Source: http://mng.bz/8MPg)

machine learning task. For instance, if the task is image classification, even if the objects appear several pixels offset from what was seen during training, the network is still able to identify the object.

Finally, to get the final probability distribution, you have several fully connected layers. But you might have suspected an issue we face here. A convolution/pooling layer produces a three-dimensional output (i.e., height, width, and channel dimensions). But a fully connected layer accepts a one-dimensional input. How do we connect the three-dimensional output of a convolution/pooling layer to a one-dimensional fully connected layer? There's a simple answer to this problem. You squash all three dimensions into a single dimension. In other words, it is analogous to unwrapping a two-dimensional RGB image to a one-dimensional vector. This provides the fully connected layer with a one-dimensional input. Finally, a softmax activation is applied to the outputs of the final fully connected layer (i.e., scores of the network) to obtain a valid probability distribution. Figure 4.8 depicts a simple CNN.

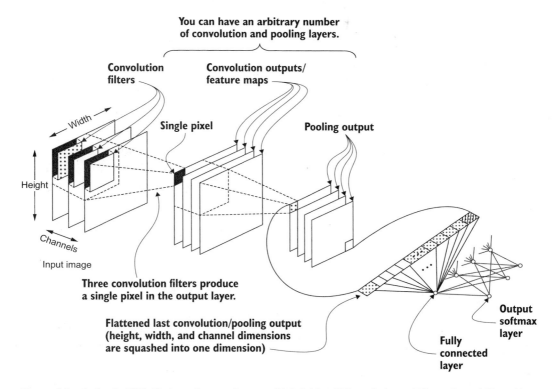

Figure 4.8   A simple CNN. First, we have an image with height, width, and channel dimensions, followed by a convolution and pooling layer. Finally, the last convolution/pooling layer output is flattened and fed to a set of fully connected layers.

With a good understanding of what a CNN comprises, we will create the following CNN using the Keras Sequential API. However, if you run this code, you will get an error. We will investigate and fix this error in the coming sections (see the next listing).

Listing 4.2   Defining a CNN with the Keras Sequential API

```
from tensorflow.keras import layers, models
import tensorflow.keras.backend as K


K.clear_session()                ◁──────
```
Clearing any existing Keras states (e.g., models) to start fresh

Defining a convolution layer; it takes parameters like filters, kernel_size, strides, activation, and padding.

```
cnn = models.Sequential(
    [layers.Conv2D(
        filters=16, kernel_size= (9,9), strides=(2,2), activation='relu',
            padding='valid', input_shape=(32,32,3)
    ),
    layers.Conv2D(
        filters=32, kernel_size= (7,7), activation='relu', padding='valid'
    ),
    layers.Conv2D(
        filters=64, kernel_size= (7,7), activation='relu', padding='valid'
    ),
    layers.Flatten(),
    layers.Dense(64, activation='relu'),
    layers.Dense(10, activation='softmax')]
)
```

Creating an intermediate fully connected layer

Final prediction layer

Before feeding the data to a fully connected layer, we need to flatten the output of the last convolution layer.

You can see that the network consists of three convolution layers and two fully connected layers. Keras provides all the layers you need to implement a CNN. As you can see, it can be done in a single line of code for our image classification network. Let's explore what is happening in this model in more detail. The first layer is specified as follows:

```
layers.Conv2D(filters=16,kernel_size=(9,9), strides=(2,2), activation='relu',
    input_shape=(32,32,3))
```

> **Hyperparameters of convolutional neural networks**
>
> In the CNN network from listing 4.2, filters, kernel_size, and strides of the Conv2D layers, the number of hidden units in the Dense layers (except the output layer) and the activation function are known as the hyperparameters of the model. Ideally, these hyperparameters need to be selected using a hyperparameter optimization algorithm, which would run hundreds (if not thousands) of models with different hyperparameter values and choose the one that maximizes a predefined metric (e.g., model accuracy). However, here we have chosen the values for these hyperparameters empirically and will not be using hyperparameter optimization.

First, the Conv2D layer is the Keras implementation of the 2D convolution operation. As you'll remember from chapter 1, we achieved this using the tf.nn.convolution operation. The Conv2D layer executes the same functionality under the hood. However, it hides some of the complexities met when using the tf.nn.convolution operation directly (e.g., defining the layer parameters explicitly) There are several important arguments you need to provide to this layer:

- filters—The number of output channels that will be present in the output.
- kernel_size—The convolution window size on the height and width dimensions, in that order.

- strides—Represents how many pixels are skipped on height and with dimensions (in that order) every time the convolution window shifts on the input. Having a higher value here helps to reduce the size of the convolution output quickly as you go deeper.
- activation—The nonlinear activation of the convolution layer.
- padding—Type of padding used for the border while performing the convolution operation. Padding borders gives more control over the size of the output.
- input_shape—A three-dimensional tuple representing the input size on (height, width, channels) dimensions, in that order. Remember that Keras adds an unspecified batch dimension automatically when specifying the shape of the data using this argument.

Let's now go over the convolution function and its parameters in more detail. We already know that the convolution operation shifts a convolution window (i.e., a kernel) over the image, while taking the sum of an element-wise product between the kernel and the portion of the image that overlaps the kernel at a given time (figure 4.9). Mathematically, the convolution operation can be stated as follows

$$y_{(i,j)} = \sum_{k=0}^{m-1} \sum_{l=0}^{m-1} f_{(k,l)} \times x_{(i+k,j+l)}$$

where x is a $n \times n$ input matrix, f is a $m \times m$ filter, and y is the output.

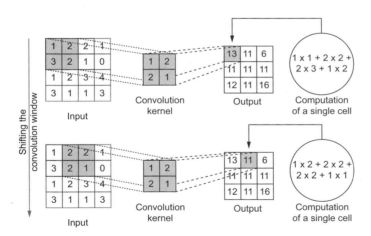

Figure 4.9   The computations that happen in the convolution operation while shifting the window

Apart from the computations that take place during the convolution operation, there are four important hyperparameters that affect the size and values produced when using the Conv2D layer in Keras:

- Number of filters
- Kernel height and width
- Kernel stride (height and width)
- Type of padding

The first aspect we will discuss is the number of filters in the layer. Typically, a single convolution layer has multiple filters. For example, think of a neural network that is trained to identify faces. One of the layers in the network might learn to identify the shape of an eye, shape of a nose, and so on. Each of these features might be learned by a single filter in the layer.

The convolution layer takes an image, which is a three-dimensional tensor of some height, width, and channels. For example, if the image is an RGB image, there will be three channels. If the image is a grayscale image, the number of channels will be one. Then, convolving this tensor with n number of filters will result in a three-dimensional output of some height, width, and n channels. This is shown in figure 4.10. When used in a CNN, the filters are the parameters of a convolution layer. These filters are initialized randomly, and over time they evolve to become meaningful features that help solve the task at hand.

As we have said before, deep neural networks process data in batches. CNNs are no exception. You can see that we have set the input_shape parameter to (32, 32, 3), where an unspecified batch dimension is automatically added, making it (None, 32, 32, 3). The unspecified dimension is denoted by None, and it means that the model can take any arbitrary number of items on that dimension. This means that a batch of data can have 3, 4, 100, or any number of images (as the computer memory permits) at run time while feeding data to the model. Therefore, the input/output of a Conv2D layer is, in fact, a four-dimensional tensor with a batch, height, width, and channel dimension. Then the filters will be another four-dimensional tensor with a kernel height, width, incoming channel, and outgoing channel dimension. Table 4.1 summarizes this information.

Table 4.1   The dimensionality of the input, filters, and the output of a Conv2D layer

	Dimensionality	Example
Input	[batch size, height, width, in channels]	[32, 64, 64, 3] (i.e., a batch of 32, 64 × 64 RGB images)
Convolution filters	[height, width, in channels, out channels]	[5, 5, 3, 16] (i.e., 16 convolution filters of size 5 × 5 with 3 incoming channels)
Output	[batch size, height, width, out channels]	[32, 64, 64, 16] (i.e., a batch of 32, 64 × 64 × 16 tensors)

Figure 4.10 depicts how the inputs and outputs look in a convolution layer.

Next, kernel height and width are the size of the filter on height and width dimensions. Figure 4.11 depicts how different kernel sizes lead to different outputs. Typically,

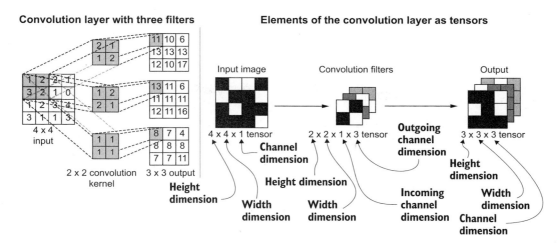

Figure 4.10   A computation of a convolution layer with multiple filters (randomly initialized). We left the batch dimension of the tensor representation to avoid clutter.

when implementing CNNs, we keep kernel height and width equal. With that, we will refer to both the height and width dimensions of the kernel generally as the *kernel size*. We can compute the output size as a function of the kernel and input size as follows:

$$size(y) = size(x) - size(f) + 1$$

For example, if the image is a 7×7 matrix and the filter is a 3×3 matrix, then the output will be a $(7 - 3 + 1, 7 - 3 + 1) = 5 \times 5$ matrix. Or, if the image is a 7×7 matrix and the filter is a 5×5 matrix, then the output will be a 3×3 matrix.

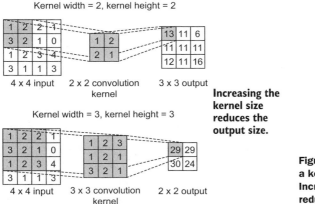

Increasing the kernel size reduces the output size.

Figure 4.11   Convolution operation with a kernel size of 2 and kernel size of 3. Increasing the kernel size leads to a reduced output size.

From a modeling perspective, increasing the kernel size (i.e., filter size) translates to an increased number of parameters. Typically, you should try to reduce the number of parameters in your network and target smaller-sized kernels. Having small kernel sizes encourages the model to learn more robust features with a small number of parameters, leading to better generalization of the model.

The next important parameter is the stride. Just like the kernel size, the stride has two components: height and width. Intuitively, the stride defines how many pixels/values you skip while shifting the convolution operation. Figure 4.12 illustrates the difference between having stride = 1 (i.e., no stride versus stride = 2). As before, we can specify the output size as a function of the input size, kernel size, and stride:

$$size(y) = \left\lceil \frac{size(x) - size(f)}{s} \right\rceil + 1$$

From a modeling perspective, striding is beneficial, as it helps you to control the amount of reduction you need in the output. You might have noticed that, even without striding, you still get an automatic dimensionality reduction during convolution. However, when using striding, you can control the reduction you want to gain without affecting the kernel size.

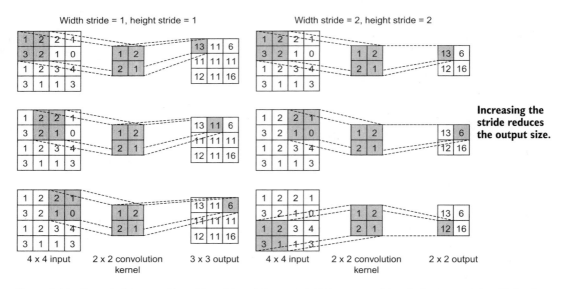

Figure 4.12   Convolution operation with stride = 1 (i.e., no stride) versus stride = 2. An increased stride leads to a smaller output.

Finally, padding decides what happens near the borders of the image. As you have already seen, when you convolve an image, you don't get a same-sized output as the input. For example, if you have a 4 × 4 matrix and a 2 × 2 kernel, you get a 3 × 3 output (i.e., following the equation $size(y) = size(x) - size(f) + 1$ we saw earlier, where x is the input size and f is the filter size). This automatic dimensionality reduction creates an issue when creating deep models. Specifically, it limits the number of layers you can have, as at some point the input will become a 1 × 1 pixel due to this automatic dimension reduction. Consequentially, this will create a very narrow bottleneck in passing information to the fully connected layers that follow, causing massive information loss.

You can use padding to alleviate this issue. With padding, you create an imaginary border of zeros around the image, such that you get the same-sized output as the input. More specifically, you append a border that is a *size(f)* – 1–thick border of zeros in order to get an output of same size as the input. For example, if you have an input of size 4 × 4 and a kernel of size 2 × 2, then you would apply a border of size 2 – 1 = 1 vertically and horizontally. This means that the kernel is essentially processing a 5 × 5 input (i.e., (4 + 1) × (4 + 1)–sized input), resulting in a 4 × 4–sized output. This is called *same padding*. Note that it does not always have to be zeros that you are padding. Though currently not supported in Keras, there are different padding strategies (some examples are available here: https://www.tensorflow.org/api_docs/python/tf/pad), such as padding with

- A constant value
- A reflection of the input
- The nearest value

If you don't apply padding, that is called *valid padding*. Not applying padding leads to the standard convolution operation we discussed earlier. The differences in padding are shown in figure 4.13.

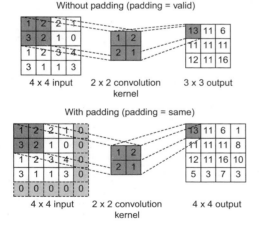

Figure 4.13 Valid versus same padding. Valid padding leads to a reduced output size, whereas same padding results in an output with equal dimensions to the input.

With that, we conclude our discussion about various hyperparameters of the `Conv2D` layer. Now let's circle back to the network we implemented. Unfortunately for you, if you try to run the code we discussed, you will be presented with a somewhat cryptic error like this:

```
-------------------------------------------------------------------
...

InvalidArgumentError: Negative dimension size caused by subtracting 7 from 6 for
'conv2d_2/Conv2D' (op: 'Conv2D') with input shapes: [?,6,6,32], [7,7,32,64].
```

What have we done wrong here? It seems TensorFlow is complaining about a negative dimension size while trying to compute the output of a convolution layer. Since we have learned all about how to compute the size of the output under various circumstances (e.g., with stride, with padding, etc.), we will compute the final output of the convolution layers. We have the following layers:

```
layers.Conv2D(16,(9,9), strides=(2,2), activation='relu', padding='valid',
input_shape=(32,32,3))
```

We are starting with an input of size $32 \times 32 \times 3$. Then, after the convolution operation, which has 16 filters, a kernel size of 9, and stride 2, we get an output of size (height and width)

```
(⌊(32 - 9) / 2⌋ + 1 = 12
```

Here, we focus only on the height and width dimensions. The next layer has 32 filters, a kernel size of 7, and no stride:

```
        layers.Conv2D(32, (7,7), activation='relu', padding='valid')
```

This layer produces an output of size

```
12 - 7 + 1 = 6
```

The final convolution layer has 64 filters, a kernel size of 7, and no stride

```
        layers.Conv2D(64, (7,7), activation='relu', padding='valid'),
```

which will produce an output of size

$$6 - 7 + 1 = 0$$

We figured it out! With our chosen configuration, our CNN is producing an invalid zero-sized output. The term *negative dimension* in the error refers to an output with invalid dimensions (i.e., less than one) being produced. The output always needs to be greater than or equal to 1.

Let's correct this network by making sure the outputs will never have negative dimensions. Furthermore, we will introduce several interleaved max-pooling layers to the CNN, which helps the network to learn translation-invariant features (see the next listing).

Listing 4.3 The corrected CNN model that has positive dimensions

The first max-pooling layer. The output size reduces from 16 to 8.

The second convolution layer. The output size stays the same as there is no stride.

The first convolution layer. The output size reduces from 32 to 16.

```
from tensorflow.keras import layers, models
import tensorflow.keras.backend as K

K.clear_session()

cnn = models.Sequential([
    layers.Conv2D(
        filters=16,kernel_size=(3,3), strides=(2,2), activation='relu',
        padding='same', input_shape=(32,32,3)),
    layers.MaxPool2D(pool_size=(2,2), strides=(2,2), padding='same'),
    layers.Conv2D(32, (3,3), activation='relu', padding='same'),
    layers.MaxPool2D(pool_size=(2,2), strides=(2,2), padding='same'),
    layers.Flatten(),
    layers.Dense(64, activation='relu'),
    layers.Dense(32, activation='relu'),
    layers.Dense(10, activation='softmax')]
)
```

The two intermediate Dense layers with ReLU activation

Squashing the height, width, and channel dimensions to a single dimension

The final output layer with softmax activation

The second max-pooling layer. The output size reduces from 8 to 4.

Max-pooling is provided by the `tensorflow.keras.layers.MaxPool2D` layer. The hyperparameters of this layer are very similar to `tensorflow.keras.layers.Conv2D`:

- `pool_size`—This is analogous to the kernel size parameter of the `Conv2D` layer. It is a tuple representing (window height, window width), in that order.
- `Strides`—This is analogous to the strides parameter of the `Conv2D` layer. It is a tuple representing (height stride, width stride), in that order.
- `Padding`—Padding can be same or valid and has the same effect as it has in the `Conv2D` layer.

Let's analyze the changes we made to our CNN:

- We used `padding='same'` for all the `Conv2D` and `MaxPool2D` layers, meaning that there won't be any automatic reduction of the output size. This eliminates the risk of mistakenly going into negative dimensions.
- We used stride parameters to control the reduction of the output size as we go deeper into the model.

You can follow the output sizes in listing 4.1 and make sure that the output will never be less than or equal to zero for the input images we have.

After the `Conv2D` and `MaxPool2D` layers, we have to have at least one `Dense` layer, as we are solving an image classification task. To get the final prediction probabilities (i.e., the probabilities of a given input belonging to the output classes), a `Dense` layer is essential. But before having a `Dense` layer, we need to flatten our four-dimensional output (i.e., [batch, height, width, channel] shaped) of the `Conv2D` or `MaxPool2D` layers to a two-dimensional input (i.e., [batch, features] shaped) to the Dense layer. That is, except for the batch dimension, everything else gets squashed to a single dimension. For this, we use the `tensorflow.keras.layers.Flatten` layer provided by Keras. For example, if the output of our last `Conv2D` layer was [None, 4, 4, 64], then the `Flatten` layer will flatten this output to a [None, 1024]–sized tensor. Finally, we add three `Dense` layers, where the first two dense layers have 64 and 32 output nodes and an activation of type ReLU. The final `Dense` layer will have 10 nodes (1 for each class) and a softmax activation.

Performance bottleneck of CNNs

Typically, in a CNN the very first `Dense` layer after the convolution/pooling layers is considered a *performance bottleneck*. This is because this layer will usually contain a large proportion of the parameters of the network. Assume you have a CNN where the last pooling layer produces an 8 × 8 × 256 output followed by a `Dense` layer with 1,024 nodes. This `Dense` layer would contain 16,778,240 (more than 16 million) parameters. If you don't pay attention to the first `Dense` layer of the CNN, you can easily run into out-of-memory errors while running the model.

It's time to test our first CNN on the data. But before that we have to compile the model with appropriate parameters. Here, we will monitor the training accuracy of the mode:

```
cnn.compile(loss='categorical_crossentropy', optimizer='adam', metrics=['acc'])
```

Finally, you can use the training data we created earlier and train the model on the data by calling

```
history = cnn.fit(tr_data,epochs=25)
```

You should get the following output:

```
Epoch 1/25
1563/1563 [==============================] - 23s 15ms/step - loss: 2.0566 - acc: 0.3195
Epoch 2/25
1563/1563 [==============================] - 13s 8ms/step - loss: 1.4664 - acc: 0.4699
...
Epoch 24/25
1563/1563 [==============================] - 13s 8ms/step - loss: 0.8070 - acc: 0.7174
Epoch 25/25
1563/1563 [==============================] - 13s 8ms/step - loss: 0.7874 - acc: 0.7227
```

It seems we are getting good at training accuracies (denoted by `acc`) and creating a steady reduction of the training loss (denoted by `loss`) for the task of identifying vehicles (around 72.2% accuracy). But we can go for far better accuracies by employing various techniques, as you will see in later chapters. This is very promising news for the team, as this means they can continue working on their full solution.

In this section, we looked at CNNs. CNNs work extremely well, especially in computer vision problems. In this instance, we looked at using a CNN to classify images to various classes (e.g., animals, vehicles, etc.) as a feasibility study for a model's ability to detect vehicles. We looked at the technical aspects of the CNN in detail, while scrutinizing various operations like convolution and pooling, as well as the impact of the parameters associated with these operations (e.g., window size, stride, padding). We saw that if we do not pay attention to how the output changes while using these parameters, it can lead to errors in our code. Next, we went on to fix the error and train the model on the data set. Finally, we saw that the model showed promising results, quickly reaching for a training accuracy above 70%. Next, we will discuss RNNs, which are heavily invested in solving time-series problems.

EXERCISE 2

Consider the following network:

```
from tensorflow.keras import layers, models

models.Sequential([
layers.Conv2D(
        filters=16, kernel_size=(5,5), padding='valid', input_shape=(64,64,3)
),
layers.MaxPool2D(pool_size=(3,3), strides=(2,2), padding='same'),
layers.Conv2D(32, (3,3), activation='relu', padding='same'),
layers.MaxPool2D(pool_size=(2,2), strides=(2,2), padding='same'),
layers.Conv2D(32, (3,3), strides=(2,2), activation='relu', padding='same')
])
```

What is the final output size (ignoring the batch dimension)?

4.3   *One step at a time: Recurrent neural networks (RNNs)*

You are working for a machine learning consultant for the National Bureau of Meteorology. They have data for CO2 concentration over the last three decades. You have been tasked with developing a machine learning model that predicts CO2 concentration for the next five years. You are planning to implement a simple RNN that takes a sequence of CO2 concentrations (in this case, the values from the last 12 months) and predicts the next in the sequence.

It can be clearly seen that what we have in front of us is a time series problem. This is quite different from the tasks we have been solving so far. In previous tasks, one input did not depend on the previous inputs. In other words, you considered each input to be *i.i.d* (independent and identically distributed) inputs. However, in this problem, that is not the case. The CO2 concentration today will depend on what the CO2 concentration was over the last several months.

Typical feed-forward networks (i.e., fully connected networks, CNNs) cannot learn from time series data without special adaptations. However, there is a special type of neural network that is designed to learn from time series data. These networks are generally known as RNNs. RNNs not only use the current input to make a prediction, but also use the *memory* of the network from past time steps, at a given time step.

How a feed-forward neural network operates

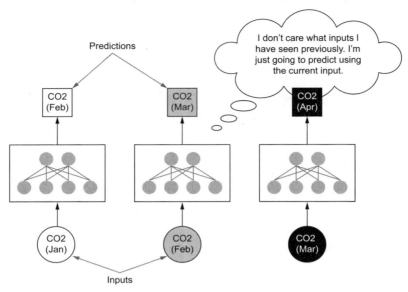

How a recurrent neural network operates

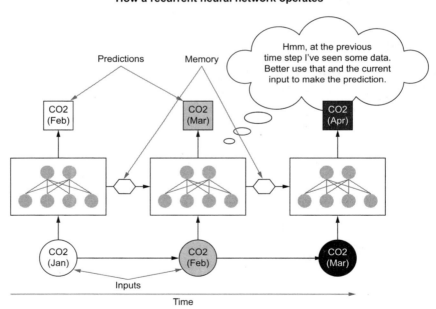

Figure 4.14   The operational difference between a feed-forward network and an RNN in terms of a CO2 concentration-level prediction task

Figure 4.14 depicts how a feed-forward network and an RNN differ in predicting CO2 concentration over the months. As you can see, if you use a feed-forward network, it has to predict the CO2 level for the next month based *only* on the previous month, whereas an RNN looks at all the previous months.

4.3.1 Understanding the data

The data set is very simple (downloaded from https://datahub.io/core/co2-ppm/r/co2-mm-gl.csv). Each datapoint has a date (YYYY-MM-DD format) and a floating-point value representing the CO2 concentration in CSV format. The data is provided to us as a CSV file. Let's download the file as follows:

```
import requests
import os

def download_data():
    """ This function downloads the CO2 data from
    https://datahub.io/core/co2-ppm/r/co2-mm-gl.csv
    if the file doesn't already exist
    """
    save_dir = "data"
    save_path = os.path.join(save_dir, 'co2-mm-gl.csv')

    # Create directories if they are not there
    if not os.path.exists(save_dir):
        os.makedirs(save_dir)

    # Download the data and save
    if not os.path.exists(save_path):
        url = "https://datahub.io/core/co2-ppm/r/co2-mm-gl.csv"
        r = requests.get(url)
        with open(save_path, 'wb') as f:
            f.write(r.content)
    else:
        print("co2-mm-gl.csv already exists. Not downloading.")
    return save_path

# Downloading the data
save_path = download_data()
```

We can easily load this data set using pandas:

```
import pandas as pd
data = pd.read_csv(save_path)
```

Now we can see what the data looks like, using the head() operation, which will provide the first few entries in the data frame:

```
data.head()
```

This will give something like figure 4.15.

	Date	Decimal Date	Average	Trend
0	1980-01-01	1980.042	338.45	337.82
1	1980-02-01	1980.125	339.14	338.10
2	1980-03-01	1980.208	339.46	338.12
3	1980-04-01	1980.292	339.86	338.24
4	1980-05-01	1980.375	340.30	338.77

Figure 4.15   Sample data in the data set

In this data set, the only two columns we are interested in are the Date column and the Average column. Out of these, the Date column is important for visualization purposes only. Let's set the Date column as the index of the data frame. This way, when we plot data, the *x*-axis will be automatically annotated with the corresponding date:

```
data = data.set_index('Date')
```

We can now visualize the data (figure 4.16) by creating a line plot with

```
data[["Average"]].plot(figsize=(12,6))
```

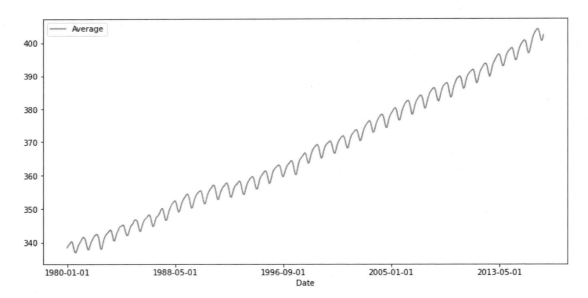

Figure 4.16   CO2 concentration plotted over time

The obvious features of the data are that it has an upward trend and short repetitive cycles. Let's see what sort of improvements we can do to this data. The clear upward trend the data is showing poses a problem. This means that the data is not distributed in a consistent range. The range increases as we go further and further down the time-line. If you feed data as it is to the model, usually the model will underperform, because any new data the model has to predict is out of the range of the data it saw during training. But if you forget the absolute values and think about this data relative to the previous value, you will see that it moves between a very small range of values (appx −2.0 to +1.5). In fact, we can test this idea easily. We will create a new column called `Average Diff`, which will contain the relative difference between two consecutive time steps:

```
data["Average Diff"]=data["Average"] - data["Average"].shift(1).fillna(method='bfill')
```

If you do a `data.head()` at this stage, you will see something similar to table 4.2.

Table 4.2   Sample data in the data set after introducing the `Average diff` column

Date	Decimal data	Average	Trend	Average diff
1980-01-01	1980.042	338.45	337.83	0.00
1980-02-01	1980.125	339.15	338.10	0.70
1980-031-01	1980.208	339.48	338.13	0.33
1980-04-01	1980.292	339.87	338.25	0.39
1980-05-01	1980.375	340.30	338.78	0.43

Here, we are subtracting a version of the `Average` column, where values are shifted forward by one time step, from the original average column. Figure 4.17 depicts this operation visually.

Finally, we can visualize how the values behave (figure 4.18) using the `data["Average Diff"].plot(figsize=(12,6))` line.

Can you see the difference? From an ever-increasing data stream, we have gone to a stream that changes within a short vertical span. The next step is creating batches of data for the model to learn. How do we create batches of data for a time series problem? Remember, we cannot just randomly sample data naively, as each input depends on its predecessors.

Let's assume we want to use 12 past $CO2$ concentration values (i.e., 12 time steps) to predict the current $CO2$ concentration value. The number of time steps is a hyperparameter you must choose carefully. In order to choose this hyperparameter confidently, you must have a solid understanding of the data and the memory limitations of the model you are using.

We first randomly choose a position in the sequence and take the 12 values from that point on as the inputs and the 13th value as the output we're interested in predicting so that the total sequence length (n_seq) you sample at a time is 13. If you do this process 10 times, you will have a batch of data with 10 elements. As you can

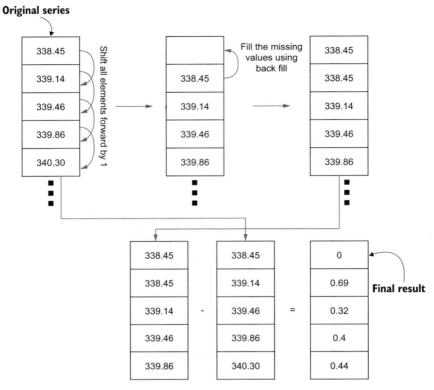

Figure 4.17   Transformations taking place going from the original Average series to the Average Diff series

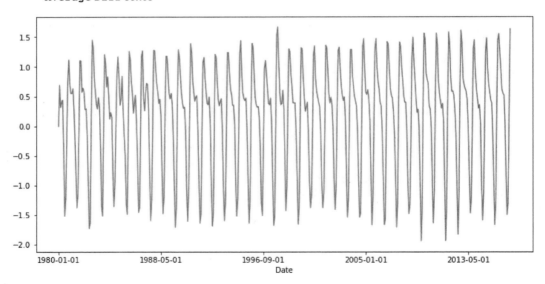

Figure 4.18   Relative change of values (i.e., Average[t]-Average[t-1]) of CO2 concentration over time

see, this process exploits the randomness while preserving the temporal characteristics of the data, and while feeding data to the model. Figure 4.19 visually describes this process.

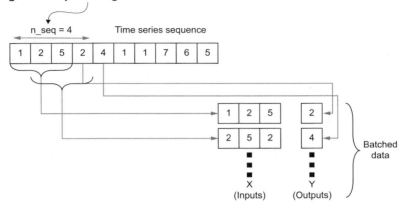

At a given time, we take three items as inputs and one as the output, giving a total sequence length of 4.

Figure 4.19   Batching time series data. n_seq represents the number of time steps we see at a given time to create a single input and an output.

To do this in Python, let's write a function that gives the data at all positions as a single data set. In other words, this function returns all possible consecutive sequences with 12 elements as x and the corresponding next value for each sequence as y. It is possible to perform the shuffling while feeding this data to the model, as the next listing shows.

Listing 4.4   The code for generating time-series data sequences for the model

```
import numpy as np

def generate_data(co2_arr,n_seq):
    x, y = [],[]
    for i in range(co2_arr.shape[0]-n_seq):
        x.append(co2_arr[i:i+n_seq-1])
        y.append(co2_arr[i+n_seq-1:i+n_seq])
    x = np.array(x)
    y = np.array(y)
    return x,y
```

Extracting a sequence of values n_seq long

Extracting the next value in the sequence as the output

Combining everything into an array

4.3.2   *Implementing the model*

With a good understanding of the data, we can start implementing the network. We will implement a network that has the following:

- A rnn layer with 64 hidden units
- A Dense layer with 64 hidden units and a ReLU activation

- A Dense layer with a single output and a linear activation

```
from tensorflow.keras import layers, models

rnn = models.Sequential([
    layers.SimpleRNN(64),
    layers.Dense(64, activation='relu'),
    layers.Dense(1)
])
```

Note that the hyperparameters of the network (e.g., number of hidden units) have been chosen empirically to work well for the given problem. The first layer is the most crucial component of the network, as it is the element that makes it possible to learn from time series data. The SimpleRNN layer encapsulates the functionality shown in figure 4.20.

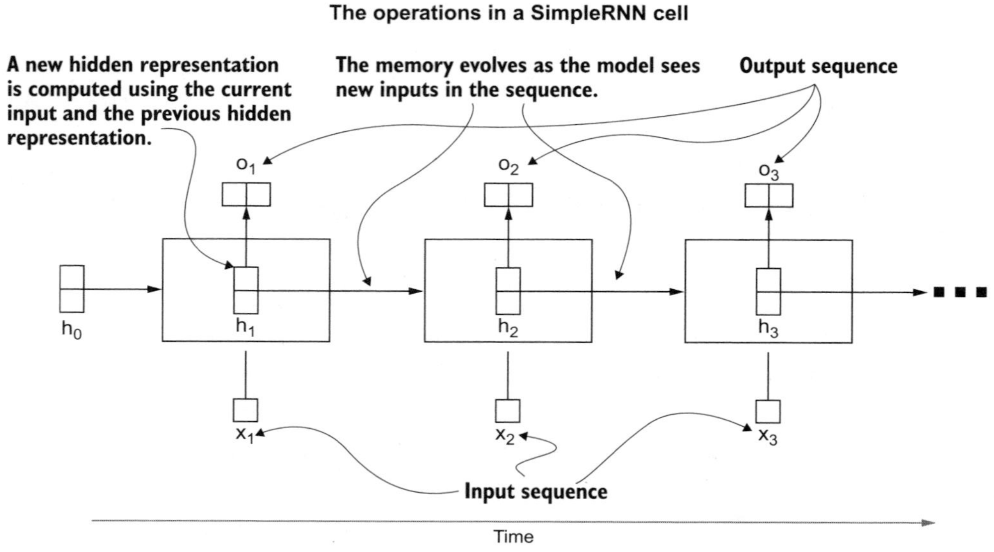

The operations in a SimpleRNN cell

Figure 4.20   **The functionality of a SimpleRNN cell. The cell goes from one input to another while producing a memory at every time step. The next step consumes the current input as well as the memory from the previous time step.**

The computations that happen in an RNN are more sophisticated than in an FCN. An RNN goes from one input to the other in the input sequence (i.e., x1, x2, x3) in the given order. At each step, the recurrent layer produces an output (i.e., o1, o2, o3) and passes the hidden computation (h0, h1, h2, h3) to the next time step. Here, the first hidden state (h0) is typically set to zero.

At a given time step, the recurrent layer computes a hidden state, just like a Dense layer. However, the specific computations involved are bit more complex and are out of the scope of this book. The hidden state size is another hyperparameter of the recurrent layer. The recurrent layer takes the current input as well as the previous hidden state computed by the cell. A larger-sized hidden state helps to maintain more memory but increases the memory requirement of the network. As the hidden state is dependent on itself from the previous time step, these networks are called RNNs.

> **The algorithm used for SimpleRNN**
>
> The computations mimicked by the `SimpleRNN` layer are also known as *Elman networks*. To learn more about specific computations taking place in recurrent layers, you can read the paper "Finding Structure in Time" by J.L. Elman (1990). For a more high-level overview of later variations of RNNs and their differences, see http://mng.bz/xnJg and http://mng.bz/Ay2g

By default, the `SimpleRNN` does not expose the hidden state to the developer and will be propagated between time steps automatically. For this task, we only need the final output produced by each time step, which is the output of that layer by default. Therefore, you can simply connect the `SimpleRNN` in the Sequential API to a `Dense` layer without any additional work.

Did you notice that we haven't provided an `input_shape` to the first layer? This is possible, as long as you provide the data in the correct shape during model fitting. Keras builds the layers lazily, so until you feed data to your model, the model doesn't need to know the input sizes. But it is always safer to set the `input_shape` argument in the first layer of the model to avoid errors. For example, in the model we defined, the first layer (i.e., the `SimpleRNN` layer) can be changed to `layers.SimpleRNN(64, input_shape=x)`, where x is a tuple containing the shape of the data accepted by the model.

Another important difference in this model is that it is a regression model, not a classification model. In a classification model, there are distinct classes (represented by output nodes), and we try to associate a given input with a distinct class (or a node). A regression model predicts a continuous value(s) as the output. Here, in our regression model, there is no notion of classes in the outputs, but a real continuous value representing CO_2 concentration. Therefore, we have to choose the loss function appropriately. In this case, we will use mean squared error (MSE) as the loss. MSE is a very common loss function for regression problems. We will compile the `rnn` with the MSE loss and the `adam` optimizer:

```
rnn.compile(loss='mse', optimizer='adam')
```

Let's cross our fingers and train our model:

```
x, y = generate_data(data["Average Diff"], n_seq=13)
rnn.fit(x, y, shuffle=True, batch_size=64, epochs=25)
```

You'll get the following exception:

```
ValueError:
    Input 0 of layer sequential_1 is incompatible with the layer:
    expected ndim=3, found ndim=2. Full shape received: [None, 12]
```

It seems we have done something wrong. The line we just ran resulted in an exception, which says something is wrong with the dimensionality of the data given to the layer sequential_1 (i.e., the SimpleRNN layer). Specifically, the sequential_1 layer expects a three-dimensional input but has a two-dimensional input. We need to investigate what's happening here and solve this.

The problem is that the SimpleRNN (or any other sequential layer in tf.keras) only accepts data in a very specific format. The data needs to be three-dimensional, with the following dimensions, in this order:

1 Batch dimension
2 Time dimension
3 Feature dimension

Even when you have a single element for any of these dimensions, they need to be present as a dimension of size 1 in the data. Let's look at what the dimensionality of x is by printing x.shape. You will get x.shape = (429, 12). Now we know what went wrong. We tried to pass a two-dimensional data set when we should have passed a three-dimensional one. In this case, we need to reshape x into a tensor of shape (492, 12, 1). Let's change our generate_data(…) function to reflect this change in the following listing.

Listing 4.5 The previous generate_data() function with data in the correct shape

```
import numpy as np

def generate_data(co2_arr,n_seq):
    x, y = [],[]
    for i in range(co2_arr.shape[0]-n_seq):
        x.append(co2_arr[i:i+n_seq-1])
        y.append(co2_arr[i+n_seq-1:i+n_seq])
    x = np.array(x).reshape(-1,n_seq-1,1)
    y = np.array(y)
    return x,y
```

Create two lists to hold input sequences and scalar output targets.

Iterate through all the possible starting points in the data for input sequences.

Create the input sequence and the output target at the ith position.

Convert x from a list to an array and make x a 3D tensor to be accepted by the RNN.

Let's try training our model now:

```
x, y = generate_data(data["Average Diff"], n_seq=13)
rnn.fit(x, y, shuffle=True, batch_size=64, epochs=25)
```

You should see the MSE of the model going down:

```
Train on 429 samples
Epoch 1/25
429/429 [==============================] - 1s 2ms/sample - loss: 0.4951
Epoch 2/25
429/429 [==============================] - 0s 234us/sample - loss: 0.0776
...
Epoch 24/25
429/429 [==============================] - 0s 234us/sample - loss: 0.0153
```

```
Epoch 25/25
429/429 [==============================] - 0s 234us/sample - loss: 0.0152
```

We start with a loss of approximately 0.5 and end up with a loss of roughly 0.015. This is a very positive sign, as it indicates the model is learning the trends present in the data.

4.3.3   Predicting future CO2 values with the trained model

Thus far, we have focused on classification tasks. It is much easier to evaluate models on classification tasks than regression tasks. In classification tasks (assuming a balanced data set), by computing the overall accuracy on the data, we can get a decent representative number on how well our model is doing. In regression tasks it's not so simple. We cannot measure an accuracy on regressed values, as the predictions are real values, not classes. For example, the magnitude of the mean squared loss depends on values we are regressing, which makes them difficult to objectively interpret. To address this, we predict the values for the next five years and visually inspect what the model is predicting (see the next listing).

> **Listing 4.6   The future CO2 level prediction logic using the trained model**

Save the very last absolute CO2 concentration value to compute the actual values from the relative predictions.

The first data sequence to start predictions from, which is reshaped to the correct shape the SimpleRNN accepts

```
history = data["Average Diff"].values[-12:].reshape(1,-1,1)      ⟵
true_vals = []
prev_true = data["Average"].values[-1]
for i in range(60):                                    ⟵   Predict for the
    p_diff = rnn.predict(history).reshape(1,-1,1)      ⟵       next 60 months.
    history = np.concatenate((history[:,1:,:],p_diff),axis=1)   ⟵
    true_vals.append(prev_true+p_diff[0,0,0])    ⟵
    prev_true = true_vals[-1]
```

Update prev_true so that the absolute CO2 concentration can be computed in the next time step.

Compute the absolute CO2 concentration.

Modify the history so that the latest prediction is included.

Make a prediction using the data sequence.

Let's review what we have done. First, we extracted the last 12 CO2 values (from the `Average Diff` column) from our training data to predict the first future CO2 value and reshaped it to the correct shape the model expects the data to be in:

```
history = data["Average Diff"].values[-12:].reshape(1,-1,1)
```

Then, we captured the predicted CO2 values in `true_vals` list. Remember that our model only predicts the relative movement of CO2 values with respect to the previous CO2 values. Therefore, after the model predicts, to get the absolute CO2 value, we need the last CO2 value. `prev_true` captures this information, which initially has the very last value in the `Average` column of the data:

```
prev_true = data["Average"].values[-1]
```

Now, for the next 60 months (or 5 years), we can recursively predict CO2 values, while making the last predicted the next input to the network. To do this we first predict a value using the `predict (…)` method provided in Keras. Then, we need to make sure the prediction is also a three-dimensional tensor (though it's a single value). Then we modify the history variable:

```
history = np.concatenate((history[:,1:,:],p_diff),axis=1)
```

We are taking all but the first value from the history and appending the last predicted value to the end. Then we append the absolute predicted CO2 value by adding the `prev_true` value to `p_diff`:

```
true_vals.append(prev_true+p_diff[0,0,0])
```

Finally, we update `prev_true` to the last absolute CO2 value we predicted:

```
prev_true = true_vals[-1]
```

By doing this set of operations recursively, we can get the predictions for the next 60 months (captured in `true_vals` variable). If we visualize the predicted values, they should look like figure 4.21.

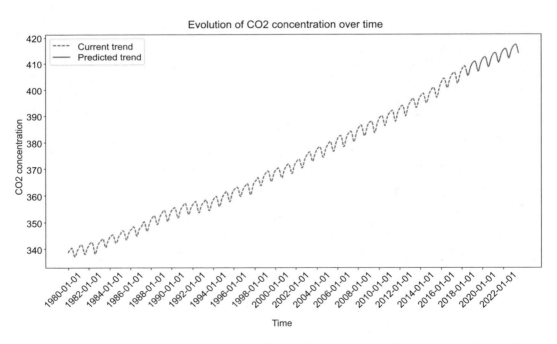

Figure 4.21   The CO2 concentration predicted over the next five years. Dashed line represents the trend from the current data, and the solid line represents the predicted trend.

Great work! Given the simplicity of the model, predictions look very promising. The model has definitely captured the annual trend of the CO2 concentration and has learned that the CO2 level is going to keep going up. You can now go to your boss and explain factually why we should be worried about climate change and dangerous levels of CO2 in the future. We end our discussion about different neural networks here.

EXERCISE 3

Impressed by your work on predicting the CO2 concentration, your boss has provided you the data and asked you to enhance the model to predict both CO2 and temperature values. Keeping the other hyperparameters the same, how would you change the model for this task? Make sure you specify the input_shape parameter for the first layer.

Summary

- Fully connected networks (FCNs) are one of the most straightforward neural networks.
- FCNs can be implemented using the Keras Dense layer.
- Convolutional neural networks (CNNs) are a popular choice for computer vision tasks.
- TensorFlow offers various layers, such as Conv2D, MaxPool2D, and Flatten, that help us implement CNNs quickly.
- CNNs have parameters such as kernel size, stride, and padding that must be set carefully. If not, this can lead to incorrectly shaped tensors and runtime errors.
- Recurrent neural networks (RNNs) are predominantly used to learn from time-series data.
- The typical RNN expects the data to be organized into a three-dimensional tensor with a batch, time, and feature dimension.
- The number of time steps the RNN looks at is an important hyperparameter that should be chosen based on the data.

Answers to exercises

Exercise 1: You can do this using the Sequential API, and you will be using only the Dense layer.

Exercise 2

```
autoencoder = models.Sequential(
    [layers.Dense(32, activation='sigmoid', input_shape=(512,)),
    layers.Dense(16, activation='sigmoid'),
    layers.Dense(512, activation='sigmoid')]
)
```

Exercise 3

```
rnn = models.Sequential([
    layers.SimpleRNN(64, input_shape=(12, 2)),
    layers.Dense(64, activation='relu'),
    layers.Dense(2)
])
```

5

State-of-the-art in deep learning: Transformers

This chapter covers

- Representing text in numerical format for machine learning models
- Building a Transformer model using the Keras sub-classing API

We have seen many different deep learning models so far, namely fully connected networks, convolutional neural networks, and recurrent neural networks. We used a fully connected network to reconstruct corrupted images, a convolutional neural network to classify vehicles from other images, and finally an RNN to predict future CO_2 concentration values. In this chapter we are going to talk about a new type of model known as the Transformer.

Transformers are the latest generation of deep networks to emerge. Vaswani et al., in their paper "Attention Is All You Need" (https://arxiv.org/pdf/1706.03762.pdf), popularized the idea. They coined the term *Transformer* and explained how it shows great promise for the future. In the years following, leading tech companies like Google, OpenAI, and Facebook implemented bigger and better Transformer models that have significantly outperformed other models in the NLP domain. Here, we will refer to the model introduced in their paper by Vaswani et al. to learn about it. Although Transformers do exist for other domains (e.g., computer vision), we will focus on how the Transformer is used in the NLP domain, particularly on a machine translation task (i.e., language translation using machine learning models). This discussion will leave out some of the details from the original Transformer paper to improve clarity, but these details will be covered in a later chapter.

Knowing the inner workings of the Transformer model is a must for anyone who wants to excel at using deep learning models to solve real-world problems. As explained, the Transformer model has proliferated the machine learning field quite rapidly. This is mainly because of the performance it has demonstrated in solving complex machine learning problems.

5.1   *Representing text as numbers*

Say you are taking part in a game show. One challenge in the game is called Word Boxes. There is a matrix of transparent boxes (3 rows, 5 columns, 10 depths). You also have balls with 0 or 1 painted on them. You are given three sentences, and your task is to fill all the boxes with 1s and 0s to represent those sentences. Additionally, you can write a short message (within a minute) that helps someone decipher this later. Later, another team member looks at the boxes and writes down as many words in the original sentences you were initially given.

The challenge is essentially how you can transform text to numbers for machine translation models. This is also an important problem you work on before learning about any NLP model. The data we have seen so far has been numerical data structures. For example, an image can be represented as a 3D array (height, width, and channel dimensions), where each value represents a pixel intensity (i.e., a value between 0 and 255). But what about text? How can we make a computer understand characters, words, or sentences? We will learn how to do this with Transformers in the context of natural language processing (NLP).

You have the following set of sentences:

- I went to the beach.
- It was cold.
- I came back to the house.

The first thing you do is assign each word in your vocabulary an ID starting from 1. We will reserve the number 0 for a special token we will see later. Say you assign the following IDs:

- I $\rightarrow$ 1
- went $\rightarrow$ 2
- to $\rightarrow$ 3
- the $\rightarrow$ 4
- beach $\rightarrow$ 5
- It $\rightarrow$ 6
- was $\rightarrow$ 7

- cold → 8
- came → 9
- back → 10
- house → 11

After mapping the words to the corresponding IDs, our sentences become the following:

- [1, 2, 3, 4, 5]
- [6, 7, 8]
- [1, 9, 10, 3, 4, 11]

Remember, you need to fill in all the boxes and have a maximum length of 5. Note that our last sentence has six words. This means all the sentences need to be represented by a fixed length. Deep learning models face a similar problem. They process data in batches, and to process it efficiently, the sequence length needs to be fixed for that batch. Real-world sentences can vary significantly in terms of their length. Therefore, we need to

- Pad short sentences with a special token <PAD> (with ID 0)
- Truncate long sentences

to make them the same length. If we pad the short sentences and truncate long sentences so that the length is 5, we get the following:

- [1, 2,   3, 4, 5]
- [6, 7,   8, 0, 0]
- [1, 9, 10, 3, 4]

Here, we have a 2D matrix of size 3×5, which represents our batch of sentences. The final thing to do is represent each of these IDs as vectors. Because our balls have 1s and 0s, you can represent each word with 11 balls (we have 10 different words and the special token <PAD>), where the ball at the position indicated by the word ID is 1 and the rest are 0s. This method is known as one-hot encoding. For example,

$$0 \to [1, 0, 0, 0, 0, 0, 0, 0, 0, 0, 0]$$

$$1 \to [0, 1, 0, 0, 0, 0, 0, 0, 0, 0, 0]$$

$$\cdots$$

$$10 \to [0, 0, 0, 0, 0, 0, 0, 0, 0, 1, 0]$$

$$11 \to [0, 0, 0, 0, 0, 0, 0, 0, 0, 0, 1]$$

Now you can fill the boxes with 1s and 0s such that you get something like figure 5.1. This way, anyone who has the word for ID mapping (provided in a sheet of paper) can decipher most of the words (except for those truncated) that were initially provided.

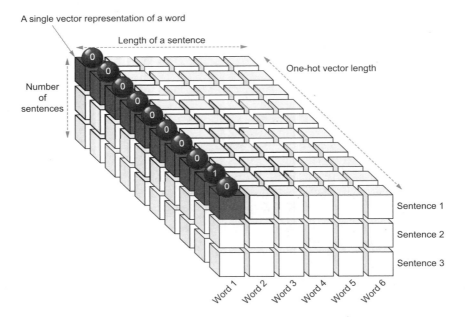

Figure 5.1   The boxes in the Word Boxes game. The shaded boxes represent a single word (i.e., the first word in the first sentence, "I," which has an ID of 1). You can see it's represented by a single ball of 1 and nine balls of 0.

Again, this is a transformation done to words in NLP problems. You might ask, "Why not feed the word IDs directly?" There are two problems:

- The value ranges the neural network sees are very large (0–100,000+) for a real-world problem. This will cause instabilities and make the training difficult.
- Feeding in IDs would falsely indicate that words with similar IDs should be alike (e.g., word ID 4 and 5). This is never the case and would confuse the model and lead to poor performance.

Therefore, it is important to bring words to some vector representation. There are many ways to turn words into vectors, such as one-hot encoding and word embeddings. You have already seen how one-hot encoding works, and we will discuss word embeddings in detail later. When we represent words as vectors, our 2D matrix becomes a 3D matrix. For example, if we set the vector length to 4, you will have a $3 \times 6 \times 4$ 3D tensor. Figure 5.2 depicts what the final matrix looks like.

Next we will discuss the various components of the popular Transformer model, which will give us a solid grounding in how these models perform internally.

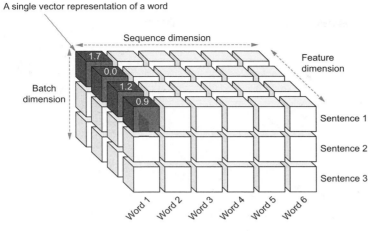

A single vector representation of a word

Figure 5.2 **3D matrix representing a batch of a sequence of words, where each word is represented by a vector (i.e., the shaded block in the matrix). There are three dimensions: batch, sequence (time), and feature.**

5.2 Understanding the Transformer model

You are currently working as a deep learning research scientist and were recently invited to conduct a workshop on Transformers at a local TensorFlow conference. Transformers are a new family of deep learning models that have surpassed their older counterparts in a plethora of tasks. You are planning to first explain the architecture of the Transformer network and then walk the participants through several exercises, where they will implement the basic computations found in Transformers as sub-classed Keras layers and finally use these to implement a basic small-scale Transformer using Keras.

5.2.1 The encoder-decoder view of the Transformer

The Transformer network is based on an encoder-decoder architecture. The encoder-decoder pattern is common in deep learning for certain types of tasks (e.g., machine translation, question answering, unsupervised image reconstruction). The idea is that the encoder takes an input and maps it to some latent (or hidden) representation (typically smaller), and the decoder constructs a meaningful output using latent representation. For example, in machine translation, a sentence from language A is mapped to a latent vector, from which the decoder constructs the translation of that sentence in language B. You can think of the encoder and decoder as two separate machine learning models, where the decoder depends on the output of the encoder. This process is depicted in figure 5.3. At a given time, both the encoder and the decoder consume a batch of a sequence of words (e.g., a batch of sentences). As machine learning models don't understand text, every word in this batch is represented by a

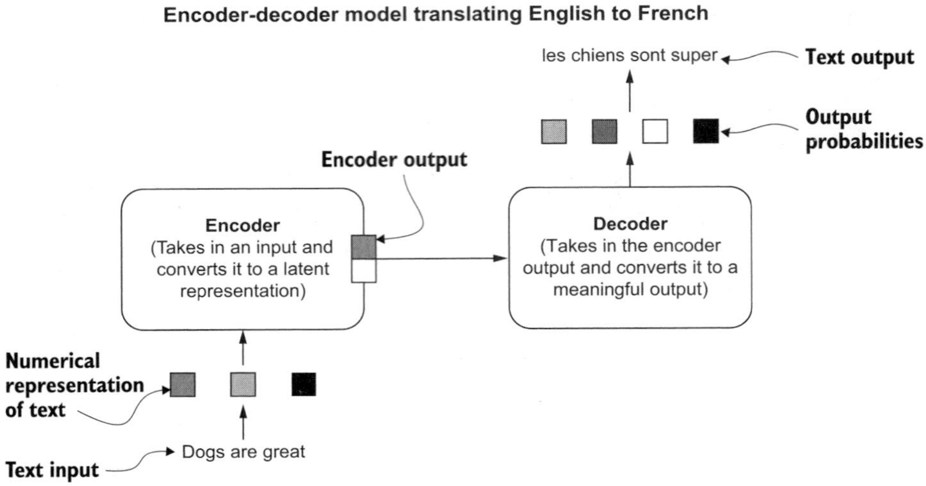

Encoder-decoder model translating English to French

Figure 5.3   The encoder-decoder architecture for a machine translation task

numerical vector. This is done by following a process such as one-hot encoding, similar to what we discussed in section 5.1.

The encoder-decoder pattern is common in real life as well. Say you are a tour guide in France and take a group of tourists to a restaurant. The waiter is explaining the menu in French, and you need to translate this to English for the group. Imagine how you would do that. When the waiter explains the dish in French, you process those words and create a mental image of what the dish is, and then you translate that mental image into a sequence of English words.

Now let's dive more into the individual components and what they are made of.

5.2.2   *Diving deeper*

Naturally, you might be asking yourself, "What do the encoder and the decoder consist of?" This is the topic of this section. Note that the encoder and decoder discussed here are quite different from the autoencoder model you saw in chapter 3. As said previously, the encoder and the decoder individually act like multilayered deep neural networks. They consist of several layers, where each layer comprises sublayers that encapsulate certain computations done on inputs to produce outputs. The output of the previous layer feeds as the input to the next layer. It is also important to note that inputs and outputs of the encoder and the decoder are sequences, such as sentences. Each layer within these models takes in a sequence of elements and outputs another sequence of elements. So, what constitutes a single layer in the encoder and the decoder?

Each encoder layer comprises two sublayers:

- Self-attention layer
- Fully connected layer

The self-attention layer produces its final output similarly to a fully connected layer (i.e., using matrix multiplications and activation functions). A typical fully connected layer will take all elements in the input sequence, process them separately, and output an element in place of each input element. But the self-attention layer can select and combine different elements in the input sequence to output a given element. This makes the self-attention layer much more powerful than a typical fully connected layer (figure 5.4).

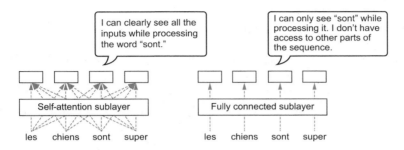

Figure 5.4   The difference between the self-attention sublayer and the fully connected sublayer. The self-attention sublayer looks at all the inputs in the sequence, whereas the fully connected sublayer only looks at the input that is processed.

Why does it pay to select and combine different input elements this way? In an NLP context, the self-attention layer enables the model to look at other words while it processes a certain word. But what does that mean for the model? This means that while the encoder is processing the word "it" in the sentence "I kicked the *ball* and *it* disappeared," the model can attend to the word "ball." By seeing both words "ball" and "it" at the same time (learning dependencies), disambiguating words is easier. Such capabilities are of paramount importance for language understanding.

We can understand how self-attention helps us solve a task conveniently through a real-world example. Assume you are playing a game with two people: person A and person B. Person A holds a question written on a board, and you need to speak the answer. Say person A reveals just one word at a time, and after the last word of the question, it is revealed that you are answering the question. For long and complex questions, this is challenging, as you cannot physically see the complete question and have to heavily rely on memory when answering the question. This is what it feels like without self-attention. On the other hand, say person B reveals the full question on the board instead of word by word. Now it is much easier to answer the question, as you can see the whole question at once. If the question is complex and requires a complex answer, you can look at different parts of the question as you provide various sections of the full answer. This is what the self-attention layer enables.

Next, the fully connected layer takes the output elements produced by the self-attention sublayer and produces a hidden representation for each output element in an element-wise fashion. This make the model deeper, allowing it to perform better.

Let's look in more detail at how data flows through the model in order to better understand the organization of layers and sublayers. Assume the task of translating the sentence "Dogs are great" (English) to "*Les chiens sont super*" (French). First, the encoder takes in the full sentence "Dogs are great" and produces an output for each word in the sentence. The self-attention layer selects the most important words for each position, computes an output, and sends that information to the fully connected layer to produce a deeper representation. The decoder produces output words iteratively, one after the other. To do that, the decoder looks at the final output sequence of the encoder and all the previous words predicted by the decoder. Assume the final prediction is <SOS> *les chiens sont super* <EOS>. Here, <SOS> marks the start of the sentence and <EOS> the end of the sentence. The first input it takes is a special tag that indicates the start of a sentence (<SOS>), along with the encoder outputs, and it produces the next word in the translation: "*les*." The decoder then consumes <SOS> and "*les*" as inputs, produces the word "*chiens*," and continues until the model reaches the end of the translation (marked by <EOS>). Figure 5.5 depicts this process.

In the original Transformer paper, the encoder has six layers, and a single layer has a self-attention sublayer and a fully connected sublayer, in that order. First, the self-attention layer takes the English words as a time-series input. However, before feeding these words to the encoder, you need to create a numerical representation of each word, as discussed earlier. In the paper, word embeddings (with some additional encoding) are used to represent the words. Each of these embeddings is a 512-long vector. Then the self-attention layer computes a hidden representation for each word of the input sentence. If we ignore some of the implementation details, this hidden representation at time step t can be thought as a weighted sum of all the inputs (in a single sequence), where the weight for position i of the input is determined by how important it is to select (or attend to) the encoder word ew_i in the input sequence while processing the word ew_t in the encoder input. The encoder makes this decision for every position t in the input sequence. For example, while processing the word "it" in the sentence "I kicked the *ball* and *it* disappeared," the encoder needs to pay more attention to the word "ball" than to the word "the." The weights in the self-attention sublayer are trained to demonstrate such properties. This way, the self-attention layer produces a hidden representation for each encoder input. We call this the *attended representation/output*.

The fully connected sublayer then takes over and is quite straightforward. It has two linear layers and a ReLU activation in between the layers. It takes the outputs of the self-attention layer and transforms to a hidden output using

$$h_1 = ReLU(xW_1 + b_1)$$

$$h_2 = h_1 W_2 + b_2$$

Note that the second layer does not have a nonlinear activation. Next, the decoder has six layers as well, where each layer has three sublayers:

- A masked self-attention layer
- An encoder-decoder attention layer
- A fully connected layer

The masked self-attention layer operates similarly to the self-attention layer. However, while processing the sth word (i.e., dw_s), it masks the words ahead of dw_s. For example, while processing the word "*chiens*," it can only attend to the words "<sos>" and "*les*." This is important because the decoder must be able to predict the correct word, given only the previous words it predicted, so it makes sense to force the decoder to attend only to the words it has already seen.

Next, the encoder-decoder attention layer takes the encoder output and the outputs produced by the masked self-attention layer and produce a series of outputs. The purpose of this layer is to compute a hidden representation (i.e., an attended representation) at time s as a weighted sum of encoder inputs, where the weight for position j is determined by how important it is to attend to encoder input ew_j, while processing the decoder word dw_s.

Finally, a fully connected layer identical to the fully connected layer from the encoder layer takes the output of the self-attention layer to produce the final output of the layer. Figure 5.5 depicts the layers and operations discussed in this section at a high level.

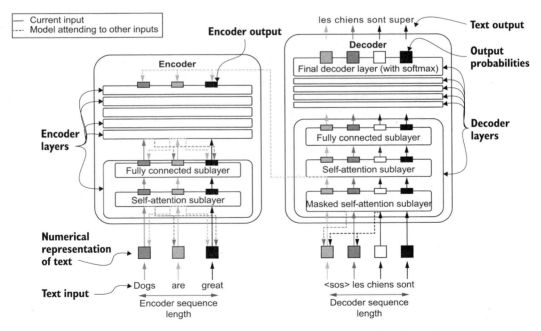

Figure 5.5 Various layers in the encoder and the decoder and various connections formed within the encoder, within the decoder, and between the encoder and the decoder. The squares represent inputs and outputs of the models. The rectangular shaded boxes represent interim outputs of the sublayers.

In the next section, we will discuss what the self-attention layer looks like.

5.2.3   *Self-attention layer*

We have covered the purpose of the self-attention layer at an abstract level of understanding. It is to, while processing the word w_t at time step t, determine how important it is to attend to the ith word (i.e., w_i) in the input sequence. In other words, the layer needs to determine the importance of all the other words (indexed by i) for every word (indexed by t). Let's now understand the computations involved in this process at a more granular level.

First, there are three different entities involved in the computation:

- A *query*—The query's purpose is to represent the word currently being processed.
- A *key*—The key's purpose is to represent the candidate words to be attended to while processing the current word.
- A *value*—The value's purpose is to compute a weighted sum of all words in the sequence, where the weight for each word is based on how important it is for understanding the current word

For a given input sequence, query, key, and value need to be calculated for every position of the input. These are calculated by an associated weight matrix with each entity.

Note that this is an oversimplification of their relationship, and the actual relationship is somewhat complex and convoluted. But this understanding provides the motivation for why we need three different entities to compute self-attention outputs.

Next, we will understand how exactly a self-attention layer goes from an input sequence to a query, key, and value tensor and finally to the output sequence. The input word sequence is first converted to a numerical representation using word embedding lookup. Word embeddings are essentially a giant matrix, where there's a vector of floats (i.e., an embedding vector) for each word in your vocabulary. Typically, these embeddings are several hundreds of elements long. For a given input sequence, we assume the input sequence is n elements long and each word vector is d_{model} elements long. Then we have a $n \times d_{model}$ matrix. In the original Transformer paper, word vectors are 512 elements long.

There are three weight matrices in the self-attention layer: query weights (W_q), key weights (W_k), and value weights (W_v), respectively used to compute the query, key, and value vectors. W_q is $d_{model} \times d_q$, W_k is $d_{model} \times d_k$, and W_v is $d_{model} \times d_v$. Let's define these elements in TensorFlow assuming a dimensionality of 512, as in the original Transformer paper. That is,

$$d_{model} = d_q = d_k = d_v = 512$$

We will first define our input x as a `tf.constant`, which has three dimensions (batch, time, feature). Wq, Wk, and Wv are declared as `tf.Variable` objects, as these are the parameters of the self-attention layer

```
import tensorflow as tf
import numpy as np

n_seq = 7
x = tf.constant(np.random.normal(size=(1,n_seq,512)))
Wq = tf.Variable(np.random.normal(size=(512,512)))
Wk = tf.Variable (np.random.normal(size=(512,512)))
Wv = tf.Variable (np.random.normal(size=(512,512)))
```

which has shapes

```
>>> x.shape=(1, 7, 512)
>>> Wq.shape=(1, 512)
>>> Wk.shape=(1, 512)
>>> Wv.shape=(1, 512)
```

Next, q, k, and v are computed as follows:

$$q = xW_q; \text{ shape transformation: } n \times d_{model}. \; d_{model} \times d_q = n \times d_q$$

$$k = xW_k; \text{ shape transformation: } n \times d_{model}. \; d_{model} \times d_k = n \times d_k$$

$$v = xW_v; \text{ shape transformation: } n \times d_{model}. \; d_{model} \times d_v = n \times d_v$$

It is evident that computing q, k, and v is a simple matrix multiplication away. Remember that there is a batch dimension in front of all the inputs (i.e., x) and output tensors (i.e,. q, k, and v) as we process batches of data. But to avoid clutter, we are going to ignore the batch dimension. Then we compute the final output of the self-attention layer as follows:

$$h = \text{softmax}\left(\frac{Q.K^T}{\sqrt{d_k}}\right) V$$

Here, the component $\text{softmax}\left(\frac{Q.K^T}{\sqrt{d_k}}\right)$ (which will be referred to as P) is a probability matrix. This is all there is in the self-attention layer. Implementing self-attention with TensorFlow is very straightforward. As good data scientists, let's create it as a reusable Keras layer, as shown in the next listing.

Listing 5.1   The self-attention sublayer

```
import tensorflow as tf
import tensorflow.keras.layers as layers

class SelfAttentionLayer(layers.Layer):

    def __init__(self, d):
        super(SelfAttentionLayer, self).__init__()        ◁── Defining the output
        self.d = d                                             dimensionality of the
                                                               self-attention outputs
```

Defining the variables for computing the query, key, and value entities

```
def build(self, input_shape):
    self.Wq = self.add_weight(
        shape=(input_shape[-1], self.d), initializer='glorot_uniform',
        trainable=True, dtype='float32'
    )
    self.Wk = self.add_weight(
        shape=(input_shape[-1], self.d), initializer='glorot_uniform',
        trainable=True, dtype='float32'
    )
    self.Wv = self.add_weight(
        shape=(input_shape[-1], self.d), initializer='glorot_uniform',
        trainable=True, dtype='float32'
    )
```

```
def call(self, q_x, k_x, v_x):
    q = tf.matmul(q_x,self.Wq)
    k = tf.matmul(k_x,self.Wk)
    v = tf.matmul(v_x,self.Wv)

    p = tf.nn.softmax(tf.matmul(q, k,
transpose_b=True)/math.sqrt(self.d))
    h = tf.matmul(p, v)
    return h,p
```

Computing the query, key, and value tensors

Computing the probability matrix

Computing the final output

Here's a quick refresher:

- __init__(self, d)—Defines any hyperparameters of the layer
- build(self, input_shape)—Creates the parameters of the layer as variables
- call(self, v_x, k_x, q_x)—Defines the computations happening in the layer

If you look at the call(self, v_x, k_x, q_x) function, it takes in three inputs: one each for computing value, key, and query. In most cases these are the same input. However, there are instances where different inputs come into these computations (e.g., some computations in the decoder). Also, note that we return both h (i.e., the final output) and p (i.e., the probability matrix). The probability matrix is an important visual aid, as it helps us understand when and where the model paid attention to words. If you want to get the output of the layer, you can do the following

```
layer = SelfAttentionLayer(512)
h, p = layer(x, x, x)
print(h.shape)
```

which will return

```
>>> (1, 7, 512)
```

EXERCISE 1

Given the following input

```
x = tf.constant(np.random.normal(size=(1,10,256)))
```

and assuming we need an output of size 512, write the code to create Wq, Wk, and Wv as tf.Variable objects. Use the np.random.normal() function to set the initial values.

5.2.4 *Understanding self-attention using scalars*

It is not yet very clear why the computations are designed the way they are. To understand and visualize what this layer is doing, we will assume a feature dimensionality of 1. That is, a single word is represented by a single value (i.e., a scalar). Figure 5.6 visualizes the computations that happen in the self-attention layer if we assume a single-input sequence and the dimensionality of inputs (d_{model}), query length (d_q), key length (d_k), and value length (d_v) is 1. As a concrete example, we start with an input sequence x, which has seven words (i.e., $n \times 1$ matrix). Under the assumptions we've made, W_q, W_k, and W_v will be scalars. The matrix multiplications used for computing q, k, and v essentially become scalar multiplications:

$$q = (q_1, q_2, \ldots, q_7), \text{ where } q_i = x_i \, W_q$$

$$k = (k_1, k_2, \ldots, k_7), \text{ where } k_i = x_i \, W_k$$

$$v = (v_1, v_2, \ldots, v_7), \text{ where } v_i = x_i \, W_v$$

Next, we need to compute the $P = \text{softmax}((Q.K^T) / \sqrt{(d_k)})$ component. $Q.K^T$ is essentially an $n \times n$ matrix that has an item representing every query and key combination (figure 5.6). The ith row and j^{th} column of $Q.K_{(i,j)}{}^T$ are computed as

$$Q.K_{(i,j)}{}^T = q_i \times k_j$$

Then, by applying the softmax, this matrix is converted to a row-wise probability distribution. You might have noted a constant $\sqrt{(d_k)}$ appearing within the softmax transformation. This is a normalization constant that helps prevent large gradient values and achieve stable gradients. In our example, you can ignore this as $\sqrt{(d_k)} = 1$.

Finally, we compute the final output $h = (h_1, h_2, \ldots, h_7)$, where

$$h_i = P_{(i,1)} \, v_1 + P_{(i,2)} \, v_2 + \ldots + P_{(i,7)} \, v_7$$

Here, we can more clearly see the relationship between q, k, and v. q and k are used to compute a soft-index mechanism for v when computing the final output. For example, when computing the fourth output (i.e., h_4), we first hard-index the fourth row (following q_4), and then mix various v values based on the soft index (i.e., probabilities) given by the columns (i.e., k values) of that row. Now it is more clear what purpose q, k, and v serve:

- *Query*—Helps build a probability matrix that is eventually used for indexing values (v). Query affects the rows of the matrix and represents the index of the current word that's being processed.

- *Key*—Helps build a probability matrix that is eventually used for indexing values (v). Key affects the columns of the matrix and represents the candidate words that need to be mixed depending on the query word.

- *Value*—Hidden (i.e., attended) representation of the inputs used to compute the final output by indexing using the probability matrix created using query and key

You can easily take the big gray box in figure 5.6, place it over the self-attention sublayer, and still have the output shape (as shown in figure 5.5) being produced (figure 5.7).

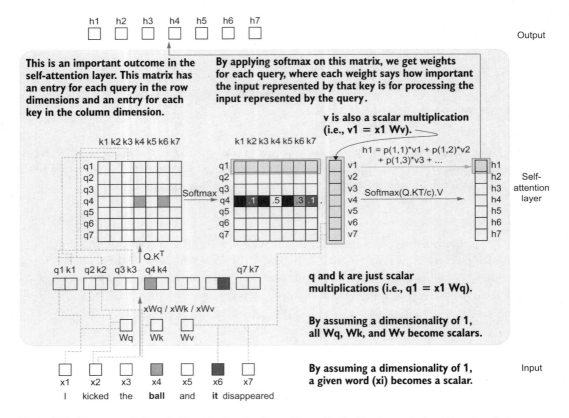

Figure 5.6   The computations in the self-attention layer. The self-attention layer starts with an input sequence and computes sequences of query, key, and value vectors. Then the queries and keys are converted to a probability matrix, which is used to compute the weighted sum of values.

Now let's scale up our self-attention layer and revisit the specific computations behind it and why they matter. Going back to our previous notation, we start with a sequence of words, which has n elements. Then, after the embedding lookup, which retrieves an

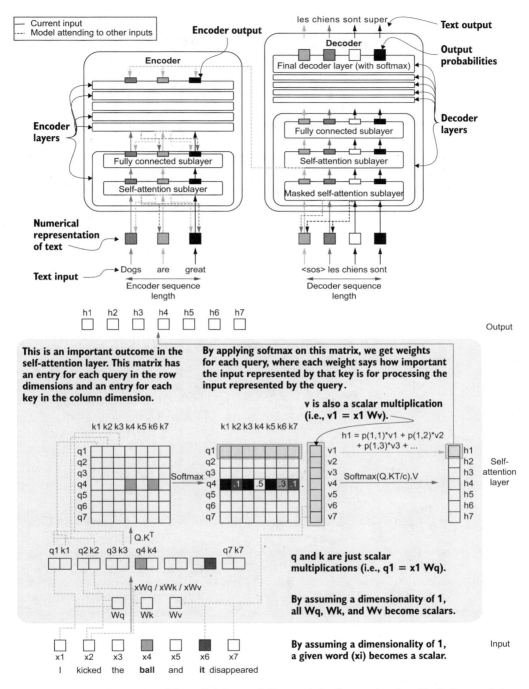

Figure 5.7   Figure 5.5 (top) and figure 5.6 (bottom). You can take the gray box from the bottom and plug it into a self-attention sublayer on the top and see that the same output sequence is being produced.

embedding vector for each word, we have a matrix of size $n \times d_{model}$. Next, we have the weights and biases to compute each of the query, key, and value vectors:

$$q = xW_q, \text{ where } x \in \mathbb{R}^{n \times d_{model}}. \ W_q \in \mathbb{R}^{d_{model} \times d_q} \text{ and } q \in \mathbb{R}^{n \times d_q}$$

$$k = xW_k, \text{ where } x \in \mathbb{R}^{n \times d_{model}}. \ W_k \in \mathbb{R}^{d_{model} \times d_k} \text{ and } k \in \mathbb{R}^{n \times d_k}$$

$$v = xW_v, \text{ where } x \in \mathbb{R}^{n \times d_{model}}. \ W_v \in \mathbb{R}^{d_{model} \times d_v} \text{ and } v \in \mathbb{R}^{n \times d_v}$$

For example, the query, or q, is a vector of size $n \times d_q$, obtained by multiplying the input x of size $n \times d_{model}$ with the weight matrix W_q of size $d_{model} \times d_q$. Also remember that, as in the original Transformer paper, we make sure that all of the input embedding of query, key, and value vectors are the same size. In other words,

$$d_{model} = d_q = d_k = d_v = 512$$

Next, we compute the probability matrix using the q and k values we obtained:

$$P = \text{softmax}\left(\frac{Q.K^T}{\sqrt{d_k}} \right)$$

Finally, we multiply this probably matrix with our value matrix to obtain the final output of the self-attention layer:

$$h = \text{softmax}\left(\frac{Q.K^T}{\sqrt{d_k}} \right) V$$

The self-attention layer takes a batch of a sequence of words (e.g., a batch of sentences of fixed length), where each word is represented by a vector, and produces a batch of a sequence of hidden outputs, where each hidden output is a vector.

How does self-attention compare to recurrent neural networks (RNNs)?

Before Transformer models, RNNs governed the domain of NLP. RNNs were popular for NLP problems because most are inherently time-series problems. You can think of a sentence/phrase as a sequence of words (i.e., each represented by a feature vector) spread across time. The RNN goes through this sequence, consuming one word at a time (while maintaining a memory/state vector), and produces some output (or a series of outputs) at the end. But you will see that RNNs perform more and more poorly as the length of the sequence increases. This is because by the time the RNN gets to the end of the sequence, it has probably forgotten what it saw at the start.

You can see that this problem is alleviated by the self-attention mechanism, which allows the model to look at the full sequence at a given time. This enables Transformer models to perform much better than RNN-based models.

5.2.5 *Self-attention as a cooking competition*

The concept of self-attention might still be a little bit elusive, making it difficult to understand what exactly is transpiring in the self-attention sublayer. The following analogy might alleviate the burden and make it easier. Say you are taking part in a cooking show with six other contestants (seven contestants in total). The game is as follows.

You are at a supermarket and are given a T-shirt with a number on it (from 1–7) and a trolley. The supermarket has seven aisles. You have to sprint to the aisle with the number on your T-shirt, and there will be a name of some beverage (e.g., apple juice, orange juice, lime juice) posted on the wall. You need to pick what's necessary to make that beverage, sprint to your allocated table, and make that beverage.

Say that you are number 4 and got orange juice, so you'll make your way to aisle 4 and collect oranges, a bit of salt, a lime, sugar, and so on. Now say the opponent next to you (number 3), had to make lime juice; they will pick limes, sugar, and salt. As you can see, you are picking different items as well as different quantities of the same item. For example, your opponent hasn't picked oranges, but you have, and you probably picked fewer limes compared to your opponent who is making lime juice.

This is quite similar to what's happening in the self-attention layer. You and your contestants are the inputs (at a single time step) to the model. The aisles are the queries, and the grocery items you have to pick are the keys. Just like indexing the probability matrix with query and keys to get the "mixing coefficients" (i.e., attention weights) for the values, you index the items you need by the aisle number allocated to you (i.e., query) and the quantity of each item in the aisle (i.e., key). Finally, the beverage you make is the value. Note that this analogy does not have 100% correspondence to the computations in the self-attention sublayer. However, you can draw significant similarities between the two processes at an abstract level. The similarities we discovered are shown in figure 5.8.

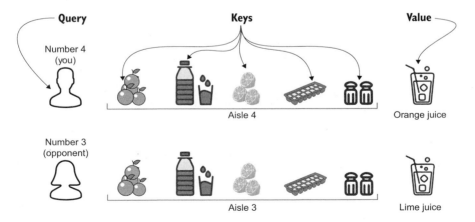

Figure 5.8 Self-attention depicted with the help of a cooking competition. The contestants are the queries, the keys are the grocery items you have to choose from, and the values are the final beverage you're making.

Next we will discuss what is meant by a masked self-attention layer.

5.2.6 *Masked self-attention layers*

As you have already seen, the decoder has a special additional self-attention sublayer called *masked self-attention*. As we have already stated, the idea is to prevent the model from "cheating" by attending to the words it shouldn't (i.e., the words ahead of the position the model has predicted for). To understand this better, assume two people are teaching a student to translate from English to French. The first person gives an English sentence, asks the student to produce the translation word by word, and provides feedback up to the word translated so far. The second person gives an English sentence and asks the student to produce the translation but provides the full translation in advance. In the second instance, it is much easier for a student to cheat, providing a good quality translation, while having very little knowledge of the languages. Now let's understand the looming danger of attending to the words it shouldn't from a machine learning point of view.

Take the task of translating the sentence "dogs are great" to "*les chiens sont super.*" When processing the sentence "Dogs are great," the model should be able to attend to any word in that sentence, as that's an input fully available to the model at any given time. But, while processing the sentence "*Les chiens sont super,*" we need to be careful about what we show to the model and what we don't. For example, while training the model, we typically feed the full output sequence at once, as opposed to iteratively feeding the words, to enhance computational efficiency. When feeding the full output sequence to the decoder, we must mask all words ahead of what is currently being processed because it is not fair for the model to predict the word "*chiens*" when it can see everything that comes after that word. It is imperative you do this. If you don't, the code will run fine. But ultimately you will have very poor performance when you bring it to the real world. The way to force this is by making the probability matrix p a lower-triangular matrix. This will essentially give zero probability for mixing any input ahead of itself during the attention/output computation. The differences between standard self-attention and masked self-attention are shown in figure 5.9.

Let's learn how we can do this in TensorFlow. We do a very simple change to the call() function by introducing a new argument, mask, which represents the items the model shouldn't see with a 1 and the rest with a 0. Then, to those elements the model shouldn't see, we add a very large negative number (i.e., -10^9) so that when softmax is applied they become zeros (listing 5.2).

Standard self-attention

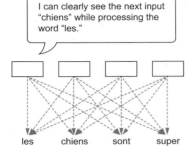

Masked standard self-attention

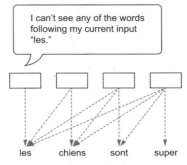

If standard attention was used in the decoder during model training, the decoder can learn poorly and still show superior performance. This is because when making predictions for the t^(th) timestep, the decoder has access to future inputs/outputs.

Masked attention will prevent the decoder from seeing any future inputs/outputs, allowing the model to generalize well during the learning task.

Figure 5.9   **Standard self-attention versus masked self-attention methods. In the standard attention method, a given step can see an input from any other timestep, regardless of whether those inputs appear before or after the current time step. However, in the masked self-attention method, the current timestep can only see the current input and what came before that time step.**

Listing 5.2   Masked self-attention sublayer

```
import tensorflow as tf

class SelfAttentionLayer(layers.Layer):

    def __init__(self, d):
        ...

    def build(self, input_shape):
        ...

    def call(self, q_x, k_x, v_x, mask=None):
        q = tf.matmul(x,self.Wq)
        k = tf.matmul(x,self.Wk)
        v = tf.matmul(x,self.Wv)

        p = tf.matmul(q, k, transpose_b=True)/math.sqrt(self.d)
        p = tf.squeeze(p)
        if mask is None:
            p = tf.nn.softmax(p)
        else:
            p += mask * -1e9
            p = tf.nn.softmax(p)
```

The call function takes an additional mask argument (i.e., a matrix of 0s and 1s).

Now, the SelfAttentionLayer supports both masked and unmasked inputs.

If the mask is provided, add a large negative value to make the final probabilities zero for the words not to be seen.

```
h = tf.matmul(p, v)
return h,p
```

Creating the mask is easy; you can use the `tf.linalg.band_part()` function to create triangular matrices

```
mask = 1 - tf.linalg.band_part(tf.ones((7, 7)), -1, 0)
```

which gives

```
>>> tf.Tensor(
    [[0. 1. 1. 1. 1. 1. 1.]
     [0. 0. 1. 1. 1. 1. 1.]
     [0. 0. 0. 1. 1. 1. 1.]
     [0. 0. 0. 0. 1. 1. 1.]
     [0. 0. 0. 0. 0. 1. 1.]
     [0. 0. 0. 0. 0. 0. 1.]
     [0. 0. 0. 0. 0. 0. 0.]], shape=(7, 7), dtype=float32)
```

We can easily verify if the masking worked by looking at the probability matrix p. It must be a lower triangular matrix

```
layer = SelfAttentionLayer(512)
h, p = layer(x, x, x, mask)
print(p.numpy())
```

which gives

```
>>> [[1.    0.    0.    0.    0.    0.    0.   ]
     [0.37  0.63  0.    0.    0.    0.    0.   ]
     [0.051 0.764 0.185 0.    0.    0.    0.   ]
     [0.138 0.263 0.072 0.526 0.    0.    0.   ]
     [0.298 0.099 0.201 0.11  0.293 0.    0.   ]
     [0.18  0.344 0.087 0.25  0.029 0.108 0.   ]
     [0.044 0.044 0.125 0.284 0.351 0.106 0.045]]
```

Now, when computing the value, the model cannot see or attend the words it hasn't seen by the time it comes to the current word.

5.2.7 Multi-head attention

The original Transformer paper discusses something called multi-head attention, which is an extension of the self-attention layer. The idea is simple once you understand the self-attention mechanism. The multi-head attention creates multiple parallel self-attention heads. The motivation for this is that, practically, when the model is given the opportunity to learn multiple attention patterns (i.e., multiple sets of weights) for an input sequence, it performs better.

Remember that in a single attention head we had all query, key, and value dimensionality set to 512. In other words,

$$d_q = d_k = d_v = 512$$

With multi-head attention, assuming we are using eight attention heads,

$$d_q = d_k = d_v = 512/8 = 64$$

Then the final outputs of all attention heads are concatenated to create the final output, which will have a dimensionality of $64 \times 8 = 512$

$$H = Concat\ (h^1, h^2, ..., h^8)$$

where h^i is the output of the ith attention head. Using the `SelfAttentionLayer` we just implemented, the code becomes

```
multi_attn_head = [SelfAttentionLayer(64) for i in range(8)]
outputs = [head(x, x, x)[0] for head in multi_attn_head]
outputs = tf.concat(outputs, axis=-1)
print(outputs.shape)
```

which gives

```
>>> (1, 7, 512)
```

As you can see, it still has the same shape as before (without multiple heads). However, this output is computed using multiple heads, which have smaller dimensionality than the original self-attention layer.

5.2.8 *Fully connected layer*

The fully connected layer is a piece of cake compared to what we just learned. So far, the self-attention layer has produced a $n \times d_v$–sized output (ignoring the batch dimension). The fully connected layer takes this input and performs the following transformation

$$h_1 = ReLU(xW_1 + b_1)$$

where W_1 is a $d_v \times d_{ff1}$ matrix and b_1 is a d_{ff1}–sized vector. Therefore, this operation gives out a $n \times d_{ff1}$–sized tensor. The resulting output is passed onto another layer, which does the following computation

$$h_2 = h_1\ W_2 + b_2$$

where W_2 is a $d_{ff1} \times d_{ff2}$–sized matrix and b_2 is a d_{ff2}–sized vector. This operation gives a tensor of size $n \times d_{ff2}$. In TensorFlow parlance, we can again encapsulate these computations as a reusable Keras layer (see the next listing).

Listing 5.3 The fully connected sublayer

```
import tensorflow as tf

class FCLayer(layers.Layer):
```

```
def __init__(self, d1, d2):
    super(FCLayer, self).__init__()
    self.d1 = d1
    self.d2 = d2

def build(self, input_shape):
    self.W1 = self.add_weight(
        shape=(input_shape[-1], self.d1), initializer='glorot_uniform',
        trainable=True, dtype='float32'
    )
    self.b1 = self.add_weight(
        shape=(self.d1,), initializer='glorot_uniform',
        trainable=True, dtype='float32'
    )
    self.W2 = self.add_weight(
        shape=(input_shape[-1], self.d2), initializer='glorot_uniform',
        trainable=True, dtype='float32'
    )
    self.b2 = self.add_weight(
        shape=(self.d2,), initializer='glorot_uniform',
        trainable=True, dtype='float32'
    )

def call(self, x):
    ff1 = tf.nn.relu(tf.matmul(x,self.W1)+self.b1)
    ff2 = tf.matmul(ff1,self.W2)+self.b2
    return ff2
```

The output dimensionality of the first fully connected computation

The output dimensionality of the second fully connected computation

Defining W1, b1, W2, and b2 accordingly. We use glorot_uniform as the initializer.

Computing the first fully connected computation

Computing the second fully connected computation

Here, you could use the `tensorflow.keras.layers.Dense()` layer to implement this functionality. However, we will do it with raw TensorFlow operations as an exercise to familiarize ourselves with low-level TensorFlow. In this setup, we will change the FCLayer, as shown in the following listing.

Listing 5.4   The fully connected layer implemented using Keras `Dense` layers

```
import tensorflow as tf
import tensorflow.keras.layers as layers

class FCLayer(layers.Layer):

    def __init__(self, d1, d2):
        super(FCLayer, self).__init__()
        self.dense_layer_1 = layer.Dense(d1, activation='relu')
        self.dense_layer_2 = layers.Dense(d2)

    def call(self, x):
        ff1 = self.dense_layer_1(x)
        ff2 = self.dense_layer_2(ff1)
        return ff2
```

Defining the first Dense layer in the __init__ function of the subclassed layer

Defining the second Dense layer. Note how we are not specifying an activation function.

Calling the second dense layer with the output of the first Dense layer to get the final output

Calling the first dense layer to get the output

Now you know what computations take place in the Transformer architecture and how to implement them with TensorFlow. But keep in mind that there are various fine-grained details explained in the original Transformer paper, which we haven't discussed. Most of these details will be discussed in a later chapter.

EXERCISE 2

Say you have been asked to experiment with a new type of multi-head attention mechanism. Instead of concatenating outputs from smaller heads (of size 64), the outputs (of size 512) are summed. Write TensorFlow code using the SelfAttentionLayer to achieve this effect. You can use the tf.math.add_n() function to sum a list of tensors element-wise.

5.2.9   *Putting everything together*

Let's bring all these elements together to create a Transformer network. Let's first create an encoder layer, which contains a set of SelfAttentionLayer objects (one for each head) and a FCLayer (see the next listing).

Listing 5.5   The encoder layer

```
import tensorflow as tf

class EncoderLayer(layers.Layer):

    def __init__(self, d, n_heads):
        super(EncoderLayer, self).__init__()
        self.d = d
        self.d_head = int(d/n_heads)
        self.n_heads = n_heads
        self.attn_heads = [
            SelfAttentionLayer(self.d_head) for i in range(self.n_heads)
        ]
        self.fc_layer = FCLayer(2048, self.d)

    def call(self, x):
        def compute_multihead_output(x):
            outputs = [head(x, x, x)[0] for head in self.attn_heads]
            outputs = tf.concat(outputs, axis=-1)
            return outputs

        h1 = compute_multihead_output(x)
        y = self.fc_layer(h1)

        return y
```

Create the fully connected layer, where the intermediate layer has 2,048 nodes and the final sublayer has d nodes.

Create multiple attention heads. Each attention head has d/n_heads–sized feature dimensionality.

Create a function that computes the multi-head attention output given an input.

Compute multi-head attention using the defined function.

Get the final output of the layer.

The EncoderLayer takes in two parameters during initialization: d (dimensionality of the output) and n_heads (number of attention heads). Then, when calling the layer, a single input x is passed. First, the attended output of the attention heads (SelfAttention-Layer) is computed, followed by the output of the fully connected layer (FCLayer). This wraps the crux of an encoder layer. Next, we create a Decoder layer (see the next listing).

Listing 5.6   The `DecoderLayer`

```
import tensorflow as tf

class DecoderLayer(layers.Layer):

    def __init__(self, d, n_heads):
        super(DecoderLayer, self).__init__()
        self.d = d
        self.d_head = int(d/n_heads)
        self.dec_attn_heads = [
            SelfAttentionLayer(self.d_head) for i in range(n_heads)
        ]
        self.attn_heads = [
            SelfAttentionLayer(self.d_head) for i in range(n_heads)
        ]
        self.fc_layer = FCLayer(2048, self.d)

    def call(self, de_x, en_x, mask=None):
        def compute_multihead_output(de_x, en_x, mask=None):
            outputs = [
                head(en_x, en_x, de_x, mask)[0] for head in
        self.attn_heads]
            outputs = tf.concat(outputs, axis=-1)
            return outputs

        h1 = compute_multihead_output(de_x, de_x, mask)
        h2 = compute_multihead_output(h1, en_x)
        y = self.fc_layer(h2)
        return y
```

Create the attention heads that process the decoder input only.

Create the attention heads that process both the encoder output and decoder input.

The final fully connected sublayer

Each head takes the first argument of the function as the query and key and the second argument of the function as the value.

Compute the first attended output. This only looks at the decoder inputs.

Compute the final output of the layer by feeding the output through a fully connected sublayer.

Compute the second attended output. This looks at both the previous decoder output and the encoder output.

The function that computes the multi-head attention. This function takes three inputs (decoder's previous output, encoder output, and an optional mask).

The decoder layer has several differences compared to the encoder layer. It contains two multi-head attention layers (one masked and one unmasked) and a fully connected layer. First, the output of the first multi-head attention layer (masked) is computed. Remember that we are masking any decoder input that is ahead of the current decoder input that's been processed. We use the decoder inputs to compute the output of the first attention layer. However, the computations happening in the second layer are a bit tricky. Brace yourselves! The second attention layer takes the encoder network's last attended output as query and key; then, to compute the value, the output of the first attention layer is used. Think of this layer as a mixer that mixes attended encoder outputs and attended decoder inputs.

With that, we can create a simple Transformer model with two encoder layers and two decoder layers). We'll use the Keras functional API (see the next listing).

Listing 5.7 The full Transformer model

Compute the output of the first encoder layer.

The encoder's input layer. It accepts a batch of a sequence of word IDs.

The embedding layer that will look up the word ID and return an embedding vector for that ID

The mask that will be used to mask decoder inputs

The hyperparameters of the Transformer model

The decoder's input layer. It accepts a batch of a sequence of word IDs.

The final prediction layer that predicts the correct output sequence

Defining the model. Note how we are providing a name for the model.

The decoder's embedding layer

Compute the output of the first decoder layer.

```
import tensorflow as tf

n_steps = 25
n_en_vocab = 300
n_de_vocab = 400
n_heads = 8
d = 512
mask = 1 - tf.linalg.band_part(tf.ones((n_steps, n_steps)), -1, 0)

en_inp = layers.Input(shape=(n_steps,))
en_emb = layers.Embedding(n_en_vocab, 512, input_length=n_steps)(en_inp)
en_out1 = EncoderLayer(d, n_heads)(en_emb)
en_out2 = EncoderLayer(d, n_heads)(en_out1)

de_inp = layers.Input(shape=(n_steps,))
de_emb = layers.Embedding(n_de_vocab, 512, input_length=n_steps)(de_inp)
de_out1 = DecoderLayer(d, n_heads)(de_emb, en_out2, mask)
de_out2 = DecoderLayer(d, n_heads)(de_out1, en_out2, mask)
de_pred = layers.Dense(n_de_vocab, activation='softmax')(de_out2)

transformer = models.Model(
    inputs=[en_inp, de_inp], outputs=de_pred, name='MinTransformer'
)
transformer.compile(
    loss='categorical_crossentropy', optimizer='adam', metrics=['acc']
)
```

Before diving into the details, let's refresh our memory with what the Transformer architecture looks like (figure 5.10).

Since we have explored the underpinning elements quite intensively, the network should be very easy to follow. All we have to do is set up the encoder model, set up the decoder model, and combine these appropriately by creating a Model object. Initially we define several hyperparameters. Our model takes n_steps-long sentences. This means that if a given sentence is shorter than n_steps, we will pad a special token to make it n_steps long. If a given sentence is longer than n_steps, we will truncate the sentence up to n_steps words. The larger the n_steps value, the more information you retain in the sentences, but also the more memory your model will consume. Next, we have the vocabulary size of the encoder inputs (i.e., the number of unique words in the data set fed to the encoder) (n_en_vocab), the vocabulary size of the decoder inputs (n_de_vocab), the number of heads (n_heads), and the output dimensionality (d).

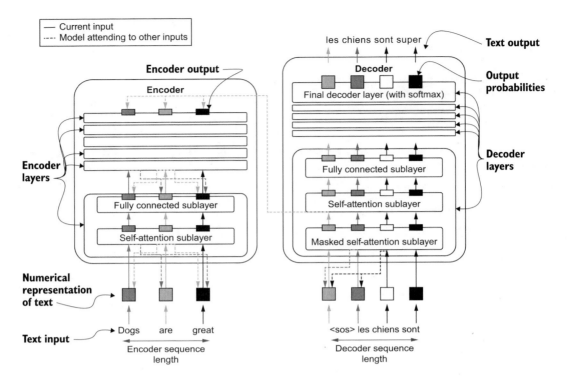

Figure 5.10   The Transformer model architecture

With that we have defined the encoder input layer, which takes a batch of n_steps–long sentences. In these sentences, each word will be represented by a unique ID. For example, the sentence "The cat sat on the mat" will be converted to [1, 2, 3, 4, 1, 5]. Next, we have a special layer called Embedding, which provides a d elements–long representation for each word (i.e., word vectors). After this transformation, you have a (batch size, n_steps, d)–sized output, which is the format of the output that should go into the self-attention layer. We discussed this transformation briefly in chapter 3 (section 3.4.3). The Embedding layer is essentially a lookup table. Given a unique ID (each ID represents a word), it gives out a vector that is d elements long. In other words, this layer encapsulates a large matrix of size (vocabulary size, d). You can see that when defining the Embedding layer:

```
layers.Embedding(n_en_vocab, 512, input_length=n_steps)
```

We need to provide the vocabulary size (the first argument) and the output dimensionality (the second argument), and finally, since we are processing an input sequence of length n_steps, we need to specify the input_length argument. With that, we can pass the output of the embedding layer (en_emb) to an Encoder layer. You can see that we have two encoder layers in our model.

Next, moving on to the decoder, everything at a high level looks identical to the encoder, except for two differences:

- The `Decoder` layer takes both the encoder output (`en_out2`) and the decoder input (`de_emb` or `de_out1`) as inputs.
- The `Decoder` layer also has a final `Dense` layer that produces the correct output sequence (e.g., in a machine translation task, these would be the translated word probabilities for each time step).

You can now define and compile the model as

```
transformer = models.Model(
    inputs=[en_inp, de_inp], outputs=de_pred, name='MinTransformer'
)
transformer.compile(
    loss='categorical_crossentropy', optimizer='adam', metrics=['acc']
)
```

Note that we can provide a name for our model when defining it. We will name our model "MinTransformer." As the final step, let's look at the model summary,

```
transformer.summary()
```

which will provide the following output:

```
Model: "MinTransformer"
```

Layer (type)	Output Shape	Param #	Connected to
input_1 (InputLayer)	[(None, 25)]	0	
embedding (Embedding)	(None, 25, 512)	153600	input_1[0][0]
input_2 (InputLayer)	[(None, 25)]	0	
encoder_layer (EncoderLayer)	(None, 25, 512)	2886144	embedding[0][0]
embedding_1 (Embedding)	(None, 25, 512)	204800	input_2[0][0]
encoder_layer_1 (EncoderLayer)	(None, 25, 512)	2886144	encoder_layer[0][0]
decoder_layer (DecoderLayer)	(None, 25, 512)	3672576	embedding_1[0][0] encoder_layer_1[0][0]
decoder_layer_1 (DecoderLayer)	(None, 25, 512)	3672576	decoder_layer[0][0] encoder_layer_1[0][0]
dense (Dense)	(None, 25, 400)	205200	decoder_layer_1[0][0]

```
Total params: 13,681,040
Trainable params: 13,681,040
Non-trainable params: 0
```

The workshop participants are going to walk out of this workshop a happy bunch. You have covered the essentials of Transformer networks while teaching the participants to implement their own. We first explained that the Transformer has an encoder-decoder architecture. We then looked at the composition of the encoder and the decoder, which are made of self-attention layers and fully connected layers. The self-attention layer allows the model to attend to other input words while processing a given input word, which is important when processing natural language. We also saw that, in practice, the model uses multiple attention heads in a single attention layer to improve performance. Next, the fully connected layer creates a nonlinear representation of the attended output. After understanding the basic elements, we implemented a basic small-scale Transformer network using reusable custom layers we created for the self-attention (`SelfAttentionLayer`) and fully connected layer (`FCLayer`).

The next step is to train this model on an NLP data set (e.g., machine translation). However, training these models is a topic for a separate chapter. There's a lot more to Transformers than what we have discussed. For example, there are pretrained transformer-based models that you can use readily to solve NLP tasks. We will revisit Transformers again in a later chapter.

Summary

- Transformer networks have outperformed other models in almost all NLP tasks.
- Transformers are an encoder-decoder–type neural network that is mainly used for learning NLP tasks.
- With Transformers, the encoder and decoder are made of two computational sublayers: self-attention layers and fully connected layers.
- The self-attention layer produces a weighted sum of inputs for a given time step, based on how important it is to attend to other positions in the sequence while processing the current position.
- The fully connected layer creates a nonlinear representation of the attended output produced by the self-attention layer.
- The decoder uses masking in its self-attention layer to make sure that the decoder does not see any future predictions while producing the current prediction.

Answers to exercises

Exercise 1

```
Wq = tf.Variable(np.random.normal(size=(256,512)))
Wk = tf.Variable (np.random.normal(size=(256,512)))
Wv = tf.Variable (np.random.normal(size=(256,512)))
```

Exercise 2

```
multi_attn_head = [SelfAttentionLayer(512) for i in range(8)]
outputs = [head(x)[0] for head in multi_attn_head]
outputs = tf.math.add_n(outputs)
```

Part 2

Look ma, no hands! Deep networks in the real world

A well-versed ML practitioner is a multifaceted individual. Not only do they need a good understanding of modern deep learning frameworks such as TensorFlow, but they also need to be able to navigate the complex APIs offered by it to implement complex deep learning models to solve some of the common machine learning problems in domains like computer vision and natural language processing.

In part 2, we look at real-world problems in both computer vision and natural language processing. First, we look at image classification and image segmentation, which are two popular computer vision tasks. For these tasks, we analyze modern complex deep learning models that have performed well on a given problem. Not only will we implement these models from scratch, we will understand the reasoning behind core design decisions and the advantages they bring about.

Next, we move to natural language processing. We first look at a sentiment analysis task and how deep learning can solve it. We also explore various corners of the solution, such as basic NLP preprocessing steps and using word vectors to enhance performance. We then look at language modeling: a pretraining task that gives the enormous language understanding enjoyed by state-of-the-art NLP models. In this discussion, we again discuss various techniques that are incorporated in language modeling to enhance the prediction quality.

Teaching machines to see: Image classification with CNNs

This chapter covers

- Exploratory data analysis on image data in Python
- Preprocessing and feeding data via image pipelines
- Using the Keras functional API to implement a complex CNN model
- Training and evaluating the CNN model

We have already done a fair bit of work on CNNs. CNNs are a type of network that can operate on two-dimensional data, such as images. CNNs use the convolution operation to create feature maps of images (i.e., a grid of pixels) by moving a kernel (i.e., a smaller grid of values) over the image to produce new values. The CNN has several of these layers that generate more and more high-level feature maps as they get deeper. You can also use max or average pooling layers between convolutional layers to reduce the dimensionality of the feature maps. The pooling layers also move a kernel over feature maps to create the smaller representation of the input. The final feature maps are connected to a series of fully connected layers, where the final layer produces the prediction (e.g., the probability of an image belonging to a certain category).

We have implemented CNN using the Keras Sequential API. We used various Keras layers such as `Conv2D`, `MaxPool2D`, and `Dense` to easily implement CNNs. We've already studied various parameters related to the `Conv2D` and `MaxPool2D` layers, such as window size, stride, and padding.

In this chapter, we will come a step closer to seeing CNNs performing on real-world data to solve an exciting problem. There's more to machine learning than implementing a simple CNN to learn from a highly curated data set, as real-world data is often messy. You will be introduced to exploratory data analysis, which is at the heart of the machine learning life cycle. You will explore an image data set, where the objective is to identify the object present in the image (known as *image classification*). We will then extensively study one of the state-of-the-art models in computer vision, known as the inception model. In deep learning, there are widely recognized neural network architectures (or templates) that perform well on a given task. The inception model is one such model that has been shown to perform well on image data. We will study the architecture of the model and the motivations behind several novel design concepts used in it. Finally, we will train the model on the data set we explored and analyze model performance by relying on metrics such as accuracy on test data.

We have come a long way. We understand the technical aspects of the main deep learning algorithms out there and can be confident in our ability to perform exploratory data analysis correctly and thus enter the model stage with confidence. However, deep networks can get very large very quickly. Complex networks drag in all sorts of computational and performance problems. So, anyone who wants to use these algorithms in real-world problems needs to learn existing models that have proven to perform well in complex learning tasks.

6.1 Putting the data under the microscope: Exploratory data analysis

You are working with a team of data scientists to build a versatile image classification model. The end goal is to use this model as a part of an intelligent shopping assistant. The user can upload a photo of the inside of their home, and the assistant will find suitable products based on their style. The team decided to start out with an image classification model. You need to come back to the group with a great data set to start with and to explain what the data looks like and why it is great. The data set contains day-to-day objects photographed in the real world, and you will do exploratory data analysis and look at various attributes of the data set (e.g., available classes, data set sizes, image attributes) to understand the data and identify and fix potential issues.

Exploratory data analysis (EDA) is the cornerstone of the technical development that you will do in a data science project. The main objective of this process is to get a high-quality clean data set by the end of the process by removing pesky problems like outliers and noise. In order to have such a data set, you need to scrutinize your data and find out if there are

- Imbalanced classes (in a classification problem)
- Corrupted data
- Missing features
- Outliers
- Features that require various transformations (e.g., normalization, one-hot encoding)

This is by no means an exhaustive list of things to look out for. The more exploration you do, the better the quality of the data.

What comes before EDA?

A machine learning problem always start with a business problem. Once the problem is properly identified and understood, you can start thinking about the data: What data do we have? What do we train the model to predict? How do these predictions translate to actionable insights that deliver benefits to the company? After you tick these boxes off, you can retrieve and start playing with the data by means of EDA. After all, every single step in a machine learning project needs to be done with a purpose.

You have already spent days researching and have found a data set that is appropriate for your problem. To develop an intelligent shopping assistant that can understand customers' style preferences, it should be able to identify as many household items as possible from the photos that customers will upload. For this, you are planning to use the `tiny-imagenet-200` (https://www.kaggle.com/c/tiny-imagenet) data set.

The ImageNet data set

Tiny ImageNet is a smaller-scale remake of the original ImageNet data set (https://www.kaggle.com/competitions/imagenet-object-localization-challenge), which is part of the annual ImageNet Large Scale Visual Recognition Challenge (ILSVRC) challenge. Each year, research teams all around the world compete to come up with state-of-the-art image classification and detection models. This data set has around 1.2 million labeled images spread across 1,000 classes and has become one of the largest labeled image data sets available in computer vision.

This data set has images belonging to 200 different classes. Figure 6.1 depicts images for some of the available classes.

First things first. We need to download the data set. The following code will create a directory called data in your working directory, download the zip file containing the

Figure 6.1   **Some sample images from the `tiny-imagenet-200`. You can see that these images belong to a wide variety of categories.**

data, and extract it for you. Finally, you should have a folder called tiny-imagenet-200 in the data folder:

```
import os
import requests
import zipfile
if not os.path.exists(os.path.join('data','tiny-imagenet-200.zip')):
    url = "http://cs231n.stanford.edu/tiny-imagenet-200.zip"
    r = requests.get(url)

    if not os.path.exists('data'):
        os.mkdir('data')

    with open(os.path.join('data','tiny-imagenet-200.zip'), 'wb') as f:
        f.write(r.content)

    with zipfile.ZipFile(
        os.path.join('data','tiny-imagenet-200.zip'), 'r'
    ) as zip_ref:
        zip_ref.extractall('data')
else:
    print("The file already exists.")
```

6.1.1   *The folder/file structure*

The data should now be available in the Ch06/data folder. Now it's time to explore the data set. The first thing we will do is manually explore the data in the folders provided to us. You'll note that there are three folders and two files (figure 6.2). Look around and explore them.

The file wnids.txt contains a set of 200 IDs (called *wnids* or WordNet IDs, based on the lexical database WordNet [https://wordnet.princeton.edu/]; figure 6.3). Each of these IDs represents a single class of images (e.g., class of gold fish).

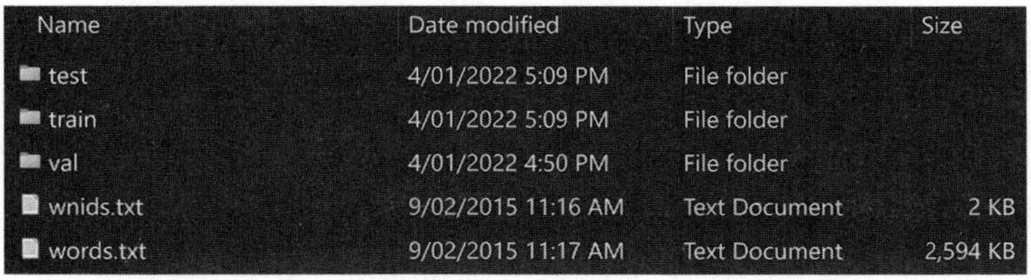

Name	Date modified	Type	Size
test	4/01/2022 5:09 PM	File folder	
train	4/01/2022 5:09 PM	File folder	
val	4/01/2022 4:50 PM	File folder	
wnids.txt	9/02/2015 11:16 AM	Text Document	2 KB
words.txt	9/02/2015 11:17 AM	Text Document	2,594 KB

Figure 6.2 The folders and files found in the `tiny-imagenet-200` data set

```
n02124075
n04067472
n04540053
n04099969
n07749582
n01641577
n02802426
n09246464
n07920052
n03970156
n03891332
```

Figure 6.3 Sample content from wnids.txt. It contains wnids (WordNet IDs), one per line.

The file words.txt provides a human touch to these IDs by giving the description of each wnid in a tab-separated-value (TSV) format (table 6.1). Note that this file contains more than 82,000 lines (well over the 200 classes we have) and comes from a much larger data set.

Table 6.1 Sample content from words.txt. It contains the wnids and their descriptions for the data found in the data set.

n00001740	entity
n00001930	physical entity
n00002137	abstraction, abstract entity
n00002452	thing
n00002684	object, physical object
n00003553	whole, unit
n00003993	congener
n00004258	living thing, animate thing
n00004475	organism, being
n00005787	benthos
n00005930	dwarf
n00006024	heterotroph
n00006150	parent

Table 6.1   (continued) Sample content from words.txt. It contains the wnids and their descriptions for the data found in the data set.

n00006269	life
n00006400	biont

The train folder contains the training data. It contains a subfolder called images, and within that, you can find 200 folders, each with a label (i.e., a wnid). Inside each of these subfolders, you'll find a collection of images representing that class. Each subfolder having a wnid as its name contains 500 images per class, 100,000 in total (in all subfolders). Figure 6.4 depicts this structure, as well as some of the data found in the train folder.

The val folder contains a subfolder called images and a collection of images (these are not divided into further subfolders like in the train folder). The labels (or wnids) for these images can be found in the val_annotations.txt file in the val folder.

The final folder is called the test folder, which we will ignore in this chapter. This data set is part of a competition, and the data is used to score the submitted models. We don't have labels for this test set.

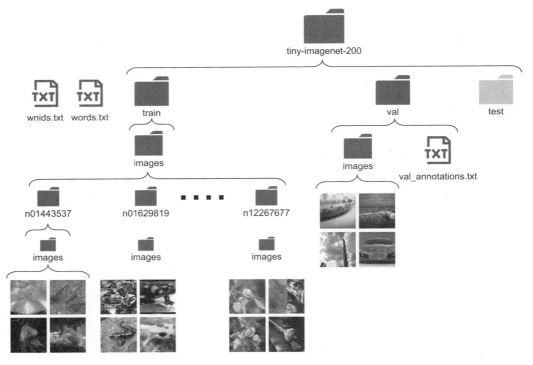

Figure 6.4   The overall structure of the `tiny-imagenet-200` data set. It has three text files (wnids.txt, words.txt, and val/val_annotations.txt) and three folders (train, val, and test). We will only use the train and val folders.

6.1.2 Understanding the classes in the data set

We have seen what kind of data we have and where it is available. For the next step, let's identify some of the classes in the data. For that, we will define a function called `get_tiny_imagenet_classes()` that reads the wnids.txt and words.txt files and creates a `pd.DataFrame` (a pandas DataFrame) with two columns: the wnid and its corresponding class description (see the next listing).

> **Listing 6.1 Getting class descriptions of the classes in the data set**

Defines a function to read the class descriptions of tiny_imagenet classes

```
import pandas as pd          Imports pandas
import os                    and os packages

data_dir = os.path.join('data', 'tiny-imagenet-200')      Defines paths of the data
wnids_path = os.path.join(data_dir, 'wnids.txt')          directory, wnids.txt, and
words_path = os.path.join(data_dir, 'words.txt')          words.txt files

def get_tiny_imagenet_classes(wnids_path, words_path):
    wnids = pd.read_csv(wnids_path, header=None, squeeze=True)
    words = pd.read_csv(words_path, sep='\t', index_col=0, header=None)
    words_200 = words.loc[wnids].rename({1:'class'}, axis=1)
    words_200.index.name = 'wnid'
    return words_200.reset_index()

labels = get_tiny_imagenet_classes(wnids_path, words_path)
labels.head(n=25)
```

Reads wnids.txt and words.txt as CSV files using pandas

Inspects the head of the data frame (the first 25 entries)

Executes the function to obtain the class descriptions

Resets the index so that it becomes a column in the data frame (which has the column name "wnid")

Sets the name of the index of the data frame to "wnid"

Gets only the classes present in the tiny-imagenet-200 data set

This function first reads the wnids.txt that contains a list of wnids that correspond to the classes available in the data set as a `pd.Series` (i.e., pandas series) object. Next, it reads the words.txt file as a `pd.DataFrame` (a pandas DataFrame), which contains a wnid to class description mapping, and assigns it to `words`. Then, it picks the items from `words` where the wnid is present in the wnids pandas series. This will return a `pd.DataFrame` with 200 rows (table 6.2). Remember that the number of items in words.txt is much larger than the actual data set, so we only need to pick the items that are relevant to us.

Table 6.2   Sample of the labels' IDs and their descriptions that we generate using the `get_tiny_imagenet_classes()` function

	wind	class
0	n02124075	Egyptian cat
1	n04067472	reel
2	n04540053	volleyball
3	n04099969	rocking chair, rocker
4	n07749582	lemon
5	n01641577	bullfrog, Rana catesbeiana
6	n02802426	basketball
7	n09246464	cliff, drop, drop-off
8	n07920052	espresso
9	n03970156	plunger, plumber's helper
10	n03891332	parking meter
11	n02106662	German shepherd, German shepherd dog, German p...
12	n03201208	dining table, board
13	n02279972	monarch, monarch butterfly, milkweed butterfly
14	n02132136	brown bear, bruin, Ursus arctos
15	n041146614	school bus

We will then compute how many data points (i.e., images) there are for each class:

```
def get_image_count(data_dir):
    # Get the count of JPEG files in a given folder (data_dir)
    return len(
        [f for f in os.listdir(data_dir) if f.lower().endswith('jpeg')]
    )

    # Apply the function above to all the subdirectories in the train folder
labels["n_train"] = labels["wnid"].apply(
    lambda x: get_image_count(os.path.join(data_dir, 'train', x, 'images'))
)
# Get the top 10 entries in the labels dataframe
labels.head(n=10)
```

This code creates a new column called n_train that shows how many data points (i.e., images) were found for each wnid. This can be achieved using the pandas pd.Series .apply() function, which applies get_image_count() to each item in the series labels["wnid"]. Specifically, get_image_count() takes in a path and returns the number of JPEG files found in that folder. When you use this get_image_count() function in conjunction with `pd.Series.apply()`, it goes to every single folder within the train folder that has a wnid as its name and counts the number of images. Once you run the line `labels.head(n=10)`, you should get the result shown in table 6.3.

Table 6.3 Sample of the data where `n_train` (number of training samples) has been calculated

	wind	class	n_train
0	n02124075	Egyptian cat	500
1	n04067472	reel	500
2	n04540053	volleyball	500
3	n04099969	rocking chair, rocker	500
4	n07749582	lemon	500
5	n01641577	bullfrog, Rana catesbeiana	500
6	n02802426	basketball	500
7	n09246464	cliff, drop, drop-off	500
8	n07920052	espresso	500
9	n03970156	plunger, plumber's helper	500

Let's quickly verify that the results are correct. Go into the n02802426 subdirectory in the train folder, which should contain images of basketballs. Figure 6.5 shows a few sample images.

Figure 6.5   Sample images for the wnid category n02802426 (i.e., basketball)

You might find these images quite the opposite of what you expected. You might have expected to see clear and zoomed-in images of basketballs. But in the real world, that's never the case. Real-life data sets are noisy. You can see the following images:

- The basketball is hardly visible (top left).
- The basketball is green (bottom left).
- The basketball is next to a baby (i.e., out of context) (top middle).

This will make you admire deep networks a bit more, as this is a hard problem for a bunch of stacked matrix multiplications (i.e., deep networks). Precise scene understanding is required to successfully solve this task. Despite the difficulty, the reward is significant. The model we develop is ultimately going to be used to identify objects in various backgrounds and contexts, such as living rooms, kitchens, and outdoors. And that is exactly what this data set trains your model for: to understand/detect objects in various contexts. You can probably imagine why the modern-day CAPTCHAs are becoming increasingly smarter and can keep up with algorithms that are able to classify objects more accurately. It is not difficult for a properly trained CNN to recognize a CAPTCHA that has cluttered backgrounds or small occlusions.

You can also quickly check the summary statistics (e.g., mean value, standard deviation, etc.) of the n_train column we generated. This provides a more digestible summary of the column than having to look through all 200 rows. This is done using the pandas describe() function:

```
labels["n_train"].describe()
```

Executing this will return the following series:

```
count    200.0
mean     500.0
std        0.0
min      500.0
25%      500.0
50%      500.0
75%      500.0
max      500.0
Name: n_train, dtype: float64
```

You can see that it returns important statistics of the column, such as the mean value, standard deviation, minimum, and maximum. Every class has 500 images, meaning the data set is perfectly class balanced. This is a handy way to verify that we have a class-balanced data set.

6.1.3   *Computing simple statistics on the data set*

Analyzing various attributes of the data is also an important step. The type of analysis will change depending on the type of data you work with. Here, we will find out the average size of images (or even the 25/50/75 percentiles).

Having this information ready by the time you get to the actual model saves you a lot of time in making certain decisions. For example, you must know basic statistics of the image size (height and width) to crop or pad images to a fixed size, as image classification CNNs can only process fixed-sized images (see the next listing).

Listing 6.2   Computing image width and height statistics

```
import os
from PIL import Image
import pandas as pd

image_sizes = []
for wnid in labels["wnid"].iloc[:25]:
    img_dir = os.path.join(
        'data', 'tiny-imagenet-200', 'train', wnid, 'images'
    )
    for f in os.listdir(img_dir):
        if f.endswith('JPEG'):
            image_sizes.append(Image.open(os.path.join(img_dir, f)).size)

img_df = pd.DataFrame.from_records(image_sizes)
img_df.columns = ["width", "height"]
img_df.describe()
```

Importing os, PIL, and pandas packages

Defining a list to hold image sizes

Looping through the first 25 classes in the data set

Looping through all the images (ending with the extension JPEG) in that directory

Creating a data frame from the tuples in the image_sizes

Appending the size of each image (i.e., a tuple of (width, height)) to image_sizes

Obtaining the summary statistics of width and height for the images we fetched

Setting column names appropriately

Defining the image directory for a particular class within the loop

Here, we take the first 25 wnids from the `labels` DataFrame we created earlier (processing all the wnids would take too much time). Then, for each wnid, we go into the subfolder that contains the data belonging to it and obtain the width and height information for each image using

```
Image.open(os.path.join(img_dir, f)).size
```

`Image.open(<path>).size` returns a tuple (width, height) for a given image. We record the width and height of all images we come across in the `image_sizes` list. Finally, the `image_sizes` list looks like the following:

```
image_sizes = [(image_1.width, image_1.height), (image_2.width,
    image_2.height), …, (image_n.width, image_n.height)]
```

For data in this format, we can use the `pd.DataFrame.from_records()` function to create a `pd.DataFrame` out of this list. A single element in `image_sizes` is a record. For example, `(image_1.width, image_1.height)` is a record. Therefore, `image_sizes` is a list of records. When you create a `pd.DataFrame` from a list of records, each record becomes a row in the pandas DataFrame, where each element in each record becomes a column. For example, since we have image width and image height as elements in each record, width and height become columns in the pandas DataFrame. Finally, we execute `img_df.describe()` to get the basic statistics on the width and height of the images we read (table 6.4).

Table 6.4 Width and height statistics of the images

	width	height
count	12500.0	12500.0
mean	64.0	64.0
std	0.0	0.0
min	64.0	64.0
25%	64.0	64.0
50%	64.0	64.0
75%	64.0	64.0
max	64.0	64.0

Next, we will discuss how we can create a data pipeline to ingest the image data we just discussed.

EXERCISE 1

Assume that while browsing through the data set, you came across some corrupted images (i.e., they have negative-valued pixels). Assuming you already have a pd.Data-Frame() called df that has a single column with the image file paths (called file-path), use the pandas apply() function to read each image's minimum value and assign it to a column called minimum. To read the image, you can assume from PIL import Image and import numpy as np have been completed. You can also use np.array(<Image>) to turn a PIL.Image into an array.

6.2   *Creating data pipelines using the Keras ImageDataGenerator*

You have explored the data set well and understand things like how many classes there are, what kind of objects are present, and the sizes of the images. Now you will create three data generators for three different data sets: training, validation, and test. These data generators retrieve data from the disk in batches and perform any preprocessing required. This way, the data is readily consumable by a model. For this, we will use the convenient tensorflow.keras.preprocessing.image.ImageDataGenerator.

We will start by defining a Keras ImageDataGenerator() to feed in data when we build the model:

```
from tensorflow.keras.preprocessing.image import ImageDataGenerator
import os

random_seed = 4321
batch_size = 128
image_gen = ImageDataGenerator(samplewise_center=True, validation_split=0.1)
```

Setting `samplewise_center=True`, the images generated will have their values normalized. Each image will be centered by subtracting the mean pixel value of that image. `validation_split` argument plays a vital role in training the data. This lets us split the training data into two subsets, training and validation, by separating a chunk (10% in this example) from the training data. Typically, in a machine learning problem, you should have three data sets:

- *Training data*—Typically the largest data set. We use this to train the model.
- *Validation data*—Held-out data set. It is not used to train the model but to monitor the performance of the model during training. Note that this validation set must remain fixed (and should not change) during training.
- *Test data*—Held-out data set. Unlike the validation data set, this is used only after the training of the model is completed. This represents how well the model will do on unseen real-world data. This is because the model has not interacted with the test data set in any way (unlike the training and validation data sets) until test time.

We will also define a random seed and a batch size for later data generation.

Once you create an `ImageDataGenerator`, you can use one of its `flow` functions to read data coming from heterogeneous sources. For example, Keras currently offers the following methods:

- `flow()`—Reads data from a NumPy array or a pandas DataFrame
- `flow_from_dataframe()`—Reads data from a file that contains filenames and their associated labels
- `flow_from_directory()`—Reads from a folder where images are organized into subfolders according to the class where they belong

First, we will look at `flow_from_directory()`, because our train directory is in the exact format `flow_from_directory()` function expects the data to be in. Specifically, `flow_from_directory()` expects the data to be in the format shown in figure 6.6.

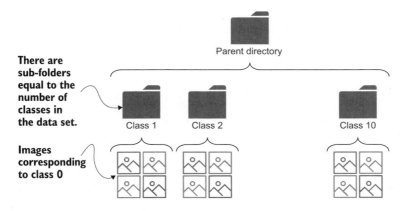

Figure 6.6   Folder structure expected by the `flow_from_directory()` method

The flow methods return data generators, which are Python generators. A generator is essentially a function that returns an iterator (called a *generator-iterator*). But to keep our discussion simple, we will refer to both the generator and the iterator as the generator. You can iterate the generator, just like a list, and return items in a sequential manner. Here's an example of a generator:

```
def simple_generator():
    for i in range(0, 100):
        yield (i, i*2)
```

Note the use of the keyword yield, which you can treat as you do the return keyword. However, unlike return, yield does not exit the function as soon as the line is executed. Now you can define the iterator as

```
iterator = simple_generator()
```

You can treat iterator like a list containing [(0, 0), (1, 2), (2, 4), …, (98, 196), (99, 198)]. However, under the hood, generators are far more memory efficient than list objects. In our case, the data generators will return a single batch of images and targets in a single iteration (i.e., a tuple of images and labels). You can directly feed these generators to a method like tf.keras.models.Model.fit() in order to train a model. The flow_from_directory() method is used to retrieve data:

```
target_size = (56,56)

train_gen = image_gen.flow_from_directory(
    directory=os.path.join('data','tiny-imagenet-200', 'train'),
    target_size=target_size, classes=None,
    class_mode='categorical', batch_size=batch_size,
    shuffle=True, seed=random_seed, subset='training'
)
valid_gen = image_gen.flow_from_directory (
    directory=os.path.join('data','tiny-imagenet-200', 'train'),
    target_size=target_size, classes=None,
    class_mode='categorical', batch_size=batch_size,
    shuffle=True, seed=random_seed, subset='validation'
)
```

You can see numerous arguments that have been set for these functions. The most important argument to note is the subset argument, which is set to "training" for train_gen and "validation" for valid_gen. The other arguments are as follows:

- directory (string)—The location of the parent directory, where data is further divided into subfolders representing classes.
- target_size (tuple of ints)—Target size of the images as a tuple of (height, width). Images will be resized to the specified height and width.
- class_mode (string)—The type of targets we are going to provide to the model. Because we want the targets to be one-hot encoded vectors representing each class, we will set it to 'categorical'. Available types include "categorical"

(default value), "binary" (for data sets with two classes, 0 or 1), "sparse" (numerical label as opposed to a one-hot encoded vector), "input" or None (no labels), and "raw" or "multi_output" (only available in special circumstances).

- batch_size (int)—The size of a single batch of data.
- shuffle (bool)—Whether to shuffle the data when fetching.
- seed (int)—The random seed for data shuffling, so we get consistent results every time we run it.
- subset (string)—If validation_split > 0, which subset you need. This needs to be set to either "training" or "validation".

Note that, even though we have 64 × 64 images, we are resizing them to 56 × 56. This is because the model we will use is designed for 224 × 224 images. Having an image size that is a factor of 224 × 224 makes adapting the model to our data much easier.

We can make our solution a bit shinier! You can see that between train_gen and valid_gen, there's a lot of repetition in the arguments used. In fact, all the arguments except subset are the same for both generators. This repetition clutters the code and creates room for errors (if you need to change arguments, you might set one and forget the other). You can use the partial function in Python to create a partial function with the repeating arguments and then use that to create both train_gen and valid_gen:

```
from functools import partial
target_size = (56,56)

partial_flow_func = partial(
        image_gen.flow_from_directory,
        directory=os.path.join('data','tiny-imagenet-200', 'train'),
        target_size=target_size, classes=None,
        class_mode='categorical', batch_size=batch_size,
        shuffle=True, seed=random_seed)

train_gen = partial_flow_func(subset='training')
valid_gen = partial_flow_func(subset='validation')
```

Here, we first create a partial_flow_function (a Python function), which is essentially the flow_from_directory function with some arguments already populated. Then, to create train_gen and valid_gen, we only pass the subset argument. This makes the code much cleaner.

Validation data check: Don't expect the framework to take care of things for you

Now that we have a training data generator and validation data generator, we shouldn't blindly commit to using them. We must make sure that our validation data, which is randomly sampled from the training data, is consistent every time we traverse the training data set. It seems like a trivial thing that should be taken care of by the framework itself, but it's better if you don't take that for granted. And if you do

(continued)

not do this check, you ultimately pay the price, so it is a good idea to make sure that we get consistent results across trials.

For this, you can iterate through the validation data generator's output multiple times for a fixed number of iterations and make sure you get the same label sequence in each trial. The code for this is available in the notebook (under the section "Validating the consistency of validation data").

We're still not done. We need to do a slight modification to the generator returned by the `flow_from_directory()` function. If you look at an item in the data generator, you'll see that it is a tuple (x, y), where x is a batch of images and y is a batch of one-hot-encoded targets. The model we use here has a final prediction layer and two additional auxiliary prediction layers. In total, the model has three output layers, so instead of a tuple (x, y), we need to return (x, (y, y, y)) by replicating y three times. We can fix this by defining a new generator `data_gen_aux()` that takes in the existing generator and modifies its output, as shown. This needs to be done for both the train data generator and validation data generator:

```
def data_gen_aux(gen):
    for x,y in gen:
        yield x,(y,y,y)

train_gen_aux = data_gen_aux(train_gen)
valid_gen_aux = data_gen_aux(valid_gen)
```

It's time to create a data generator for test data. Recall that we said the test data we are using (i.e., the `val` directory) is structured differently than the train and tran_val data folders. Therefore, it requires special treatment. The class labels are found in a file called val_annotations.txt, and the images are placed in a single folder with a flat structure. Not to worry; Keras has a function for this situation too. In this case, we will first read the val_annotations.txt as a `pd.DataFrame` using the `get_test_labels_df()` function. The function simply reads the val_annotations.txt file and creates a `pd.DataFrame` with two columns, the filename of an image and the class label:

```
def get_test_labels_df(test_labels_path):
    test_df = pd.read_csv(test_labels_path, sep='\t', index_col=None,
      header=None)
    test_df = test_df.iloc[:,[0,1]].rename({0:"filename", 1:"class"}, axis=1)
    return test_df

test_df = get_test_labels_df(os.path.join('data','tiny-imagenet-200', 'val',
    'val_annotations.txt'))
```

Next, we will use the `flow_from_dataframe()` function to create our test data generator. All you need to do is pass the `test_df` we created earlier (for the `dataframe` argument) and point at the directory where the images can be found (for the `directory` argument). Note that we are setting `shuffle=False` for test data, as we would like feed test data in the same order so that the performance metrics we monitor will be the same unless we change the model:

```
test_gen = image_gen.flow_from_dataframe(
    dataframe=test_df, directory=os.path.join('data','tiny-imagenet-
    200', 'val', 'images'), target_size=target_size,
class_mode='categorical', batch_size=batch_size, shuffle=False
    )
```

Next, we are going to define one of the complex computer vision models using Keras and eventually train it on the data we have prepared.

EXERCISE 2

As part of the testing process, say you want to see how robust the model is against corrupted labels in the training data. For this, you plan to create a generator that sets the label to 0 with 50% probability. How would you change the following generator for this purpose? You can use `np.random.normal()` to draw a value randomly from a normal distribution with zero mean and unit variance:

```
def data_gen_corrupt(gen):
    for x,y in gen:
        yield x,(y,y,y)
```

6.3   *Inception net: Implementing a state-of-the-art image classifier*

You have analyzed the data set and have a well-rounded idea of what the data looks like. For images, you inarguably turn to CNNs, as they are the best in the business. It's time to build a model to learn customers' personal tastes. Here, we will replicate one of the state-of-the-art CNN models (known as *Inception net*) using the Keras functional API.

Inception net is a complex CNN that has made its mark by delivering state-of-the art performance. Inception net draws its name from the popular internet meme "We need to go deeper" that features Leonardo De Caprio from the movie *Inception*.

The Inception model has six different versions that came out over the course of a short period of time (approximately 2015–2016). That is a testament to how popular the model was among computer vision researchers. To honor the past, we will implement the first inception model that came out (i.e., Inception net v1) and later compare it to other models. As this is an advanced CNN, a good understanding of its architecture and some design decisions is paramount. Let's look at the Inception model, how is it different from a typical CNN, and most importantly, why it is different.

The Inception model (or Inception net) isn't a typical CNN. Its prime characteristic is complexity, as the more complex (i.e., more parameters) the model is, the higher the accuracy. For example, Inception net v1 has close to 20 layers. But there are two main problems that rear their heads when it comes to complex models:

- If you don't have a big enough data set for a complex model, it is likely the model will overfit the training data, leading to poor overall performance on real-world data.
- Complex models lead to more training time and more engineering effort to fit those models into relatively small GPU memory.

This demands a more pragmatic way to approach this problem, such as by answering the question "How can we introduce *sparsity* in deep models (i.e., having fewer parameters) so that the risk of overfitting as well as the appetite for memory goes down?" This is the main question answered in the Inception net model.

What is overfitting?

Overfitting is an important concept in machine learning and can be notoriously hard to avoid. Overfitting refers to the phenomenon where the model learns to represent training data very well (i.e., high train accuracy) but performs poorly on unseen data (i.e., low test accuracy). This happens when the model tries to remember training samples rather than learn generalizable features from the data. This is prevalent in deep networks, as they usually have more parameters than the amount of data. Overfitting will be discussed in more detail in the next chapter.

Let's remind ourselves of the basics of CNNs.

6.3.1 Recap on CNNs

CNNs are predominantly used to process images and solve computer vision problems (e.g., image classification, object detection, etc.). As depicted in figure 6.7, a CNN has three components:

- Convolution layers
- Pooling layers
- Fully connected layers

The convolution operation shifts a small kernel (also called a filter) with a fixed size over the width and height dimensions of the input. While doing so, it produces a single value at each position. The convolution operation consumes an input with some width, height, and a number of channels and produces an output that has some width, height, and a single channel. To produce a multichannel output, a convolution layer stacks many of these filters, leading to as many outputs as the number of filters. A convolution layer has the following important parameters:

- *Number of filters*—Decides the channel depth (or the number of feature maps) of the output produced by the convolution layer

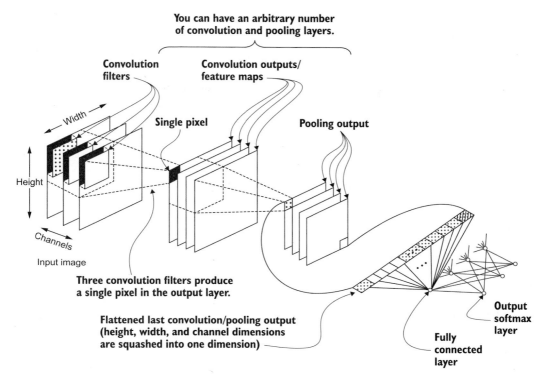

Figure 6.7 A simple convolutional neural network. First, we have an image with height, width, and channel dimensions, followed by a convolution and a pooling layer. Finally, the last convolution/pooling layer output is flattened and fed to a set of fully connected layers.

- *Kernel size*—Also known as the receptive field, it decides the size (i.e., height and width) of the filters. The larger the kernel size, the more of the image the model sees at a given time. But larger filters lead to longer training times and larger memory requirements.
- *Stride*—Determines how many pixels are skipped while convolving the image. A higher stride leads to a smaller output size (stride is typically used only on height and width dimensions).
- *Padding*—Prevents the automatic dimensionality reductions that take place during the convolution operation by adding an imaginary border of zeros, such that the output has the same height and width as the input.

Figure 6.8 shows the working of the convolution operation.

The pooling operation exhibits the same behavior as the convolution operation when processing an input. However, the exact computations involved are different. There are two different types of pooling: max and average. Max pooling takes the maximum value found in the dark gray box shown in figure 6.9 as the window moves

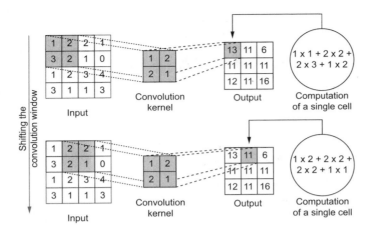

Figure 6.8   The computations that happen in the convolution operation while shifting the window

over the input. Average pooling takes the average value of the dark gray box as the window moves over the input.

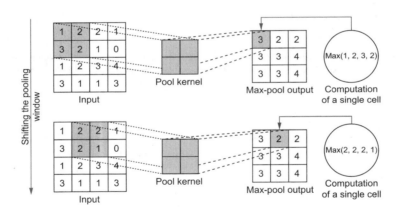

Figure 6.9   How the pooling operation computes the output. It looks at a small window and takes the maximum of the input in that window as the output for the corresponding cell.

NOTE   CNNs use average pooling as the closest to the output and max pooling layers everywhere else. This configuration has been found to deliver better performance.

The benefit of the pooling operation is that it makes CNNs translation invariant. Translation invariance means that the model can recognize an object regardless of where it appears. Due to the way max pooling is computed, the feature maps generated are similar, even when objects/features are offset by a small number of pixels from what the model was trained on. This means that if you are training a model to classify dogs, the network will be resilient against where exactly the dog appears (only to a certain extent).

Finally, you have a fully connected layer. As we are mostly interested in classification models right now, we need to output a probability distribution over the classes we have for any given image. We do that by connecting a small number of fully connected layers to the end of the CNNs. The fully connected layers will take the last convolution/pooling output as the input and produce a probability distribution over the classes in the classification problem.

As you can see, CNNs have many hyperparameters (e.g., number of layers, convolution window size, strides, fully connected hidden layer sizes, etc.). For optimal results, they need to be selected using a hyperparameter optimization technique (e.g., grid search, random search).

6.3.2 Inception net v1

Inception net v1 (also called GoogLeNet) (http://mng.bz/R4GD) takes CNNs to another level. It is not a typical CNN and requires more effort to implement compared to a standard CNN. At first glance, Inception net might look a bit scary (see figure 6.10). But there are only a handful of new concepts that you need to grok to understand this model. It's mostly the repetitive application of those concepts that makes the model sophisticated.

Let's first understand what's in the Inception model at a macro level, as shown in figure 6.10, temporarily ignoring the details, such as layers and their parameters. We will flesh these out once we develop a strong macro-level understanding.

Inception net starts with something called a *stem*. The stem consists of convolution and pooling layers identical to the convolution and pooling layers of a typical CNN. In other words, the stem is a sequence of convolution and pooling layers organized in a specific order.

Next you have several *Inception blocks* interleaved by max pooling layers. An inception block contains a parallel set of sub-convolution layers with varying kernel sizes. This enables the model to look at the input with different-sized receptive fields at a given depth. We will study the details and motivations behind this in detail.

Finally, you have a fully connected layer, which resembles the final prediction layer you have in a typical CNN. You can also see that there are two more interim fully connected layers. These are known as *auxiliary output layers*. Just like the final prediction layer, they consist of fully connected layers and a softmax activation that outputs a probability distribution over the classes in the data set. Though they have the same appearance as the final prediction layer, they do not contribute to the final output of the model but do play an important role in stabilizing the model during training. Stable training becomes more and more strenuous as the model gets deeper (mostly due to the limited precision of numerical values in a computer).

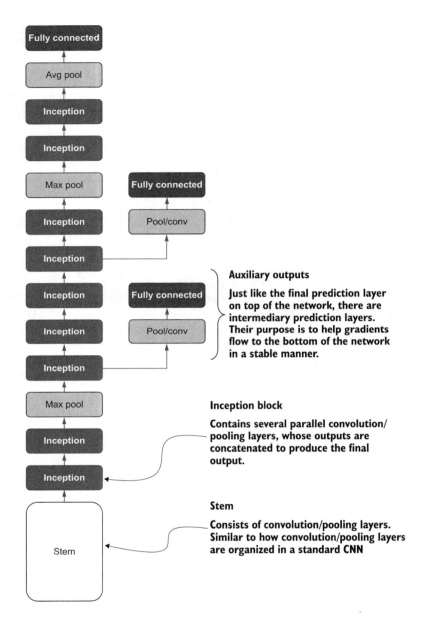

Auxiliary outputs

Just like the final prediction layer on top of the network, there are intermediary prediction layers. Their purpose is to help gradients flow to the bottom of the network in a stable manner.

Inception block

Contains several parallel convolution/pooling layers, whose outputs are concatenated to produce the final output.

Stem

Consists of convolution/pooling layers. Similar to how convolution/pooling layers are organized in a standard CNN

Figure 6.10   Abstract architecture of Inception net v1. Inception net starts with a stem, which is an ordinary sequence of convolution/pooling layers that is found in a typical CNN. Then Inception net introduces a new component known as an Inception block. Finally, Inception net also makes use of auxiliary output layers.

Let's implement a version of the original Inception net from scratch. While doing so, we will discuss any new concepts we come across.

> ### Caveat! We are going to build a slightly different Inception net v1
>
> We are implementing something slightly different from the original Inception net v1 model to deal with a certain practical limitation. The original Inception net is designed to process inputs of size 224 × 224 × 3 belonging to 1,000 classes, whereas we have 64 × 64 × 3 inputs belonging to 200 classes, which we will resize to 56 × 56 × 3 such that it is a factor of 224 (i.e., 56 × 4 = 224). Therefore, we will make some changes to the original Inception net. You can safely ignore the details that follow for the moment if you like. But if you are interested, we specifically make the following changes:
>
> - Make stride 1 for the first three layers that have stride 2 (in the stem) so that we enjoy the full depth of the model for the smaller input images we have.
> - Change the size of the last fully connected classification layer from 1,000 to 200 as we only have 200 classes.
> - Remove some regularization (i.e., dropout, loss weighting; these will be reintroduced in the next chapter).
>
> If you are comfortable with the model discussed here, there will be no issue with understanding the original Inception v1 model.

First let's define a function that creates the stem of Inception net v1. The stem is the first few layers of Inception net and looks like nothing more than the typical convolution/pooling layers you find in a typical CNN. But there is a new layer (called a *lambda layer*) that performs something known as *local response normalization* (LRN). We will discuss the purpose of this layer in more detail soon (see the next listing).

Listing 6.3 Defining the stem of Inception net

```
def stem(inp):
    conv1 = Conv2D(
        64, (7,7), strides=(1,1), activation='relu', padding='same'
    )(inp)
maxpool2 = MaxPool2D((3,3), strides=(2,2), padding='same')(conv1)
lrn3 = Lambda(
    lambda x: tf.nn.local_response_normalization(x)
)(maxpool2)

conv4 = Conv2D(
    64, (1,1), strides=(1,1), padding='same'
)(lrn3)
conv5 = Conv2D(
    192, (3,3), strides=(1,1), activation='relu', padding='same'
)(conv4)
    lrn6 = Lambda(lambda x: tf.nn.local_response_normalization(x))(conv5)
```

The output of the first convolution layer

The output of the first max pooling layer

The first local response normalization layer. We define a lambda function that encapsulates LRN functionality.

Subsequent convolution layers

The second LRN layer

```
maxpool7 = MaxPool2D((3,3), strides=(1,1), padding='same')(lrn6)
```

```
return maxpool7
```
← Returns the final output (i.e., output of the max pooling layer)

Max pooling layer

Most of this code should be familiar to you by now. It is a series of layers, starting from an input to produce an output.

Lambda layers (tf.keras.layers.Lambda)

Lambda layers in Keras have a similar purpose to standard Python lambda functions. They encapsulate some computations that are not typically available as a standard layer in Keras when written as a standard lambda function. For example, you can define a Keras layer that takes the maximum over axis 1 as follows. However, you can only use TensorFlow/Keras computations in the Keras lambda function:

```
x = tf.keras.layers.Input(shape=(10,))
max_out = tf.keras.layers.Lambda(lambda x: tf.reduce_max(x, axis=1))(x)
```

You might notice that the purpose of a lambda layer is almost identical to the sub-classing API of Keras. Well, yes, but the lambda layer does not require the amount of code scaffolding required in the sub-classing API. For layers with complex operations (e.g., if-else conditions, for loops, etc.), you might find the sub-classing API easier.

Specifically, we define the following layers:

- A convolution layer
  - 64 filters, (7,7) kernel size, (2,2) strides, activation ReLU, same padding
- A local response normalization layer
  - This is specified using a tf.keras.layers.Lambda layer. This layer provides you an easy way to define a Keras layer that encapsulates TensorFlow/Keras computations that are not readily available. Local response normalization is a technique to normalize a given input.
- Second convolution layer
  - 192 filters, (3,3) kernel size, (2, 2) strides, ReLU activation, same padding
- A local response normalization layer
- A max pool layer
  - (3,3) kernel size, (2,2) stride, and same padding

Local response normalization

Local response normalization (LRN) is an early layer normalization technique introduced in the paper "ImageNet Classification with Deep CNNs" (http://mng.bz/EWPr).

This technique is inspired by the lateral inhibition (http://mng.bz/N6PX) exhibited in a biological system. This refers to the phenomenon where excited neurons suppress the activity of neighboring neurons (e.g., observed in retinal receptors). Essentially, the LRN layer normalizes each value of a convolution output by dividing it by the values found in its neighborhood (the neighborhood is parametrized by a radius, which is a hyperparameter of the layer). This normalization creates competition among neurons and leads to slightly better performance. We will not discuss the exact equation involved in this computation, as this method has fallen out of fashion and better and more promising regularization techniques, such as batch normalization, have taken over.

GOING DEEPER INTO THE INCEPTION BLOCK

As stated earlier, one of the main breakthroughs in Inception net is the Inception block. Unlike a typical convolution layer that has a fixed kernel size, the Inception block is a collection of parallel convolutional layers with different kernel sizes. Specifically, the Inception block in Inception v1 contains a 1×1 convolution, a 3×3 convolution, a 5×5 convolution, and pooling. Figure 6.11 shows the architecture of an Inception block.

Let's understand why these parallel convolution layers are better than having a giant block of convolution filters with the same kernel size. The main advantage is that the Inception block is highly parameter efficient compared to a single convolution block. We can crunch some numbers to assure ourselves that this is the case. Let's say we have two convolution blocks: one Inception block and a standard convolution block. Assume that the Inception block has the following:

- A 1×1 convolution layer with 32 filters
- A 3×3 convolution layer with 16 filters
- A 5×5 convolution layer with 16 filters

If you were to design a standard convolution layer that has the representational power of the Inception block, you'd need

- A 5×5 convolution layer with 64 filters

Assuming we're processing an input with a single channel, the inception block has 576 parameters given by

$$1 \times 1 \times 1 \times 32 + 3 \times 3 \times 1 \times 16 + 5 \times 5 \times 1 \times 16 = 576$$

The standard convolution block has 1,600 parameters:

$$5 \times 5 \times 1 \times 64 = 1,600$$

In other words, the Inception block has a 64% reduction in the number of parameters compared to a standard convolution layer that has the representational power of the Inception block.

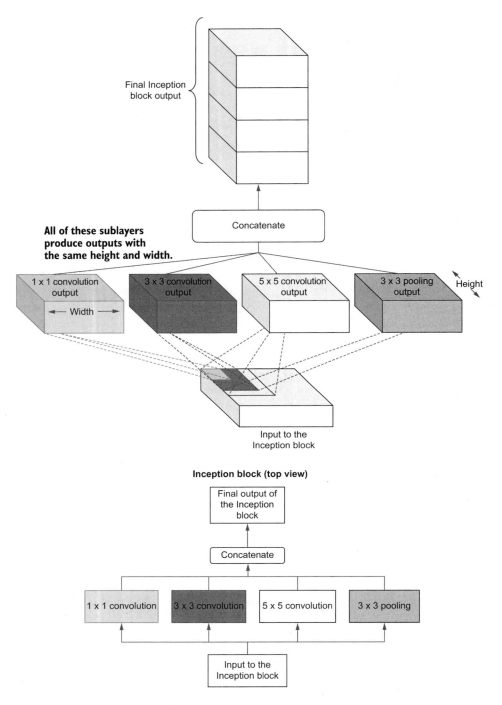

Figure 6.11   The computations in the Inception block, which is essentially a set of parallel convolution/pooling layers with different kernel sizes

CONNECTION BETWEEN INCEPTION BLOCK AND SPARSITY

For the curious minds out there, there might still be a lingering question: How does the Inception block introduce sparsity? Think of the following two scenarios where you have three convolution filters. In one scenario, you have three 5 × 5 convolution filters, whereas in the other you have a 1 × 1, 3 × 3 and 5 × 5 convolution filter. Figure 6.12 illustrates the difference between the two scenarios.

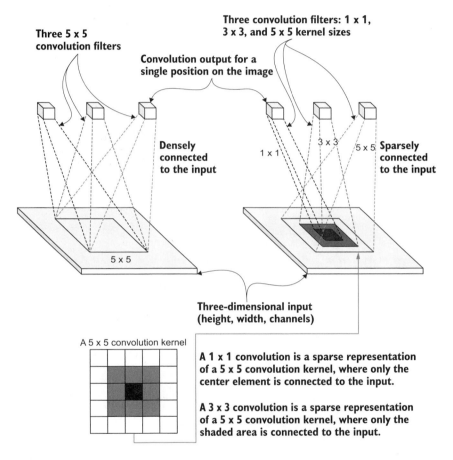

Figure 6.12 How the Inception block encourages sparsity in the model. You can view a 1 × 1 convolution as a highly sparse 5 × 5 convolution.

It is not that hard to see that when you have three 5 × 5 convolution filters, it creates a very dense connection between the convolution layer and the input. However, when you have a 1 × 1, 3 × 3, and 5 × 5 convolution layer, the connections between the input and the layer are sparser. Another way to think about this is that a 1 × 1 convolution is essentially a 5 × 5 convolution layer, where all the elements are switched off except for the center element. Therefore, a 1×1 convolution is a highly sparse 5×5 convolution layer. Similarly, a 3×3 convolution is a sparse 5×5 convolution layer. And by enforcing sparsity, we make the CNN parameter efficient and reduce the chances of overfitting. This explanation is motivated by the discussion found at http://mng.bz/Pn8g.

1×1 CONVOLUTIONS AS A DIMENSIONALITY REDUCTION METHOD

Usually, the deeper your model is, the higher the performance (given that you have enough data). As we already know, the depth of a CNN comes at a price. The more layers you have, the more parameters it creates. Therefore, you need to be extra cautious of the parameter count of deep models.

Being a deep model, Inception net leverages 1×1 convolution filters within Inception blocks to suppress a large increase in parameters. This is done by using 1×1 convolution layers to produce smaller outputs from a larger input and feed those smaller outputs as inputs to the convolution sublayers in the Inception blocks (figure 6.13). For example, if you have a $10 \times 10 \times 256$–sized input, by convolving it with a 1×1 convolution layer with 32 filters, you get a $10 \times 10 \times 32$–sized output. This output is eight times smaller than the original input. In other words, a 1×1 convolution reduces the channel depth/dimension of large inputs. Thus, it is considered a dimensionality reduction method. The weights of these 1×1 convolutions can be treated just like parameters of the network and let the network learn the best values for these filters to solve a given task.

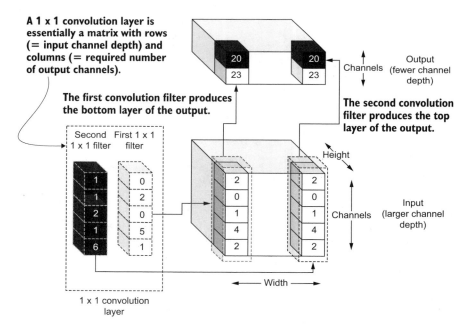

Figure 6.13   The computations of a 1×1 convolution and how it enables reduction of a channel dimension of an input

Now it's time to define a function that represents this new and improved Inception block, as shown in the following listing.

Listing 6.4   Defining the Inception block of the Inception net

```
def inception(inp, n_filters):

    # 1x1 layer
    out1 = Conv2D(
        n_filters[0][0], (1,1), strides=(1,1), activation='relu',
    padding='same'
    )(inp)

    # 1x1 followed by 3x3
    out2_1 = Conv2D(
        n_filters[1][0], (1,1), strides=(1,1), activation='relu',
    padding='same')
(inp)
    out2_2 = Conv2D(
        n_filters[1][1], (3,3), strides=(1,1), activation='relu',
    padding='same'
)(out2_1)

# 1x1 followed by 5x5
out3_1 = Conv2D(
    n_filters[2][0], (1,1), strides=(1,1), activation='relu',
    padding='same'
)(inp)
out3_2 = Conv2D(
    n_filters[2][1], (5,5), strides=(1,1), activation='relu',
    padding='same'
)(out3_1)

# 3x3 (pool) followed by 1x1
out4_1 = MaxPool2D(
    (3,3), strides=(1,1), padding='same'
)(inp)
out4_2 = Conv2D(
    n_filters[3][0], (1,1), strides=(1,1), activation='relu',
    padding='same'
)(out4_1)

out = Concatenate(axis=-1)([out1, out2_2, out3_2, out4_2])
return out
```

The `inception()` function takes in some input (four-dimensional: batch, height, width, channel, dimensions) and a list of filter sizes for the convolution sublayers in the Inception block. This list should have the filter sizes in the following format:

```
[(1x1 filters), (1x1 filters, 3x3 filters), (1x1 filters, 5x5 filters), (1x1
    filters)]
```

The outer loop corresponds to the vertical pillars in the Inception block, and the inner loops correspond to the convolution layers in each pillar (figure 6.14).

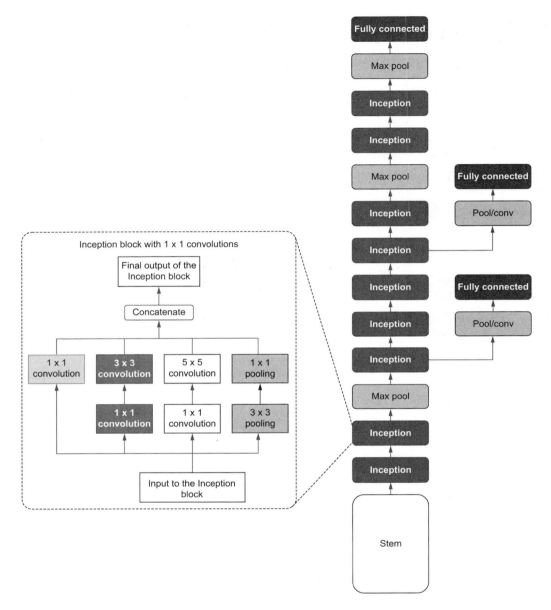

Figure 6.14   The Inception block alongside the full architecture of the Inception net model

We then define the four vertical streams of computations that finally get concatenated to one at the end:

- The 1×1 convolution
- The 1×1 convolution followed by a 3×3 convolution

- The 1 × 1 convolution followed by a 5 × 5 convolution
- The 3 × 3 pooling layer followed by a 1 × 1 convolution

Mathematical view of dimensionality reduction using 1 × 1 convolutions

If you are not a fan of the picturesque method, here's a more concise and mathematical view of how 1 × 1 convolutions reduce dimensions. Say you have an input of size 10 × 10 × 256. Say you have a 1 × 1 convolution layer of size 1 × 1 × 32:

- Size (input) = 10 × 10 × 256
- Size (layer) = 1 × 1 × 32

You can represent your convolution layer as a 1 × 32 matrix. Next, repeat the columns on axis = 0 (i.e., row dimension), 256 times which gives us

- Size (input) = 10 × 10 × 256
- Size (layer) = 256 × 32

Now you can multiply the input with the convolution filter

- Size (output) = (10 × 10 × 256) (256 × 32)

which gives us an output of size

- Size (output) = 10 × 10 × 32

which is much smaller than the original input.

Finally, we concatenate all the outputs of these streams into one on the last axis (denoted by axis = −1). Note the last dimension is the channel dimension of all the outputs. In other words, we are stacking these outputs on the channel dimension. Figure 6.14 illustrates how the Inception block sits in the overall Inception net model. Next, we will discuss another component of the Inception net model known as auxiliary output layers.

AUXILIARY OUTPUT LAYERS

Finally, we have two auxiliary output layers that help stabilize our deep CNN. As mentioned earlier, the auxiliary outputs are there to stabilize the training of deep networks. In Inception net, the auxiliary output layer has the following (figure 6.15).

- A 5 × 5 average pooling layer
- A 1 × 1 convolution layer
- A Dense layer with ReLU activation that consumes the flattened output from the 1 × 1 convolution layer
- A Dense layer with softmax that outputs the probabilities of the classes

We define a function that produces the auxiliary output predictions as follows (listing 6.5).

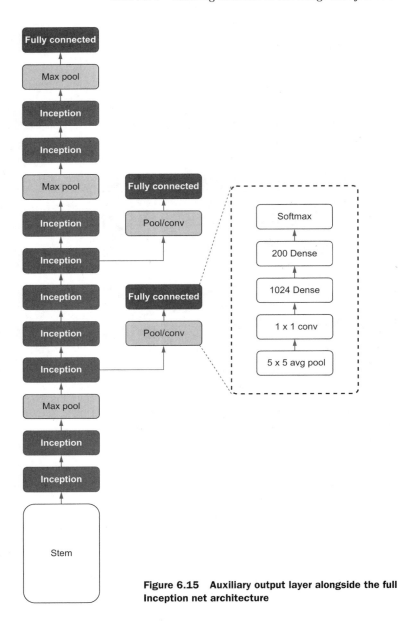

Figure 6.15   Auxiliary output layer alongside the full Inception net architecture

---

Listing 6.5   Defining the auxiliary output as a Python function

1 × 1 convolution layer's output

The output of the average pooling layer. Note that it uses valid pooling, which results in a 4 × 4–sized output for the next layer.

```
def aux_out(inp,name=None):
    avgpool1 = AvgPool2D((5,5), strides=(3,3), padding='valid')(inp)
    conv1 = Conv2D(128, (1,1), activation='relu', padding='same')(avgpool1)
```

```
flat = Flatten()(conv1)
dense1 = Dense(1024, activation='relu')(flat)
aux_out = Dense(200, activation='softmax', name=name)(dense1)
return aux_out
```

Flattens the output of the convolution layer so that it can be fed to a Dense layer

The final prediction for Dense layer's output

The first Dense layer's output

The aux_out() function defines the auxiliary output layer. It starts with an average pool layer with a kernel size of (5,5) and strides (3,3) and valid padding. This means that the layer does not try to correct for the dimensionality reduction introduced while pooling (as done in same padding). Then it's followed by a convolution layer with 128 filters, (1,1) kernel size, ReLU activation, and same padding. Then, a Flatten() layer is needed before feeding the output to a Dense layer. Remember that the Flatten() layer flattens the height, width, and channel dimension to a single dimension. Finally, a Dense layer with 200 nodes and a softmax activation is applied. With that, we have all the building blocks to build our very own Inception net.

6.3.3 Putting everything together

We have come a long way. Let's catch our breath and reflect on what we have achieved so far:

- The abstract architecture and components of the Inception net model consist of a stem, Inception blocks, and auxiliary outputs.
- Precise details of these components. Stem resembles the stem (everything except the fully connected layers) of a standard CNN. The Inception blocks carry sub-convolution layers with different kernel sizes that encourage sparsity and reduce overfitting.
- The auxiliary outputs make the network training smoother and rid the network of any undesirable numerical errors during training.

We also defined methods to encapsulate these so that we can call these methods and build the full Inception net. Now we can define the full Inception model (see the next listing). Additionally, you can find the exact Inception block specifications (as per the original paper) summarized in table 6.5.

Listing 6.6 Defining the full Inception net model

```
def inception_v1():

    K.clear_session()

    inp = Input(shape=(56,56,3))
    stem_out = stem(inp)
```

Defines an input layer. It takes a batch of 64 × 64 × 3–sized inputs.

To define the stem, we use the previously defined stem() function.

Defines Inception blocks. Note that each Inception block has different numbers of filters.

```
inc_3a = inception(stem_out, [(64,),(96,128),(16,32),(32,)])
inc_3b = inception(inc_3a, [(128,),(128,192),(32,96),(64,)])

maxpool = MaxPool2D((3,3), strides=(2,2), padding='same')(inc_3b)

inc_4a = inception(maxpool, [(192,),(96,208),(16,48),(64,)])
inc_4b = inception(inc_4a, [(160,),(112,224),(24,64),(64,)])
```

Defines auxiliary outputs

```
aux_out1 = aux_out(inc_4a, name='aux1')

inc_4c = inception(inc_4b, [(128,),(128,256),(24,64),(64,)])
inc_4d = inception(inc_4c, [(112,),(144,288),(32,64),(64,)])
inc_4e = inception(inc_4d, [(256,),(160,320),(32,128),(128,)])

maxpool = MaxPool2D((3,3), strides=(2,2), padding='same')(inc_4e)

aux_out2 = aux_out(inc_4d, name='aux2')

inc_5a = inception(maxpool, [(256,),(160,320),(32,128),(128,)])
inc_5b = inception(inc_5a, [(384,),(192,384),(48,128),(128,)])
avgpool1 = AvgPool2D((7,7), strides=(1,1), padding='valid')(inc_5b)

flat_out = Flatten()(avgpool1)
out_main = Dense(200, activation='softmax', name='final')(flat_out)

model = Model(inputs=inp, outputs=[out_main, aux_out1, aux_out2])
model.compile(loss='categorical_crossentropy',
              optimizer='adam', metrics=['accuracy'])
return model
```

The Flatten layer flattens the average pooling layer and prepares it for the fully connected layers.

The final pooling layer is defined as an Average pooling layer.

When compiling the model, we use categorical cross-entropy loss for all the output layers and the optimizer adam.

The final prediction layer that has 200 output nodes (one for each class)

You can see that the model has nine Inception blocks following the original paper. In addition, it has the stem, auxiliary outputs, and a final output layer. The specifics of the layers are listed in table 6.5.

Table 6.5   Summary of the filter counts of the Inception modules in the Inception net v1 model. C(nxn) represents a nxn convolution layer, whereas MaxP(mxm) represents a mxm max-pooling layer.

Inception layer	C(1 × 1)	C(1 × 1); before C(3 × 3)	C(3 × 3)	C(1 × 1); before C(5 × 5)	C(5 × 5)	C(1 × 1); after MaxP(3 × 3)
Inc_3a	64	96	128	16	32	32
Inc_3b	128	128	192	32	96	64
Inc_4a	192	96	208	16	48	64
Inc_4b	160	112	224	24	64	64
Inc_4c	128	128	256	24	64	64

Table 6.5 Summary of the filter counts of the Inception modules in the Inception net v1 model. C(nxn) represents a nxn convolution layer, whereas MaxP(mxm) represents a mxm max-pooling layer. *(continued)*

Inception layer	C(1 × 1)	C(1 × 1); before C(3 × 3)	C(3 × 3)	C(1 × 1); before C(5 × 5)	C(5 × 5)	C(1 × 1); after MaxP(3 × 3)
Inc_4d	112	144	288	32	64	64
Inc_4e	256	160	320	32	128	128
Inc_5a	256	160	320	32	128	128
Inc_5b	384	192	384	48	128	128

The layer definitions will be quite similar to what you have already seen. However, the way we define the model and the compilation will be new to some of you. As we discussed, Inception net is a multi-output model. You can define the Keras model with multiple outputs by passing a list of outputs instead of a single output:

```
model = Model(inputs=inp, outputs=[out_main, aux_out1, aux_out2])
```

When compiling the model, you can define loss as a list of a single string. If you define a single string, that loss will be used for all the outputs. We compile the model using the categorical cross-entropy loss (for both the final output layer and auxiliary outputs) and the optimizer adam, which is a state-of-the-art optimizer widely used to optimize models and that can adapt the learning rate appropriately as the model trains. In addition, we will inspect the accuracy of the model:

```
model.compile(loss='categorical_crossentropy', optimizer='adam',
    metrics=['accuracy'])
```

With the inception_v1() function defined, you can create a model as follows:

```
model = inception_v1()
```

Let's take a moment to reflect on what we have achieved so far. We have downloaded the data, dissected it, and analyzed the data to understand the specifics. Then we created an image data pipeline using tensorflow.keras.preprocessing.image.Image-DataGenerator. We split the data into three parts: training, validation, and testing. Finally, we defined our model, which is a state-of-the art image classifier known as Inception net. We will now look at other Inception models that have emerged over the years.

6.3.4 *Other Inception models*

We successfully implemented an Inception net model, which covers most of the basics we need to understand other Inception models. There have been five more Inception nets since the v1 model. Let's go on a brief tour of the evolution of Inception net.

INCEPTION V1

We have already discussed Inception net v1 in depth. The biggest breakthroughs introduced in Inception net v1 are as follows:

- The concept of an Inception block, which allows the CNN to have different receptive fields (i.e., kernels sizes) at the same depth of the model. This encourages sparsity in the model, leading to fewer parameters and fewer chances of overfitting.
- With the 20 layers in the Inception model, the memory of a modern GPU can be exhausted if you are not careful. Inception net mitigates this problem by using 1×1 convolution layers to reduce output channel depth whenever it increases too much.
- The deeper the networks are, the more they are prone to having instable gradients during model training. This is because the gradients must travel a long way (from the top to the very bottom), which can lead to instable gradients. Auxiliary output layers introduced in the middle of the network as regularizers alleviate this problem, leading to stable gradients.

INCEPTION V2

Inception net v2 came not long after Inception net v1 was released ("Rethinking the Inception Architecture for Computer Vision," https://arxiv.org/pdf/1512.00567 .pdf). The main contributions of this model are as follows.

A representational bottle neck occurs when a layer does not have enough capacity (i.e., parameters) to learn a good representation of the input. This can happen if you decrease the size of the layers too fast as you go deep. Inception v2 rejigged the architecture to ensure that no representational bottlenecks are present in the model. This is mostly achieved by changing the layer sizes while keeping the rest of the details the same.

Minimizing the parameters of the network further to reduce overfitting was reinforced. This is done by replacing higher-order convolutions (e.g., 5×5 and 7×7) with 3×3 convolutions (also known as factorizing large convolution layers). How is that possible? Let me illustrate that for you (figure 6.16).

Replacing a 5 x 5 convolution layer with two 3 x 3 convolution layers

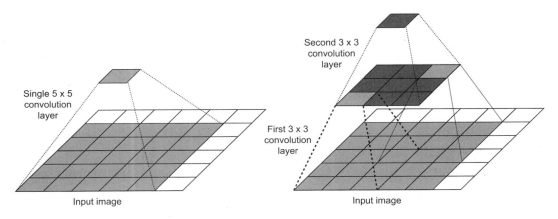

Figure 6.16 A 5 × 5 convolution layer (left) with two 3 × 3 convolution layers (right)

By representing 5×5 convolution with two smaller 3×3 convolution operations, we enjoy a reduction of 28% in parameters. Figure 6.17 contrasts Inception v1 block with Inception v2 block.

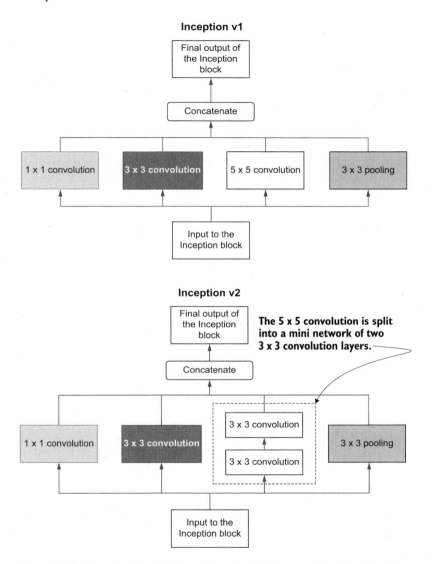

Figure 6.17   Inception block in Inception net v1 (left) versus Inception block in Inception net v2 (right)

Here's what the TensorFlow code looks like:

```
# 1x1 layer
out1 = Conv2D(64, (1,1), strides=(1,1), activation='relu', padding='same')(inp)
```

```
# 1x1 followed by 3x3
out2_1 = Conv2D(
    96, (1,1), strides=(1,1), activation='relu', padding='same'
)(inp)
out2_2 = Conv2D(
    128, (3,3), strides=(1,1), activation='relu', padding='same'
)(out2_1)

# 1x1 followed by 5x5
# Here 5x5 is represented by two 3x3 convolution layers
out3_1 = Conv2D(
    16, (1,1), strides=(1,1), activation='relu', padding='same'
)(inp)
out3_2 = Conv2D(
    32, (3,3), strides=(1,1), activation='relu', padding='same'
)(out3_1)
out3_3 = Conv2D(
    32, (3,3), strides=(1,1), activation='relu', padding='same'
)(out3_2)

# 3x3 (pool) followed by 1x1
out4_1 = MaxPool2D((3,3), strides=(1,1), padding='same')(inp)
out4_2 = Conv2D(
    32, (1,1), strides=(1,1), activation='relu', padding='same'
)(out4_1)

out = Concatenate(axis=-1)([out1, out2_2, out3_3, out4_2])
```

But we don't have to stop here. We can factorize any n × n convolution operation to two 1 × n and n × 1 convolution layers, for example, giving 33% parameter reduction for a 3 × 3 convolution layer (figure 6.18). Empirically, it has been found that factorizing n × n operation to two 1 × n and n × 1 operations is useful only in higher layers. You can refer to the paper to understand when and where these types of factorizations are used.

Replacing a 3 x 3 convolution layer with two 3 x 1 and 1 x 3 convolution layers

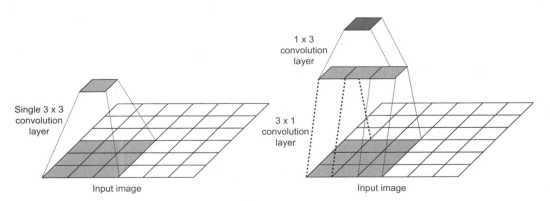

Figure 6.18   A 3 × 3 convolution layer (left) with 3 × 1 and 1 × 3 convolution layers (right)

INCEPTION V3

Inception v3 was introduced in the same paper as Inception net v2. The primary contribution that sets v3 apart from v2 is the use of batch normalization layers. Batch normalization ("Batch Normalization: Accelerating Deep Network Training by Reducing Internal Covariate Shift," http://proceedings.mlr.press/v37/ioffe15.pdf) normalizes the outputs of a given layer x by subtracting the mean ($E(x)$) and standard deviation ($\sqrt{Var(x)}$) from the outputs:

$$\hat{x} = \frac{x - E(x)}{\sqrt{Var(x)}}$$

This process helps the network stabilize its output values without letting them become too large or too small. Next, it has two trainable parameters, γ and β, that scale and offset the normalized output:

$$y = \gamma\hat{x} + \beta$$

This way, the network has the flexibility to learn its own variation of the normalization by learning optimal γ and β in case $\hat{x}$ is not the optimal normalization configuration. At this time, all you need to understand is that batch normalization normalizes the output of a given layer in the network. We will discuss how batch normalization is used within the Inception net model in more detail in the next chapter.

INCEPTION V4

Inception-v4 was introduced in the paper "Inception-v4, Inception-ResNet and the Impact of Residual Connections on Learning" (http://mng.bz/J28P) and does not introduce any new concepts, but rather focuses on making the model simpler without sacrificing performance. Mainly, v4 simplifies the stem of the network and other elements. As this is mostly grooming the network's hyperparameters for better performance and not introducing any new concepts, we will not dive into this model in great detail.

INCEPTION-RESNET V1 AND INCEPTION-RESNET V2

Inception-ResNet v1 and v2 were introduced in the same paper and were its main contributions. Inception-ResNet simplifies the Inception blocks that are used in the model and removes some cluttering details. More importantly, it introduces residual connections. *Residual connections* (or *skip connections*) were introduced in the paper by Kaiming He et al. titled "Deep Residual Learning for Image Recognition" (https://arxiv.org/pdf/1512.03385.pdf). It's an elegantly simple concept, yet very powerful, and it has been responsible for many of the top-performing models in many different domains.

As shown in figure 6.19, residual connections represent simply adding a lower input (close to the input) to a higher-level input (further from the input). This creates a shortcut between the lower input and a higher input, essentially creating another shortcut from the resulting output to the lower layer. We will not dive into too much detail here, as we will discuss Inception-ResNet models in detail in the next chapter. Next, we will train the model we just defined on the image data we have prepared.

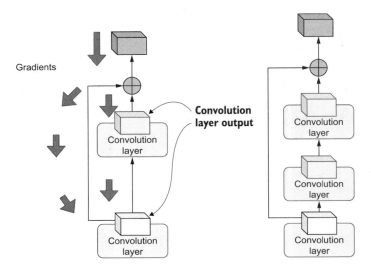

Figure 6.19   How residual connections are introduced to a network. It is a simple operation, where you add a lower output (closer to input) of a layer to a higher output (further from input). Skip connections can be designed in such a way to skip any number of layers you like. The figure also highlights the flow of gradients; you can see how skip connections allow gradients to bypass certain layers and travel to lower layers.

EXERCISE 3

As a part of research, you are testing a new technique called *poolception*. Conceptually similar to an Inception block, poolception has three parallel pooling layers with the following specifications:

- A 3×3 max pooling layer with stride 2 and same padding
- A 5×5 max pooling layer with stride 2 and same padding
- A 3×3 average pooling layer with stride 2 and same padding

Finally, the outputs of these layers are concatenated on the channel axis. Can you implement this as a Python function called `poolception` that takes the previous layer's input x as an argument?

6.4   *Training the model and evaluating performance*

Great work! You have defined one of the state-of-the-art model architectures that has delivered great performance on similar (and larger) data sets. Your next task is to train this model and analyze its performance.

Model training is an imperative step if you need a model that performs well once it's time to use it. Training the model optimizes (i.e., changes) the parameters of the model in such a way that it can produce the correct prediction given an input. Typically, model training is done for several epochs, where each epoch can consist of thousands of iterations. This process can take anywhere from hours to even weeks depending on the size of the data set and the model. As we have already discussed, deep neural networks, due to their well-known memory requirements, consume data in small batches. A step where the model is optimized with a single data batch is known as an *iteration*. When you traverse the full data set in such batches, it's known as an *epoch*.

Finally, once the training is done, you need to ensure that the model performs well on unseen data. This unseen data must not have had any interaction with the model during the training. The most common evaluation metric for deep learning networks is accuracy. Therefore, we measure the test accuracy to ensure the model's sturdiness.

In order to train the model, let us first define a function that computes the number of steps or iterations per epoch, given the size of the data set and batch size. It's always a good idea to run for a predefined number of steps for every epoch. There can be instances where Keras is unable to figure out the number of steps, in which case it can leave the model running until you stop it:

```
def get_steps_per_epoch(n_data, batch_size):
    if n_data%batch_size==0:
        return int(n_data/batch_size)
    else:
        return int(n_data*1.0/batch_size)+1
```

It's a very simple calculation. The number of steps for an epoch is the number of data points (n_data) divided by batch size (batch_size). And if n_data is not divisible by batch_size, you need to add 1 to the returned value to make sure you're not leaving any data behind. Now let's train the model in the following listing.

Listing 6.7   Training the Inception net

```
from tensorflow.keras.callbacks import CSVLogger
import time
import os

if not os.path.exists('eval'):
    os.mkdir('eval')

csv_logger = CSVLogger(os.path.join('eval','1_eval_base.log'))

history = model.fit(
    x=train_gen_aux,
    validation_data=valid_gen_aux,
    steps_per_epoch=get_steps_per_epoch(0.9*500*200,batch_size),
    validation_steps=get_steps_per_epoch(0.1*500*200,batch_size),
    epochs=50,
    callbacks=[csv_logger]
)

if not os.path.exists('models'):
    os.mkdir("models")
model.save(os.path.join('models', 'inception_v1_base.h5'))
```

Creates a directory called eval to store the performance results

This is a Keras callback that you pass to the fit() function. It writes the metrics data to a CSV file.

By fitting the model, you can see that we are passing the train and validation data generators to the function.

Saves the model to disk so it can be brought up again if needed

When training the model, the following steps are generally followed:

- Train the model for a number of epochs.
- At the end of every training epoch, measure performance on the validation data set.
- After all the training epochs have finished, measure the performance on the test set.

When `model.fit()` is called in the code, it takes care of the first two steps. We will look at the `model.fit()` function in a bit more detail. We pass the following arguments to the function:

- x—Takes the train data generator to the model, which contains both inputs (x) and targets (y).
- y—Typically takes in the targets. Here we do not specify y, as x already contains the targets.
- `validation_data`—Takes the validation data generator.
- `steps_per_epoch`—Number of steps (iterations) per epoch in training.
- `validation_steps`—Number of steps (iterations) per epoch in validation.
- epochs—Number of epochs.
- `callbacks`—Any callbacks that need to be passed to the model (for a full list of callbacks visit http://mng.bz/woEW).

You should get something like the following after training the model:

```
Train for 704 steps, validate for 79 steps
Epoch 1/50
704/704 [==============================] - 196s 279ms/step - loss: 14.6223
   - final_loss: 4.9449 - aux1_loss: 4.8074 - aux2_loss: 4.8700 -
   final_accuracy: 0.0252 - aux1_accuracy: 0.0411 - aux2_accuracy: 0.0347
   - val_loss: 13.3207 - val_final_loss: 4.5473 - val_aux1_loss: 4.3426 -
   val_aux2_loss: 4.4308 - val_final_accuracy: 0.0595 - val_aux1_accuracy:
   0.0860 - val_aux2_accuracy: 0.0765
...
Epoch 50/50
704/704 [==============================] - 196s 279ms/step - loss: 0.6361 -
   final_loss: 0.2271 - aux1_loss: 0.1816 - aux2_loss: 0.2274 -
   final_accuracy: 0.9296 - aux1_accuracy: 0.9411 - aux2_accuracy: 0.9264
   - val_loss: 27.6959 - val_final_loss: 7.9506 - val_aux1_loss: 10.4079 -
   val_aux2_loss: 9.3375 - val_final_accuracy: 0.2703 - val_aux1_accuracy:
   0.2318 - val_aux2_accuracy: 0.2361
```

NOTE On an Intel Core i5 machine with an NVIDIA GeForce RTX 2070 8GB, the training took approximately 2 hours and 45 minutes. You can reduce the training time by cutting down the number of epochs.

Finally, we will test the trained model on the test data (i.e., the data in the val folder). You can easily get the model's test performance by calling `model.evaluate()` by passing the test data generator (test_gen_aux) and the number of steps (iterations) for the test set:

```
model = load_model(os.path.join('models','inception_v1_base.h5'))
test_res = model.evaluate(test_gen_aux, steps=get_steps_per_epoch(200*50,
➥ batch_size))
test_res_dict = dict(zip(model.metrics_names, test_res))
```

You will get the following output:

```
196/196 [==============================] - 17s 88ms/step - loss: 27.7303 -
➥ final_loss: 7.9470 - aux1_loss: 10.3892 - aux2_loss: 9.3941 -
➥ final_accuracy: 0.2700 - aux1_accuracy: 0.2307 - aux2_accuracy: 0.2367
```

We can see that the model reaches around 30% validation and test accuracy and a whopping ~94% training accuracy. This is a clear indication that we haven't steered clear from overfitting. But this is not entirely bad news. Thirty percent accuracy means that the model did recognize around 3,000/10,000 images in the validation and test sets. In terms of the sheer data amount, this corresponds to 60 classes out of 200.

> **NOTE** An overfitted model is like a student who memorized all the answers for an exam, whereas a generalized model is a student who worked hard to understand concepts that will be tested on the exam. The student who memorized answers will only perform well in the exam and fail in the real world, whereas the student who understood concepts can generalize their knowledge both to the exam and the real world.

Overfitting can happen for a number of reasons:

- The model architecture is not optimal for the data set we have.
- More regularization is needed to reduce overfitting, such as dropout and batch normalization.
- We are not using a pretrained model that has already been trained on similar data.

We are going to address each of these concerns in the next chapter, where it will be exciting to see how much things improve.

EXERCISE 4

If you train a model for 10 epochs with a data set that has 50,000 samples with a batch size of 250, how many iterations would you train the model for? Assuming you are given the inputs as a variable x and labels as a variable y, populate the necessary arguments in model.fit() to train the model according to this specification. When not using a data generator, you can set the batch size using the batch_size argument and ignore the steps_per_epoch argument (automatically inferred) in model.fit().

Summary

- Exploratory data analysis (EDA) is a crucial step in the machine learning life cycle that must be performed before starting on any modeling.
- The more aspects of the data you analyze, the better.
- The Keras data generator can be used to read images from disk and load them into memory to train the model.
- Inception net v1 is one of the state-of-the-art computer vision models for image classification designed for reducing overfitting and memory requirements of deep models.
- Inception net v1 consists of a stem, several inception blocks, and auxiliary outputs.
- An Inception block is a layer in the Inception net that consists of several sub-convolution layers with different kernel sizes, whereas the auxiliary output ensures smoothness in model training.
- When training a model, there are three data sets: training, validation, and test.
- Typically, we train the model on training data for several epochs, and at the end of every epoch, we measure the performance on the validation set. Finally, after the training has finished, we measure performance on the test data set.
- A model that overfits is like a student who memorized all the answers for an exam. It can do very well on the training data but will do poorly in generalizing its knowledge to analyze unseen data.

Answers to exercises

Exercise 1

```python
def get_img_minimum(path):
    img = np.array(Image.open(path))
    return np.min(img)

df["minimum"] = df["filepath"].apply(lambda x: get_img_minimum(x))
```

Exercise 2

```python
def data_gen_corrupt(gen):
    for x,y in gen:
        if np.random.normal()>0:
            y = 0
        yield x,(y,y,y)
```

Exercise 3

```python
def poolception(x):
    out1 = MaxPool2D(pool_size=(3,3), strides=(2,2), padding='same')(x)
    out2 = MaxPool2D(pool_size=(5,5), strides=(2,2), padding='same')(out1)
    out3 = AvgPool2D(pool_size=(3,3), strides=(2,2), padding='same')(out2)
```

```
out = Concatenate(axis=-1)([out1, out2, out3])
return out
```

Exercise 4: Total number of iterations = (data set size/batch_size) * epochs = (50,000/250) * 10 = 2,000

```
model.fit(x=x, y=y, batch_size=250, epochs=10)
```

Teaching machines to see better: Improving CNNs and making them confess

This chapter covers

- Reducing overfitting of image classifiers
- Boosting model performance via better model architectures
- Image classification using pretrained models and transfer learning
- Modern ML explainability techniques to dissect image classifiers

We have developed and trained a state-of-the-art image classifier known as the Inception net v1 on an object classification data set. Inception net v1 is a well-recognized image classification model in computer vision. You learned how Inception blocks are created by aggregating convolution windows at multiple scales, which encourages sparsity in the model. You further saw how 1 × 1 convolutions are employed to keep the dimensionality of layers to a minimum. Finally, we observed how Inception net v1 uses auxiliary classification layers in the middle of the network to stabilize and maintain the gradient flow throughout the network. However, the results didn't really live up to the reputation of the model, which was heavily overfit with ~30% validation and test accuracies and a whopping ~94% training accuracy. In this chapter, we will discuss improving the model by reducing overfitting and improving validation and test accuracies, which will ultimately leave us with a model that reaches ~80% accuracy (equivalent to being able to accurately identify 160/200 classes of objects) on validation and test sets. Furthermore, we will look at techniques that allow us to probe the model's brain to gain insights.

This chapter takes you through an exciting journey where we turn a suboptimal machine learning model to a significantly superior model. This process will be reminiscent of what we did in the previous chapter. We will add an additional step to explain/interpret the decisions the model made. We will use special techniques to see which part of the image the model paid most attention to in order to make a prediction. This helps us to build trust in the model. During this process, we identify lurking issues in the model and systematically fix them to increase performance. We will discuss several important techniques, including the following:

- Augmenting the data by using various image transformation techniques such as brightness/contrast adjustment, rotation, and translation to create more labeled data for the model
- Implementing a variant of Inception net that is more suited for the size and type of data used
- Using transfer learning to leverage a model already trained on a larger data set and fine-tuning it to perform well on the data set we have

This chapter might deeply resonate with you if you have ever had to implement a deep learning solution to an unfamiliar problem. Typically, implementing "some" deep network will not place you on the apex of success. The novelty of the problem or the bespoke nature of the problem at hand can impede your progress if you are not careful. Such problems send you into uncharted territory where you need to tread carefully to find a solution without exhausting yourself. This chapter will provide guidance for anyone who might come face-to-face with such situations in computer vision.

7.1 Techniques for reducing overfitting

We are pursuing the ambitious goal of developing an intelligent shopping assistant app that will use an image/object classifier as a vital component. For this, we will use the data set `tiny-imagenet-200`, which is a smaller version of the large ImageNet image classification data set, and consists of images and a class that represents the object present in that image. The data set has a training subset and a testing subset. You split the training subset further into a training set (90% of the original) and a validation set (10% of the original).

You have developed a model based on the famous Inception net model, but it is overfitting heavily. Overfitting needs to be alleviated, as it leads to models that perform exceptionally well on training data but poorly on test/real-world data. You know several techniques to reduce overfitting, namely data augmentation (creating more data out of existing data; for images this includes creating variants of the same image by introducing random brightness/contrast adjustments, translations, rotations, etc.), dropout (i.e., turning nodes randomly in the network during training), and early stopping (i.e., terminating model training before overfitting takes place). You wish to leverage these methods with the Keras API to reduce overfitting.

Usually, reducing overfitting requires close scrutiny of the machine learning pipeline end to end. This involves looking at the data fed in, the model structure, and the model training. In this section, we will look at all these aspects and see how we can place guards against overfitting. The code for this is available at Ch07-Improving-CNNs-and-Explaining/7.1.Image_Classification_Advance.ipynb.

7.1.1 *Image data augmentation with Keras*

First in line is augmenting data in the training set. Data augmentation is a prevalent method for increasing the amount of data available to deep learning networks without labeling new data. For example, in an image classification problem, you can create multiple data points from a single image by creating various transformed versions of the same image (e.g., shift the image, change brightness) and having the same label as for the original image (figure 7.1). As previously stated, more data conduces the strength of deep learning models by increasing generalizability (and reducing overfitting), leading to reliable performance in the real world. For image data, there are many different augmentation techniques you can use:

- Randomly adjusting brightness, contrast, and so on
- Randomly zooming in/out, rotations, translations, and so on

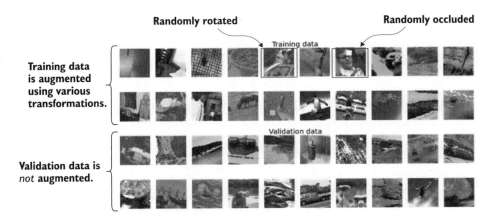

Figure 7.1 Difference between training data and validation data after the augmentation step. The figure clearly shows various transformations applied on the training data and not on the validation data, as we expected.

Such augmentation can be easily applied by providing several additional parameters to the ImageDataGenerator that we used earlier. Let's define a new Keras ImageData-Generator with data augmentation capability. In Keras you can perform most of these augmentations, and there's hardly a need to look elsewhere. Let's look at various options an `ImageDataGenerator` provides (only the most important parameters are shown). Figure 7.2 illustrates the effects of the different parameters listed here.

```
data_gen = tf.keras.preprocessing.image.ImageDataGenerator(
    featurewise_center=False, samplewise_center=False,
    featurewise_std_normalization=False, samplewise_std_normalization=False,
    zca_whitening=False, rotation_range=0, width_shift_range=0.0,
    height_shift_range=0.0, brightness_range=None, shear_range=0.0,
    zoom_range=0.0,
    channel_shift_range=0.0, horizontal_flip=False,
    vertical_flip=False, fill_mode="nearest", rescale=None,
    preprocessing_function=None, validation_split=0.0
)
```

where

- `featurewise_center` specifies whether the images are centered by subtracting the mean value of the whole data set (e.g., `True`/`False`).
- `samplewise_center` specifies whether the images are centered by subtracting individual mean values of each image (e.g., `True`/`False`).
- `featurewise_std_normalization` is the same as `featurewise_center`, but instead of subtracting, the mean images are divided by the standard deviation (`True`/`False`).
- `samplewise_std_normalization` is the same as `samplewise_center`, but instead of subtracting, the mean images are divided by the standard deviation (`True`/`False`).
- `zca_whitening` is a special type of image normalization that is geared toward reducing correlations present in the image pixels (see http://mng.bz/DgP0) (`True`/`False`).
- `rotation_range` specifies the bounds of the random image rotations (in degrees) done during data augmentation. There is a float with values between (0, 360); for example, 30 means a range of −30 to 30; 0 is disabled.
- `width_shift_range` specifies the bounds for random shifts (as proportions or pixels) done on the width axis during data augmentation.
  A tuple with values between (−1, 1) is considered as a proportion of the width (e.g., (−0.4, 0.3)).
  A tuple with values between (-inf, inf) is considered as pixels (e.g., (−150, 250)).
- `height_shift_range` is the same as `width_shift_range` except for the height dimension.
- `brightness_range` specifies the bounds of the random brightness adjustments made to data during data augmentation.
  A tuple with values between (-inf, inf) is, for example, (−0.2, 0.5) or (−5, 10); `0` is disabled.

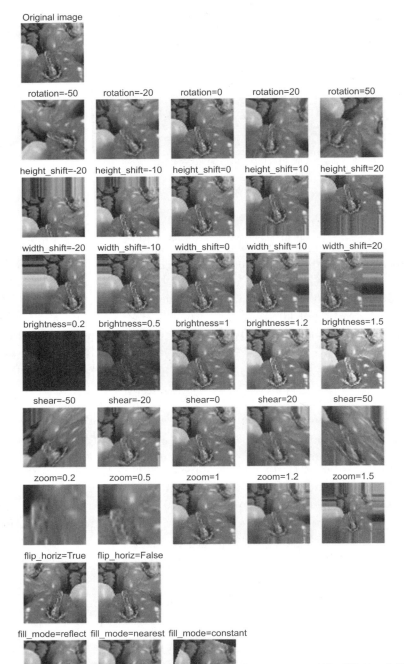

Figure 7.2   Effects of different augmentation parameters and their values of the `ImageDataGenerator`

- shear_range is the same as brightness_range but for shearing (i.e., skewing) images during data augmentation
  A float in degrees is, for example, 30.0.
- zoom_range is the same as brightness_range except for scaling the images during data augmentation.
- horizontal_flip specifies whether to randomly flip images horizontally during data augmentation (True/False).
- vertical_flip is the same as horizontal_flip but flips vertically (True/False)
- fill_mode defines how the empty spaces created by various image transformations (e.g., translating the image to the left creates an empty space on the right) are handled. Possible options are "reflect," "nearest," and "constant." The last row of figure 7.2 depicts the differences.
- rescale rescales the inputs by a constant value.
- preprocessing_function takes a Python function that can be used to introduce additional data augmentation/preprocessing steps that are not readily available.
- validation_split addresses how much data should be used as validation data. We don't use this parameter, as we create a data generator for the validation set separately because we do not want an augmentations app. A float is, for example, 0.2.

With a good understanding of different parameters, we will define two image data generators: one with data augmentation (training data) and the other without (testing data). For our project, we will augment the data in the following ways:

- Randomly rotate images
- Randomly translate on width dimension
- Randomly translate on height dimension
- Randomly adjust brightness
- Randomly shear
- Randomly zoom
- Randomly flip images horizontally
- Random gamma correct (custom implementation)
- Random occlude (custom implementation)

The following listing shows how the ImageDataGenerator is defined with a validation split.

> **Listing 7.1 Defining the ImageDataGenerator with validation split**

```
image_gen_aug = ImageDataGenerator(
    samplewise_center=False,
    rotation_range=30,
    width_shift_range=0.2, height_shift_range=0.2,
    brightness_range=(0.5,1.5),
    shear_range=5,
    zoom_range=0.2,
    horizontal_flip=True,
    fill_mode='reflect',
```

Various augmentation arguments previously discussed (set empirically)

Defines the ImageDataGenerator for training/validation data

We will switch off samplewise_center temporarily and reintroduce it later.

```
                    validation_split=0.1
)
image_gen = ImageDataGenerator(samplewise_center=False)
```

**Uses a 10% portion of training
data as validation data**

**Defines a separate
ImageDataGenerator
for testing data**

We chose the parameters for these arguments empirically. Feel free to experiment with
other arguments and see the effect they have on the model's performance. One important thing to note is that, unlike previous examples, we set `samplewise_center=False`.
This is because we are planning to do few custom preprocessing steps before the normalization. Therefore, we will turn off the normalization in the `ImageDataGenerator`
and reintroduce it later (through a custom function). Next, we will define the training
and testing data generators (using a flow function). Following a similar pattern as the
previous chapter, we will get the training and validation data generators through the
same data generator (using the `validation_split` and `subset` arguments; see the following listing).

Listing 7.2   Defining the data generators for training, validation, and testing sets

```
partial_flow_func = partial(
        image_gen_aug.flow_from_directory,
        directory=os.path.join('data','tiny-imagenet-200', 'train'),
        target_size=target_size, classes=None,
        class_mode='categorical', batch_size=batch_size,
        shuffle=True, seed=random_seed
)
train_gen = partial_flow_func(subset='training')

valid_gen = partial_flow_func(subset='validation')

test_df = get_test_labels_df(
        os.path.join('data','tiny-imagenet-200',  'val',
'val_annotations.txt')
)
test_gen = image_gen.flow_from_dataframe(
        test_df, directory=os.path.join('data','tiny-imagenet-200',  'val',
'images'),
        target_size=target_size, classes=None,
        class_mode='categorical', batch_size=batch_size, shuffle=False
)
```

**Define a partial function that has
all the arguments fixed except
for the subset argument.**

**Get the training
data subset.**

**Get the validation
data subset.**

**Read in the test labels
stored in a txt file.**

Define the test data generator.

To refresh our memory, the `flow_from_directory`(...) has the following function
signature:

```
image_gen.flow_from_directory (
    directory=<directory where the images are>,
    target_size=<height and width or target image>,
    classes=None,
    class_mode=<type of targets generated such as one hot encoded, sparse, etc.>,
    batch_size=<size of a single batch>,
```

```
    shuffle=<whether to shuffle data or not>,
    seed=<random seed to be used in shuffling>,
    subset=<set to training or validation>
)
```

The `train_gen` and `valid_gen` uses `image_gen_aug` (with data augmentation) to retrieve data. `train_gen` and `valid_gen` are defined as partial functions of the original `image_gen.flow_from_directory()`, where they share all the arguments except for the `subset` argument. However, it is important to keep in mind that augmentation is only applied to training data and must not be applied on the validation subset. This is the desired behavior we need, as we want the validation data set to remain fixed across epochs. Next, `test_gen` uses `image_gen` (without data augmentation).

> ### Why should we not augment validation/test data?
>
> When augmenting data, you should only augment the training data set and not the validation and test sets. Augmentation on validation and test sets will lead to inconsistent results between trials/runs (due to the random modifications introduced by data augmentation). We want to keep our validation and testing data sets consistent from the start to the end of training. Therefore, data augmentation is only done to the training data.

Remember that Inception Net v1 has three output layers; therefore, the output of the generator needs to be a single input and three outputs. We do this by defining a new Python generator off the Keras generator that modifies the content accordingly (see the next listing).

Listing 7.3 Defining the data generator with several modifications

```
def data_gen_augmented_inceptionnet_v1(gen, random_gamma=False,
  random_occlude=False):
    for x,y in gen:
        if random_gamma:
            # Gamma correction
            # Doing this in the image process fn doesn't help improve
performance
            rand_gamma = np.random.uniform(0.9, 1.08, (x.shape[0],1,1,1))
            x = x**rand_gamma
        if random_occlude:
            # Randomly occluding sections in the image
            occ_size = 10
            occ_h, occ_w = np.random.randint(0, x.shape[1]-occ_size),
np.random.randint(0, x.shape[2]-occ_size)
            x[:,occ_h:occ_h+occ_size,occ_w:occ_w+occ_size,:] =
np.random.choice([0.,128.,255.])
```

Check if the Gamma correction augmentation is needed.

Define a new function that introduces two new augmentation techniques and modifies the format of the final output.

Perform Gamma correction-related augmentation.

Check if random occlusion augmentation is needed.

Defines the starting x/y pixels randomly for occlusion

Apply a white/gray/black color randomly to the occlusion.

Makes sure we replicate the target (y) three times

```
# Image centering
x -= np.mean(x, axis=(1,2,3), keepdims=True)

yield x, (y,y,y)
```

Perform the sample-wise centering that was switched off earlier.

```
train_gen_aux = data_gen_augmented_inceptionnet_v1(
    train_gen, random_gamma=True, random_occlude=True
)
valid_gen_aux = data_gen_augmented_inceptionnet_v1(valid_gen)
test_gen_aux = data_gen_augmented_inceptionnet_v1(test_gen)
```

Training data is augmented with random gamma correction and occlusions.

Validation/testing sets are not augmented.

You can see how the `data_gen_augmented_inceptionnet_v1` returns a single input (`x`) and three replicas of the same output (`y`). In addition to modifying the format of the output, this `data_gen_augmented_inceptionnet_v1` will include two extra data augmentation steps using a custom implementation (which are not available as built-ins):

- *Gamma correction*—A standard computer vision transformation performed by raising the pixel values to the power of some value (http://mng.bz/lxdz). In our case, we chose this value randomly between 0.9 and 1.08.
- *Random occlusions*—We will occlude a random patch on the image (10 × 10) with white, gray, or black pixels (chosen randomly).

You also need to center the images, as we set the `samplewise_center` argument to `False` when we defined the `ImageDataGenerator`. This is done by subtracting the mean pixel value of each image from its pixels. With the `data_gen_augmented_inceptionnet_v1` function defined, we can create the modified data generators `train_gen_aux`, `valid_gen_aux`, and `test_gen_aux` for training/validation/testing data, respectively.

> **Check, check, check to avoid model performance defects**
>
> If you don't check to see if just the training data is augmented, you can be in trouble. If it doesn't work as intended, it can easily fly under the radar. Technically, your code is working and free of functional bugs. But this will leave you scratching your head for days trying to figure out why the model is not performing as intended in the real world.

Finally, the most important step in this process is verifying that the data augmentation is working as we expect and not corrupting the images in unexpected ways, which would impede the learning of the model. For that, we can plot some of the samples generated by the train data generator as well as the validation data generator. Not only do we need to make sure that the data augmentation is working properly, but we also need to make sure that data augmentation is not present in the validation set. Figure 7.3 ensures that this is the case.

Next, we discuss another regularization technique called dropout.

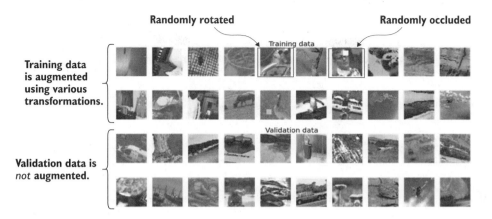

Figure 7.3   Difference between training data and validation data after the augmentation step. The figure clearly shows various transformations applied on the training data and not on the validation data, as we expected.

7.1.2   *Dropout: Randomly switching off parts of your network to improve generalizability*

We will now learn a technique called *dropout* to reduce further overfitting. Dropout was part of Inception net v1, but we avoided dropout in the previous chapter to improve clarity.

Dropout is a regularization technique for deep networks. A regularization technique's job is to control the deep network in such a way that the network is rid of numerical errors during training or troublesome phenomena like overfitting. Essentially, regularization keeps the deep network well behaved.

Dropout switches off output neurons randomly during each training iteration. This helps the model learn redundant features during training as it will not always have the previously learned features at its disposal. In other words, the network only has a subset of parameters of the full network to learn at a given time, and it forces the network to learn multiple (i.e., redundant) features to classify objects. For example, if the network is trying to identify cats, in the first iteration it might learn about whiskers. Then, if the nodes that correspond to the knowledge on whiskers are switched off, it might learn about cats' pointy ears (figure 7.4). This leads to a network that learns redundant/different features like whiskers, two pointed ears, and so on, leading to better performance at test time.

The nodes are switched off by applying a random mask of 1s and 0s on each layer you want to apply dropout on (figure 7.5). There is also a vital normalization step you perform on the active nodes during training. Let's assume we are training a network with 50% dropout (i.e., dropping half of the nodes on every iteration). When 50% of your network is switched off, conceptually your network's total output is reduced by half, compared to having the full network on. Therefore, you need to multiply the

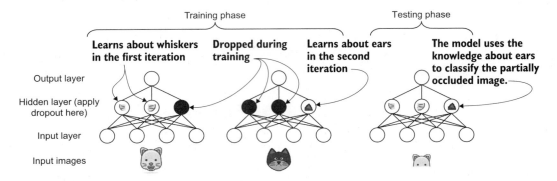

Figure 7.4 **How dropout might change the network when learning to classify cat images. In the first iteration, it might learn about whiskers. In the second iteration, as the part containing information about whiskers is turned off, the network might learn about pointy ears. This leads the network to having knowledge about both whiskers and ears when it's time for testing. That's good in this case, because in the test image, you cannot see the cat's whiskers!**

output by a factor of 2 to make sure the total output remains constant. Such computational details of dropout are highlighted in figure 7.5. The good news is that you don't have to implement any of the computational details, as dropout is provided as a layer in TensorFlow.

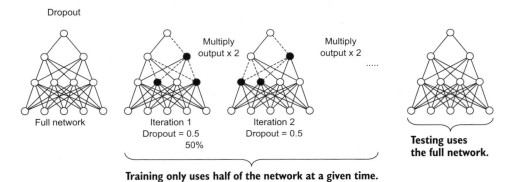

Training only uses half of the network at a given time.

Figure 7.5 **A computational perspective on how dropout works. If dropout is set to 50%, then half the nodes in every layer (except for the last layer) will be turned off. But at testing time, all the nodes are switched on.**

Inception net v1 (figure 7.6) only has dropout for fully connected layers and the last average pooling layer. Remember not to use dropout on the last layer (i.e., the layer that provides final predictions). There are two changes to perform:

- Apply 70% dropout to the intermediate fully connected layer in the auxiliary outputs.
- Apply 40% dropout to the output of the last average pooling layer.

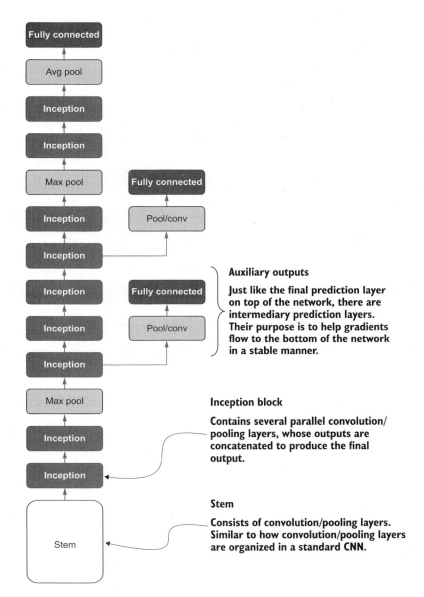

Auxiliary outputs

Just like the final prediction layer on top of the network, there are intermediary prediction layers. Their purpose is to help gradients flow to the bottom of the network in a stable manner.

Inception block

Contains several parallel convolution/ pooling layers, whose outputs are concatenated to produce the final output.

Stem

Consists of convolution/pooling layers. Similar to how convolution/pooling layers are organized in a standard CNN.

Figure 7.6 Abstract architecture of Inception net v1. Inception net starts with a stem, which is an ordinary sequence of convolution/pooling layers that you will find in a typical CNN. Then Inception net introduces a new component known as Inception block. Finally, Inception net also makes use of auxiliary output layers.

In TensorFlow, applying dropout is as easy as writing a single line. Once you get the output of the fully connected layer, `dense1`, you can apply dropout with

```
dense1 = Dropout(0.7)(dense1)
```

Here, we're using a 70% dropout rate (as suggested in the original Inception net v1 paper) for the auxiliary output.

Dropout on convolution layers

Dropout is mostly applied to dense layers, so one cannot help but wonder, "Why are we not applying dropout on convolution layers?" It is still an open debate. For example, the original dropout paper by Nitish Srivastava et al. (http://mng.bz/o2Nv) argues that using dropout on lower convolution layers provides a performance boost. In contrast, the paper "Bayesian CNNs with Bernoulli Approximate Variational Inference" by Yarin Gal et al. (https://arxiv.org/pdf/1506.02158v6.pdf) argues that dropout on convolution layers doesn't help much as, due to their low number of parameters (compared to a dense layer), they are already regularized well. Consequentially, dropout can hinder the learning in convolution layers. One thing you need to take into account is the time of publication. The dropout paper was written two years before the Bayesian CNN paper. Regularization and other improvements introduced in that duration could have had a major impact on improving deep networks, so the benefit of having dropout in convolution layers could become negligible. You can find a more casual discussion on http://mng.bz/nNQ4.

The final code for the auxiliary output is shown in the following listing.

Listing 7.4   Modifying the auxiliary output of Inception net

```
def aux_out(inp,name=None):
    avgpool1 = AvgPool2D((5,5), strides=(3,3), padding='valid')(inp)
    conv1 = Conv2D(128, (1,1), activation='relu', padding='same')(avgpool1)
    flat = Flatten()(conv1)
    dense1 = Dense(1024, activation='relu')(flat)
    dense1 = Dropout(0.7)(dense1)          ⟵  Applying a dropout layer
    aux_out = Dense(200, activation='softmax', name=name)(dense1)     with 70% dropout
    return aux_out
```

Next, we will apply dropout to the output of the last average pooling layer before the final prediction layer. We must flatten the output of the average pooling layer (flat_out) before feeding into a fully connected (i.e., dense) layer. Then dropout is applied on flat_out using

```
flat_out = Dropout(0.4)(flat_out)
```

We are using a dropout rate of 40% for this layer, as prescribed by the paper. The final code (starting from the average pooling layer) looks like this:

```
avgpool1 = AvgPool2D((7,7), strides=(1,1), padding='valid')(inc_5b)

flat_out = Flatten()(avgpool1)
flat_out = Dropout(0.4)(flat_out)
out_main = Dense(200, activation='softmax', name='final')(flat_out)
```

This concludes the discussion on dropout. One final note to keep in mind is that you should not naively set the dropout rate. It should be chosen via a hyperparameter optimization technique. A very high dropout rate can leave your network severely crippled, whereas a very low dropout rate will not contribute to reducing overfitting.

7.1.3 *Early stopping: Halting the training process if the network starts to underperform*

The final technique we will be looking at is called early stopping. As the name suggests, early stopping stops training the model when the validation accuracy stops increasing. You may be thinking, "What? I thought the more training we do the better." Until you reach a certain point, more training is better, but then training starts to reduce the model's generalizability. Figure 7.7 depicts the typical training accuracy and validation accuracy curves you will obtain over the course of training a model. As you can see, after a point, the validation accuracy stops increasing and starts dropping. This is the start of overfitting. You can see that the training accuracy keeps going up, regardless of the validation accuracy. This is because modern deep learning models have more than enough parameters to "remember" data instead of learning features and patterns present in the data.

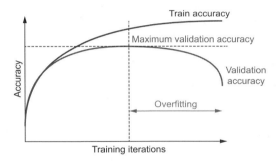

Figure 7.7 An illustration of overfitting. At the start, as the number of training iterations increases, both training and validation accuracies increase. But after a certain point, the validation accuracy plateaus and starts to go down, while the training accuracy keeps going up. This behavior is known as overfitting and should be avoided.

The early stopping procedure is quite simple to understand. First, you define a maximum number of epochs to train for. Then the model is trained for one epoch. After the training, the model is evaluated on the validation set using an evaluation metric (e.g., accuracy). If the validation accuracy has gone up and hasn't reached the maximum epoch, the training is continued. Otherwise, training is stopped, and the model is finalized. Figure 7.8 depicts the early stopping workflow.

Implementing early stopping requires minimal changes to your code. First, as before, we will set up a function that computes the number of steps:

```
def get_steps_per_epoch(n_data, batch_size):
    """ Given the data size and batch size, gives the number of steps to
 travers the full dataset """
    if n_data%batch_size==0:
        return int(n_data/batch_size)
    else:
        return int(n_data*1.0/batch_size)+1
```

Next, we will use the EarlyStopping callback provided by Keras (http://mng.bz/v6lr) to enable early stopping during the training. A Keras callback is an easy way to make

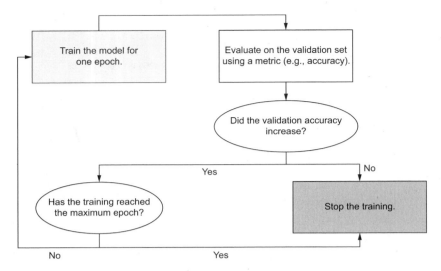

Figure 7.8   The workflow followed during early stopping. First the model is trained for one epoch. Then, the validation accuracy is measured. If the validation accuracy has increased and the training hasn't reached maximum epoch, training is continued. Otherwise, training is halted.

something happen at the end of each epoch during training. For example, for early stopping, all we need to do is analyze the validation accuracy at the end of each epoch and, if it hasn't shown any improvement, terminate the training. Callbacks are ideal for achieving this. We have already used the CSVLogger callback to log the metric quantities over the epochs. The EarlyStopping callback has several arguments:

- monitor—Which metric needs to be monitored in order to terminate the training. You can get the list of defined metric names using the model.metric_names attribute of a Keras model. In our example, this will be set to val_loss (i.e., the loss value computed on the validation data).
- min_delta—The minimum change required in the monitored metric to be considered an improvement (i.e., any improvement < min_delta will be considered a "no improvement" [defaults to zero]).
- patience—If there's no improvement after this many epochs, training will stop (defaults to zero).
- mode—Can be auto/min/max. In min, training will stop if the metric has stopped decreasing (e.g., loss). In max, training will stop if the metric has stopped increasing (e.g., accuracy). The mode will be automatically inferred from the metric name (defaults to auto).
- baseline—Baseline value for the metric. If the metric doesn't improve beyond the baseline, training will stop (defaults to none).
- restore_best_weights—Restores the best weight result in between the start of the training and the termination that showed the best value for the chosen metric (defaults to false).

First, we will create a directory called `eval` if it doesn't exist. This will be used to store the CSV, returned by the `CSVLogger`:

```
# Create a directory called eval which stores model performance
if not os.path.exists('eval'):
    os.mkdir('eval')
# Logging the performance metrics to a CSV file
csv_logger = CSVLogger(os.path.join('eval','2_eval_data_aug_early_stopping.log'))
```

Then we define the `EarlyStopping` callback. We chose `val_loss` as the metric to monitor and a `patience` of five epochs. This means the training will tolerate a "no improvement" for five epochs. We will leave the other parameters in their defaults:

```
# Early stopping callback
es_callback = EarlyStopping(monitor='val_loss', patience=5)
```

Finally call `model.fit()` with the data and the appropriate callbacks. Here, we use the previously defined `train_gen_aux` and `valid_gen_aux` as the training and validation data (respectively). We also set epochs to 50 and the training steps and the validations steps using the `get_steps_per_epoch` function. Finally, we provide the `EarlyStopping` and `CSVLogger` callbacks, so the training stops when there's no improvement under the specified conditions:

```
history = model.fit(
    train_gen_aux, validation_data=valid_gen_aux,
    steps_per_epoch=get_steps_per_epoch(int(0.9*(500*200)),batch_size),
    validation_steps=get_steps_per_epoch(int(0.1*(500*200)),batch_size),
    epochs=50, callbacks=[es_callback, csv_logger]
)
```

The next listing shows a summary of the training logs.

> **Listing 7.5 Training logs provided during training the model**

Because we used a high dropout rate of 70% for some layers, TensorFlow warns us about it, as unintended high dropout rates can hinder model performance.

```
Train for 703 steps, validate for 78 steps
Epoch 1/50
WARNING:tensorflow:Large dropout rate: 0.7 (>0.5). In TensorFlow 2.x,
   dropout() uses dropout rate instead of keep_prob. Please ensure that
   this is intended.                                                        ◄─┐
WARNING:tensorflow:Large dropout rate: 0.7 (>0.5). In TensorFlow 2.x,         │
   dropout() uses dropout rate instead of keep_prob. Please ensure that       │
   this is intended.                                                        ◄─┤
WARNING:tensorflow:Large dropout rate: 0.7 (>0.5). In TensorFlow 2.x,         │
   dropout() uses dropout rate instead of keep_prob. Please ensure that       │
   this is intended.                                                        ◄─┘
703/703 [==============================] - 196s 279ms/step - loss: 15.4462
   - final_loss: 5.1507 - aux1_loss: 5.1369 - aux2_loss: 5.1586 -
   final_accuracy: 0.0124 - aux1_accuracy: 0.0140 - aux2_accuracy: 0.0119
   - val_loss: 14.8221 - val_final_loss: 4.9696 - val_aux1_loss: 4.8943 -
```

```
⮞ val_aux2_loss: 4.9582 - val_final_accuracy: 0.0259 - val_aux1_accuracy:
⮞ 0.0340 - val_aux2_accuracy: 0.0274
...
Epoch 38/50
703/703 [==============================] - 194s 276ms/step - loss:
⮞ 9.4647 - final_loss: 2.8825 - aux1_loss: 3.3037 - aux2_loss: 3.2785 -
⮞ final_accuracy: 0.3278 - aux1_accuracy: 0.2530 - aux2_accuracy: 0.2572
⮞ - val_loss: 9.7963 - val_final_loss: 3.1555 - val_aux1_loss: 3.3244 -
⮞ val_aux2_loss: 3.3164 - val_final_accuracy: 0.2940 - val_aux1_accuracy:
⮞ 0.2599 - val_aux2_accuracy: 0.2590
```

It seems the model doesn't see a benefit in training the model for 50 epochs. After epoch 38, it has decided to terminate the training. This is evident by the fact that training stopped before reaching epoch 50 (as shown in the line `Epoch 38/50`). The other important observation is that you can see that the training accuracy doesn't explode to large values, as we saw in the last chapter. The training accuracy has remained quite close to the validation accuracy (~30%). Though we don't see much of a performance increase, we have managed to reduce overfitting significantly. With that, we can focus on getting the accuracy higher.

NOTE On an Intel Core i5 machine with an NVIDIA GeForce RTX 2070 8GB, the training took approximately 1 hour and 30 minutes to run 38 epochs.

Next, we will revisit our model. We will dig into some research and implement a model that has proven to work well for this specific classification problem.

EXERCISE 1
You have the following model presented to you, and you see that it is heavily underfitting. Underfitting occurs when your model is not approximating the distribution of the data closely enough. Suggest how you can change the dropout layer to reduce underfitting. You can choose between 20%, 50%, and 80% as dropout rates:

```
model = tf.keras.models.Sequential([
tf.keras.layers.Dense(100, activation='relu', input_shape=(250,)),
tf.keras.layers.Dropout(0.5),
tf.keras.layers.Dense(10, activation='softmax')
])
model.compile
    (loss='categorical_crossentropy', optimizer='adam', metrics=['accuracy'])
model.fit(X, y, epochs=25)
```

EXERCISE 2
Define an early stopping callback to terminate the training if the validation loss value (i.e., `val_loss`) has not increased by 0.01 after five epochs. Use `tf.keras.callbacks.EarlyStopping` callback for this purpose.

7.2   *Toward minimalism: Minception instead of Inception*

We now have a model where overfitting is almost nonexistent. However, test performance of the model is still not where we want it to be. You feel like you need a fresh perspective on this problem and consult a senior data scientist on your team. You explain how you have trained an Inception net v1 model on the `tiny-imagenet-200` image classification data set, as well as the poor performance of the model. He mentions that he recently read a paper (cs231n.stanford.edu/reports/2017/pdfs/930.pdf) that uses a modified version of the Inception net that's motivated by Inception-ResNet v2 and has achieved better performance on the data set.

He further explains two new techniques, batch normalization and residual connections (that are used in the modified inception net as well as Inception-ResNet v2), and the significant impact they have in helping the model training, especially in deep models. Now you will implement this new modified model and see if it will improve performance.

We have seen a slight increase in the validation and test accuracies. But we still have barely scratched the surface when it comes to performance. For example, there are reports of ~85% test accuracy for this data set (http://mng.bz/44ev). Therefore, we need to look for other ways to improve the model.

That session you had with the senior data scientist on your team couldn't have been more fruitful. We are going to try the new network he read about.

This network is predominantly inspired by the Inception-Resnet-v2 network that was briefly touched on in the previous chapter. This new network (which we will call Minception) leverages all the state-of-the-art components used in the Inception-ResNet v2 model and modifies them to suit the problem at hand. In this section, you will learn this new model in depth. Particularly, Minception net has the following elements:

- A stem
- Inception-ResNet block A
- Inception-ResNet block B
- Reduction blocks (a new type of block to reduce output size)
- Average pooling layer
- Final prediction layer

Just like other Inception models, this has a stem and Inception blocks. However, Minception differs from Inception Net v1 because it does not have auxiliary outputs, as they have other techniques to stabilize the training. Another notable difference is that Minception has two types of Inception blocks, whereas Inception Net v1 reuses the same format throughout the network. While discussing the different aspects of Minception, we will compare it to Inception Net v1 (which we implemented) in more detail. In a later section, we will discuss the architecture of the Inception-ResNet v2 model in more detail and compare that to Minception. The code for this is available at `Ch07-Improving-CNNs-and-Explaining/7.1.Image_Classification_Advance.ipynb`.

7.2.1   *Implementing the stem*

First and foremost, we should focus on the stem of the model. To refresh our knowledge, a stem is a sequence of convolution and pooling layers and resembles a typical CNN. Minception, however, has a more complex layout, as shown in figure 7.9.

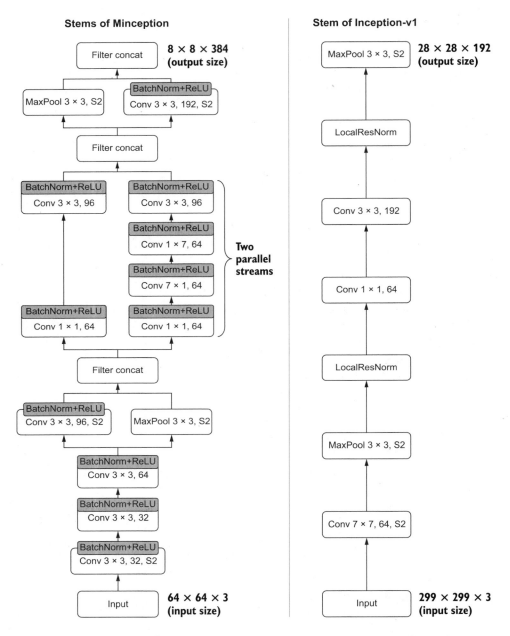

Figure 7.9   Comparing the stems of Minception and Inception-v1. Note how Minception separates the nonlinear activation of convolution layers. This is because batch normalization must be inserted in between the convolution output and the nonlinear activation.

You can see that it has parallel streams of convolution layers spread across the stem. The stem of the Minception is quite different from Inception Net v1. Another key difference is that Minception does not use local response normalization (LRN) but something far more powerful known as *batch normalization.*

Batch normalization: A versatile normalization technique to stabilize and accelerate the training of deep networks

Batch normalization (BN) was introduced in the paper "Batch Normalization: Accelerating Deep Network Training by Reducing Internal Covariate Shift" by Sergey Ioffe et al. (http://proceedings.mlr.press/v37/ioffe15.pdf). As the name suggests, it is a normalization technique that normalizes the intermediate outputs of deep networks.

"Why is this important?" you might ask. It turns out deep networks can cause massive headaches if not properly cared for. For example, a batch of improperly scaled/anomalous inputs during training or incorrect weight initialization can lead to a poor model. Furthermore, such problems can amplify along the depth of the network or over time, leading to changes to the distribution of the inputs received by each layer over time. The phenomenon where the distribution of the inputs is changed over time is known as a *covariate shift*. This is very common, especially in streaming data problems. Batch normalization was invented to solve this problem. Let's understand how BN solves this problem. The batch normalization layer does the following things:

- Normalize $x^{(k)}$, the outputs of the kth layer of the network using

$$\hat{x}^{(k)} = \frac{x^{(k)} - E[x^{(k)}]}{\sqrt{Var(x^{(k)})}}$$

  Here, $E[x^{(k)}]$ represents the mean of the output, and $Var[x^{(k)}]$ is the variance of the output. Both $E[x^{(k)}]$ and $Var[x^{(k)}]$ are vectors. For a fully connected layer with n nodes, both $E[x^{(k)}]$ and $Var[x^{(k)}]$ are n-long vectors (computed by taking mean-over-batch dimension). For a convolutional layer with f filters/kernels, $E[x^{(k)}]$ and $Var[x^{(k)}]$ will be f-long vectors (computed by taking mean over batch, height, and width dimensions).

- Scale and offset the normalized output using two trainable hyperparameters, γ and β (defined separately for each layer), as

$$y^{(k)} = \gamma^{(k)}\hat{x}^{(k)} + \beta^{(k)}$$

  In this process, computing E(x) and Var(x) gets a bit tricky, as these need to be treated differently in the training and testing phases.

- During training, following the stochastic (i.e., looking at a random batch of data instead of the full data set at a given time) nature of the training for each batch, E(x) and Var(x) are computed using only that batch of data. Therefore, for each batch, you can compute E(x) (mean) and Var(x) (variance) without worrying about anything except the current batch.

(continued)

- Then, using each E(x) and Var(x) computed for each batch of data, we estimate E(x) and Var(x) for the population. This is achieved by computing the running mean of E(x) and Var(x). We will not discuss how the running mean works. But you can imagine the running mean as an efficiently computed approximate representation of the true mean for a large data set.
- During the testing phase, we use the population-based E(x) and Var(x) that we computed earlier and perform the earlier defined computations to get $y^{(k)}$.

Due to the complex steps involved in the batch normalization, it will take quite some effort to implement this from the scratch. Luckily, you don't have to. There is a batch normalization layer provided in TensorFlow (http://mng.bz/Qv0Q). If you have the output of some dense layer (let's call it dense1) to inject batch normalization, all you need to do is

```
dense1_bn = BatchNormalization()(dense1)
```

Then TensorFlow will automatically take care of all the complex computations that need to happen under the hood for batch normalization to work properly. Now it's time to use this powerful technique in our Minception model. In the next listing, you can see the implementation of the stem of Minception net. We will write a function called stem, which allows us to turn on/off batch normalization at will.

Listing 7.6   Defining the stem of Minception

```
def stem(inp, activation='relu', bn=True):          ◁——  Defines the function. Note
                                                          that we can switch batch
                                                          normalization on and off.
    conv1_1 = Conv2D(
 ┌─▷    32, (3,3), strides=(2,2), activation=None,
        kernel_initializer=init, padding='same'
 │  )(inp) #62x62
 │  if bn:                                                 Note that first batch
 │      conv1_1 = BatchNormalization()(conv1_1)   ◁——     normalization is applied
 │      conv1_1 = Activation(activation)(conv1_1)  ◁——┐   before applying the
 │                                                    │   nonlinear activation.
 │      conv1_2 = Conv2D(                             │
 ├─▷        32, (3,3), strides=(1,1), activation=None,│   Nonlinear activation
 │          kernel_initializer=init, padding='same'  │   is applied to the layer
 │      )(conv1_1) # 31x31                            ┘   after the batch
 │      if bn:                                            normalization step.
 │          conv1_2 = BatchNormalization()(conv1_2)
 │      conv1_2 = Activation(activation)(conv1_2)
 │
 │      conv1_3 = Conv2D(
 └─▷        64, (3,3), strides=(1,1), activation=None,
            kernel_initializer=init, padding='same'
        )(conv1_2) # 31x31
```

The first part of the stem until the first split

```
if bn:
    conv1_3 = BatchNormalization()(conv1_3)
conv1_3 = Activation(activation)(conv1_3)

maxpool2_1 = MaxPool2D((3,3), strides=(2,2),
padding='same')(conv1_3)

conv2_2 = Conv2D(
    96, (3,3), strides=(2,2), activation=None,
    kernel_initializer=init, padding='same'
)(conv1_3)
if bn:
    conv2_2 = BatchNormalization()(conv2_2)
conv2_2 = Activation(activation)(conv2_2)

out2 = Concatenate(axis=-1)([maxpool2_1, conv2_2])

conv3_1 = Conv2D(
    64, (1,1), strides=(1,1), activation=None,
    kernel_initializer=init, padding='same'
)(out2)
if bn:
    conv3_1 = BatchNormalization()(conv3_1)
conv3_1 = Activation(activation)(conv3_1)

conv3_2 = Conv2D(
    96, (3,3), strides=(1,1), activation=None,
    kernel_initializer=init, padding='same'
)(conv3_1)
if bn:
    conv3_2 = BatchNormalization()(conv3_2)
conv3_2 = Activation(activation)(conv3_2)

conv4_1 = Conv2D(
    64, (1,1), strides=(1,1), activation=None,
    kernel_initializer=init, padding='same'
)(out2)
if bn:
    conv4_1 = BatchNormalization()(conv4_1)
conv4_1 = Activation(activation)(conv4_1)

conv4_2 = Conv2D(
    64, (7,1), strides=(1,1), activation=None,
    kernel_initializer=init, padding='same'
)(conv4_1)
if bn:
    conv4_2 = BatchNormalization()(conv4_2)

conv4_3 = Conv2D(
    64, (1,7), strides=(1,1), activation=None,
    kernel_initializer=init, padding='same'
)(conv4_2)
if bn:
    conv4_3 = BatchNormalization()(conv4_3)
conv4_3 = Activation(activation)(conv4_3)
```

The two parallel streams of the first split

Concatenates the outputs of the two parallel streams in the first split

First stream of the second split

Second stream of the second split

```
conv4_4 = Conv2D(
    96, (3,3), strides=(1,1), activation=None,
    kernel_initializer=init, padding='same'
) (conv4_3)
if bn:
    conv4_4 = BatchNormalization()(conv4_4)
conv4_4 = Activation(activation)(conv4_4)

out34 = Concatenate(axis=-1)([conv3_2, conv4_4])

maxpool5_1 = MaxPool2D((3,3), strides=(2,2), padding='same')(out34)
conv6_1 = Conv2D(
    192, (3,3), strides=(2,2), activation=None,
    kernel_initializer=init, padding='same'
) (out34)
if bn:
    conv6_1 = BatchNormalization()(conv6_1)
conv6_1 = Activation(activation)(conv6_1)

out56 = Concatenate(axis=-1)([maxpool5_1, conv6_1])

return out56
```

Second stream of the second split → (points to the `conv4_4 = Conv2D(...)` block)

Concatenates the outputs of the two streams in the second split → (points to the `out34 = Concatenate(...)` line)

The third (final split) and the concatenation of the outputs → (points to the `maxpool5_1`/`conv6_1`/`out56` block)

A key change you should note is that the nonlinear activation of each layer is separated from the layers. This is so that batch normalization can be inserted in between the output of the layer and the nonlinear activation. This is the original way to apply batch normalization, as discussed in the original paper. But whether BN should come before or after the nonlinearity is an ongoing discussion. You can find a casual discussion on this topic at http://mng.bz/XZpp.

7.2.2 *Implementing Inception-ResNet type A block*

With the stem of the network behind us, let's move forward to see what the Inception blocks look like in Minception net. Let's quickly revisit what the Inception block is and why it was developed. The Inception block was developed to maximize the representational power of convolution layers while encouraging sparsity in model parameters and without shooting the memory requirements through the roof. It does this by having several parallel convolution layers with varying receptive field sizes (i.e., kernel sizes). The Inception block in Minception net uses mostly the same framework. However, it introduces one novel concept, known as *residual connections.*

Residual/skip connections: Shortcuts to stable gradients

We have already touched lightly on residual connections, which introduce one of the simplest operations you can think of in mathematics: element-wise adding of an input to an output. In other words, you take a previous output of the network (call it x) and add it to the current output (call it y), so you get the final output z as z = x + y.

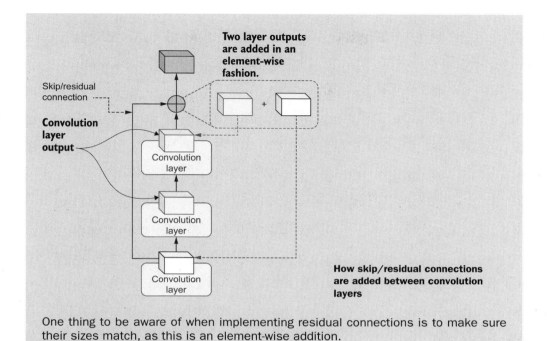

Two layer outputs are added in an element-wise fashion.

Skip/residual connection

Convolution layer output

How skip/residual connections are added between convolution layers

One thing to be aware of when implementing residual connections is to make sure their sizes match, as this is an element-wise addition.

What is residual about residual connections? Mathematical view

It might not be obvious at first, but it's not clear what is residual about skip connections. Assume the following scenario. You have an input x; next you have some layer, $F(x) = y$, that takes an input x and maps it to y. You implement the following network.

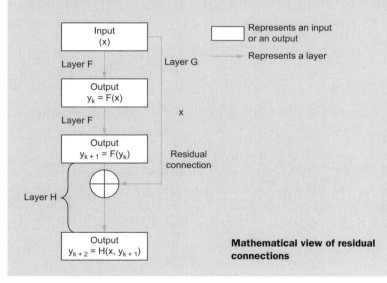

Mathematical view of residual connections

(continued)

$$y_k = F(x)$$

$$y_{k+1} = F(y_k)$$

$$y_{k+2} = y_{k+1} + x$$

$y_{k+2} = y_{k+1} + G(x)$; let us consider the residual connections as a layer that does identity mapping and call it G.

$$y_{k+2} - y_{k+1} = G(x) \text{ or}$$

$G(x) = y_{k+2} - y_{k+1}$; G, in fact, represents the residual between the final output and the previous output.

By considering final output as a layer H that takes x and y_{k+1} as inputs, we obtain the following equation:

$$G(x) = H(x, y_{k+1}) - F(y_k)$$

You can see how the residual enters the picture. Essentially, G(x) is a residual between the final layer output and the previous layer's output

It could not be easier to implement residual connections. Assume you have the following network:

```
from tensorflow.keras.layers import Dense, Input, Add

inp = Input(shape=(10,))
d1 = Dense(20, activation='relu')(inp)
d2 = Dense(20, activation='relu')(d1)
d3 = Dense(20, activation='relu')(d2)
```

You'd like to create a residual connection from d1 to d3. Then all you need to do is

```
d4 = d3 + d1
```

or, if you want to use a Keras layer (equivalent to the previous operation), you can do

```
d4 = Add()([d3, d1])
```

There you have it: d4 is the output of a residual connection. You might remember that I said the output sizes must match in order for the residual connections to be added. Let's try adding two incompatible shapes. For example, let's change the Dense layer to have 30 nodes instead of 20:

```
inp = Input(shape=(10,))
d1 = Dense(20, activation='relu')(inp)
d2 = Dense(20, activation='relu')(d1)
d3 = Dense(30, activation='relu')(d2)
d4 = Add()([d3, d1])
```

If you try to run this code, you'll get the following error:

```
--------------------------------------------------------------------------
ValueError                                Traceback (most recent call last)
...
----> d4 = Add()([d3, d1])
...
ValueError: Operands could not be broadcast together with shapes (30,) (20,)
```

As you can see, TensorFlow is complaining that it was not able to broadcast (in this context, this means performing element-wise addition) two tensors with shapes 30 and 20. This is because TensorFlow doesn't know how to add a (batch_size, 20) tensor to (batch_size, 30). If you see a similar error when trying to implement residual connections, you should go through the network outputs and make sure they match. To get rid of this error, all you need to do is change the code as follows:

```
inp = Input(shape=(10,))
d1 = Dense(20, activation='relu')(inp)
d2 = Dense(20, activation='relu')(d1)
d3 = Dense(20, activation='relu')(d2)
d4 = Add()([d3, d1])
```

Minception has two types of Inception blocks (type A and type B). Now let's write Inception-ResNet block (type A) as a function inception_resnet_a. Compared to the Inception block you implemented earlier, this new inception block has the following additions:

- Uses batch normalization
- Uses a residual connection from the input to the final output of the block

Figure 7.10 compares Inception-ResNet block type A of Minception to Inception Net v1. An obvious difference is that Inception Net v1 does not harness the power of residual connections.

Let's now implement the Minception-ResNet block A. Figure 7.11 shows the type of computations and their connectivity that need to be implemented (listing 7.7).

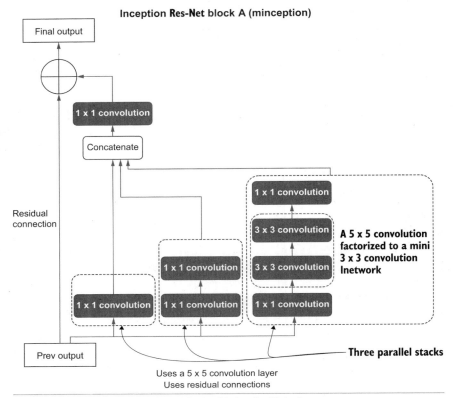

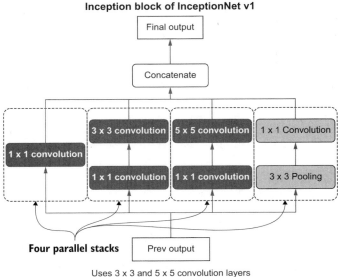

Figure 7.10   Comparison between Inception-ResNet block A (Minception) and Inception net v1's Inception block

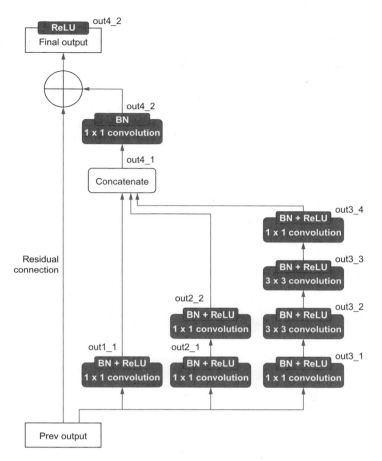

Figure 7.11   Illustration of the Minception-ResNet block A with annotations from code listing 7.7

Listing 7.7   Implementation of Minception-ResNet block A

```
def inception_resnet_a(inp, n_filters, initializer, activation='relu',
    bn=True, res_w=0.1):
    out1_1 = Conv2D(
        n_filters[0][0], (1,1), strides=(1,1),
    activation=None,
        kernel_initializer=initializer,
    padding='same'
    )(inp)                                        ◁
    if bn:                                           The first parallel
        out1_1 = BatchNormalization()(out1_1)       stream in the block
    out1_1 = Activation(activation)(out1_1)       ◁
```

```
out2_1 = Conv2D(
    n_filters[1][0], (1,1), strides=(1,1),
activation=None,
    kernel_initializer=initializer, padding='same'
)(inp)
if bn:
    out2_1 = BatchNormalization()(out2_1)
out2_1 = Activation(activation)(out2_1)

out2_2 = Conv2D(
    n_filters[1][1], (1,1), strides=(1,1), activation=None,
    kernel_initializer=initializer, padding='same'
)(out2_1)
if bn:
    out2_2 = BatchNormalization()(out2_2)
out2_2 = Activation(activation)(out2_2)

out2_3 = Conv2D(
    n_filters[1][2], (1,1), strides=(1,1), activation=None,
    kernel_initializer=initializer, padding='same'
)(out2_2)

out3_1 = Conv2D(
    n_filters[2][0], (1,1), strides=(1,1), activation=None,
    kernel_initializer=initializer, padding='same'
)(inp)
if bn:
    out3_1 = BatchNormalization()(out3_1)
out3_1 = Activation(activation)(out3_1)

out3_2 = Conv2D(
    n_filters[2][1], (3,3), strides=(1,1), activation=None,
    kernel_initializer=initializer, padding='same'
)(out3_1)
if bn:
    out3_2 = BatchNormalization()(out3_2)
out3_2 = Activation(activation)(out3_2)

out3_3 = Conv2D(
    n_filters[2][2], (3,3), strides=(1,1), activation=None,
    kernel_initializer=initializer, padding='same'
)(out3_2)
if bn:
    out3_3 = BatchNormalization()(out3_3)
out3_3 = Activation(activation)(out3_3)

out3_4 = Conv2D(
    n_filters[2][3], (1,1), strides=(1,1), activation=None,
    kernel_initializer=initializer, padding='same'
)(out3_3)
if bn:
    out3_4 = BatchNormalization()(out3_4)
out3_4 = Activation(activation)(out3_4)
```

The second parallel stream in the block

The third parallel stream in the block

```
out4_1 = Concatenate(axis=-1)([out1_1, out2_2, out3_4])        ◁┐   Concatenate
out4_2 = Conv2D(                                                    the outputs
    n_filters[3][0], (1,1), strides=(1,1), activation=None,        of the three
    kernel_initializer=initializer, padding='same'                 separate
)(out4_1)                                                          streams.
if bn:
    out4_2 = BatchNormalization()(out4_2)

out4_2 += res_w * inp                         │   Incorporate the residual
out4_2 = Activation(activation)(out4_2)       │   connection (which is
                                              │   multiplied by a factor to
    return out4_2                             │   improve the gradient flow).
```

Though the function appears long, it is mostly playing Legos with convolution layers. Figure 7.11 provides you the mental map between the visual inception layer and the code. A key observation is how the batch normalization and the nonlinear activation (ReLU) are applied in the top part of the block. The last 1×1 convolution uses batch normalization, not nonlinear activation. Nonlinear activation is only applied after the residual connections.

We are now going to see how to implement the Inception-ResNet B block.

7.2.3 *Implementing the Inception-ResNet type B block*

Next up is the Inception-ResNet type B block in the Minception network. We will not talk about this at length as it is very similar to the Inception-ResNet A block. Figure 7.12 depicts the Inception-ResNet B block and compares it to Inception-ResNet A block. Block B looks relatively simpler than block A, with only two parallel streams. The code-related annotations help you map the mental model of the Inception block to the code, as shown in the following listing.

Listing 7.8   The implementation of Minception-ResNet block B

```
def inception_resnet_b(inp, n_filters, initializer, activation='relu',
⇒ bn=True, res_w=0.1):
    out1_1 = Conv2D(
        n_filters[0][0], (1,1), strides=(1,1), activation=None,
        kernel_initializer=initializer, padding='same'
    )(inp)
    if bn:
        out1_1 = BatchNormalization()(out1_1)
    out1_1 = Activation(activation)(out1_1)

    out2_1 = Conv2D(
        n_filters[1][0], (1,1), strides=(1,1), activation=activation,
        kernel_initializer=initializer, padding='same'
    )(inp)
    if bn:
        out2_1 = BatchNormalization()(out2_1)
    out2_1 = Activation(activation)(out2_1)
```

The first parallel stream in the block

Inception Res-Net block A

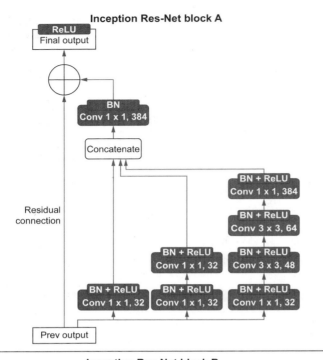

Inception Res-Net block B

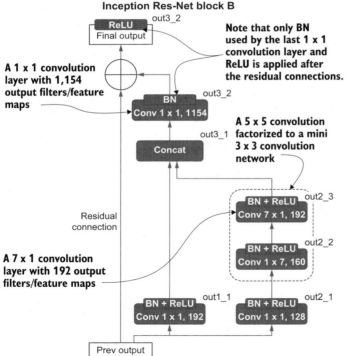

Note that only BN used by the last 1 x 1 convolution layer and ReLU is applied after the residual connections.

A 1 x 1 convolution layer with 1,154 output filters/feature maps

A 5 x 5 convolution factorized to a mini 3 x 3 convolution network

A 7 x 1 convolution layer with 192 output filters/feature maps

Figure 7.12   Minception's Inception-ResNet block B (left) and Minception's Inception-ResNet block A (right) side by side

```
        out2_2 = Conv2D(
            n_filters[1][1], (1,7), strides=(1,1), activation=None,
            kernel_initializer=initializer, padding='same'
        )(out2_1)
        if bn:
            out2_2 = BatchNormalization()(out2_2)
        out2_2 = Activation(activation)(out2_2)

        out2_3 = Conv2D(
            n_filters[1][2], (7,1), strides=(1,1), activation=None,
            kernel_initializer=initializer, padding='same'
        )(out2_2)
        if bn:
            out2_3 = BatchNormalization()(out2_3)
        out2_3 = Activation(activation)(out2_3)

        out3_1 = Concatenate(axis=-1)([out1_1, out2_3])
        out3_2 = Conv2D(
            n_filters[2][0], (1,1), strides=(1,1), activation=None,
            kernel_initializer=initializer, padding='same'
        )(out3_1)
        if bn:
            out3_2 = BatchNormalization()(out3_2)

        out3_2 += res_w * inp
        out3_2 = Activation(activation)(out3_2)

        return out3_2
```

The second parallel stream in the block → (annotation pointing to `out2_2 = Activation(activation)(out2_2)` through `out2_3 = Activation(activation)(out2_3)`)

Concatenate the results from the two parallel streams. ← (annotation pointing to `out3_1 = Concatenate(axis=-1)([out1_1, out2_3])`)

The final convolution layer on top of the concatenated result ← (annotation pointing to `out3_2 = BatchNormalization()(out3_2)`)

Applies the weighted residual connection ← (annotation pointing to `out3_2 += res_w * inp`)

This is quite similar to the function `inception_resnet_a(...)`, with two parallel streams and residual connections. The differences to note are that the type A block has a larger number of convolution layers than the type B block. In addition, the type A block uses a 5 × 5 convolution (factorized to two 3 × 3 convolution layers) and type B uses a 7 × 7 convolution (factorized to 1 × 7 and 7 × 1 convolution layers). I will leave it up to the reader to explore the function in detail.

7.2.4 *Implementing the reduction block*

Inspired by Inception-ResNet models, Minception also uses reduction blocks. Reduction blocks are quite similar to Resnet blocks, with the exception of not having residual connections in the blocks (see the next listing).

Listing 7.9 Implementation of the reduction block of Minception

```
def reduction(inp, n_filters, initializer, activation='relu', bn=True):
    # Split to three branches
    # Branch 1
```

```
out1_1 = Conv2D(
    n_filters[0][0], (3,3), strides=(2,2),
    kernel_initializer=initializer, padding='same'
)(inp)
if bn:
    out1_1 = BatchNormalization()(out1_1)
out1_1 = Activation(activation)(out1_1)

out1_2 = Conv2D(
    n_filters[0][1], (3,3), strides=(1,1),
    kernel_initializer=initializer, padding='same'
)(out1_1)
if bn:
    out1_2 = BatchNormalization()(out1_2)
out1_2 = Activation(activation)(out1_2)

out1_3 = Conv2D(
    n_filters[0][2], (3,3), strides=(1,1),
    kernel_initializer=initializer, padding='same'
)(out1_2)
if bn:
    out1_3 = BatchNormalization()(out1_3)
out1_3 = Activation(activation)(out1_3)

# Branch 2
out2_1 = Conv2D(
    n_filters[1][0], (3,3), strides=(2,2),
    kernel_initializer=initializer, padding='same'
)(inp)
if bn:
    out2_1 = BatchNormalization()(out2_1)
out2_1 = Activation(activation)(out2_1)

# Branch 3
out3_1 = MaxPool2D((3,3), strides=(2,2), padding='same')(inp)

# Concat the results from 3 branches
out = Concatenate(axis=-1)([out1_3, out2_1, out3_1])

return out
```

First parallel stream of convolutions ▷

Second parallel stream of convolutions ◁

Third parallel stream of pooling ▷

Concatenates all the outputs ◁

I will let figure 7.13 speak for itself in terms of explaining listing 7.9. But as you can see, at an abstract level it uses the same types of connections and layers as the Inception blocks we discussed.

Now we're going to see how we can complete the puzzle of Minception by collating all the different elements we have implemented thus far.

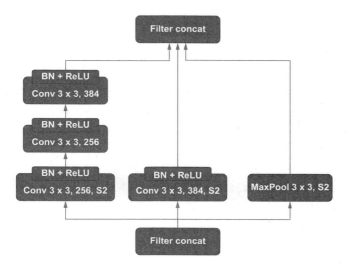

Figure 7.13 Illustration of the reduction block

7.2.5 *Putting everything together*

Great work so far. With all the basic blocks ready, our Minception model is taking shape. Next, it's a matter of putting things where they belong. The final model uses the following components:

- A single stem
- 1x Inception-ResNet block A
- 2x Inception-ResNet block B
- Average pooling
- Dropout
- Final prediction layer with 200 nodes and softmax activation

In addition, we will make a few more changes to the inputs of the model. According to the original paper, the model takes in a $56 \times 56 \times 3$–sized input instead of a $64 \times 64 \times 3$–sized input. This is done by the following:

- *Training phase*—Randomly cropping a $56 \times 56 \times 3$–sized image from the original $64 \times 64 \times 3$–sized image
- *Validation/testing phase*—Center cropping a $56 \times 56 \times 3$–sized image from the original image

Furthermore, we will introduce another augmentation step to randomly contrast images during the training (as used in the paper). Unfortunately, you cannot achieve either of these steps with the ImageDataGenerator. The good news is that since TensorFlow 2.2, there have been several new image preprocessing layers introduced (http://mng.bz/yvzy). We can incorporate these layers just like any other layer in the model. For example, we start with the input just like before:

```
inp = Input(shape=(64,64,3))
```

Then you import the `RandomCrop` and `RandomContrast` layers and use them as follows:

```
from tensorflow.keras.layers.experimental.preprocessing import RandomCrop,
➥ RandomContrast
# Cropping the image to a 56x56 sized image
crop_inp = RandomCrop(56, 56, seed=random_seed)(inp)
# Provide a random contrast between 0.7 and 1.3 where 1.0 is the original
➥ contrast
crop_inp = RandomContrast(0.3, seed=random_seed)(crop_inp)
```

The final model looks like the following listing.

Listing 7.10   The final Minception model

```
import tensorflow as tf
from tensorflow.keras.layers import Input, Conv2D, MaxPool2D, Dropout,
➥ AvgPool2D, Dense, Concatenate, Flatten, BatchNormalization, Activation
➥ from tensorflow.keras.layers.experimental.preprocessing import RandomCrop,
➥ RandomContrast
from tensorflow.keras.models import Model
from tensorflow.keras.losses import CategoricalCrossentropy
import tensorflow.keras.backend as K
from tensorflow.keras.callbacks import EarlyStopping, CSVLogger
```

Define the 64 × 64 Input layer.
```
inp = Input(shape=(64,64,3))
```
Perform random cropping on the input (randomness is only activated during training).

```
crop_inp = RandomCrop(56, 56, seed=random_seed)(inp)
crop_inp = RandomContrast(0.3, seed=random_seed)(crop_inp)
```

Define the output of the stem.
```
stem_out = stem(crop_inp)
```
Perform random contrast on the input (randomness is only activated during training).

Define the Inception-ResNet block (type A).
```
inc_a = inception_resnet_a(stem_out, [(32,),(32,32), (32, 48, 64,
➥ 384),(384,)], initializer=init)

red = reduction(inc_a, [(256,256,384),(384,)], initializer=init)
```
Define a reduction layer.

Define 2 Inception-ResNet block (type B).
```
inc_b1 = inception_resnet_b(red, [(192,),(128,160,192),(1152,)],
➥ initializer=init)
inc_b2 = inception_resnet_b(inc_b1,  [(192,),(128,160,192),(1152,)],
➥ initializer=init)

avgpool1 = AvgPool2D((4,4), strides=(1,1), padding='valid')(inc_b2)
flat_out = Flatten()(avgpool1)
dropout1 = Dropout(0.5)(flat_out)
out_main = Dense(200, activation='softmax',  kernel_initializer=init,
➥ name='final')(flat_out)
```
Define the model.
```
minception_resnet_v2 = Model(inputs=inp, outputs=out_main)
minception_resnet_v2.compile(loss='categorical_crossentropy',
➥ optimizer='adam', metrics=['accuracy'])
```
Define the final prediction layer.

Compile the model with categorical crossentropy loss and the adam optimizer.

Finally, our Minception model is ready for battle. It takes in a $64 \times 64 \times 3$–sized input (like the other models we implemented). It then randomly (during training) or center (during validation/testing) crops the image and applies random contrast adjustments (during training). This is taken care of automatically. Next, the processed input goes into the stem of the network, which produces the output `stem_out`, which goes into an Inception-ResNet block of type A and flows into a reduction block. Next, we have two Inception-ResNet type B blocks, one after the other. This is followed by an average pooling layer, a `Flatten` layer that squashes all dimensions except the batch dimension to 1. Then a dropout layer with 50% dropout is applied on the output. Finally, a dense layer with 200 nodes (one for each class) with softmax activation produces the final output. Lastly, the model is compiled using the categorical cross-entropy loss and the `adam` optimizer.

This ends our conversation about the Minception model. Do you want to know how much this will boost our model's performance? In the next section, we will train the Minception model we defined.

7.2.6 *Training Minception*

Now we're on to training the model. The training process is very similar to what you already did for the Inception Net v1 model, with one difference. We are going to use a learning rate reduction schedule to further reduce overfitting and improve generalizability. In this example, the learning rate scheduler will reduce the learning rate if the model's performance doesn't improve within a predefined duration (see the next listing).

Listing 7.11 Training the Minception model

```
import time
from tensorflow.keras.callbacks import EarlyStopping, CSVLogger
from functools import partial

n_epochs=50                                              Sets up an early
                                                         stopping callback
es_callback = EarlyStopping(monitor='val_loss', patience=10)
csv_logger = CSVLogger(os.path.join('eval','3_eval_minception.log'))
lr_callback = tf.keras.callbacks.ReduceLROnPlateau(
    monitor='val_loss', factor=0.1, patience=5, verbose=1, mode='auto'
)                                                        Sets up a learning
                                                         rate control callback
history = model.fit(
    train_gen_aux, validation_data=valid_gen_aux,
    steps_per_epoch=get_steps_per_epoch(int(0.9*(500*200)), batch_size),
    validation_steps=get_steps_per_epoch(int(0.1*(500*200)), batch_size),
    epochs=n_epochs,                                     Sets up a CSV logger
    callbacks=[es_callback, csv_logger, lr_callback]     to record metrics
)
```

Trains the model →

When training deep networks, using a learning rate schedule instead of a fixed learning rate is quite common. Typically, we get better performance by using a higher learning rate at the beginning of the model training and then using a smaller learning rate as the model progresses. This is because, as the model converges during the optimization process, you should make the step size smaller (i.e., the learning rate). Otherwise, large step sizes can make the model behave erratically. We can be smart about this process and reduce the learning rate whenever we do not see an increase in an observed metric instead of reducing the learning rate in fixed intervals. In Keras you can easily incorporate this into model training via the callback `ReduceLROnPlateau` (http://mng.bz/M5Oo):

```
lr_callback = tf.keras.callbacks.ReduceLROnPlateau(
    monitor='val_loss', factor=0.1, patience=5, verbose=1, mode='auto'
)
```

When using the callback, you need to set the following keyword arguments:

- `monitor`—Defines the observed metric. In our example, we will decide when to reduce the learning rate based on validation loss.
- `factor`—The multiplicative factor to reduce the learning rate by. If the learning rate is 0.01, a factor of 0.1, this means, on reduction, that the learning rate will be 0.001.
- `patience`—Similar to early stopping, how many epochs to wait before reducing the learning rate with no improvement in the metric.
- `mode`—Similar to early stopping, whether the metric minimization/maximization should be considered as an improvement.

When you train your model, you should get an output like the following:

```
Train for 703 steps, validate for 78 steps
Epoch 1/50
703/703 [==============================] - 158s 224ms/step - loss: 4.9362 -
➥ accuracy: 0.0544 - val_loss: 13.1802 - val_accuracy: 0.0246
...
Epoch 41/50
702/703 [=============================>.] - ETA: 0s - loss: 2.5830 -
➥ accuracy: 0.6828
Epoch 00041: ReduceLROnPlateau reducing learning rate to 0.00010000000474974513.
703/703 [==============================] - 136s 194ms/step - loss: 2.5831 -
➥ accuracy: 0.6827 - val_loss: 3.4446 - val_accuracy: 0.4316
...
Epoch 47/50
702/703 [=============================>.] - ETA: 0s - loss: 2.3371 -
➥ accuracy: 0.7859
Epoch 00047: ReduceLROnPlateau reducing learning rate to 1.0000000474974514e-05.
703/703 [==============================] - 139s 197ms/step - loss: 2.3372 -
➥ accuracy: 0.7859 - val_loss: 3.2988 - val_accuracy: 0.4720
...
Epoch 50/50
703/703 [==============================] - 137s 194ms/step - loss: 2.3124 -
➥ accuracy: 0.7959 - val_loss: 3.3133 - val_accuracy: 0.4792
```

Amazing! We get a tremendous accuracy boost just by tweaking the model architecture. We now have a model that has around 50% accuracy on the validation set (which is equivalent to identifying 100/200 classes of objects accurately, or 50% of images classified that are accurate for each class). You can see the interventions made by the ReduceLROnPlateau callback in the output.

Finally, we save the model using

```
if not os.path.exists('models'):
    os.mkdir("models")
model.save(os.path.join('models', 'minception_resnet_v2.h5'))
```

Next, we can measure the model's performance on the test set:

```
# Load the model from disk
model = load_model(os.path.join('models','minception_resnet_v2.h5'))

# Evaluate the model
test_res = model.evaluate(test_gen_aux, steps=get_steps_per_epoch(500*50,
    batch_size))
```

This should give around 51% accuracy on the test set. That's very exciting news. We have almost doubled the performance of the previous model by paying more attention to the structure of the model.

This is a good lesson that teaches us the vital role played by the model architecture in deep learning. There's a misconception that deep learning is the silver bullet that solves anything. It is not. For example, you shouldn't expect any random architecture that's put together to work as well as some of the state-of-the-art results published. Getting a well-performing deep network can be a result of days or even weeks of hyper-parameter optimization and empirically driven choices.

In the next section, we will leverage transfer learning to reach a higher degree of accuracy faster. We will download a pretrained model and finetune it on the specific data set.

NOTE On an Intel Core i5 machine with an NVIDIA GeForce RTX 2070 8GB, the training took approximately 1 hour and 54 minutes to run 50 epochs.

EXERCISE 3

You have the following convolution block that you are using to implement an image classifier:

```
def my_conv_block(input, activation):
    out_1 = tf.keras.layers.Conv2D(n_filters[0][2], (3,3), strides=(1,1),
                kernel_initializer=initializer, padding='same')(input)
    out_final = tf.keras.layers.BatchNormalization()(out_1)
    out_final = tf.keras.layers.Activation(activation)(out_final)
    return out_final
```

You would like to make the following two changes:

- Introduce batch normalization after applying the activation
- Create a residual connection from the output of the convolution layer to the output of the batch normalization layers output.

7.3   *If you can't beat them, join 'em: Using pretrained networks for enhancing performance*

So far, you have developed a good image classification model, which uses various methods to prevent overfitting. The company was happy until your boss let out the news that there's a new competitor in town that is performing better than the model you developed. Rumor is that they have a model that's around 70% accurate. So, it's back to the drawing board for you and your colleagues. You believe that a special technique known as transfer learning can help. Specifically, you intend to use a pretrained version of Inception-ResNet v2 that is already trained on the original ImageNet image classification data set; fine-tuning this model on the `tiny-imagenet-200` data set will provide better accuracy than all the models implemented thus far.

If you want to come close to state of the art, you must use every bit of help you can get. A great way to begin this quest is to start with a pretrained model and then fine-tune it for your task. A pretrained model is a model that has already being trained on a similar task. This process falls under the concept of *transfer learning*. For example, you can easily find models that have been pretrained on the ILSVRC task.

7.3.1   *Transfer learning: Reusing existing knowledge in deep neural networks*

Transfer learning is a massive topic and is something for a separate chapter (or even a book). There are many variants of transfer learning. To understand different facets of transfer learning, refer to https://ruder.io/transfer-learning/. One method is to use a pretrained model and fine-tune it for the task to be solved. The process looks like figure 7.14.

First, you train the model on a task for which you already have a large labeled data set (known as the pretrained task). For example, in image classification, you have several large labeled data sets, including the ImageNet data set. Once you train a model on the large data set, you get the weights of the network (except for the final prediction layer) and fit a new prediction layer that matches the new task. This gives a very good starting point for the network to solve the new task. You are then able to solve the new task with a smaller data set, as you have already trained your model on similar, larger data sets.

How can we use transfer learning to solve our problem? It is not that difficult. Keras provides a huge model repository for image classification tasks (http://mng.bz/aJdo). These models have been trained predominantly on the ImageNet image classification task. Let's tame the beast produced in the lineage of Inception networks: Inception-ResNet v2. Note that the code for this section can be found at `Ch07-Improving-CNNs-and-Explaining/7.2.Transfer_Learning.ipynb`.

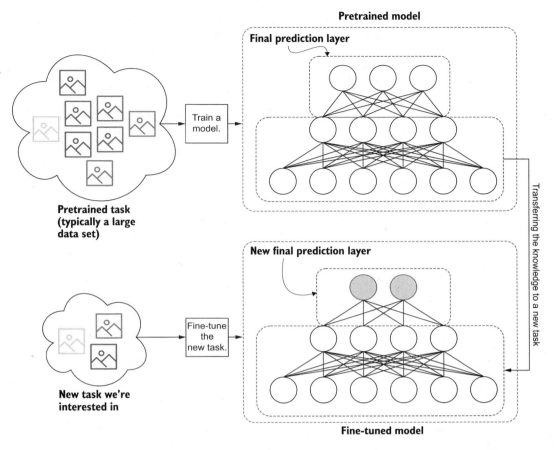

Figure 7.14   How transfer learning works. First, we start with a model that is pretrained on a larger data set that is solving a similar/relevant task to the one we're interested in. Then we transfer the model weights (except the last layer) and fit a new prediction layer on top of the existing weights. Finally, we fine-tune the model on a new task.

Inception-ResNet v2

We briefly touched on the Inception-ResNet v2 model. It was the last Inception model produced. Inception-ResNet v2 has the following characteristics that set it apart from other inception models:

- Redesigned stem that removes any representational bottlenecks
- Inception blocks that use residual connections
- Reduction modules that reduce the height/width dimensions of the inputs
- Does not use auxiliary outputs as in the early Inception nets

(continued)

As you can see, the redesigned stem, Inception-ResNet blocks, and reduction modules are being used in the Minception model. And if you compare the diagrams of Minception that are provided to the diagrams in the original paper, you will see how many similarities they share. Therefore, we will not repeat our discussion of these components. If you still want to see the specific details and illustrations of the different components, refer to the original paper (https://arxiv.org/pdf/1602.07261.pdf). However, the high-level architecture of Inception-ResNet v2 looks like the following figure.

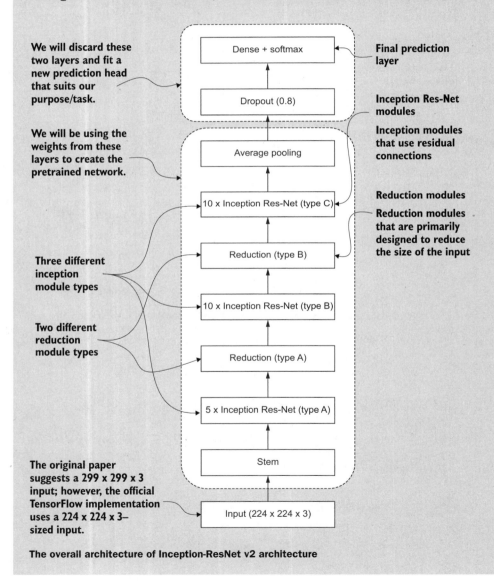

The overall architecture of Inception-ResNet v2 architecture

You can download the Inception-ResNet v2 model with a single line:

```
InceptionResNetV2(include_top=False, pooling='avg')
```

Here, `include_top=False` means that the final prediction layer will be discarded. It is necessary because the original inception net is designed for 1,000 classes. However, we only have 200 classes. `pooling='avg'` ensures that the last pooling layer in the model is an average pooling layer. Next, we will create a new model that encapsulates the pretrained Inception-ResNet v2 model as the essence but is modified to solve the tiny-ImageNet classification task, as shown in the next listing.

Listing 7.12 Implementing a model based on the pretrained Inception-ResNet v2 model

```
from tensorflow.keras.applications import InceptionResNetV2        Some important
from tensorflow.keras.models import Sequential                     imports
from tensorflow.keras.layers import Input, Dense, Dropout

model = Sequential([                    Defining an input layer
    Input(shape=(224,224,3)),           for a 224 × 224 image          The pretrained
    InceptionResNetV2(include_top=False, pooling='avg'),            weights of the
    Dropout(0.4),                                                   Inception-ResNet
    Dense(200, activation='softmax')       Final prediction layer   v2 model
])                                         with 200 classes

adam = tf.keras.optimizers.Adam(learning_rate=0.0001)
model.compile(loss='categorical_crossentropy', optimizer=adam,
  metrics=['accuracy'])             Using a smaller learning rate since the
model.summary()                     network is already trained on ImageNet
                                    data (chosen empirically)
```

Apply 40% dropout

Here, you can see that we are defining a sequential model that

- First defines an input layer of size 224 × 224 × 3 (i.e., height = 224, width = 224, channels = 3)
- Defines the Inception-ResNet v2 model as a layer
- Uses a dropout of 40% on the last average pooling layer
- Defines a dense layer that uses softmax activation and has 200 nodes

One crucial challenge we need to deal with is that the original input Inception-ResNet v2 is designed to consume is size 224 × 224 × 3. Therefore, we will need to find a way to present our inputs (i.e., 64 × 64 × 3) in a way that complies with Inception-ResNet v2's requirements. In order to do that, we will make some changes to the `ImageData-Generator`, as the following listing shows.

Listing 7.13 The modified ImageDataGenerator that produces 224 × 224 images

```
def get_train_valid_test_data_generators(batch_size, target_size):

    image_gen_aug = ImageDataGenerator(
        samplewise_center=False, rotation_range=30, width_shift_range=0.2,
```

```
        height_shift_range=0.2, brightness_range=(0.5,1.5), shear_range=5,
        zoom_range=0.2, horizontal_flip=True, validation_split=0.1
    )
    image_gen = ImageDataGenerator(samplewise_center=False)
```

> Defines a data-augmenting image data generator and a standard image data generator

```
    partial_flow_func = partial(
        image_gen_aug.flow_from_directory,
        directory=os.path.join('data','tiny-imagenet-200', 'train'),
        target_size=target_size,
        classes=None,
        class_mode='categorical',
        interpolation='bilinear',
        batch_size=batch_size,
        shuffle=True,
        seed=random_seed)
```

Defines a partial function to avoid repeating arguments

Uses a target size of 224 × 224

Uses bilinear interpolation to make images bigger

```
    # Get the training data subset
    train_gen = partial_flow_func(subset='training')
    # Get the validation data subset
    valid_gen = partial_flow_func(subset='validation')
```

Defines the data generators for training and validation sets

```
    # Defining the test data generator
    test_df = get_test_labels_df(os.path.join('data','tiny-imagenet-200',
'val', 'val_annotations.txt'))
    test_gen = image_gen.flow_from_dataframe(
        test_df,
        directory=os.path.join('data','tiny-imagenet-200',  'val', 'images'),
        target_size=target_size,
        classes=None,
        class_mode='categorical',
        interpolation='bilinear',
        batch_size=batch_size,
        shuffle=False
    )
    return train_gen, valid_gen, test_gen
```

Defines the test data generator

Uses a target size of 224 × 224 and bilinear interpolation

```
batch_size = 32
target_size = (224,224)
```

Defines the batch size and target size

```
# Getting the train,valid, test data generators
train_gen, valid_gen, test_gen =
  get_train_valid_test_data_generators(batch_size, target_size)

train_gen_aux = data_gen_augmented(train_gen, random_gamma=True,
  random_occlude=True)

valid_gen_aux = data_gen_augmented(valid_gen)
test_gen_aux = data_gen_augmented(test_gen)
```

Gets the train/valid/test modified data generators using the data_gen_augmented function

Finally, it's time for the grand unveil! We will train the best model we've come up with:

```
from tensorflow.keras.callbacks import EarlyStopping, CSVLogger
es_callback = EarlyStopping(monitor='val_loss', patience=10)
```

```
csv_logger = CSVLogger(os.path.join('eval','4_eval_resnet_pretrained.log'))
n_epochs=30
lr_callback = tf.keras.callbacks.ReduceLROnPlateau(
    monitor='val_loss', factor=0.1, patience=5, verbose=1, mode='auto'
)

history = model.fit(
    train_gen_aux, validation_data=valid_gen_aux,
    steps_per_epoch=int(0.9*(500*200)/batch_size),
     validation_steps=int(0.1*(500*200)/batch_size),
    epochs=n_epochs, callbacks=[es_callback, csv_logger, lr_callback]
)
```

The training will be identical to the earlier training configuration we used when training the Minception model. We will not repeat the details. We are using the following:

- Metric logging
- Early stopping
- Learning rate scheduling

NOTE   On an Intel Core i5 machine with an NVIDIA GeForce RTX 2070 8GB, the training took approximately 9 hours and 20 minutes to run 23 epochs.

You should get a result similar to the following:

```
Epoch 1/50
2813/2813 [==============================] - 1465s 521ms/step - loss:
➥ 2.0031 - accuracy: 0.5557 - val_loss: 1.5206 - val_accuracy: 0.6418
...
Epoch 23/50
2813/2813 [==============================] - ETA: 0s - loss: 0.1268 -
➥ accuracy: 0.9644
Epoch 00023: ReduceLROnPlateau reducing learning rate to
➥ 9.999999974752428e-08.
2813/2813 [==============================] - 1456s 518ms/step - loss:
➥ 0.1268 - accuracy: 0.9644 - val_loss: 1.2681 - val_accuracy: 0.7420
```

Isn't this great news? We have reached around 74% validation accuracy by combining all we have learned. Let's quickly look at the test accuracy of the model:

```
# Evaluate the model
test_res = model.evaluate(test_gen_aux, steps=get_steps_per_epoch(500*50,
➥ batch_size))
```

This should show you around ~79% accuracy. It hasn't been an easy journey, but you obviously have surpassed your competitor's model of ~70% accuracy.

In the next section, we will look at the importance of model explainability. We will learn about a technique that we can use to explain the knowledge embedded in our model.

Inception-ResNet v2 versus Minception

The stem of the Minception and Inception-Resnet-v2 are identical in terms of the innovations they introduce (e.g., Inception-ResNet blocks, reduction blocks, etc.). However, there are the following low-level differences:

- Inception-ResNet v2 has three different Inception block types; Minception has only two.
- Inception-ResNet v2 has two different types of reduction blocks; Minception has only one.
- Inception-ResNet v2 has 25 Inception layers, but Minception (the version we implemented) has only three.

There are also other minor differences, such as the fact that Inception-ResNet v2 uses valid padding in a few layers of the model. Feel free to consult the Inception-ResNet v2 paper if you want to know the details. Another notable observation is that neither the Minception nor the Inception-ResNet v2 uses local response normalization (LRN), as they use something far more powerful: batch normalization.

EXERCISE 4

You want to implement a network using a different pretrained network known as VGG-Net (16 layers). You can obtain the pretrained network from `tf.keras.applications .VGG16`. Next, you discard the top layer and introduce a max pooling layer on top. Then you want to add two dense layers on top of the pretrained network with 100 (`ReLU` activation) and 50 (`Softmax` activation) nodes. Implement this network.

7.4 *Grad-CAM: Making CNNs confess*

The company can't be happier about what you have done for them. You have managed to build a model that not only beat the performance of the competitor, but also is one of the best in production. However, your boss wants to be certain that the model is trustworthy before releasing any news on this. Accuracy alone is not enough! You decide to demonstrate how the model makes predictions using a recent model interpretation technique known as *Grad-CAM*. Grad-CAM uses the magnitude of the gradients generated for a given input with respect to the model's predictions to provide visualizations of where the model focused. A large magnitude of gradients in a certain area of an image means that the image focuses more in that area. And by superimposing the gradient magnitudes depicted as a heatmap, you are able to produce an attractive visualization of what the model is paying attention to in a given input.

Grad-CAM (which stands for gradient class activation map) is a model interpretation technique introduced for deep neural networks by Ramprasaath R. Selvaraju et al. in "Grad-CAM: Visual Explanations from Deep Networks via Gradient-based Localization" (https://arxiv.org/pdf/1610.02391.pdf). Deep networks are notorious for their inexplicable nature and are thus termed *black boxes*. Therefore, we must do some analysis and ensure that the model is working as intended.

The following code delineates how Grad-CAM works its magic, and the implementation is available in the notebook Ch07-Improving-CNNs-and-Explaining/7.3 .Interpreting_CNNs_GradCAM.ipynb. In the interest of conserving the length of this chapter, we will discuss only the pseudocode of this approach and will leave the technical details to appendix B (see the next listing).

Listing 7.14 Pseudocode of Grad-CAM computations

```
Define: model (Trained Inception Resnet V2 model)
Define: probe_ds (A list of image, class(integer) tuples e.g. [(image,
    class-int), (image, class-int), …]) that we will use to interpret the model
Define: last_conv (Last convolution layer of the model - closest to the
    prediction layer)
Load the model (inceptionnet_resnet_v2.h5)

For img, cls in probe_ds:

    # Computing the gradient map and its associated weights
    Compute the model's final output (out) and last_conv layer's output
    (conv_out)
    Compute the gradient d (out[cls]) / d (conv_out) and assign to grad
    Compute channel weights by taking the mean of grad over width and
    height dimensions (Results in a [batch size(=1), 1, 1, # channels in
    last_conv] tensor)

    # Creating the final gradient heatmap
    grad = grad * weights # Multiply grad with weights
    grad = tf.reduce_sum(grad, axis=-1) # Take sum over channels
    grad = tf.nn.relu(grad) # Apply ReLU activation to obtain the gradient
    heatmap

    # Visualizing the gradient heatmap
    Resize the gradient heatmap to a size of 224x224
    Superimpose the gradient heatmap on the original image (img)
    Plot the image and the image with the gradient heatmap superimposed
    side by side
```

The key computation that is performed by Grad-CAM is, given an input image, taking the gradient of the node that corresponds to the true class of the image with respect to the last convolution output of the model.

The magnitude of the gradient at each pixel of the images represents the contribution that pixel made to the final outcome. Therefore, by representing Grad-CAM output as a heatmap, resizing to match the original image, and superimposing that on the original image, you can get a very attractive and informative plot of where the model focused to find different objects. The plots are self-explanatory and show whether the model is focusing on the correct object to produce a desired prediction. In figure 7.15, we show which areas the model focuses on strongly (red/dark = highest focus, blue/light = less focus).

Figure 7.15 (i.e., visualization of Grad-CAM) shows that our model is truly an intelligent model. It knows where to focus to find a given object, even in cluttered

Figure 7.15   Visualization of the Grad-CAM output for several probe images. The redder/darker an area in the image, the more the model focuses on that part of the image. You can see that our model has learned to understand some complex scenes and separate the model that it needs to focus on.

environments (e.g., classifying the dining table). As mentioned earlier, the redder/darker the area, the more the model focuses on that area to make a prediction. Now it's time for you to demonstrate the results to your boss and build the needed confidence to go public with the new model!

We will end our discussion about image classification here. We have learned about many different models and techniques that can be used to solve the problem effectively. In the next chapter, we will discuss a different facet of computer vision known as image segmentation.

Summary

- Image augmentation, dropout, and early stopping are some of the common techniques used to prevent overfitting in vision deep networks.
- Most of the common image augmentation steps can be achieved through the Keras `ImageDataGenerator`.
- It is important to pay attention to the architecture of the model chosen for a given problem. One should not randomly choose an architecture but research and identify an architecture that has worked for a similar problem. Otherwise, choose the architecture through hyperparameter optimization. The Minception model's architecture has been proven to work well on the same data we used in this chapter.
- Transfer learning enables us to use already trained models to solve new tasks with better accuracy.
- In Keras you can get a given model with a single line of code and adapt it to the new task.
- Various pretrained networks are available at http://mng.bz/M5Oo.
- Grad-CAM (gradient class activation map) is an effective way to interpret your CNN.
- Grad-CAM computes where the model focused the most based on the magnitude of gradients produced with respect to the prediction made by the model.

Answers to exercises

Exercise 1

1 You should reduce the dropout rate to keep more nodes switched during training if underfitting is occurring:

```
model = tf.keras.models.Sequential([
tf.keras.layers.Dense(100, activation='relu', input_shape=(250,)),
tf.keras.layers.Dropout(0.2),
tf.keras.layers.Dense(10, activation='softmax')
])
model.compile(loss='categorical_crossentropy', optimizer='adam',
➥ metrics=['accuracy'])
model.fit(X, y, epochs=25)
```

2 Early stopping is introduced using the `EarlyStopping` callback:

```
es_callback = tf.keras.callbacks.EarlyStopping(monitor='val_loss',
➥ patience=5, min_delta=0.1)
model.fit(X, y, epochs=25, callbacks=[es_callback])
```

Exercise 2

```
tf.keras.callbacks.EarlyStopping(monitor='val_loss', min_delta=0.01, patience=5)
```

Exercise 3

```
def my_conv_block(input, activation):
    out_1 = tf.keras.layers.Conv2D(n_filters[0][2], (3,3), strides=(1,1),
                   kernel_initializer=initializer, activation=activation,
                   padding='same')(input)

    out_final = tf.keras.layers.BatchNormalization()(out_1)

    out = out_final + out_1
    return out
```

Exercise 4

```
model = tf.keras.models.Sequential([
    tf.keras.layers.Input(shape=(224,224,3)),
    tf.keras.applications.VGG16(include_top=False, pooling='max'),
    tf.keras.layers.Dense(100, activation='relu'),
    tf.keras.layers.Dense(50, activation='softmax')
])
```

Telling things apart: Image segmentation

This chapter covers

- Understanding segmentation data and working with it in Python
- Implementing a fully fledged segmentation data pipeline
- Implementing an advanced segmentation model (DeepLab v3)
- Compiling models with custom-built image segmentation loss functions/metrics
- Training the image segmentation model on the clean and processed image data
- Evaluating the trained segmentation model

In the last chapter, we learned about various advanced computer vision models and techniques to push the performance of an image classifier. We learned about the architecture of Inception net v1 as well as its successors (e.g., Inception net v2, v3, and v4). Our objective was to lift the performance of the model on an image classification data set with 64 × 64–sized RGB images of objects belonging to 200 different classes. While trying to train a model on this data set, we learned many important concepts:

- *Inception blocks*—A way to group convolutional layers having different-sized windows (or kernels) to encourage learning features at different scales while making the model parameter efficient due to the smaller-sized kernels.
- *Auxiliary outputs*—Inception net uses a classification layer (i.e., a fully connected layer with softmax activation) not only at the end of the network, but also in the middle of the network. This enables the gradients from the final layer to flow strongly all the way to the first layer.
- *Augmenting data*—Using various image transformation techniques (adjusting brightness/contrast, rotating, translating, etc.) to increase the amount of labeled data using the `tf.keras.preprocessing.image.ImageDataGenerator`.
- *Dropout*—Switching on and off nodes in the layers randomly. This forces the neural networks to learn more robust features as the network does not always have all the nodes activated.
- *Early stopping*—Using the performance on the validation data set as a way to control when the training stops. If the validation performance has not increased in a certain number of epochs, training is halted.
- *Transfer learning*—Downloading and using a pretrained model (e.g., Inception-ResNet v2) trained on a larger, similar data set as the initialization and fine-tuning it to perform well on the task at hand.

In this chapter, we will learn about another important task in computer vision: image segmentation. In image classification, we only care if an object exists in a given image. Image segmentation, on the other hand, recognizes multiple objects in the same image as well as where they are in the image. It is a very important topic of computer vision, and applications like self-driving cars live and breathe image segmentation models. Self-driving cars need to precisely locate objects in their surroundings, which is where image segmentation comes into play. As you might have guessed already, they also have their roots in many other applications:

- Image retrieval
- Identifying galaxies (http://mng.bz/gwVx)
- Medical image analysis

If you are a computer vision/deep learning engineer/researcher working on image-related problems, there is a high chance that your path will cross with image segmentation. Image segmentation models classify each pixel in the image to one of a predefined set of object categories. Image segmentation has ties to the image classification task we saw earlier. Both solve a classification task. Additionally, pretrained image classification models are used as the backbone of segmentation models, as they can provide crucial image features at different granularities to solve the segmentation task better and faster. A key difference is that image classifiers are solving a sparse prediction task, where each image has a single class label associated, as opposed to segmentation models that solve a dense prediction task that has a class label associated with every pixel in the image.

Any image segmentation algorithm can be classified as one of the following:

- *Semantic segmentation*—The algorithm is only interested in identifying different categories of objects present in the image. For example, if there are multiple persons in the image, the pixels corresponding to all of them will be tagged with the same class.
- *Instance segmentation*—The algorithm is interested in identifying different objects separately. For example, if there are multiple persons in the image, pixels belonging to each person are represented by a unique class. Instance-based segmentation is considered more difficult than semantic segmentation.

Figure 8.1 depicts the difference between the data found in a semantic segmentation task and an instance-based segmentation task. In this chapter, we will focus on semantic segmentation (http://mng.bz/5QAZ).

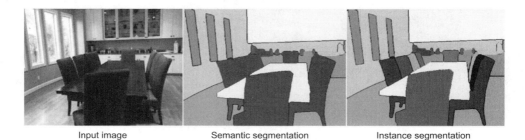

Input image   Semantic segmentation   Instance segmentation

Figure 8.1   Semantic segmentation versus instance segmentation

In the next section, we will look at the data we are dealing with more closely.

8.1 *Understanding the data*

You are experimenting with a startup idea. The idea is to develop a navigation algorithm for small remote-control (RC) toys. Users can choose between how safe or adventurous the navigation needs to be. As the first step, you plan to develop an image segmentation model. The output of the image segmentation model will later feed to a different model that will predict the navigation path depending on what the user requests.

For this task, you feel the Pascal VOC 2012 data set will be a good fit as it mostly comprises indoor and outdoor images that are found in urban/domestic environments. It contains pairs of images: an input image containing some objects and an annotated image. In the annotated image, each pixel has an assigned color, depending on which object that pixel belongs to. Here, you plan to download the data set and load the data successfully into Python.

After having a good understanding/framing of the problem you want to solve, your next focus point should be understanding and exploring the data. Segmentation data is different from the image classification data sets we've seen thus far. One major difference is that both the input and target are images. The input image is a standard image, similar to what you'd find in an image classification task. Unlike in image classification, the target is not a label, but an image, where each pixel has a color from a predefined palette of colors. In other words, each object we're interested in segmenting is assigned a color. Then a pixel corresponding to that object in the input image is colored with that color. The number of available colors is the same as the number of different objects (plus background) that you're interested in identifying (figure 8.2).

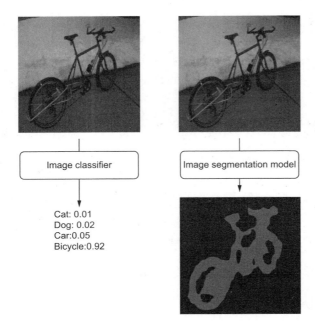

Figure 8.2   Inputs and outputs of an image classifier versus an image segmentation model

For this task, we will be using the PASCAL VOC 2012 data set, which is popular and consists of real-world scenes. The data set has labels for 22 different classes, as outlined in table 8.1.

Table 8.1   Different classes and their respective labels in the PASCAL VOC 2012 data set

Class	Assigned Label	Class	Assigned Label
Background	0	Dining table	11
Aeroplane	1	Dog	12
Bicycle	2	Horse	13

Table 8.1   Different classes and their respective labels in the PASCAL VOC 2012 data set *(continued)*

Class	Assigned Label	Class	Assigned Label
Bird	3	Motorbike	14
Boat	4	Person	15
Bottle	5	Potted plant	16
Bus	6	Sheep	17
Car	7	Sofa	18
Cat	8	Train	19
Chair	9	TV/monitor	20
Cow	10	Boundaries/unknown object	255

The white pixels represent object boundaries or unknown objects. Figure 8.3 illustrates the data set by showing a sample for every single object class present.

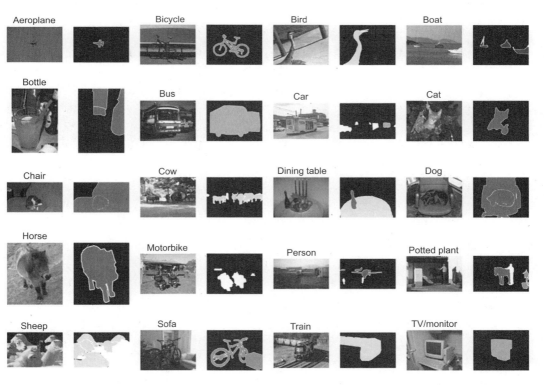

Figure 8.3   Samples from the PASCAL VOC 2012 data set. The data set shows a single example image, along with the annotated segmentation of it for the 20 different object classes.

In figure 8.4, diving a bit deeper, you can see a single sample datapoint (best viewed in color) up close. It has two objects: a chair and a dog. As it is shown, different colors are assigned to different object categories. While the figure is best viewed in color, you still can distinguish different objects by paying attention to the white border that outlines the objects in the figure.

Original image

Segmented annotations

 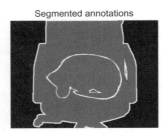

Figure 8.4   An original input image in image segmentation and the corresponding target annotated/segmented image

First, we'll download the data set, if it does not exist, from http://mng.bz/6XwZ (see the next listing).

Listing 8.1   Downloading data

```
import os
import requests
import tarfile

# Retrieve the data
if not os.path.exists(os.path.join('data','VOCtrainval_11-May-2012.tar')):
    url = "http://host.robots.ox.ac.uk/pascal/VOC/voc2012/VOCtrainval_11-
May-2012.tar"
    # Get the file from web
    r = requests.get(url)

    if not os.path.exists('data'):
        os.mkdir('data')

    # Write to a file
    with open(os.path.join('data','VOCtrainval_11-May-2012.tar'), 'wb') as f:
        f.write(r.content)
else:
    print("The tar file already exists.")

if not os.path.exists(os.path.join('data', 'VOCtrainval_11-May-2012')):
    with tarfile.open(os.path.join('data','VOCtrainval_11-May-2012.tar'),
      'r') as tar:
        tar.extractall('data')
else:
    print("The extracted data already exists")
```

Check if the file is already downloaded. If so, don't download again.

Get the content from the URL.

Save the file to disk.

If the file exists but is not extracted, extract the file.

The data set download is quite similar to our past experience. The data exists as a tarfile. We download the file if it doesn't exist and extract it. Next, we will discuss how to use the image library Pillow and NumPy to load the images into memory. Here, the target images will need special treatment, as you will see that they are not stored using the conventional approach. There are no surprises involved with loading input images to memory. Using the PIL (i.e., Pillow) library, they can be loaded with a single line of code:

```
from PIL import Image

orig_image_path = os.path.join('data', 'VOCtrainval_11-May-2012',
  'VOCdevkit', 'VOC2012', 'JPEGImages', '2007_000661.jpg')

orig_image = Image.open(orig_image_path)
```

Next, you can inspect the image's attributes:

```
print("The format of the data {}".format(orig_image.format))
>>> The format of the data JPEG

print("This image is of size: {}".format(orig_image.shape))
>>> This image is of size: (375, 500, 3)
```

It's time to load the corresponding annotated/segmented target images. As mentioned earlier, target images require special attention. The target images are not stored as standard images but as *palettized* images. Palettization is a technique to reduce memory footprint while storing images with a fixed number of colors in the image. The crux of the method is to maintain a palette of colors. The palette is stored as a sequence of integers, which has a length of the number of colors or the number of channels. (E.g., in the case of RGB, where a pixel is made of three values corresponding to red, green, and blue, the number of channels is three. A grayscale image has a single channel, where each pixel is made of a single value). The image itself then stores an array of indices (size = height × width), where each index maps to a color in the palette. Finally, by mapping the palette indices from the image to palette colors, you can compute the original image. Figure 8.5 provides a visual exposition of this discussion.

The next listing shows the code for reconstructing the original image pixels from the palettized image.

Listing 8.2 Reconstructing the original image from a palettized image

The palette is stored as a vector. We reshape it to an array, where each row represents a single RGB color.

```
def rgb_image_from_palette(image):

    """ This function restores the RGB values form a palletted PNG image """
    palette = image.get_palette()          ◁———  Get the color
                                                  palette from
                                                  the image.
    palette = np.array(palette).reshape(-1,3)
    if isinstance(image, PngImageFile):
        h, w = image.height, image.width
        # Squash height and width dimensions (makes slicing easier)
        image = np.array(image).reshape(-1)    ◁———
```

Convert the palettized image stored as an array to a vector (helps with our next steps).

Get the image's height and width.

```
elif isinstance(image, np.ndarray):
    h, w = image.shape[0], image.shape[1]
    image = image.reshape(-1)
```
Get the image as a vector if the image is provided as an array instead of a Pillow image.

```
rgb_image = np.zeros(shape=(image.shape[0],3))
rgb_image[(image != 0),:] = pallette[image[(image != 0)], :]
rgb_image = rgb_image.reshape(h, w, 3)

return rgb_image
```
Restore the original shape.

We first define a vector of zeros that has the same length as our image. Then, for all the indices found in the image, we gather corresponding colors from the palette and assign them to the same position in the rgb_image.

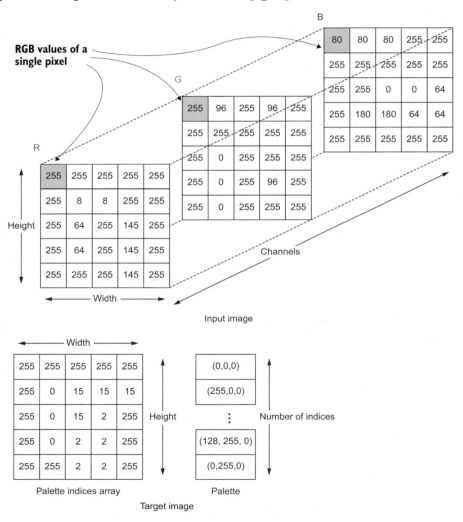

Figure 8.5   **The numerical representation of input images and target images in the PASCAL VOC 2012 data set**

Here, we first obtain the palette of the image using the `get_palette()` function. This will be present as a one-dimensional array (of length number of classes × number of channels). Next, we need to reshape the array to a (number of classes, number of channels)–sized array. In our case, this will be converted to a (22,3)–sized array. As we define the first dimension of the reshape as –1, it will be automatically inferred from the original size of the data and the other dimensions of the reshape operation. Finally, we define an array of zeros, which will ultimately store the actual colors the indices found in the image. To do that, we index the `rgb_image` vector using the `image` (which contains indices) and assign matching colors from the palette to those indices.

With the data we have looked at thus far, let's define a TensorFlow data pipeline that can transform and convert the data to a format acceptable by the model.

EXERCISE 1

You have been provided with an `rgb_image` in RGB format, where each pixel belongs to one of n distinctive colors and has been given a palette called palette, which is a [n,3]–sized array. How would you convert the `rgb_image` to a palettized image?

> **HINT** You can create the naïve solution by using three `for` loops: two loops to get a single pixel of `rgb_image` and then a final loop to traverse each color in the palette.

8.2 *Getting serious: Defining a TensorFlow data pipeline*

So far, we have discussed the data that will help us build a navigation algorithm for the RC toy. Before building a model, an important task to complete is having a scalable data ingestion method from disk to the model. Doing this upfront will save us a lot of time when we're ready to scale or productionize. You think the best way is to implement a `tf.data` pipeline to retrieve images from the disk, preprocess them, transform them, and have them ready for the model to grab them. This pipeline should read images in, reshape them to a fixed size (in the case of variable-sized images), augment them (during the training stage), batch them, and repeat this process for a desired number of epochs. Finally, we will define three pipelines: a training data pipeline, a validation data pipeline, and a testing data pipeline.

Our goal at the end of the data exploration stage should be to build a reliable data pipeline from the disk to the model. This is what we will be looking at here. At a high level, we will build a TensorFlow data pipeline that will perform the following tasks:

- Get the filenames belonging to a certain subset (e.g., training, validation, or testing).
- Read the specified images from the disk.
- Preprocess the images (this involves normalizing/resizing/cropping images).
- Perform augmentation on the images to increase the volume of data.
- Batch the data in small batches.
- Optimize data retrieval using several built-in optimization techniques.

As the first step, we will write a function that returns a generator that will generate file-names of the data that we want to be fetched. We will also provide the ability to specify which subset the user wants to be fetched (e.g., training, validation, or testing). Returning data through a generator will make writing a `tf.data` pipeline easier (see the following listing).

Listing 8.3   Retrieving the filenames for a given subset of data

For validation/test subsets, perform a one-time shuffle to make sure we get a good mix with a fixed seed.

```
def get_subset_filenames(orig_dir, seg_dir, subset_dir, subset):
    """ Get the filenames for a given subset (train/valid/test) """

    if subset.startswith('train'):                          Read the CSV file
        ser = pd.read_csv(                                  that contains the
            os.path.join(subset_dir, "train.txt"),          training instance
            index_col=None, header=None, squeeze=True       filenames.
        ).tolist()
    elif subset.startswith('val') or subset.startswith('test'):

        random.seed(random_seed)                    Read the CSV file that
                                                    contains validation/test
        ser = pd.read_csv(                          filenames.
            os.path.join(subset_dir, "val.txt"),
            index_col=None, header=None, squeeze=True
        ).tolist()

        random.shuffle(ser)              Shuffle the data after
                                         fixing the seed.

        if subset.startswith('val'):        Get the first half as
            ser = ser[:len(ser)//2]         the validation set.
        else:
            ser = ser[len(ser)//2:]             Get the second
    else:                                       half as the test
        raise NotImplementedError("Subset={} is not        set.
 recognized".format(subset))

    orig_filenames = [os.path.join(orig_dir,f+'.jpg') for f in ser]
    seg_filenames = [os.path.join(seg_dir, f+'.png') for f in ser]
                                                                        Return the
    for o, s in zip(orig_filenames, seg_filenames):                     filename pairs
        yield o, s                                                      (input and
                            Form absolute paths                         annotations) as
 Form absolute paths to the input   to the segmented                    a generator.
 image files we captured (depending  image files.
 on the subset argument).
```

You can see that we're passing a few arguments when reading the CSV files. These arguments characterize the file we're reading. These files are extremely simple and contain just a single image filename on a single line. `index_col=None` means that the file does not have an index column, `header=None` means there is no header in the file, and `squeeze=True` means that the output will be presented as a pandas `Series`, not a pandas `Dataframe`. With that, we can define a TensorFlow data set (`tf.data.Dataset`) as follows:

```
filename_ds = tf.data.Dataset.from_generator(
    subset_filename_gen_func, output_types=(tf.string, tf.string)
)
```

TensorFlow has several different functions for generating data sets using different sources. As we have defined the function `get_subset_filenames()` to return a generator, we will use the `tf.data.Dataset.from_generator()` function. Note that we need to provide the format as well as the datatypes of the returned data, by the generator, using the `output_types` argument. The function `subset_filename_gen_func` returns two strings; therefore, we define output types as a tuple of two `tf.string` elements.

One other important aspect is the different txt files we read from depending on the subset. There are three different files in the relative path: the `data\VOCtrainval_11-May-2012\VOCdevkit\VOC2012\ImageSets\Segmentation` folder; train.txt, val.txt, and `trainval.txt`. Here, train.txt contains the filenames of the training images, whereas `val.txt` contains the filenames of the validation/testing images. We will use these files to create different pipelines that produce different data.

Where does tf.data come from?

TensorFlow's tf.data pipeline can consume data from various sources. Here are some of the commonly used methods to retrieve data:

`tf.data.Dataset.from_generator(gen_fn)`—You have already seen this function in action. If you have a generator (i.e., `gen_fn`) that produces data, you want it to be processed through a `tf.data` pipeline. This is the easiest method to use.

`tf.data.Dataset.from_tensor_slices(t)`—This is a very useful function if you have data already loaded as a big matrix. t can be an N-dimensional matrix, and this function will extract element by element on the first dimension. For example, assume that you have loaded a tensor t of size 3 × 4 to memory:

```
t = [ [1,2,3,4],
      [2,3,4,5],
      [6,7,8,9] ]
```

Then you can easily set up a `tf.data` pipeline as follows. `tf.data.Dataset.from_tensor_slices(t)` will return [1,2,3,4], then [2,3,4,5], and finally [6,7,8,9] when you iterate this data pipeline. In other words, you are seeing one row (i.e., a slice from the batch dimension, hence the name `from_tensor_slices`) at a time. You can now incorporate functions like `tf.data.Dataset.batch()` to get a batch of rows.

Now it's time to read in the images found in the file paths we obtained in the previous step. TensorFlow has support to easily load an image, where the path to a filename is img_filename, using the functions tf.io.read_file and tf.image.decode_image. Here, img_filename is a tf.string (i.e., a string in TensorFlow):

```
tf.image.decode_jpeg(tf.io.read_file(image_filename))
```

We will use this pattern to load input images. However, we need to implement a custom image load function to load the target image. If you use the previous approach, it will automatically convert the image to an array with pixel values (instead of palette indices). But if we don't perform that conversion, we will have a target array that is in the exact format we need because the palette indices that are in the target image are the actual class labels for each corresponding pixel in the input image. We will use PIL.Image within our TensorFlow data pipeline to load the image as a palettized image and avoid converting it to RGB:

```
from PIL import Image

def load_image_func(image):
    """ Load the image given a filename """

    img = np.array(Image.open(image))
    return img
```

However, you can't yet use custom functions as part of the tf.data pipeline. They need to be streamlined with the data-flow graph of the data pipeline by wrapping it as a TensorFlow operation. This can be easily achieved by using the tf.numpy_function operation, which allows you to wrap a custom function that returns a NumPy array as a TensorFlow operation. If we have the target image's file path represented by y, you can use the following code to load the image into TensorFlow with a custom image-loading function:

```
tf.numpy_function(load_image_func, inp=[y], Tout=[tf.uint8])
```

The dark side of tf.numpy_function

NumPy has larger coverage for various scientific computations than TensorFlow, so you might think that tf.numpy_funtion makes things very convenient. This is not quite true, as you can infest your TensorFlow code with terrible performance degradations. When TensorFlow executes NumPy code, it can create very inefficient data flow graphs and introduce overheads. Therefore, always try to stick to TensorFlow operations and use custom NumPy code only if you have to. In our case, since there is no alternative way for us to load a paletized image without mapping paletized values to actual RGB, we used a custom function.

Notice how we're passing both the input (i.e., inp=[y]) and its data type (i.e., Tout=[tf.uint8]) to this function. They both need to be in the form of a Python list. Finally, let's collate everything we discussed in one place:

```
def load_image_func(image):
    """ Load the image given a filename """

    img =  np.array(Image.open(image))
    return img

# Load the images from the filenames returned by the above step
    image_ds = filename_ds.map(lambda x,y: (
        tf.image.decode_jpeg(tf.io.read_file(x)),
        tf.numpy_function(load_image_func, [y], [tf.uint8])
    ))
```

The `tf.data.Dataset.map()` function will be used quite heavily throughout this discussion. You can find a lengthy explanation of the `map()` function in the sidebar.

A Refresher: tf.data.Dataset.map() function

This `tf.data` pipeline will make extensive use of the `tf.data.Dataset.map()` function. Therefore, it is extremely helpful for us to remind ourselves what this function accomplishes.

The `td.data.Dataset.map()` function applies a given function or functions across all the records in a data set. In other words, it transforms the data points in the data set using a specified transformation. For example, assume the `tf.data.Dataset`

```
dataset = tf.data.Dataset.from_tensor_slices([1, 2, 3, 4])
```

to get the square of each element, you can use the map function as

```
dataset = dataset.map(lambda x: x**2)
```

If you have multiple elements in a single record, leveraging the flexibility of `map()`, you can transform them individually:

```
dataset = tf.data.Dataset.from_tensor_slices([[1,3], [2,4], [3,5], [4,6]])
dataset = dataset.map(lambda x, y: (x**2, y+x))
which will return,
[[1, 4], [4, 6], [9, 8], [16, 10]]
```

As a normalization step we will bring the pixel values to [0,1] range by using

```
image_ds = image_ds.map(lambda x, y: (tf.cast(x, 'float32')/255.0, y))
```

Note that we are keeping our target image (y) as it is. Before I continue with any more steps in our pipeline, I want to direct your attention to an important matter. This is a caveat that is quite common, and it is thus worthwhile to be aware of it. After the step we just completed, you might feel like, if you want, you can batch the data and feed it to the model. For example

```
image_ds = image_ds.batch(10)
```

If you do that for this data set, you will get an error like the following:

```
InvalidArgumentError: Cannot batch tensors with different shapes in
component 0. First element had shape [375,500,3] and element 1 had
shape [333,500,3]. [Op:IteratorGetNext]
```

This is because you ignored a crucial characteristic and a sanity check of the data set. Unless you're using a curated data set, you are unlikely to find images with the same dimensions. If you look at images in the data set, you will notice that they are not of the same size; they have different heights and widths. In TensorFlow, unless you use a special data structure like tf.RaggedTensor, you cannot batch unequally sized images together. That is exactly what TensorFlow is complaining about in the error.

To alleviate the problem, we need to bring all the images to a standard size (see listing 8.4). To do that, we will define the following function. It will either

- Resize the image to a larger size (resize_to_before_crop) and then crop the image to the desired size (input_size) or
- Resize the image to the desired size (input_size)

Listing 8.4   Bringing images to a fixed size using random cropping or resizing

```python
def randomly_crop_or_resize(x,y):
    """ Randomly crops or resizes the images """

    def rand_crop(x, y):
        """ Randomly crop images after enlarging them """
        x = tf.image.resize(x, resize_to_before_crop, method='bilinear')
        y = tf.cast(
            tf.image.resize(
                tf.transpose(y,[1,2,0]),
                resize_to_before_crop, method='nearest'
            ),
            'float32'
        )

        offset_h = tf.random.uniform(
            [], 0, x.shape[0]-input_size[0], dtype='int32'
        )
        offset_w = tf.random.uniform(
            [], 0, x.shape[1]-input_size[1], dtype='int32'
        )
        x = tf.image.crop_to_bounding_box(
            image=x,
            offset_height=offset_h, offset_width=offset_w,
            target_height=input_size[0], target_width=input_size[1]
        )
        y = tf.image.crop_to_bounding_box(
            image=y,
            offset_height=offset_h, offset_width=offset_w,
            target_height=input_size[0], target_width=input_size[1]
        )
```

Annotations:

- Define a function to randomly crop images after resizing.
- Resize the input image using bilinear interpolation to a larger size.
- Resize the target image using the nearest interpolation to a larger size.
- To resize, we first swap the axis of y as it has the shape [1, height, width]. We convert this back to [height, width, 1] (i.e., a single channel image) using the tf.transpose() function.
- Define a random variable to offset images on height during cropping.
- Define a random variable to offset images on width during cropping.
- Crop the input image and the target image using the same cropping parameters.

```
        return x, y

    def resize(x, y):
        """ Resize images to a desired size """
        x = tf.image.resize(x, input_size, method='bilinear')
        y = tf.cast(
                tf.image.resize(
                    tf.transpose(y,[1,2,0]),
                    input_size, method='nearest'
                ),
                'float32'
            )

        return x, y

    rand = tf.random.uniform([], 0.0,1.0)

    if augmentation and \
        (input_size[0] < resize_to_before_crop[0] or \
        input_size[1] < resize_to_before_crop[1]):
        x, y = tf.cond(
                rand < 0.5,
                lambda: rand_crop(x, y),
                lambda: resize(x, y)
            )
    else:
        x, y = resize(x, y)

    return x, y
```

Resize both the input image and the target image to a desired size (no cropping).

Define a random variable (used to perform augmentations).

If augmentation is enabled and the resized image is larger than the input size we requested, perform augmentation.

During augmentation, the rand_crop or resize function is executed randomly.

If augmentation is disabled, only resize images.

Here, we define a function called randomly_crop_or_resize, which has two nested functions, rand_crop and resize. The rand_crop first resizes the image to the size specified in resize_to_before_crop and creates a random crop. It is imperative to check that you applied the exact same crop to both the input and the target. For example, same-crop parameters should be used to crop both the input and the target. In order to crop images, we use

```
x = tf.image.crop_to_bounding_box(
    image=x,
    offset_height=offset_h, offset_width=offset_w,
    target_height=input_size[0], target_width=input_size[1]
)
y = tf.image.crop_to_bounding_box(
    image=y,
    offset_height=offset_h, offset_width=offset_w,
    target_height=input_size[0], target_width=input_size[1]
)
```

The arguments are self-explanatory: image takes an image to be cropped, offset_height and offset_width decide the starting point for the crop, and target_height and target_width specify the final size after the crop. The resize function will simply resize the input and the target to a specified size using the tf.image.resize operation.

When resizing, we use *bilinear interpolation* for the input images and *nearest interpolation* for targets. Bilinear interpolation resizes the images by computing the resulting pixels, as an average of neighboring pixels, whereas nearest interpolation computes the output pixel as the nearest most common pixel from the neighbors. Bilinear interpolation leads to a smoother result after resizing. However, you must use nearest interpolation for the target image, as bilinear interpolation will lead to fractional outputs, corrupting the integer-based annotations. The interpolation techniques described are visualized in figure 8.6.

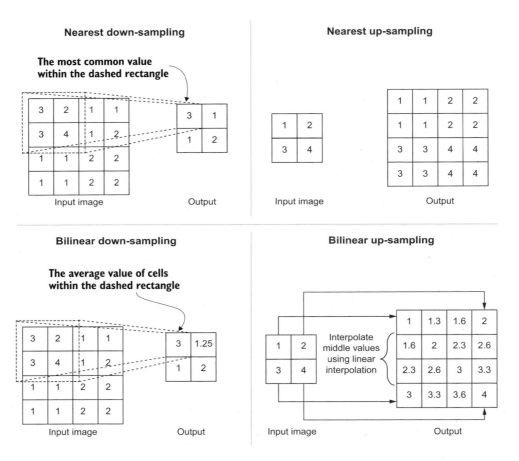

Figure 8.6   Nearest interpolation and bilinear interpolation for both up-sampling and down-sampling tasks

Next, we will introduce an additional step to the way we're going to use these two nested functions. If augmentation is enabled, we want the cropping or resizing to take place randomly within the pipeline. We will define a random variable (drawn from a uniform distribution between 0 and 1) and perform crop or resize depending on the value of the random variable at a given time. This conditioning can be achieved using the tf.cond function, which takes three arguments and returns output according to these arguments:

- Condition—This is a computation that results in a Boolean value (i.e., is the random variable rand greater than 0.5).
- true_fn—If the condition is true, then this function will be executed (i.e., perform rand_crop on both x and y)
- false_fn—If the condition is false, then this function will be executed (i.e., perform a resize on both x and y)

If augmentation is disabled (i.e., by setting the augmentation variable to False), only resizing is performed. With the details fleshed out, we can use the randomly_crop_ or_resize function in our data pipeline as follows:

```
image_ds = image_ds.map(lambda x,y: randomly_crop_or_resize(x,y))
```

At this point, we have a globally fixed-sized image coming out of our pipeline. The next thing we address is very important. Factors such as variable size of images and custom NumPy functions used to load images make it impossible for TensorFlow to infer the shape of its final tensor (though it's a fixed-sized tensor) after a few steps. If you check the shapes of the tensors produced at this point, you will probably perceive them as

```
(None, None, None)
```

This means that TensorFlow was unable to infer the shape of the tensors. To avoid any ambiguities or problems moving forward, we will set the shape of the output we have in the pipeline. For a tensor t, if the shape is ambiguous but you know the shape, you can set the shape manually using

```
t.set_shape([<shape of the tensor>])
```

In our data pipeline, we can set the shape as

```
def fix_shape(x, y, size):
    """ Set the shape of the input/target tensors """

    x.set_shape((size[0], size[1], 3))
    y.set_shape((size[0], size[1], 1))

    return x, y

image_ds = image_ds.map(lambda x,y: fix_shape(x,y, target_size=input_size))
```

We know that the outputs following the resize or crop are going to be

- *Input image*—An RGB image with input_size height and width
- *Target image*—A single-channel image with input_size height and width

We will set the shape accordingly using the `tf.data.Dataset.map()` function. We cannot underestimate the power of data augmentation, so we will introduce several data augmentation steps to our data pipeline (see the next listing).

Listing 8.5   Functions used for random augmentation of images

```
def randomly_flip_horizontal(x, y):
    """ Randomly flip images horizontally. """           Define a
                                                          random
    rand = tf.random.uniform([], 0.0,1.0)      ◄──        variable.

    def flip(x, y):
        return tf.image.flip_left_right(x), tf.image.flip_left_right(y)   ◄──

    x, y = tf.cond(rand < 0.5, lambda: flip(x, y), lambda: (x, y))   ◄──

    return x, y

    if augmentation:
        image_ds = image_ds.map(lambda x, y: randomly_flip_horizontal(x,y))

    image_ds = image_ds.map(lambda x, y: (tf.image.random_hue(x, 0.1), y))

    image_ds = image_ds.map(lambda x, y: (tf.image.random_brightness(x, 0.1), y))   ◄──

    image_ds = image_ds.map(lambda x, y: (tf.image.random_contrast(x, 0.8, 1.2), y))
```

Define a function to flip images deterministically.

Using the same pattern as before, we use tf.cond to randomly perform horizontal flipping.

Randomly flip images in the data set.

Randomly adjust the contrast of the input image (target stays the same).

Randomly adjust the hue (i.e., color) of the input image (target stays the same).

Randomly adjust the brightness of the input image (target stays the same).

In listing 8.5, we perform the following translations:

- Randomly flipping images horizontally
- Randomly changing the hue of the images (up to 10%)
- Randomly changing the brightness of the images (up to 10%)
- Randomly changing the contrast of the images (up to 20%)

By using the `tf.data.Dataset.map()` function, we can easily perform the specified random augmentation steps, should the user enable augmentation in the pipeline (i.e., by setting the augmentation variable to `True`). Note that we're performing some augmentations (e.g., random hue, brightness, and contrast adjustments) on the input image only. We will also give the user the option to have different-sized inputs and targets (i.e., outputs). This is achieved by resizing the output to a desired size, defined by the `output_size` argument. The model we use for this task has different-sized input and output dimensions:

```
if output_size:
    image_ds = image_ds.map(
                    lambda x, y: (
```

```
                            x,
                            tf.image.resize(y, output_size, method='nearest')
                    )
        )
```

Again, here we use the nearest interpolation to resize the target. Next, we will shuffle the data (if the user set the shuffle argument to True):

```
if shuffle:
    image_ds = image_ds.shuffle(buffer_size=batch_size*5)
```

The shuffle function takes an important argument called buffer_size, which determines how many samples are loaded to memory in order to select a sample randomly. The higher the buffer_size, the more randomness you are introducing. On the other hand, a higher buffer_size implies higher memory consumption. It's now time to batch the data, so instead of a single data point, we get a batch of data when we iterate:

```
image_ds = image_ds.batch(batch_size).repeat(epochs)
```

This is done using the tf.data.Dataset.batch() function and passing the desired batch size as the argument. When using the tf.data pipeline, if you are running it for multiple epochs, you also need to use the tf.data.Dataset.repeat() function to repeat the pipeline for a given number of epochs.

Why do we need tf.data.Dataset.repeat()?

tf.data.Dataset is a generator. A unique characteristic of a generator is that you only can iterate it once. After the generator reaches the end of the sequence it's iterating, it will exit by throwing an exception. Therefore, if you need to iterate through a generator multiple times, you need to redefine the generator as many times as needed. By adding tf.data.Dataset.repeat(epochs), the generate is redefined as many times as we would like (epochs times in this example).

One more step is needed before our tf.data pipeline is done and dusted. If you look at the shape of the target (y) output, you will see that it has a channel dimension of 1. However, for the loss function we will be using, we need to get rid of that dimension:

```
image_ds = image_ds.map(lambda x, y: (x, tf.squeeze(y)))
```

For this, we will use the tf.squeeze() operation, which removes any dimensions that are of size 1 and returns a tensor. For example, if you squeeze a tensor of size [1,3,2,1,5], you will get a [3,2,5] sized tensor. The final code is provided in listing 8.6. You might notice two steps that are highlighted. These are two popular optimization steps available: caching and prefetching.

Listing 8.6   The final tf.data pipeline

```
def get_subset_tf_dataset(
    subset_filename_gen_func, batch_size, epochs,
    input_size=(256, 256), output_size=None, resize_to_before_crop=None,
    augmentation=False, shuffle=False
):

    if augmentation and not resize_to_before_crop:
        raise RuntimeError(
            "You must define resize_to_before_crop when augmentation is enabled."
        )

    filename_ds = tf.data.Dataset.from_generator(
        subset_filename_gen_func, output_types=(tf.string, tf.string)
    )

    image_ds = filename_ds.map(lambda x,y: (
        tf.image.decode_jpeg(tf.io.read_file(x)),
        tf.numpy_function(load_image_func, [y], [tf.uint8])
    )).cache()

    image_ds = image_ds.map(lambda x, y: (tf.cast(x, 'float32')/255.0, y))


    def randomly_crop_or_resize(x,y):
        """ Randomly crops or resizes the images """
        ...

        def rand_crop(x, y):
            """ Randomly crop images after enlarging them """
            ...

        def resize(x, y):
            """ Resize images to a desired size """
            ...

    image_ds = image_ds.map(lambda x,y: randomly_crop_or_resize(x,y))
    image_ds = image_ds.map(lambda x,y: fix_shape(x,y, target_size=input_size))

    if augmentation:
        image_ds = image_ds.map(lambda x, y: randomly_flip_horizontal(x,y))
        image_ds = image_ds.map(lambda x, y: (tf.image.random_hue(x, 0.1), y))
        image_ds = image_ds.map(lambda x, y: (tf.image.random_brightness(x, 0.1), y))
        image_ds = image_ds.map(
            lambda x, y: (tf.image.random_contrast(x, 0.8, 1.2), y)
        )

    if output_size:
        image_ds = image_ds.map(
            lambda x, y: (x, tf.image.resize(y, output_size, method='nearest'))
        )

    if shuffle:
        image_ds = image_ds.shuffle(buffer_size=batch_size*5)
```

- Return a list of filenames depending on the subset of data requested.
- If augmentation is enabled, resize_to_before_crop needs to be defined.
- Load the images into memory. cache() is an optimization step and will be discussed in the text.
- Normalize the input images.
- The function that randomly crops or resizes images
- Set the shape of the resulting images.
- Perform random crop or resize on the images.
- Randomly perform various augmentations on the data.
- Resize the output image if needed.
- Shuffle the data using a buffer.

```
image_ds = image_ds.batch(batch_size).repeat(epochs)

image_ds = image_ds.prefetch(tf.data.experimental.AUTOTUNE)

image_ds = image_ds.map(lambda x, y: (x, tf.squeeze(y)))

return image_ds
```

Batch the data and repeat the process for a desired number of epochs.

This is an optimization step discussed in detail in the text.

Remove the unnecessary dimension from target images.

Get the final tf.data pipeline.

It wasn't an easy journey, but it was a rewarding one. We have learned some important skills in defining the data pipeline:

- Defining a generator that returns the filenames of the data to be fetched
- Loading images within a `tf.data` pipeline
- Manipulating images (resizing, cropping, brightness adjustment, etc.)
- Batching and repeating data
- Defining multiple pipelines for different data sets with different requirements

Next, we will look at some optimization techniques to turn our mediocre data pipeline into an impressive data highway.

8.2.1   *Optimizing tf.data pipelines*

TensorFlow is a framework meant for consuming large data sets, where consuming data in an efficient manner is a key priority. One thing still missing from our conversation is what kind of optimization steps are available for `tf.data` pipelines, so let us nudge this discussion in that direction. Two steps were set in bold in listing 8.6: caching and prefetching. If you are interested in other optimization techniques, you can read more at https://www.tensorflow.org/guide/data_performance.

Caching will store the data in memory as it flows through the pipeline. This means that, when cached, that step (e.g., loading the data from the disk) happens only in the first epoch. The subsequent epochs will read from the cached data that's held in memory. Here, you can see that we're caching the images after we load them to memory. This way, TensorFlow loads the images in the first epoch only:

```
image_ds = filename_ds.map(lambda x,y: (
        tf.image.decode_jpeg(tf.io.read_file(x)),
        tf.numpy_function(load_image_func, [y], [tf.uint8])
)).cache()
```

Prefetching is another powerful weapon you have at your disposal, and it allows you to leverage the multiprocessing power of your device:

```
image_ds = image_ds.prefetch(tf.data.experimental.AUTOTUNE)
```

The argument provided to the function decides how much data is prefetched. By setting it to AUTOTUNE, TensorFlow will decide the best amount of data to be fetched depending on the resources available. Assume a simple data pipeline that loads images from the disk and trains a model. Then, the data read and model training will happen in interleaved steps. This leads to significant idling time, as the model idles while the data is loading, and vice versa.

However, thanks to prefetching, this doesn't need to be the case. Prefetching employs background threads and an internal buffer to load the data in advance while the model is training. When the next iteration comes, the model can seamlessly continue the training as data is already fetched into the memory. The differences between sequential execution and prefetching are shown in figure 8.7.

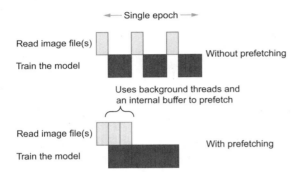

Figure 8.7   Sequential execution versus pre-fetching-based execution in model training

Next, we will look at the finished `tf.data` pipeline for the image segmentation problem.

8.2.2   The final tf.data pipeline

Finally, you can define the data pipeline(s) using the functions we have defined so far. Here, we define three different data pipelines for three different purposes: training, validation, and testing (see the following listing).

Listing 8.7   Creating the train/validation/test data pipelines instances

```
orig_dir = os.path.join(
    'data', 'VOCtrainval_11-May-2012', 'VOCdevkit', 'VOC2012', 'JPEGImages'
)
seg_dir = os.path.join(
    'data', 'VOCtrainval_11-May-2012', 'VOCdevkit', 'VOC2012',
    'SegmentationClass'
)
subset_dir = os.path.join(
    'data', 'VOCtrainval_11-May-2012', 'VOCdevkit', 'VOC2012', 'ImageSets',
    'Segmentation'
)

partial_subset_fn = partial(
    get_subset_filenames, orig_dir=orig_dir, seg_dir=seg_dir,
    subset_dir=subset_dir
)
```

Directory where the input images are

Directory where the annotated images (targets) are

Directory where the text files containing train/validation/test filenames are

Define a reusable partial function from get_subset_filenames.

Define input image size.

```
train_subset_fn = partial(partial_subset_fn, subset='train')
val_subset_fn = partial(partial_subset_fn, subset='val')
test_subset_fn = partial(partial_subset_fn, subset='test')

input_size = (384, 384)

tr_image_ds = get_subset_tf_dataset(
    train_subset_fn, batch_size, epochs,
    input_size=input_size, resize_to_before_crop=(444,444),
    augmentation=True, shuffle=True
)
val_image_ds = get_subset_tf_dataset(
    val_subset_fn, batch_size, epochs,
    input_size=input_size,
    shuffle=False
)
test_image_ds = get_subset_tf_dataset(
    test_subset_fn, batch_size, 1,
    input_size=input_size,
    shuffle=False
)
```

Define three generators for train/validation/test data.

Define a train data pipeline that uses data augmentation and shuffling.

Define a validation data pipeline that doesn't use data augmentation or shuffling.

Define a test data pipeline.

First, we define several important paths:

- orig_dir—Directory containing input images
- seg_dir—Directory containing the target images
- subset_dir—Directory containing text files (train.txt, val.txt) that enlist training and validation instances, respectively

Then we will define a partial function from the get_subset_filenames() function we defined earlier so that we can get a generator just by setting the subset argument of the function. Using this technique, we will define three generators: train_subset_fn, val_subset_fn, and test_subset_fn. Finally, we will define three tf.data.Datasets using the get_subset_tf_dataset() function. Our pipelines will have the following characteristics:

- *Training pipeline*—Performs data augmentation and data shuffling on every epoch
- *Validation pipeline and test pipeline*—No augmentation or shuffling

The model we will define expects a 384 × 384–sized input and an output. In the training data pipeline, we will resize images to 444 × 444 and then randomly crop a 384 × 384–sized image. Following this, we will look at the core part of the solution: defining the image segmentation model.

EXERCISE 2

You have been given a small set of data that contains two tensors: tensor a contains 100 64 × 64 × 3–sized images (i.e., 100 × 64 × 64 × 3 shaped), and tensor b contains 100 32 × 32 × 1–sized segmentation masks (i.e., 100 × 32 × 32 × 1 shaped). You have been asked to define a tf.data.Dataset using the functions discussed that will

- Resize the segmentation masks to match the input image size (using nearest interpolation)
- Normalize the input images using the transformation (x − 128)/255 where a single image is x
- Batch the data to batches of 32 and repeat for five epochs
- Prefetch the data with an auto-tuning feature

8.3   *DeepLabv3: Using pretrained networks to segment images*

It's now time to create the brains of the pipeline: the deep learning model. Based on feedback from a colleague at a self-driving car company working on similar problems, you will implement a DeepLab v3 model. This is a model built on the back of a pretrained ResNet 50 model (trained on image classification) but with the last several layers changed to perform *atrous convolution* instead of standard convolution. It uses a pyramidal aggregation module that uses atrous convolution at different scales to generate image features at different scales to produce the final output. Finally, it uses a bilinear interpolation layer to resize the final output to a desired size. You are confident that DeepLab v3 can deliver good initial results.

Deep neural network–based segmentation models can be broadly categorized into two types:

- Encoder decoder models (e.g., U-Net model)
- Fully convolutional network (FCN) followed by a pyramidal aggregation module (e.g., DeepLab v3 model)

A well-known example of the encoder-decoder model is the U-Net model. In other words, U-Net has an encoder that gradually creates smaller, coarser representations of the input. This is followed by a decoder that takes the representations the encoder built and gradually up-samples (i.e., increases the size of) the output until it reaches the size of the input image. The up-sampling is achieved through an operation known as *transpose convolution*. Finally, you train the whole structure end to end, where an input is the input image and the target is the segmentation mask for the corresponding image. We will not discuss this type of model in this chapter. However, I have included a detailed walkthrough in appendix B (along with an implementation of the model).

The other type of segmentation models introduces a special model that replaces the decoder. We call this module a *pyramidal aggregation module.* Its purpose is to garner spatial information at different scales (e.g., different-sized outputs from various interim convolution layers) that provides fine-grained contextual information about the objects present in the image. DeepLab v3 is a prime example of this approach. We will put the DeepLab v3 model under the microscope and use it to excel at the segmentation task.

Researchers and engineers gravitate toward methods that use pyramidal aggregation modules more. There could be many reasons for this. One lucrative reason is that there are less parameters in networks that use pyramidal aggregation than an encoder-decoder based counterpart. Another reason may be that, typically, introducing a novel module offers more flexibility (compared to an encoder-decoder) to engineer efficient and accurate feature extraction methods at multiple scales.

How important is the pyramidal aggregation module? To know that, we have to first understand what the fully convolutional part of the network looks like. Figure 8.8 illustrates the generic structure of such a segmentation model.

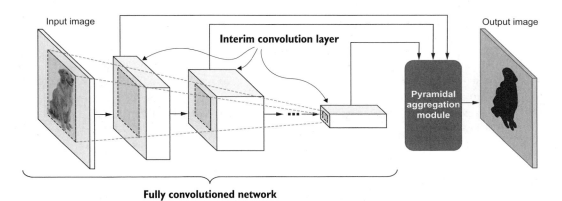

Figure 8.8   General structure and organization of a fully convolutional network that uses a pyramidal aggregation module

The best way to understand the importance of the pyramidal aggregation module is to see what happens if we don't have it. If that is the case, then the last convolutional layer will have the enormous and unrealistic responsibility of building the final segmentation mask (which is typically 16–32x times larger than the layer output). It is no surprise that there is a massive representational bottleneck between the final convolution layer and the final segmentation mask, leading to poor performance. The pyramidal structure typically enforced in CNNs results in a very small output width and height in the final layer.

The pyramidal aggregation module bridges this gap. It does so by combining several different interim outputs. This way, the network has ample fine-grained (from earlier layers) and coarser (from deeper layers) details to construct the desired segmentation mask. Fine-grained representations provide spatial/contextual information about the image, whereas the coarser representations provide high-level information about the image (e.g., what objects are present). By fusing both types of these representations, the task of generating the final output becomes more achievable.

Why not a skyscraper instead of a pyramid?

You might be tempted to ponder, if making the outputs smaller as you go causes loss of information, "Why not keep it the same size?" (hence the term *skyscraper*). This is an impractical solution for two main reasons.

First, decreasing the size of the outputs through pooling or striding is an important regularization method that forces the network to learn translation-invariant features (as we discussed in chapter 6). By taking this away, we can hinder the generalizability of the network.

Second, not decreasing the output size will increase the memory footprint of the model significantly. This will, in turn, restrict the depth of the network dramatically, making it more difficult to create deeper networks.

DeepLab v3 is the golden child of a lineage of models that emerged from and was introduced in the paper "Rethinking Atrous Convolution for Semantic Image Segmentation" (https://arxiv.org/pdf/1706.05587.pdf) by several researchers from Google.

Most segmentation models face an adverse side effect caused by a common and beneficial design principle. Vision models incorporate stride/pooling to make network translation invariant. But an ill-favored outcome of that is the compounding reduction of the size of the outputs produced. This typically leads to a final output that is 16–32 times smaller than the input. Being a dense prediction task, image segmentation tasks suffer heavily from this design idea. Therefore, most of the groundbreaking networks that have surfaced have been about solving this. The DeepLab model came into the world for exactly that purpose. Let's now see how DeepLab v3 solves this problem.

DeepLab v3 uses a ResNet-50 (https://arxiv.org/pdf/1512.03385.pdf) pretrained on an ImageNet image classification data set as its backbone for extracting features of an image. It is one of the pioneering residual networks that made waves in the computer vision community a few years ago. DeepLab v3 introduces several architectural changes to the model to alleviate this issue. Furthermore, DeepLab v3 introduces a shiny new component called *atrous spatial pyramid pooling* (ASPP). We will discuss each of these in more detail in the coming sections.

8.3.1   A quick overview of the ResNet-50 model

The ResNet-50 model consists of several convolution blocks, followed by a global average pooling layer and a fully connected final prediction layer with softmax activation. The convolution block is the innovative part of the model. The original model has 16 convolution blocks organized into five groups. A single block consists of three convolution layers (1×1 convolution layer with stride 2, 3×3 convolution layer, and 1×1 convolution layer), batch normalization, and residual connections. We discussed residual connections in depth in chapter 7. Next, we will discuss a core computation used throughout the model known as atrous convolution.

8.3.2   Atrous convolution: Increasing the receptive field of convolution layers with holes

Compared to the standard ResNet-50, a major change that DeepLab v3 boasts is the use of atrous convolutions. Atrous (meaning "holes" in French) convolution, also known as dilated convolution, is a variant of the standard convolution. Atrous convolution works by inserting "holes" in between the convolution parameters. The increase in the receptive field is controlled by a parameter called *dilation rate*. A higher dilation rate means more holes between actual parameters in the convolution. A major benefit of atrous convolution is the ability to increase the size of the receptive field without compromising the parameter efficiency of a convolution layer.

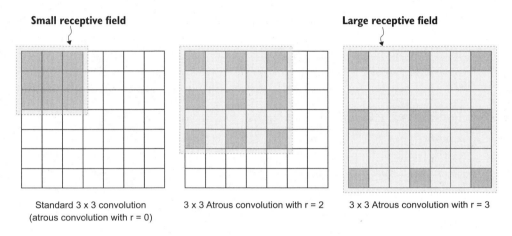

Figure 8.9   Atrous convolution compared to standard convolution. Standard convolution is a special case of atrous convolution, where the rate is 1. As you increase the dilation rate, the receptive field of the layer increases.

Figure 8.9 shows how a large dilation rate leads to a larger receptive field. The number of shaded gray boxes represents the number of parameters, whereas the dashed, lightly shaded box represents the size of the receptive field. As you can see, the number of parameters stays constant, while the receptive field increases. Computationally, it is quite straightforward to extend standard convolution to atrous convolution. All you need to do is insert zeros for the holes in the atrous convolution operation.

Wait! How does atrous convolution help segmentation models?

As we discussed, the main issue presented by the pyramidal structure of CNNs is that the output gets gradually smaller. The easiest solution, leaving the learned parameters untouched, is to reduce the stride of the layers. Though technically that will increase output size, conceptually there is a problem.

(continued)

To understand it, assume the ith layer of a CNN has a stride of 2 and gets a h × w–sized input. Then the i+1th layer gets a h/2 × w/2–sized input. By removing the stride of the ith layer, it gets a h × w–sized output. However, the kernel of the i+1th layer has been trained to see a smaller output, so by increasing the size of the input, we are disrupting (or reducing) the receptive field of the layer. By introducing atrous convolution, we compensate for that reduction of the receptive field.

Let's now see how the ResNet-50 is repurposed for image segmentation. First, we download it from the `tf.keras.applications` module. The architecture of the ResNet-50 model has the following format. To start, it has a stride 2 convolution layer and a stride 2 pooling layer. After that, it has sequence of convolution blocks and finally an average pooling layer and fully connected output layer. These convolution blocks have a hierarchical organization of convolution layers. Each convolution block consists of several subblocks, which consist of three convolution layers (i.e., a 1 × 1 convolution, a 3 × 3 convolution, and a 1 × 1 convolution) along with batch normalization.

8.3.3 *Implementing DeepLab v3 using the Keras functional API*

The network starting from the input up to the `conv4` block remains unchanged. Following the notation from the original ResNet paper, these blocks are identified as `conv2`, `conv3`, and `conv4` block groups. Our first task is to create a model containing the input layer up to the `conv4` block of the original ResNet-50 model. After that, we will focus on recreating the final convolution block (i.e., `conv5`) as per the DeepLab v3 paper:

```
# Pretrained model and the input
inp = layers.Input(shape=target_size+(3,))
resnet50 = tf.keras.applications.ResNet50(
    include_top=False, input_tensor=inp,pooling=None
)

for layer in resnet50.layers:
    if layer.name == "conv5_block1_1_conv":
        break
    out = layer.output

resnet50_upto_conv4 = models.Model(resnet50.input, out)
```

As shown here, we find the last layer in the ResNet-50 model just before the `"conv5_block1_1_conv"`, which would be the last layer of the `conv4` block group. With that, we can define a makeshift model that contains layers from the input to the final output of the `conv4` block group. Later, we will focus on augmenting this model by introducing modifications and novel components from the paper. We will redefine the `conv5` block with dilated convolutions. To do this, we need to understand the composition of a ResNet block (figure 8.10). We can assume it has three different levels.

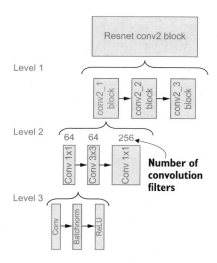

Figure 8.10 Anatomy of a convolution block in ResNet-50. For this example, we show the very first convolution block of ResNet-50. The organization of a convolution block group consists of three different levels.

Let's now implement a function to represent each level while using dilated convolution. In order to convert a standard convolution layer to a dilated convolution, we just have to pass in the desired rate to the dilation_rate parameter in the tf.keras .layers.Conv2D layer. First, we will implement a function that represents a level 3 block, as shown in the following listing.

Listing 8.8 A level 3 convolution block in ResNet-50

Here, inp takes a 4D input having shape [batch size, height, width, channels].

```
def block_level3(
    inp, filters, kernel_size, rate, block_id, convlayer_id, activation=True
):
    """ A single convolution layer with atrous convolution and batch
     normalization
    inp: 4-D tensor having shape [batch_size, height, width, channels]
    filters: number of output filters
    kernel_size: The size of the convolution kernel
    rate: dilation rate for atrous convolution
    block_id, convlayer_id - IDs to distinguish different convolution blocks
     and layers
    activation: If true ReLU is applied, if False no activation is applied
    """

    conv5_block_conv_out = layers.Conv2D(
        filters, kernel_size, dilation_rate=rate, padding='same',
        name='conv5_block{}_{}_conv'.format(block_id, convlayer_id)
    )(inp)

    conv5_block_bn_out = layers.BatchNormalization(
        name='conv5_block{}_{}_bn'.format(block_id, convlayer_id)
    )(conv5_block_conv_out)
```

Perform 2D convolution on the input with a given number of filters, kernel_size, and dilation rate.

Perform batch normalization on the output of the convolution layer.

```
if activation:
    conv5_block_relu_out = layers.Activation(
        'relu', name='conv5_block{}_{}_relu'.format(block_id, convlayer_id)
    )(conv5_block_bn_out)

    return conv5_block_relu_out
else:
    return conv5_block_bn_out
```

Apply ReLU activation if activation is set to True.

Return the output without an activation if activation is set to False.

A level 3 block has a single convolution layer with a desired dilation rate and a batch normalization layer followed by a nonlinear ReLU activation layer. Next, we will write a function for the level 2 block (see the next listing).

Listing 8.9   A level 2 convolution block in ResNet-50

```
def block_level2(inp, rate, block_id):
    """ A level 2 resnet block that consists of three level 3 blocks """

    block_1_out = block_level3(inp, 512, (1,1), rate, block_id, 1)
    block_2_out = block_level3(block_1_out, 512, (3,3), rate, block_id, 2)
    block_3_out = block_level3(
        block_2_out, 2048, (1,1), rate, block_id, 3, activation=False
    )

    return block_3_out
```

A level 2 block consists of three level 3 blocks with a given dilation rate that have convolution layers with the following specifications:

- 1 × 1 convolution layer having 512 filters and a desired dilation rate
- 3 × 3 convolution layer having 512 filters and a desired dilation rate
- 1 × 1 convolution layer having 2048 filters and a desired dilation rate

Apart from using atrous convolution, this is identical to a level 2 block of the original conv5 block in the ResNet-50 model. With all the building blocks ready, we can implement the fully fledged conv5 block with atrous convolution (see the next listing).

Listing 8.10   Implementing the final ResNet-50 convolution block group (level 1)

```
def resnet_block(inp, rate):
    """ Redefining a resnet block with atrous convolution """

    block0_out = block_level3(
        inp, 2048, (1,1), 1, block_id=1, convlayer_id=0, activation=False
    )
    block1_out = block_level2(inp, 2, block_id=1)
    block1_add = layers.Add(
        name='conv5_block{}_add'.format(1))([block0_out, block1_out]
    )
    block1_relu = layers.Activation(
        'relu', name='conv5_block{}_relu'.format(1)
    )(block1_add)
```

Create a level 3 block (block0) to create residual connections for the first block.

Define the first level 2 block, which has a dilation rate of 2 (block1).

Create a residual connection from block0 to block1.

Apply ReLU activation to the result.

The second
level 2
block with
a dilation
rate of 2
(block2)

```
block2_out = block_level2 (block1_relu, 2, block_id=2) # no relu
block2_add = layers.Add(
    name='conv5_block{}_add'.format(2)
)([block1_add, block2_out])
block2_relu = layers.Activation(
    'relu', name='conv5_block{}_relu'.format(2)
)(block2_add)

block3_out = block_level2 (block2_relu, 2, block_id=3)
block3_add = layers.Add(
    name='conv5_block{}_add'.format(3)
)([block2_add, block3_out])
block3_relu = layers.Activation(
    'relu', name='conv5_block{}_relu'.format(3)
)(block3_add)

return block3_relu
```

**Create a residual connection
from block1 to block2.**

**Apply ReLU
activation.**

**Apply a similar
procedure to
block1 and block2
to create block3.**

There's no black magic here. The function `resnet_block` lays the outputs of the functions we already discussed to assemble the final convolution block. Particularly, it has three level 2 blocks with residual connections going from the previous block to the next. Finally, we can get the final output of the `conv5` block with a dilation rate of 2 by calling the `resnet_block` function with the output of the interim model (`resnet50_upto_conv4`) we defined as the input and a dilation rate of 2:

```
resnet_block4_out = resnet_block(resnet50_upto_conv4.output, 2)
```

8.3.4 *Implementing the atrous spatial pyramid pooling module*

Here, we will discuss the most exciting innovation of the DeepLab v3 model. The atrous spatial pyramid pooling (ASPP) module serves two purposes:

- Aggregates multiscale information about an image, obtained through outputs produced using different dilation rates
- Combines highly summarized information obtained through global average pooling

The ASPP module gathers multiscale information by performing different convolutions on the last ResNet-50 output. Specifically, the ASPP module performs 1×1 convolution, 3×3 convolution (r = 6), 3×3 convolution (r = 12), and 3×3 convolution (r = 18), where r is the dilation rate. All of these convolutions have 256 output channels and are implemented as level 3 blocks (provided by the function `block_level3()`).

ASRP captures high-level information by performing global average pooling, followed by a 1×1 convolution with 256 output channels to match the output size of multiscale outputs, and finally a bilinear up-sampling layer to up-sample the height and width dimensions shrunk by the global average pooling. Remember that bilinear interpolation up-samples the images by computing the resulting pixels as an average of neighboring pixels. Figure 8.11 illustrates the ASPP module.

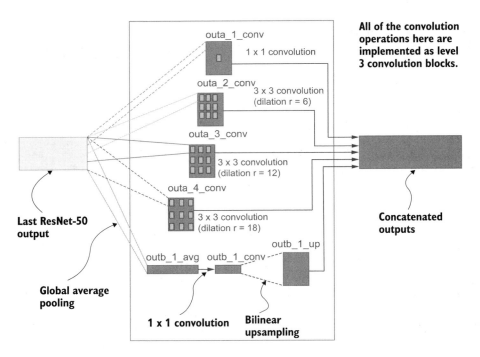

Figure 8.11   The ASPP module used in the DeepLab v3 model

The job of the ASPP module can be summarized as a concise function. We have all the tools we need to implement this function from the previous work we have done (see the following listing).

Listing 8.11   Implementing ASPP

```
def atrous_spatial_pyramid_pooling(inp):
    """ Defining the ASPP (Atrous spatial pyramid pooling) module """

    # Part A: 1x1 and atrous convolutions
    outa_1_conv = block_level3(
        inp, 256, (1,1), 1, '_aspp_a', 1, activation='relu'
    )
    outa_2_conv = block_level3(
        inp, 256, (3,3), 6, '_aspp_a', 2, activation='relu'
    )
    outa_3_conv = block_level3(
        inp, 256, (3,3), 12, '_aspp_a', 3, activation='relu'
    )
    outa_4_conv = block_level3(
        inp, 256, (3,3), 18, '_aspp_a', 4, activation='relu'
    )

    # Part B: global pooling
    outb_1_avg = layers.Lambda(
```

Define a 1 × 1 convolution.

Define a 3 x 3 convolution with 256 filters and a dilation rate of 6.

Define a 3 x 3 convolution with 256 filters and a dilation rate of 12.

Define a 3 x 3 convolution with 256 filters and a dilation rate of 18.

```
                    lambda x: K.mean(x, axis=[1,2], keepdims=True)
                )(inp)
            outb_1_conv = block_level3(
                outb_1_avg, 256, (1,1), 1, '_aspp_b', 1, activation='relu'
            )
            outb_1_up = layers.UpSampling2D((24,24),
                interpolation='bilinear')(outb_1_avg)
            out_aspp = layers.Concatenate()(
                [outa_1_conv, outa_2_conv, outa_3_conv, outa_4_conv, outb_1_up]
            )
            return out_aspp

        out_aspp = atrous_spatial_pyramid_pooling(resnet_block4_out)
```

Define a global average pooling layer. → `)(inp)`

Define a 1 × 1 convolution with 256 filters. →

Up-sample the output using bilinear interpolation. ←

Concatenate all the outputs. →

Create an instance of ASPP. →

The ASPP module consists of four level 3 blocks, as outlined in the code. The first block comprises a 1 × 1 convolution with 256 filters without dilation (this produces outa_1_conv). The latter three blocks consist of 3 × 3 convolutions with 256 filters but with varying dilation rates (i.e., 6, 12, 18; they produce outa_2_conv, outa_3_conv, and outa_4_conv, respectively). This covers aggregating features from the image at multiple scales. However, we also need to preserve the global information about the image, similar to a global average pooling layer (outb_1_avg). This is achieved through a lambda layer that averages the input over the height and width dimensions:

```
outb_1_avg = layers.Lambda(lambda x: K.mean(x, axis=[1,2], keepdims=True))(inp)
```

The output of the averaging is then followed by a 1 × 1 convolution filter with 256 filters. Then, to bring the output to the same size as previous outputs, an up-sampling layer that uses bilinear interpolation is used (this produces outb_1_up):

```
outb_1_up = layers.UpSampling2D((24,24), interpolation='bilinear')(outb_1_avg)
```

Finally, all these outputs are concatenated to a single output using a Concatenate layer to produce the final output out_aspp.

8.3.5 Putting everything together

Now it's time to collate all the different components to create one majestic segmentation model. The next listing outlines the steps required to build the final model.

Listing 8.12 The final DeepLab v3 model

```
inp = layers.Input(shape=target_size+(3,))

resnet50= tf.keras.applications.ResNet50(
    include_top=False, input_tensor=inp,pooling=None
)

for layer in resnet50.layers:
    if layer.name == "conv5_block1_1_conv":
```

Define the RGB input layer. ←

Download and define the resnet50. ←

```
        break
    out = layer.output                          ◁──┐  Get the output of the last
                                                    │  layer we're interested in.
                                                                                      ┌─ Define the
                                                                                      │  removed
    resnet50_upto_conv4 = models.Model(resnet50.input, out)                           │  conv5 resnet
                                                                                      │  block.
    resnet_block4_out = resnet_block(resnet50_upto_conv4.output, 2)   ◁──────────────┘

    out_aspp = atrous_spatial_pyramid_pooling(resnet_block4_out)   ◁──┐  Define the
                                                                      │  ASPP module.

    out = layers.Conv2D(21, (1,1), padding='same')(out_aspp)                │  Define the
    final_out = layers.UpSampling2D((16,16), interpolation='bilinear')(out) │  final output.

    deeplabv3 = models.Model(resnet50_upto_conv4.input, final_out)   ◁──┐  Define the
                                                                         │  final model.
```

**Define an interim model from the input
up to the last layer of the conv4 block.**

Note how the model has a linear layer that does not have any activation present (e.g., sigmoid or softmax). This is because we are planning to use a special loss function that uses logits (unnormalized scores obtained from the last layer before applying softmax) instead of normalized probability scores. Due to that, we will keep the last layer a linear output with no activation.

We have one final housekeeping step to perform: copying the weights from the original conv5 block to the newly created conv5 block in our model. To do that, first we need to store the weights from the original model as follows:

```
w_dict = {}
for l in ["conv5_block1_0_conv", "conv5_block1_0_bn",
          "conv5_block1_1_conv", "conv5_block1_1_bn",
          "conv5_block1_2_conv", "conv5_block1_2_bn",
          "conv5_block1_3_conv", "conv5_block1_3_bn"]:
    w_dict[l] = resnet50.get_layer(l).get_weights()
```

We cannot copy the weights to the new model until we compile the model, as weights are not initialized until the model is compiled. Before we do that, we need to learn loss functions and evaluation metrics that are used in segmentation tasks. To do that, we will need to implement custom loss functions and metrics and use them to compile the model. This will be discussed in the next section.

EXERCISE 3

You want to create a new pyramidal aggregation module called aug-ASPP. The idea is similar to the ASPP module we implemented earlier, but with a few differences. Let's say you have been given two interim outputs from the model: out_1 and out_2 (same size). You have to write a function, aug_aspp, that will take these two outputs and do the following:

- Perform atrous convolution with r = 16, 128 filters, 3 × 3 convolution, stride 1, and ReLU activation on out_1 (output will be called atrous_out_1)
- Perform atrous convolution with r = 8, 128 filters, 3 × 3 convolution, stride 1, and ReLU activation on both out_1 and out_2 (output will be called atrous_out_2_1 and atrous_out_2_2)

- Concatenate `atrous_out_2_1` and `atrous_out_2_2` (output will be called `atrous_out_2`)
- Apply 1 × 1 convolution with 64 filters to both `atrous_out_1` and `atrous_out_2` and concatenate (output will be called `conv_out`)
- Use bilinear up-sampling to double the size of `conv_out` (on height and width dimensions) and apply sigmoid activation

8.4 Compiling the model: Loss functions and evaluation metrics in image segmentation

In order to finalize the DeepLab v3 model (built using mostly the ResNet-50 structure and the ASPP module), we have to define a suitable loss function and metrics to measure the performance of the model. Image segmentation is quite different from image classification tasks, so the loss function and metrics don't necessarily translate to the segmentation problem. One key difference is that there is typically a large class imbalance in segmentation data, as a "background" class typically dominates an image compared to other object-related pixels. To get started, you read a few blog posts and research papers and identify weighted categorical cross-entropy loss and dice loss as good candidates. You focus on three different metrics: pixel accuracy, mean (class-weighted) accuracy, and mean IoU.

Loss functions and evaluation metrics used in image segmentation models are different from what is used in image classifiers. To start, image classifiers take in a single class label for a single image, whereas a segmentation model predicts a class for every single pixel in the image. This highlights the necessity of not only reimagining existing loss functions and metrics, but also inventing new losses and evaluation metrics that are more appropriate for the output produced by segmentation models. We will first discuss loss functions and then metrics.

8.4.1 Loss functions

A *loss function* is what is used to optimize the model whose purpose is to find the parameters that minimize a defined loss. A loss function used in a deep network must be *differentiable*, as the minimization of the loss happens with the help of gradients. The loss functions we'll use comprise two loss functions:

- Cross-entropy loss
- Dice loss

CROSS-ENTROPY LOSS

Cross-entropy loss is one of the most common losses used in segmentation tasks and can be implemented with just one line in Keras. We already used cross-entropy loss quite a few times but didn't analyze it in detail. However, it is worthwhile to review the underpinning mechanics that govern cross-entropy loss.

Cross-entropy loss takes in a predicted target and a true target. Both these tensors are of shape [batch size, height, width, object classes]. The object class dimension is a one-hot encoded representation of which object class a given pixel belongs to. The cross-entropy loss is then computed for every pixel independently using

$$CE(i, j) = -\left(\sum_{k=1}^{c} y_k \log(\hat{y}_k) + (1 - y_k) \log(1 - \hat{y}_k) \right)$$

where $CE(i, j)$ represents the cross-entropy loss for pixel at position (i, j) on the image, c is the number of classes, and y_k and $\hat{y}_k$ represent the elements in the one-hot encoded vector and the predicted probability distribution over classes of that pixel. This is then summed across all the pixels to get the final loss.

Beneath the simplicity of the method, a critical issue lurks. Class imbalance is almost certain to rear its ugly head in image segmentation problems. You will find hardly any real-world images where each object occupies an equal area in the image. The good news is it is not very difficult to deal with this issue. This can be mitigated by assigning a weight for each pixel in the image, depending on the dominance of the class it represents. Pixels belonging to large objects will have smaller weights, whereas pixels belonging to smaller objects will have larger weights, providing an equal say despite the size in the final loss. The next listing shows how to do this in TensorFlow.

Listing 8.13 Computing the label weights for a given batch of data

```
def get_label_weights(y_true, y_pred):                                          Get the total pixels
                                                                                per-class in y_true.
    weights = tf.reduce_sum(tf.one_hot(y_true, num_classes), axis=[1,2])   ◁──

    tot = tf.reduce_sum(weights, axis=-1, keepdims=True)          Compute the weights
                                                                  per-class. Rarer classes
    weights = (tot - weights) / tot   # [b, classes]       ◁───   get more weight.

    y_true = tf.reshape(y_true, [-1, y_pred.shape[1]*y_pred.shape[2]])

    y_weights = tf.gather(params=weights, indices=y_true, batch_dims=1)    ◁─
    y_weights = tf.reshape(y_weights, [-1])    ◁──

    return y_weights                          Make y_weights        Create a weight
                                              a vector.             vector by gathering the
                                                                    weights corresponding
                                                                    to indices in y_true.
```

Get the total pixels in y_true.

Reshape y_true to a [batch size, height*width]–sized tensor.

Here, for a given batch, we compute the weights as a sequence/vector that has a number of elements equal to y_true. First, we get the total number of pixels for each class by computing the sum over the width and height of the one-hot encoded y_true (i.e., has dimensions batch, height, width, and class). Here, a class that has a value larger than num_classes will be ignored. Next, we compute the total number of pixels per sample by taking the sum over the class dimension resulting in *tot* (a [batch size, 1]– sized tensor). Now the weights can be computed per sample and per class using

$$w_i = \frac{n - n_i}{n_i}$$

where n is the total number of pixels and n^i is the total number of pixels belonging to the ith class. After that, we reshape y_true to shape [batch size, -1] as preparation for an important step in weight computation. As the final output, we want to create a tensor out of weights, where we gather elements from the y_weights that correspond to elements in y_true. In other words, we fetch the value from y_weights, where the index to fetch is given by the values in y_true. At the end, the result will be of the same shape and size as y_true. This is all we need to weigh the samples: multiply weights element-wise with the loss value for each pixel. To achieve this, we will use the function tf.gather(), which gathers the elements from a given tensor (params) while taking a tensor that represents indices (indices) and returns a tensor that is of the same shape as the indices:

```
y_weights = tf.gather(params=weights, indices=y_true, batch_dims=1)
```

Here, to ignore the batch dimension during performing the gather, we pass the argument batch_dims indicating how many batch dimensions we have. With that, we will define a function that outputs the weighted cross-entropy loss given a batch of predicted and true targets.

With the weights ready, we can now implement our first segmentation loss function. We will implement weighted cross-entropy loss. At a glance, the function masks irrelevant pixels (e.g., pixels belonging to unknown objects) and unwraps the predicted and true labels to get rid of the height and width dimensions. Finally, we can compute the cross-entropy loss using the built-in function in TensorFlow (see the next listing).

Listing 8.14   Implementing the weighted cross-entropy loss

```
def ce_weighted_from_logits(num_classes):

    def loss_fn(y_true, y_pred):
        """ Defining cross entropy weighted loss """

        valid_mask = tf.cast(
            tf.reshape((y_true <= num_classes - 1), [-1,1]), 'int32'
        )

        y_true = tf.cast(y_true, 'int32')
        y_true.set_shape([None, y_pred.shape[1], y_pred.shape[2]])

        y_weights = get_label_weights(y_true, y_pred)
        y_pred_unwrap = tf.reshape(y_pred, [-1, num_classes])
        y_true_unwrap = tf.reshape(y_true, [-1])

        return tf.reduce_mean(
            y_weights * tf.nn.sparse_softmax_cross_entropy_with_logits(
                y_true_unwrap * tf.squeeze(valid_mask),
                y_pred_unwrap * tf.cast(valid_mask, 'float32'))
        )
    return loss_fn
```

Annotations:
- Define the valid mask, masking unnecessary pixels.
- Some initial setup that casts y_true to int and sets the shape
- Get the label weights.
- Unwrap y_pred and y_true so that batch, height, and width dimensions are squashed.
- Compute the cross-entropy loss with y_true, y_pred, and the mask.
- Return the function that computes the loss.

You might be thinking, "Why is the loss defined as a nested function?" This is a standard pattern we have to follow if we need to include extra arguments to our loss function (i.e., num_classes). All we are doing is capturing the computations of the loss function in the loss_fn function and then creating an outer function ce_weighted_from_logits() that will return the function that encapsulates the loss computations (i.e., loss_fn).

Specifically, a valid mask is created to indicate whether the labels in y_true are less than the number of classes. Any label that has a value larger than the number of classes is ignored (e.g., unknown objects). Next, we get the weight vector and indicate a weight for each pixel using the get_label_weights() function. We will unwrap y_pred to a [-1, num_classes]–sized tensor, as y_pred contains *logits* (i.e., unnormalized probability scores output by the model) across all classes in the data set. y_true will be unwrapped to a vector (i.e., a single dimension), as y_true only contains the class label. Finally, we use tf.nn.sparse_softmax_cross_entropy_with_logits() to compute the loss over masked predicted and true targets. The function takes two arguments, labels and logits, which are self-explanatory. We can make two salient observations:

- We are computing sparse cross-entropy loss (i.e., not standard cross-entropy loss).
- We are computing cross-entropy loss from logits.

When using sparse cross entropy, we don't have to one-hot encode the labels, so we can skip this, which leads to a more memory-efficient data pipeline. This is because one-hot encoding is handled internally by the model. By using a sparse loss, we have less to worry about.

Computing the loss from logits (i.e., unnormalized scores) instead of from normalized probabilities leads to better and more stable gradients. Therefore, whenever possible, make sure to use logits instead of normalized probabilities.

DICE LOSS
The second loss we will discuss is called the *dice loss*, which is computed as

$$DiceLoss = 1 - \frac{2\ \text{Intersection}}{\text{Intersection} | \text{Union}}$$

Here, the intersection between the prediction and target tensors can be computed with element-wise multiplication, whereas the union can be computed using element-wise addition between the prediction and the target tensors. You might be thinking that using element-wise operations is a strange way to compute intersection and union. To understand the reason behind this, I want to refer to a statement made earlier: a loss function used in a deep network must be *differentiable*.

This means that we cannot use the standard conventions we use to compute intersection and union from a given set of values. Rather, we need to resort to a differentiable computation, leading to intersection and union between two tensors. Intersection can be computed by taking element-wise multiplication between the predicted and true targets. Union can be computed by taking the element-wise addition between the predicted and true targets. Figure 8.12 clarifies how these operations lead to intersection and union between two tensors.

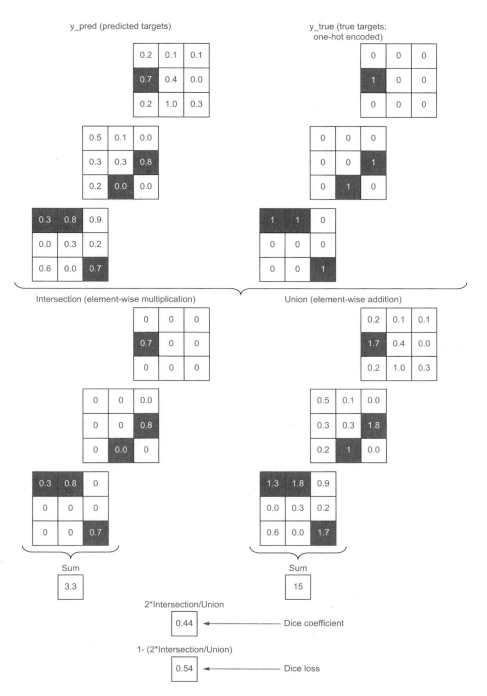

Figure 8.12 Computations involved in dice loss. The intersection can be computed as a differentiable function by taking element-wise multiplication, whereas union can be computed as the element-wise sum.

This loss is predominantly focused on maximizing the intersection between the predicted and true targets. The multiplier of 2 is used to balance out the duplication of values that comes from the overlap between the intersection and the union, found in the denominator (see the following listing).

Listing 8.15   Implementing the dice loss

```
def dice_loss_from_logits(num_classes):
    """ Defining the dice loss 1 - [(2* i + 1)/(u + i)]"""

    def loss_fn(y_true, y_pred):

        smooth = 1.

        # Convert y_true to int and set shape
        y_true = tf.cast(y_true, 'int32')
        y_true.set_shape([None, y_pred.shape[1], y_pred.shape[2]])

        # Get pixel weights
        y_weights = tf.reshape(get_label_weights(y_true, y_pred), [-1, 1])

        # Apply softmax to logits
        y_pred = tf.nn.softmax(y_pred)

        y_true_unwrap = tf.reshape(y_true, [-1])
        y_true_unwrap = tf.cast(
            tf.one_hot(tf.cast(y_true_unwrap, 'int32'), num_classes),
            'float32'
        )
        y_pred_unwrap = tf.reshape(y_pred, [-1, num_classes])

        intersection = tf.reduce_sum(y_true_unwrap * y_pred_unwrap * y_weights)

        union = tf.reduce_sum((y_true_unwrap + y_pred_unwrap) * y_weights)

        score = (2. * intersection + smooth) / ( union + smooth)

        loss = 1 - score

        return loss

    return loss_fn
```

- **Initial setup for y_true**
- **Apply softmax on y_pred to get normalized probabilities.**
- **Compute intersection using element-wise multiplication.**
- **Compute the dice coefficient.**
- **Get the label weights and reshape it to a [-1, 1] shape.**
- **Unwrap y_pred and one-hot–encoded y_true to the [-1, num_classes] shape.**
- **Compute union using element-wise addition.**
- **Compute the dice loss.**

Here, smooth is a smoothing parameter that we'll use to avoid potential NaN values resulting in division by zero. After that we do the following:

- Obtain weights for each y_true label
- Apply a softmax activation to y_pred
- Unwrap y_pred to the [-1, num_classes] tensor and y_true to a [-1]–sized vector

Then intersection and union are computed for y_pred and y_true. Specifically, intersection is computed as the result of element-wise multiplication of y_pred and y_true and the union as the result of the element-wise addition of y_pred and y_true.

Focal loss

Focal loss is a relatively novel loss introduced in the paper "Focal Loss for Dense Object Prediction" (https://arxiv.org/pdf/1708.02002.pdf). Focal loss was introduced to combat the severe class imbalance found in segmentation tasks. Specifically, it solves a problem in many easy examples (e.g., samples from common classes with smaller loss), over-powering small numbers of hard examples (e.g., samples from rare classes with larger loss). Focal loss solves this problem by introducing a modulating factor that will down-weight easy examples, so, naturally, the loss function focuses more on learning hard examples.

The loss function we will use to optimize the segmentation model will be the loss resulting from addition of sparse cross-entropy loss and dice loss (see the next listing).

Listing 8.16   Final combined loss function

```
def ce_dice_loss_from_logits(num_classes):

    def loss_fn(y_true, y_pred):
        # Sum of cross entropy and dice losses
        loss = ce_weighted_from_logits(num_classes)(
            tf.cast(y_true, 'int32'), y_pred
        ) + dice_loss_from_logits(num_classes)(
            y_true, y_pred
        )

        return loss

    return loss_fn
```

Next, we will discuss evaluation metrics.

8.4.2   Evaluation metrics

Evaluation metrics play a vital role in model training as a health check for the model. This means low performance/issues can be quickly identified by making sure evaluation metrics behave in a reasonable way. Here we will discuss three different metrics:

- Pixel
- Mean accuracy
- Mean IoU

We will implement these as custom metrics by leveraging some of the existing metrics in TensorFlow, where you have to subclass from the tf.keras.metrics.Metric class or one of the existing metrics. This means that you create a new Python class, which inherits from the base `tf.keras.metrics.Metric` base class of one of the existing concrete metrics classes:

```
class MyMetric(tf.keras.metrics.Metric):

  def __init__(self, name='binary_true_positives', **kwargs):
    super(MyMetric, self).__init__(name=name, **kwargs)

    # Create state related variables

  def update_state(self, y_true, y_pred, sample_weight=None):

    # update state in this function

  def result(self):

    # We return the result computed from the state

  def reset_states():
    # Do what's required to reset the maintained states
    # This function is called between epochs
```

The first thing you need to understand about a metric is that it is a stateful object, meaning it maintains a state. For example, a single epoch has multiple iterations and assumes you're interested in computing the accuracy. The metric needs to accumulate the values required to compute the accuracy over all the iterations so that at the end, it can compute the average accuracy for that epoch. When defining a metric, there are three functions you need to be mindful of: `__init__`, `update_state`, `result`, and `reset_states`.

Let's get concrete by assuming that we are implementing an accuracy metric (i.e., the number of elements in `y_pred` that matched `y_true` as a percentage). It needs to maintain a total: the sum of all the accuracy values we passed and the count (number of accuracy values we passed). With these two state elements, we can compute the mean accuracy at any time. When implementing the accuracy metric, you implement these functions:

- `__init__`—Defines two states; total and count
- `update_state`—Updates total and count based on `y_true` and `y_pred`
- `result`—Computes the mean accuracy as total/count
- `reset_states`—Resets both the total and count (this needs to happen at the beginning of an epoch)

Let's see how this knowledge translates to the evaluation metrics we're interested in solving.

PIXEL AND MEAN ACCURACIES

Pixel accuracy is the simplest metric you can think of. It measures the pixel-wise accuracy between the prediction and the true target (see the next listing).

Listing 8.17   Implementing the pixel accuracy metric

```
class PixelAccuracyMetric(tf.keras.metrics.Accuracy):

    def __init__(self, num_classes, name='pixel_accuracy', **kwargs):
        super(PixelAccuracyMetric, self).__init__(name=name, **kwargs)

    def update_state(self, y_true, y_pred, sample_weight=None):

        y_true.set_shape([None, y_pred.shape[1], y_pred.shape[2]])
        y_true = tf.reshape(y_true, [-1])

        y_pred = tf.reshape(tf.argmax(y_pred, axis=-1), [-1])

        valid_mask = tf.reshape((y_true <= num_classes - 1), [-1])

        y_true = tf.boolean_mask(y_true, valid_mask)
        y_pred = tf.boolean_mask(y_pred, valid_mask)

        super(PixelAccuracyMetric, self).update_state(y_true, y_pred)
```

Reshape y_true to a vector. (annotation pointing to `y_true = tf.reshape(y_true, [-1])`)

Set the shape of y_true (in case it is undefined). (annotation pointing to `y_true.set_shape(...)`)

Reshape y_pred after taking argmax to a vector. (annotation pointing to `y_pred = tf.reshape(...)`)

Define a valid mask (mask out unnecessary pixels). (annotation pointing to `valid_mask = ...`)

Gather pixels/labels that satisfy the valid_mask condition. (annotation pointing to the boolean_mask lines)

With the processed y_true and y_pred, compute the accuracy using the update_state() function. (annotation pointing to `super(...).update_state(...)`)

Pixel accuracy computes the one-to-one match between predicted pixels and true pixels. To compute this, we subclass from `tf.keras.metrics.Accuracy` as it has all the computations we need. To do this, we override the `update_state` function as shown. There are a few things we need to take care of:

- We need to set the shape of `y_true` as a precaution. This is because when working with `tf.data.Dataset`, sometimes the shape is lost.
- Reshape `y_true` to a vector.
- Get the class labels of `y_pred` by performing `tf.argmax()` and reshape it to a vector.
- Define a valid mask that ignores unwanted classes (e.g., unknown objects).
- Get the pixels that satisfy only the `valid_mask` filter.

Once we complete these tasks, we simply call the parent object's (i.e., `tf.keras.metrics.Accuracy`) `update_state` method with the corresponding arguments. We don't have to override `result()` and `reset_states()` functions, as they already contain the correct computations.

We said that class imbalance is prevalent in image segmentation problems. Typically, background pixels will spread in a large region of the image, potentially leading to misguided conclusions. Therefore, a slightly better approach might be to compute the accuracy individually per class and then average it. Enter mean accuracy, which prevents the undesired characteristics of pixel accuracy (see the next listing).

Listing 8.18   Implementing the mean accuracy metric

```
class MeanAccuracyMetric(tf.keras.metrics.Mean):

    def __init__(self, num_classes, name='mean_accuracy', **kwargs):
        super(MeanAccuracyMetric, self).__init__(name=name, **kwargs)

    def update_state(self, y_true, y_pred, sample_weight=None):

        smooth = 1

        y_true.set_shape([None, y_pred.shape[1], y_pred.shape[2]])

        y_true = tf.reshape(y_true, [-1])
        y_pred = tf.reshape(tf.argmax(y_pred, axis=-1),[-1])

        valid_mask = tf.reshape((y_true <= num_classes - 1), [-1])

        y_true = tf.boolean_mask(y_true, valid_mask)
        y_pred = tf.boolean_mask(y_pred, valid_mask)

        conf_matrix = tf.cast(
            tf.math.confusion_matrix(y_true, y_pred, num_classes=num_classes),
            'float32'
        )
        true_pos = tf.linalg.diag_part(conf_matrix)

        mean_accuracy = tf.reduce_mean(
            (true_pos + smooth)/(tf.reduce_sum(conf_matrix, axis=1) + smooth)
        )

        super(MeanAccuracyMetric, self).update_state(mean_accuracy)
```

Initial setup

Compute the confusion matrix using y_true and y_pred.

Get the true positives (elements on the diagonal).

Compute the mean accuracy using true positives and true class counts for each class.

Compute the average of mean_accuracy using the update_state() function.

The MeanAccuracyMetric will branch out from tf.keras.metrics.Mean, which computes the average over a given sequence of values. The plan is to compute the mean_accuracy within the update_state() function and then pass the value to the parent's update_state() function so that we get the average value of mean accuracy. First, we perform the initial setup and clean-up of y_true and y_pred we discussed earlier.

Afterward, we compute the confusion matrix (figure 8.13) from predicted and true targets. A confusion matrix for an n-way classification problem (i.e., a classification problem with n possible classes) is defined as a $n \times n$ matrix. Here, the element at the (i, j) position indicates how many instances were predicted as belonging to the ith class but actually belong to the jth class. Figure 8.13 portrays this type of confusion matrix. We can get the true positives by extracting the diagonal (i.e., (i, i) elements in the matrix for all $1 <= i <= n$). We can now compute the mean accuracy in two steps:

1 Perform element-wise division on the true positive count by actual counts for all the classes. This produces a vector whose elements represents per-class accuracy.
2 Compute the vector mean that resulted from step 1.

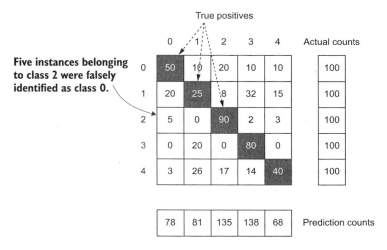

Figure 8.13   Illustration of a confusion matrix for a five-class classification problem. The shaded boxes represent true positives.

Finally, we pass the mean accuracy to its parent's `update_state()` function.

MEAN IOU

Mean IoU (mean intersection over union) is a popular evaluation metric pick for segmentation tasks and has close ties to the dice loss we discussed earlier, as they both use the concept of intersection and union to compute the final result (see the next listing).

Listing 8.19   Implementing the mean IoU metric

```
class MeanIoUMetric(tf.keras.metrics.MeanIoU):

    def __init__(self, num_classes, name='mean_iou', **kwargs):
        super(MeanIoUMetric, self).__init__(num_classes=num_classes, name=name,
        **kwargs)

    def update_state(self, y_true, y_pred, sample_weight=None):

        y_true.set_shape([None, y_pred.shape[1], y_pred.shape[2]])
        y_true = tf.reshape(y_true, [-1])

        y_pred = tf.reshape(tf.argmax(y_pred, axis=-1), [-1])

        valid_mask = tf.reshape((y_true <= num_classes - 1), [-1])
```

```
# Get pixels corresponding to valid mask
y_true = tf.boolean_mask(y_true, valid_mask)
y_pred = tf.boolean_mask(y_pred, valid_mask)

super(MeanIoUMetric, self).update_state(y_true, y_pred)
```

> **After the initial setup of y_true and y_pred, all we need to do is call the parent's update_state() function.**

The mean IoU computations are already found in `tf.keras.metrics.MeanIoU`. Therefore, we will use that as our parent class. All we need to do is perform the aforementioned setup for `y_true` and `y_pred` and then call the parent's `update_state()` function. Mean IoU is computed as

$$IoU = \frac{\text{True Positives}}{(\text{True Positives} + \text{False Positives} + \text{False Negatives})}$$

Various elements used in this computation are depicted in figure 8.14.

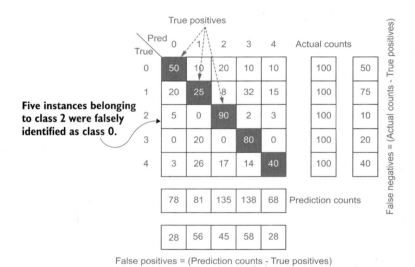

Figure 8.14   Confusion matrix and how it can be used to compute false positives, false negatives, and true positives

We now understand the loss functions and evaluation metrics that are available to us and have already implemented them. We can incorporate these losses to compile the model:

```
deeplabv3.compile(
    loss=ce_dice_loss_from_logits(num_classes),
    optimizer=optimizer,
    metrics=[
        MeanIoUMetric(num_classes),
        MeanAccuracyMetric(num_classes),
        PixelAccuracyMetric(num_classes)
    ])
```

Remember that we stored the weights from a convolution block we removed earlier. Now that we have compiled the model, we can copy the weights to the new model using the following syntax:

```
# Setting weights for newly added layers
for k, w in w_dict.items():
    deeplabv3.get_layer(k).set_weights(w)
```

We now move on to training the model with the data pipeline and the model we defined.

EXERCISE 4

You are coming up with a new loss function that computes the disjunctive union between y_true and y_pred. The disjunctive union between two sets A and B is the set of elements that are in either A or B but not in the intersection. You know you can compute the intersection with element-wise multiplication and union with element-wise addition of y_true and y_pred. Write the equation to compute the disjunctive union as a function of y_true and y_pred.

8.5   *Training the model*

You're coming to the final stages of the first iteration of your product. Now it's time to put the data and knowledge you garnered to good use (i.e., train the model). We will train the model for 25 epochs and monitor the pixel accuracy, mean accuracy, and mean IoU metrics. During the training, we will measure the performance on validation data set.

Training the model is the easiest part, as we have done the hard work that leads up to training. It is now just a matter of calling fit() with the correct parameters on the DeepLab v3 we just defined, as the following listing shows.

Listing 8.20   Training the model

```
if not os.path.exists('eval'):
    os.mkdir('eval')

csv_logger = tf.keras.callbacks.CSVLogger(
    os.path.join('eval','1_pretrained_deeplabv3.log'))

monitor_metric = 'val_loss'
mode = 'min' if 'loss' in monitor_metric else 'max'
print("Using metric={} and mode={} for EarlyStopping".format(monitor_metric,
    mode))
lr_callback = tf.keras.callbacks.ReduceLROnPlateau(
    monitor=monitor_metric, factor=0.1, patience=3, mode=mode, min_lr=1e-8
)
es_callback = tf.keras.callbacks.EarlyStopping(
    monitor=monitor_metric, patience=6, mode=mode
)
```

Train logger

Set the mode for the following callbacks automatically by looking at the metric name.

Learning rate scheduler

Early stopping callback

```
# Train the model
deeplabv3.fit(
    x=tr_image_ds, steps_per_epoch=n_train,
    validation_data=val_image_ds, validation_steps=n_valid,
    epochs=epochs, callbacks=[lr_callback, csv_logger, es_callback])
```

Train the model while using the validation set for learning rate adaptation and early stopping.

First, we will define a directory called eval if it does not exist. The training logs will be saved in this directory. Next, we define three different callbacks to be used during the training:

- csv_logger—Logs the training loss/metrics and validation loss/metrics
- lr_callback—Reduces the learning rate by a factor of 10, if the validation loss does not decrease within three epochs
- es_callback—Performs early stopping if the validation loss does not decrease within six epochs

NOTE On an Intel Core i5 machine with an NVIDIA GeForce RTX 2070 8GB, the training took approximately 45 minutes to run 25 epochs.

With that, we call deeplabv3.fit() with the following parameters:

- x—The tf.data pipeline producing training instances (set to tr_image_ds).
- steps_per_epoch—Number of steps per epoch. This is obtained by computing the number of training instances and dividing it by the batch size (set to n_train).
- validation_data—The tf.data pipeline producing validation instances. This is obtained by computing the number of validation instances and dividing it by the batch size (set to val_image_ds).
- epochs—Number of epochs (set to epochs).
- callbacks—The callbacks we set up earlier (set to [lr_callback, csv_logger, es_callback]).

After the model is trained, we will evaluate it on the test set. We will also visualize segmentations generated by the model.

EXERCISE 5

You have a data set of 10,000 samples and have split it into 90% training data and 10% validation data. You use a batch size of 10 for training and a batch size of 20 for validation. How many training and validation steps will be there in a single epoch?

8.6 *Evaluating the model*

Let's take a moment to reflect on what we have done so far. We defined a data pipeline to read images and prepare them as inputs and targets for the model. Then we defined a model known as DeepLab v3 that uses a pretrained ResNet-50 as its backbone and a special module called atrous spatial pyramid pooling to predict the final segmentation mask. Then we defined task-specific losses and metrics to make sure we could evaluate the model with a variety of metrics. Afterward, we trained the model. Now it's time for the ultimate reveal. We will measure the performance on an unseen test data set to see how well the model does. We will also visualize the model outputs and compare them against the real targets by plotting them side by side.

We can run the model over the unseen test images and gauge how well it is performing. To do that, we execute the following:

```
deeplabv3.evaluate(test_image_ds, steps=n_valid)
```

The size of the test set is the same as the validation set, as we split the images listed in val.txt into two equal validation and test sets. This will return around

- 62% mean IoU
- 87% mean accuracy
- 91% pixel accuracy

These are very respectable scores given our circumstances. Our training data set consists of less than 1,500 segmented images. Using this data, we were able to train a model that achieves around 62% mean IoU on a test data set of approximately size 725.

What does state of the art look like?

The state-of-the-art performance on Pascal VOC 2012 reports around 90% mean IoU (http://mng.bz/o2m2). However, these are models that are much larger and complex than what we used here. Furthermore, they are typically trained with significantly more data by using an auxiliary data set known as the semantic boundary data set (SBD) (introduced in the paper http://mng.bz/nNve). This will push the training datapoint count to over 10,000 (close to seven times the size of our current training set).

You can further investigate the model by visually inspecting some of the results our module produces. After all, it is a vision model that we are developing. Therefore, we should not rely solely on numbers to make decisions and conclusions. We should also visually analyze the results before settling on a conclusion.

What would the results from a U-Net based network look like?

Under similar conditions provided for the DeepLab v3 model, the U-Net model built with a pretrained ResNet-50 model as the encoder was only able to achieve approximately 32.5% mean IoU, 78.5% mean accuracy, and 81.5% pixel accuracy. The implementation is provided in the Jupyter notebook in the ch08 folder.

On an Intel Core i5 machine with an NVIDIA GeForce RTX 2070 8GB, the training took approximately 55 minutes to run 25 epochs.

There is a detailed explanation of the U-Net model in appendix B.

To complete this investigation, we will get a random sample from the test set and ask the model to predict the segmentation map for each of those images. Then we will plot the results side by side to ensure that our model is doing a good job (figure 8.15).

Figure 8.15   Comparing the true annotated targets to model predictions. You can see that the model is quite good at separating objects from different backgrounds.

We can see that unless it is an extremely difficult image (e.g., the top-left image, where there's a car obscured by a gate), our model does a very good job. It can identify almost all the images found in the sample we analyzed with high accuracy. The code for visualizing the images is provided in the notebook.

This concludes our discussion of image segmentation. In the next few chapters, we will discuss several natural language processing problems.

EXERCISE 6

You are given

- A model (called model)
- A batch of images called `batch_image` (already preprocessed and ready to be fed to a model)
- A corresponding batch of targets, `batch_targets` (the true segmentation mask in one-hot encoded format)

Write a function called `get_top_bad_examples`(model, batch_images, batch_targets, n) that will return the top n indices of the hardest (highest loss) images in `batch_images`. Given a predicted mask and a target mask, you can use the sum over element-wise multiplication as the loss of a given image.

You can use the `model.predict()` function to make a prediction on `batch_images`, and it will return a predicted mask as the same size as `batch_targets`. Once you compute the losses for the batch (`batch_loss`), you can use the `tf.math.top_k(batch_loss, n)` function to get the indices of elements with the highest value. `tf.math.top_k()` returns a tuple containing the top values and indices of a given vector, in that order.

Summary

- Segmentation models fall into two broad categories: semantic segmentation and instance segmentation.
- The `tf.data` API provides various functionality to implement complex data pipelines, such as using custom NumPy functions, performing quick transformations using `tf.data.Dataset.map()`, and I/O optimization techniques like prefetch and cache.
- DeepLab v3 is a popular segmentation model that uses a pretrained ResNet-50 model as its backbone and atrous convolutions to increase the receptive field by inserting holes (i.e., zeros) between the kernel weights.
- The DeepLab v3 model uses a module known as atrous spatial pyramid pooling to aggregate information at multiple scales, which helps to create a fine-grained segmented output.
- In segmentation tasks, cross entropy and dice loss are two popular losses, whereas pixel accuracy, mean accuracy, and mean IoU are popular evaluation metrics.
- In TensorFlow, loss functions can be implemented as stateless functions. But metrics must be implemented as stateful objects by subclassing from the `tf.keras.metrics.Metric` base class or a suitable class.
- The DeepLab v3 model achieved a very good accuracy of 62% mean IoU on the Pascal VOC 2010 data set.

Answers to exercises

Exercise 1

```
palettized_image = np.zeros(shape=rgb_image.shape[:-1])
for i in range(rgb_image.shape[0]):
    for j in range(rgb_image.shape[1]):
        for k in range(palette.shape[0]):
            if (palette[k] == rgb_image[i,j]).all():
                palettized_image[i,j] = k
                break
```

Exercise 2

```
dataset_a = tf.data.Dataset.from_tensor_slices(a)
dataset_b = tf.data.Dataset.from_tensor_slices(b)

image_ds = tf.data.Dataset.zip((dataset_a, dataset_b))

image_ds = image_ds.map(
        lambda x, y: (x, tf.image.resize(y, (64,64),  method='nearest'))
    )

image_ds = image_ds.map(
        lambda x, y: ((x-128.0)/255.0, tf.image.resize(y, (64,64),
    method='nearest'))
    )

image_ds = image_ds.batch(32).repeat(5).prefetch(tf.data.experimental.AUTOTUNE)
```

Exercise 3

```
import tensorflow.keras.layers as layers

def aug_aspp(out_1, out_2):

    atrous_out_1 = layers.Conv2D(128, (3,3), dilation_rate=16,
 padding='same', activation='relu')(out_1)

    atrous_out_2_1 = layers.Conv2D(128, (3,3), dilation_rate=8,
 padding='same', activation='relu')(out_1)
    atrous_out_2_2 = layers.Conv2D(128, (3,3), dilation_rate=8,
 padding='same', activation='relu')(out_2)
    atrous_out_2 = layers.Concatenate()([atrous_out_2_1, atrous_out_2_2])

    tmp1 = layers.Conv2D(64, (1,1), padding='same',
     activation='relu')(atrous_out_1)
    tmp2 = layers.Conv2D(64, (1,1), padding='same',
     activation='relu')(atrous_out_2)
    conv_out = layers.Concatenate()([tmp1,tmp2])

    out = layers.UpSampling2D((2,2), interpolation='bilinear')(conv_out)
    out = layers.Activation('sigmoid')(out)

    return out
```

Exercise 4

```
out = (y_pred - (y_pred * y_true)) + (y_true - (y_pred * y_true))
```

Exercise 5

```
9000 and 500
```

Exercise 6

```
def get_top_n_bad_examples(model, batch_images, batch_targets, n):

    batch_pred = model.predict(batch_images)

    batch_loss = tf.reduce_sum(batch_pred*batch_targets, axis=[1,2,3])

    _, hard_inds = tf.math.top_k(batch_loss, n)

    return hard_inds
```

Natural language processing with TensorFlow: Sentiment analysis

This chapter covers

- Preprocessing text with Python
- Analyzing text-specific attributes important for the model
- Creating a data pipeline to handle text sequences with TensorFlow
- Analyzing sentiments with a recurrent deep learning model (LSTM)
- Training the model on imbalanced product reviews
- Implementing word embeddings to improve model performance

In the previous chapters, we looked at two compute-vision-related applications: image classification and image segmentation. Image classification focuses on recognizing if an object belonging to a certain class is present in an image. Image segmentation tasks look not only at recognizing the objects present in the image, but also which pixels in the image belong to a certain object. We also anchored our discussions around learning the backbone of complex convolutional neural networks such as Inception net (image classification) and DeepLab v3 (image segmentation) models. If we look beyond images, text data is also a prominent modality of data. For example, the world wide web is teeming with text data. We can safely assume that it is the most common modality of data available in the web. Therefore, natural language processing (NLP) has been and will be a deeply rooted topic, enabling us to harness the power of the freely available text (e.g., through language modeling) and build machine learning products that can leverage textual data to produce meaningful outcomes (e.g., sentiment analysis).

NLP is a term that we give to the overarching notion that houses a plethora of tasks having to do with text. Everything from simple tasks, such as changing the case of text (e.g., converting uppercase to lowercase), to complex tasks, such as translating languages and word sense disambiguation (inferring the meaning of a word with the same spelling depending on the context) falls under the umbrella of NLP. Following are some of the notable tasks that you will experience if you enter the realm of NLP:

- *Stop word removal*—Stop words are uninformative words that frequent text corpora (e.g., "and," "it," "the," "am," etc.). Typically, these words add very little or nothing to the semantics (or meaning) of text. To reduce the feature space, many tasks remove stop words in early stages before feeding text to the model.
- *Lemmatization*—This is another technique to reduce the feature space the model has to deal with. Lemmatization will convert a given word to its base form (e.g., buses to bus, walked to walk, went to go, etc.), which reduces the size of the vocabulary and, in turn, the dimensionality of data the model needs to learn from.
- *Part of speech (PoS) tagging*—PoS tagging does exactly what it says: it tags every word in a given text with a part of speech (e.g., noun, verb, adjective, etc.). The Penn Treebank project provides one of the most popular and comprehensive list of PoS tags available. To see the full list, go to http://mng.bz/mO1W.
- *Named entity recognition (NER)*—NER is responsible for extracting various entities (e.g., Names of people/companies, geo locations, etc.) from text.
- *Language modeling*—Language modeling is the task of predicting the nth word given $1, \ldots, w-1^{th}$ word. Language modeling can be used to generate songs, movie scripts, and stories by training the model on relevant data. Due to the highly accessible nature of the data needed for language modeling (i.e., it does not require any labeled data), it commonly serves as a pretraining method to inject language understanding for decision-support NLP models.
- *Sentiment analysis*—Sentiment analysis is the task of identifying the sentiment given a piece of text. For example, a sentiment analyzer can analyze product/movie reviews and automatically produce a score to indicate how good the product is.
- *Machine translation*—Machine translation is the task of converting a phrase/sentence in a source language to a phrase/sentence in a target language. These models are trained using bilingual parallel text corpora.

It is rare that you will not come across an NLP task as a data scientist or a ML researcher. To solve NLP tasks quickly and successfully, it is important to understand processing data, standard models used, and so on.

In this chapter, you will learn how to develop a sentiment analyzer for video game review classification. You will start by exploring the data and learn about some common NLP preprocessing steps. You will also note that the data set is imbalanced (i.e., does not have a roughly equal number of samples for all the classes) and learn what can be done about that. We will then develop a TensorFlow data pipeline with which we will pipe data to our model to train. Here, you'll encounter a new machine learning model known as a *long short-term memory* (LSTM) model that has made its mark in the NLP domain. LSTM models can process sequences (e.g., a sentence—a sequence of words in a particular order) by going through each element iteratively to produce some outcome at the end. In this task, the model will output a binary value (0 for negative reviews and 1 for positive reviews). While traversing the sequence, an LSTM model maintains the memory of what it has seen so far. This makes LSTM models very powerful and able to process long sequences and learn patterns in them. After the model is trained, we will evaluate it on some test data to make sure it performs well and then save it. The high-level steps we will follow to develop this model include the following:

1 Download the data. We will use a video game review corpus from Amazon.
2 Explore and clean the data. Incorporate some text cleaning steps (e.g., lemmatization) to clean the data and prepare the corpus for the modeling task.
3 Create a data pipeline to convert raw text to a numerical format understood by machine learning models.
4 Train the model on the data produced by the data pipeline.
5 Evaluate the model on validation, and test data to ensure model's generalizability.
6 Save the trained model, and write the performance results.

9.1 *What the text? Exploring and processing text*

You are building a sentiment analyzer for a popular online video game store. They want a bit more than the number of stars, as the number of stars might not reflect the sentiment accurately due to the subjectivity of what a star means. The executives believe the text is more valuable than the number of stars. You've been asked to develop a sentiment analyzer that can determine how positive or negative a review is, given the text.

You have decided to use an Amazon video game review data set for this. It contains various reviews posted by users along with the number of stars. Text can be very noisy due to the complexity of language, spelling mistakes, and so on. Therefore, some type of preprocessing will act as the gatekeeper for producing clean data. In this section, we will examine the data and some basic statistics. Then we will perform several preprocessing steps: comprising, lowering the case (e.g., convert "John" to "john"), removing punctuation/numbers, removing stop words (i.e., uninformative words like "to," "the," "a," etc.) and lemmatization (converting words to their base form; e.g., "walking" to "walk").

As the very first step, let's download the data set in the next listing.

> **Listing 9.1 Downloading the Amazon review data set**

```
import os
import requests
import gzip
import shutil

# Retrieve the data
if not os.path.exists(os.path.join('data','Video_Games_5.json.gz')):
    url =
 "http://deepyeti.ucsd.edu/jianmo/amazon/categoryFilesSmall/Video_Games_
 5.json.gz"
    # Get the file from web
    r = requests.get(url)

    if not os.path.exists('data'):
        os.mkdir('data')

    # Write to a file
    with open(os.path.join('data','Video_Games_5.json.gz'), 'wb') as f:
        f.write(r.content)
else:
    print("The tar file already exists.")

if not os.path.exists(os.path.join('data', 'Video_Games_5.json')):
    with gzip.open(os.path.join('data','Video_Games_5.json.gz'), 'rb') as f_in:
        with open(os.path.join('data','Video_Games_5.json'), 'wb') as f_out:
            shutil.copyfileobj(f_in, f_out)
else:
    print("The extracted data already exists")
```

If the gzip file has not been downloaded, download it and save it to the disk.

If the gzip file is located in the local disk, don't download it.

If the gzip file exists but has not been extracted, extract it.

This code will download the data to a local folder if it doesn't already exist and extract the content. It will have a JSON file that will contain the data. JSON is a format for representing data and is predominately used to transfer data in web requests. It allows us to define data as key-value pairs. If you look at the JSON file, you will see that it has one record per line, where each record is a set of key-value pairs, and key is the column name and value is the value of that column for that record. You can see a few records extracted from the data:

```
{"overall": 5.0, "verified": true, "reviewTime": "10 17, 2015",
 "reviewerID": "xxx", "asin": "0700026657", "reviewerName": "xxx",
 "reviewText": "This game is a bit hard to get the hang of, but when you
 do it's great.", "summary": "but when you do it's great.",
 "unixReviewTime": 1445040000}
{"overall": 4.0, "verified": false, "reviewTime": "07 27, 2015",
 "reviewerID": "xxx", "asin": "0700026657", "reviewerName": "xxx",
 "reviewText": "I played it a while but it was alright. The steam was a
 bit of trouble. The more they move … looking forward to anno 2205 I
 really want to play my way to the moon.", "summary": "But in spite of
 that it was fun, I liked it", "unixReviewTime": 1437955200}
```

```
{"overall": 3.0, "verified": true, "reviewTime": "02 23, 2015",
➥ "reviewerID": "xxx", "asin": "0700026657", "reviewerName": "xxx",
➥ "reviewText": "ok game.", "summary": "Three Stars", "unixReviewTime":
➥ 1424649600}
```

Next, we will further explore the data we have:

```
import pandas as pd

# Read the JSON file
review_df = pd.read_json(
    os.path.join('data', 'Video_Games_5.json'), lines=True, orient='records'
)
# Select on the columns we're interested in
review_df = review_df[["overall", "verified", "reviewTime", "reviewText"]]
review_df.head()
```

The data is in JSON format. pandas provides a pd.read_json() function to read JSON data easily. When reading JSON data, you have to make sure that you set the orient argument correctly. This is because the orient argument enables pandas to understand the structure of JSON data. JSON data is unstructured compared to CSV files, which have a more consistent structure. Setting orient='records' will enable pandas to read data structured in this way (one record per line) correctly into a pandas DataFrame. Running the previous code snippet will produce the output shown in table 9.1.

Table 9.1 Sample data from the Amazon review data set

	overall	verified	reviewTime	reviewText
0	5	True	10 17, 2015	This game is a bit hard to get the hang of, bu...
1	4	False	07 27, 2015	I played it a while but it was alright. The st...
2	3	True	02 23, 2015	ok game.
3	2	True	02 20, 2015	found the game a bit too complicated, not what...
4	5	True	12 25, 2014	great game, I love it and have played it since...

We will now remove any records that have an empty or null value in the reviewText column:

```
review_df = review_df[~review_df["reviewText"].isna()]
review_df = review_df[review_df["reviewText"].str.strip().str.len()>0]
```

As you may have already noticed, there's a column that says whether the review is from a verified buyer. To preserve the integrity of our data, let's only consider the reviews from verified buyers. But before that, we have to make sure that we have enough data after filtering unverified reviews. To do that, let's see how many records there are for different values (i.e., `True` and `False`) of the verified column. For that, we will use panda's built-in `value_counts()` function as follows:

```
review_df["verified"].value_counts()
```

This will return

```
True     332504
False    164915
Name: verified, dtype: int64
```

That's great news. It seems we have more data from verified buyers than unverified users. Let's create a new DataFrame called `verified_df` that only contains verified reviews:

```
verified_df = review_df.loc[review_df["verified"], :]
```

Next, out of the verified reviews, we will evaluate the number of reviews for each different rating in the overall column:

```
verified_df["overall"].value_counts()
```

This will give

```
5    222335
4     54878
3     27973
1     15200
2     12118
Name: overall, dtype: int64
```

This is an interesting finding. Typically, we want to have equal amounts of data for each different rating. But that's never the case in the real world. For example, here, we have four times more 5-star reviews than 4-star reviews. This is known as *class imbalance*. Real-world data is often noisy, imbalanced, and dirty. We will see these characteristics as we look further into the data. We will circle back to the issue of class imbalance in the data when we are developing our model.

Sentiment analysis is designed as a classification problem. Given the review (as a sequence of words, for example), the model predicts a class out of a set of discrete classes. We are going to focus on two classes: positive or negative. We will make the assumption that 5 or 4 stars indicate a positive sentiment, whereas 3, 2, or 1 star mean a negative sentiment. Astute problem formulation, such as reducing the number of classes, can make the classification task easier. To do this, we can use the convenient built-in pandas function `map()`. `map()` takes a dictionary, where the key indicates the current value, and the value indicates the value the current value needs to be mapped to:

```
verified_df["label"]=verified_df["overall"].map({5:1, 4:1, 3:0, 2:0, 1:0})
```

Now let's check the number of instances for each class after the transformation

```
verified_df["label"].value_counts()
```

which will return

```
1    277213
0     55291
Name: label, dtype: int64
```

There's around 83% positive samples and 17% negative samples. That's a significant discrepancy in terms of the number of samples. The final step of our simple data exploration is to make sure there's no order in the data. To shuffle the data, we will use panda's `sample()` function. `sample()` is technically used to sample a small fraction of data from a large data set. But by setting `frac=1.0` and a fixed random seed, we can get the full data set shuffled in a random manner:

```
verified_df = verified_df.sample(frac=1.0, random_state=random_seed)
```

Finally, we will separate the inputs and labels into two separate variables, as this will make processing easier for the next steps:

```
inputs, labels = verified_df["reviewText"], verified_df["label"]
```

Next, we will focus on an imperative task, which will ultimately improve the quality of the data that is going into the model: cleaning and preprocessing the text. Here we will focus on performing the following subtasks. You will learn more details about every subtask in the coming discussion:

- Lower the case of words.
- Treat shortened forms of words (e.g., "aren't," "you'll," etc.).
- Tokenize text into words (known as *tokenization*).
- Remove uninformative text, such as numbers, punctuation, and stop words. Stop words are words that are frequent in text corpora but do not justify the value of their presence enough for most NLP tasks (e.g., "and," "the," "am," "are," "it," "he," "she," etc.).
- Lemmatize words. Lemmatization is the process of converting words to their base-form (e.g., plural nouns to singular nouns and past-tense verbs to present-tense verbs).

To do most of these tasks, we will rely on a famous and well-known Python library for text processing known as NLTK (Natural Language Toolkit). If you have set up the development environment, you should have the NLTK library installed. But our job is not done yet. To perform some of the subtasks, we need to download several external resources provided by NLTK:

- averaged_perceptron_tagger—Identifies part of speech
- wordnet and omw-1.4-_Will be used to lemmatize (i.e., convert words to their base form)
- stopwords—Provides the list of stop words for various languages
- punkt—Used to tokenize text to smaller components (e.g., words, sentences, etc.)

Let's first do that:

```
import nltk

nltk.download('averaged_perceptron_tagger', download_dir='nltk')
nltk.download('wordnet', download_dir='nltk')
nltk.download('omw-1.4', download_dir='nltk')
nltk.download('stopwords', download_dir='nltk')
nltk.download('punkt', download_dir='nltk')
nltk.data.path.append(os.path.abspath('nltk'))
```

We can now continue with our project. To understand the various preprocessing steps that'll be laid out here, we will zoom in on a single review, which is simply a Python string (i.e., a sequence of characters). Let's call this single review doc.

First we can convert a string to lowercase simply by calling the function lower() on a string. lower() is a Python built-in function available for strings that will convert characters in a given string to lowercase characters:

```
doc = doc.lower()
```

Next, we will expand the "n't" to "not" if it's present:

```
import re

doc = re.sub(pattern=r"\w+n\'t ", repl="not ", string=doc)
```

To do so, we will use regular expressions. Regular expressions give us a way to match arbitrary patterns and manipulate them in various ways. Python has a built-in library to handle regular expressions, known as re. Here, re.sub() will substitute words that match a certain pattern (i.e., any sequence of alphabetical characters followed by "n't; e.g., "don't," "can't") and replace them with a string passed as repl (i.e., "not ") in the string doc. For example, "won't" will be replaced with "not." We do not care about the prefix "will," as it will be removed anyway during the stop word removal we will perform later. If you're interested, you can read more about regular expression syntax at https://www.rexegg.com/regex-quickstart.html.

We will remove shortened forms such as 'll, 're, 'd, and 've. You might notice that this will result in uncomprehensive phrases like "wo" (i.e., "won't" becomes "wo" + "not"); we can safely ignore them. Notice that we are treating the shortened form of "not" quite differently from other shortened forms. This is because, unlike the other shortened forms, if present, "not" can have a significant impact on what a review actually conveys. We will talk about this again in just a little while:

```
doc = re.sub(pattern=r"(?:\'ll |\'re |\'d |\'ve )", repl=" ", string=doc)
```

Here, to replace the shortened forms of 'll, 're, 'd, and 've, we are again using regular expressions. Here, `r"(?:\'ll |\'re |\'d |\'ve )"` is a regular expression in Python that essentially identifies any occurrence of 'll/'re/'d/'ve in doc. Then we will remove any digits in doc using the `re.sub()` function like before:

```
doc = re.sub(pattern=r"/d+", repl="", string=doc)
```

We will remove stop words and any punctuation as our next step. As mentioned earlier, stop words are words that appear in text but add very little value to the meaning of the text. In other words, even if the stop words are missing from the text, you'll still be able to infer the meaning of what's being said. The library NLTK provides a list of stop words, so we don't have to come up with them:

```
from nltk.corpus import stopwords
from nltk import word_tokenize
import string

EN_STOPWORDS = set(stopwords.words('english')) - {'not', 'no'}

tokens = [w for w in word_tokenize(doc) if w not in EN_STOPWORDS and w not in
    string.punctuation]
```

Here, to access the stop words, all you have to do is call `from nltk.corpus import stopwords` and then call `stopwords.words('english')`. This will return a list. If you look at the words present in the list of stop words, you'll observe almost all the common words (e.g., "I," "you," "a," "the," "am," "are," etc.) you'd encounter while reading a text. But as we stressed earlier, the word "not" is a special word, especially in the context of sentiment analysis. The presence of words like "no" and "not" can completely flip the meaning of a text in our case.

Also note the use of the function `word_tokenize()`. This is a special processing step known as *tokenization*. Here, passing a string to `word_tokenize()` returns a list, with each word being an element. Word tokenization might look very trivial for a language like English, where words are delimited by a space character or a period. But this can be a complex task in other languages (e.g., Japanese) where separation between tokens is not explicit.

Do "not" let stop words fool you!

If you look at most stop word lists, you will see that the words "no" and "not" are considered stop words as they are common words to see in a text corpus. However, for our task of sentiment analysis, these words play a significant role in changing the meaning (and possibly the label) of a review. The review "this is a great video game" means the opposite of "this is not a great video game" or "this game is no good." For this reason, we specifically remove the words "no" and "not" from the list of stop words.

Next, we have another treatment known as *lemmatization*. Lemmatization truncates/stems a given word to a base form, for example, converting plural nouns to singular nouns or past tense verbs to present tense, and so on. This can be done easily using a lemmatizer object shipped with the NLTK package:

```
lemmatizer = WordNetLemmatizer()
```

Here we are downloading the `WordNetLemmatizer`. `WordNetLemmatizer` is a lemmatizer built on the well-renowned WordNet database. If you haven't heard of WordNet, it is a famous lexical database (in the form of a network/graph) that you can utilize for tasks such as information retrieval, machine translation, text summarization, and so on. WordNet comes in many sizes and flavors (e.g., Multilingual WordNet, Non-English WordNet, etc.). You can explore more about WordNet and browse the database online at https://wordnet.princeton.edu/:

```
pos_tags = nltk.pos_tag(tokens)
    clean_text = [
        lemmatizer.lemmatize(w, pos=p[0].lower()) \
        if p[0]=='N' or p[0]=='V' else w \
        for (w, p) in pos_tags
    ]
```

By calling the function `lemmatizer.lemmatize()`, you can convert any given word to its base form (if it is not already in base form). But when calling the function, you need to pass in an important argument called `pos`. `pos` refers to the PoS tag (part-of-speech tag) of that word. PoS tagging is a special NLP task, where the task is to classify a given word to a PoS tag from a given set of discrete PoS tags. Here are a few examples of PoS tags:

- *DT*—Determiner (e.g., a, the)
- *JJ*—Adjective (e.g., beautiful, delicious)
- *NN*—Noun, singular or mass (e.g., person, dog)
- *NNS*—Noun, plural (e.g., people, dogs)
- *NNP*—Proper noun, singular (e.g., I, he, she)
- *NNPS*—Proper noun, plural (e.g., we, they)
- *VB*—Verb, base form (e.g., go, eat, walk)
- *VBD*—Verb, past tense (e.g., went, ate, walked)
- *VBG*—Verb, gerund or present participle (e.g., going, eating, walking)
- *VBN*—Verb, past participle (e.g., gone, eaten, walked)

- *VBP*—Verb, non-third-person singular present
- *VBZ*—Verb, third-person singular present

You can find the full list of PoS tags at http://mng.bz/mO1W. A note-worthy observation is how the tags are organized. You can see that if you consider only the first two characters of the tags, you get a broader set of classes (e.g., NN, VB), where all the nouns will be classified with NN and verbs will be classified with VB, and so on. We will use this property to make our lives easier.

Back to our code: let's assimilate how we are using PoS tags to lemmatize words. When lemmatizing words, you have to pass in the PoS tag for the word you are lemmatizing. This is important as the lemmatization logic is different for different types of words. We will first get a list that has (<word>, <pos>) elements for the words in tokens (returned by the tokenization process). Then we iterate through the `pos_tags` list and call the `lemmatizer.lemmatize()` function with the word and the PoS tag. We will only lemmatize verbs and nouns to save computational time.

More about WordNet

Word net is a lexical database (sometimes called a lexical ontology) that is in the form of an interconnected network. These connections are based on how similar two words are. For example, the words "car" and "automobile" have a smaller distance, whereas "dog" and "volcano" are far apart.

The words in WordNet are grouped into *synsets* (short for synonym sets). A synset captures the words that share a common meaning (e.g., dog, cat, hamster). Each word can belong to one or multiple synsets. Each synset has *lemmas*, which are the words in that synset.

Going a level up, there are relationships between synsets. There are four different relationships:

- *Hypernyms*—A hypernym synset is the synset that is more general than a given synset. For example, "animal" is a hypernym synset of "pet."
- *Hyponyms*—A hyponym synset is a more specific synset than a given synset. For example, "car" is a hyponym synset of the "vehicle" synset.
- *Holonyms*—A holonym synset is a synset that a given synset is a part of (is-part-of relationship). For example, "engine" is a holonym synset of the "car" synset.
- *Meronyms*—A meronym synset is a synset that a given synset is made of (is-made-of relationship). For example, "leaf" is a meronym synset of the "plant" synset.

Due to this organization of interconnected synsets, using WordNet you can measure the distance between two words as well. Similar words will have a smaller distance, whereas disparate words will have a larger distance.

You can experiment with these ideas in NLTK by importing WordNet from `nltk.corpus import wordnet`. For more information refer to https://www.nltk.org/howto/wordnet.html.

This concludes the series of steps we are incorporating to build the preprocessing workflow for our text. We will encapsulate these steps in a function called `clean_text()`, as in the following listing.

Listing 9.2 Preprocessing logic for reviews in the dataset

```
def clean_text(doc):
    """ A function that cleans a given document (i.e. a text string)"""

    doc = doc.lower()
    doc = doc.replace("n\'t ", ' not ')
    doc = re.sub(r"(?:\'ll |\'re |\'d |\'ve )", " ", doc)
    doc = re.sub(r"/d+","", doc)

    tokens = [
        w for w in word_tokenize(doc) if w not in EN_STOPWORDS and w not in
    string.punctuation
    ]

    pos_tags = nltk.pos_tag(tokens)
    clean_text = [
        lemmatizer.lemmatize(w, pos=p[0].lower()) \
        if p[0]=='N' or p[0]=='V' else w \
        for (w, p) in pos_tags
    ]

    return clean_text
```

Turn to lower case.

Remove digits.

Get the PoS tags for the tokens in the string.

Expand the shortened form n't to "not."

Remove shortened forms like 'll, 're, 'd, 've, as they don't add much value to this task.

Break the text into tokens (or words); while doing that, ignore stop words from the result.

To lemmatize, get the PoS tag of each token; if it is N (noun) or V (verb) lemmatize, else keep the original form.

You can check the processing done in the function by calling it on a sample text

```
sample_doc = 'She sells seashells by the seashore.'
print("Before clean: {}".format(sample_doc))
print("After clean: {}".format(clean_text(sample_doc)))
```

which returns

```
Before clean: She sells seashells by the seashore.
After clean: ["sell", "seashell", "seashore"]
```

We will leverage this function along with panda's `apply` function to apply this processing pipeline on each row of text that we have in our `data` DataFrame:

```
inputs = inputs.apply(lambda x: clean_text(x))
```

You might want to leave your computer for a while to grab a coffee or to check on your friends. It might take close to an hour to run this one-liner. The final result looks like table 9.2.

Table 9.2   Original text versus preprocessed text

Original text	Clean text (tokenized)
Worked perfectly on Wii and GameCube. No issues with compatibility or loss of memory.	`['work', 'perfectly', 'wii', 'gamecube', 'no', 'issue', 'compatibility', 'loss', 'memory']`
Loved the game, and the other collectibles that came with it are well made. The mask is big, and it almost fits my face, so that was impressive.	`['loved', 'game', 'collectible', 'come', 'well', 'make', 'mask', 'big', 'almost', 'fit', 'face', 'impressive']`
It's an okay game. To be honest, I am very bad at these types of games and to me it's very difficult! I am always dying, which depresses me. Maybe if I had more skill I would enjoy this game more!	`["'s", 'okay', 'game', 'honest', 'bad', 'type', 'game', '--', "'s", 'difficult', 'always', 'die', 'depresses', 'maybe', 'skill', 'would', 'enjoy', 'game']`
Excellent product as described.	`['excellent', 'product', 'describe']`
The level of detail is great; you can feel the love for cars in this game.	`['level', 'detail', 'great', 'feel', 'love', 'car', 'game']`
I can't play this game.	`['not', 'play', 'game']`

Finally, to avoid overdosing on coffee or pestering your friends by running this too many times, we will save the data to the disk:

```
inputs.to_pickle(os.path.join('data','sentiment_inputs.pkl'))
labels.to_pickle(os.path.join('data','sentiment_labels.pkl'))
```

Now, we are going to define a data pipeline to transform the data to a format that is understood by the model and can be used to train and evaluate the model.

EXERCISE 1
Given the string s, "i-purchased-this-game-for-99-i-want-a-refund," you'd like to replace the dash "-" with a space and then lemmatize only the verbs in the text. How would you do that?

9.2   *Getting text ready for the model*

You have a clean data set with text stripped of any unnecessary or unwarranted linguistic complexities for the problem we're solving. Additionally, the binary labels have been generated from the number of stars given for each review. Before pushing ahead with the model training and evaluation, we have to do some further processing of our data set. Specifically, we will create three subsets of data—training, validation and testing—which will be used to train and evaluate the model. Next, we will look at two important characteristics of our data sets: the vocabulary size and the distribution of the sequence length (i.e., the number of words) in the examples we have. Finally, you will convert the words to numbers (or numerical IDs), as machine learning models do not understand strings but numbers.

In this section, we will further prepare the data to be consumed by the model. Right now, we have a very nice layout of processing steps to go from a noisy, inconsistent review to a simple, consistent text string that preserves the semantics of the review. But we haven't addressed the elephant in the room! That is, machine learning models understand numerical data, not textual data. The string "not a great game" does not mean anything to a model if you present it as is. We have to further refine our data so that we end up with a number sequence instead of a word sequence. In our journey to get the data ready for the model, we will perform the following subtasks:

- Check the size of the vocabulary/word frequency after preprocessing. This will later be used as a hyperparameter of the model.
- Check the summary statistics of the sequence length (mean, median, and standard deviation). This will later be used as a hyperparameter of the model.
- Create a dictionary that will map each unique word to a unique ID (we will call this a tokenizer).

9.2.1 Splitting training/validation and testing data

A word of caution! When performing these tasks, you might inadvertently create oozing data leakages in our model. We have to make sure we perform these tasks *using only the training data set* and keep the validation and testing data separate. Therefore, our first goal should be separating training/validation/test data.

> **The lurking data leakages in NLP**
>
> You might be thinking, "Great! All I have to do is load the processed text corpus and perform the analysis or tasks on that." Not so fast! That is the incorrect way to do it. Before doing any data-specific processing/analysis, such as computing the vocabulary size or developing a tokenizer, you have to separate the data into training/validation and test sets, and then perform this processing/analysis on the training data.
>
> The purpose of the validation data is to act as a compass for choosing hyperparameters and to determine when to stop training. The test data set is your benchmark on how well the model is going to perform in the real world. Given the nature of the purpose fulfilled by the validation/test data, they should not be part of your analysis, but only be used to evaluate performance. Using validation/test data in your analysis to develop a model gives you an unfair advantage and causes what's known as *data leakage*. Data leakage refers to directly or indirectly providing access to the examples you evaluate the model on. If the validation/test data is used for any analysis we do, we are providing access to those data sets before the evaluation phase. Models with data leakages can lead to poor performance in the real world.

We know we have an imbalanced data set. Despite having an imbalanced data set, we have to make sure our model is good at identifying both positive and negative reviews.

This means the data sets we'll be evaluating on need to be balanced. To achieve this, here's what we will do:

- Create balanced (i.e., equal count of positive and negative samples) validation and test sets
- Assign the remaining datapoints to the training set

Figure 9.1 depicts this process.

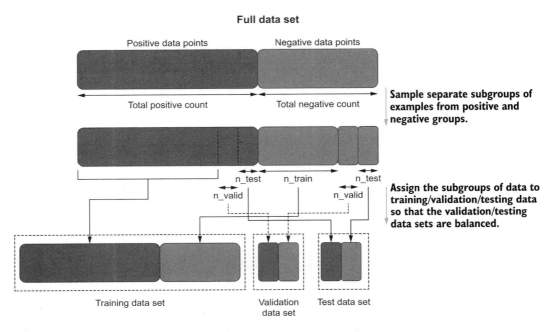

Figure 9.1 The process for splitting training/valid/test data

We will now see how we can do this in Python. First, we start by identifying the indices that correspond to positive labels and negative labels separately:

```
neg_indices = pd.Series(labels.loc[(labels==0)].index)
pos_indices = pd.Series(labels.loc[(labels==1)].index)
```

Stratified sampling: An alternative to imbalanced data sets

Your design of validation and test sets will dictate how you will define performance metrics to evaluate the trained model. If you create equally balanced validation/test sets, then you can safely use accuracy as a metric to evaluate the trained model. That is what we will do here: create balanced validation/test data sets, and then use accuracy as a metric to evaluate the model. But you might not be so lucky all the time. There can be scenarios where the minority class is so scary you can't afford to create balanced data sets.

> In such instances, you can use *stratified sampling*. Stratified sampling creates individual data sets, roughly maintaining the original class ratios in the full data set. When this is the case, you have to carefully choose your metric, because standard accuracy can no longer be trusted. For example, if you care about identifying positive samples with high accuracy at the cost of a few false positives, then you should use recall (or F1 score with higher weight given to recall) as the performance metric.

Next, we will define the size of our validation/test set as a function of `train_fraction` (a user-defined argument that determines how much data to leave for the training set). We will use a default value of 0.8 for the `train_fraction`:

```
n_valid = int(
    min([len(neg_indices), len(pos_indices)]) * ((1-train_fraction)/2.0)
)
```

It might look like a complex computation, but it is, in fact, a simple one. We will use the valid fraction as half of the fraction of data left for training data (the other half is used for the testing set). And finally, to convert the fractional value to the actual number of samples, we multiply the fraction by the smallest of counts of positive and negative samples. This way, we make sure the underrepresented class stays as the focal point during the data split. We keep the validation set and the test set equal. Therefore

```
n_test = n_valid
```

Next, we define the three sets of indices (for train/validation/test datasets) for each label type (positive and negative). We will create a funneling process to assign data points to different data sets. First, we do the following:

1 Randomly sample `n_test` number of indices from the negative indices (`neg_test_indices`).
2 Then randomly sample `n_valid` indices from the remaining indices (`neg_valid_inds`).
3 The remaining indices are kept as the training instances (`neg_train_inds`).

The same process is then repeated for positive indices to create three index sets for training/validation/test data sets:

```
neg_test_inds = neg_indices.sample(n=n_test, random_state=random_seed)
neg_valid_inds = neg_indices.loc[
    ~neg_indices.isin(neg_test_inds)
].sample(n=n_test, random_state=random_seed)
neg_train_inds = neg_indices.loc[
    ~neg_indices.isin(neg_test_inds.tolist()+neg_valid_inds.tolist())
]

pos_test_inds = pos_indices.sample(n=n_test, random_state=random_seed
)
```

```
pos_valid_inds = pos_indices.loc[
    ~pos_indices.isin(pos_test_inds)
].sample(n=n_test, random_state=random_seed)
pos_train_inds = pos_indices.loc[
    ~pos_indices.isin(pos_test_inds.tolist()+pos_valid_inds.tolist())
]
```

With the negative and positive indices to slice the inputs and labels, now it's time to create actual data sets:

```
tr_x = inputs.loc[
    neg_train_inds.tolist() + pos_train_inds.tolist()
].sample(frac=1.0, random_state=random_seed)
tr_y = labels.loc[
    neg_train_inds.tolist() + pos_train_inds.tolist()
].sample(frac=1.0, random_state=random_seed)

v_x = inputs.loc[
    neg_valid_inds.tolist() + pos_valid_inds.tolist()
].sample(frac=1.0, random_state=random_seed)
v_y = labels.loc[
    neg_valid_inds.tolist() + pos_valid_inds.tolist()
].sample(frac=1.0, random_state=random_seed)

ts_x = inputs.loc[
    neg_test_inds.tolist() + pos_test_inds.tolist()
].sample(frac=1.0, random_state=random_seed)
ts_y = labels.loc[
    neg_test_inds.tolist() + pos_test_inds.tolist()
].sample(frac=1.0, random_state=random_seed)
```

Here, (tr_x, tr_y), (v_x, v_y), and (ts_x, ts_y) represent the training, validation, and testing data sets, respectively. Here, the data sets suffixed with _x come from the inputs, and the data sets suffixed with _y come from the labels. Finally, we can wrap the logic we discussed in a single function as in the following listing.

Listing 9.3 Splitting training/validation/testing data sets

```
def train_valid_test_split(inputs, labels, train_fraction=0.8):
    """ Splits a given dataset into three sets; training, validation and test """

    neg_indices = pd.Series(labels.loc[(labels==0)].index)      Separate indices of negative
    pos_indices = pd.Series(labels.loc[(labels==1)].index)      and positive data points.

    n_valid = int(min([len(neg_indices), len(pos_indices)])
        * ((1-train_fraction)/2.0))                             Compute the valid and test data
    n_test = n_valid                                            set sizes (for minority class).

    neg_test_inds = neg_indices.sample(n=n_test, random_state=random_seed)
    neg_valid_inds = neg_indices.loc[~neg_indices.isin(
        neg_test_inds)].sample(n=n_test, random_state=random_seed)
```

Get the indices of the minority class that goes to the test set.   **Get the indices of the minority class that goes to the validation set.**

```
                neg_train_inds = neg_indices.loc[~neg_indices.isin(
                    neg_test_inds.tolist()+neg_valid_inds.tolist())]
```

The rest of the indices in the minority class belong to the training set.

Compute the majority class indices for the test/validation/train sets

```
                pos_test_inds = pos_indices.sample(n=n_test)
                pos_valid_inds = pos_indices.loc[
                    ~pos_indices.isin(pos_test_inds)].sample(n=n_test)
                pos_train_inds = pos_indices.loc[
                    ~pos_indices.isin(pos_test_inds.tolist()+pos_valid_inds.tolist())
                ]
```

Get the training/valid/test data sets using the indices created.

```
                tr_x = inputs.loc[neg_train_inds.tolist() +
                pos_train_inds.tolist()].sample(frac=1.0, random_state=random_seed)
                tr_y = labels.loc[neg_train_inds.tolist() +
                pos_train_inds.tolist()].sample(frac=1.0, random_state=random_seed)
                v_x = inputs.loc[neg_valid_inds.tolist() +
                pos_valid_inds.tolist()].sample(frac=1.0, random_state=random_seed)
                v_y = labels.loc[neg_valid_inds.tolist() +
                pos_valid_inds.tolist()].sample(frac=1.0, random_state=random_seed)
                ts_x = inputs.loc[neg_test_inds.tolist() +
                pos_test_inds.tolist()].sample(frac=1.0, random_state=random_seed)
                ts_y = labels.loc[neg_test_inds.tolist() +
                pos_test_inds.tolist()].sample(frac=1.0, random_state=random_seed)

                print('Training data: {}'.format(len(tr_x)))
                print('Validation data: {}'.format(len(v_x)))
                print('Test data: {}'.format(len(ts_x)))

                return (tr_x, tr_y), (v_x, v_y), (ts_x, ts_y)
```

Then simply call the function to generate training/validation/testing data:

```
(tr_x, tr_y), (v_x, v_y), (ts_x, ts_y) = train_valid_test_split(data, labels)
```

Next, we're going to examine the corpus a bit more to explore the vocabulary size and sequence length with respect to the reviews we have in the training set. These will be used as hyperparameters to the model later on.

9.2.2 *Analyze the vocabulary*

Vocabulary size is an important hyperparameter for the model. Therefore, we have to find the optimal vocabulary size that will allow us to capture enough information to solve the task accurately. To do that, we will first create a long list, where each element is a word:

```
data_list = [w for doc in tr_x for w in doc]
```

This line goes through each `doc` in `tr_x` and then through each word (`w`) in that doc and creates a flattened sequence of words that are present in all the documents. Because we have a Python list, where each element is a word, we can utilize Python's built-in `Counter` objects to get a dictionary, where each word is mapped to a key and the value represents the frequency of that word in the corpus. Note how we are using the training data set only for this analysis in order to avoid data leakage:

```
from collections import Counter
cnt = Counter(data_list)
```

With our word frequency dictionary out of the way, let's look at some of the most common words in our corpus:

```
freq_df = pd.Series(
    list(cnt.values()),
    index=list(cnt.keys())
).sort_values(ascending=False)

print(freq_df.head(n=10))
```

This will return the following result, where you can see the top words that appear in the text. Looking at the results, it makes sense. It's no surprise that words like "game," "like," and "play" get priority in terms of frequency over the other words:

```
game     407818
not      248244
play     128235
's       127844
get      108819
like     100279
great     97041
one       89948
good      77212
time      63450
dtype: int64
```

Going a step forward, let's compute the summary statistics on the text corpus. By doing this, we can see the average frequency of words, standard deviation, minimum, maximum, and so on:

```
print(freq_df.describe())
```

This will give some important basic statistics about the frequency of words. For example, from this we can say the average frequency of words is ~76 with a standard deviation of ~1754:

```
count    133714.000000
mean         75.768207
std        1754.508881
min           1.000000
25%           1.000000
50%           1.000000
75%           4.000000
max      408819.000000
dtype: float64
```

We will then create a variable called n_vocab that will hold the size of the vocabulary containing the words appearing at least 25 times in the corpus. You should get a value close to 11,800 for n_vocab:

```
n_vocab = (freq_df >= 25).sum()
```

9.2.3 *Analyzing the sequence length*

Remember that tr_x is a pandas Series object, where each row contains a review and each review is a list of words. When the data is in this format, we can use the pd.Series.str.len() function to get the length of each row (or the number of words in each review):

```
seq_length_ser = tr_x.str.len()
```

When computing the basic statistics, we will do things a bit differently. Our goal here is to find three bins of sequence lengths so we can bin them to short, medium, and long sequences. We will use these bucket boundaries when defining our TensorFlow data pipeline. To do that, we will first identify the cut-off points (or quantiles) to remove the top and bottom 10% of data. This is because top and bottom slices are full of outliers, and, as you know, they will skew the statistics like mean. In pandas, you can get the quantiles with the quantile() function, where you pass a fractional value to indicate which quantile you're interested in:

```
p_10 = seq_length_ser.quantile(0.1)
p_90 = seq_length_ser.quantile(0.9)
```

Then you simply filter the data between those quantiles. Next, we use the describe function with the 33% percentile and 66% percentile, as we want to bin to three different categories:

```
seq_length_ser[(seq_length_ser >= p_10) & (seq_length_ser <
    p_90)].describe(percentiles=[0.33, 0.66])
```

If you run this code, you'll get the following output:

```
count    278675.000000
mean         15.422596
std          16.258732
min           1.000000
33%           5.000000
50%          10.000000
66%          16.000000
max          74.000000
Name: reviewText, dtype: float64
```

Following the results, we will use 5 and 15 as our bucket boundaries. In other words, reviews are classified according to the following logic:

- Review length in [0, 5) are short reviews.
- Review length in [5, 15) are medium reviews.
- Review length in [15, inf) are long reviews.

The last two subsections conclude our analysis to find the vocabulary size and sequence length. The outputs presented here provided all the information to pick our hyperparameters with a principled mind-set.

9.2.4   *Text to words and then to numbers with Keras*

We have a clean, processed corpus of text as well as the vocabulary size and sequence length parameters we'll use later. Our next task is to convert text to numbers. There are two standard steps in converting text to numbers:

1 Split text to tokens (e.g., characters/words/sentences).
2 Create a dictionary that maps each unique token to a unique ID.

For example, if you have the sentence

```
the cat sat on the mat
```

we will first tokenize this into words, resulting in

```
[the, cat, sat, on, the, mat]
```

and have the dictionary

```
{the: 1, cat: 2, sat: 3, on: 4, mat: 5}
```

Then you can create the following sequence to represent the original text:

```
[1,2,3,4,1,5]
```

The Keras `Tokenizer` object supports exactly this functionality. It takes a corpus of text, tokenizes it with some user-defined parameters, builds the dictionary automatically, and saves it as a state. This way, you can use the `Tokenizer` to convert any arbitrary text as many times as you like to numbers. Let's look at how we can do this using the Keras `Tokenizer`:

```
from tensorflow.keras.preprocessing.text import Tokenizer

tokenizer = Tokenizer(
    num_words=n_vocab,
    oov_token='unk',
    lower=False,
    filters='!"#$%&()*+,-./:;<=>?@[\\]^_`{|}~\t\n',
    split=' ',
    char_level=False
)
```

You can see there are several arguments passed to the Tokenizer. Let's look at these arguments in a bit more detail:

- num_words—This defines the vocabulary size to limit the size of the dictionary. If num_words is set to 1,000, it will consider the most common 1,000 words in the corpus and assign them unique IDs.
- oov_token—This argument treats the words that fall outside the defined vocabulary size. The words that appear in the corpus but are not captured within the most common num_words words will be replaced with this token.
- lower—This determines whether to perform case lowering on the text. Since we have already done that, we will set it to False.
- filter—This defines any character(s) you want removed from the text before tokenizing.
- split—This is the separator character that will be used to tokenize your text. We want individual words to be tokens; therefore, we will use space, as words are usually separated by a space.
- char_level—This indicates whether to perform character-level tokenization (i.e., each character is a token).

Before we move forward, let's remind ourselves what our data looks like in the current state. Remember that we have

- Cleaned data
- Preprocessed data
- Split each review into individual words

By the end of this process, we have data as shown. First, we have the input, which is a pd.Series object that contains the list of clean words. The number in front of the text is the index of that record in the pd.Series object:

```
122143     [work, perfectly, wii, gamecube, issue, compat...
444818     [loved, game, collectible, come, well, make, m...
79331      ['s, okay, game, honest, bad, type, game, --, ...
97250                      [excellent, product, describe]
324411        [level, detail, great, feel, love, car, game]
...
34481      [not, actually, believe, write, review, produc...
258474     [good, game, us, like, movie, franchise, hard,...
466203     [fun, first, person, shooter, nice, combinatio...
414288                       [love, amiibo, classic, color]
162670     [fan, halo, series, start, enjoy, game, overal...
Name: reviewText, dtype: object
```

Next, we have the labels, where each label is a binary label to indicate whether the review is a positive review or a negative review:

```
122143     1
444818     1
79331      0
```

```
97250      1
324411     1
...
34481      1
258474     1
466203     1
414288     1
162670     0
Name: label, dtype: int64
```

In a way, that first step of tokenizing the text has already happened. The Keras `Tokenizer` is smart enough to skip that step if it has already happened. To build the dictionary of the `Tokenizer`, you can call the `tf.keras.preprocessing.text.Tokenizer` `.fit_on_texts()` function, as shown:

```
tokenizer.fit_on_texts(tr_x.tolist())
```

The `fit_on_texts()` function accepts a list of strings, where each string is a single entity of what you're processing (e.g., a sentence, a review, a paragraph, etc.) or a list of lists of tokens, where a token can be a word, a character, or even a sentence. As you fit the `Tokenizer` on some text, you can inspect some of the internal state variables. You can check the word to ID mapping using

```
tokenizer.word_index["game"]
```

which will return

```
2
```

You also can check the ID to word mapping (i.e., the reverse operation of mapping a word to an ID) using

```
tokenizer.index_word[4]
```

which will return

```
"play"
```

To convert a text corpus to a sequences of indices, you can use the `texts_to_sequences()` function. It takes a list of lists of tokens and returns a list of lists of IDs:

```
tr_x = tokenizer.texts_to_sequences(tr_x.tolist())
v_x = tokenizer.texts_to_sequences(v_x.tolist())
ts_x = tokenizer.texts_to_sequences(ts_x.tolist())
```

Let's see some of the results of the `text_to_sequences()` function that converted some samples:

```
Text: ['work', 'perfectly', 'wii', 'gamecube', 'issue', 'compatibility',
➥ 'loss', 'memory']
Sequence: [14, 295, 83, 572, 121, 1974, 2223, 345]
```

```
Text: ['loved', 'game', 'collectible', 'come', 'well', 'make', 'mask',
 ⟹ 'big', 'almost', 'fit', 'face', 'impressive']
Sequence: [1592, 2, 2031, 32, 23, 16, 2345, 153, 200, 155, 599, 1133]

Text: ["'s", 'okay', 'game', 'honest', 'bad', 'type', 'game', '--', "'s",
 ⟹ 'difficult', 'always', 'die', 'depresses', 'maybe', 'skill', 'would',
 ⟹ 'enjoy', 'game']
Sequence: [5, 574, 2, 1264, 105, 197, 2, 112, 5, 274, 150, 354, 1, 290,
 ⟹ 400, 19, 67, 2]

Text: ['excellent', 'product', 'describe']
Sequence: [109, 55, 501]

Text: ['level', 'detail', 'great', 'feel', 'love', 'car', 'game']
Sequence: [60, 419, 8, 42, 13, 265, 2]
```

Great! We can see that text is converted to ID sequences perfectly. We will now proceed to defining the TensorFlow pipeline using the data returned by the Keras `Tokenizer`.

EXERCISE 2

Given the string s, "a_b_B_c_d_a_D_b_d_d", can you define a tokenizer, `tok`, that lowers the text, splits by the underscore character "_", has a vocabulary size of 3, and fits the `Tokenizer` on s. If the `Tokenizer` ignores the out-of-vocabulary index words starting from 1, what would be the output if you call `tok.texts_to_sequences([s])`?

9.3 *Defining an end-to-end NLP pipeline with TensorFlow*

You have defined a clean data set that is in the numerical format the model expects it to be in. Here, we will define a TensorFlow data set pipeline to produce batches of data from the data we have defined. In the data pipeline, you will generate a batch of data, where the batch consists of a tuple `(x, y)`. `x` represents a batch of text sequences, where each text sequence is an arbitrarily long sequence of token IDs. `y` is a batch of labels corresponding to the text sequences in the batch. When generating a batch of examples, first the text sequences are assigned to buckets depending on the sequence length. Each bucket has a predefined allowed sequence length interval. Examples in a batch consist only of examples in the same bucket.

We are now in a great position. We have done quite a lot of preprocessing on the data and have converted text to machine readable numbers. In the next step, we will build a `tf.data` pipeline to convert the output of the `Tokenizer` to a model-friendly output.

As the first step, we are going to concatenate the target label (having a value of 0/1) to the input. This way, we can shuffle the data in any way we want and still preserve the relationship between inputs and the target label:

```
data_seq = [[b]+a for a,b in zip(text_seq, labels) ]
```

Next, we will create a special type of `tf.Tensor` object known as a *ragged tensor* (i.e., `tf.RaggedTensor`). In a standard tensor, you have fixed dimensions. For example, if you define a 3 × 4–sized tensor, every single row needs to have four columns (i.e., four values). Ragged tensors are a special type of tensor that supports variable-sized tensors. For example, it is perfectly fine to have data like this as a ragged tensor:

```
[
  [1,2],
  [3,2,5,9,10],
  [3,2,3]
]
```

This tensor has three rows, where the first row has two values, the second five values, and the final row three values. In other words, it has a variable second dimension. This is a perfect data structure for our problem because each review has a different number of words, leading to variable-sized ID sequences corresponding to each review:

```
max_length = 50
tf_data = tf.ragged.constant(data_seq)[:,:max_length]
```

Primer on tf.RaggedTensor

`tf.RaggedTensor` objects are a special type of tensor that can have variable-sized dimensions. You can read more about ragged tensors at http://mng.bz/5QZ8. There are many ways to define a ragged tensor.

We can define a ragged tensor by passing a nested list containing values to the `tf.ragged.constant()` function:

```
a = tf.ragged.constant([[1, 2, 3], [1,2], [1]])
```

You can also define a flat sequence of values and define where to split the rows:

```
b = tf.RaggedTensor.from_row_splits([1,2,3,4,5,6,7], row_splits=[0, 3,
    3, 6, 7])
```

Here, each value in the `row_splits` argument defines where subsequent rows in the resulting tensor end. For example, the first row will contain elements from index 0 to 3 (i.e., 0, 1, 2). This will output

```
<tf.RaggedTensor [[1, 2, 3], [], [4, 5, 6], [7]]>
```

You can get the shape of the tensor using `b.shape`, which will return

```
[4, None]
```

You can even have multidimensional ragged tensors, where you have more than one variable-sized dimension as follows:

```
c = tf.RaggedTensor.from_nested_row_splits(
    flat_values=[1,2,3,4,5,6,7,8,9],
    nested_row_splits=([0,2,3],[0,4,6,9]))
```

Here, the `nested_row_splits` is a list of 1D tensors, where the ith tensor represents the row split for the ith dimension. c will look as follows:

```
<tf.RaggedTensor [[[1, 2, 3, 4], [5, 6]], [[7, 8, 9]]]>
```

You can perform slicing and indexing on ragged tensors, similar to how you do on normal tensors:

```
print(c[:1, :, :])
```

This will return

```
<tf.RaggedTensor [[[1, 2, 3, 4], [5, 6]]]>
```

where

```
print(c[:,:1,:])
```

This will return

```
<tf.RaggedTensor [[[1, 2, 3, 4]], [[7, 8, 9]]]>
```

Finally, with

```
print(c[:, :, :2])
```

you will get

```
<tf.RaggedTensor [[[1, 2], [5, 6]], [[7, 8]]]>
```

We will limit the maximum length of the reviews to `max_length`. This is done under the assumption that `max_length` words are adequate to capture the sentiment in a given review. This way, we can avoid final data being excessively long because of one or two extremely long comments present in the data. The higher the `max_length`, the better, in terms of capturing the information in the review. But a higher `max_length` value comes with a hefty price tag in terms of required computational power:

```
text_ds = tf.data.Dataset.from_tensor_slices(tf_data)
```

We will create a data set using the `tf.data.Dataset.from_tensor_slices()` function. This function on the ragged tensor, which we just created, will extract one row (i.e., a single review) at a time. It's important to remember that each row will have a different size. We will filter any reviews that are empty. You could do this using the `tf.data.Dataset.filter()` function:

```
text_ds = text_ds.filter(lambda x: tf.size(x)>1)
```

Essentially, we are saying here that any review that has a size smaller than or equal to 1 will be discarded. Remember that each record will have at least a single element (which is the label). This is an important step because having empty reviews can cause problems in the model down the track.

Next, we will address an extremely important step and the highlight of our impressive data pipeline. In sequence processing, you might have heard the term *bucketing* (or *binning*). Bucketing refers to, when batching data, using similar-sized inputs. In other words, a single batch of data includes similar-sized reviews and will not have reviews with drastically different lengths in the same batch. The following sidebar explains the process of bucketing in more detail.

Bucketing: Similar length sequences stick together!

Let's look at an example. Assume that you have a list of reviews, [r1(5), r2(11), r3(6), r4(4), r5(15), r6(18), r7(25), r8(29), r9(30)], where the code `rx` represents the review ID and the number within brackets represents the number of words in the review. If you select a batch size of 3, it makes sense to batch data the following way:

```
[r1, r3, r4]
[r2, r5, r6]
[r7, r8, r9]
```

You can see that the similar-length reviews are batched together. This is implemented practically by a process known as bucketing. First, we create several buckets with predefined boundaries. For instance, in our example, there can be three buckets with the following intervals:

```
[[0,11), [11, 21), [21, inf))
```

Then, depending on the length of the review, each review is assigned to a bucket. Finally, when getting batches of data, a batch (randomly sampled) from a single bucket at random is selected.

After identifying the buckets, we have to batch the data so that we end up with a fixed-sequence length. This is achieved by padding zeros to the end until we have all sequences in that batch with equal lengths. Let's assume the reviews r1, r3, and r4 have the following word ID sequences:

```
[10, 12, 48, 21,  5]
[ 1, 93, 28,  8, 20, 10]
[32, 20,  1,  2]
```

To batch these sequences, we will pad zeros to the end of short sequences, resulting in

```
[10, 12, 48, 21,  5,  0]
[ 1, 93, 28,  8, 20, 10]
[32, 20,  1,  2,  0,  0]
```

You can see that now we have a batch of data with fixed-sequence lengths that can be converted to a `tf.Tensor`.

Fortunately, all we need to worry about in order to use bucketing is understanding the syntax of a convenient TensorFlow function that is already provided: `tf.data` `.experimental.bucket_by_sequence_length()`. The experimental namespace is a special namespace allocated for TensorFlow functionality that has not been fully tested. In other words, there might be edge cases where these functions might fail. Once the functionality is well tested, these cases will move out of the experimental namespace into a stable one. Note that this function returns another function that performs the bucketing on a data set. Therefore, you have to use this function in conjunction with `tf.data.Dataset.apply()` in order to execute the returned function. The syntax can be slightly cryptic at first glance. But things will be clearer when we take a deeper look at the arguments. You can see that we're using the bucket boundaries we identified earlier when analyzing the sequence lengths of the reviews:

```
bucket_boundaries=[5,15]
batch_size = 64
bucket_fn = tf.data.experimental.bucket_by_sequence_length(
        element_length_func = lambda x: tf.cast(tf.shape(x)[0],'int32'),
        bucket_boundaries=bucket_boundaries,
        bucket_batch_sizes=[batch_size,batch_size,batch_size],
        padding_values=0,
        pad_to_bucket_boundary=False
    )
```

Let's examine the arguments provided to this function:

- `elment_length_func`—This is at the heart of the bucketing function as it tells the function how to compute the length of a single record or instance coming in. Without the length of the record, bucketing is impossible.
- `bucket_boundaries`—Defines the upper bound of bucket boundaries. This argument accepts a list of values in increasing order. If you provided `bucket_bounderies` [x, y, z], where x < y < z, then the bucket intervals would be [0, x), [x, y), [y, z), [z, inf).
- `bucket_batch_sizes`—Batch size for each bucket. You can see that we have defined the same batch size for all the buckets. But you can also use other strategies, such as higher batch size for shorter sequences.
- `padded_values`—This defines, when bringing sequences to the same length, what to pad the short sequences with. Padding with zero is a very common method. We will stick with that.
- `pad_to_bucket_boundary`—This is a special Boolean argument that will decide the final size of the variable dimension of each batch. For example, assume you have a bucket with the interval [0, 11) and a batch of sequences with lengths [4, 8, 5]. If `pad_to_bucket_boundary=True`, the final batch will have the variable dimension of 10, which means every sequence is padded to the maximum limit. If `pad_to_bucket_boundary=False`, you'll have the variable dimension of 8 (i.e., the length of the longest sequence in the batch).

Remember that we had a `tf.RaggedTensor` initially fed to the `tf.data.Dataset` `.from_tensor_slices` function. When returning slices, it will return slices with the same data type. Unfortunately, `tf.RaggedTensor` objects are not compatible with the bucketing function. Therefore, we perform the following hack to convert slices back to `tf.Tensor` objects. We simply call the map function with the lambda function `lambda x: x`. With that, you can call the `tf.data.Dataset.apply()` function with the `bucket_fn` as the argument:

```
text_ds = text_ds.map(lambda x: x).apply(bucket_fn)
```

At this point, we have done all the hard work. By now, you have implemented the functionality to accept a data set with arbitrary length sequences and to sample a batch of sequences from that using the bucketing strategy. The bucketing/binning strategy used here makes sure that we don't group sequences with large differences in their lengths, which will lead to excessive padding.

As we have done many times, let's shuffle the data to make sure we observe enough randomness during the training phase:

```
if shuffle:
    text_ds = text_ds.shuffle(buffer_size=10*batch_size)
```

Remember that we combined the target label and the input to ensure correspondence between inputs and targets. Now we can safely split the target and input into two separate tensors using tensor slicing syntax as shown:

```
text_ds = text_ds.map(lambda x: (x[:,1:], x[:,0]))
```

Now we can let out a sigh of relief. We have completed all the steps of the journey from raw unclean text to clean semi-structured text that can be consumed by our model. Let's wrap this in a function called `get_tf_pipeline()`, which takes a `text_seq` (list of lists of word IDs), `labels` (list of integers), `batch_size` (int), `bucket_boundaries` (list of ints), `max_length` (int), and `shuffle` (Boolean) arguments (see the following listing).

Listing 9.4 The `tf.data` pipeline

```
def get_tf_pipeline(
    text_seq, labels, batch_size=64, bucket_boundaries=[5,15],
    max_length=50, shuffle=False
):
    """ Define a data pipeline that converts sequences to batches of data """

    data_seq = [[b]+a for a,b in zip(text_seq, labels) ]          ◁──┐ Concatenate the
                                                                       label and the input
    tf_data = tf.ragged.constant(data_seq)[:,:max_length]            sequence so that
                                                                       we don't mess up
    Define the variable sequence                                      the order when
    data set as a ragged tensor.                                      we shuffle.
```

```
text_ds = tf.data.Dataset.from_tensor_slices(tf_data)
```
Create a data set out of the ragged tensor.

```
bucket_fn = tf.data.experimental.bucket_by_sequence_length(
    lambda x: tf.cast(tf.shape(x)[0],'int32'),
    bucket_boundaries=bucket_boundaries,
    bucket_batch_sizes=[batch_size,batch_size,batch_size],
    padded_shapes=None,
    padding_values=0,
    pad_to_bucket_boundary=False
)
```
Bucket the data (assign each sequence to a bucket depending on the length).

For example, for bucket boundaries [5, 15], you get buckets [0, 5], [5, 15], [15,inf].

```
text_ds = text_ds.map(lambda x: x).apply(bucket_fn)
```
Apply bucketing.

Shuffle the data.
```
if shuffle:
    text_ds = text_ds.shuffle(buffer_size=10*batch_size)
```

```
text_ds = text_ds.map(lambda x: (x[:,1:], x[:,0]))

return text_ds
```
Split the data to inputs and labels.

It's been a long journey. Let's reflect on what we have done so far. With the data pipeline done and dusted, let's learn about the models that can consume this type of sequential data. Next, we will define the sentiment analyzer model that we've been waiting to implement.

EXERCISE 3

If you want have the buckets (0, 10], (10, 25], (25, 50], [50, inf) and always return padded to the boundary of the bucket, how would you modify this bucketing function? Note that the number of buckets has changed from the number we have in the text.

9.4 *Happy reviews mean happy customers: Sentiment analysis*

Imagine you have converted the reviews to numbers and defined a data pipeline that generates batches of inputs and labels. Now it's time to crunch them using a model to train a model that can accurately identify sentiments in a posted review. You have heard that long short-term memory models (LSTMs) are a great starting point for processing textual data. The goal is to implement a model based on LSTMs that produces one of two possible outcomes for a given review: a negative or a positive sentiment.

If you have reached this point, you should be happy. You have ploughed through a lot. Now it's time to reward yourself with information about a compelling family of models known as deep sequential models. Some example models of this family are as follows:

- Simple recurrent neural networks (RNNs)
- Long short-term memory (LSTM) networks
- Gated recurrent units (GRUs)

9.4.1   LSTM Networks

Previously we discussed a simple recurrent neural network and its application in predicting CO2 concentration levels in the future. In this chapter, we will look at the mechanics of LSTM networks. LSTMs models were very popular for almost a decade. They are a great choice for processing sequential data and typically have three important dimensions:

- A batch dimension
- A time dimension
- A feature dimension

If you think about the data returned by the NLP pipeline we discussed, it has all these dimensions. The batch dimension is represented by each different review sampled into that batch. The time dimension is represented by the sequence of word IDs appearing in a single review. Finally, you can think of feature dimension being 1, as a single feature is represented by a single numerical value (i.e., an ID; see figure 9.2). The feature dimension has values corresponding to features on that dimension. For example, if you have a weather model that has three features (e.g., temperature, precipitation, wind speed), the input to the model would be [<batch size>, <sequence length>, 3]–sized input.

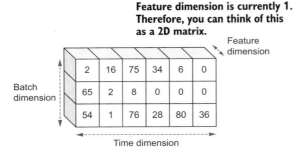

Figure 9.2   3D view of sequential data. Typically, sequential data is found with three dimensions; batch size, sequence/time, and feature.

The LSTM takes an input with the three dimensions discussed. Let's zoom in a bit more to see how an LSTM operates on such data. To keep the discussion simple, assume a batch size of 1 or a single review. If we assume a single review r that has n words it can be written as

$$r = w_1, w_2, \ldots, w_t, \ldots, w_n,$$ where w_t represents the ID of the word in the tth position.

At time step t, the LSTM model starts with

- The previous output state vector h_{t-1}
- The previous cell state vector c_{t-1}

and computes

- The current cell state c_t using the current input w_t and the previous cell state c_{t-1} and output state h_{t-1} and
- The current output state h_t using the current input w_t and the previous state h_{t-1} and the current cell state c_t

This way, the model keeps iterating over all the timesteps (in our example, it's word IDs in the sequence) until it reaches the end. While iterating this way, the model keeps producing a cell state and an output state (figure 9.3).

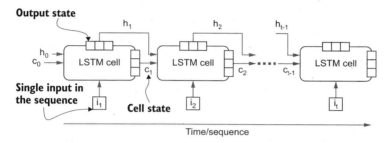

Figure 9.3 High-level longitudinal view of an LSTM cell. At a given time step t, the LSTM cell takes in two previous states (h_{t-1} and c_{t-1}), along with the input, and produces two states (h_t and c_t).

With a good high-level understanding of the LSTM cell, let's look at the equations that are cranking the gears of this model. The LSTM takes three inputs:

- x_t—The input at timestep t
- h_{t-1}—The output state at timestep $t–1$
- c_{t-1}—The cell state at timestep $t–1$

With that, the LSTM produces two outputs:

- (c_t)—The cell state at timestep t
- (h_t)—The output state at timestep t

To produce these outputs, the LSTM model leverages a gating mechanism. These gates determine how much information flows through them to the next stage of computations. The LSTM cell has three gates:

- *An input gate* (i_t)—Determines how much of the current input will affect the subsequent computations
- *A forget gate* (f_t)—Determines how much of the previous cell state is discarded when computing the new cell state
- *An output gate* (o_t)—Determines how much of the current cell state contributes to the final output

These gates are made of trainable weights. This means that when training an LSTM model on a certain task, the gating mechanism will be jointly optimized to produce the optimal flow of information required to solve that task.

What carries long-term and short-term memories in LSTMs?

The cell state preserves the long-term information and relationships as the model progresses through the input over the time dimension. In fact, it has been found that LSTMs can remember up to hundreds of timesteps when learning time-series problems.

On the other hand, the output state can be thought as the short-term memory where it will look at the input, the long-term memory stored in the cell state, and decide the optimal amount of information required at that stage of the computation.

You might still be wondering, "What is this gating mechanism actually achieving?" Let me illustrate that with a sentence. To solve almost all NLP tasks, capturing syntactic and semantic information as well parsing dependencies correctly in a given text input is imperative. Let's see how an LSTM can help us to achieve that. Assume you've been given the sentence:

the dog ran after the green ball and it got tired and barked at a plane

In your mind, picture an LSTM model hopping from one word to another, processing them. Then assume you query the model for answers to questions at various stages of processing the sentence. Say you ask the question "Who ran?" while it's processing the phrase "the dog ran." The model will probably have its input gate widely open to absorb as much information as the model can, because the model starts with no prior knowledge about what language looks like. And if you think about it, the model does not really need to pay attention to its memory because the answer is one word away from the word "ran."

Next, you ask "Who got tired?" When processing "it got tired," the model might want to tap into its cell state instead of focusing on the input, as the only clue in this phrase is "it." If the model is to identify the relationship between it and dog, it will need to close the input gate slightly and open the forget gate so that more information flows from the past memory (about the dog) into the current memory.

Finally, let's say you ask "What was barked at?" by the time the model reaches the "barked at a plane" section. To produce the final output, you don't need much information from past memory, so you might tighten the output gate to avoid too much information coming from the past memory. I hope these walkthroughs were useful in order to grok the purpose of these gates. Remember that this is just an analogy to understand the purpose of these gates. But in practice, the actual behavior can differ. It is also worth noticing that these gates are not binary; rather, the output of the gate is controlled by a sigmoidal function, meaning that it leads to a soft open/close state at a given time rather than a hard open/close state.

To complete our discussion, let's inspect the equations that drive the computations in an LSTM cell. But you don't have to memorize or understand these equations in detail, as it's not a requirement to use LSTMs. But to make our discussion holistic, let's look at them. The first computation computes the input gate:

$$i_t = \sigma(W_{ih}h_{t-1} + W_{ix}x_t + b_f)$$

Here, W_{ih} and W_{ix} are trainable weights that produce the gate value, where b_i is the bias. The computations here closely resemble the computations of a fully connected layer. This gate results in a vector for a given input whose values are between 0 and 1. You can see its resemblance to a gate (assuming 0 means closed and 1 means open). The rest of the gates follow a similar pattern of computations. The forget gate is computed as

$$f_t = \sigma(W_{fh}h_{t-1} + W_{fx}x_t + b_f)$$

Then the cell state is computed. Cell state is computed from a two-fold computation:

$$\tilde{C}_t = \tanh(W_{ch}h_{t-1} + W_{cx}x_t = b_c)$$

$$c_t = f_t h_{t-1} + i_t\tilde{C}_t$$

The computation is quite intuitive. It uses the forget gate to control the previous cell state, where it uses the input gate to control $\tilde{C}_t$ computed using x_t (the current input). Finally, the output gate and the state are computed as

$$o_t = \sigma(W_{oh}h_{t-1} + W_{ox}x_t + b_0)$$

$$h_t = o_t tanh(c_t)$$

Here, c_t is computed using the inputs controlled via the forget gate and the input gate. Therefore, in a way, o_t gets to control how much the current input, the current cell state, the previous cell state, and the previous output state contribute to the final state output of the LSTM cell. In TensorFlow and Keras, you can define an LSTM with

```
import tensorflow as tf
tf.keras.layers.LSTM(units=128, return_state=False, return_sequences=False)
```

The first argument units is a hyperparameter of the LSTM layer. Similar to how the number of units defines the output size of a fully connected layer, the units argument defines the output, state, and gate vector dimensionality. The higher this number, the more representative power the model possesses. Next, the return_state=False means only the output state will be returned when the layer is called on an input. If return_state=True, both the cell state and the output state are returned. Finally, `return_sequences=False` means that only the final state(s) after processing the whole sequence is returned. If `return_sequences=True`, all the state(s) returned during processing every element in the sequence are returned. Figure 9.4 depicts the differences in these arguments' results.

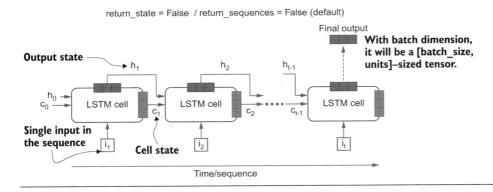

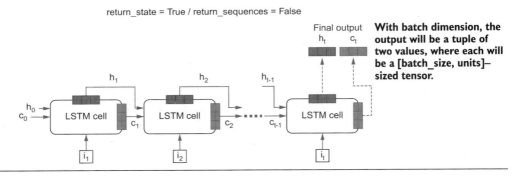

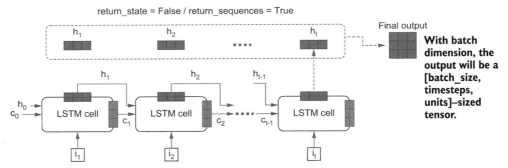

Figure 9.4 The changes to the output of the LSTM layer resulted in changes to the `return_state` and `return_sequences` arguments.

Next, let's define the final model.

9.4.2   *Defining the final model*

We will define the final model using the Sequential API. Our model will have the following layers (figure 9.5):

- *A masking layer*—This layer plays an important role in which input elements in the sequence will contribute to the training. We will learn more about this soon.
- *A one-hot encoding layer*—This layer will convert the word IDs to one-hot encoded sequences. This is an important transformation we have to perform before feeding our inputs to the model.
- *An LSTM layer*—The LSTM layer will return the final output state as the output.
- *A* Dense *layer with 512 nodes (ReLU activation)*—A Dense layer takes the output of the LSTM cell and produces an interim hidden output.
- *A* Dropout *layer*—Dropout is a regularization technique that randomly switches outputs during the training process. We discussed the purpose of Dropout and how it works in chapter 7.
- *A final output layer with a single node (sigmoid activation)*—Note that we only need a single node to represent the output. If the value of the output is 0, it's a negative sentiment. If the value is 1, it's a positive sentiment.

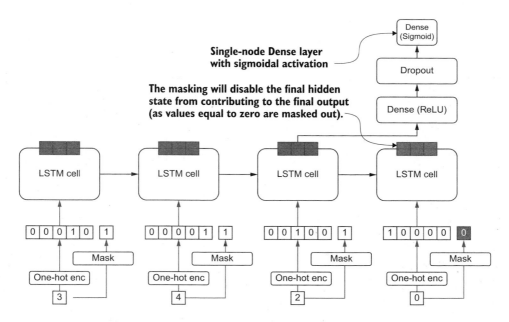

Figure 9.5   The high-level model architecture of the sentiment analyzer

Our tf.data pipeline produces a [<batch size>, <sequence length>]–shaped 2D tensor. In practice, they would both be None. In other words, it will be a [None, None]–sized tensor as we have to support variable-sized batches and variable-sized sequence lengths in our model. A dimension of size None means that the model can accept any sized tensor on that dimension. For example, with a [None, None] tensor, when actual data is retrieved, it can be a [5, 10]–, [12, 54]–, or [102, 14]–sized tensor. As the entry point to the model, we will use a reshaping layer wrapped in a lambda layer as follows:

```
tf.keras.layers.Lambda(lambda x: tf.expand_dims(x, axis=-1),
    input_shape=(None,)),
```

This layer takes our [None, None] input produced by the data pipeline and reshapes it to a [None, None, 1]–sized tensor. This reshaping is necessary for the next layer in line, making it a perfect opportunity to discuss the next layer. The next layer is a masking layer that serves a very special purpose. We have not seen a masking layer used in previous chapters. However, masking is commonly used in NLP problems. The need for masking arises from the padding operation we perform on the inputs during the bucketing of input sequences. In NLP data sets, you will seldom see text appearing with a fixed length. Typically, each text record has a different length. To batch these variable-sized text records together for the model, padding plays an essential role. Figure 9.6 illustrates what the data looks like after padding.

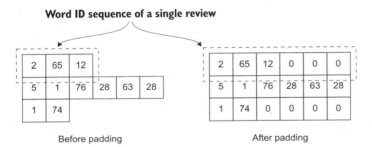

Figure 9.6   Text sequences before and after padding

But this introduces an extra burden. The values introduced by padding (typically zero) do not carry any information. Therefore, they should be ignored in any computation that happens in the model. For example, the LSTM model should halt processing and return that last state just before encountering padded values when padding is used in the input. The tf.keras.layers.Masking layer helps us to do exactly that. The input to the masking layer must be a [batch size, sequence length, feature dimension]–sized 3D tensor. This alludes to our last point about reshaping the output of our tf.data pipeline to a 3D tensor. In TensorFlow you define a mask as follows:

```
tf.keras.layers.Masking(mask_value=0)
```

The masking layer creates a special mask, and this mask is propagated to the subsequent layers in the model. Layers like the LSTM layer know what to do if a mask is passed from a layer below. More specifically, the LSTM model will output its state values just before it encountered zeros (if a mask is provided). It is also worth paying attention to the `input_shape` argument. The input to our model will be a two-dimensional tensor: an arbitrary-sized batch with an arbitrary-sized sequence length (due to bucketing). Therefore, we cannot specify a sequence length in the `input_shape` argument, so the model expects a (None, None, 1)–sized tensor as the input (the extra None is added automatically to represent the batch dimension).

With the mask defined, we will convert the word IDs to one-hot vectors using a custom layer. This is an essential step before feeding data to the LSTM. This can be achieved as follows:

```
class OnehotEncoder(tf.keras.layers.Layer):
    def __init__(self, depth, **kwargs):
        super(OnehotEncoder, self).__init__(**kwargs)
        self.depth = depth


    def build(self, input_shape):
        pass


    def call(self, inputs):

        inputs = tf.cast(inputs, 'int32')

        if len(inputs.shape) == 3:
            inputs = inputs[:,:,0]

        return tf.one_hot(inputs, depth=self.depth)


    def compute_mask(self, inputs, mask=None):
        return mask


    def get_config(self):
        config = super().get_config().copy()
        config.update({'depth': self.depth})
        return config
```

Then call it with

```
OnehotEncoder(depth=n_vocab),
```

The layer is a mouthful, so let's break it down. First you define a user-defined parameter called `depth`. This defines the feature dimension of the final result. Next, you have to define the `call()` function. The `call()` function takes in the inputs, casts them to `'int32'`, and then removes the final dimension if the input is three-dimensional. This is because the masking layer we defined has a dimension of size 1 to represent the feature dimension. This dimension is not understood by the `tf.one_hot()` function that we use to generate one-hot encoded vectors. Therefore, it must be removed. Finally, we return the result of the `tf.one_hot()` function. Remember to provide the depth parameter when using `tf.one_hot()`. If it is not provided, TensorFlow tries to automatically infer the value, which leads to inconsistently sized tensors between different batches. We define the `compute_mask()` function to make sure we propagate the mask to the next layer. The layer simply takes the mask and passes it to the next layer. Finally, we define a `get_config()` function to update the parameters in that layer. It is essential for config to return the correct set of parameters; otherwise, you will run into problems saving the model. We define the LSTM layer as the next layer of the model:

```
tf.keras.layers.LSTM(units=128, return_state=False, return_sequences=False)
```

More about propagating masks within models

It is important to remember a few things when using a masking layer. First, it is better to avoid using lambda layers in your model when using masking. This is because there have been several issues raised when using masking in conjunction with lambda layers (e.g., https://github.com/tensorflow/tensorflow/issues/40085). The best option is to write a custom layer as we have done. After defining a custom layer, you have to override the `compute_mask()` function to return the mask (with modifications, if required) for the next layer.

We have to be extra careful here. Depending on the arguments you provide when defining this layer, you will get vastly different outputs. To define our sentiment analyzer, we only want the final output state of the model. This means we're not interested in the cell state, nor all the output states computed during processing the sequence. Therefore, we have to set the arguments accordingly. According to our requirements, we must set `return_state=False` and `return_sequences=False`. Finally, the final state output goes to a `Dense` layer with 512 units and ReLU activation:

```
tf.keras.layers.Dense(512, activation='relu'),
```

The dense layer is followed by a `Dropout` layer that will drop 50% of the inputs of the previous `Dense` layer during training.

```
tf.keras.layers.Dropout(0.5)
```

Finally, the model is crowned with a `Dense` layer having a single unit and sigmoidal activation, which will produce the final prediction. If the produced value is less than 0.5, it is considered label 0 and 1 otherwise:

```
tf.keras.layers.Dense(1, activation='sigmoid')
```

We can define the full model as shown in the next listing.

Listing 9.5 Implementation of the full sentiment analysis model

After creating the mask, convert
inputs to one-hot encoded inputs.

```
model = tf.keras.models.Sequential([                          Create a mask to mask
                                                              out zero inputs.
    tf.keras.layers.Masking(mask_value=0.0, input_shape=(None,1)),
    OnehotEncoder(depth=n_vocab),
    tf.keras.layers.LSTM(128, return_state=False, return_sequences=False),
    tf.keras.layers.Dense(512, activation='relu'),
    tf.keras.layers.Dropout(0.5),
    tf.keras.layers.Dense(1, activation='sigmoid')
])
```

Define an LSTM
layer that returns
the last state
output vector
(from unmasked
inputs).

**Define a Dropout layer
with 50% dropout.**

**Define a final
prediction layer
with a single node
and sigmoidal
activation.**

**Define a Dense layer
with ReLU activation.**

Next, we're off to compiling the model. Again, we have to be careful about the loss function we will be using. So far, we have used the `categorical_crossentropy` loss. This loss is used for multiclass classification problems (greater than two classes). Since we're solving a binary classification problem, we must switch to `binary_crossentropy` instead. Using the wrong loss function can lead to numerical instabilities and inaccurately trained models:

```
model.compile(loss='binary_crossentropy', optimizer='adam',
    metrics=['accuracy'])
```

Finally, let's examine the model by printing out the summary by running `model.summary()`:

```
Model: "sequential"
```

Layer (type)	Output Shape	Param #
masking (Masking)	(None, None)	0
lambda (Lambda)	(None, None, 11865)	0
lstm (LSTM)	(None, 128)	6140928
dense (Dense)	(None, 512)	66048
dropout (Dropout)	(None, 512)	0
dense_1 (Dense)	(None, 1)	513

```
Total params: 6,207,489
Trainable params: 6,207,489
Non-trainable params: 0
```

This is our first encounter with a sequential model. Let's review the model summary in more detail. First, we have a masking layer that returns an output of the same size as the input (i.e., [None, None]–sized tensor). Then a one-hot encoding layer returns a tensor with a feature dimension of 11865 (which is the vocabulary size). This is because, unlike the input that had a word represented by a single integer, one-hot encoding converts it to a vector of zeros, of the size of the vocabulary, and sets the value indexed by the word ID to 1. The LSTM layer returns a [None, 128]–sized tensor. Remember that we are only getting the final state output vector, which will be a [None, 128]–sized tensor, where 128 is the number of units. This last output returned by the LSTM goes to a Dense layer with 512 nodes and ReLU activation. A dropout layer with 50% dropout follows it. Finally, a Dense layer with one node produces the final prediction: a value between 0 and 1.

In the following section, we will train the model on training data and evaluate it on validation and testing data to assess the performance of the model.

EXERCISE 4

Define a model that has a single LSTM layer and a single Dense layer. The LSTM model has 32 units and accepts a (None, None, 30)-sized input (this includes the batch dimension) and produces all the state outputs (instead of the final one). Next, a lambda layer should sum up the states on the time dimension to produce a (None, 32)-sized output. This output goes to the Dense layer with 10 nodes and softmax activation. You can use the tf.keras.layers.Add layer to sum up the state vectors. You will need to use the functional API to implement this.

9.5   *Training and evaluating the model*

We're all set to train the model we just defined. As the first step, let's define two pipelines: one for the training data and one for the validation data. Remember that we split our data and created three different sets: training (tr_x and tr_y), validation (v_x and v_y), and testing (ts_x and ts_y). We will use a batch size of 128:

```
# Using a batch size of 128
batch_size =128

train_ds = get_tf_pipeline(tr_x, tr_y, batch_size=batch_size, shuffle=True)
valid_ds = get_tf_pipeline(v_x, v_y, batch_size=batch_size)
```

Then comes a very important calculation. In fact, doing or not doing this computation can decided whether your model is going to work or not. Remember that we noticed a significant class imbalance in our data set in section 9.1. Specifically, there are more positive classes than negative classes in the data set. Here we will define a weighing factor to assign a greater weight to negative samples when computing the loss and updating weights of the model. To do that, we will define the weighing factor:

$$weight_{neg} = count(positive\ samples)/count(negative\ samples)$$

This will result in a > 1 factor as there are more positive samples than negative samples. We can easily compute this using the following logic:

```
neg_weight = (tr_y==1).sum()/(tr_y==0).sum()
```

This results in $weight_{neg}$~6 (i.e., approximately 6). Next, we will define the training step as follows:

```
model.fit(
    x=train_ds,
    validation_data=valid_ds,
    epochs=10,
    class_weight={0:neg_weight, 1:1.0}
)
```

Here, `train_ds` is passed to `x`, but in fact contains both the inputs and targets. `valid_ds`, containing validation samples, is passed to `validation_data` argument. We will run this for 10 epochs. Finally, note that we are using the `class_weight` argument to tell the model that negative samples must be prioritized over positive samples (due to the under-representation in the data set). `class_weight` is defined as a dictionary, where the key is the class label and the value represents the weight given to the samples of that class. When passed, during the loss computations the losses resulting from negative classes will be multiplied by a factor of `neg_weight`, leading to more attention being given to negative samples during the optimization process. In practice, we are going to follow the same pattern as in other chapters and run the training process with three callbacks:

- A CSV logger
- A learning rate scheduler
- Early stopping

The full code looks like the following listing.

Listing 9.6 Training procedure for the sentiment analyzer

```
os.makedirs('eval', exist_ok=True)

csv_logger = tf.keras.callbacks.CSVLogger(          ◁─── Log the performance
        os.path.join('eval','1_sentiment_analysis.log'))      metrics to a CSV file.

monitor_metric = 'val_loss'
mode = 'min'
print("Using metric={} and mode={} for EarlyStopping".format(monitor_metric,
    mode))
                                                    The learning rate
                                                    reduction callback
lr_callback = tf.keras.callbacks.ReduceLROnPlateau(
    monitor=monitor_metric, factor=0.1, patience=3, mode=mode, min_lr=1e-8    ◁───
)
```

```
es_callback = tf.keras.callbacks.EarlyStopping(
    monitor=monitor_metric, patience=6, mode=mode, restore_best_weights=False
)
```

The early stopping callback

```
model.fit(
    train_ds,
    validation_data=valid_ds,
    epochs=10,
    class_weight={0:neg_weight, 1:1.0},
    callbacks=[es_callback, lr_callback, csv_logger])
```

Train the model.

You should get similar results:

```
Using metric=val_loss and mode=min for EarlyStopping
Epoch 1/10
2427/2427 [==============================] - 72s 30ms/step - loss: 0.7640 -
accuracy: 0.7976 - val_loss: 0.4061 - val_accuracy: 0.8193 - lr: 0.0010

...

Epoch 7/10
2427/2427 [==============================] - 73s 30ms/step - loss: 0.2752 -
accuracy: 0.9393 - val_loss: 0.7474 - val_accuracy: 0.8026 - lr: 1.0000e-04
Epoch 8/10
2427/2427 [==============================] - 74s 30ms/step - loss: 0.2576 -
accuracy: 0.9439 - val_loss: 0.8398 - val_accuracy: 0.8041 - lr: 1.0000e-04
```

It seems that by the end of the training, we have reached above 80% validation accuracy. That's great news, because we made sure that the validation data set is a balanced data set. But we can't be too sure. We will need to test our model on a data set that it hasn't had the chance to see: the testing set. Before that, let's save the model:

```
os.makedirs('models', exist_ok=True)
tf.keras.models.save_model(model, os.path.join('models',
    '1_sentiment_analysis.h5'))
```

We have already created the test data set and have defined the NLP pipeline to process the data, so it's a matter of calling the get_tf_pipeline() function with the data:

```
test_ds = get_tf_pipeline(ts_x, ts_y, batch_size=batch_size)
```

It's now as simple as calling the following one-liner to get the test performance of the model:

```
model.evaluate(test_ds)
```

The final result looks like this:

```
87/87 [==============================] - 2s 27ms/step - loss: 0.8678 -
accuracy: 0.8038
```

We can now go to sleep knowing our model's performance on unseen data is on par with the validation performance we saw during training.

Is good accuracy all we're after?

The short answer is no. Solving a machine learning task involves many tasks working in harmony. And during the execution of these tasks, we perform various transformations/computations on inputs as well as outputs. The complexity of the whole process means that there are more chances for things to go wrong. Therefore, we should check as many things as we can during the process.

Speaking solely about testing, we have to make sure that the test data is correctly processed while going through the data pipeline. Furthermore, we should check the final predictions. Among many other checks, you can check the topmost positive predictions and negative predictions to make sure the model's decisions are sensible. You can simply visually inspect the input text and the corresponding prediction. We will discuss the specifics in a coming section.

It will only slightly increase the time spent on your model. But it can save you hours of debugging as well as embarrassment or loss of reputation from releasing an inaccurate model.

In the next section, we will further enhance our model by using word vectors to represent tokens fed into the model. Word vectors help machine learning models understand language better.

EXERCISE 5

Assume you have three classes in your training data set: A, B and C. You have 10 records for A, 25 for B, and 50 for C. What do you think will be good weights for the three classes? Remember that the majority class should get a smaller weight.

9.6 *Injecting semantics with word vectors*

You have built a model that can measure sentiments with ~80% accuracy, but you want to improve further. You believe word embeddings will provide the edge required to attain a higher accuracy. Word embeddings are a way to encode words as a feature vector. Word embeddings learn feature vectors for the words in the vocabulary jointly with the model training. An embedding layer introduces a trainable matrix, where each row represents a trainable vector for a single word in the vocabulary. This is much better than one-hot encoding because one-hot encoding suffers from the curse of dimensionality, which means that as the number of words grows, so does the dimensionality of the inputs to the model.

You should feel proud about having a reasonable model that can accurately classify positive and negative sentiments; 80% accuracy is a great starting point. But let's see what we can improve in the already good model we have.

A bottleneck that's staring us right in the face is the one-hot encoding layer that's in our model. One-hot encoding, despite its simplicity, is a very inefficient representation of words. It is a localized representation of words, meaning only one element (set to value 1) in the representation carries information. In other words, it's a very sparse representation that has a very large number of elements set to zero and does not contribute with information. One-hot encoding also suffers from the curse of dimensionality. Finally, one-hot encoding completely disregards the valuable semantics present in the text. With one-hot encoding, you can't say if a cat is more similar to a dog than it is to a volcano. Now the question is, are there better ways to represent words?

9.6.1   *Word embeddings*

It's time to usher in a new era of word representations known as *word embeddings*. Word embeddings, sometimes called word vectors, are a very information-rich and efficient representation of words. As opposed to the localized representations like one-hot vectors, word vectors provide a distributed representation. This means that all the elements in the vector play a role in defining the word represented by the vector. In other words, word vectors have dense representations, in contrast to the sparse representation of one-hot vectors. The dimensionality of word vectors does not depend on the size of vocabulary, which allows you to save memory and computational time. Finally, but most importantly, word vectors capture the semantics or similarity of words. With word vectors, you know that a cat is more similar to a dog than to a volcano. Before understanding word vectors, you have to understand the important role played by the context around a word. Word vectors heavily rely on the context of words to generate rich representations of words. The importance of the context is subliminally captured by a famous quote by J.R. Firth, an English linguist:

> *You shall know a word by the company it keeps.*

To expand on this a little more, the context of a word plays an important role in defining the semantics of that word. For example, take the following sentence:

> Our pet Toby is a ____; he enjoys playing with a ball.

What do you think is the right word here? We see words like "pet," "playing," and "ball" in the context. Most likely it's a cat or a dog. This means that only a certain type of words (i.e., a type of pet) will appear in this context. Using this property, word vectors can generate vectors that preserve the semantics of the text. In this example, word vectors will capture that cats and dogs are very similar (not biologically, of course, but in the way we interact with or perceive them). In a more technical stance, the objective of word vector algorithms is as follows: if word w_i and w_j appear in the same context, for some distance measure $Dist(a,b)$, that measures the distance between two vectors a and b:

$$Dist(w_i, w_j) \sim 0$$

The actual word vector algorithms are out of scope for this book. A few note-worthy algorithms are Skip-gram, CBoW (Continuous Bag-of-Words), GloVe (global vectors) and ELMo (Embeddings from Language Models). You can read more details about the Skip-gram and CBoW algorithms by reading the paper "Efficient Estimation of Word Representations in Vector Space" by Tomas Mikolov et al. (https://arxiv.org/pdf/1301.3781.pdf).

Show me the word vector algorithms

Word vector algorithms train in an unsupervised manner. The training algorithm specifics will differ depending on the algorithm. The Skip-gram algorithm generates input target pairs by picking a probe word as the input and the context words as the targets. For example, from the sentence "I went to buy flowers" it will generate input target pairs such as [(went, I), (went, to), (to, went), (to, buy), . . .]. Then it will solve the classification task of predicting the context of a probe word, which will lead to identifying good word vectors. However, word vector algorithms like Skip-gram suffer from the lack of a global view of the corpus because the algorithm only considers the small context around a word.

GloVe, on the other hand, uses both local and global information to generate word vectors. To extract global information of a corpus, it leverages a co-occurrence matrix, which contains how many times the word "i" appeared in the context of "j" in the corpus. You can read more about this in the paper, "GloVe: Global Representations for Word Vectors" by Pennington et al. (https://nlp.stanford.edu/pubs/glove.pdf). GloVe still does not address the problem of ambiguous words. By ambiguous words, I mean words that have different meanings depending on the context. For example, the word "bank" in the sentences "I went to the bank to deposit money" and "I walked on the river bank" has entirely different meanings. GloVe would give the same vector for both cases, which is not accurate.

Enter ELMo! ELMo was introduced in the paper "Deep Contextualized Word Representations" by Peters et al. (https://arxiv.org/pdf/1802.05365.pdf). ELMo uses bidirectional LSTM models to generate word vectors. A bidirectional LSTM is similar to a standard LSTM but reads the sequence both forward and backward.

The final output of a word vector algorithm is a V × d–sized embedding matrix. The ith row of this matrix represents the word vector for the word represented by the ID i. d is typically < 300 and is selected using a hyperparameter algorithm. Figure 9.7 depicts the word embedding matrix.

We will now enhance our sentiment analyzer model with word embeddings.

9.6.2 Defining the final model with word embeddings

In general, any deep sequential model can benefit from word embeddings. As an added benefit, most of the time you don't need to worry about the word vector algorithms themselves and can enjoy good performance by introducing a randomly initialized embedding space. Then the embeddings can be trained jointly with the other parts of the models during the specific NLP task we're solving. Following the same pattern, let's introduce a randomly initialized embedding space to our sentiment analyzer.

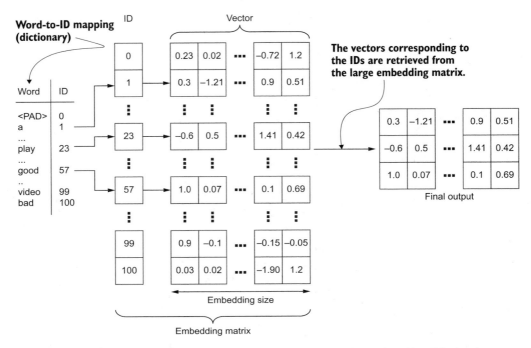

Figure 9.7   An overview of how the embedding matrix is used to obtain word vectors. A lookup is performed using the input word IDs to fetch the vectors corresponding to those indices. The actual values of the vectors are learned during the model training.

Let's remind ourselves of the previous model we implemented. The model consisted of a masking layer, a one-hot encoder layer, and an LSTM layer followed by two Dense layers (with dropout in between):

```
model = tf.keras.models.Sequential([
    # Create a mask to mask out zero inputs
    tf.keras.layers.Masking(mask_value=0.0, input_shape=(None,1)),
    # After creating the mask, convert inputs to onehot encoded inputs
    OnehotEncoder(depth=n_vocab),
    # Defining an LSTM layer
    tf.keras.layers.LSTM(128, return_state=False, return_sequences=False),
    # Defining a Dense layer
    tf.keras.layers.Dense(512, activation='relu'),
    tf.keras.layers.Dropout(0.5),
    tf.keras.layers.Dense(1, activation='sigmoid')
])
```

The model will remain more or less the same, except for two changes:

- We will replace the one-hot encoder layer with an tf.keras.layers.Embedding layer.
- The masking functionality will be absorbed into the tf.keras.layers.Embedding layer by setting the mask_zero=True in the layer.

The `tf.keras.layers.Embeddings` layer introduces a large trainable matrix into the model. This matrix is a `(V+1) x d`–sized matrix, where `V` is the vocabulary size. The additional one is required as we use the special reserved ID zero. `d` is chosen through a hyperparameter optimization algorithm. In the following model, we will set `d = 128` empirically. The line that has changed has been highlighted in bold in the listing.

Listing 9.7 Implementing the sentiment analyzer with word embeddings

Add an Embedding layer. It will look up word vectors for the word IDs passed in as the input.

Create a mask to mask out zero inputs.

```
model = tf.keras.models.Sequential([

    tf.keras.layers.Embedding(input_dim=n_vocab+1, output_dim=128, mask_zero=True),

    tf.keras.layers.LSTM(128, return_state=False, return_sequences=False),
    tf.keras.layers.Dense(512, activation='relu'),
    tf.keras.layers.Dropout(0.5),
    tf.keras.layers.Dense(1, activation='sigmoid')
])

model.compile(loss='binary_crossentropy', optimizer='adam', metrics=['accuracy'])
model.summary()
```

Define an LSTM layer.

Define Dense layers.

Define a Dropout layer.

Define the final Dense layer with sigmoidal activation.

Compile the model with binary cross-entropy as the loss.

Empty inputs, the mask, and the LSTM layer

We made sure that we don't have any empty reviews in our data set by introducing a filter to filter out the empty reviews. It is worth understanding why we did this. In addition to playing a role as a data cleaning step, it serves an important purpose. Having empty reviews in the data set will result in an all-zero vector in our data pipeline. For example, an empty review if the sequence length is 5 will return [0,0,0,0,0]. When using a Masking layer, all the inputs will be ignored. This is a problematic edge case for the LSTM layer and will raise the following error:

```
UnknownError: [_Derived_] CUDNN_STATUS_BAD_PARAM
in tensorflow/stream_executor/cuda/cuda_dnn.cc(1496):
 'cudnnSetRNNDataDescriptor( data_desc.get(), data_type, layout,
 max_seq_length, batch_size, data_size, seq_lengths_array,
 (void*)&padding_fill)'
 [[{{node cond_38/then/_0/CudnnRNNV3}}]]
 [[sequential/lstm/StatefulPartitionedCall]]
 [[gradient_tape/sequential/embedding/embedding_lookup/Reshape/_42]]
 [Op:__inference_train_function_8225]

Function call stack:
train_function -> train_function -> train_function
```

For this reason, you must make sure that the empty reviews are filtered from the data before feeding the data to the model.

With that, we will train the model we defined.

9.6.3 *Training and evaluating the model*

Training and evaluation code are identical to the implementation we discussed earlier. Therefore, we will not reiterate the discussion. When you train the new model, you will see a result similar to the following.

When you train the model, you will reach a validation accuracy that is slightly above the previous validation accuracy we experienced:

```
Epoch 1/25
2427/2427 [==============================] - 30s 12ms/step - loss: 0.7552 -
➡ accuracy: 0.7949 - val_loss: 0.3942 - val_accuracy: 0.8277 - lr: 0.0010
Epoch 2/25


...


Epoch 8/25
2427/2427 [==============================] - 29s 12ms/step - loss: 0.3059 -
➡ accuracy: 0.9312 - val_loss: 0.6839 - val_accuracy: 0.8130 - lr: 1.0000e-04
```

Evaluating the model can be done by running the following:

```
test_ds = get_tf_pipeline(ts_x, ts_y, batch_size=128)
model.evaluate(test_ds)
```

It seems that adding an embedding layer leads to a slightly higher testing performance as well:

```
87/87 [==============================] - 0s 5ms/step - loss: 0.7214 -
accuracy: 0.8111
```

Remember that we said we wouldn't trust the accuracy alone. Now let's dig in a bit deeper and see if our model is giving out sensible predictions. An easy way to do this is to check the top-k positive reviews and the top-k negative reviews in the test set and do a visual inspection. We exhausted the tf.data pipeline when we finished the evaluation. Therefore, we need to redefine the data pipeline:

```
test_ds = get_tf_pipeline(ts_x, ts_y, batch_size=128)
```

Then we will go batch by batch, and for each batch, we will store the inputs, predictions, and targets in three separate lists: test_x, test_pred, and test_y, respectively:

```
test_x = []
test_pred = []
test_y = []
for x, y in test_ds:
    test_x.append(x)
    test_pred.append(model.predict(x))
    test_y.append(y)
```

```
test_x = [doc for t in test_x for doc in t.numpy().tolist()]
test_pred = tf.concat(test_pred, axis=0).numpy()
test_y = tf.concat(test_y, axis=0).numpy()
```

We will use argsort to get the indices of the sorted prediction array. This way, the start of the array will have the indices of the most negative reviews, whereas the end of the array will contain the most positive review indices. Let's take the five top-most and five bottom-most reviews to visually check:

```
sorted_pred = np.argsort(test_pred.flatten())
min_pred = sorted_pred[:5]
max_pred = sorted_pred[-5:]

print("Most negative reviews\n")
print("="*50)
for i in min_pred:
    print(" ".join(tokenizer.sequences_to_texts([test_x[i]])), '\n')

print("\nMost positive reviews\n")
print("="*50)
for i in max_pred:
    print(" ".join(tokenizer.sequences_to_texts([test_x[i]])), '\n')
```

Let's check the results:

```
Most negative reviews
==================================================
buy game high rating promise gameplay saw youtube story so-so graphic
➡ mediocre control terrible could not adjust control option preference …

attempt install game quad core windows 7 pc zero luck go back forth try
➡ every suggestion rockstar support absolutely useless game …

way product 5 star 28 review write tone lot review similar play 2 song
➡ expert drum say unless play tennis shoe fact screw not flush mean feel
➡ every kick specifically two screw leave plus pedal completely torn
➡ mount screw something actually go wrong pedal instal unscrew send back
➡ ea

unk interactive stranger unk unk genre develop operation flashpoint various
➡ real-life computer sims military folk unk know come deliver good
➡ recreation ultra deadly unk modern combat engagement arma attempt
➡ simulate `` unk firepower '' soldier combine arm warfare set fictional
➡ sprawl island nation conveniently mirror terrain middle eastern country

not cup tea


Most positive reviews
==================================================
find something love every final fantasy game play thus far ff13 different
➡ really appreciate square enix 's latest trend shake gameplay new
➡ release still hammer best look …
```

know little squad base game genre know game fun not unk fun obliterate
➥ enemy mobile suit satisfy blow zombie head resident evil graphic
➥ presentation solid best franchise yes …

okay hdtv monitor cause ps3 switch game movie widescreen fullscreen every 5
➥ minute someone tell need get hd component cable look price saw brand
➥ name sony much money basically name brand pay fancy retail packaging
➥ generic cable get quality without fancy packaging name brand embed
➥ cable favor save money

absolutely phenomenal gaming mouse love programmable size button mouse
➥ surprising ergonomic design …

first motorstorm come unk racing type one pioneer physic base race every
➥ track lot branch path every branch suitable different class vehicle
➥ take next level race much bigger apart mud also obstacles individual
➥ vehicle class small vehicle get stuck plant unk hazard time lot physic
➥ people complain vehicle slide

We can confidently say that our sentiment analyzer was a success! The negative and positive reviews identified by the model seem like they're in the correct places. We had to overcome many obstacles having to do with data quality, data preparation, and model design. Through them all, we persevered! In the next chapter, we will discuss another NLP task known as language modeling.

EXERCISE 6
Word vector algorithms like Skip-gram use an embedding layer directly connected to a Dense layer that has the same size as the vocabulary. If you have a vocabulary of size 500, want to produce 32 dimensional word vectors, and have a dense layer with 500 units and a softmax activation, how would you implement a model? The model accepts a (None, 500)–sized (batch dimension is None) one-hot encoded vectors of words.

Summary

- The NLTK library provides an API to perform various text preprocessing tasks, such as tokenizing to words, removing stop words, lemmatization, and so on.
- Preprocessing tasks need to be applied with care. For example, when removing stop words, the word "not" should not be removed. This is because in a sentiment analysis task, the word "not" carries very important information.
- tensorflow.keras.preprocessing.text.Tokenizer can be used to convert text to numbers. This is done by the Tokenizer first building a dictionary that maps each unique word to a unique ID. Then a given text can be converted to a sequence of IDs.
- Padding is a technique used to bring variable-length text to the same length.
- Padding works by padding all sequences in a given text corpus to a fixed length by inserting zeros (at the end or at the beginning).

- When processing variable-length sequences like text, there's another strategy known as bucketing that is used to batch similar-length text sequences together. This helps the model keep the memory footprint small as well as to not waste computation on excessing padding.
- In TensorFlow, you can use `tf.data.experimental.bucket_by_sequence_length()` to bucket text sequences.
- LSTM (long short-term memory) models have shown superior performance in solving NLP tasks.
- LSTM models work by going from one timestep to the next, while processing the input at that time step to produce an output for each timestep.
- LSTM models have a mechanism to store both long-term and short-term memory. This is achieved through a gating mechanism that controls the flow of information in the LSTM cell.
- Word embeddings are a text encoding method that is superior to one-hot encoding and that has the ability to preserve the semantics of words when generating the numerical representation of words.

Answers to exercises

Exercise 1

```
s = s.replace("-", ' ')
  tokens = word_tokenize(s)
pos_tags = nltk.pos_tag(tokens)
clean_text = [
        lemmatizer.lemmatize(w, pos=p[0].lower()) if p[0]=='V' else w
        for (w, p) in pos_tags
]
```

Exercise 2

```
s = "a_b_B_c_d_a_D_b_d_d"
tok = Tokenizer(num_words = 3, split="_", lower=True)
tok.fit_on_texts([s])
```

Most common words get the lowest word ID (starting from 1).
➥ `tok.texts_to_sequences([s])` will produce `[[3,2,2,1,3,1,2,1,1]]`

Exercise 3

```
bucket_fn = tf.data.experimental.bucket_by_sequence_length(
        lambda x: tf.cast(tf.shape(x)[0],'int32'),
        bucket_boundaries=[10, 25, 30],
        bucket_batch_sizes=[batch_size,batch_size,batch_size, batch_size],
        padded_shapes=None,
        padding_values=0,
        pad_to_bucket_boundary=True
    )
```

Exercise 4

```
inp = tf.keras.layers.Input(shape=(None, 30))
lstm_out = tf.keras.layers.LSTM(32, return_sequences=True)(inp)
sum_out = tf.keras.layers.Add(axis=1)(lstm_out)
dense_out = tf.keras.layers.Dense(10, activation='softmax')(sum_out)
```

Exercise 5

```
A - (25+50)/(10+25+50)
B - (10+50)/(10+25+50)
C - (10+25)/(10+25+50)
```

Exercise 6

```
tf.keras.models.Sequential(
[
    tf.keras.layers.Embedding(input_dim=500, output_dim=32,
     input_shape=(500,)),
    tf.keras.layers.Dense(500, activation='softmax')
])
```

10

Natural language processing with TensorFlow: Language modeling

This chapter covers

- Implementing an NLP data pipeline with TensorFlow
- Implementing a GRU-based language model
- Using a perplexity metric for evaluating language models
- Defining an inference model to generate new text from the trained model
- Implementing beam search to uplift the quality of generated text

In the last chapter, we discussed an important NLP task called sentiment analysis. In that chapter, you used a data set of video game reviews and trained a model to predict whether a review carried a negative or positive sentiment by analyzing the text. You learned about various preprocessing steps that you can perform to improve the quality of the text, such as removing stop words and lemmatizing (i.e., converting words to a base form; e.g., plural to singular). You used a special type of model known as long short-term memory (LSTM). LSTM models can process sequences such as sentences and learn the relationships and dependencies in them to produce an outcome. LSTM models do this by maintaining a state (or memory) containing information about the past, as it processes a sequence one element at a time. The LSTM model can use the memory of past inputs it has seen along with the current input to produce an output at any given time.

In this chapter, we will discuss a new task known as *language modeling*. Language modeling has been at the heart of NLP. Language modeling refers to the task of predicting the next word given a sequence of previous words. For example, given the sentence, "I went swimming in the ____," the model would predict the word "pool." Ground-shattering models like BERT (bidirectional encoder representation from Transformers, which is a type of Transformer-based model) are trained using language modeling tasks. This is a prime example of how language modelling can help to actualize innovative models that go on to be used in a plethora of areas and use cases.

In my opinion, language modeling is an underdog in the world of NLP. It is not appreciated enough, mostly due to the limited use cases the task itself helps to realize. However, language modeling can provision the much-needed linguistic knowledge (e.g., semantics, grammar, dependency parsing, etc.) to solve other downstream use cases (e.g., information retrieval, question answering, machine translation, etc.). Therefore, as an NLP practitioner, you must understand the language modeling task.

In this chapter, you will build a language model. You will learn about the various preprocessing steps involved, such as using n-grams instead of full words as features for the model to reduce the size of the vocabulary. You can convert any text to n-grams by splitting it every n characters (e.g., if you use bi-grams, aabbbccd becomes aa, bb, bc, and cd). You will define a `tf.data` pipeline that will do most of this preprocessing for us. Next, you will use a close relative of the LSTM model known as *gated recurrent unit* (GRU) to do the language modeling task. GRU is much simpler than the LSTM model, making it faster to train while maintaining similar performance to the LSTM model. We will use a special metric called perplexity to measure how good our model is. Perplexity measures how surprised the model was to see the next word in the corpus given the previous words. You will learn more about this metric later in the chapter. Finally, you will learn about a technique known as *beam search*, which can uplift the quality of the text generated by the model by a significant margin.

10.1   Processing the data

You've been closely following a new generation of deep learning models that have emerged, known as Transformers. These models have been trained using language modeling. It is a technique that can be used to train NLP models to generate stories/ Python code/movie scripts, depending on the training data used. The idea is that when a sequence of n words, predict the n + 1 word. The training data can easily be generated from a corpus of text by taking a sequence of text as the input and shifting it right by 1 to generate the targets. This can be done at a character level, word level, or n-gram level. We will use two-grams for the language modeling task. We will use a children's story data set from Facebook known as bAbI (https://research.fb.com/downloads/babi/). You will create a TensorFlow data pipeline that performs these transformations to generate inputs and targets from text.

10.1.1   *What is language modeling?*

We have briefly discussed the task of language modeling. In a nutshell, language modeling, for the text w_1, w_2, ..., w_{n-1}, w_n, where w_i is the ith word in the text, computes the probability of w_n given w_1, w_2, ..., w_{n-1}. In mathematical notation

$$P(w_n | w_1, w_2, ..., w_{n-1})$$

In other words, it predicts w_n given w_1, w_2, ..., w_{n-1}. When training the model, we train it to maximize this probability; in other words

$$\text{argmax}_W P(w_n | w_1, w_2, ..., w_{n-1})$$

where the probability is computed using a model that has the trainable weights/parameters W. This computation becomes computationally infeasible for large texts, as we need to look at it from the current word all the way to the very first word. To make this computationally realizable, let's use the *Markov property*, which states that you can approximate this sequence with limited history; in other words

$$P(w_n | w_1, w_2, ..., w_{n-1}) \approx P(w_n | w_k, w_{k+1}, ..., w_{n-1}) \text{ for some } k$$

As you can imagine, the smaller the k, the better the approximation is.

> **Cloze task**
>
> Transformer models like BERT use a variant of language modeling called m*asked language modeling*. Masked language modeling is inspired by the *Cloze* task or the Cloze test. The idea is to ask the student, when given a sentence with one or more blanks, to fill in the blanks. This has been used in language assessment tests to measure the linguistic competency of students. In masked language modeling, the model becomes the student. Words are removed from inputs at random, and the model is asked to predict the missing word. This forms the foundation of the training process used in models like BERT.

10.1.2   *Downloading and playing with data*

As the very first step, let's download the data set using the code in the following listing.

> **Listing 10.1   Downloading the Amazon review data set**

```
import os
import requests
import tarfile

import shutil
```

```
# Retrieve the data
if not os.path.exists(os.path.join('data', 'lm','CBTest.tgz')):    ◁
    url = "http://www.thespermwhale.com/jaseweston/babi/CBTest.tgz"
    # Get the file from web
    r = requests.get(url)                                              If the tgz file
                                                                     containing data has
    if not os.path.exists(os.path.join('data','lm')):               not been downloaded,
        os.mkdir(os.path.join('data','lm'))                          download the data.

    # Write to a file
    with open(os.path.join('data', 'lm', 'CBTest.tgz'), 'wb') as f:    ◁
        f.write(r.content)
                                                                      Write the
else:                                                                downloaded
    print("The tar file already exists.")                       data to the disk.

if not os.path.exists(os.path.join('data', 'lm', 'CBTest')):      ◁
    # Write to a file
    tarf = tarfile.open(os.path.join("data","lm","CBTest.tgz"))
    tarf.extractall(os.path.join("data","lm"))
else:                                                     If the tgz file is available but has
    print("The extracted data already exists")            not been extracted, extract it to
                                                              the given directory.
```

Listing 10.1 will download the data to a local folder if it doesn't already exist and extract the content. If you look in the data folder (specifically, data/lm/CBTest/data), you will see that it has three text files: cbt_train.txt, cbt_valid.txt, and cbt_test.txt. Each file contains a set of stories. We are going to read these files into memory. We will define a simple function to read these files into memory in the next listing.

Listing 10.2   Reading the stories in Python

```
def read_data(path):
    stories = []                    ◁      Define a list to hold
                                            all the stories.

    with open(path, 'r') as f:
        s = []                      ◁      Define a list to      Whenever, we encounter
        for row in f:                      hold a story.         a line that starts with
                                                                 _BOOK_TITLE_, it's a
            if row.startswith("_BOOK_TITLE_"):    ◁              new story.
                if len(s)>0:
  Reset the list          stories.append(' '.join(s).lower())    ◁
containing the      └▷  s = []                            If we saw the
current story.                                            beginning of a new
                             Append the                   story, add the already
            s.append(row)    ◁    current row of          existing story to the
                                  text to the list s.     list stories.

    if len(s)>0:
        stories.append(' '.join(s).lower())    ◁
                                       Handle the edge case of the
    return stories                     last story remaining in s
                                       once the loop is over.
```

This code opens a given file and reads it row by row. We do have some additional logic to break the text into individual stories. As said earlier, each file contains multiple stories. And we want to create a list of strings at the end, where each string is a single story. The previous function does that. Next, we can read the text files and store them in variables like this:

```
stories = read_data(os.path.join('data','lm','CBTest','data','cbt_train.txt'))
val_stories = read_data(os.path.join('data','lm','CBTest','data','cbt_valid.txt'))
test_stories = read_data(os.path.join('data','lm','CBTest','data','cbt_test.txt'))
```

Here, stories will contain the training data, val_stories will contain the validation data, and finally, test_stories will contain test data. Let's quickly look at some high-level information about the data set:

```
print("Collected {} stories (train)".format(len(stories)))
print("Collected {} stories (valid)".format(len(val_stories)))
print("Collected {} stories (test)".format(len(test_stories)))
print(stories[0][:100])
print('\n', stories[10][:100])
```

This code checks how many stories are in each data set and prints the first 100 characters in the 11th story in the training set:

```
Collected 98 stories (train)
Collected 5 stories (valid)
Collected 5 stories (test)

chapter i. -lcb- chapter heading picture : p1.jpg -rcb- how the fairies
➥ were not invited to court .


 a tale of the tontlawald long , long ago there stood in the midst of a
➥ country covered with lakes a
```

Out of curiosity, let's also analyze the vocabulary size we have to work with. To analyze the vocabulary size, we will first convert our list of strings to a list of lists of strings, where each string is a single word. Then we can leverage the built-in Counter object to get the word frequency of the text corpus. After that, we will create a pandas Series object with the frequencies as the values and words as indices and see how many words occur more than 10 times:

```
from collections import Counter
# Create a large list which contains all the words in all the reviews
data_list = [w for doc in stories for w in doc.split(' ')]

# Create a Counter object from that list
# Counter returns a dictionary, where key is a word and the value is the
    frequency
cnt = Counter(data_list)

# Convert the result to a pd.Series
freq_df = pd.Series(
```

```
    list(cnt.values()), index=list(cnt.keys())
).sort_values(ascending=False)

# Count of words >= n frequent
n=10
print("Vocabulary size (>={} frequent): {}".format(n, (freq_df>=n).sum()))
```

This will return

```
,       348650
the     242890
.\n     192549
and     179205
to      120821
a       101990
of       96748
i        79780
he       78129
was      66593
dtype: int64

Vocabulary size (>=10 frequent): 14473
```

Nearly 15,000 words; that's quite a vocabulary—and that's just the words that appear more than 10 times. In the previous chapter, we dealt with a vocabulary of approximately 11,000 words. So why should we be worried about the extra 4,000? Because more words mean more features for the model, and that means a larger number of parameters and more chances of overfitting. The short answer is it really depends on your use case.

For example, in the sentiment analysis model we had in the last chapter, the final prediction layer was a single-node fully connected layer, regardless of the vocabulary size. However, in language modeling, the final prediction layer's dimensionality depends on the vocabulary size, as the final goal is to predict the next word. This is done through a softmax layer that represents the probabilistic likelihood of the next word over the whole vocabulary, given a sequence of words. Not only the memory requirement, but also the computational time, increase as the softmax layer grows. Therefore, it is worthwhile investigating other techniques to reduce the vocabulary size.

Is large vocabulary size the ultimate weakness of the softmax layer?

A major weakness of the softmax layer is its computational complexity. The softmax layer needs to first perform a matrix multiplication to get the logits (i.e., unnormalized scores output by the final layer of the network). Then it needs to sum over the last axis to compute softmax probabilities of the output. Specifically, for the input h, the logits of the softmax layer are computed as

$$s = h. W + b \text{ where } W \in R^{|h| \times |V|} \wedge b \in R^{|V|}$$

where W is the weight matrix, b is the bias of that final layer, $|h|$ is the size of the input, and $|v|$ is the size of the vocabulary. Then softmax normalization is applied as

$$\hat{y} = \frac{s}{\Sigma_{i=1}^{V} s_i}$$

These computations should make it evident to you that a large vocabulary (whose size can easily reach hundreds of thousands for a real-world application) will create problems in executing this computation in a limited time during model training. Having to do this for thousands of batches of data makes the problem even worse. Therefore, better techniques to compute the loss without using all the logits have emerged. Two popular choices are

- Noise contrastive estimation (NCE) loss
- Hierarchical softmax

Noise contrastive estimation (NCE)

We will look at the prime motivation that drives these methods but not delve into the specifics, as this is considered out of scope for this book. For the details on these topics, refer to https://ruder.io/word-embeddings-softmax. NCE only uses the logit indexed by the true target and a small sample of k random set of logits (termed *noise*) to compute the loss. The more you match the true data distribution in the noise sample, the better the results will be. Specifically, if the true target is s and the logit at the index s is termed s_i, the following loss is used:

$$J = (1 - \sigma(s_i)) + k \sum_{j=1}^{k} \sigma(s_j) \text{ where } j \sim P_n$$

Here, σ denotes that the sigmoidal activation is a common activation function used in neural networks and is computed as $\sigma(x) = 1/(1 + e^{-x})$, where s_i represents the logit value of the true target i, and j represents an index sampled from a predefined distribution over the vocabulary P_n.

Hierarchical softmax

Unlike standard softmax, which has a flat structure where each node represents an element in the vocabulary, hierarchical softmax represents the words in the vocabulary as the leaf nodes in a binary tree, and the task becomes choosing whether to go left or right in order to reach the right node. The following figure depicts the formation of the layer when hierarchical softmax is used. As is evident, to infer the probability of a word given the previous sequence of words, the layer only has to go through three steps of computation at max (shown by the dark path), as opposed to evaluating across all seven possible words.

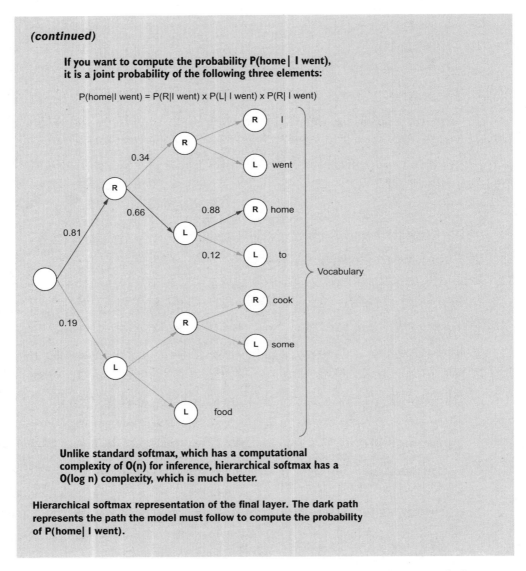

(continued)

If you want to compute the probability P(home| I went), it is a joint probability of the following three elements:

P(home|I went) = P(R|I went) x P(L| I went) x P(R| I went)

> Vocabulary

Unlike standard softmax, which has a computational complexity of O(n) for inference, hierarchical softmax has a O(log n) complexity, which is much better.

Hierarchical softmax representation of the final layer. The dark path represents the path the model must follow to compute the probability of P(home| I went).

Next, we will see how we can deal with language in the case of a large vocabulary.

10.1.3   *Too large vocabulary? N-grams to the rescue*

Here, we start the first step of defining various text preprocessors and the data pipeline. We suspect that going forward with a large vocabulary size can have adverse repercussions on our modeling journey. Let's find some ways to reduce the vocabulary size. Given that children's stories use a relatively simple language style, we can represent text as n-grams (at the cost of the expressivity of our model). N-grams are an approach where a word is decomposed to finer sub-words of fixed length. For example, the bigrams (or two-grams) of the sentence

```
I went to the bookshop
```

are

```
"I ", " w", "we", "en", "nt", "t ", " t", "to", "o ", "th", "he", "e ", " b",
"bo", "oo", "ok", "ks", "sh", "ho", "op"
```

where three grams would be

```
"I w", " we", "wen", "ent", "nt ", "t t", " to", "to ", "o t", " th", "the",
"he ", "e b", " bo", "boo", "ook", "oks", "ksh", "sho", "hop"
```

The unigrams (or one-grams) would simply be the individual characters. In other words, we are moving a window of fixed length (with a stride of 1), while reading the characters within that window at a time. You could also generate n-grams without overlaps by moving the window at a stride equal to the length of the window. For example, bigrams without overlapping would be

```
"I ", "we", "nt", " t", "o ", "th", "e ", "bo", "ok", "sh", "op"
```

Which one to use depends on your use case. For the language modeling task, it makes sense to use the non-overlapping approach. This is because by joining the n-grams that we generated, we can easily generate readable text. For certain use cases, the non-overlapping approach can be disadvantageous as it leads to a coarser representation of text because it doesn't capture all the different n-grams that appear in text.

By using bigrams instead of words to develop your vocabulary, you can cut down the size of the vocabulary by a significant factor. There are many other advantages that come with the n-gram approach, as we will see soon. We will write a function to generate n-grams given a text string:

```
def get_ngrams(text, n):
    return [text[i:i+n] for i in range(0,len(text),n)]
```

All we do here is go from the beginning to the end of the text with a stride equal to n and read the sequence of characters from position i to i+n. We can test how this performs on sample text:

```
test_string = "I like chocolates"
print("Original: {}".format(test_string))
for i in list(range(3)):
    print("\t{}-grams: {}".format(i+1, get_ngrams(test_string, i+1)))
```

This will print the following output:

```
Original: I like chocolates
    1-grams: ['I', ' ', 'l', 'i', 'k', 'e', ' ', 'c', 'h', 'o', 'c',
    'o', 'l', 'a', 't', 'e', 's']
```

```
2-grams: ['I ', 'li', 'ke', ' c', 'ho', 'co', 'la', 'te', 's']
3-grams: ['I l', 'ike', ' ch', 'oco', 'lat', 'es']
```

Let's now repeat the process for analyzing the vocabulary size, but with n-grams instead of words:

```
from itertools import chain
from collections import Counter

# Create a counter with the bi-grams
ngrams = 2

text = chain(*[get_ngrams(s, ngrams) for s in stories])
cnt = Counter(text)

# Create a pandas series with the counter results
freq_df = pd.Series(list(cnt.values()),
    index=list(cnt.keys())).sort_values(ascending=False)
```

Now, if we check the number of words that appear at least 10 times in the text

```
n_vocab = (freq_df>=10).sum()
print("Size of vocabulary: {}".format(n_vocab))
```

we will see

```
Size of vocabulary: 735
```

Wow! Compared to the 15,000 words we had, 735 is much smaller and more manageable.

Advantages of n-grams

Here are some of the main advantages of using n-grams over words:

- The limited number of n-grams for small n limits the vocabulary size, leading to both memory and computational advantages.
- N-grams lead to fewer chances of out-of-vocabulary words, as an unseen word can usually be constructed using n-grams seen in the past.

10.1.4   *Tokenizing text*

We will *tokenize* the text now (i.e., split a string into a list of smaller tokens—words). By the end of this section, you will have defined and fitted a tokenizer on the bigrams generated for your text. First, let's import the Tokenizer from TensorFlow:

```
from tensorflow.keras.preprocessing.text import Tokenizer
```

We don't have to do any preprocessing and want to convert text to word IDs as it is. We will define the num_words argument to limit the vocabulary size as well as an oov_token that will be used to replace all the n-grams that appear less than 10 times in the training corpus:

```
tokenizer = Tokenizer(num_words=n_vocab, oov_token='unk', lower=False)
```

Let's generate n-grams from the stories in training data. `train_ngram_stories` will be a list of lists of strings, where the inner list represents a list of bigrams for a single story and the outer list represents all the stories in the training data set:

```
train_ngram_stories = [get_ngrams(s,ngrams) for s in stories]
```

We will fit the `Tokenizer` on the two-grams of the training stories:

```
tokenizer.fit_on_texts(train_ngram_stories)
```

Now convert all training, validation, and testing stories to sequences of IDs, using the already fitted `Tokenizer` trained using two-grams from the training data:

```
train_data_seq = tokenizer.texts_to_sequences(train_ngram_stories)

val_ngram_stories = [get_ngrams(s,ngrams) for s in val_stories]
val_data_seq = tokenizer.texts_to_sequences(val_ngram_stories)

test_ngram_stories = [get_ngrams(s,ngrams) for s in test_stories]
test_data_seq = tokenizer.texts_to_sequences(test_ngram_stories)
```

Let's analyze how the data looks after converting to word IDs by printing some test data. Specifically, we'll print the first three story strings (`test_stories`), n-gram strings (`test_ngram_stories`), and word ID sequences (`test_data_seq`):

```
Original: the yellow fairy book the cat and the mouse in par
n-grams: ['th', 'e ', 'ye', 'll', 'ow', ' f', 'ai', 'ry', ' b', 'oo', 'k ',
➥ 'th', 'e ', 'ca', 't ', 'an', 'd ', 'th', 'e ', 'mo', 'us', 'e ', 'in',
➥ ' p', 'ar']
Word ID sequence: [6, 2, 215, 54, 84, 35, 95, 146, 26, 97, 123, 6, 2, 128,
➥ 8, 15, 5, 6, 2, 147, 114, 2, 17, 65, 52]


Original: chapter i. down the rabbit-hole alice was beginnin
n-grams: ['ch', 'ap', 'te', 'r ', 'i.', ' d', 'ow', 'n ', 'th', 'e ', 'ra',
➥ 'bb', 'it', '-h', 'ol', 'e ', 'al', 'ic', 'e ', 'wa', 's ', 'be', 'gi',
➥ 'nn', 'in']
Word ID sequence: [93, 207, 57, 19, 545, 47, 84, 18, 6, 2, 126, 344,
➥ 38, 400, 136, 2, 70, 142, 2, 66, 9, 71, 218, 251, 17]


Original: a patent medicine testimonial `` you might as well
n-grams: ['a ', 'pa', 'te', 'nt', ' m', 'ed', 'ic', 'in', 'e ', 'te', 'st',
➥ 'im', 'on', 'ia', 'l ', '``', ' y', 'ou', ' m', 'ig', 'ht', ' a', 's ',
➥ 'we', 'll']
Word ID sequence: [60, 179, 57, 78, 33, 31, 142, 17, 2, 57, 50, 125, 43,
➥ 266, 56, 122, 92, 29, 33, 152, 149, 7, 9, 103, 54]
```

10.1.5 *Defining a tf.data pipeline*

Now the preprocessing has happened, and we have text converted to word ID sequences. We can define the tf.data pipeline that will deliver the final processed data ready to be consumed by the model. The main steps involved in the process are illustrated in figure 10.1.

As we did before, let's define the word ID corpus as a tf.RaggedTensor object, as the sentences in the corpus have variable sequence lengths:

```
text_ds = tf.data.Dataset.from_tensor_slices(tf.ragged.constant(data_seq))
```

Remember that a ragged tensor is a tensor that has variable-sized dimensions. Then we will shuffle the data so that stories come at a random order if shuffle is set to True (e.g., training time):

```
if shuffle:
    text_ds = text_ds.shuffle(buffer_size=len(data_seq)//2)
```

Now comes the tricky part. In this section, we will see how to generate fixed-sized windowed sequences from an arbitrarily long text. We will do that through a series of steps. This section can be slightly complex compared to the rest of the pipeline. This is because there will be interim steps that result in data sets nested up to three levels. Let's try to go through this in as much detail as possible.

First, let's make it clear what we need to achieve. The first steps we need to perform are to do the following for each individual story S:

- Create a tf.data.Dataset() object containing the word IDs of the story S as its items.
- Call the tf.data.Dataset.window() function to window word IDs with a n_seq+1–sized window and a predefined shift. The window() function returns a WindowDataset object for each story S.

After this, you will have a three-level nested data structure having the specification

```
tf.data.Dataset(                     # <- From the original dataset
  tf.data.Dataset(     # <- From inner dataset containing word IDs of story S only
    tf.data.WindowDataset(…)  # <- Dataset returned by the window() function
  )
)
```

We will need to flatten this data set and untangle the nesting in our data set to end up with a flat tf.data.Dataset. You can remove these inner nestings using the tf.data .Dataset.flat_map() function. We will soon see how to use the flat_ map() function. To be specific, we have to use two flat_map calls to remove two levels of nesting so that we end up with only the flat original data set containing simple

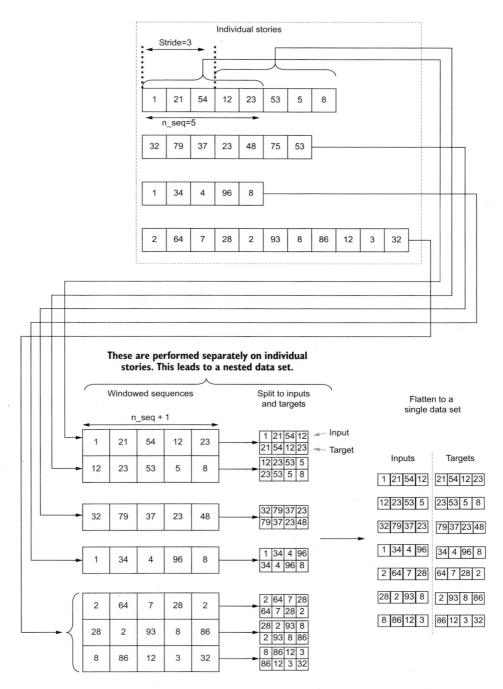

Figure 10.1   The high-level steps of the data pipeline we will be developing. First the individual stories are broken down to fixed-length sequences (or windows). Then, from the windowed sequences, inputs and targets are generated.

tensors as elements. In TensorFlow, this process can be achieved using the following line of code:

```
text_ds = text_ds.flat_map(
    lambda x: tf.data.Dataset.from_tensor_slices(
        x
    ).window(
        n_seq+1,shift=shift
    ).flat_map(
        lambda window: window.batch(n_seq+1, drop_remainder=True)
    )
  )
  )
```

This is what we are doing here: first, we create a `tf.data.Dataset` object from a single story (`x`) and then call the `tf.data.Dataset.window()` function on that to create the windowed sequences. This windowed sequence contains windows, where each window is a sequence with n_seq+1 consecutive elements in the story x.

Then we call the `tf.data.Dataset.flat_map()` function, where, for each `window` element, we get all the individual IDs as a single batch. In other words, a single window element produces a single batch with all the elements in that window. Make sure you use `drop_remainder=True`; otherwise, the data set will return smaller subwindows within that window that contain fewer elements. Using `tf.data.Dataset.flat_map()` instead of map makes sure that the inner-most nesting will be removed. This whole thing is called with a `tf.data.Dataset.flat_map()` call, which gets rid of the next level of nesting immediately following the innermost nesting we removed. It is quite a complex process for a single liner. I suggest you go through it again if you have not fully understood the process.

You might notice that we are defining the window size as n_seq+1 and not n_seq. The reason for this will become evident later, but using n_seq+1 makes our life so much easier when we have to generate inputs and targets from the windowed sequences.

Difference between map and flat_map in tf.data.Dataset

Both functions `tf.data.Dataset.map()` and `tf.data.Dataset.flat_map()` achieve the same result but with different data set specifications. For example, assume the data set

```
ds = tf.data.Dataset.from_tensor_slices([[1,2,3], [5,6,7]])
```

Using the `tf.data.Dataset.map()` function to square the elements as

```
ds = ds.map(lambda x: x**2)
```

will result in a data set that has the elements

```
[[1, 4, 9], [25, 36, 49]]
```

As you can see, the result has the same structure as the original tensor. Using the `tf.data.Dataset.flat_map()` function to square the elements as

```
ds = ds.flat_map(lambda x: x**2)
```

will result in a data set that has

```
[1,4,9,25,36,49]
```

As you can see, that inner-most nesting has been flattened to produce a flat sequence of elements.

The hardest part of our data pipeline is done. By now, you have a flat data set, and each item is n_seq+1 consecutive word IDs belonging to a single story. Next, we will perform a window-level shuffle on the data. This is different from the first shuffle we did as that was on the story level (i.e., not the window level):

```
# Shuffle the data (shuffle the order of n_seq+1 long sequences)
if shuffle:
    text_ds = text_ds.shuffle(buffer_size=10*batch_size)
```

We're then going to batch the data so that we will get a batch of windows every time we iterate the data set:

```
# Batch the data
text_ds = text_ds.batch(batch_size)
```

Finally, the reason we chose the sequence length as n_seq+1 will become clearer. Now we will split the sequences into two versions, where one sequence will be the other shifted to the right by 1. In other words, the targets to this model will be inputs shifted to the right by 1. For example, if the sequence is [0,1,2,3,4], then the two resulting sequences will be [0,1,2,3] and [1,2,3,4]. Furthermore, we will use prefetching to speed up the data ingestion:

```
# Split each sequence to an input and a target
text_ds = tf.data.Dataset.zip(
    text_ds.map(lambda x: (x[:,:-1], x[:, 1:]))
).prefetch(buffer_size=tf.data.experimental.AUTOTUNE)
```

Finally, the full code can be encapsulated in a function as in the next listing.

Listing 10.3 The `tf.data` pipeline from free text sequences

```
def get_tf_pipeline(data_seq, n_seq, batch_size=64, shift=1, shuffle=True):
    """ Define a tf.data pipeline that takes a set of sequences of text and
    convert them to fixed length sequences for the model """
```

Define a tf.dataset from a ragged tensor created from data_seq.

```
text_ds = tf.data.Dataset.from_tensor_slices(tf.ragged.constant(data_seq))

if shuffle:
    text_ds = text_ds.shuffle(buffer_size=len(data_seq)//2)
```

If shuffle is set, shuffle the data (shuffle story order).

```
text_ds = text_ds.flat_map(
    lambda x: tf.data.Dataset.from_tensor_slices(
        x
    ).window(
        n_seq+1, shift=shift
    ).flat_map(
        lambda window: window.batch(n_seq+1, drop_remainder=True)
    )
)

if shuffle:
    text_ds = text_ds.shuffle(buffer_size=10*batch_size)
```

Shuffle the data (shuffle the order of the windows generated).

```
text_ds = text_ds.batch(batch_size)
```

Batch the data.

```
text_ds = tf.data.Dataset.zip(
    text_ds.map(lambda x: (x[:,:-1], x[:, 1:]))
).prefetch(buffer_size=tf.data.experimental.AUTOTUNE)

return text_ds
```

Split each sequence into an input and a target and enable pre-fetching.

Here we create windows from longer sequences, given a window size and a shift, and then use a series of flat_map operations to remove the nesting that's created in the process.

All this hard work wouldn't mean as much as it should unless we looked at the generated data

```
ds = get_tf_pipeline(train_data_seq, 5, batch_size=6)

for a in ds.take(1):
    print(a)
```

which will show you

```
(
<tf.Tensor: shape=(6, 5), dtype=int32, numpy=
array([[161,  12,  69, 396,  17],
       [  2,  72,  77,  84,  24],
       [ 87,   6,   2,  72,  77],
       [276, 484,  57,   5,  15],
       [ 75, 150,   3,   4,  11],
       [ 11,  73, 211,  35, 141]])>,
<tf.Tensor: shape=(6, 5), dtype=int32, numpy=
array([[ 12,  69, 396,  17,  44],
       [ 72,  77,  84,  24,  51],
       [  6,   2,  72,  77,  84],
       [484,  57,   5,  15,  67],
       [150,   3,   4,  11,  73],
       [ 73, 211,  35, 141,  98]])>
)
```

Great, you can see that we get a tuple of tensors as a single batch: inputs and targets. Moreover, you can validate the correctness of the results, as we can clearly see that the targets are the input shifted to the right by 1. One last thing: we will save the same hyperparameters to the disk. Particularly

- n in n-grams
- Vocabulary size
- Sequence length

```
print("n_grams uses n={}".format(ngrams))
print("Vocabulary size: {}".format(n_vocab))

n_seq=100
print("Sequence length for model: {}".format(n_seq))

with open(os.path.join('models', 'text_hyperparams.pkl'), 'wb') as f:
    pickle.dump({'n_vocab': n_vocab, 'ngrams':ngrams, 'n_seq': n_seq}, f)
```

Here, we are defining the sequence length n_seq=100; this is the number of bigrams we will have in a single input/label sequence.

In this section, we learned about the data used for language modeling and defined a capable `tf.data` pipeline that can convert sequences of text into input label sequences that can be used to train the model directly. Next, we will define a machine learning model to generate text with.

EXERCISE 1

You are given a sequence x that has values [1,2,3,4,5,6,7,8,9,0]. You have been asked to write a `tf.data` pipeline that generates an input and target tuple, and the target is the input shifted two elements to the right (i.e., the target of the input 1 is 3). You have to do this so that a single input/target has three elements and no overlap between the consecutive input sequences. For the previous sequence it should generate [([1,2,3], [3,4,5]), ([6,7,8], [8,9,0])].

10.2   GRUs in Wonderland: Generating text with deep learning

Now we're on to the rewarding part: implementing a cool machine learning model. In the last chapter, we talked about deep sequential models. Given the sequential nature of the data, you probably have guessed that we're going to use one of the deep sequential models like LSTMs. In this chapter, we will use a slightly different model called *gated recurrent units* (GRUs). The principles that drive the computations in the model remain the same as LSTMs. To maintain the clarity of our discussion, it's worthwhile to remind ourselves how LSTM models work.

LSTMs are a family of deep neural networks that are specifically designed to process sequential data. They process a sequence of inputs, one input at a time. An LSTM cell goes from one input to the next while producing outputs (or states) at each time step (figure 10.2). Additionally, to produce the outputs of a given time step, LSTMs uses previous outputs (or states) it produced. This property is very important for LSTMs and gives them the ability to memorize things over time.

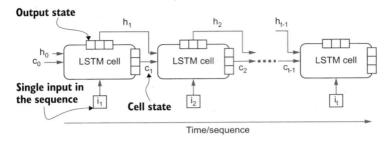

Figure 10.2   Overview of the LSTM model and how it processes a sequence of inputs spread over time

Let's summarize what we learned about LSTMs in the previous chapter, as that will help us to compare LSTMs and GRUs. An LSTM has two states known as the cell state and the output state. The cell state is responsible for maintaining long-term memory, whereas the output state can be thought of as the short-term memory. The outputs and interim results within an LSTM cell are controlled by three gates:

- *Input gate*—Controls the amount of the current input that will contribute to the final output at a given time step
- *Forget gate*—Controls how much of the previous cell state affects the current cell state computation
- *Output gate*—Controls how much the current cell state contributes to the final output produced by the LSTM model

The GRU model was introduced in the paper "Learning Phrase Representations using RNN Encoder–Decoder for Statistical Machine Translation" by Cho et al. (https://arxiv.org/pdf/1406.1078v3.pdf). The GRU model can be considered a simplification of the LSTM model while preserving on-par performance. The GRU cell has two gates:

- *Update gate* (z_t)—Controls how much of the previous hidden state is carried to the current hidden state
- *Reset gate* (r_t)—Controls how much of the hidden state is reset with the new input

Unlike the LSTM cell, a GRU cell has only one state vector. In summary, there are two major changes in a GRU compared to an LSTM model:

- Both the input gate and forget gate are combined into a single gate called the update gate (z_t). The input gate is computed as ($1-z_t$), whereas the forget gate stays z_t.

- There's only one state (h_t) in contrast to the two states found in an LSMT cell (i.e., cell state and the output state).

Figure 10.3 depicts the various components of the GRU cell. Here is the full list of equations that make a GRU spin:

$$r_t = \sigma(W_{rh}h_{t-1} + W_{rx}x_t + b_r)$$

$$z_t = \sigma(W_{zh}h_{t-1} + W_{zx}x_t + b_z)$$

$$\tilde{h}_t = \tanh(W_h(rh_{t-1}) + W_x x_t + b)$$

$$h_t = (z_{th}h_{t-1} + (1 - z_t)\tilde{h}_t$$

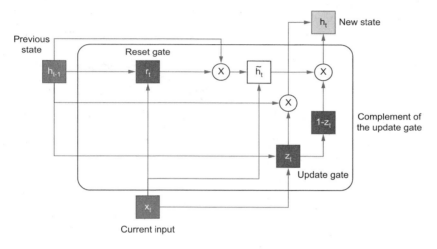

Figure 10.3   Overview of the computations transpiring in a GRU cell

This discussion was immensely helpful to not only understand the GRU model but also to learn how it's different from an LSTM cell. You can define a GRU cell in TensorFlow as follows:

```
tf.keras.layers.GRU(units=1024, return_state=False, return_sequences=True)
```

The parameter units, `return_state` and `return_sequences`, have the same meaning as they do in the context of an LSTM cell. However, note that the GRU cell has only one state; therefore, if `return_state=true`, the same state is duplicated to mimic the output state and the cell state of the LSTM layer. Figure 10.4 shows what these parameters do for a GRU layer.

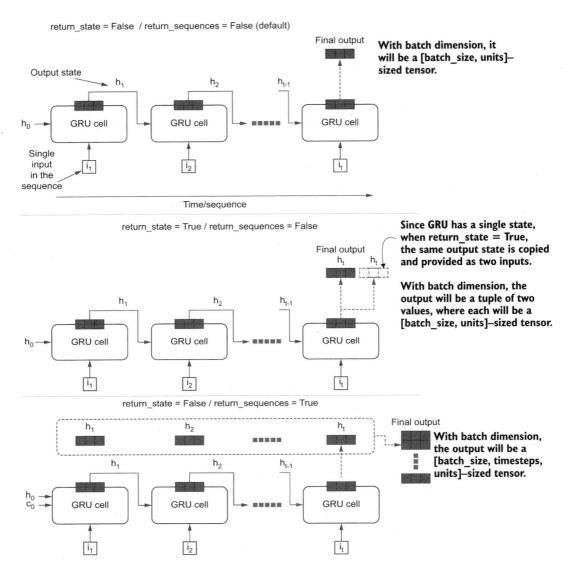

Figure 10.4   Changes in results depending on the `return_state` and `return_sequences` arguments of the GRU cell

We now know everything we need to define the final model (listing 10.4). Our final model will consist of

- An embedding layer
- A GRU layer (1,024 units) that returns all the final state vectors as a tensor that has shape [batch size, sequence length, number of units]

- A Dense layer with 512 units and ReLU activation
- A Dense layer with n_vocab units and softmax activation

Listing 10.4   Implementing the language model

Define an embedding layer
to learn word vectors
of the bigrams.

```
model = tf.keras.models.Sequential([
    tf.keras.layers.Embedding(
        input_dim=n_vocab+1, output_dim=512,input_shape=(None,)
    ),
    tf.keras.layers.GRU(1024, return_state=False, return_sequences=True),

    tf.keras.layers.Dense(512, activation='relu'),

    tf.keras.layers.Dense(n_vocab, name='final_out'),
    tf.keras.layers.Activation(activation='softmax')
])
```

Define
an LSTM
layer.

Define a
Dense
layer.

Define a final Dense layer
and softmax activation.

You will notice that the Dense layer after the GRU receives a three-dimensional tensor (as opposed to the typical two-dimensional tensor passed to Dense layers). Dense layers are smart enough to work with both two-dimensional and three-dimensional inputs. If the input is three-dimensional (like in our case), then a Dense layer that accepts a [batch size, number of units] tensor is passed through all the steps in the sequence to generate the Dense layer's output. Also note how we are separating the softmax activation from the Dense layer. This is actually an equivalent of

```
tf.keras.layers.Dense(n_vocab, activation='softmax', name='final_out')
```

We will not prolong the conversation by reiterating what's shown in listing 10.4, as it is self-explanatory.

EXERCISE 2

You have been given the model as follows and have been asked to add another GRU layer with 512 units that returns all the state outputs, on top of the existing GRU layer. What changes would you make to the following code?

```
model = tf.keras.models.Sequential([
    tf.keras.layers.Embedding(
        input_dim=n_vocab+1, output_dim=512,input_shape=(None,)
    ),
    tf.keras.layers.GRU(1024, return_state=False, return_sequences=True),
    tf.keras.layers.Dense(n_vocab, activation='softmax', name='final_out'), ])
```

In this section, we learned about gated recurrent units (GRUs) and how they compare to LSTMs. Finally, we defined a language model that can be trained on the data we downloaded and processed earlier. In the next section, we are going to learn about evaluation metrics for assessing the quality of generated text.

10.3   *Measuring the quality of the generated text*

Performance monitoring has been an integral part of our modeling journey in every chapter. It is no different here. Performance monitoring is an important aspect of our language model, and we need to find metrics that are suited for language models. Naturally, given that this is a classification task, you might be thinking, "Wouldn't accuracy be a good choice for a metric?" Well, not quite in this task.

For example, if the language model is given the sentence "I like my pet dog," then when asked to predict the missing word given "I like my pet ____," the model might predict "cat," and the accuracy would be zero. But that's not correct; "cat" makes as much sense as "dog" in this example. Is there a better solution here?

Enter perplexity! Intuitively, *perplexity* measures how "surprised" the model was to see a target given the previous word sequence. Before understanding perplexity, you need to understand what "entropy" means.

Entropy is a term coined by the famous Claude Shannon, who is considered the father of information theory. Entropy measures the surprise/uncertainty/randomness of an event. The event can have some outcome generated by an underlying probability distribution over all the possible outcomes. For example, if you consider tossing a coin (with a probability p of landing on heads) an event, if p = 0.5, you will have the maximum entropy, as that is the most uncertain scenario for a coin toss. If p = 1 or p = 0, then you have the minimum entropy, as you know what the outcome is before tossing the coin.

The original interpretation of entropy is the expected value of the number of bits required to send a signal or a message informing of an event. A bit is a unit of memory, which can be 1 or 0. For example, you are the commander of an army that's at war with countries A and B. Now you have four possibilities: A and B both surrender, A wins and B loses, A loses and B wins, and both A and B win. If all these events are equally likely to happen, you need two bits to send a message, where each bit represents whether that country won. Entropy of a random variable X is quantified by the equation

$$H(X) = -\sum_{x \vee X} p(x) \log(p(x))$$

where x is an outcome of X. Believe it or not, we have been using this equation without knowing it every time we used the categorical cross-entropy loss. The crux of the categorical cross entropy is this equation. Coming back to the perplexity measure, perplexity is simply

$$Perplexity = 2^{H(X)}$$

Since perplexity is a function of entropy, it measures how surprised/uncertain the model was to see the target word, given the sequence of previous words. Perplexity can also be thought of as the number of all possible combinations of a given signal.

For example, assume you are sending a message with two bits, where all the events are equally likely; then the entropy = 2, which means perplexity = 2^2 = 4. In other words, there are four combinations two bits can be in: 00, 01, 10, and 11.

In more of a modeling perspective, you can think of perplexity as the number of different targets that the model thinks fit the blank as the next word, given a sequence of previous words. The smaller this number, the better, as that means the model is trying to find a word from a smaller subset, indicating signs of language understanding.

To implement perplexity, we will define a custom metric. The computation is very simple. We compute the categorical cross entropy and then exponentiate it to get the perplexity. The categorical cross entropy is simply an extension of the entropy to measure entropy in classification problems with more than two classes. For an input example (x_i, y_i), it is typically defined as

$$\text{CategoricalCrossEntropy}(\hat{y}_i, y_i) = -\sum_{c=1}^{c} y_{i,c} \log(\hat{y}_{i,c})$$

where y_i denotes the one-hot encoded vector representing the true class the example belongs to and $\hat{y}_i$ is the predicted class probability vector of C elements, with $\hat{y}_{i,c}$ denoting the probability of the example belonging to class c. Note that in practice, an exponential (natural) base is used instead of base, 2 as the computations are faster. The following listing delineates the process.

Listing 10.5 Implementation of the perplexity metric

```
import tensorflow.keras.backend as K

class PerplexityMetric(tf.keras.metrics.Mean):

    def __init__(self, name='perplexity', **kwargs):
        super().__init__(name=name, **kwargs)
        self.cross_entropy = tf.keras.losses.SparseCategoricalCrossentropy(
            from_logits=False, reduction='none'
        )

    def _calculate_perplexity(self, real, pred):          ◁── Define a function to compute perplexity given real and predicted targets.

        loss_ = self.cross_entropy(real, pred)            ◁── Compute the categorical cross-entropy loss.

        mean_loss = K.mean(loss_, axis=-1)    ▷ Compute the mean of the loss.
        perplexity = K.exp(mean_loss)          ◁── Compute the exponential of the mean loss (perplexity).

        return perplexity

    def update_state(self, y_true, y_pred, sample_weight=None):
        perplexity = self._calculate_perplexity(y_true, y_pred)
        super().update_state(perplexity)
```

What we're doing is very simple. First, we subclass the tf.keras.metrics.Mean class. The tf.keras.metrics.Mean class will keep track of the mean value of any outputted metric passed into its `update_state()` function. In other words, when we subclass the `tf.keras.metrics.Mean` class, we don't specifically need to manually compute the mean of the accumulated perplexity metric as the training continues. It will be automatically done by that parent class. We will define the loss function we will use in the `self.cross_entropy` variable. Then we write the function `_calculate_perplexity()`, which takes the real targets and the predictions from the model. We compute the sample-wise loss and then compute the mean. Finally, to get the perplexity, we exponentiate the mean loss. With that, we can compile the model:

```
model.compile(
    loss='sparse_categorical_crossentropy',
    optimizer='adam',
    metrics=['accuracy', PerplexityMetric()]
)
```

In this section, we learned about the performance metrics, such as entropy and perplexity, used to evaluate language models. Furthermore, we implemented a custom perplexity metric that is used to compile the final model. Next, we'll train our model on the data we have prepared and evaluate the quality of generated text.

EXERCISE 3

Imagine a classification problem that has three outputs. There are two scenarios with different predictions:

Scenario A: Labels [0, 2, 1]

Predictions: [[0.6, 0.2, 0.2], [0.1, 0.1, 0.8], [0.3, 0.5, 0.2]]

Scenario B: Labels [0, 2, 1]

Predictions: [[0.3, 0.3, 0.4], [0.4, 0.3, 0.3], [0.3, 0.3, 0.4]]

Which one will have the lowest perplexity?

10.4 *Training and evaluating the language model*

In this section, we will train the model. Before training the model, let's instantiate the training and validation data sets using the previously implemented `get_tf_pipeline()` function. We will only use the first 50 stories (out of a total of 98) in the training set to save time. We will take a sequence of 100 bigrams at a time and hop the story by shifting the window by 25 bigrams. This means the starting index of the sequences for a single story is 0, 25, 50, . . ., and so on. We will use a batch size of 128:

```
n_seq = 100
train_ds = get_tf_pipeline(
    train_data_seq[:50], n_seq, stride=25, batch_size=128
)
valid_ds = get_tf_pipeline(
    val_data_seq, n_seq, stride=n_seq, batch_size=128
)
```

To train the model, we will define the callbacks as before. We will define

- A CSV logger that will log performance over time during training
- A learning rate scheduler that will reduce the learning rate when performance has plateaued
- An early stopping callback to terminate the training if the performance is not improving

```
os.makedirs('eval', exist_ok=True)

csv_logger =
➥ tf.keras.callbacks.CSVLogger(os.path.join('eval','1_language_modelling.
➥ log'))

monitor_metric = 'val_perplexity'
mode = 'min'
print("Using metric={} and mode={} for
  EarlyStopping".format(monitor_metric, mode))


lr_callback = tf.keras.callbacks.ReduceLROnPlateau(
    monitor=monitor_metric, factor=0.1, patience=2, mode=mode, min_lr=1e-8
)

es_callback = tf.keras.callbacks.EarlyStopping(
    monitor=monitor_metric, patience=5, mode=mode,
➥ restore_best_weights=False
)
```

Finally, it's time to train the model. I wonder what sort of cool stories I can squeeze out from the trained model:

```
model.fit(train_ds, epochs=50,  validation_data = valid_ds,
➥ callbacks=[es_callback, lr_callback, csv_logger])
```

> **NOTE** On an Intel Core i5 machine with an NVIDIA GeForce RTX 2070 8 GB, the training took approximately 1 hour and 45 minutes to run 25 epochs.

After training the model, you will see a validation perplexity close to 9.5. In other words, this means that, for a given word sequence, the model thinks there can be 9.5 different next words that are the right word (not exactly, but it is a close-enough approximation). Perplexity needs to be judged carefully as the goodness of the measure tends to be subjective. For example, as the size of the vocabulary increases, this number can go up. But this doesn't necessarily mean that the model is bad. The number can go up because the model has seen more words that fit the occasion compared to when the vocabulary was smaller.

  We will evaluate the model on the test data to gauge how well our model can anticipate some of the unseen stories without being surprised:

```
batch_size = 128
test_ds = get_tf_pipeline(
    test_data_seq, n_seq, shift=n_seq, batch_size=batch_size
)
model.evaluate(test_ds)
```

This will give you approximately

```
61/61 [==============================] - 2s 39ms/step - loss: 2.2620 -
➡ accuracy: 0.4574 - perplexity: 10.5495
```

which is on par with the validation performance we saw. Finally, save the model with

```
os.makedirs('models', exist_ok=True)
tf.keras.models.save_model(model, os.path.join('models', '2_gram_lm.h5'))
```

In this section, you learned to train and evaluate the model. You trained the model on the training data set and evaluated the model on validation and testing sets. In the next section, you will learn how to use the trained model to generate new children's stories. Then, in the following section, you will learn how to generate text with the model we just trained.

EXERCISE 4

Assume you want to use the validation accuracy (val_accuracy) instead of validation perplexity (val_perlexity) to define the early stopping callback. How would you change the following callback?

```
es_callback = tf.keras.callbacks.EarlyStopping(
    monitor='val_perlexity', patience=5, mode='min',
➡ restore_best_weights=False
)
```

10.5 Generating new text from the language model: Greedy decoding

One of the coolest things about a language model is the generative property it possesses. This means that the model can generate new data. In our case, the language model can generate new children's stories using the knowledge it garnered from the training phrase.

But to do so, we have to use some extra elbow grease. The text-generation process is different from the training process. During the training, we had the full sequence end to end. This means you can process a sequence of arbitrary length in one go. But when generating new text, you don't have a sequence of text available to you; in fact, you are trying to generate one. You start with a random word or words and get an output word, and then recursively feed the current output as the next input to generate new text. In order to facilitate this process, we need to define a new version of the trained model. Let's flesh out the generative process a bit more. Figure 10.5 compares the training process versus the generation/inference process.

Training model

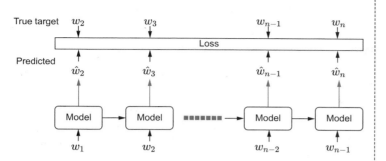

Inference model

The predicted word at time step t is used as the next input to the inference model.

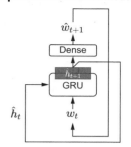

We also pass the hidden state at time step t as the previous hidden state for the next time step.

Figure 10.5   Comparison between the language model at training time and the inference/decoding phrase. In the inference phase, we predict one time step at a time. In each time step, we get the predicted word as the input and the new hidden state as the previous hidden state for the next time step.

- Define an initial word w_t (random word from the vocabulary).
- Define an initial state vector h_t (initialized with zeros).
- Define a list, words, to hold the predicted words and initialize it with the initial word.
- For t from 1 to n:
  - Get the next word (w_{t+1}) and the state vector (h_{t+1}) from the model and assign to w_t and h_t, respectively. This creates a recursive process, enabling us to generate as many words as we like.
  - Append the new word to words.

We will use the Keras functional API to build this model, as shown in the next listing. First, let's define two inputs.

Listing 10.6   Implementation of the inference/decoding language model

Define an input that can take an arbitrarily long sequence of word IDs.

Define another input that will feed in the previous state.

```
inp = tf.keras.layers.Input(shape=(None,))
inp_state = tf.keras.layers.Input(shape=(1024,))
```

Define an embedding layer.

```
emb_layer = tf.keras.layers.Embedding(
    input_dim=n_vocab+1, output_dim=512, input_shape=(None,)
)
emb_out = emb_layer(inp)
```

Get the embedding vectors from the input word ID.

```
gru_layer = tf.keras.layers.GRU(
    1024, return_state=True, return_sequences=True
)
gru_out, gru_state = gru_layer(emb_out, initial_state=inp_state)

dense_layer = tf.keras.layers.Dense(512, activation='relu')
dense_out = dense_layer(gru_out)

final_layer = tf.keras.layers.Dense(n_vocab, name='final_out')
final_out = final_layer(dense_out)
softmax_out = tf.keras.layers.Activation(activation='softmax')(final_out)

infer_model = tf.keras.models.Model(
    inputs=[inp, inp_state], outputs=[softmax_out, gru_state]
)
```

Get the GRU output and the state from the model.

Compute the first fully connected layer output.

Define a final layer that is the same size as the vocabulary and get the final output of the model.

Define a GRU layer that returns both the output and the state. However, note that they will be the same for a GRU.

Define the final model that takes an input and a state vector as the inputs and produces the next word prediction and the new state vector as the outputs.

We have to perform an important step after defining the model. We must transfer the weights from the trained model to the newly defined inference model. For that, we have to identify layers with trainable weights, get the weights for those layers from the trained model, and assign them to the new model:

```
# Copy the weights from the original model
emb_layer.set_weights(model.get_layer('embedding').get_weights())
gru_layer.set_weights(model.get_layer('gru').get_weights())
dense_layer.set_weights(model.get_layer('dense').get_weights())
final_layer.set_weights(model.get_layer('final_out').get_weights())
```

To get weights of a specific layer in the trained model, you can call

```
model.get_layer(<layer name>).get_weights()
```

This will return a NumPy array with the weights. Next, to assign those weights to a layer, call

```
layer.set_weights(<weight matrix>)
```

We can now call the newly defined model recursively to generate as many bigrams as we like. We will discuss the process to do that in more detail. Instead of starting with a single random word, let's start with a sequence of text. We will convert the text to bigrams and subsequently to word IDs using the Tokenizer:

```
text = get_ngrams(
    "CHAPTER I. Down the Rabbit-Hole Alice was beginning to get very tired
➡ of sitting by her sister on the bank ,".lower(),
    ngrams
)

seq = tokenizer.texts_to_sequences([text])
```

Next, let's reset the states of the model (this is not needed here because we're starting fresh, but it's good to know that we can do that). We will define a state vector with all zeros:

```
# Reset the state of the model initially
model.reset_states()
# Defining the initial state as all zeros
state = np.zeros(shape=(1,1024))
```

Then we will recursively predict on each bigram in the seq variable to update the state of the GRU model with the input sequence. Once we sweep through the whole sequence, we will get the final predicted bigram (that will be our first predicted bigram) and append that to the original bigram sequence:

```
# Recursively update the model by assining new state to state
for c in seq[0]:
    out, state = infer_model.predict([np.array([[c]]), state])

# Get final prediction after feeding the input string
wid = int(np.argmax(out[0],axis=-1).ravel())
word = tokenizer.index_word[wid]
text.append(word)
```

We will define a new input x with the last word ID that was predicted:

```
# Define first input to generate text recursively from
x = np.array([[wid]])
```

The fun begins now. We will predict 500 bigrams (i.e., 1,000 characters) using the approach discussed earlier. In every iteration, we predict a new bigram and the new state with the infer_model using the input x and the state vector state. The new bigram and the new state recursively replace x and state variables with these new outputs (see the next listing).

> **Listing 10.7 Recursively predicting a new word using the previous word as an input**

```
for _ in range(500):

    out, state = infer_model.predict([x, state])

    out_argsort = np.argsort(out[0], axis=-1).ravel()
    wid = int(out_argsort[-1])
    word = tokenizer.index_word[wid]


    if word.endswith(' '):
        if np.random.normal()>0.5:
            width = 3
            i = np.random.choice(
                list(range(-width,0)),
                p=out_argsort[-width:]/out_argsort[-width:].sum()
            )
            wid = int(out_argsort[i])
            word = tokenizer.index_word[wid]
```

Get the next output and state.

Get the word ID and the word from out.

If the word ends with space, we introduce a bit of randomness to break repeating text.

Essentially pick one of the top three outputs for that timestep depending on their likelihood.

```
    text.append(word)          ◄─┐   Append the prediction
                                 │   cumulatively to text.
┌─▷  x = np.array([[wid]])
│
Recursively make the current
prediction the next input.
```

Note that a little bit of work is required to get the final value of x as the model predicts a probability prediction (assigned to out) as its output, not a word ID. Furthermore, we're going to use some additional logic to improve the randomness (or entropy, one could say) in the generated text by picking a word randomly from the top three words. But we don't pick them with equal probability. Rather, let's use their predicted probabilities to predict the word. To make sure we don't get too much randomness and to avoid getting random tweaks in the middle of words, let's do this only when the last character is a space character. The final word ID (picked either as the word with the highest probability or at random) is assigned to the variable x. This process will repeat for 500 steps, and by the end, you'll have a cool machine-generated story on your hands. You can print the final text and see how it looks. To do that, simply join the bigrams in the text sequence as follows:

```
# Print the final output
print('\n')
print('='*60)
print("Final text: ")
print(''.join(text))
```

This will display

```
Final text:
chapter i. down the rabbit-hole alice was beginning to get very tired of
⇒ sitting by her sister on the bank , and then they went to the shore ,
⇒ and then the princess was so stilling that he was a little girl ,

...

  it 's all right , and i 'll tell you how young things would n't be able to
⇒ do it .
  i 'm not goin ' to think of itself , and i 'm going to be sure to see you .
  i 'm sure i can notice them .
  i 'm going to see you again , and i 'll tell you what i 've got , '
```

It's certainly not bad for a simple single layer GRU model. Most of the time, the model spits out actual words. But there are occasional spelling mistakes and more frequent grammatical errors haunting the text. Can we do better? In the next section, we are going to learn about a new technique to generate text called beam search.

EXERCISE 5

Assume you have the following code that chooses the next word greedily without randomness. You run this code and realize that the results are very bad:

```
for _ in range(500):

    out, new_s = infer_model.predict([x, s])

    out_argsort = np.argsort(out[0], axis=-1).ravel()
    wid = int(out_argsort[-1])
    word = tokenizer.index_word[wid]

    text.append(word)

    x = np.array([[wid]])
```

What do you think is the reason for the poor performance?

10.6   Beam search: Enhancing the predictive power of sequential models

We can do better that greedy decoding. Beam search is a popular decoding algorithm used in sequential/time-series tasks like this to generate more accurate predictions. The idea behind beam search is very simple. Unlike in greedy decoding, where you predict a single timestep, with beam search you predict several time steps ahead. In each time step, you get the top k predictions and branch out from them. Beam search has two important parameters: beam width and beam depth. Beam width controls how many candidates are considered at each step, whereas beam depth determines how many steps to search. For example, for a beam width of 3 and a beam depth of 5, the number of possible options become $3^5 = 243$. Figure 10.6 further illustrates how beam search works.

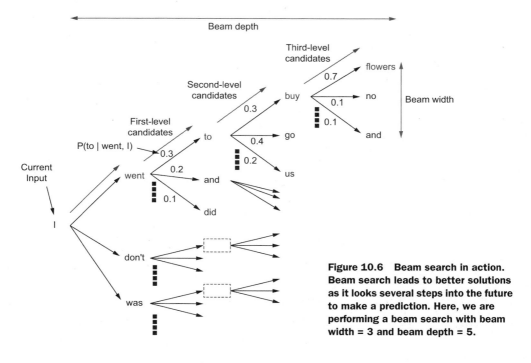

Figure 10.6   Beam search in action. Beam search leads to better solutions as it looks several steps into the future to make a prediction. Here, we are performing a beam search with beam width = 3 and beam depth = 5.

First let's define a function that will take a model, input, and state and return the output and the new state:

```
def beam_one_step(model, input_, state):
    """ Perform the model update and output for one step"""
    output, new_state = model.predict([input_, state])
    return output, new_state
```

Then, using this function, we will define a recursive function (recursive_fn) that will recursively predict the next word from the previous prediction for a predefined depth (defined by beam_depth). At each time step, we consider the top k candidates (defined by beam_width) to branch out from. The recursive_fn function will populate a variable called results. results will contain a list of tuples, where each tuple represents a single path in the search. Specifically, each tuple contains the

- Elements in the path
- The joint log probability of that sequence
- The final state vector to pass to the GRU

This function is outlined in the following listing.

Listing 10.8   Implementation of the beam search as a recursive function

Define an outer wrapper for the computational function of beam search.

Define an inner function that is called recursively to find the beam paths.

```
def beam_search(
    model, input_, state, beam_depth=5, beam_width=3, ignore_blank=True
):
    """ Defines an outer wrapper for the computational function of beam
    search """

    def recursive_fn(input_, state, sequence, log_prob, i):
        """ This function performs actual recursive computation of the long
        string"""

        if i == beam_depth:
            """ Base case: Terminate the beam search """
            results.append((list(sequence), state, np.exp(log_prob)))
            return sequence, log_prob, state
        else:
            """ Recursive case: Keep computing the output using the
            previous outputs"""
            output, new_state = beam_one_step(model, input_, state)

            # Get the top beam_widht candidates for the given depth
            top_probs, top_ids = tf.nn.top_k(output, k=beam_width)
            top_probs, top_ids = top_probs.numpy().ravel(),
            top_ids.numpy().ravel()

            # For each candidate compute the next prediction
            for p, wid in zip(top_probs, top_ids):
                new_log_prob = log_prob + np.log(p)
```

Define the base case for terminating the recursion.

Append the result we got at the termination so we can use it later.

During recursion, get the output word and the state by calling the model.

Get the top k candidates for that step.

For each candidate, compute the joint probability. We will do this in log space to have numerical stability.

Penalize joint probability whenever the same symbol repeats.

```
if len(sequence)>0 and wid == sequence[-1]:
    new_log_prob = new_log_prob + np.log(1e-1)
```

Append the current candidate to the sequence that maintains the current search path at the time.

```
sequence.append(wid)
_ = recursive_fn(
    np.array([[wid]]), new_state, sequence, new_log_prob, i+1
)
sequence.pop()
```

Call the function recursively to find the next candidates.

Make a call to the recursive function to trigger the recursion.

```
results = []
sequence = []
log_prob = 0.0
recursive_fn(input_, state, sequence, log_prob, 0)

results = sorted(results, key=lambda x: x[2], reverse=True)

return results
```

Sort the results by log probability.

Finally, we can use this `beam_search` function as follows: we will use a beam depth of 7 and a beam width of 2. Up until the `for` loop, things are identical to how we did things using greedy decoding. In the `for` loop, we get the results list (sorted high to low on joint probability). Then, similar to what we did previously, we'll get the next prediction randomly from the top 10 predictions based on their likelihood as the next prediction. The following listing delineates the code to do so.

Listing 10.9 Implementation of beam search decoding to generate a new story

```
text = get_ngrams(
    "CHAPTER I. Down the Rabbit-Hole Alice was beginning to get very tired
    of sitting by her sister on the bank ,".lower(),
    ngrams
)
```

Define a sequence of ngrams from an initial sequence of text.

Convert the bigrams to word IDs.

```
seq = tokenizer.texts_to_sequences([text])

state = np.zeros(shape=(1,1024))
for c in seq[0]:
    out, state = infer_model.predict([np.array([[c]]), state
```

Build up model state using the given string.

```
wid = int(np.argmax(out[0],axis=-1).ravel())
word = tokenizer.index_word[wid]
text.append(word)
```

Get the predicted word after processing the sequence.

```
x = np.array([[wid]])

for i in range(100):
```

Predict for 100 time steps.

```
    result = beam_search(infer_model, x, state, 7, 2)
```

Get the results from beam search.

```
    n_probs = np.array([p for _,_,p in result[:10]
    p_j = np.random.choice(list(range(
        n_probs.size)), p=n_probs/n_probs.sum())
```

Get one of the top 10 results based on their likelihood.

```
        best_beam_ids, state, _ = result[p_j]      |  Replace x and state with
        x = np.array([[best_beam_ids[-1]]])        |  the new values computed.

        text.extend([tokenizer.index_word[w] for w in best_beam_ids])

print('\n')
print('='*60)
print("Final text: ")
print(''.join(text))
```

Running the code in listing 10.9, you should get text similar to the following:

```
Final text:

chapter i. down the rabbit-hole alice was beginning to get very tired of
➡ sitting by her sister on the bank , and there was no reason that her
➡ father had brought him the story girl 's face .
`` i 'm going to bed , '' said the prince , `` and you can not be able
➡ to do it . ''
`` i 'm sure i shall have to go to bed , '' he answered , with a smile
➡ .
`` i 'm so happy , '' she said .
`` i do n't know how to bring you into the world , and i 'll be sure
➡ that you would have thought that it would have been a long time .
there was no time to be able to do it , and it would have been a
➡ little thing . ''
`` i do n't know , '' she said .

...

`` what is the matter ? ''
`` no , '' said anne , with a smile .
`` i do n't know what to do , '' said mary .
`` i 'm so glad you come back , '' said mrs. march , with
```

The text generated with beam search reads much better than the text we saw with greedy decoding. You see improved grammar and less spelling mistakes when text is generated with beam search.

Diverse beam search

Different alternatives to beam search have surfaced over time. One popular alternative is called *diverse beam search*, introduced in the paper, "Diverse Beam Search: Decoding Diverse Solutions from Neural Sequence Models" by Vijayakumar et al. (https://arxiv.org/pdf/1610.02424.pdf). Diverse beam search overcomes a critical limitation of vanilla beam search. That is, if you analyze the most preferred candidate sequences proposed by beam search, you'll find that they differ only by a few elements. This also can lead to repeating text that lacks variety. Diverse beam search comes up with an optimization problem that incentivizes diversity of the proposed candidates during the search. You can read more about this in the paper.

This concludes our discussion on language modeling. In the next chapter, we will learn about a new type of NLP problem known as a sequence-to-sequence problem. Let's summarize the key highlights of this chapter.

EXERCISE 6

You used the line `result = beam_search(infer_model, x, state, 7, 2)` to perform beam search. You want to consider five candidates at a given time and search only three levels deep into the search space. How would you change the line?

Summary

- Language modeling is the task of predicting the next word given a sequence of words.
- Language modeling is the workhorse of some of the top-performing models in the field, such as BERT (a type of Transformer-based model).
- To limit the size of the vocabulary and avoid computational issues, n-gram representation can be used.
- In n-gram representation, text is split into fixed-length tokens, as opposed to doing character-level or word-level tokenization. Then, a fixed sized window is moved over the sequence of text to generate inputs and targets for the model. In TensorFlow, you can use the `tf.data.Dataset.window()` function to implement this functionality.
- The gated recurrent unit (GRU) is a sequential model that operates similarly to an LSTM, where it jumps from one input to the next in a sequence while generating a state at each time step.
- The GRU is a compact version of an LSTM model that maintains a single state and two gates but delivers on-par performance.
- Perplexity measures how surprised the model was to see the target word given the input sequence.
- The computation of the perplexity measure is inspired by information theory, in which the measure entropy is used to quantify the uncertainty in a random variable that represents an event where the outcomes are generated with some underlying probability distribution.
- The language models after training can be used to generate new text. There are two popular techniques—greedy decoding and beam search decoding:
  - Greedy decoding predicts one word at a time, where the predicted word is used as the input in the next time step.
  - Beam search decoding predicts several steps into the future and selects the sequence that gives the highest joint probability.

Answers to exercises

Exercise 1

```
ds = tf.data.Dataset.from_tensor_slices(x)
ds = ds.window(5,shift=5).flat_map(
    lambda window: window.batch(5, drop_remainder=True)
)
ds = ds.map(lambda xx: (xx[:-2], xx[2:]))
```

Exercise 2

```
model = tf.keras.models.Sequential([
    tf.keras.layers.Embedding(
        input_dim=n_vocab+1, output_dim=512,input_shape=(None,)
    ),

    tf.keras.layers.GRU(1024, return_state=False, return_sequences=True),
    tf.keras.layers.GRU(512, return_state=False, return_sequences=True),
    tf.keras.layers.Dense(n_vocab, activation='softmax', name='final_out'),
])
```

Exercise 3

Scenario A will have the lowest perplexity.

Exercise 4

```
es_callback = tf.keras.callbacks.EarlyStopping(
    monitor='val_accuracy', patience=5, mode='max',
     restore_best_weights=False
)
```

Exercise 5

The line out, new_s = infer_model.predict([x, s]), is wrong. The state is not recursively updated in the inference model. This will lead to a working model but with poor performance. It should be corrected as out, s = infer_model.predict([x, s]).

Exercise 6

```
result = beam_search(infer_model, x, state, 3, 5)
```

Part 3

Advanced deep networks
for complex problems

Deep learning has come a long way since the introduction of models like convolutional neural networks, LSTMs, and so on. Transformer-based models encompassing billions of parameters have out-performed the aforementioned models across the board. Another topic that has gained popularity, due to the demand for better models and agility in developing ML models, is tracking and productionizing ML models.

In part 3, we will first discuss a more complex variant of RNN based models known as sequence-to-sequence models. Then we will discuss Transformer-based models in more detail and see firsthand how they can be used for tasks like spam classification and question answering. You will also learn how you can leverage high-level libraries like Hugging Face's Transformers to implement solutions quickly.

Then, you will learn how to use the TensorBoard to track the performance of models. You will learn about easily visualizing model performance over time and advanced capabilities like performance profiling. Finally, we introduce TFX, a library that standardizes the productionization of ML models. You will develop an end-to-end pipeline that manages the ML workflow end to end, from data to the deployment.

11

Sequence-to-sequence learning: Part 1

This chapter covers

- Understanding sequence-to-sequence data
- Building a sequence-to-sequence machine translation model
- Training and evaluating sequence-to-sequence models
- Repurposing the trained model to generate translations for unseen text

In the previous chapter, we discussed solving an NLP task known as language modeling with deep recurrent neural networks. In this chapter, we are going to further our discussion and learn how we can use recurrent neural networks to solve more complex tasks. We will learn about a variety of tasks in which an arbitrary-length input sequence is mapped to another arbitrary-length sequence. Machine translation is a very appropriate example of this that involves converting a sequence of words in one language to a sequence of words in another.

In this chapter, our primary focus is on building an English-to-German machine translator. To arrive at that, we will first download a machine translation data set, look at the structure of that data set, and apply some processing to prepare it for the model. Then we will define a machine translation model that can learn to map arbitrarily long sequences to other arbitrarily long sequences. This is an encoder-decoder-based model, meaning there is an encoder that takes in one sequence (e.g., an English phrase) to produce a latent representation of the sequence and a decoder that decodes that information to produce a target sequence (e.g., a German phrase). A special characteristic of this model will be its ability to take in raw strings and convert them to numerical representations internally. Therefore, this model is more end-to-end than other NLP models we have created in previous chapters. Once the model is defined, we will train it using the data set we processed and evaluate it on two metrics: per-word accuracy of the sequences produced and BLEU (biLingual evaluation understudy). BLEU is a more advanced metric than accuracy that mimics how a human would evaluate the quality of a translation. Finally, we will define a slightly modified decoder that can recursively produce words (starting from an initial seed) while taking the previous prediction as the input for the current time step. In the first section, we will discuss the data a bit before diving into modeling.

11.1 *Understanding the machine translation data*

You are developing a machine translation service for tourists who are visiting Germany. You found a bilingual parallel corpus of English and German text (available at http://www.manythings.org/anki/deu-eng.zip). It contains English text and a corresponding German translation side by side in a text file. The idea is to use this to train a sequence-to-sequence model, and before doing that, you have to understand the organization of the data, load it into memory, and analyze the vocabulary size and the sequence length. Furthermore, you will process the text so that it has the special token "sos" (denotes "start of sentence") at the beginning of the German translation and "eos" (denotes "end of sentence") at the end of the translation. These are important tags that will help us at the time of generating translations from the model.

Let's first download the data set and take a tour of it. You will need to manually download this data set (available at http://www.manythings.org/anki/deu-eng.zip), as this web page does not support automatic retrieval through script. Once downloaded, we will extract the data, which has a text file containing the data:

```
import os
import requests
import zipfile

# Make sure the zip file has been downloaded
if not os.path.exists(os.path.join('data','deu-eng.zip')):
    raise FileNotFoundError(
        "Uh oh! Did you download the deu-eng.zip from
➡ http:/ /www.manythings.org/anki/deu-eng.zip manually and place it in the
➡ Ch11/data folder?"
    )

else:
    if not os.path.exists(os.path.join('data', 'deu.txt')):
```

```
        with zipfile.ZipFile(os.path.join('data','deu-eng.zip'), 'r') as
    zip_ref:
            zip_ref.extractall('data')
    else:
        print("The extracted data already exists")
```

If you open the text file, it will have entries as follows:

```
Go.     Geh.     CC-BY 2.0 (France) Attribution: tatoeba.org
➡ #2877272 (CM) & #8597805 (Roujin)
Hi.     Hallo!     CC-BY 2.0 (France) Attribution: tatoeba.org
➡ #538123 (CM) & #380701 (cburgmer)
Hi.     Grüß Gott!     CC-BY 2.0 (France) Attribution:
➡ tatoeba.org #538123 (CM) & #659813 (Esperantostern)
...
If someone who doesn't know your background says that you sound like
➡ a native speaker, ... . In other words, you don't really sound like
➡ a native speaker.     Wenn jemand, der nicht weiß, woher man
➡ kommt, sagt, man erwecke doch den Eindruck, Muttersprachler zu sein,
➡ ... - dass man diesen Eindruck mit anderen Worten eigentlich nicht
➡ erweckt.     CC-BY 2.0 (France) Attribution: tatoeba.org #953936
➡ (CK) & #8836704 (Pfirsichbaeumchen)
Doubtless there exists in this world precisely the right woman for
➡ any given man to marry and vice versa; ..., that probably, since
➡ the earth was created, the right man has never yet met the right
➡ woman.     Ohne Zweifel findet sich auf dieser Welt zu jedem Mann
➡ genau die richtige Ehefrau und umgekehrt; ..., dass seit Erschaffung
➡ ebenderselben wohl noch nie der richtige Mann der richtigen Frau
➡ begegnet ist.     CC-BY 2.0 (France) Attribution: tatoeba.org
➡ #7697649 (RM) & #7729416 (Pfirsichbaeumchen)
```

The data is in tab-separated format and has a <German phrase><tab><English phrase><tab><Attribution> format. We really care about the first two tab-separated values in a record. Once the data is downloaded, we can easily load the data to a pandas DataFrame. Here we will load the data, set up column names, and extract the columns that are of interest to us:

```
import pandas as pd

# Read the csv file
df = pd.read_csv(
    os.path.join('data', 'deu.txt'), delimiter='\t', header=None
)
# Set column names
df.columns = ["EN", "DE", "Attribution"]
df = df[["EN", "DE"]]
```

We can also compute the size of the DataFrame through

```
print('df.shape = {}'.format(df.shape))
```

which will return

```
df.shape = (227080, 2)
```

NOTE   The data here is updated over time. Therefore, you can get slightly different results (e.g., data set size, vocabulary size, vocabular distribution, etc.) than shown here.

We have around 227,000 examples in our data set. Each example contains an English phrase/sentence/paragraph and the corresponding German translation. We will do one more cleaning step. It seems that some of the entries in the text file have some Unicode issues. These are handled fine by pandas, but are problematic for some downstream TensorFlow components. Therefore, let's run the following cleanup step to ignore those problematic lines in the data:

```
clean_inds = [i for i in range(len(df)) if b"\xc2" not in
    df.iloc[i]["DE"].encode("utf-8")]

df = df.iloc[clean_inds]
```

Let's analyze some of the samples by calling df.head() (table 11.1) and df.tail() (table 11.2). df.head() returns the contents of table 11.1, whereas df.tail() produces the contents of table 11.2.

Table 11.1   Some of the examples at the beginning of the data

	EN	DE
0	Go.	Geh.
1	Hi.	Hallo!
2	Hi.	Grüß Gott!
3	Run!	Lauf!
4	Run.	Lauf!

Table 11.2   Some of the examples at the end of the data

	EN	DE
227075	Even if some by non-native speakers...	Auch wenn Sätze von Nichtmutterspra-chlern mitu...
227076	If someone who doesn't your background sa...	Wenn jemand, der deine Herkunft nicht kennt, s...
227077	If someone who doesn't your background sa...	Wenn jemand Fremdes dir sagt, dass du dich wie...
227078	If someone who doesn't your background sa...	Wenn jemand, der nicht weiß, woher man kommt, ...
227079	Doubtless there exists in this world pre-cisely...	Ohne Zweifel findet sich auf dieser Welt zu je...

The examples are sorted by their length, and you can see that they start with examples of a single word and end up with examples with approximately 50 words. We will only use a sample of 50,000 phrases from this data set to speed up our workflow:

```
n_samples = 50000
df = df.sample(n=n_samples, random_state=random_seed)
```

We set the random seed as `random_seed=4321`.

Finally, we will introduce two special tokens to the German translations: `sos` and `eos`. `sos` marks the start of the translation, whereas `eos` marks the end of the translation. As you will see, these tokens serve an important purpose when it comes to generating translations after the model trained. But for consistency during training and inference (or generation), we will introduce these tokens to all of our examples. This can be easily done as follows:

```
start_token = 'sos'
end_token = 'eos'
df["DE"] = start_token + ' ' + df["DE"] + ' ' + end_token
```

> ## SOS and EOS tokens
> The choice of SOS and EOS is just a convenience, and technically they could be represented by any two unique tokens, as long as they are not words from the corpus itself. It is important to make these tokens unique, as they play an important role when generating translations from previously unseen English sentences. The specifics of the role will be discussed in a later section.

It's a very straightforward transformation. This will convert the phrase `"Grüß Gott!"` to `"sos Grüß Gott! eos"`. Next, we're going to generate a training/validation/test subset from the data we sampled:

```
# Randomly sample 10% examples from the total 50000 randomly
test_df = df.sample(n=n=int(n_samples/10), random_state=random_seed)
# Randomly sample 10% examples from the remaining randomly
valid_df = df.loc[~df.index.isin(test_df.index)].sample(
    n=n=int(n_samples/10), random_state=random_seed
)
# Assign the rest to training data
train_df = df.loc[~(df.index.isin(test_df.index) |
➡  df.index.isin(valid_df.index))]
```

We will keep 10% of the data as test data, another 10% as validation data, and the remaining 80% as training data. The data will be randomly sampled (without replacement) for the data sets. We then move on to analyze two important characteristics of text data sets, as we have done over and over again: the vocabulary size (listing 11.1) and the sequence length (listing 11.2).

Listing 11.1 Analyzing the vocabulary size

```
from collections import Counter

en_words = train_df["EN"].str.split().sum()        ◁——  Create a flattened list
de_words = train_df["DE"].str.split().sum()        ◁——  from English words.
                                                         Create a flattened list
                                                         of German words.
n=10      ◁———  Get the vocabulary size of words
                appearing more than or equal to 10 times.

def get_vocabulary_size_greater_than(words, n, verbose=True):

    """ Get the vocabulary size above a certain threshold """

    counter = Counter(words)        ◁——  Generate a counter object (i.e., dict
                                          word -> frequency).

    freq_df = pd.Series(            ◁——  Create a pandas series from the counter,
        list(counter.values()),          and then sort most frequent to least.
        index=list(counter.keys())
    ).sort_values(ascending=False)

    if verbose:                          Print the most
        print(freq_df.head(n=10))   ◁——  common words.

    n_vocab = (freq_df>=n).sum()    ◁——  Get the count of words that
                                          appear at least 10 times.
    if verbose:
        print("\nVocabulary size (>={} frequent): {}".format(n, n_vocab))

    return n_vocab

print("English corpus")
print('='*50)
en_vocab = get_vocabulary_size_greater_than(en_words, n)

print("\nGerman corpus")
print('='*50)
de_vocab = get_vocabulary_size_greater_than(de_words, n)
```

which will return

```
English corpus
==================================================
Tom     9427
to      8673
I       8436
the     6999
you     6125
a       5680
is      4374
in      2664
of      2613
was     2298
dtype: int64

Vocabulary size (>=10 frequent): 2238
```

```
German corpus
==================================================
sos        40000
eos        40000
Tom         9928
Ich         7749
ist         4753
nicht       4414
zu          3583
Sie         3465
du          3112
das         2909
dtype: int64

Vocabulary size (>=10 frequent): 2497
```

Next, sequence analysis is done in the following function.

Listing 11.2 Analyzing the sequence length

```
def print_sequence_length(str_ser):

    """ Print the summary stats of the sequence length """

    seq_length_ser = str_ser.str.split(' ').str.len()      ◁──  Create a pd.Series,
                                                                 which contains the
                                                                 sequence length for
                                                                 each review.

    print("\nSome summary statistics")
    print("Median length: {}\n".format(seq_length_ser.median()))     Get the median as
    print(seq_length_ser.describe())                                 well as summary
                                                                     statistics of the
                                                                     sequence length.
    print(
        "\nComputing the statistics between the 1% and 99% quantiles (to
⇢  ignore outliers)"
    )
    p_01 = seq_length_ser.quantile(0.01)     Get the quantiles at given marks
    p_99 = seq_length_ser.quantile(0.99)     (i.e., 1% and 99% percentiles).

    print(
        seq_length_ser[
            (seq_length_ser >= p_01) & (seq_length_ser < p_99)
        ].describe()      ◁──  Print the summary stats of the data
    )                          between the defined quantiles.
```

Next, call this function on the data to get the statistics:

```
print("English corpus")
print('='*50)
print_sequence_length(train_df["EN"])

print("\nGerman corpus")
print('='*50)
print_sequence_length(train_df["DE"])
```

This produces

```
English corpus
==================================================
```

```
Some summary statistics
Median length: 6.0

count    40000.000000
mean         6.360650
std          2.667726
min          1.000000
25%          5.000000
50%          6.000000
75%          8.000000
max        101.000000
Name: EN, dtype: float64

Computing the statistics between the 1% and 99% quantiles (to ignore outliers)
count    39504.000000
mean         6.228002
std          2.328172
min          2.000000
25%          5.000000
50%          6.000000
75%          8.000000
max         14.000000
Name: EN, dtype: float64

German corpus
===================================================

Some summary statistics
Median length: 8.0

count    40000.000000
mean         8.397875
std          2.652027
min          3.000000
25%          7.000000
50%          8.000000
75%         10.000000
max         77.000000
Name: DE, dtype: float64

Computing the statistics between the 1% and 99% quantiles (to ignore outliers)
count    39166.000000
mean         8.299035
std          2.291474
min          5.000000
25%          7.000000
50%          8.000000
75%         10.000000
max         16.000000
Name: DE, dtype: float64
```

Next, let's print out the vocabulary size and the sequence length parameters for the two languages:

```
print("EN vocabulary size: {}".format(en_vocab))
print("DE vocabulary size: {}".format(de_vocab))

# Define sequence lengths with some extra space for longer sequences
en_seq_length = 19
de_seq_length = 21

print("EN max sequence length: {}".format(en_seq_length))
print("DE max sequence length: {}".format(de_seq_length))
```

This will return

```
EN vocabulary size: 359
DE vocabulary size: 336
EN max sequence length: 19
DE max sequence length: 21
```

Now we have the language-specific parameters needed to define the model. In the next section, we'll look at how we can define a model to translate between languages.

EXERCISE 1

You have been given a pandas Series ser in the following format:

```
0      [a, b, c]
1         [d, e]
2    [f, g, h, i]
...

dtype: object
```

Write a function called vocab_size(ser) to return the vocabulary size.

11.2 Writing an English-German seq2seq machine translator

You have a clean data set that is ready to go into a model. You will be using a sequence-to-sequence deep learning model as the machine translation model. It consists of two parts: an encoder that produces a hidden representation of the English (source) text and a decoder that decodes that representation to German (target) text. Both the encoder and the decoder are recurrent neural networks. Moreover, the model will accept raw text and will convert the raw text to token IDs using a TextVectorization layer provided in TensorFlow. These token IDs will go to an embedding layer that will return word vectors of the token IDs.

We have the data prepared and ready to go. Now let's learn about the model that can consume this data. Sequence-to-sequence learning maps an arbitrarily long sequence to another arbitrarily long sequence. This poses a unique challenge for us, as the model not only needs to be able to consume a sequence of arbitrary length, but also needs to be able to produce a sequence of arbitrary length as the output. For example, in machine translation, it is very common for translations to have fewer or more words than the input. Because of this, they require a special type of model. These models are known as *encoder-decoder* or *seq2seq* (short for sequence-to-sequence) models.

Encoder-decoder models are, in fact, two different models interconnected in a certain way. Conceptually, the encoder takes in a sequence and produces a context vector (or a thought vector) that embeds the information present in the input sequence. The decoder takes in the representation produced by the encoder and decodes it to generate another sequence. Since the two parts (i.e., the encoder and the decoder) operate on separate things (i.e., the encoder consumes the input sequence while the decoder generates the output sequence), encoder-decoder models are well suited for solving sequence-to-sequence tasks. Another way to understand what the encoder and the decoder do is as follows: the encoder processes the source language input (i.e., the language to translate from), and the decoder processes the target language input (i.e., the language to translate to). This is depicted in figure 11.1.

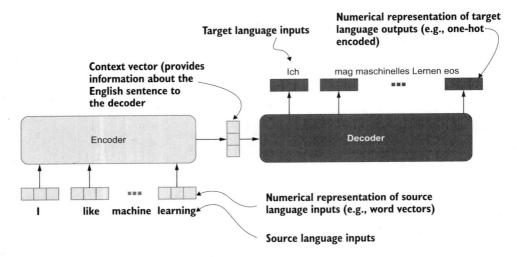

Figure 11.1 High-level components of the encoder-decoder architecture in the context of machine translation

Particularly, the encoder contains a recurrent neural network. We will be using a gated recurrent unit (GRU) model. It goes through the input sequence and produces a final output, which is the final output of the GRU cell after it processes the last element in the input sequence.

Thought vector

A *thought vector* is a term popularized by Geoffery Hinten, a luminary in deep learning who has been involved since its inception. A thought vector refers to a vectorized representation of a thought. The ability to generate accurate numerical representations of

> thoughts would revolutionize the way we search documents or search on the web (e.g., Google). This is similar to how a numerical representation of a word is called a *word vector*. In the context of machine translation, the context vector can be called a thought vector as it captures the essence of a sentence or a phrase in a single vector.
>
> You can read more about this at https://wiki.pathmind.com/thought-vectors.

Next, we have the decoder, which also consists of a GRU model and several `Dense` layers. The purpose of the `Dense` layers is to generate a final prediction (a word from the target vocabulary). The weights of the `Dense` layers present in the decoder are shared across time. This means that, just as the GRU layer updates the same weights as it moves from one input to the other, the `Dense` layer reuses the same weights across the time steps. This process is depicted in figure 11.2.

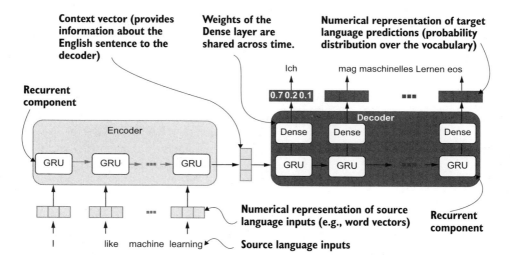

Figure 11.2 Specific components in the encoder and decoder modules. The encoder has a GRU layer, and the decoder consists of a GRU layer followed by one or more `Dense` layers, whose weights are shared across time.

Up until now, when solving NLP tasks, converting string tokens to numerical IDs was considered a preprocessing step. In other words, we would perform the tokens-to-ID conversion and input the IDs to the model. But it doesn't have to be that way. We can define more versatile models that do such text processing internally as well as learn to solve the tasks. Keras provides certain layers that can plug into your model to be more end-to-end. The `tensorflow.keras.layers.experimental.preprocessing.Text-Vectorization` layer is one such layer. Let's examine the usage of this layer.

11.2.1 *The TextVectorization layer*

The `TextVectorization` layer takes in a string, tokenizes it, and converts the tokens to IDs by means of a vocabulary (or dictionary) lookup. It takes a list of strings (or an array of strings) as the input, where each string can be a word/phrase/sentence (and so on). Then it learns the vocabulary from that corpus. Finally, the layer can be used to convert a list of strings to a tensor that contains a sequence of token IDs for each string in the list provided. Let's see this layer in action. First import the layer with

```
from tensorflow.keras.layers.experimental.preprocessing import
    TextVectorization
```

Then define the layer as follows. Here we're defining the layer for the English language. Keep in mind that we need two `TextVectorization` layers in our model, one for English and one for German:

```
en_vectorize_layer = TextVectorization(
    max_tokens=en_vocab,
    output_mode='int',
    output_sequence_length=None
)
```

It's worthwhile to stop here and look at the different arguments we're providing:

- `max_tokens`—Specifies the number of words in the vocabulary. Any word that is not present in the vocabulary (i.e., an out-of-vocabulary word) is converted to `[UNK]`.
- `output_mode`—Specifies the type of the final output. Can be one of `"int"`, `"binary"`, `"count"`, and `"tf-idf"`. `"int"` means the layer will output a token ID for each token. `"binary"` implies that the output will be a [<batch size>, <vocab size>] tensor, where a value of 1 is given at an index, if the token indicated by that index is present in that example. `"count"` gives a similar output as `"binary"`, but instead of 1s, it contains the number of times a token appeared in that example. `"tf-id"` gives a similar output as `"binary"`, but the TF-IDF value at each position.
- `output_sequence_length`—Specifies the length of the batched input sequence after converting to token IDs. If set to `None`, it means the sequence length will be set to the length of the longest sequence in the batch. The shorter sequences are padded with a special token (special token defaults to `""`).

To make the best out of this layer, we have to fit it on a text corpus so that it can learn the vocabulary. Calling the `adapt()` function and passing the list of strings (or an array of strings) to it achieves that. In other words, `adapt()` yields the same results as the `fit()` method of a scikit-learn model (http://mng.bz/aJmB). It takes in some data and trains (or adapts) the model according to the data. In the case of the tokenizer, among other things, it builds out a dictionary (a mapping from word to ID):

```
en_vectorize_layer.adapt(np.array(train_df["EN"].tolist()).astype('str'))
```

After fitting the layer, you can get the vocabulary

```
print(en_vectorize_layer.get_vocabulary()[:10])
```

which prints

```
['', '[UNK]', 'tom', 'to', 'you', 'the', 'i', 'a', 'is', 'that']
```

In other words, the vocabulary is a list of tokens where the ID corresponds to their indexes in the list. You can compute the size of the vocabulary by

```
print(len(en_vectorize_layer.get_vocabulary()))
```

which returns

```
2238
```

Next, to use this layer to convert strings to numerical IDs, we must wrap it in a model. To do so, let's first define a Keras Sequential model. Let's name the model toy_model as this will only be used to learn the behavior of the text vectorizer:

```
toy_model = tf.keras.models.Sequential()
```

Define an input layer, set its size to accept a tensor with a single column (i.e., a list of strings), and set the data type to tf.string:

```
toy_model.add(tf.keras.Input(shape=(1,), dtype=tf.string))
```

Then add the text vectorization layer we defined:

```
toy_model.add(en_vectorize_layer)
```

You can use this just like any other Keras model and convert arbitrary text to numerical ID sequences. Specifically, you use the model.predict() function on some input data, which takes in the input and transforms it accordingly depending on the layers used in the model:

```
input_data = [["run"], ["how are you"],["ectoplasmic residue"]]
pred = toy_model.predict(input_data)
```

Finally, print the inputs and results as follows

```
print("Input data: \n{}\n".format(input_data))
print("\nToken IDs: \n{}".format(pred))
```

which gives

```
Input data:
[['run'], ['how are you'], ['ectoplasmic residue']]

Token IDs:
[[427   0   0]
 [ 40  23   4]
 [  1   1   0]]
```

The layer does everything accordingly. Let's first looks at the shape of the output. The shape, since we set the `output_sequence_length=None`, pads all the examples in the input up to the length of the longest input in the inputs. Here, "how are you" is the longest and has three words in it. Therefore, all the rows are padded with zeros, such that each example has three columns. Generally, the layer returns a [<batch size>, sequence_length]–sized output.

If the word is found in the vocabulary, it is converted to some number (e.g., "run" is converted to 427). If the word is not found in the vocabulary (e.g., "ectoplasmic"), it is replaced with a special ID (1) that corresponds to out-of-vocabulary words.

11.2.2 Defining the TextVectorization layers for the seq2seq model

With a good understanding of the `TextVectorization` layer, let's define a function to return a text vectorization layer wrapped in a `Keras Model` object. This function, named `get_vectorizer()`, takes in the following arguments:

- `corpus`—Accepts a list (or array) of strings (i.e., a corpus to build the vocabulary).
- `n_vocab`—Vocabulary size. The most common n_vocab words are kept to build the vocabulary.
- `max_length` (optional)—Length of the resulting token sequences. It defaults to `None`, in which case the sequence length will be the length of the longest text sequence.
- `return_vocabulary` (optional)—Whether to return the vocabulary (i.e., list of string tokens).
- `name` (optional)—String to set the model name

It defines an input layer that accepts a batch of strings (having a total shape of [None, 1]). Next, the function defines a text vectorizer layer. Note that the layer has a vocabulary size of n_vocab + 2. The extra 2 is necessary to accommodate the special tokens `" "` and `"[UNK]"`. The layer is fitted with the text corpus passed into the function. Finally, we define a Keras model with the input layer (inp) and the output of the text vectorization layer (vectorize_out). If the return_vocabulary is set to `True`, it will also return the vocabulary of the vectorize_layer, as shown in the next listing.

> **Listing 11.3   Defining the text vectorizers for the encoder-decoder model**

```
def get_vectorizer(
    corpus, n_vocab, max_length=None, return_vocabulary=True, name=None
):

    """ Return a text vectorization layer or a model """

    inp = tf.keras.Input(shape=(1,), dtype=tf.string, name='encoder_input')    ⟵

    vectorize_layer =
 ⇒ tf.keras.layers.experimental.preprocessing.TextVectorization(
```

Define an input layer that takes a list of strings (or an array of strings).

```
        max_tokens=n_vocab+2,
        output_mode='int',
        output_sequence_length=max_length,
    )
```

When defining the vocab size, we use n_vocab + 2 ,as there are two special tokens, "(Padding)" and "[UNK]", added automatically.

Fit the vectorizer layer on the data.

```
    vectorize_layer.adapt(corpus)

    vectorized_out = vectorize_layer(inp)
```

Get the token IDs for the data fed to the input.

```
    if not return_vocabulary:
        return tf.keras.models.Model(
            inputs=inp, outputs=vectorized_out, name=name
        )
    else:
        return tf.keras.models.Model(
            inputs=inp, outputs=vectorized_out, name=name
        ), vectorize_layer.get_vocabulary()
```

Return the model only. The model takes an array of strings and outputs a tensor of token IDs.

Return the vocabulary in addition to the model.

Since we have defined the function, let's use it and define two vectorizers, one for the English inputs and one for the German inputs:

```
# Get the English vectorizer/vocabulary
en_vectorizer, en_vocabulary = get_vectorizer(
    corpus=np.array(train_df["EN"].tolist()), n_vocab=en_vocab,
    max_length=en_seq_length, name='en_vectorizer'
)
# Get the German vectorizer/vocabulary
de_vectorizer, de_vocabulary = get_vectorizer(
    corpus=np.array(train_df["DE"].tolist()), n_vocab=de_vocab,
    max_length=de_seq_length-1, name='de_vectorizer'
)
```

Here, the corpus takes in a list or an array of text. Each text is a string containing an English or German phrase/sentence. n_vocab defines the size of the vocabulary, and max_length defines the sequence length to which we should pad the data. Note how we use de_seq_length-1 for the decoder. This Subtraction of 1 here is a necessity due to the way data is presented to the decoder during the model training. We will discuss the specific details when we reach model training. Finally, we can define a name to keep track of different layers.

11.2.3 Defining the encoder

Moving on to the encoder, we will use a GRU model at the core of our encoder. The encoder is responsible for processing the source input sequence. Its responsibility is to process the source input and produce a *context vector* (sometimes called a *thought vector*). This vector captures the essence of the input sequence in a compact, vectorized representation. Normally, this context vector would be the GRU cell's last output state after it processes the full input sequence.

Let's see the steps involved in getting the encoder ready. For this, we will use the Keras Functional layer. Sequence-to-sequence models are not sequential and involve nonlinear connections between the encoder and the decoder. Therefore, we cannot use the Keras Sequential API. First, we define the input layer:

```
# The input is (None,1) shaped and accepts an array of strings
inp = tf.keras.Input(shape=(1,), dtype=tf.string, name='e_input')
```

The input accepts a list of strings. Note how we are setting the shape to (1,) to make sure the model accepts a tensor with just one column and dtype to tf.string. Next, we vectorize the text input fed forward by inp:

```
# Vectorize the data (assign token IDs)
vectorized_out = en_vectorizer(inp)
```

Here, the vectorizer is a model that performs text vectorization, which is output by the get_vectorizer() function we defined earlier.

Next, we define an embedding layer that will convert the token IDs returned by the vectorizer to word vectors. This is a layer that has trainable weights. Therefore, during the training, the model will tune the word embeddings to reflect useful representations to solve the task at hand:

```
# Define an embedding layer to convert IDs to word vectors
emb_layer = tf.keras.layers.Embedding(
    input_dim=n_vocab+2, output_dim=128, mask_zero=True, name='e_embedding'
)
# Get the embeddings of the token IDs
emb_out = emb_layer(vectorized_out)
```

When defining the embedding layer, you need to always pass the vocabulary size (input_dim) and the output_dim. Note that the vocabulary size has been increased by 2 to accommodate the two special tokens (i.e., UNK and PAD) that are introduced. We will set the output_dim to 128. We also want to mask excessive zeros that were padded from the final computations and thus set mask_zero=True. Finally, we will also pass a name to identify the layer easily.

Now we are coming to the core of our model: the recurrent neural network (RNN). As mentioned earlier, we will use a GRU model but with an added twist! We are going to make our GRU model bidirectional! A bidirectional RNN is a special type of RNN that processes a sequence both forward and backward. This is in contrast to a standard RNN, which only processes the sequence forward:

```
gru_layer = tf.keras.layers.Bidirectional(tf.keras.layers.GRU(128))
```

Then we get the output of the gru_layer and assign it to gru_out:

```
gru_out = gru_layer(emb_out)
```

Bidirectional RNN: Reading text forward and backward

The standard RNN reads the text forward, one time step at a time, and outputs a sequence of outputs. Bidirectional RNNs, as the name suggests, not only read the text forward, but read it backward. This means that bidirectional RNNs have two sequences of outputs. Then these two sequences are combined using a combination strategy (e.g., *concatenation*) to produce the final output. Bidirectional RNNs typically outperform standard RNNs because they understand relationships in text both forward and backward, as shown in the following figure.

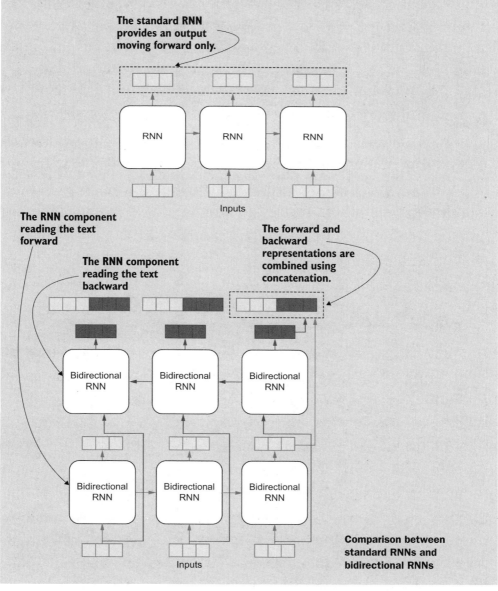

The standard RNN provides an output moving forward only.

Inputs

The RNN component reading the text forward

The RNN component reading the text backward

The forward and backward representations are combined using concatenation.

Inputs

Comparison between standard RNNs and bidirectional RNNs

(continued)

Why does reading text backward help? There are some languages that are read backward (e.g., Arabic, Hebrew). Unless the text is specifically processed to account for this writing style, a standard RNN would have a very difficult time understanding the language. By having a bidirectional RNN, you are removing the model's dependency on a language to always be left to right or right to left.

If we consider the English language, there can be instances where it's impossible to infer a relationship going only forward. Consider the two sentences

John went toward the bank on Clarence Street.

John went towards the bank of the river.

Since the two sentences are identical up to the word "bank," it is not possible to know if the bank is referring to the financial institution or a river bank until you read the rest. For a bidirectional RNN, this is trivial.

Finally, we define the encoder model as a `tf.keras.models.Model` object. It takes `inp` (i.e., a single-column tensor of type `tf.string`) and outputs `gru_out` (i.e., the final state of the bidirectional GRU model). This final state of the GRU model is what is considered the context vector that provides the decoder information about the source language sentence/phrase input:

```
encoder = tf.keras.models.Model(inputs=inp, outputs=gru_out)
```

You can observe the step-by-step build of the encoder model encapsulated in a function, as shown in the following listing.

Listing 11.4   The function that returns the encoder

```
def get_encoder(n_vocab, vectorizer):
    """ Define the encoder of the seq2seq model"""

    inp = tf.keras.Input(shape=(1,), dtype=tf.string, name='e_input')

    vectorized_out = vectorizer(inp)

    emb_layer = tf.keras.layers.Embedding(
        n_vocab+2, 128, mask_zero=True, name='e_embedding'
    )

    emb_out = emb_layer(vectorized_out)

    gru_layer = tf.keras.layers.Bidirectional(
        tf.keras.layers.GRU(128, name='e_gru'),
        name='e_bidirectional_gru'
    )
```

The input is (None,1) shaped and accepts an array of strings.

Vectorize the data (assign token IDs)

Define an embedding layer to convert IDs to word vectors.

Get the embeddings of the token IDs.

Define a bidirectional GRU layer. The encoder looks at the English text (i.e., the input) both backward and forward.

```
gru_out = gru_layer(emb_out)
```
Get the output of the gru the last (the last output state vector returned by the model).

```
encoder = tf.keras.models.Model(
    inputs=inp, outputs=gru_out, name='encoder'
)
```
Define the encoder model; it takes in a list/array of strings and returns the last output state of the GRU model.

```
    return encoder
```

After defining the function, you can simply call it to build the encoder model:

```
encoder = get_encoder(en_vocab, en_vectorizer)
```

11.2.4 Defining the decoder and the final model

The encoder is done and dusted, and it's time to look at the decoder. The decoder is going to look slightly more complex than the encoder. The core model of the decoder is again a GRU model. It is then followed by a fully connected hidden layer and a fully connected prediction layer. The prediction layer outputs a word from the German vocabulary (by computing probability over all the words in the vocabulary) for each time step.

During model training, the decoder predicts the next word in a given target sequence. For example, the decoder, given the target sequence [A, B, C, D], will train the model for three time steps on the following input-output tuples: (A, B), (B, C), and (C, D). In other words, given the token A, predict token B; given the token B, predict token C; and so on. If you think about the end-to-end process of the encoder-decoder model, the following steps take place:

1 The encoder processes the source input sequence (i.e., English) and produces a context vector (i.e., the last output state of the GRU model).
2 The decoder uses the context vector produced by the encoder as its initial state for the recurrent component.
3 The decoder takes in the target input sequence (i.e., German) and predicts the next token given the previous token. For each time step, it predicts a token over the complete target vocabulary using a fully connected layer and a softmax layer.

This way of training the model is known as *teacher forcing*, as you are guiding the decoder with the target sequence (i.e., the teacher). Using teacher forcing quickly leads to better performance, compared to not using teacher forcing during the training of encoder-decoder-type models. Let's look at the decoder and see how the encoder and the decoder tie in to create the final model in more depth, shown in figure 11.3.

It's time to discuss the specifics of building the decoder and the final model. The first thing we have to do is get the encoder's output by passing an input. We define an input layer identical to the input of the encoder and pass that to the encoder model we defined earlier:

```
e_inp = tf.keras.Input(shape=(1,), dtype=tf.string, name='e_input_final')
```

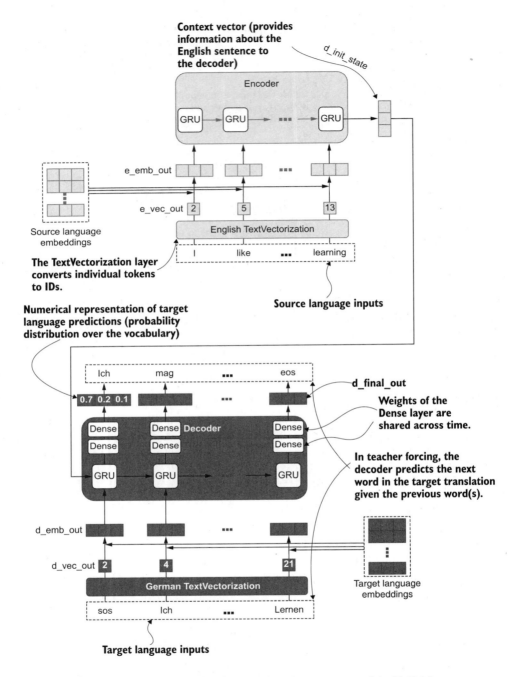

Figure 11.3   The implementation of the final sequence-to-sequence model with the focus on various layers and outputs involved

Then we pass the e_inp to the encoder model, which will give us the last output state of the GRU model as the output. This is an important input for the decoder:

```
d_init_state = encoder(e_inp)
```

As the starting point of the decoder, we define an input layer with identical specifications to the encoder's input:

```
d_inp = tf.keras.Input(shape=(1,), dtype=tf.string, name='d_input')
```

We then pass the input to a text vectorization model given the get_vectorizer() function:

```
vectorized_out = de_vectorizer(inp)
```

We define an embedding layer as we did with the encoder so that token IDs produced by the text vectorization layer are converted to word vectors. Note that we have two separate embedding layers for the encoder and the decoder, as they use sequences from two different languages:

```
emb_layer = tf.keras.layers.Embedding(
    input_dim=n_vocab+2, output_dim=128, mask_zero=True, name='d_embedding'
)
emb_out = emb_layer(vectorized_out)
```

It's now time to implement the recurrent component of the decoder. Similar to the encoder, we are using a GRU model to process the sequence:

```
gru_layer = tf.keras.layers.GRU(256, return_sequences=True)
```

But note that, in contrast to the encoder, in the decoder we are not using a bidirectional wrapper on the GRU model. The decoder cannot rely on a backward reading capability because it should generate the next output depending only on the previous and the current input. Note also that we have set return_sequences=True:

```
gru_out = gru_layer(emb_out, initial_state=d_init_state)
```

Finally, passing the output of the embedding layer to the gru_layer, we get the output. We stated earlier that the d_init_state (i.e., the encoder's output) is one of the important inputs to the decoder. Here, we pass the d_init_state as the initial state to the decoder's GRU layer. This means that, instead of starting out with a zero-initialized state vector, the decoder will use the encoder's context vector as the initial state. Since we have set return_sequences=True, the output will contain output state vectors from all the time steps, not just the last one. This means the output will be of size [<batch size>, <time steps>, 256].

Listing 11.5   Defining the decoder and the final model

The input is (None,1) shaped and accepts an array of strings.
We feed the German sequence as the input and ask the model
to predict it with the words offset by 1 (i.e., the next word).

```
def get_final_seq2seq_model(n_vocab, encoder, vectorizer):
    """ Define the final encoder-decoder model """
    e_inp = tf.keras.Input(
        shape=(1,), dtype=tf.string, name='e_input_final'
    )
    d_init_state = encoder(e_inp)

    d_inp = tf.keras.Input(shape=(1,), dtype=tf.string, name='d_input')

    d_vectorized_out = vectorizer(d_inp)

    d_emb_layer = tf.keras.layers.Embedding(
        n_vocab+2, 128, mask_zero=True, name='d_embedding'
    )
    d_emb_out = d_emb_layer(d_vectorized_out)

    d_gru_layer = tf.keras.layers.GRU(
        256, return_sequences=True, name='d_gru'
    )

    d_gru_out = d_gru_layer(d_emb_out, initial_state=d_init_state)

    d_dense_layer_1 = tf.keras.layers.Dense(
        512, activation='relu', name='d_dense_1'
    )
    d_dense1_out = d_dense_layer_1(d_gru_out)

    d_dense_layer_final = tf.keras.layers.Dense(
        n_vocab+2, activation='softmax', name='d_dense_final'
    )
    d_final_out = d_dense_layer_final(d_dense1_out)

    seq2seq = tf.keras.models.Model(
        inputs=[e_inp, d_inp], outputs=d_final_out, name='final_seq2seq'
    )

    return seq2seq
```

Define an encoder input layer and get the encoder output (i.e., the context vector).

Get the decoder's vectorized output.

Define an embedding layer to convert IDs to word vectors. This is a different layer from the encoder's embedding layer.

Define a GRU layer. Unlike the encoder, we cannot define a bidirectional GRU for the decoder.

Get the output of the GRU layer of the decoder.

Define an intermediate Dense layer and get the output.

The final prediction layer with softmax

Define the full model.

We can now define everything needed for our final model as

```
# Get the English vectorizer/vocabulary
en_vectorizer, en_vocabulary = get_vectorizer(
    corpus=np.array(train_df["EN"].tolist()), n_vocab=en_vocab,
    max_length=en_seq_length, name='e_vectorizer'
)
# Get the German vectorizer/vocabulary
de_vectorizer, de_vocabulary = get_vectorizer(
```

```
        corpus=np.array(train_df["DE"].tolist()), n_vocab=de_vocab,
        max_length=de_seq_length-1, name='d_vectorizer'
)

# Define the final model
encoder = get_encoder(n_vocab=en_vocab, vectorizer=en_vectorizer)
    final_model = get_final_seq2seq_model(
        n_vocab=de_vocab, encoder=encoder, vectorizer=de_vectorizer
    )
```

Here, we are defining the English and German vectorizers (en_vectorizer and de_vectorizer, respectively). An encoder is then defined using the English vocabulary size and the English vectorizer. Finally, the final encoder-decoder model is defined using the German vocabulary size (de_vocab) encoder and the German vectorizer (de_vectorizer).

11.2.5 *Compiling the model*

The last thing to do have the model ready for training is compile the model. We will use sparse categorical cross-entropy loss, the Adam optimizer, and the accuracy as metrics:

```
from tensorflow.keras.metrics import SparseCategoricalAccuracy

final_model.compile(
    loss='sparse_categorical_crossentropy',
    optimizer='adam',
    metrics=['accuracy']
)
```

Finally, let's print the model summary

```
final_model.summary()
```

which will output

```
Model: "final_seq2seq"
```

Layer (type)	Output Shape	Param #
➡ Connected to		
===		
d_input (InputLayer)	[(None, 1)]	0
d_vectorizer (Functional)	(None, 20)	0
➡ d_input[0][0]		
e_input_final (InputLayer)	[(None, 1)]	0
d_embedding (Embedding)	(None, 20, 128)	319872
➡ d_vectorizer[0][0]		
encoder (Functional)	(None, 256)	484864
➡ e_input_final[0][0]		

d_gru (GRU) ➡ d_embedding[0][0] ➡ encoder[0][0]	(None, 20, 256)	296448
d_dense_1 (Dense) ➡ d_gru[0][0]	(None, 20, 512)	131584
d_dense_final (Dense) ➡ d_dense_1[0][0]	(None, 20, 2499)	1281987

```
================================================================
Total params: 2,514,755
Trainable params: 2,514,755
Non-trainable params: 0
```

In the next section, we will learn how the model we just defined can be trained with the data we prepared.

EXERCISE 2

In contrast to teacher forcing, another technique used to define encoder-decoder models is by defining a model where

- The encoder takes in the English token sequence
- The decoder takes in the context vector repeated on the time axis as inputs so that the same context vector is fed to the decoder for every time step

You have been provided the following encoder. Define the decoder that has a GRU layer and two fully connected hidden layers and the final model that starts with en_inp, and produce the final predictions:

```
en_inp = tf.keras.Input(shape=(1,), dtype=tf.string, name='e_input')
en_vectorized_out = en_vectorizer(inp)
en_emb_layer = tf.keras.layers.Embedding(
    en_vocab+2, 128, mask_zero=True, name='e_embedding'
)
en_emb_out = emb_layer(vectorized_out)
en_gru_layer = tf.keras.layers.GRU(256, name='e_gru')
en_gru_out = gru_layer(emb_out)
```

You can use the tf.keras.layers.RepeatVector layer to repeat the context vector for any number of times. For example, if you pass a [None, 32]–sized tensor to the tf.keras.layers.RepeatVector(5) layer, it returns a [None, 5, 32]–sized tensor by repeating the [None, 32] tensor five times on the time dimension.

11.3 *Training and evaluating the model*

You have defined an end-to-end model that can consume raw text and generate translations. Next, you will train this model on the data that was prepared earlier. You will use the training set to train the model and the validation set to monitor the performance as it trains. Finally, the model will be tested on test data. To evaluate the model, we will use two metrics: accuracy and BLEU. BLEU is a popular metric used in sequence-to-sequence problems to measure the quality of the output sequence (e.g., translation).

We have defined and compiled the model. We will now train the model on training data and evaluate its performance on validation and testing data across several metrics. We will use a performance metric known as BLEU to measure the performance of our model. It is not a standard metric provided in Keras and will be implemented using standard Python/NumPy functions. Due to this, we will write custom train/evaluation loops to train and evaluate the model, respectively.

To facilitate the model training and evaluation, we are going to create several helper functions. First, we will create a function to create inputs and targets from the Python DataFrame objects we defined at the beginning (see the next listing).

Listing 11.6   Preparing the training/validation/test data for model training and evaluation

```
def prepare_data(train_df, valid_df, test_df):
    """ Create a data dictionary from the dataframes containing data """

    data_dict = {}                          ⟵  Define a dictionary for containing
    for label, df in zip(                       train/validation/test data.
        ['train', 'valid', 'test'], [train_df, valid_df, test_df]
    ):
        en_inputs = np.array(df["EN"].tolist())     ⟵  Define the encoder inputs
        de_inputs = np.array(                           as the English text.
            df["DE"].str.rsplit(n=1, expand=True).iloc[:,0].tolist()      ⟵
        )
        de_labels = np.array(
            df["DE"].str.split(n=1, expand=True).iloc[:,1].tolist()
        )
        data_dict[label] = {
            'encoder_inputs': en_inputs,
            'decoder_inputs': de_inputs,
            'decoder_labels': de_labels
        }

    return data_dict
```

Iterate through the train, valid, and test DataFrames.

Define the decoder outputs as all of the German text but the first token.

Define the decoder inputs as all of the German text but the last token.

Update the dictionary with encoder inputs, decoder inputs, and the decoder outputs.

This function takes in the three data frames, `train_df`, `valid_df`, and `test_df`, and performs some transformations on them to return a dictionary that contains three keys: `train`, `valid`, and `test`. Under each key, you will find the following:

- Encoder inputs (i.e., an English word sequence)
- Decoder inputs (i.e., a German word sequence)
- Decoder outputs (i.e., a German word sequence)

As we stated earlier, we are using a technique known as teacher forcing to lift the model's performance. Therefore, the decoder's object becomes predicting the next word given the previous word(s). For instance, for the example ("I want a piece of chocolate cake", "Ich möchte ein Stück Schokoladenkuchen"), encoder inputs, decoder inputs, and decoder outputs become the following:

- ["I", "want", "a", "piece", "of", "chocolate", "cake"] (encoder inputs)
- ["Ich", "möchte", "ein", "Stück"] (decoder inputs)
- ["möchte", "ein", "Stück", "Schokoladenkuchen"] (decoder outputs)

As can be seen, at every time step, the decoder is predicting the next word given the previous word(s). The prepare_data(...) function does this, as the next listing shows. Then we will write a function to shuffle the data. This function will then be used to shuffle data at the beginning of every epoch during training.

Listing 11.7 Shuffling the training data

```
def shuffle_data(en_inputs, de_inputs, de_labels, shuffle_indices=None):
    """ Shuffle the data randomly (but all of inputs and labels at ones)"""

    if shuffle_indices is None:
        shuffle_indices =
    np.random.permutation(np.arange(en_inputs.shape[0]))      ◁──┐ If shuffle_indices are not
    else:                                                          passed, create shuffled
        shuffle_indices = np.random.permutation(shuffle_indices)   ◁── indices automatically.

                                                               Shuffle the provided
    return (                                                   shuffle_indices.
        en_inputs[shuffle_indices],
        de_inputs[shuffle_indices],
        de_labels[shuffle_indices]          ◁──┐ Return
    ), shuffle_indices                             shuffled data.
```

The shuffle_data() function takes the data output by the prepare_data function (i.e., encoder inputs, decoder inputs, and decoder outputs). Optionally, it takes in a shuffled representation of the data indices. We allow the shuffle indices to be passed into the function so that, by shuffling the already shuffled indices, you get a new permutation of the order of the data. This is useful for generating different shuffle configurations in every epoch during the training.

The shuffle_data() function, if shuffle_indices is not passed, will generate a random permutation of the data indices. Data indices are generated by np.arange(en_inputs.shape[0]), which creates an ordered number sequence from 0 to the number of examples in en_inputs. A random permutation of a given array can be generated by calling the np.random.permutation() function on the array. If an array has been passed to the shuffle_indices argument, then the array passed into shuffle_indices will be shuffled, generating a new shuffled data configuration. Finally, we return encoder inputs (en_inputs), decoder inputs (de_inputs), and decoder outputs (de_labels) shuffled, as determined by the shuffle_indices array.

Next, we will write a function to evaluate the model. In this function, we evaluate a given model on given data using the defined batch_size. Particularly, we evaluate the machine translation model on three metrics:

- *Cross-entropy loss*—The standard multiclass cross-entropy loss calculated between the prediction probabilities and true targets.
- *Accuracy*—Standard accuracy measured on whether the model predicts the same word as the true target at a given time step. In other words, the prediction must match the true target exactly, from word to word.
- *BLEU score*—A more powerful metric than the accuracy that is based on precision but takes into account many n-grams for different values of n.

Bilingual Evaluation Understudy (BLEU)

BLEU is a metric used to measure the quality of generated text sequences (e.g., translations) by measuring how close the translation is to a given ground truth (or multiple ground truths per translation, as the same thing can be said differently in languages). It was introduced in the paper "BLEU: A Method for Automatic Evaluation of Machine Translation" by Papineni et al. (https://www.aclweb.org/anthology/P02 -1040.pdf). A BLEU score is a variant of the precision metric that is used to compute the similarity between a candidate text (i.e., prediction) against *multiple* reference translations (i.e., ground truths).

To understand the BLEU metric, let's consider the following candidates and references:

Candidate 1 (C1): the cat was on the red mat

Candidate 2 (C2): the cat the cat the cat the

Reference 1: the cat is on the floor

Reference 2: there was a cat on the mat

The precision for candidate 1 and 2 can be computed as

precision = Number of words matched any reference/Number of words in the candidate

which means

Precision(C1) = 6/7 and Precision(C2) = 7/7

This contradicts intuition. Obviously, C1 is a much better choice as a match for the references. But the precision tells another story. Therefore, BLEU introduces a modified precision. In modified precision, for a given unique word in the candidate, you compute the number of times that the word appears in any single reference and take the maximum of it. Then you sum this value for all the unique words in the candidate text. For example, for C1 and C2, modified unigram precision is

ModPrecision(C1) = (2 + 1 + 1 + 2 + 0 + 1) /7 = 5/7 and ModPrecision(C2) = (2 + 1)/7 = 3/7

This is much better: C1 has a higher precision than C2, which is what we wanted. BLEU extends the modified unigram precision to modified n-gram precision and computes the modified precision for several n-grams (e.g., unigrams, bigrams, trigrams, etc.). Computing modified precision over many different n-grams enables BLEU to favor translations or candidates that have longer subsequences matching the reference.

We will define an object called BLEUMetric, which will compute the BLEU score for a given batch of predictions and targets, as shown in the following listing.

Listing 11.8   Defining the `BLEUMetric` **for evaluating the machine translation model**

```
class BLEUMetric(object):

    def __init__(self, vocabulary, name='perplexity', **kwargs):
        """ Computes the BLEU score (Metric for machine translation) """
        super().__init__()
        self.vocab = vocabulary                    ← Get the vocabulary from
        self.id_to_token_layer = StringLookup(       the fitted TextVectorizer.
            vocabulary=self.vocab, invert=True,
            num_oov_indices=0
        )                                          ← Define a StringLookup layer, which
                                                     can convert token IDs to words.

    def calculate_bleu_from_predictions(self, real, pred):
        """ Calculate the BLEU score for targets and predictions """

        pred_argmax = tf.argmax(pred, axis=-1)     ← Get the predicted
                                                     token IDs.

        pred_tokens = self.id_to_token_layer(pred_argmax)    Convert token IDs
        real_tokens = self.id_to_token_layer(real)           to words using the
                                                             vocabulary and the
        def clean_text(tokens):                              StringLookup.

            """ Clean padding and [SOS]/[EOS] tokens to only keep meaningful
        words """
            t = tf.strings.strip(              ← Strip the string of any
                    tf.strings.regex_replace(    extra white spaces.          Join all the tokens
                        tf.strings.join(                            ←          to one string in
                            tf.transpose(tokens), separator=' '                each sequence.
                        ),
                    "eos.*", ""),
                )
            t = np.char.decode(t.numpy().astype(np.bytes_), encoding='utf-8')  ←
            t = [doc if len(doc)>0 else '[UNK]' for doc in t ]

            t = np.char.split(t).tolist()

            return t

        pred_tokens = clean_text(pred_tokens)      ←
        real_tokens = [[r] for r in clean_text(real_tokens)]    ←

        bleu, precisions, bp, ratio, translation_length, reference_length = \
    compute_bleu(real_tokens, pred_tokens, smooth=False)    ←

        return bleu
```

Get the vocabulary from the fitted TextVectorizer.

Define a StringLookup layer, which can convert token IDs to words.

Get the predicted token IDs.

Convert token IDs to words using the vocabulary and the StringLookup.

Strip the string of any extra white spaces.

Join all the tokens to one string in each sequence.

Replace everything after the EOS token with a blank.

Decode the byte stream to a string.

If the string is empty, add a [UNK] token. If not, it can lead to numerical errors.

Split the sequences into individual tokens.

Get the clean versions of the predictions and real sequences.

We have to wrap each real sequence in a list to make use of a third-party function to compute BLEU.

Get the BLEU value for the given batch of targets and predictions.

First, we define an __init__ (...) function and several attributes of this class, such as vocab, which will have the decoder's vocabulary returned by the TextVectorization layer. Next, we define a TensorFlow StringLookup layer that can return the string token given the token ID, and vice versa. All that is required by the StringLookup function is the vocabulary of the decoder's TextVectorization layer. By default, the StringLookup layer converts a given string token to a token ID. Setting invert=true means that this layer will convert a given token ID to a string token. We also need to say that we don't want this layer to automatically add representations for out-of-vocabulary words. For that we set num_oov_indices=0.

Next, we define a function called calculate_bleu_from_predictions(...) that takes a batch of true targets and a batch of prediction probabilities given by the model to compute the BLEU score for that batch. First, it computes the predicted token IDs by taking the maximum index of each probability vector for each time step:

```
pred_argmax = tf.argmax(pred, axis=-1)
```

Next, the string tokens are generated using the StringLookup layer defined earlier:

```
pred_tokens = self.id_to_token_layer(pred_argmax)
real_tokens = self.id_to_token_layer(real)
```

Specifically, we pass the token ID matrices (predicted and target) to the StringLookup layer. For example, if

```
real = [
    [4,1,0],
    [8,2,21]
]
```

```
vocabulary = ['', '[UNK]', 'sos', 'eos', 'tom', 'ich', 'nicht', 'ist', 'du', 'sie']
```

then

```
real_tokens = tf.Tensor([
    [b'tom' b'[UNK]' b'']
    [b'du' b'sos' b'[UNK]']
], shape=(2, 3), dtype=string)
```

After that, we define a function to perform some cleaning. The defined function will truncate the predictions such that everything after the EOS token is removed (inclusive) and will tokenize the sentences into lists of words. The input to this function is a tensor, where each row is a list of tokens (i.e., pred_tokens). Let's make this an opportunity to hone our understanding of the TensorFlow string operations. TensorFlow has a namespace known as tf.strings (http://mng.bz/gw7E) that provides a variety of basic string manipulation functionality:

```
def clean_text(tokens):

    """ Clean padding and [SOS]/[EOS] tokens to only keep meaningful words """
```

```
    # 3. Strip the string of any extra white spaces
    translations_in_bytes = tf.strings.strip(
        # 2. Replace everything after the eos token with blank
        tf.strings.regex_replace(
            # 1. Join all the tokens to one string in each sequence
            tf.strings.join(tf.transpose(tokens), separator=' '),
            "eos.*", ""
        ),
    )

    # Decode the byte stream to a string
    translations = np.char.decode(
        translations_in_bytes.numpy().astype(np.bytes_), encoding='utf-8'
    )

    # If the string is empty, add a [UNK] token
    # Otherwise get a Division by zero error
    translations = [sent if len(sent)>0 else '[UNK]' for sent in translations ]

    # Split the sequences to individual tokens
    translations = np.char.split(translations).tolist()

    return translations
```

Let's look at the first line of code that calls several tf.string operations on the inputs:

```
translations_in_bytes = tf.strings.strip(
        # 2. Replace everything after the eos token with blank
        tf.strings.regex_replace(
            # 1. Join all the tokens to one string in each sequence
            tf.strings.join(tf.transpose(tokens), separator=' '),
            "eos.*", ""
        ),
    )
```

It executes a sequence of transformations on the input string tensor. First, calling tf.strings.join() on tokens will join all the tokens in one column using a given separator. For example

```
[
    ['a','b','c'],
    ['d', 'e', 'f']
]
```

becomes

```
['ad', 'be', 'cf']
```

Since our sentences are across the rows, we first need to transpose tokens, such that sentences are in the columns. Next, tf.strings.regex_replace() is called on the tensor, where each item is a sentence resulting from the join. It will remove everything followed by the EOS token. This string pattern is captured by the eos.* regex. Finally, we strip any starting and ending spaces from the resulting strings.

TensorFlow keeps strings in byte format. In order to convert the string to UTF-8 encoding, we have a series of conversions to get it into the correct format:

1 First, we have to convert the array to a NumPy array. The elements in this array would be in Object format.
2 Next, we convert this to an array of bytes by calling translations_in_bytes .numpy().astype(np.bytes_).
3 Finally, we decode the array of bytes and convert it to a desired encoding (in our case, UTF-8).

The rest of the code is straightforward to understand and has been delineated in the code as annotations.

Finally, we call the clean_text() function on both predicted and real token tensors and feed the final results to a third-party implementation of the BLEU metric:

```
pred_tokens = clean_text(pred_tokens)
real_tokens = [[r] for r in clean_text(real_tokens)]

bleu, precisions, bp, ratio, translation_length, reference_length =
    compute_bleu(real_tokens, pred_tokens)
```

The clean_text() function will convert both predicted translations and true translations (sometimes referred to as *references*) to a list of a list of tokens. Here, the outer list represents individual examples, whereas the inner list represents the tokens in a given example. As the final step, we will wrap each reference in another list structure so that real_tokens becomes a list of a list of a list of tokens. This is a necessity, as we will be using a third-party implementation of the BLEU metric. compute_bleu, used here, is a third-party implementation found in the TensorFlow repository (http://mng.bz/e7Ev). The compute_bleu() function expects two main arguments:

- *Translation*—A list of a list of tokens.
- *References*—A list of a list of list of tokens. In other words, each translation can have multiple references, where each reference is a list of tokens.

Then it returns

- bleu—BLEU score for a given batch of candidate reference pairs.
- precisions—Individual n-gram precisions that build up the final BLEU score.
- bp—Brevity penalty (special part of BLEU score that penalizes short candidates).
- ratio—Candidate length divided by reference length.
- translation_length—Sum of lengths of candidates in the batch.
- reference_length—Sum of lengths of references in the batch. In the case of multiple references per candidate, minimum is selected.

Let's test the compute_bleu() function in action. Let's imagine a translation and a reference. In the first scenario, the translation has [UNK] tokens appearing at the beginning and the remaining match the reference completely. In the second scenario, we again have two [UNK] tokens, but they appear at the beginning and in the middle. Let's see the result:

```
translation = [['[UNK]', '[UNK]', 'mÃssen', 'wir', 'in', 'erfahrung',
➡ 'bringen', 'wo', 'sie', 'wohnen']]
reference = [[['als', 'mÃssen', 'mÃssen', 'wir', 'in', 'erfahrung',
➡ 'bringen', 'wo', 'sie', 'wohnen']]]

bleu1, _, _, _, _, _ = compute_bleu(reference, translation)

translation = [['[UNK]', 'einmal', 'mÃssen', '[UNK]', 'in', 'erfahrung',
➡ 'bringen', 'wo', 'sie', 'wohnen']]
reference = [[['als', 'mÃssen', 'mÃssen', 'wir', 'in', 'erfahrung',
➡ 'bringen', 'wo', 'sie', 'wohnen']]]


bleu2, _, _, _, _, _ = compute_bleu(reference, translation)

print("BLEU score with longer correctly predict phrases: {}".format(bleu1))
print("BLEU score without longer correctly predict phrases:
➡ {}".format(bleu2))
```

This will print

```
BLEU score with longer correctly predict phrases: 0.7598356856515925
BLEU score without longer correctly predict phrases: 0.537284965911771
```

If you were to compute the word-to-word accuracy of the translation compared to the reference, you would get the same result, as only the two [UNK] tokens are mismatched. However, the BLEU score is different for the two instances. It clearly shows that BLEU prefers the translation that gets more words continuously right, without breaks.

We have all the bells and whistles we need to write the training and evaluation loops for the model. Let's first write the evaluation loop (see the next listing), as it will be used in the training loop to evaluate the model.

Listing 11.9   Evaluating the encoder-decoder model

```
def evaluate_model(
    model, vectorizer, en_inputs_raw, de_inputs_raw, de_labels_raw, batch_size
):
    """ Evaluate the model on various metrics such as loss, accuracy and BLEU """

    bleu_metric = BLEUMetric(de_vocabulary)          ◁─── Define the metric.

    loss_log, accuracy_log, bleu_log = [], [], []
                                                          ┐ Get the number
    n_batches = en_inputs_raw.shape[0]//batch_size   ◁───┘ of batches.
    print(" ", end='\r')
                                      ┐ Evaluate one
                                      │ batch at a time.
    for i in range(n_batches):   ◁───┘                        Status update ┐
                                                                            │
        print("Evaluating batch {}/{}".format(i+1, n_batches), end='\r')  ◁─┘
```

```
              x = [
                  en_inputs_raw[i*batch_size:(i+1)*batch_size],
                  de_inputs_raw[i*batch_size:(i+1)*batch_size]
              ]
              y = de_vectorizer(de_labels_raw[i*batch_size:(i+1)*batch_size])

              loss, accuracy = model.evaluate(x, y, verbose=0)
              pred_y = model.predict(x)
                  bleu = bleu_metric.calculate_bleu_from_predictions(y, pred_y)

          loss_log.append(loss)
          accuracy_log.append(accuracy)
          bleu_log.append(bleu)

      return np.mean(loss_log), np.mean(accuracy_log), np.mean(bleu_log)
```

Get the inputs and targets.

Get the evaluation metrics.

Get the predictions to compute BLEU.

Compute the BLEU metric.

Update logs that contain loss, accuracy, and BLEU metrics.

The evaluate_model() function takes in several important arguments:

- model—The encoder-decoder model we defined.
- en_inputs_raw—The encoder inputs (text). This will be an array of strings, where each string is an English sentence/phrase.
- de_inputs_raw—The decoder inputs (text). This will be an array of strings. It will have all the words but the last word in every German translation.
- de_labels_raw—The decoder labels (text). This will be an array of strings. It will have all the words but the first one in every German translation.
- de_vectorizer—The decoder vectorizer to convert decoder_labels_raw (text) to token IDs.

The function defines a BLEUMetric object we defined earlier. It defines placeholders for accumulating loss, accuracy, and BLEU scores for each batch in the given data set. Then it goes through each batch of data and does the following:

- Creates the batch input as the corresponding batch of data from en_inputs_ raw and de_inputs_raw
- Creates the targets as token IDs using de_labels_raw
- Evaluates the model using batch inputs and targets to get the loss and accuracy scores of the batch
- Computes the BLEU score using the true targets and predictions
- Accumulates the metrics in the placeholders defined earlier

Finally, after the model has iterated through all the batches of data, it will return the mean loss, accuracy, and BLEU scores as the final evaluation benchmark for the data set.

With that, we jump into defining the training loop (see the next listing). We will define a function called train_model() that will do following four core tasks:

- Train the model with the training data.
- Evaluate the model with the training data.
- Evaluate the model with validation data.
- Evaluate the model with testing data.

Listing 11.10   Training the model using a custom training/evaluation loop

```
def train_model(model, vectorizer, train_df, valid_df, test_df, epochs,
    batch_size):
    """ Training the model and evaluating on validation/test sets """

    bleu_metric = BLEUMetric(de_vocabulary)      ⟵─┤ Define the metric.

    data_dict = prepare_data(train_df, valid_df, test_df)    ⟵─┤ Define the data.

    shuffle_inds = None


    for epoch in range(epochs):

        bleu_log = []            │ Reset metric logs at
        accuracy_log = []        │ the beginning of
        loss_log = []            │ every epoch.

        (en_inputs_raw,de_inputs_raw,de_labels_raw), shuffle_inds  =
    ⟹  shuffle_data(
            data_dict['train']['encoder_inputs'],
            data_dict['train']['decoder_inputs'],
            data_dict['train']['decoder_labels'],
            shuffle_inds
        )
        n_train_batches = en_inputs_raw.shape[0]//batch_size

        for i in range(n_train_batches):    ⟵─┤ Train one batch
                                                at a time.
            print("Training batch {}/{}".format(i+1, n_train_batches),
    ⟹  end='\r')

            x = [    ⟵─┤ Get a batch of inputs (English and
                          German sequences).
                en_inputs_raw[i*batch_size:(i+1)*batch_size],
                de_inputs_raw[i*batch_size:(i+1)*batch_size]
            ]
            y = vectorizer(de_labels_raw[i*batch_size:(i+1)*batch_size])    ⟵─
                                                 Get a batch of
                                                 targets (German
                                                 sequences
                                                 offset by 1).
            model.train_on_batch(x, y)    ⟵─┤ Train for a single step.
            loss, accuracy = model.evaluate(x, y, verbose=0)
            pred_y = model.predict(x)
            bleu = bleu_metric.calculate_bleu_from_predictions(y, pred_y)

            loss_log.append(loss)            │ Update the epoch's
            accuracy_log.append(accuracy)    │ log records of the
            bleu_log.append(bleu)            │ metrics.


        val_en_inputs = data_dict['valid']['encoder_inputs']    │ Define
        val_de_inputs = data_dict['valid']['decoder_inputs']    │ validation
        val_de_labels = data_dict['valid']['decoder_labels']    │ data.
```

Annotations (left margin, top to bottom):

Shuffle data at the beginning of every epoch.

Get the number of training batches.

Status update

Evaluate the model to get the metrics.

Get the final prediction to compute BLEU.

Compute the BLEU metric.

```
        val_loss, val_accuracy, val_bleu = evaluate_model(
            model,
            vectorizer,
            val_en_inputs,
            val_de_inputs,
            val_de_labels,
            epochs,
            batch_size
        )
```

Evaluate the
model on
validation
data.

Print the
evaluation
metrics of
each epoch.

```
        print("\nEpoch {}/{}".format(epoch+1, epochs))
        print(
            "\t(train) loss: {} - accuracy: {} - bleu: {}".format(
                np.mean(loss_log), np.mean(accuracy_log), np.mean(bleu_log)
            )
        )
        print(
            "\t(valid) loss: {} - accuracy: {} - bleu: {}".format(
                val_loss, val_accuracy, val_bleu
            )
        )


    test_en_inputs = data_dict['test']['encoder_inputs']
    test_de_inputs = data_dict['test']['decoder_inputs']
    test_de_labels = data_dict['test']['decoder_labels']

    test_loss, test_accuracy, test_bleu = evaluate_model(
            model,
            vectorizer,
            test_en_inputs,
            test_de_inputs,
            test_de_labels,
            epochs,
            batch_size
    )

    print("\n(test) loss: {} - accuracy: {} - bleu: {}".format(
        test_loss, test_accuracy, test_bleu)
    )
```

Let's analyze the function in listing 11.10 to understand its behavior. If you take a step back, all it's doing is calling the functions we defined earlier and displaying results. First it prepares the data (using the prepare_data() function) by presenting it as a dictionary that has train, valid, and test keys. Next, it goes through several epochs of training. In each epoch, it shuffles the training data and goes through the data batch by batch. For every training batch, the model is trained on the data and evaluated on the same batch. The train data evaluation logs are used to compute the training performance, just as we saw in the evaluate_model() function. Then, after the training loop finishes, the model is evaluated on the validation data. Finally, at the end of training the model, the model is evaluated on the test data. You can call the train_model() function as shown:

```
epochs = 5
batch_size = 128

train_model(final_model, de_vectorizer, train_df, valid_df, test_df,
➥ epochs, batch_size)
```

This will output a result similar to the following:

```
Evaluating batch 39/39
Epoch 1/5
    (train) loss: 1.7741597780050375 - accuracy: 0.2443966139585544 –
➥ bleu: 0.0014343267864378607
    (valid) loss: 1.4453194752717629 - accuracy: 0.3318057709779495 –
➥ bleu: 0.010740537197906803
Evaluating batch 39/39

...

Epoch 5/5
    (train) loss: 0.814081399104534 - accuracy: 0.5280381464041196 –
➥ bleu: 0.1409178724874819
    (valid) loss: 0.8876287539800009 - accuracy: 0.514901713683055 –
➥ bleu: 0.1285171513954398
Evaluating batch 39/39
(test) loss: 0.9077589313189188 - accuracy: 0.5076315150811122 - bleu:
➥ 0.12664703414801345
```

> **NOTE** On an Intel Core i5 machine with an NVIDIA GeForce RTX 2070
> 8 GB, the training took approximately 4 minutes and 10 seconds to run five
> epochs.

The first observation we can make is that the training has progressed in the right direction. Both training and validation metrics have improved over time. The model has kicked off with a training accuracy of 24% and a BLEU score of 0.001, and ended up with an accuracy of 52% and a BLEU score of 0.14. During validation, the model has increased the accuracy from 33% to 51%, whereas the BLEU score has gone from 0.01 to 0.12. As we did before, let's save the model so that it can later be used in the real world. We will save the model as well as the vocabulary:

```
## Save the model
os.makedirs('models', exist_ok=True)
tf.keras.models.save_model(final_model, os.path.join('models', 'seq2seq'))

import json
os.makedirs(os.path.join('models', 'seq2seq_vocab'), exist_ok=True)

# Save the vocabulary files
with open(os.path.join('models', 'seq2seq_vocab', 'en_vocab.json'), 'w') as f:
    json.dump(en_vocabulary, f)
with open(os.path.join('models', 'seq2seq_vocab', 'de_vocab.json'), 'w') as f:
    json.dump(de_vocabulary, f)
```

When training the model, we used the target (i.e., target language tokens) to provide an input to the decoder. This is not possible when using the model to translate where the target is unknown. For this, in the following section, we modify our trained model while using the same model parameters.

EXERCISE 3

You have the following function for training a model. Here, `en_inputs_raw` represents the encoder inputs, `de_inputs_raw` represents decoder inputs, and `de_labels_raw` represents decoder labels:

```
for epoch in range(epochs):

    bleu_log = []

    n_train_batches = en_inputs_raw.shape[0]//batch_size

    for i in range(n_train_batches):

        print("Training batch {}/{}".format(i+1, n_train_batches), end='\r')

        x = [
            en_inputs_raw[i*batch_size:(i+1)*batch_size],
            de_inputs_raw[i*batch_size:(i+1)*batch_size]
        ]
        y = vectorizer(de_labels_raw[i*batch_size:(i+1)*batch_size])

        model.train_on_batch(x, y)
        pred_y = model.predict(x)

        bleu_log.append(bleu_metric.calculate_bleu_from_predictions(y, pred_y))

    mean_bleu = np.mean(bleu_log)
```

You want to change the code so that, if the mean training BLEU score of a given epoch is smaller than the last epoch, the training is stopped. How would you change the code?

11.4   From training to inference: Defining the inference model

You have trained a sequence-to-sequence machine translation model and plan to use it to generate German translations for some unseen English phrases. It has been trained using teacher forcing, meaning that the words in the translation have been fed as inputs. You realize that this is not possible during inference, as the task itself is to generate the translation. Therefore, you are going to create a new encoder-decoder model using the trained weights of the original model. In this model, the decoder operates recursively, where it feeds its previous prediction as the input in the next time step. The decoder starts off with the SOS token and continues in this manner until it outputs the EOS token.

The ultimate objective of training a machine translator is to use it in the real world to translate unseen source language sentences (e.g., English) to a target language (e.g., German). However, unlike most of the other models we trained, we cannot take this off of the shelf and use it straight away for inference. There's extra effort required to bridge the gap between using a trained model for inference. Before coming up with a solution, let's first understand the underlying problem.

During model training, we used teacher forcing to improve the performance of the model. In teacher forcing, the decoder is provided target language inputs (e.g., German) and asked to predict the next word in the sequence at each time step. This means that the trained model relies on two inputs: English sequences and German sequences. However, during inference, we don't have access to the German sequences. Our task is to generate those German sequences for given English sequences. Therefore, we need to repurpose our trained model to be able to generate German translations without relying on whole German sequences to be available.

The solution is to keep the encoder as it is and introduce several modifications to the decoder. We will make our decoder a recursive decoder. By that, we mean that the decoder will use its previous predicted word as an input to the next time step, until it reaches the end of the sequence (figure 11.4). Specifically, we do the following. For a given English sequence

- Get the context vector by inputting the English sequence to the encoder.
- We first input the SOS token (x_0^d) (denoted by start_token in the code) along with the context vector (si_1^d) and get the decoder's prediction ($\hat{y}_1^d$) and the output state (so_1^d).
- Until the decoder's prediction ($\hat{y}_{t+1}^d$) is EOS (denoted by end_token in the code)
  - Feed the decoder's prediction ($\hat{y}_t^d$) and the output state (so_t^d) at time t as the input (x_{t+1}^d) and the initial state (si_{t+1}^d) for the next time step (t + 1).
  - Get the decoder's prediction ($\hat{y}_{t+1}^d$) and the output state (so_{t+1}^d) in the next time step.

To achieve this, we have to introduce two major changes to the trained model:

- Separate the encoder and the decoder as separate models.
- Change the decoder such that it takes an input token and an initial state as the input and outputs the predicted token and the next state as the output.

Let's see how we can do this in TensorFlow. First, we will load the model we just saved:

```
model = tf.keras.models.load_model(save_path)
```

It's very easy to get the encoder model because we have encapsulated the encoder as a nested model in the final model. It can be taken out by calling

```
en_model = model.get_layer("encoder")
```

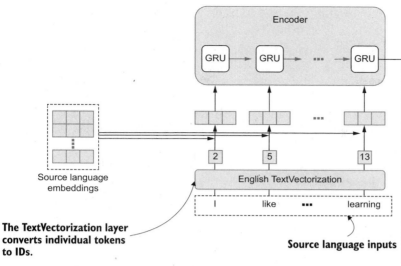

The TextVectorization layer
converts individual tokens
to IDs.

Source language inputs

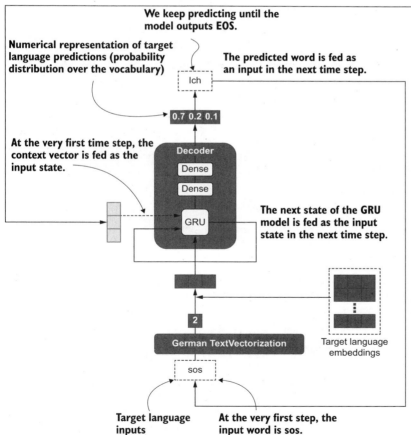

We keep predicting until the
model outputs EOS.

Numerical representation of target
language predictions (probability
distribution over the vocabulary)

The predicted word is fed as
an input in the next time step.

At the very first time step, the
context vector is fed as the
input state.

The next state of the GRU
model is fed as the input
state in the next time step.

Target language
inputs

At the very first step, the
input word is sos.

Figure 11.4   Using the
sequence-to-sequence
model for inference
(i.e., generating
translations from
English inputs)

After that, we define two inputs to represent the two inputs of the decoder:

```
d_inp = tf.keras.Input(shape=(1,), dtype=tf.string, name='d_infer_input')
d_state_inp = tf.keras.Input(shape=(256,), name='d_infer_state')
```

As we discussed earlier, we define two inputs: one to represent the input to the decoder (d_inp) and another to represent the state input to the decoder's GRU layer (d_state_inp). Analyzing the shapes, d_inp takes in an array of strings, just like before. d_state_inp represents the state vector of the GRU model and has 256 feature dimensionality.

After we define the inputs, we will retrace all the steps we followed during the decoder build in the trained model. However, instead of creating new randomly initialized layers, we will get layers from the trained model. Particularly, we will have the following layers to flow the inputs through:

- Decoder's vectorization layer (produces d_vectorized_out)
- Decoder's embedding layer (produces d_emb_out)
- Decoder's GRU layer (produces d_gru_out)
- Decoder's fully connected hidden layer (produces d_dense1_out)
- Final prediction layer (produces d_final_out)

It is worth highlighting an important change we are introducing to the GRU model. Note that we are setting return_sequences=False to make sure the decoder GRU only returns the last output (i.e., not a sequence of outputs). In other words, the output of the GRU layer is a [None, 256]–sized tensor. This helps us match the shape of the output to the d_state_inp we defined earlier, making it easier to build a recursive model. Furthermore, the GRU layer takes d_state_inp as the initial_state in the model. This way, we can feed the output state vector as a recursive input to the decoder:

```
# Generate the vectorized output of inp
d_vectorizer = model.get_layer('d_vectorizer')
d_vectorized_out = d_vectorizer(d_inp)

# Generate the embeddings from the vectorized input
d_emb_out = model.get_layer('d_embedding')(d_vectorized_out)

# Get the GRU layer
d_gru_layer = model.get_layer("d_gru")
# Since we generate one word at a time, we will not need the return_sequences
d_gru_layer.return_sequences = False
# Get the GRU out while using d_state_inp from earlier, as the initial state
d_gru_out = d_gru_layer(d_emb_out, initial_state=d_state_inp)

# Get the dense output
d_dense1_out = model.get_layer("d_dense_1")(d_gru_out)

# Get the final output
d_final_out = model.get_layer("d_dense_final")(d_dense1_out)
```

It's time to define the final decoder model:

```
de_model = tf.keras.models.Model(
    inputs=[d_inp, d_state_inp], outputs=[d_final_out, d_gru_out]
)
```

The model takes the `d_inp` and `d_state_inp` as inputs and produces `d_final_out` (i.e., the final prediction) and `d_gru_out` (i.e., the GRU output state) as the output. Finally, let's take a step back and encapsulate the work we did in a single function called `get_inference_model()`, as shown in the next listing.

Listing 11.11   Defining the recursive inference model for the machine translation model

Define the first input to the new inference decoder, an input layer that takes a batch of strings.

Define the second input to the new inference decoder, an input layer that takes an initial state to pass to the decoder GRU as the input state.

```
import tensorflow.keras.backend as K
K.clear_session()

def get_inference_model(save_path):
    """ Load the saved model and create an inference model from that """

    model = tf.keras.models.load_model(save_path)          ← Load the saved
                                                             trained model.

    en_model = model.get_layer("encoder")        ← Get the encoder model from
                                                   the loaded model by calling
                                                   the get_layer() function.
    d_inp = tf.keras.Input(
        shape=(1,), dtype=tf.string, name='d_infer_input'
    )
    d_state_inp = tf.keras.Input(shape=(256,), name='d_infer_state')  ←

    d_vectorizer = model.get_layer('d_vectorizer')     | Generate the vectorized output
    d_vectorized_out = d_vectorizer(d_inp)             | of the string input to the decoder.

    d_emb_out = model.get_layer('d_embedding')(d_vectorized_out)   ←

    d_gru_layer = model.get_layer("d_gru")                  Generate the embeddings
    d_gru_layer.return_sequences = False                    from the vectorized input.
    d_gru_out = d_gru_layer(d_emb_out, initial_state=d_state_inp)  ←

    d_dense1_out = model.get_layer("d_dense_1")(d_gru_out)   ←

    d_final_out = model.get_layer("d_dense_final")(d_dense1_out)   ←

    de_model = tf.keras.models.Model(
        inputs=[d_inp, d_state_inp], outputs=[d_final_out, d_gru_out]
    )
                                                        Get the final output.
    return en_model, de_model
                                                        Get the dense output.
```

Get the decoder's GRU layer.

Define the final decoder.

Since we generate one word at a time, we will not need the return_sequences.

Get the GRU out while using d_state_inp from earlier as the initial state.

We will then define a function to load back the vocabularies we just saved. We saved the vocabularies using the JSON format, and all we need to do to load the vocabularies is call `json.load()` with the opened vocabulary files:

```
def get_vocabularies(save_dir):
    """ Load the vocabulary files from a given path"""

    with open(os.path.join(save_dir, 'en_vocab.json'), 'r') as f:
        en_vocabulary = json.load(f)

    with open(os.path.join(save_dir, 'de_vocab.json'), 'r') as f:
        de_vocabulary = json.load(f)

    return en_vocabulary, de_vocabulary

print("Loading vocabularies")
en_vocabulary, de_vocabulary = get_vocabularies(
    os.path.join('models', 'seq2seq_vocab')
)

print("Loading weights and generating the inference model")
en_model, de_model = get_inference_model(os.path.join('models', 'seq2seq'))
print("\tDone")
```

Steaming ahead, we now have everything to generate new translations. As discussed, we are going to create a process/function where we input the English sentence (denoted by `sample_en_text`) to the encoder to produce the context vector. Next, make a prediction with the SOS token and the context vector to get the first German token prediction and the next state output. Finally, recursively feed the outputs of the decoder as inputs to the decoder until the predicted token is EOS. The following listing delineates this functionality using the inference model we just built.

Listing 11.12   Generating translations with the new inference model

```
def generate_new_translation(en_model, de_model, de_vocabulary,
    sample_en_text):
    """ Generate a new translation """

    start_token = 'sos'                                          Get the initial
    print("Input: {}".format(sample_en_text))                    state for the
                                                                  decoder.

    d_state = en_model.predict(np.array([sample_en_text]))

    de_word = start_token              The first input word to the decoder
                                       will always be the start_token
    de_translation = []                (i.e., it has the value sos).

    while de_word != end_token:        Keep predicting until we get the
                                       end_token (i.e., it has the value eos).
```

Print the input.

We collect the translation in this list.

```
de_pred, d_state = de_model.predict([np.array([de_word]), d_state])
de_word = de_vocabulary[np.argmax(de_pred[0])]
de_translation.append(de_word)

print("Translation: {}\n".format(' '.join(de_translation)))
```

Get the actual word from the
token ID of the prediction.

Add that to the
translation.

Override the previous state
input with the new state.

Let's run this for several test inputs in our data set and see what we get:

```
for i in range(5):
    sample_en_text = test_df["EN"].iloc[i]
    generate_new_translation(en_model, de_model, de_vocabulary, sample_en_text)
```

This will output

```
Input: The pleasure's all mine.
Translation: die [UNK] [UNK] mir eos

Input: Tom was asking for it.
Translation: tom sprach es zu tun eos

Input: He denied having been involved in the affair.
Translation: er [UNK] sich auf das [UNK] [UNK] eos

Input: Is there something in particular that you want to drink?
Translation: gibt es etwas [UNK] wenn du etwas [UNK] eos

Input: Don't run. Walk slowly.
Translation: [UNK] nicht zu fuß eos
```

You can run these English phrases/sentences against Google Translate and see how closely our model is getting them. For a model trained on a relatively simple and small data set, our model is doing very well. The [UNK] token is present in the translation because all the less-frequent words are replaced with [UNK] in the corpus. Therefore, when the model is uncertain of the word that should be filled in a certain position, it is likely to output [UNK].

EXERCISE 4

Instead of using the GRU model, you have decided to use an LSTM model. As you know, an LSTM model has two states: a cell state and an output state. You have built the encoder and are now building the decoder. You are planning to adapt the following code to use an LSTM model:

```
d_inp = tf.keras.Input(shape=(1,), dtype=tf.string)
d_state_inp = tf.keras.Input(shape=(256,))

d_vectorized_out = de_vectorizer(d_inp)
```

```
d_emb_out = tf.keras.layers.Embedding(de_vocab+2, 128,
    mask_zero=True)(d_vectorized_out)

d_gru_out = tf.keras.layers.GRU(256)(d_emb_out, initial_state=d_state_inp)

d_final_out = tf.keras.layers.Dense(
    de_vocab+2, activation='softmax'
)(d_gru_out)

de_model = tf.keras.models.Model(
    inputs=[d_inp, d_state_inp], outputs=[d_final_out, d_gru_out]
)
```

If you set `return_state=True` in an LSTM layer and call it on some compatible input x, the output is as follows

```
lstm_out, state_h, state_c = tf.keras.layers.LSTM(256, return_state=True)(x)
```

where `state_h` and `state_c` represent the output state and the cell state respectively.

We have trained a machine translation model using the sequence-to-sequence architecture. In the next chapter, we will look at how we can improve this model further by using a technique known as attention.

Summary

- The encoder-decoder pattern is common for sequence-to-sequence tasks such as machine translation.
- The encoder takes in source language inputs and produces a context vector.
- The context vector is used by the decoder to produce target language outputs (i.e., translation).
- The `tf.keras.layers.experimental.preprocessing.TextVectorization` layer allows you to integrate tokenization (i.e., converting strings to list of tokens and then to token IDs) into your model. This enables the model to take in strings rather than numerical values.
- When training models on sequence-to-sequence tasks, you can employ teacher forcing:
  - In teacher forcing, the encoder consumes the source language input and produces the context vector as usual. Then the decoder consumes and predicts the words in the translation. In other words, the decoder is trained in such a way that the decoder predicts the next word given the previous word(s) in the translation.
- The quality of translations produced by a machine translation model is measured using the BLEU score:
  - The BLEU score uses a modified version of the precision metric along with measuring precision on different n-grams of the translation to come up with a score.

- Once a model is trained using teacher forcing, a separate inference model needs to be defined using the trained weights:
  - This inference model has the same encoder, but the decoder takes in the previously predicted word as an input for the next step and recursively predicts words until a predefined ending criterion is met.

Answers to exercises

Exercise 1

```
def vocab_size(ser):

    cnt = Counter(ser.sum())
    return len(cnt)
```

Exercise 2

```
# The decoder
en_repeat_out = tf.keras.layers.RepeatVector(de_seq_length)(en_gru_out)
d_gru_layer = tf.keras.layers.GRU(256, return_sequences=True, name='d_gru')
d_gru_out = d_gru_layer(en_repeat_out, initial_state=gru_out)
d_dense_layer_1 = tf.keras.layers.Dense(512, activation='relu', name='d_dense_1')
d_dense1_out = d_dense_layer_1(d_gru_out)
d_dense_layer_final = tf.keras.layers.Dense(
    de_vocab+2, activation='softmax', name='d_dense_final'
)
d_final_out = d_dense_layer_final(d_dense1_out)

# Define the full model
model = tf.keras.models.Model(
    inputs=inp, outputs=d_final_out, name='final_seq2seq'
)
```

Exercise 3

```
prev_bleu = None

for epoch in range(epochs):

    bleu_log = []

    n_train_batches = en_inputs_raw.shape[0]//batch_size

    for i in range(n_train_batches):

        print("Training batch {}/{}".format(i+1, n_train_batches), end='\r')


        x = [
            en_inputs_raw[i*batch_size:(i+1)*batch_size],
            de_inputs_raw[i*batch_size:(i+1)*batch_size]
        ]
        y = vectorizer(de_labels_raw[i*batch_size:(i+1)*batch_size])
```

```
        model.train_on_batch(x, y)
        pred_y = model.predict(x)

        bleu_log.append(bleu_metric.calculate_bleu_from_predictions(y,
     pred_y))

    mean_bleu = np.mean(bleu_log)

    # The termination criteria
    if prev_bleu and prev_bleu > mean_bleu:
        break

    prev_bleu = mean_bleu
```

Exercise 4

```
d_inp = tf.keras.Input(shape=(1,), dtype=tf.string)
d_state_h_inp = tf.keras.Input(shape=(256,))
d_state_c_inp = tf.keras.Input(shape=(256,))

d_vectorized_out = de_vectorizer(d_inp)

d_emb_out = tf.keras.layers.Embedding(
    de_vocab+2, 128, mask_zero=True
)(d_vectorized_out)

d_lstm_out, d_state_h, d_state_c = tf.keras.layers.LSTM(
    256, return_state=True
)(d_emb_out, initial_state=[d_state_h_inp, d_state_c_inp])

d_final_out = tf.keras.layers.Dense(
    de_vocab+2, activation='softmax'
)(d_lstm_out)

de_model = tf.keras.models.Model(
    inputs=[d_inp, d_state_h_inp, d_state_c_inp],
    outputs=[d_final_out, d_state_h, d_state_c]
)
de_model.summary()
```

Sequence-to-sequence learning: Part 2

This chapter covers

- Implementing the attention mechanism for the seq2seq model
- Generating visualizations from the attention layer to glean insights from the model

In the previous chapter, we built an English-to-German machine translator. The machine learning model was a sequence-to-sequence model that could learn to map arbitrarily long sequences to other arbitrarily long sequences. It had two main components: an encoder and a decoder. To arrive at that, we first downloaded a machine translation data set, examined the structure of that data set, and applied some processing (e.g., adding SOS and EOS tokens) to prepare it for the model. Next, we defined the machine translation model using standard Keras layers. A special characteristic of this model is its ability to take in raw strings and convert them to numerical representations internally. To achieve this, we used the Keras's Text-Vectorization layer. When the model was defined, we trained it using the data set we processed and evaluated it on two metrics: per-word accuracy of the sequences produced and BLEU. BLEU is a more advanced metric than accuracy that mimics how a human would evaluate the quality of a translation. To train the model, we used a technique known as teacher forcing. When teacher forcing is used, we feed the decoder, with the target translation offset by 1. This means the decoder predicts the next word in the target sequence given the previous word(s), instead of trying to predict the whole target sequence without any knowledge of the target sequence. This leads to better performance. Finally, we had to redefine our model to suit inference. This is because we had to modify the decoder such that it predicted one word at a time instead of a sequence. This way, we can create a recursive decoder at inference time, which predicts a word and feeds the predicted word as an input to predict the next word in the sequence.

In this chapter, we will explore ways to increase the accuracy of our model. To do that, we will use the attention mechanism. Without attention, machine translation models rely on the last output produced after processing the input sequence. Through the attention mechanism, the model is able to obtain rich representations from all the time steps (while processing the input sequence) during the generation of the translation. Finally, we will conclude the chapter by visualizing the attention mechanisms that will give insights into how the model pays attention to words provided to it during the translation process.

The data and the processing we do in this chapter are going to be identical to the last chapter. Therefore, we will not discuss data in detail. You have been provided all the code necessary to load and process data in the notebook. But let's refresh the key steps we performed:

- Download the data set manually from http://www.manythings.org/anki/deu -eng.zip.
- The data is in tab-separated format and `<German phrase><tab><English phrase><tab><Attribution>` format. We really care about the first two tab-separated values in a record. We are going to predict the German phrase given the English phrase.
- We randomly sample 50,000 data points from the data set and use 5,000 (i.e., 10%) as validation data and another 5,000 (i.e., 10%) as test data.
- We add a start token (e.g., SOS) and an end token (e.g., EOS) to each German phrase. This is an important preprocessing step, as this helps us to recursively infer words from our recursive decoder at inference time (i.e., provide SOS as the initial seed and keep predicting until the model outputs EOS or reaches a maximum length).
- We look at summary statistics of vocabulary size and sequence length, as these hyperparameters are very important for our `TextVectorization` layer (the layer can be found at tensorflow.keras.layers.experimental.preprocessing.Text-Vectorization).
- The vocabulary size is set as the number of unique words that appear more than 10 times in the corpus for both languages, and the sequence length is set as the 99% quantile (plus a buffer of 5) for both languages.

12.1 Eyeballing the past: Improving our model with attention

You have a working prototype of the translator but still think you can push the accuracy up by using attention. Attention provides a richer output from the encoder to the decoder by allowing the decoder to look at all the outputs produced by the encoder over the entire input sequence. You will modify the previously implemented model to incorporate an attention layer that takes all the encoder outputs (one for each time step) and produces a sequence of outputs for each decoder step that will be concatenated with the standard output produced by the decoder.

We have a working machine translator model that can translate from English to German. Performance of this model can be pushed further using something known as *Bahdanau attention*. Bahdanau attention was introduced in the paper "Neural Machine Translation by Jointly Learning to Align and Translate" by Bahdanau et al. (https://arxiv.org/pdf/1409.0473.pdf). We already discussed self-attention in chapter 5. The underlying principle between the two attention mechanisms is the same. They both allow the model to get a rich representation of historical/future input in a sequence to facilitate the model in understanding the language better. Let's see how the attention mechanism can be tied in with the encoder-decoder model we have.

The attention mechanism produces an output for each decoder time step, similar to how the decoder's GRU model produces an output at each time step. The attention output is combined with the decoder's GRU output and fed to the subsequent hidden layer in the decoder. The attention output produced at each time step of the decoder combines the encoder's outputs from all the time steps, which provides valuable information about the English input sequence to the decoder. The attention layer is allowed to mix the encoder outputs differently to produce the output for each decoder time step, depending on which part of the translation the decoder model is working on at a given moment. You should be able to see how powerful the attention mechanism is. Previously, the context vector was the only input from the encoder that was accessible to the decoder. This is a massive performance bottleneck, as it is impractical for the encoder to encode all the information present in a sentence using a small-sized vector.

Let's probe a bit more to understand the specific computations that transpire during the computation of the attention outputs. Let's assume that the encoder output at position j $(1 < j < T_e)$ is denoted by h_j, and the decoder RNN output state at time i $(1 < i < T_d)$ is denoted by s_i; then the attention output c_i for the ith decoding step is computed by

$$e_{ij} = v^T \, tanh(s_{i-1} \; W + h_j U)$$

$$\alpha_{ij} = \frac{\exp(e_{ij})}{\sum_{k=1}^{T_d} \exp(e_{ik})}$$

$$c_i = \sum_{j=1}^{T_e} \alpha_{ij} h_i$$

Here, W, U, and v are weight matrices (initialized randomly just like neural network weights). Their shapes are defined in accordance with the dimensionality of hidden representations s and h, which will be discussed in detail soon. In summary, this set of equations, for a given decoder position

- Computes energy values representing how important each encoder output is for that decoding step using a small fully connected network whose weights are W, U, and v
- Normalizes energies to represent a probability distribution over the encoder steps
- Computes a weighted sum of encoder outputs using the probability distribution

12.1.1 *Implementing Bahdanau attention in TensorFlow*

Unfortunately, TensorFlow does not have a built-in layer to readily use in our models to enable the attention mechanism. Therefore, we will implement an `Attention` layer using the Keras subclassing API. We will call this the `DecoderRNNAttentionWrapper` and will have to implement the following functions:

- `__init__`—Defines various initializations that need to happen before the layer can operate correctly
- `build()`—Defines the parameters (e.g., trainable weights) and their shapes associated with the computation
- `call()`—Defines the computations and the final output that should be produced by the layer

The `__init__()` function initializes the layer with any attributes it requires to operate correctly. In this case, our `DecoderRNNAttentionWrapper` takes in a `cell_fn` as the argument. `cell_fn` needs to be a Keras layer object that implements the `tf.keras.layers.AbstractRNNCell` interface (http://mng.bz/pO18). There are several options, such as `tf.keras.layers.GRUCell`, `tf.keras.layers.LSTMCell`, and `tf.keras.layers.RNNCell`. In this case, we will use the `tf.keras.layers.GRUCell`.

Difference between tf.keras.layers.GRUCell and tf.keras.layers.GRU

The `GRUCell` can be thought of as an abstraction of the GRU layer. The `GRUCell` encompasses the most minimalist computation you can think of in an RNN layer. Given an input and a previous state, it computes the next output and the next state. This is the most primitive computation that governs an RNN layer:

```
output, next_state = tf.keras.layers.GRUCell(input, state)
```

> In other words, a GRUCell encapsulates the computations required to compute a sin-
> gle time step in an input sequence. The GRU layer is a fully fledged implementation
> of the GRUCell that can process the whole sequence. Furthermore, the GRU layer
> gives options like return_state and return_sequence to control the output pro-
> duced by the GRU layer.
>
> In short, the GRU layer provides the convenience for processing input sequences,
> and the GRUCell exposes the more fine-grained implementation details that allow
> one to process a single time step in the sequence.

Here, we have decided to go with GRU, as the GRU model is a lot simpler than an
LSTM (meaning there is reduced training time) but achieves roughly similar results
on NLP tasks:

```python
def __init__(self, cell_fn, units, **kwargs):
    self._cell_fn = cell_fn
    self.units = units
    super(DecoderRNNAttentionWrapper, self).__init__(**kwargs)
```

Next, the build() function is defined. The build function declares the three weight
matrices used in the attention computation: W, U and v. The argument input_shape
contains the shapes of the inputs. Our input will be a tuple containing encoder outputs and the decoder RNN inputs:

```python
def build(self, input_shape):


    self.W_a = self.add_weight(
        name='W_a',
        shape=tf.TensorShape((input_shape[0][2], input_shape[0][2])),
        initializer='uniform',
        trainable=True
    )

    self.U_a = self.add_weight(
        name='U_a',
        shape=tf.TensorShape((self._cell_fn.units, self._cell_fn.units)),
        initializer='uniform',
        trainable=True
    )

    self.V_a = self.add_weight(
        name='V_a',
        shape=tf.TensorShape((input_shape[0][2], 1)),
        initializer='uniform',
        trainable=True
    )


    super(DecoderRNNAttentionWrapper, self).build(input_shape)
```

The most important argument to note in the weight definitions is the shape argument. We are defining them so that

- `W_a` (representing W) has a shape of [<encoder hidden size>, <attention hidden size>]
- `U_a` (representing U) has a shape of [<decoder hidden size>, <attention hidden size>]
- `V_a` (representing v) has a shape of [<attention hidden size>, 1]

Here, the <encoder hidden size> and <decoder hidden size> are the number of units in the final output of the RNN layer of the encoder or the decoder, respectively. We typically keep the encoder and decoder RNN sizes the same to simplify the computations. The <attention hidden size> is a hyperparameter of the layer that can be set to any value and represents the dimensionality of internal computations of the attention. Finally, we define the `call()` method (see listing 12.1). The `call()` method encapsulates the computations that take place when the layer is called with inputs. This is where the heavy lifting required to compute the attention outputs happens. At a high level, the attention layer needs to traverse all the encoder inputs (i.e., each time step) for each decoder input.

Listing 12.1   Attention computation in the `DecoderRNNAttentionWrapper`

When calling the _step function, we are passing encoder_outputs as a constant, as we need access to the full encoder sequence. Here we access it within the _step function.

Computes the energies and normalizes them. Produces a [batch_size, en_seq_len] sized output

```
def call(self, inputs, initial_state, training=False):

    def _step(inputs, states):
        """ Step function for computing energy for a single decoder state
        inputs: (batchsize * de_in_dim)
        states: [(batchsize * de_latent_dim)]
        """
        encoder_full_seq = states[-1]

        W_a_dot_h = K.dot(encoder_outputs, self.W_a)

        U_a_dot_s = K.expand_dims(K.dot(states[0], self.U_a), 1)

        Wh_plus_Us = K.tanh(W_a_dot_h + U_a_dot_s)

        e_i = K.squeeze(K.dot(Wh_plus_Us, self.V_a), axis=-1)
        a_i = K.softmax(e_i)

        c_i = K.sum(encoder_outputs * K.expand_dims(a_i, -1), axis=1)
```

Computes S.Wa where S represents all the encoder outputs and S=[s0, s1, ..., si]. This produces a [batch size, en_seq_len, hidden size]–sized output.

Computes tanh(S.Wa + hj.Ua). This produces a [batch_size, en_seq_len, hidden size]–sized output

Computes hj.Ua, where hj represent the jth decoding step. This produces a [batch_size, 1, hidden size]–sized output

Computes the final attention output (c_i) as a weighted sum of h_j (for all j), where weights are denoted by a_i. Produces a [batch_size, hidden_size] output

```
        s, states = self._cell_fn(K.concatenate([inputs, c_i], axis=-1),
    states)

        return (s, a_i), states

    """ Computing outputs """

    encoder_outputs, decoder_inputs = inputs

    _, attn_outputs, _ = K.rnn(
        step_function=_step, inputs=decoder_inputs,
    initial_states=[initial_state], constants=[encoder_outputs]
    )

    # attn_out => (batch_size, de_seq_len, de_hidden_size)
    # attn_energy => (batch_size, de_seq_len, en_seq_len)
    attn_out, attn_energy = attn_outputs

        return attn_out, attn_energy
```

The inputs to the attention layer are encoder outputs and decoder RNN inputs.

The K.rnn() function executes the _step() function for every input in the decoder inputs to produce attention outputs for all the decoding steps.

The final output is two-fold: attention outputs of a [batch size, de_seq_len, hidden size]–sized output and attention energies [batch dize, de_seq_len, en_seq_len]–sized outputs

Concatenate sthe current input and c_i and feeds it to the decoder RNN to get the output

Let's demystify what's done in this function. The input to this layer is an iterable of two elements: encoder output sequence (encoder_outputs) and decoder RNN input sequence (decoder_inputs). Next, we use a special backend function of Keras called K.rnn() (http://mng.bz/OoPR) to iterate through these inputs while computing the final output required. In our example, it is called as

```
_, attn_outputs, _ = K.rnn(
        step_function=_step, inputs=decoder_inputs,
    initial_states=[initial_state], constants=[encoder_outputs],
    )
```

Here, it applies the step_function to each time step slice of the inputs tensor. For example, the decoder_inputs is a [<batch size>, <decoder time steps>, <embedding size>]–sized input. Then the K.rnn() function applies the step_function to every [<batch size>, <embedding size>] output for <decoder time steps> number of times. The update this function does is a recurrent update, meaning that it takes an initial state and produces a new state until it reaches the end of the input sequence. For that, initial_states provides the starting states. Finally, we are passing encoder_outputs as a constant to the step_function. This is quite important as we need the full sequence of the encoder's hidden outputs to compute attention at each decoding step. Within the step_function, constants gets appended to the value of the states argument. So, you can access encoder_outputs as the last element of states.

The _step function does the computations we outlined in listing 12.1 for a single decoder time step. It takes inputs (a slice of the time dimension of the original input) and states (initialized with the initial_states value in the K.rnn() function). Next, using these two entities, the normalized attention energies (i.e., α_{ij}) for a single time step are computed (a_i). Following that, c_i is computed, which is a weighted sum of encoder_outputs weighted by a_i. Afterward, it updates the cell_fn (i.e., GRUCell) with the current input and the state. Note that the current input to the cell_fn is a concatenation of the decoder input and c_i (i.e., the weighted sum of encoder inputs). The cell function then outputs the output state along with the next state. We return this information out. In other words, the _step() function outputs the output for that time step (i.e., a tuple of decoder RNN output and normalized energies that computed the weighted sum of encoder inputs) and the next state of the decoder RNN.

Finally, you can obtain the full output of the _step function for all the decoder time steps using the K.rnn() function as shown. We are only interested in the output itself (denoted by attn_outputs) and will ignore the other things output by the function.

The K.rnn() function outputs the following outputs when called:

- last_output—The last output produced by the _step_function after it reaches the end of the sequence
- outputs—All the outputs produced by the step_function
- new_states—The last states produced by the step_function after it reaches the end of the sequence

Finally, the call() function produces two outputs:

- attn_out—Holds all the attention outputs for all the decoding steps
- attn_energy—Provides the normalized energy values for a batch of data, where the energy matrix for one example contains energy values for all the encoder time steps for every decoder time step

We have discussed the most important functions of the DecoderRNNAttentionWrapper layer. If you want to see the full sub-classed implementation of the DecoderRNN-AttentionWrapper, please refer to the code at Ch11/11.1_seq2seq_machine_translation .ipynb.

12.1.2 Defining the final model

When defining the final model, the get_vectorizer() and get_encoder() functions remain identical to what was shown in the previous section. All the modifications required need to happen in the decoder. Therefore, let's define a function, get_final_seq2seq_model_with_attention(), that provides us the decoder with Bahdanau attention in place, as shown in the next listing.

> **Listing 12.2 Defining the final sequence-to-sequence model with attention**

```
def get_final_seq2seq_model_with_attention(n_vocab, encoder, vectorizer):
    """ Define the final encoder-decoder model """

    e_inp = tf.keras.Input(shape=(1,), dtype=tf.string, name='e_input_final')
    fwd_state, bwd_state, en_states = encoder(e_inp)

    d_inp = tf.keras.Input(shape=(1,), dtype=tf.string, name='d_input')
```

Get the encoder outputs for all the timesteps.

The input is (None,1) shaped and accepts an array of strings.

```
d_vectorized_out = vectorizer(d_inp)
```
Vectorize the data
(assign token IDs).

```
d_emb_layer = tf.keras.layers.Embedding(
    n_vocab+2, 128, mask_zero=True, name='d_embedding'
)
d_emb_out = d_emb_layer(d_vectorized_out)
```
Define an embedding
layer to convert IDs
to word vectors.

```
d_init_state = tf.keras.layers.Concatenate(axis=-1)([fwd_state, bwd_state])

gru_cell = tf.keras.layers.GRUCell(256)
attn_out, _   = DecoderRNNAttentionWrapper(
    cell_fn=gru_cell, units=512, name="d_attention"
)([en_states, d_emb_out], initial_state=d_init_state)

d_dense_layer_1 = tf.keras.layers.Dense(512, activation='relu',
  name='d_dense_1')
d_dense1_out = d_dense_layer_1(attn_out)

d_final_layer = tf.keras.layers.Dense(
    n_vocab+2, activation='softmax', name='d_dense_final'
)
d_final_out = d_final_layer(d_dense1_out)

seq2seq = tf.keras.models.Model(
    inputs=[e_inp, d_inp], outputs=d_final_out,
    name='final_seq2seq_with_attention'
)

return seq2seq
```

Define a GRUCell, which
will then be used for the
Attention layer.

Define the
intermediate
and final Dense
layer outputs.

Get the attention
outputs. The GRUCell is
passed as the cell_fn,
where the inputs are
en_states (i.e., all of the
encoder states) and
d_emb_out (input to the
decoder RNN).

Define a model that
takes encoder and
decoder inputs as
inputs and outputs
the final predictions
(d_final_out).

Define the initial state to the decoder as
the concatenation of the last forward
and backward encoder states.

We already have done all the hard work. Therefore, changes to the decoder can be summarized in two lines of code:

```
gru_cell = tf.keras.layers.GRUCell(256)
attn_out, _   = DecoderRNNAttentionWrapper(
    cell_fn=gru_cell, units=512, name="d_attention"
)(
    [en_states, d_emb_out], initial_state=d_init_state
)
```

We first define a GRUCell object with 256 hidden units. Then we define the Decoder-RNNAttentionWrapper, where the cell_fn is the GRUCell we defined and units is set to 512. units in the DecoderRNNAttentionWrapper defines the dimensionality of the weights and the intermediate attention outputs. We pass en_states (i.e., encoder output sequence) and d_emb_out (i.e., decoder input sequence to the RNN) and set the initial state as the final state of the encoder (i.e., d_init_state).

Next, as before, we have to define a get_vectorizer() function (see the next listing) to get the English/German vectorizers.

Listing 12.3   Defining the `TextVectorizers` for the encoder-decoder model

```
def get_vectorizer(
    corpus, n_vocab, max_length=None, return_vocabulary=True, name=None
):
```
> Define an input layer that takes a list of strings (or an array of strings).

```
    """ Return a text vectorization layer or a model """

    inp = tf.keras.Input(shape=(1,), dtype=tf.string, name='encoder_input')    ◁

    vectorize_layer =
      tf.keras.layers.experimental.preprocessing.TextVectorization(
        max_tokens=n_vocab+2,                    ◁
        output_mode='int',
        output_sequence_length=max_length,
        name=name
    )
```
> When defining the vocab size, there are two special tokens, (Padding) and '[UNK]' (OOV tokens), added automatically.

```
    vectorize_layer.adapt(corpus)    ◁
```
> Fit the vectorizer layer on the data.

```
    vectorized_out = vectorize_layer(inp)    ◁
```
> Get the token IDs for the data fed to the input.

> **Return the vocabulary in addition to the model.**

```
    if not return_vocabulary:
        return tf.keras.models.Model(inputs=inp, outputs=vectorized_out)    ◁
    else:
        return tf.keras.models.Model(
            inputs=inp, outputs=vectorized_out
        ), vectorize_layer.get_vocabulary()
```
> Return only the model, which takes an array of a string and outputs a tensor of token IDs.

The `get_encoder()` function shown in the following listing builds the encoder. As these have been discussed in detail, they will not be repeated here.

Listing 12.4   The function that returns the encoder

```
def get_encoder(n_vocab, vectorizer):
    """ Define the encoder of the seq2seq model"""
```
> The input is (None,1) shaped and accepts an array of strings.

> **Vectorize the data (assign token IDs).**

```
    inp = tf.keras.Input(shape=(1,), dtype=tf.string, name='e_input')    ◁

    vectorized_out = vectorizer(inp)
```
> Define an embedding layer to convert IDs to word vectors.

> **Get the embeddings of the token IDs**

```
    emb_layer = tf.keras.layers.Embedding(
        n_vocab+2, 128, mask_zero=True, name='e_embedding'    ◁
    )

    emb_out = emb_layer(vectorized_out)

    gru_layer = tf.keras.layers.Bidirectional(
        tf.keras.layers.GRU(128, name='e_gru'),    ◁
        name='e_bidirectional_gru'
    )
```
> Define a bidirectional GRU layer. The encoder looks at the English text (i.e., the input) both backward and forward; this leads to better performance.

```
    gru_out = gru_layer(emb_out)    ◁
```
> Get the output of the GRU layer (the last output state vector returned by the model).

```
encoder = tf.keras.models.Model(
    inputs=inp, outputs=gru_out, name='encoder'
)
return encoder
```

◁───── **Define the encoder model; this takes in a list/array of strings as the input and returns the last output state of the GRU model as the output.**

As the very last step, we define the final model and compile it using the same specifications we used for the earlier model:

```
# Get the English vectorizer/vocabulary
en_vectorizer, en_vocabulary =
➥ get_vectorizer(np.array(train_df["EN"].tolist()), en_vocab,
    max_length=en_seq_length, name='e_vectorizer')
# Get the German vectorizer/vocabulary
de_vectorizer, de_vocabulary =
➥ get_vectorizer(np.array(train_df["DE"].tolist()), de_vocab,
➥ max_length=de_seq_length-1, name='d_vectorizer')

# Define the final model with attention
encoder = get_encoder_with_attention(en_vocab, en_vectorizer)
final_model_with_attention =
➥ get_final_seq2seq_model_with_attention(de_vocab, encoder, de_vectorizer)

# Compile the model
final_model_with_attention.compile(
    loss='sparse_categorical_crossentropy',
    optimizer='adam',
    metrics=['accuracy']
)
```

12.1.3 *Training the model*

Training the model is quite straightforward as it remains the same as before. All we need to do is call the `train_model()` function with the arguments model (a Keras model to be trained/evaluated), vectorizer (a target language vectorizer to convert token IDs to text), `train_df` (training data), `valid_df` (validation data), `test_df` (testing data), epochs (an `int` to represent how many epochs the model needs to be trained) and `batch_size` (size of a training/evaluation batch):

```
epochs = 5
batch_size = 128

train_model(final_model_with_attention, de_vectorizer, train_df, valid_df,
➥ test_df, epochs, batch_size)
```

This will output

```
Evaluating batch 39/39
Epoch 1/5
    (train) loss: 2.096887740951318 - accuracy: 0.6887444907274002 -
➥ bleu: 0.00020170408678925458
    (valid) loss: 1.5872839291890461 - accuracy: 0.7375801282051282 -
➥ bleu: 0.002304922518160425
```

...

```
Evaluating batch 39/39
Epoch 5/5
    (train) loss: 0.7739567615282841 - accuracy: 0.8378756006176655 –
➡ bleu: 0.20010080750506093
    (valid) loss: 0.8180131682982812 - accuracy: 0.837830534348121 –
➡ bleu: 0.20100039279462362
Evaluating batch 39/39
(test) loss: 0.8390972828253721 - accuracy: 0.8342147454237326 - bleu:
➡ 0.19782372616582572
```

Compared to the last model we had, this is quite an improvement. We have almost doubled the validation and testing BLEU scores. All this was possible because we introduced the attention mechanism to alleviate a huge performance bottleneck in the encoder-decoder model.

NOTE On an Intel Core i5 machine with an NVIDIA GeForce RTX 2070 8 GB, the training took approximately five minutes to run five epochs.

Finally, for later use, we save the trained model, along with the vocabularies:

```
## Save the model
os.makedirs('models', exist_ok=True)
tf.keras.models.save_model(final_model_with_attention,
➡ os.path.join('models', 'seq2seq_attention'))

# Save the vocabulary
import json
os.makedirs(
    os.path.join('models', 'seq2seq_attention_vocab'), exist_ok=True
)
with open(os.path.join('models', 'seq2seq_attention_vocab',
➡ 'de_vocab.json'), 'w') as f:
    json.dump(de_vocabulary, f)

with open(os.path.join('models', 'seq2seq_attention_vocab',
➡ 'en_vocab.json'), 'w') as f:
    json.dump(en_vocabulary, f)
```

State-of-the-art results for English-German translation

One way to know where our model stands is to compare it to the state-of-the-art result that has been achieved on English-German translation. In 2021, at the time of writing this book, a BLEU score of 0.3514 has been achieved by one of the models. The model is introduced in the paper "Lessons on Parameter Sharing across Layers in Transformers" by Takase et al. (https://arxiv.org/pdf/2104.06022v1.pdf).

This should not be taken as an exact comparison to our model, as the benchmarked models are typically trained on the WMT English-German data set (https://nlp.stanford .edu/projects/nmt/), which is a much larger and more complex data set. However, given that we have a relatively simple model with no special training time optimizations, 0.1978 is a decent score.

With that, we will discuss how we can visualize the attention weights to see the attention patterns the model uses when decoding inputs.

EXERCISE 1

You have invented a novel attention mechanism called AttentionX. Unlike Bahdanau attention, this attention mechanism takes encoder inputs and the decoder's RNN outputs to produce the final output. The fully connected layers take this final output instead of the usual decoder's RNN output. Given that, you've implemented the new attention mechanism in a layer called `AttentionX`. For encoder input x and decoder's RNN output y, it can be called as

```
z = AttentionX()([x, y])
```

where the final output z is a [<batch size>, <decoder time steps>, <hidden size>]–sized output. How would you change the following decoder to use this new attention mechanism?

```
e_inp = tf.keras.Input(shape=(1,), dtype=tf.string, name='e_input_final')
fwd_state, bwd_state, en_states = encoder(e_inp)

d_inp = tf.keras.Input(shape=(1,), dtype=tf.string, name='d_input')

d_vectorized_out = vectorizer(d_inp)

d_emb_layer = tf.keras.layers.Embedding(
    n_vocab+2, 128, mask_zero=True, name='d_embedding'
)
d_emb_out = d_emb_layer(d_vectorized_out)

d_init_state = tf.keras.layers.Concatenate(axis=-1)([fwd_state, bwd_state])

gru_out = tf.keras.layers.GRU(256, return_sequences=True)(
    d_emb_out, initial_state=d_init_state
)

d_dense_layer_1 = tf.keras.layers.Dense(512, activation='relu',
    name='d_dense_1')
d_dense1_out = d_dense_layer_1(attn_out)

d_final_layer = tf.keras.layers.Dense(
    n_vocab+2, activation='softmax', name='d_dense_final'
)
d_final_out = d_final_layer(d_dense1_out)
```

12.2 *Visualizing the attention*

You have determined that the attention-based model works better than the one without attention. But you are skeptical and want to understand if the attention layer is producing meaningful outputs. For that, you are going to visualize attention patterns generated by the model for several input sequences.

Apart from the performance, one of the lucrative advantages of the attention mechanism is the interpretability it brings along to the model. The normalized energy values, one of the interim outputs of the attention mechanism, can provide powerful insights into the model. Since the normalized energy values represent how much each encoder output contributed to decoding/translating at each decoding timestep, it can be used to generate a heatmap, highlighting the most important words in English that correspond to a particular German word.

If we go back to the DecoderRNNAttentionWrapper, by calling it on a certain input, it produces two outputs:

- Decoder RNN output sequence
- Alpha (i.e., normalized energy values) for all the encoder positions for every decoder position

The second output is what we are after. That tensor holds the key to unlocking the powerful interpretability brought by the attention mechanism.

Let's write a function called the attention_visualizer() that will load the saved model and outputs not only the predictions of the model, but also the attention energies that will help us generate the final heatmap. In this function, we will load the model and create outputs by using the trained layers to retrace the interim and final outputs of the decoder, as shown in the next listing. This is similar to how we retraced the various steps in the model to create an inference model from the trained model.

> **Listing 12.5 A model that visualizes attention patterns from input text**

```
def attention_visualizer(save_path):
    """ Define the attention visualizer model """

    model = tf.keras.models.load_model(save_path)          ← Load the model.

    e_inp = tf.keras.Input(
        shape=(1,), dtype=tf.string, name='e_input_final'
    )                                                        Define the encoder input for
    en_model = model.get_layer("encoder")                    the model and get the final
    fwd_state, bwd_state, en_states = en_model(e_inp)        outputs of the encoder.

    e_vec_out = en_model.get_layer("e_vectorizer")(e_inp)   ← Get the encoder
                                                               vectorizer (required
    d_inp = tf.keras.Input(                                    to interpret the
        shape=(1,), dtype=tf.string, name='d_infer_input'     final output).
    )

    d_vec_layer = model.get_layer('d_vectorizer')           Get the decoder
    d_vec_out = d_vec_layer(d_inp)                          vectorizer and the output.
```

Define the decoder input.

```
d_emb_out = model.get_layer('d_embedding')(d_vec_out)

d_attn_layer = model.get_layer("d_attention")

d_init_state = tf.keras.layers.Concatenate(axis=-1)(
    [fwd_state, bwd_state]
)

attn_out, attn_states = d_attn_layer(
    [en_states, d_emb_out], initial_state=d_init_state
)

d_dense1_out = model.get_layer("d_dense_1")(attn_out)

d_final_out = model.get_layer("d_dense_final")(d_dense1_out)

visualizer_model = tf.keras.models.Model(
    inputs=[e_inp, d_inp],
    outputs=[d_final_out, attn_states, e_vec_out, d_vec_out]
)

return visualizer_model
```

The next few steps just reiterate the steps in the trained model. We simply get the corresponding layers and pass the output of the previous step to the current step.

Here we define the final model to visualize attention patterns; we are interested in the attn_states output (i.e., normalized energy values). We will also need the vectorized token IDs to annotate the visualization.

Note how the final model we defined returns four different outputs, as opposed to the trained model, which only returned the predictions. We will also need a get_vocabulary() function that will load the saved vocabularies:

```
def get_vocabularies(save_dir):
    """ Load the vocabularies """

    with open(os.path.join(save_dir, 'en_vocab.json'), 'r') as f:
        en_vocabulary = json.load(f)

    with open(os.path.join(save_dir, 'de_vocab.json'), 'r') as f:
        de_vocabulary = json.load(f)

    return en_vocabulary, de_vocabulary
```

Finally, call these functions so that we have the vocabularies and the model ready:

```
print("Loading vocabularies")
en_vocabulary, de_vocabulary = get_vocabularies(
    os.path.join('models', 'seq2seq_attention_vocab')
)

print("Loading weights and generating the inference model")
visualizer_model = attention_visualizer(
    os.path.join('models', 'seq2seq_attention')
)
print("\tDone")
```

Next, we'll move on to visualizing the outputs produced by the `visualizer_model`; we will be using the Python library `matplotlib` to visualize attention patterns for several examples. Let's define a function called `visualize_attention()` that takes in the `visualizer_model`, the two vocabularies, a sample English sentence, and the corresponding German translation (see the next listing). Then it will make a prediction on the inputs, retrieve the attention weights, generate a heatmap, and annotate the two axes with the English/German tokens.

Listing 12.6 Visualizing attention patterns using input text

```
import matplotlib.pyplot as plt
%matplotlib inline

def visualize_attention(visualizer_model, en_vocabulary, de_vocabulary,
    sample_en_text, sample_de_text, fig_savepath):
    """ Visualize the attention patterns """

    print("Input: {}".format(sample_en_text))

    d_pred, attention_weights, e_out, d_out = visualizer_model.predict(
        [np.array([sample_en_text]), np.array([sample_de_text])]
    )

    d_pred_out = np.argmax(d_pred[0], axis=-1)

    y_ticklabels = []
    for e_id in e_out[0]:
        if en_vocabulary[e_id] == "":
            break
        y_ticklabels.append(en_vocabulary[e_id])

    x_ticklabels = []
    for d_id in d_pred_out:
        if de_vocabulary[d_id] == 'eos':
            break
        x_ticklabels.append(de_vocabulary[d_id])

    fig, ax = plt.subplots(figsize=(14, 14))

    attention_weights_filtered = attention_weights[
        0, :len(y_ticklabels), :len(x_ticklabels)
    ]

    im = ax.imshow(attention_weights_filtered)

    ax.set_xticks(np.arange(attention_weights_filtered.shape[1]))
    ax.set_yticks(np.arange(attention_weights_filtered.shape[0]))
    ax.set_xticklabels(x_ticklabels)
    ax.set_yticklabels(y_ticklabels)

    ax.tick_params(labelsize=20)
    ax.tick_params(axis='x', labelrotation=90)
```

Get the model predictions. → `d_pred, attention_weights, e_out, d_out = visualizer_model.predict(...)`

Get the token IDs of the predictions of the model. → `d_pred_out = np.argmax(d_pred[0], axis=-1)`

Our y tick labels will be the input English words. We stop as soon as we see padding tokens.

Our x tick labels will be the predicted German words. We stop as soon as we see the EOS token.

We are going to visualize only the useful input and predicted words so that things like padded values and anything after the EOS token are discarded.

Generate the attention heatmap.

Set the x ticks, y ticks, and tick labels.

```
plt.colorbar(im)
plt.subplots_adjust(left=0.2, bottom=0.2)
```
Generate the color bar to understand the value range found in the heat map.

Save the figure to the disk.
```
save_dir, _ = os.path.split(fig_savepath)
if not os.path.exists(save_dir):
    os.makedirs(save_dir, exist_ok=True)
plt.savefig(fig_savepath)
```

First, we input the English and German input text to the model to generate a prediction. We need to input both the English and German inputs as we are still using the teacher-forced model. You might be wondering, "Does that mean I have to have the German translation ready and can only visualize attention patterns in the training mode?" Of course not! You can have an inference model defined, like we did in a previous section in this chapter, and still visualize the attention patterns. We are using the trained model itself to visualize patterns, as I want to focus on visualizing attention patterns rather than defining the inference model (which we already did for another model).

Once the predictions and attention weights are obtained, we define two lists: x_ticklabels and y_ticklabels. They will be the labels (i.e., English/German words) you see on the two axes in the heatmap. We will have the English words on the row dimension and German words in the column dimension (figure 12.1). We will also do a simple filtering to get rid of paddings (i.e., "") and German text appearing after the EOS token and get the attention weights within the range that satisfy these two criteria. You can then simply call the matplotlib's imshow() function to generate the heatmap and set the axes' ticks and the labels for those ticks. Finally, the figure is saved to the disk.

Let's give this a trial run! Let's take a few examples from our test DataFrame and visualize attention patterns. We will create 10 visualizations and will also make sure that those 10 examples we choose have at least 10 English words to make sure we don't visualize very short phrases:

```
# Generate attention patterns for a few inputs
i = 0
j = 0
while j<9:
    sample_en_text = test_df["EN"].iloc[i]
    sample_de_text = test_df["DE"].iloc[i:i+1].str.rsplit(n=1,
 expand=True).iloc[:,0].tolist()
    i += 1

    if len(sample_en_text.split(" ")) > 10:
        j += 1
    else:
        continue

    visualize_attention(
        visualizer_model, en_vocabulary, de_vocabulary, sample_en_text,
        sample_de_text, os.path.join('plots','attention_{}.png'.format(i))
    )
```

If you run this code successfully, you should get 10 attention visualizations shown and stored on the disk. In figures 12.1 and 12.2, we show two such visualizations.

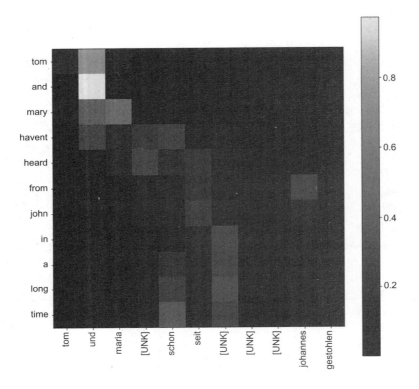

Figure 12.1   Attention patterns visualized for an input English text

In the figures, the lighter the color, the more the model has paid attention to that word. In figure 12.1, we can see that, when translating the words, "und" and "maria," the model has mostly paid attention to "and" and "mary," respectively. If you go to Google Translate and do the German translations for the word "and," for example, you will see that this is, in fact, correct. In figure 12.2, we can see that when generating "hast keine nicht," the model has paid attention to the phrase "have no idea." The other observation we can make is that the attention pattern falls roughly diagonally. This makes sense as both these languages roughly follow the same writing style.

This concludes our discussion about sequence-to-sequence models. In the next chapter, we will discuss a family of models that has been writing the state-of-the-art of machine learning for a few years: Transformers.

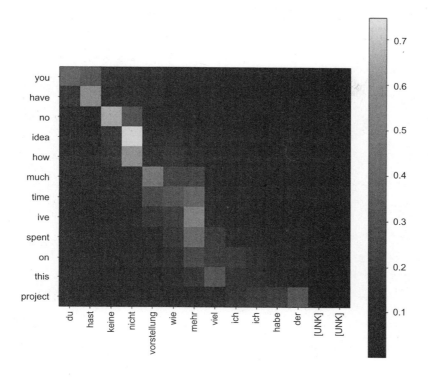

Figure 12.2 Attention patterns visualized for an input English text

EXERCISE 2

You have an attention matrix given by `attention_matrix`, with English words given by `english_text_labels` and German words given by `german_text_labels`. How would you create a visualization similar to figure 12.1? Here, you will need to use the `imshow()`, `set_xticks()`, `set_yticks()`, `set_xticklabels()`, and `set_yticklabels()` functions.

Summary

- Using attention in sequence-to-sequence models can greatly help shoot their performance up.
- Using attention at each decoding time step, the decoder gets to see all the historical outputs of the encoder and select and mix these outputs to come up with an aggregated (e.g., summed) representation of that, which gives a holistic view of what was in the encoder input.
- One of the intermediate products in the attention computation is the normalized energy values, which give a probability distribution of how important each encoded position was for decoding a given time step for every decoding step. In

other words, this is a matrix that has a value for every encoder time step and decoder time step combination. This can be visualized as a heatmap and can be used to interpret which words the decoder paid attention to when translating a certain token in the decoder.

Answers to exercises

Exercise 1

```
e_inp = tf.keras.Input(
    shape=(1,), dtype=tf.string, name='e_input_final'
)
fwd_state, bwd_state, en_states = encoder(e_inp)

d_inp = tf.keras.Input(shape=(1,), dtype=tf.string, name='d_input')

d_vectorized_out = vectorizer(d_inp)

d_emb_layer = tf.keras.layers.Embedding(
    n_vocab+2, 128, mask_zero=True, name='d_embedding'
)
d_emb_out = d_emb_layer(d_vectorized_out)

d_init_state = tf.keras.layers.Concatenate(axis=-1)([fwd_state, bwd_state])

gru_out = tf.keras.layers.GRU(256, return_sequences=True)(
    d_emb_out, initial_state=d_init_state
)

attn_out = AttentionX()([en_states, gru_out])

d_dense_layer_1 = tf.keras.layers.Dense(
    512, activation='relu', name='d_dense_1'
)
d_dense1_out = d_dense_layer_1(attn_out)

d_final_layer = tf.keras.layers.Dense(
    n_vocab+2, activation='softmax', name='d_dense_final'
)
d_final_out = d_final_layer(d_dense1_out)
```

Exercise 2

```
im = ax.imshow(attention_matrix)

ax.set_xticks(np.arange(attention_matrix.shape[1]))
ax.set_yticks(np.arange(attention_matrix.shape[0]))

ax.set_xticklabels(german_text_labels)
ax.set_yticklabels(english_text_labels)
```

13 Transformers

This chapter covers

- Implementing a full Transformer model with all the components
- Implementing a spam classifier using a pretrained BERT model from TFHub
- Implementing a question-answering model using Hugging Face's Transformer library

In chapters 11 and 12, you learned about sequence-to-sequence models, a powerful family of models that allows us to map an arbitrary-length sequence to another arbitrary-length sequence. We exemplified this ability through a machine translation task. Sequence-to-sequence models consist of an encoder and a decoder. The encoder takes in the input sequence (a sentence in the source language) and creates a compact representation of that (known as the context vector). The decoder takes in the context vector to produce the final target (i.e., a sentence in the target language). But we saw how limiting the context vector makes the model and looked at two techniques to improve model performance. First, teacher forcing allows the decoder to see not only the context vector but also the previous words in the target at a given time. This provides the decoder much more information to produce

453

the final prediction accurately. Second, the attention mechanism allows the decoder to peek into any part of the encoder history of outputs and use that information to produce the output as well. However, LSTM and GRU models are still quite restrictive as they can only see one output in the sequence at a given time and need to rely on a limited state vector (i.e., memory) to remember what they have seen.

But there's a new rival in town. If there's one word that most recent state-of-the-art NLP and computer vision research have been brimming with, it's Transformer. Transformer models are the latest type of deep learning models that made an unforgettable entrance by being crowned as state of the art for many NLP tasks, beating previous leaders such as LSTM- and GRU-based models. Inspired by their unprecedented success in NLP, they are now being introduced to solve various computer vision problems.

By design, Transformer models make remembering or using information present in long sequences of data (e.g., a sequence of words) trivial. Unlike LSTM models, which have to look at one time step at a time, Transformer models can see the full sequence at once. This enables Transformer models to understand language better than other models. Furthermore, Transformer models enjoy high parallelizability due to the minimization of longitudinal (i.e., temporal) computations that require sequential processing of text.

In this chapter, continuing our conversation from chapter 5, we will discuss some more details of the Transformer model so that our understanding of it is holistic. We will see how the Transformer model employs several embeddings to represent tokens as well as the position of those tokens in the sequence. Then we will learn BERT, a variant of the Transformer model that has been trained on a large corpus of text, ready to be used as a base layer to solve downstream NLP tasks easily without the need for complex models. BERT is essentially the encoder section of the Transformer model pretrained on large amounts of text using two techniques: masked language modeling (i.e., words in the sequence are randomly masked where BERT must predict the masked words) and next-sentence prediction (i.e., given two sentences, A and B, predict whether B entails A). We will see BERT in action when we use it to implement a spam classifier in TensorFlow. Next, Hugging Face's `transformers` library (https://huggingface.co/transformers/) is a popular choice for implementing state-of-the-art Transformer models with ease. It is one of the most valuable libraries to look at if you are planning to implement Transformer models in TensorFlow. For this reason, we will implement a question-answering model using the Transformers library by Hugging Face. Finally, we will end the chapter with a discussion about how Transformer models are used in computer vision.

As the first step, let's revisit what we have already learned about Transformer models (see figure 13.1) and expand our understanding a bit further.

The high-level purpose of these elements is to generate an attended representation (i.e., a latent or hidden representation for a given token that is enriched by the information in other tokens of the input sequence) of a given input token. To do that, the model

- Generates a query for each position in the input sequence
- For each query, determines how much each key should contribute (the key also represents individual tokens)
- Based on the contributions of the keys for a given query, mixes the values corresponding to those keys to generate the final attended representation

All three of the query, key, and values are generated by multiplying a trainable weight matrix with an input token's numerical representation. All this needs to happen in a differentiable way to ensure the gradients can be backpropagated through the model. The paper proposes the following computation to compute the final representation of the self-attention layer for the input tokens:

$$h = \text{softmax}\left(\frac{Q.K^T}{\sqrt{d_k}}\right)V$$

Here, Q represents the queries, K represents the keys, and V represents values for all the inputs and all the tokens in each input in a batch of data. This is what makes Transformer models so powerful: unlike LSTM models, Transformer models aggregate looking at all tokens in a sequence to a single matrix multiplication, making these models highly parallelizable.

13.1.2 Embeddings in the Transformer

One thing we overlooked when discussing the Transformer model is the embeddings used in it. We briefly touched on the word embeddings used. Let's discuss this topic in more detail here. Word embeddings provide a semantic-preserving representation of words based on the context in which words are used. In other words, if two words are used in the same context, they will have similar word vectors. For example, the words "cat" and "dog" will have similar representations, whereas "cat" and "volcano" will have vastly different representations.

Word vectors were initially introduced in the paper titled "Efficient Estimation of Word Representations in Vector Space" by Mikolov et al. (https://arxiv.org/pdf/1301 .3781.pdf). It came in two variants, skip-gram and continuous bag-of-words (CBOW). Because skip-gram is somewhat more widely accepted than CBOW, let's discuss the crux of the skip-gram algorithm.

The first step is to define a large matrix of size V × E, where V is the size of the vocabulary and E is the size of the embeddings. The size of the embeddings (E) is a user-defined hyperparameter, where a larger E typically leads to more powerful word embeddings. In practice, you do not need to increase the size of embeddings beyond 300.

Next, you create inputs and targets in a completely unsupervised manner. Given a large corpus of text, you select a word form as the input (probe word) and the words surrounding the probe word as targets. The surrounding words are captured by defining a fixed-sized window around the probe word. For example, for a window size of 2 (on each side of the probe word), you can generate the following input-target pairs from the sentence "angry John threw a pizza at me."

```
(John, angry), (John, threw), (John, a), (threw, angry), (threw, John),
(threw, a), (threw, pizza), …, (at, a), (at, pizza), (at, me)
```

With the labeled data, you can frame the problem of learning word embeddings as a classification problem. In other words, you train a model (i.e., a function of the word-embedding matrix) to predict the target word, given the input word. The model consists of two components, the embedding matrix and a fully connected layer with a softmax activation to output the predictions. Once the embeddings are learned, you can discard the other things around it (e.g., the fully connected layer) and use the embedding matrix for a downstream NLP task such as sentiment analysis, machine translation, and so on. You just have to look up the embedding vector corresponding to a word in order to obtain a numerical representation for this word.

Motivated by the original word vector algorithms, modern deep learning models combine learning word embeddings and the actual decision-support NLP problem to a single model training task. In other words, the following general approach is taken to incorporate word embeddings to a machine learning model:

- Define a randomly initialized word-embedding matrix (or pretrained embeddings available to download for free).
- Define the model (randomly initialized) that uses word embeddings as the inputs and produces an output (e.g., sentiment, a language translation, etc.).
- Train the whole model (embeddings + the model) end to end on the task.

The same technique is used in Transformer models. However, in Transformer models, there are two different embeddings:

- Token embeddings (which provide a unique representation for each token seen by the model in an input sequence)
- Positional embeddings (which provide a unique representation for each position in the input sequence)

The token embeddings have a unique embedding vector for each token (e.g., character, word, sub-word), depending on the model's tokenizing mechanism.

The positional embeddings are used to signal the model where a token is appearing. The primary purpose is for the positional embeddings server to tell the Transformer model where a word is appearing. This is because, unlike LSTMs/GRUs, Transformer models don't have a notion of sequence, as they process the whole text at once. Furthermore, a change to the position in word can alter the meaning of a sentence or a word. For example, in the two versions of

```
Ralph loves his tennis ball. It likes to chase the ball
Ralph loves his tennis ball. Ralph likes to chase it
```

the word "it" refers to different things, and the position of the word "it" can be used as a cue to identify this difference. The original Transformer paper uses the following equations to generate positional embeddings:

$$PE(pos,2i) = \sin(pos/10000^{2i/d_{\text{model}}})$$

$$PE(pos,2i+1) = \cos(pos/10000^{2i/d_{\text{model}}})$$

where pos denotes the position in the sequence and i denotes the ith feature dimension ($0 \le i < d_{\text{model}}$). Even-numbered features use a sine function, whereas odd-numbered features use a cosine function. Figure 13.2 presents how positional embeddings change as the time step and the feature position change. It can be seen that feature

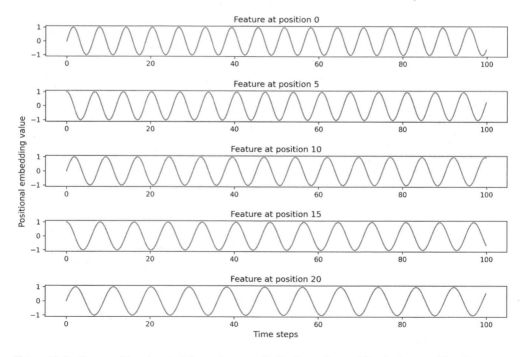

Figure 13.2 How positional embeddings change with the time step and the feature position. Even-numbered feature positions use the sine function, whereas odd-numbered positions use the cosine function. Additionally, the frequency of the signals decreases as the feature position increases.

positions with higher indices have lower frequency sinusoidal waves. It is not entirely clear how the authors came up with the exact equation. However, they do mention that they did not see a significant performance difference between the previous equation and letting the model learn positional embeddings jointly during the training.

It is important to note that both token and positional embeddings will have the same dimensionality (i.e., d_{model}). Finally, as the input to the model, the token embeddings and the positional embeddings are summed to form a single hybrid embedding vector (figure 13.3).

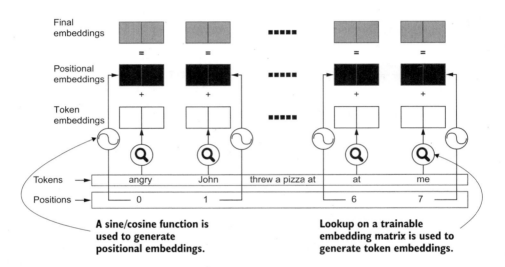

Figure 13.3   The embeddings generated in a Transformer model and how the final embeddings are computed

13.1.3 *Residuals and normalization*

Another important characteristic of the Transformer models is the existence of the residual connections and the normalization layers in between the individual layers. We discussed residual connections in depth in chapter 7 when we discussed advance techniques for image classification. Let's briefly revisit the mechanics and the motivation for residual connections.

Residual connections are formed by adding a given layer's output to the output of one or more layers ahead. This, in turn, forms "shortcut connections" through the model and provides a stronger gradient flow by reducing the changes of the phenomenon known as the *vanishing gradients* (figure 13.4). Vanishing gradients cause the gradients in the layers closest to the inputs to be very small so that the training in those layers is hindered.

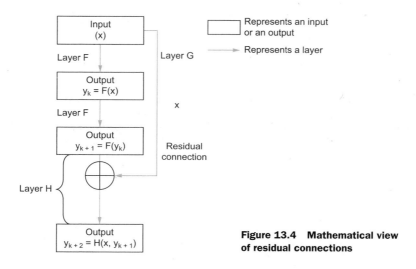

Figure 13.4 Mathematical view of residual connections

In Transformer models, in each layer, residual connections are created in the following way:

- The input to the multi-head self-attention sublayer is added to the output of the multi-head self-attention sublayer.
- The input to the fully connected sublayer is added to the output of the fully connected sublayer.

Next, the output reinforced by residual connections goes through a layer normalization layer. *Layer normalization,* similar to batch normalization, is a way to reduce the "covariate shift" in neural networks, allowing them to be trained faster and achieve better performance. Covariate shift refers to changes in the distribution of neural network activations (caused by changes in the data distribution) that transpire as the model goes through model training. Such changes in the distribution hurt consistency during model training and negatively impact the model. Layer normalization was introduced in the paper "Layer Normalization" by Ba et al. (https://arxiv.org/pdf/1607.06450.pdf).

Batch normalization computes the mean and variance of activations as an average over the samples in the batch, causing its performance to rely on mini batch sizes, which are used to train the model.

However, layer normalization computes the mean and variance (i.e., the normalization terms) of the activations in such a way that the normalization terms are the same for every hidden unit. In other words, layer normalization has a single mean and a variance value for all the hidden units in a layer. This is in contrast to batch normalization, which maintains individual mean and variance values for each hidden unit in a layer. Moreover, unlike batch normalization, layer normalization does not average over the samples in the batch, but rather leaves the averaging out and has different normalization terms for different inputs. By having a mean and variance per sample, layer normalization gets rid of the dependency on the mini batch size. For more details about this method, please refer to the original paper.

> ### Layer normalization in TensorFlow/Keras
> TensorFlow provides a convenient implementation of the layer normalization algorithm at http://mng.bz/YGRB. You can use this layer with any model you define using TensorFlow Keras APIs.

Figure 13.5 depicts how residual connections and layer normalization are used in Transformer models.

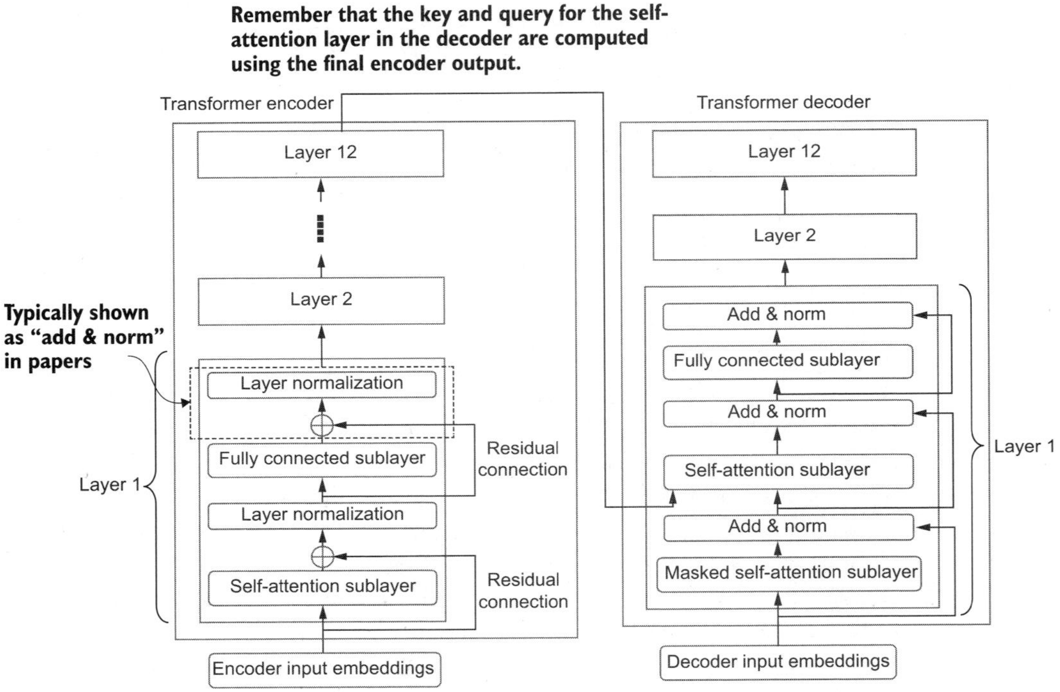

Figure 13.5   How residual connections and layer normalization layers are used in the Transformer model

With that, we end the discussion about the components in the Transformer model. We have discussed all the bells and whistles of the Transformer model, namely self-attention layers, fully connected layers, embeddings (token and positional), layer normalization, and residual connections. In the next section, we will discuss how we can use a pretrained Transformer model known as BERT to solve a spam classification task.

EXERCISE 1

You are given the following code for the Transformer encoder

```
import tensorflow as tf

# Defining some hyperparameters
n_steps = 25 # Sequence length
n_en_vocab = 300 # Encoder's vocabulary size
n_heads = 8 # Number of attention heads
d = 512 # The feature dimensionality of each layer

# Encoder input layer
en_inp = tf.keras.layers.Input(shape=(n_steps,))
# Encoder input embedddings
en_emb = tf.keras.layers.Embedding(
    n_en_vocab, d, input_length=n_steps
) (en_inp)

# Two encoder layers
en_out1 = EncoderLayer(d, n_heads)(en_emb)
en_out2 = EncoderLayer(d, n_heads)(en_out1)

model = tf.keras.models.Model(inputs=en_inp, output=en_out2)
```

where the `EncoderLayer` defines a typical Transformer encoder layer that has a self-attention sublayer and a fully connected sublayer. You are asked to integrate positional encoding using the equation

$$PE(pos,2i) = \sin(pos/10000^{2i/d_{model}})$$

pos goes from 0 to 511 (d=512 features) and *i* goes from 0 to 24 (n_steps=25 time steps) and denotes the time step. In other words, our positional encoding will be a tensor of shape [n_steps, d]. You can use `tf.math.sin()` to generate the sin value element-wise for a tensor. You can define the positional embeddings as a tensor and not the product of a `tf.keras.layers.Layer`. The final embedding should be generated by summing the token embeddings and the positional embeddings. How would you do that?

13.2 Using pretrained BERT for spam classification

You are working as a data scientist for a mail service company, and the company is dying to implement a spam classification functionality. They want to implement this functionality in house and save dollars. Having read about BERT and how powerful it is for solving NLP tasks, you explain to the team that all you need to do is download the BERT model, fit a classification layer on top of BERT, and train the whole model end to end on labeled data. The labeled data consists of a spam message and a label indicating whether the message is spam or ham (i.e., not spam). You have been put in charge of implementing this model.

Now that we have discussed all the moving elements of the Transformer architecture, it puts us in a very strong position to understand BERT. BERT is a Transformer-based model introduced in the paper "BERT: Pre-Training of Deep Bidirectional Transformers for Language Understanding" by Devlin et al. (https://arxiv.org/pdf/1810.04805.pdf), and it represents a very important milestone in the history of NLP as it's a pioneering model that proved the ability to apply "transfer learning" in the domain of NLP.

BERT is a Transformer model that is pretrained on large amounts of textual data in an unsupervised fashion. Therefore, you can use BERT as the basis to get rich, semantically sound numerical representations for textual input sequences that can be readily fed to your downstream NLP models. Because of the rich textual representations provided by BERT, you're relieving your decision support model of the need to understand the language and instead can directly focus on the problem at hand. From a technical perspective, if you're solving a classification problem with BERT, all you need to do is

- Fit a classifier(s) (e.g., a logistic regression layer) on top of BERT, which takes BERT's output(s) as the input(s)
- Train the model (i.e., BERT + classifier(s)) end to end on the discriminative task

History of BERT

Before models like BERT, solving natural language processing (NLP) tasks was both repetitive and time-consuming. Every time, you had to train a model from scratch. And to exacerbate this suboptimal way of tackling problems, most models struggled with long sequences of text, limiting their ability to understand language.

In 2017, Transformer models for NLP tasks were proposed in the paper "Attention Is All You Need" (https://arxiv.org/pdf/1706.03762.pdf). Transformer models beat previous dominants like LSTMs and GRUs across the board on a collection of NLP tasks. Transformer models, unlike recurrent models that look at one word at a time and maintain a state (i.e., memory), look at the whole sequence at once.

Then, in 2018, the "ImageNet moment" arrived for NLP (i.e., transfer learning in NLP). The ImageNet moment refers to the moment when ML practitioners realized that using a computer vision model that is already trained on the large ImageNet image classification data set on other tasks (e.g., object detection, image segmentation) yields better performance faster. This essentially gave rise to the concept of transfer learning that is heavily used in the computer vision domain. So, until 2018, the NLP domain did not have a very good way to employ transfer learning to uplift the performance on tasks. The paper "Universal Language Model Fine-Tuning for Text Classification" (https://arxiv.org/pdf/1801.06146.pdf) introduced the idea of using pretraining on a language modeling task and then training the model on a discriminative task (e.g., a classification problem). The advantage of this approach was that you did not need as many samples as if you were to train the model from scratch.

In 2018, BERT was introduced. It was a marriage of two of the finest moments in the history of NLP. In other words, BERT is a Transformer model that is pretrained on large amounts of textual data in an unsupervised fashion.

We will now examine the BERT model in more detail.

13.2.1 Understanding BERT

Let's now inspect BERT more microscopically. As I alluded to earlier, BERT is a Transformer model. To be exact, it's the encoder part of the Transformer model. This means that BERT takes an input sequence (a collection of tokens) and produces an encoded output sequence. Figure 13.6 depicts the high-level architecture of BERT.

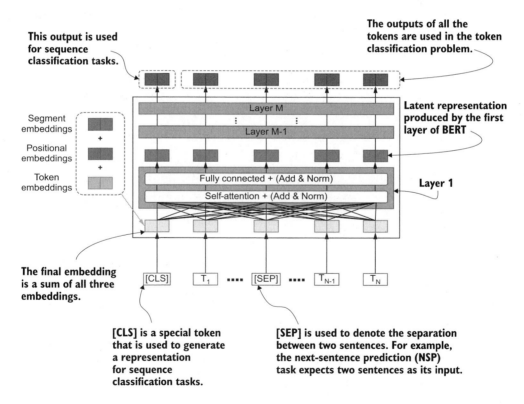

Figure 13.6   The high-level architecture of BERT. It takes a set of input tokens and produces a sequence of hidden representations generated using several hidden layers.

When BERT takes an input, it inserts some special tokens into the input. First, at the beginning, it inserts a [CLS] (an abbreviated form of the term classification) token that is used to generate the final hidden representation for certain types of tasks (e.g., sequence classification). It represents the output after attending to all the tokens in the sequence. Next, it also inserts an [SEP] (i.e., "separation") token depending on the type of input. The [SEP] token marks the end and beginning of different sequences in the input. For example, in question answering, the model takes a question and a context (e.g., paragraph) that may have the answer as an input, and [SEP] is used in between the question and the context.

Next, the final embedding of the tokens is generated using three different embedding spaces. The token embedding has a unique vector for each token in the vocabulary. The positional embeddings encode the position of each token, as discussed earlier. Finally, the segment embedding provides a distinct representation for each subcomponent in the input when the input consists of multiple components. For example, in question answering, the question will have a unique vector as its segment embedding vector, whereas the context will have a different embedding vector. This is done by having n different embedding vectors for the n different components in the input sequence. Depending on the component index specified for each token in the input, the corresponding segment-embedding vector is retrieved. n needs to be specified in advance.

The real value of BERT comes from the fact that it has been pretrained on a large corpus of data in a self-supervised fashion. In the pretraining stage, BERT is trained on two different tasks:

- Masked language modeling (MLM)
- Next-sentence prediction (NSP)

The masked language modeling (MLM) task is inspired by the *Cloze task* or the *Cloze test*, where a student is given a sentence with one or more blanks and is asked to fill the blanks. Similarly, given a text corpus, words are masked from sentences and then the model is asked to predict the masked tokens. For example, the sentence

```
I went to the bakery to buy bread
```

might become

```
I went to the [MASK] to buy bread
```

NOTE   There has been a plethora of Transformer-based models, each building on the previous. You can read more about these models in appendix C.

Figure 13.7 illustrates the main components of BERT during the training of the masked language modeling task. BERT uses a special token ([MASK]) to represent masked words. Then the target for the model will be the word "bakery." But this introduces a practical issue to the model. The special token [MASK] does not appear in

Pretraining BERT

BERT is pretrained on two self-supervised tasks: masked language modelling (MLM) and next-sentence prediction (NSP).

- In MLM, input tokens are randomly masked and the model is asked to predict the missing tokens.
- In NSP, two sentences are provided as the input and asked to predict if the second sentence is the next sentence of the first sentence.

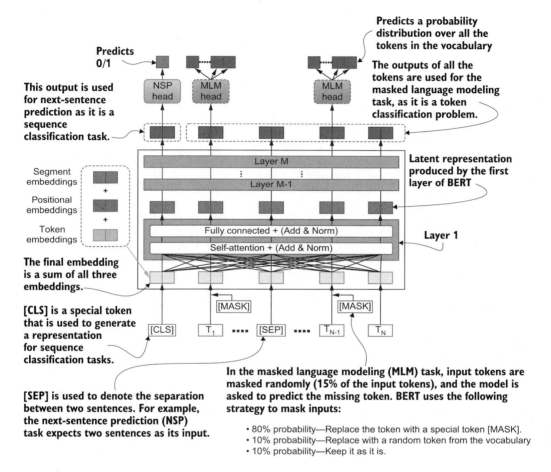

Figure 13.7   The methodology used for pretraining BERT. BERT is pretrained on two tasks: a masked language modeling task and the next sentence prediction task. In the masked language modeling task, the tokens in the input are masked and the model is asked to predict masked tokens. In the next sentence prediction task, the model is asked to predict if given two sentences are next to each other.

the actual text. This means that the text the model will see during the fine-tuning phase (i.e., when training on a classification problem) will be different than what it will see during pretraining. This is sometimes referred to as the *pretraining–fine-tuning discrepancy*. Therefore, the authors of BERT suggest the following approach to cope with the issue. When masking a word, do one of the following:

- Use the [MASK] token as it is (with 80% probability).
- Use a random word (with 10% probability).
- Use the true word (with 10% probability).

Next, in the next sentence prediction task, the model is given a pair of sentences, A and B (in that order), and is asked to predict whether B is the next sentence after A. This can be done by fitting a binary classifier on top of BERT and training the whole model end to end on selected pairs of sentences. Generating pairs of sentences as inputs to the model is not hard and can be done in an unsupervised manner:

- A sample with the label TRUE is generated by picking two sentences that are adjacent to each other.
- A sample with the label FALSE is generated by picking two sentences randomly that are not adjacent to each other.

Following this approach, a labeled data set is generated for the next sentence prediction task. Then BERT, along with the binary classifier, is trained end to end using the labeled data set. Figure 13.7 highlights the data and the model architecture in the next sentence prediction task.

You might have noticed in figure 13.6 that the input to BERT has special tokens. There are two special tokens (in addition to the [MASK] token we already discussed) that serve special purposes.

The [CLS] token is appended to any input sequence fed to BERT. This denotes the beginning of the input. It also forms the basis for the input fed into the classification head used on top of BERT to solve your NLP task. As you know, BERT produces a hidden representation for each input token in the sequence. As a convention, the hidden representation corresponding to the [CLS] token is used as the input to the classification model that sits on top of BERT.

The task-specific NLP tasks solved by BERT can be classified into four different categories. These are based on the tasks found in the General Language Understanding Evaluation (GLUE) benchmark task suite (https://gluebenchmark.com):

- *Sequence classification*—Here, a single input sequence is given and the model is asked to predict a label for the whole sequence (e.g., sentiment analysis, spam identification).
- *Token classification*—Here, a single input sequence is given and the model is asked to predict a label for each token in the sequence (e.g., named entity recognition, part-of-speech tagging).
- *Question answering*—Here, the input consists of two sequences: a question and a context. The question and the context are separated by an [SEP] token. The model is trained to predict the starting and ending indices of the span of tokens belonging to the answer.
- *Multiple choice*—Here the input consists of multiple sequences: a question followed by multiple candidates that may or may not be the answer to the question.

These multiple sequences are separated by the token [SEP] and provided as a single input sequence to the model. The model is trained to predict the correct answer (i.e., the class label) for that question.

BERT is designed in such a way that it can be used to solve these tasks without any modifications to the base model. In tasks that involve multiple sequences (e.g., question answering, multiple-choice questions), you need to tell the model different inputs separately (e.g., which tokens are the question and which tokens are the context in the question-answering task). In order to make that distinction, the [SEP] token is used. An [SEP] token is inserted between the different sequences. For example, if you are solving a question-answering task, you might have an input as follows:

```
Question: What color is the ball?
Paragraph: Tippy is a dog. She loves to play with her red ball.
```

Then the input to BERT might look like

```
[CLS] What color is the ball [SEP] Tippy is a dog She loves to play with her
red ball [SEP]
```

BERT also uses a segment-embedding space to denote which sequence a token belongs to. For example, inputs having only one sequence have the same segment-embedding vector for all the tokens (e.g., spam classification task). Inputs having two or more sequences use the first or second space depending on which sequence the token belongs to. For example, in question answering, the model will use a unique segment-embedding vector to encode tokens of the question, where it will use a different segment-embedding vector to encode the tokens of the context. Now we have discussed all the elements of BERT needed to use it successfully to solve a downstream NLP task. Let's reiterate the key points about BERT:

- BERT is an encoder-based Transformer that is pretrained on large amounts of text.
- BERT uses masked language modeling and next-sentence prediction tasks to pretrain the model.
- BERT outputs a hidden representation for every token in the input sequence.
- BERT has three embedding spaces: token embedding, positional embedding, and segment embedding.
- BERT uses a special token [CLS] to denote the beginning of an input and is used as the input to a downstream classification model.
- BERT is designed to solve four types of NLP tasks: sequence classification, token classification, free-text question answering, and multiple-choice question answering.
- BERT uses the special token [SEP] to separate sequence A and sequence B.

Next, we will learn how we can classify spam messages with BERT.

13.2.2   *Classifying spam with BERT in TensorFlow*

It's now time to show off your skills by implementing a spam classifier with minimal effort. First, let's download data. The data we will use for this exercise is a collection of spam and ham (non-spam) SMS messages available at http://mng.bz/GE9v. The Python code for downloading the data has been provided in the Ch13-Transformers-with-TF2-and-Huggingface/13.1_Spam_Classification_with_BERT.ipynb notebook.

UNDERSTANDING THE DATA

Once you download the data and extract it, we can quickly look at what's in the data. It will be a single tab-separated text file. The first three entries of the file are as follows:

```
ham     Go until jurong point, crazy.. Available only in bugis n great
➡ world la e buffet... Cine there got amore wat...
ham     Ok lar... Joking wif u oni...
spam            Free entry in 2 a wkly comp to win FA Cup final tkts 21st
➡ May 2005 …
```

As shown, each line starts with the word ham or spam, indicating whether it's safe or spam. Then the text in the message is given, followed by a tab. Our next task is to load this data into memory and store the inputs and labels in NumPy arrays. The following listing shows the steps to do so.

Listing 13.1   Loading the data from the text file into NumPy arrays

```
inputs = []          ◁——— Inputs (messages) are stored here.
labels = []

n_ham, n_spam = 0,0          ◁——— Counts the total number of ham/spam examples
with open(os.path.join('data', 'SMSSpamCollection'), 'r') as f:
    for r in f:          ◁——— Read every row in the file.
        if r.startswith('ham'):          ◁——— If the line starts with spam, it's spam.
            label = 0          ◁——— Assign it a label of 0.
            txt = r[4:]          ◁——— Input is the text in the line (except for the word starting ham).
            n_ham += 1
        # Spam input
        elif r.startswith('spam'):
            label = 1
            txt = r[5:]          ◁——— Input is the text in the line (except for the word that starts spam).
            n_spam += 1
        inputs.append(txt)
        labels.append(label)          ◁——— Append the labels to labels.
    # Convert them to arrays
    inputs = np.array(inputs).reshape(-1,1)          ◁——— Convert inputs to a NumPy array (and reshape it to a matrix with one column).
    labels = np.array(labels)
```

The label (0/1) is stored here.

If the line starts with ham, it's a ham example.

Increase the count n_ham.

Assign it a label of 1.

Append the input text to inputs.

Convert the labels list to a NumPy array.

You can print the n_ham and n_spam variables and verify that there are 4,827 ham examples and 747 spam examples. In other words, there are fewer spam examples than ham examples. Therefore, we have to make sure to account for this imbalance when training the model.

TREATING CLASS IMBALANCE IN THE DATA

To counteract class imbalance, let's create balanced training/validation and testing data sets. To do that, we will use the `imbalanced-learn` library, which is a great library for manipulating imbalanced data sets (e.g., sampling various amounts of data from different classes). There are two primary strategies for restoring balance in a data set:

- Undersampling the majority class (fewer samples from that class are selected for the final data set)
- Oversampling the minority class (more samples from that class are generated for the final data set)

We will use the first strategy here (i.e., undersampling the majority class). More specifically, we will first

- Create balanced testing and validation data sets by randomly sampling data from the data set (n examples per each class)
- Assign the rest of the data to a training set and undersample the majority class in the training set using an algorithm known as the *near-miss* algorithm

The creation of the training validation and testing data is illustrated in figure 13.8.

First, let's import a few under-samplers from the library and the NumPy library:

```
from imblearn.under_sampling import  NearMiss, RandomUnderSampler
import numpy as np
```

Next, we will define a variable, n, which denotes how many examples per class we will keep in the validation and testing data sets:

```
n=100 # Number of instances for each class for test/validation sets
random_seed = 4321
```

Then we will define a random under-sampler. The most important parameter is the `sampling_strategy` parameter, which takes a dictionary with the label as the key and the number of samples required for that label as the value. We will also pass `random_seed` to the `random_state` argument to make sure we get the same result every time we run the code:

```
rus = RandomUnderSampler(
    sampling_strategy={0:n, 1:n}, random_state=random_seed
)
```

Then we call the `fit_resample()` function of the under-sampler, with the inputs and labels arrays we created, to sample data:

```
rus.fit_resample(inputs, labels)
```

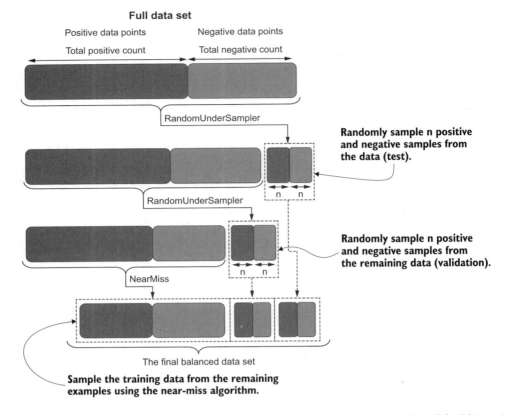

Figure 13.8   How the training, validation, and testing data sets are created from the original data set

Once you fit the under-sampler, you can get the indices of the selected samples using the under-sampler's `sample_indices_` attribute. Using those indices, we will create a new pair of arrays, `test_x` and `test_y`, to hold the test data:

```
test_inds = rus.sample_indices_
test_x, test_y = inputs[test_inds], np.array(labels)[test_inds]
```

The indices that are not in the test data set are assigned to separate arrays: `rest_x` and `rest_y`. These will be used to create the validation data set and the training data set:

```
rest_inds = [i for i in range(inputs.shape[0]) if i not in test_inds]
rest_x, rest_y = inputs[rest_inds], labels[rest_inds]
```

Following the same approach, we undersample data from `rest_x` and `rest_y` to create the validation data set (`valid_x` and `valid_y`). Note that we are not using the inputs and labels arrays, but rather the remaining data of those arrays after separating the test data:

```
rus.fit_resample(rest_x, rest_y)
valid_inds = rus.sample_indices_
valid_x, valid_y = rest_x[valid_inds], rest_y[valid_inds]
```

Finally, we create the training data set, which will hold all the remaining elements after creating the test and validation data sets:

```
train_inds = [i for i in range(rest_x.shape[0]) if i not in valid_inds]
train_x, train_y = rest_x[train_inds], rest_y[train_inds]
```

We also have to make sure that the training data set is balanced. In order to do that, let's use a smarter way to undersample data than randomly selecting elements. The undersampling algorithm we will use here is called the near-miss algorithm. The near-miss algorithm removes samples from the majority class that are too close to the samples in the minority class. This helps to increase the distance between minority and majority class examples. Here, the minority class refers to the class having less data and the majority class refers to the class that has more data. To use the near-miss algorithm, it needs to able to compute the distance between two samples. Therefore, we need to convert our text into some numerical representation. We will represent each message as a bag-of-words representation. By using scikit-learn's `CountVectorizer`, we can easily do that:

```
from sklearn.feature_extraction.text import CountVectorizer

countvec = CountVectorizer()
train_bow = countvec.fit_transform(train_x.reshape(-1).tolist())
```

`train_bow` will contain the bag-of-word representations of our data. Then we can pass this to a `NearMiss` instance. The way to obtain the data is the same as before:

```
from imblearn.under_sampling import NearMiss

oss = NearMiss()
x_res, y_res = oss.fit_resample(train_bow, train_y)
train_inds = oss.sample_indices_

train_x, train_y = train_x[train_inds], train_y[train_inds]
```

Let's print the sizes of our data sets and see if they have the sizes we wanted in the first place:

```
Test dataset size
1    100
0    100
dtype: int64

Valid dataset size
1    100
0    100
dtype: int64
```

```
Train dataset size
1    547
0    547
dtype: int64
```

Excellent! Our data sets are all balanced, and we are ready to press ahead with the rest of the workflow.

DEFINING THE MODEL

With the data prepared and ready, we will download the model. The BERT model we will use is from the TensorFlow hub (https://www.tensorflow.org/hub). The Tensor-Flow hub is a model repository for various models trained on various tasks. You can get models for a multitude of tasks, including image classification, object detection, language modeling, question answering, and so on. To see the full list of available models, check out https://tfhub.dev/.

In order for us to successfully use BERT for an NLP task, we need three important things to work:

- *A tokenizer*—Determines how to split the provided input sequence to tokens
- *An encoder*—Takes in the tokens, computes numerical representations, and finally generates a hidden representation for each token as well as a pooled representation (a single representation of the whole sequence)
- *A classification head*—Takes in the pooled representation and generates a label for the input

First, let's examine the tokenizer. The tokenizer takes a single input string or a list of strings and converts it to a list of strings or a list of lists of strings, respectively. It does this by breaking each string into smaller elements. For example, a sentence can be broken into words by splitting it on the space character. The tokenizer in BERT uses an algorithm known as the *WordPiece* algorithm (http://mng.bz/z40B). It uses an iterative approach to find sub-words (i.e., parts of words) that appear commonly in a data set. The details of the WordPiece algorithm are out of scope for this book. Feel free to consult the original paper to learn more details. The most important characteristic of the tokenizer for this discussion is that it will break a given input string (e.g., a sentence) into a list of smaller tokens (e.g., sub-words).

Advantage of sub-word approaches like the WordPiece algorithm

Sub-word approaches like the WordPiece algorithm learn smaller, commonly occurring parts of words and use them to define the vocabulary. There are two main advantages to this approach compared to having whole words in our vocabulary.

Using sub-words often reduces the size of the vocabulary. Assume the words ["walk", "act", "walked", "acted", "walking", "acting"]. If individual words are used, each word needs to be a single item in the vocabulary. However, if a sub-word approach is used, the vocabulary can be reduced to ["walk", "act", "##ed", "##ing"], which only has four words. Here, the ## means that it needs to be prefixed with another sub-word.

Secondly, a sub-word approach can handle out-of-vocabulary words. This means the sub-word approach can represent words that appear in the test data set, but not in the training set. A word-based approach will not be able to do so and will simply replace the unseen word with a special token. Assume the sub-word vocabulary ["walk", "act", "##ed", "##ing", "develop"]. Even if the words "developed" or "developing" don't appear in the training data, the vocabulary can still represent these words by combining two sub-words from the vocabulary (e.g., developed = develop + ##ed).

To set up the tokenizer, let's first import the `tf-models-official` library:

```
import tensorflow_models as tfm
```

Then you can define a tokenizer as follows:

```
vocab_file = os.path.join("data", "vocab.txt")

do_lower_case = True

tokenizer = tfm.nlp.layers.FastWordpieceBertTokenizer(
    vocab_file=vocab_file, lower_case=do_lower_case
)
```

Here, you first get the location of the vocabulary file and define some configurations, such as whether the text should be converted to lowercase before tokenizing it. The vocabulary file is a text file with one sub-word in each line. This tokenizer uses Fast WordPiece Tokenization (https://arxiv.org/abs/2012.15524.pdf), an efficient implementation of the original WordPiece algorithm. Note that the `vocab_file` and `do_lower_case` are settings found in the model artifacts we will be downloading from TensorFlow hub in the next step. But for ease of understanding, we define them as constants here. You will find the code to automatically extract them from the model in the notebook. Next, we can use the tokenizer as follows

```
tokens = tf.reshape(
    tokenizer(["She sells seashells by the seashore"]), [-1])
print("Tokens IDs generated by BERT: {}".format(tokens))
ids = [tokenizer._vocab[tid] for tid in tokens]
print("Tokens generated by BERT: {}".format(ids))
```

which returns

```
Tokens IDs generated by BERT: [ 2016 15187 11915 18223  2015  2011  1996
    11915 16892]
Tokens generated by BERT: ['she', 'sells', 'seas', '##hell', '##s', 'by',
    'the', 'seas', '##hore']
```

You can see here how BERT's tokenizer is tokenizing the sentence. Some words are kept as they are, whereas some words are split into sub-words (e.g., seas + ##hell + ##s). As discussed earlier, the ## means that it does not mark the beginning of a word. In other words, ## shows that this sub-word needs to be prefixed with another sub-word to get an actual word. Now, let's look at the special tokens that are used by the BERT model and what IDs are assigned to them. This also validates that these tokens exist in the tokenizer:

```
special_tokens = ['[CLS]', '[SEP]', '[MASK]', '[PAD]']
ids = [tokenizer._vocab.index(tok) for tok in special_tokens]
for t, i in zip(special_tokens, ids):
    print("Token: {} has ID: {}".format(t, i))
```

This returns

```
Token: [CLS] has ID: 101
Token: [SEP] has ID: 102
Token: [MASK] has ID: 103
Token: [PAD] has ID: 0
```

Here, the [PAD] is another special token used by BERT to denote padded tokens (0s). Padding is used very commonly in NLP to bring sentences with different lengths to the same length by padding the sentences with zeros. Here, the [PAD] token corresponds to zero.

With the basic functionality of the tokenizer understood, we can define a function called encode_sentence() that will encode a given sentence to an input understood by the BERT model (see the next listing).

Listing 13.2   Encoding a given input string using BERT's tokenizer

```
def encode_sentence(s):
    """ Encode a given sentence by tokenizing it and adding special tokens """

    tokens = list(
        tf.reshape(tokenizer(["CLS" + s + "[SEP]"]), [-1])
    )
    return tokens          ◁─── Add the special [CLS] and
                                [SEP] tokens to the sequence
                                and get the token IDs.
```

Return the token IDs.

In this function, we return the tokenized output, first adding the [CLS] token, then tokenizing the given string to a list of sub-words, and finally adding the [SEP] token to mark the end of the sentence/sequence. For example, the sentence "I like ice cream"

```
encode_sentence("I like ice cream")
```

will return

```
[101, 1045, 2066, 3256, 6949, 102]
```

As we can see, token ID 101 (i.e., [CLS]) is at the beginning, and 102 (i.e., [SEP]) is at the end. The rest of the token IDs correspond to the actual string we input. It is not enough to tokenize inputs for BERT; we also have to define some extra inputs to the model. For example, the sentence

```
"I like ice cream"
```

should return a data structure like the following:

```
{
    'input_word_ids': [[ 101, 1045, 2066, 3256, 6949,  102,   0,   0]],
    'input_mask': [[1., 1., 1., 1., 1., 1., 0., 0.]],
    'input_type_ids': [[0, 0, 0, 0, 0, 0, 0, 0]]
}
```

Let's discuss the various elements in this data structure. BERT takes in an input in the form of a dictionary where

- The key input_ids represents the token_ids obtained from the encode_ sentence function previously defined
- The key input_mask represents a mask the same size as the input_ids of 1s and 0s, where ones indicate values that should not be masked (e.g., actual tokens in the input sequence and special tokens like [CLS] token ID 101 and [SEP] token ID 102), and where zero indicates tokens that should be masked (e.g., the [PAD] token ID 0).
- The key input_type_ids is a matrix/vector of 1s and 0s having the same size as input_ids. This indicates which sentence each token belongs to. Remember that BERT can take two types of inputs: inputs with one sequence and inputs with two sequences, A and B. The input_type_ids matrix denotes which sequence (A or B) each token belongs to. Since we only have one sequence in our inputs, we simply create a matrix of zeros having the same size as input_ids.

The function get_bert_inputs() will generate the input in this format using a set of documents (i.e., a list of strings, where each string is an input; see the next listing).

Listing 13.3   Formatting a given input to the format BERT accepts

```
def get_bert_inputs(tokenizer, docs,max_seq_len=None):
    """ Generate inputs for BERT using a set of documents """

    packer = tfm.nlp.layers.BertPackInputs(
        seq_length=max_seq_length,
        special_tokens_dict = tokenizer.get_special_tokens_dict()
    )

    packed = packer(tokenizer(docs))
```

Use BertPackInputs to generate token IDs, mask and segment IDs.

Generate outputs for all the messages in docs.

```
packed_numpy = dict(
    [(k, v.numpy()) for k,v in packed.items()]
)
# Final output
return packed_numpy
```

⭠ Return the
result.

⭠ Convert the output of
BertPackInputs to a
dictionary with keys as
string and value as a
numpy array.

Here we are using the `BertPackInputs` object that takes in an array where each item is a string containing the message. Then `BertPackInputs` generates a dictionary that contains the following processed outputs:

- `input_word_ids`—Token IDs with [CLS] and [SEP] token IDs automatically added.
- `input_mask`—An integer array with each element representing whether it is a real token (1) or a padded token (0) at that position.
- `input_type_ids`—An integer array with each element representing which segment each token belongs to. It will be an array of all zeros in this case.

`BertPackInputs` does a lot of different preprocessing required by the BERT model. You can read about various inputs accepted by this layer at https://www.tensorflow.org/api_docs/python/tfm/nlp/layers/BertPackInputs.

To generate the prepared training, validation, and testing data for the model, simply call the `get_bert_inputs()` function:

```
train_inputs = get_bert_inputs(train_x, max_seq_len=80)
valid_inputs = get_bert_inputs(valid_x, max_seq_len=80)
test_inputs = get_bert_inputs(test_x, max_seq_len=80)
```

After this, let's shuffle the data in `train_inputs` as a precaution. Currently, the data is ordered such that spam messages appear after ham messages:

```
train_inds = np.random.permutation(len(train_inputs["input_word_ids"]))
train_inputs = dict(
    [(k, v[train_inds]) for k, v in train_inputs.items()]
)
train_y = train_y[train_inds]
```

Remember to use the same shuffling for both inputs and labels to maintain their association. We have done everything to prepare the inputs for the model. Now it's time for the grand unveiling of the model. We need to define BERT with a classification head so that the model can be trained end to end on the classification data set we have. We will do this in two steps. First, we will download the encoder part of BERT from TensorFlow hub and then use the `tfm.nlp.models.BertClassifier` object in the `tensorflow-models-official` library to generate the final BERT model with the classifier head. Let's examine how we do the first part:

```
import tensorflow_hub as hub

hub_bert_url = "https://tfhub.dev/tensorflow/bert_en_uncased_L-12_H-768_A-12/4"
max_seq_length = 60
```

```
# Contains input token ids
input_word_ids = tf.keras.layers.Input(
    shape=(max_seq_length,), dtype=tf.int32, name="input_word_ids"
)
# Contains input mask values
input_mask = tf.keras.layers.Input(
    shape=(max_seq_length,), dtype=tf.int32, name="input_mask"
)
input_type_ids = tf.keras.layers.Input(
    shape=(max_seq_length,), dtype=tf.int32, name="input_type_ids"
)

# BERT encoder downloaded from TF hub
bert_layer = hub.KerasLayer(hub_bert_url, trainable=True)

# get the output of the encoder
output = bert_layer({
    "input_word_ids":input_word_ids,
    "input_mask": input_mask,
    "input_type_ids": input_type_ids
})

# Define the final encoder as with the Functional API
hub_encoder = tf.keras.models.Model(
    inputs={
        "input_word_ids": input_word_ids,
        "input_mask": input_mask,
        "input_type_ids": input_type_ids
    },
    outputs={
        "sequence_output": output["sequence_output"],
        "pooled_output": output["pooled_output"]
    }
)
```

Here, we first define three input layers, where each input layer has one of the outputs of the BertPackInputs mapped to. For example, the input_word_ids input layer will receive the output found at the key input_word_ids in the dictionary produced by the function get_bert_inputs(). Next, we download the pretrained BERT encoder by passing a URL to the hub.KerasLayer object. This layer produces two outputs: sequence_output, which contains hidden representations of all the time steps, and pooled_output, which contains the hidden representation corresponding to the position of the [CLS] token. For this problem, we need the latter to pass it to a classification head sitting on top of the encoder. We will finally define a Keras model using the Functional API. This model needs to have a specific input and output signature defined via dictionaries as shown previously. We will use this model to define a classifier model based on this encoder:

```
# Generating a classifier and the encoder
bert_classifier = tfm.nlp.models.BertClassifier(
    network=hub_encoder, num_classes=2
)
```

As you can see, it's quite straightforward to define the classifier. We simply pass our hub_encoder to the BertClassifier and say we have two classes, spam and ham (i.e. num_classes=2).

Alternative way to get the BERT encoder

There's another method you can use to get a BERT encoder. However, it requires manually loading pretrained weights; therefore, we will keep this method as an alternative. Firstly, you start with a configuration file containing the encoder model's various hyperparameters. I have provided you with the original configuration used for the model as a YAML file (Ch12/data/ bert_en_uncased_base.yaml). It contains various hyperparameters used by BERT (e.g., hidden dimension size, nonlinear activation, etc.). Feel free to look at them to understand the different parameters used for the model. We will load these configurations using the yaml library as a dictionary and store it in config_dict. Next, we generate encoder_config, an EncoderConfig object initiated with the configuration we loaded. With encoder_config defined, we will build an encoder BERT model that is able to generate feature representations of tokens, and then call bert.bert_models.classifier_model() with this encoder as the network. Note that this method gets a randomly initialized BERT model:

```
import yaml

with open(os.path.join("data", "bert_en_uncased_base.yaml"), 'r') as stream:
    config_dict = yaml.safe_load(stream)['task']['model']['encoder']['bert']

encoder_config = tfm.nlp.encoders.EncoderConfig({
    'type':'bert',
    'bert': config_dict
})

bert_encoder = tfm.nlp.encoders.build_encoder(encoder_config)

bert_classifier = tfm.nlp.models.BertClassifier(
    network=bert_encoder, num_classes=2
)
```

If you want a pretrained version of BERT like this, then you need to download the TensorFlow checkpoint. You can do this by going to the link found in bert_url and then clicking download. Finally, you load the weights with

```
checkpoint = tf.train.Checkpoint(encoder=bert_encoder)
checkpoint.read(<path to .ckpt>).assert_consumed()
```

Now you have a pretrained BERT encoder.

Next, let's discuss how we can compile the built model.

COMPILING THE MODEL

Here we will define the optimizer to train the model. So far, we have not changed much from the default optimizer options provided in TensorFlow/Keras. This time, let's use the optimizer provided in the tf-models-official library. The optimizer can be instantiated by calling the `nlp.optimization.create_optimizer()` function. This is outlined in the next listing.

Listing 13.4   Optimizing BERT on the spam classification task

```
epochs = 3
batch_size = 56
eval_batch_size = 56

train_data_size = train_x.shape[0]
steps_per_epoch = int(train_data_size / batch_size)
num_train_steps = steps_per_epoch * epochs
warmup_steps = int(num_train_steps * 0.1)

init_lr = 3e-6
end_lr = 0.0

linear_decay = tf.keras.optimizers.schedules.PolynomialDecay(
    initial_learning_rate=init_lr,
    end_learning_rate=end_lr,
    decay_steps=num_train_steps)

warmup_schedule = tfm.optimization.lr_schedule.LinearWarmup(
    warmup_learning_rate = 1e-10,
    after_warmup_lr_sched = linear_decay,
    warmup_steps = warmup_steps
)

optimizer = tf.keras.optimizers.experimental.Adam(
    learning_rate = warmup_schedule
)
```

As the default optimizer, *Adam with weight decay* (https://arxiv.org/pdf/1711.05101 .pdf) is used. Adam with weight decay is a variant of the original Adam optimizer we used, but with better generalization properties. The `num_warmup_steps` denotes the duration of the learning rate warm-up. During the warm-up, the learning rate is brought up linearly from a small value to `init_lr` (defined in `linear_decay`) within `num_warmup_steps`. After that, the learning rate is decayed all the way to `end_lr` (defined in `linear_decay`) during `num_train_steps` using a polynomial decay (http://mng.bz/06lN). This is depicted in figure 13.9.

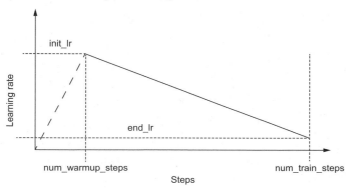

Figure 13.9   The behavior of the learning rate as training progresses through iterations (i.e., steps)

Now we can compile the model just like we did before. We will define a loss (sparse categorical cross-entropy loss) and a metric (accuracy computed using labels rather than one-hot vectors) and then pass the optimizer, loss, and metric to the hub_ classifier.compile() function:

```
metrics = [tf.keras.metrics.SparseCategoricalAccuracy('accuracy',
➥ dtype=tf.float32)]
loss = tf.keras.losses.SparseCategoricalCrossentropy(from_logits=True)

hub_classifier.compile(
    optimizer=optimizer,
    loss=loss,
    metrics=metrics)
```

TRAINING THE MODEL

We've come a long way, and now all that's left is training the model. Model training is quite simple and similar to how we trained models using the tf.keras.Model.fit() function:

```
hub_classifier.fit(
    x=train_inputs,
    y=train_y,
    validation_data=(valid_inputs, valid_y),
    validation_batch_size=eval_batch_size,
    batch_size=batch_size,
    epochs=epochs)
```

We are passing the train_inputs we prepared using the get_bert_inputs() function to the argument x and train_y (i.e., a vector of 1s and 0s indicating whether the input is a spam or a ham, respectively) to y. Similarly, we define validation_data as a tuple containing valid_inputs and valid_y. We also pass in the batch_size (training batch size), validation_batch_size, and the number of epochs to train for.

EVALUATING AND INTERPRETING THE RESULTS

When you run the training, you should get a result close to the following. Here you can see the training loss and the accuracy as well as the validation loss and the accuracy:

```
Epoch 1/3
18/18 [==============================] - 544s 29s/step - loss: 0.7082 -
➥ accuracy: 0.4555 - val_loss: 0.6764 - val_accuracy: 0.5150
Epoch 2/3
18/18 [==============================] - 518s 29s/step - loss: 0.6645 -
➥ accuracy: 0.6589 - val_loss: 0.6480 - val_accuracy: 0.8150
Epoch 3/3
18/18 [==============================] - 518s 29s/step - loss: 0.6414 -
➥ accuracy: 0.7608 - val_loss: 0.6391 - val_accuracy: 0.8550
```

The console output clearly shows that the training loss went down steadily, whereas the accuracy rose from 45% to 76%. The model has reached a validation accuracy of 85%. This clearly shows the power of a model like BERT. If you were to train an NLP model from scratch, it would be impossible to reach a validation accuracy of 85% in such a short time. Since BERT has very strong language understanding, the model can focus on learning the task at hand. Note that you may get a different level of accuracy from what's shown here as our validation and testing sets are quite small (each having only 200 records).

> **NOTE** On an Intel Core i5 machine with an NVIDIA GeForce RTX 2070 8 GB, the training took approximately 40 seconds to run 3 epochs.

Finally, let's test the model on the test data by calling the `evaluate()` function

```
hub_classifier.evaluate(test_inputs, test_y)
```

which will return

```
7/7 [==============================] - 22s 3s/step - loss: 0.6432 - accuracy:
    0.7950
```

Again, it's a great result. After just three epochs and no fancy parameter tweaking, we have achieved 79.5% accuracy on the test data. And all we did was fit a logistic regression layer on top of BERT.

The next section will discuss how we can define a model that can find answers to a given question from a paragraph. To do this, we will use one of the most popular libraries for Transformer models to date: Hugging Face's `transformers` library.

EXERCISE 2
You have a classification problem that has five classes, and you would like to modify the `bert_classifier`. Given the data in the correct format, how would you change the `bert_classifier` object defined?

13.3 *Question answering with Hugging Face's Transformers*

Your friend is planning to kick off a start-up that uses ML to find answers to open-domain questions. Lacking the ML background, he turns to you to ask whether it is feasible to do so using ML. Knowing that question answering is machine learnable given labeled data, you decide to create a question-answering prototype using a BERT variant and demonstrate it. You will be using the SQUAD v1 question-answering data set and training a DistilBERT (a variant of BERT) on the data set. For this, you are going to use the Hugging Face's `transformers` library (https://huggingface.co/transformers/). Hugging Face's `transformers` library provides implementations of different Transformer models and easy-to-use APIs to train/evaluate models on data sets.

BERT is designed to solve two different types of tasks:

- Tasks having a single sequence of text as the input
- Tasks having two sequences of text (A and B) as the input

Spam classification falls under the first type. Question answering is a type of task that has two input sequences. In question answering, you have a question and a context (a paragraph, a sentence, etc.), which may contain the answer to the question. Then a model is trained to predict the answer for a given question and a context. Let's get to know the process a bit better. Each record in the data set will consist of following elements:

- A question (a sequence of text)
- A context (a sequence of text)
- A starting index of the answer from the context (an integer)
- An ending index of the answer from the context (an integer)

First, we need to combine the question and the context and add several special tokens. At the beginning, we need to add a [CLS] token and then a [SEP] to separate the question and the context, as well as an [SEP] to mark the end of the input. Furthermore, the question and the context are broken down into tokens (i.e., sub-words) using the model's tokenizer. For the input having

Question: `What did the dog barked at`

Answer: `The dog barked at the mail man`

if we assume individual words as tokens, the input will look as follows:

```
[CLS], What, did, the, dog, barked, at, [SEP], The, dog, barked, at, the,
⇨ mailman, [SEP]
```

Next, these tokens are converted to IDs and fed to the BERT model. The output of the BERT model is connected to two downstream classification layers: one layer predicts the starting index of the answer, whereas the other layer predicts the ending index of the answer. Each of these two classification layers has its own weights and biases.

The BERT model will output a hidden representation for each token in the input sequence. The token output representations across the entire span of the context are fed to the downstream models. Each classification layer then predicts the probability of each token being the starting/ending token of the answer. The weights of these layers are shared across the time dimension. In other words, the same weight matrix is applied to every output representation to predict the probabilities.

For this section, we are going to use Hugging Face's `transformers` library. Please refer to the sidebar for more details.

Hugging Face's `transformers` library

Hugging Face is a company that focuses on solving NLP problems. The company provides libraries to train NLP models as well as host data sets and train models in a publicly accessible repository. We will use two Python libraries provided by Hugging Face: `transformers` and `datasets`.

At the time of writing this book, the `transformers` library (https://huggingface.co/transformers/) is the most versatile Python library that provides instant access to many Transformer models that have been released (e.g., BERT, XLNet, DistilBERT, Albert, RoBERT, etc.) as well as to community-released NLP models (https://huggingface.co/models). The `transformers` library supports both TensorFlow and PyTorch deep learning frameworks. PyTorch (https://pytorch.org/) is another deep learning framework like TensorFlow that offers a comprehensive suite of functionality to implement and productionize deep learning models. The following are the key advantages I see in the `transformers` library:

- An easy-to-understand API to pretrain and fine-tune models that is consistent across all the models
- The ability to download TensorFlow versions of various Transformer models and use them as Keras models
- The ability to convert TensorFlow and PyTorch models
- Powerful features such as the Trainer (http://mng.bz/Kx9j), which allows users to create and train models with lot of flexibility
- Highly active community-contributing models and data sets

13.3.1 Understanding the data

As mentioned, we will use the SQuAD v1 data set (https://rajpurkar.github.io/SQuAD-explorer/). It's a question-answering data set created by Stanford University. You can easily download the data set using Hugging Face's `datasets` library as follows:

```
from datasets import load_dataset
dataset = load_dataset("squad")
```

Let's print the data set and see the available attributes:

```
print(dataset)
```

This will return

```
DatasetDict({
    train: Dataset({
        features: ['id', 'title', 'context', 'question', 'answers'],
        num_rows: 87599
    })
    validation: Dataset({
        features: ['id', 'title', 'context', 'question', 'answers'],
        num_rows: 10570
    })
})
```

There are 87,599 training examples and 10,570 validation samples. We will use these examples to create the train/validation/test split. We are interested in the last three columns in the features section only (i.e., context, question, and answers). From these, context and question are simply strings, whereas answers is a dictionary. Let's analyze answers a bit further. You can print a few answers with

```
dataset["train"]["answers"][:5]
```

which gives

```
[{'answer_start': [515], 'text': ['Saint Bernadette Soubirous']},
 {'answer_start': [188], 'text': ['a copper statue of Christ']},
 {'answer_start': [279], 'text': ['the Main Building']},
 {'answer_start': [381], 'text': ['a Marian place of prayer and reflection']},
 {'answer_start': [92], 'text': ['a golden statue of the Virgin Mary']}]
```

We can see that each answer has a starting index (character based) and a text containing the answer. With this information, we can easily calculate the answer's ending index (i.e., end index = start index + len(text)).

GLUE benchmark task suite

The GLUE benchmark (https://gluebenchmark.com/tasks) is a popular collection of tasks for evaluating NLP models. It tests the natural language understanding of models on a variety of tasks. The following tasks are included in the GLUE tasks collection.

Task	Type	Description
The Corpus of Linguistic Acceptability	Binary classification	Contains sentences followed by labels (0/1) to indicate the grammatical correctness of that sentence.
The Stanford Sentiment Treebank	Multi-class classification	Contains movie reviews followed by labels (1–5) to indicate the sentiment of the reviews.
Microsoft Research Paraphrase Corpus	Binary classification	Contains pairs of sentences, where the second sentence may be a paraphrased/semantic representation of the first sentence, as well as labels (0/1) to indicate if the two sentences are related.
Semantic Textual Similarity Benchmark	Regression	Contains pairs of sentences followed by a continuous target (0–5) indicating how similar the two sentences are.
Quora Question Pairs	Binary classification	Contains pairs of questions and labels (0/1) to indicate whether one is a duplicate of the other.
MultiNLI Matched and MultiNLI Mismatched	Multi-class classification	Contains pairs of sentences and labels to indicate if the second sentence entails/contradicts/is neutral given the first sentence.
Recognizing Textual Entailment	Multi-class classification	Contains pairs of sentences and labels to indicate if the second sentence entails/contradicts/is neutral given the first sentence.
Question NLI	Multi-class classification	Based on the popular question-answering data set SQuAD, which contains pairs of questions and reading passages. The targets are the starting and ending positions of the answer in the reading passage.
Winograd NLI	Multi-class classification	A word-sense disambiguation task, where a pair of sentences are given along with a label (0/1) indicating if the second sentence resolves the ambiguity in the first sentence correctly. For example, "I stuck a pin through a carrot. When I pulled the pin out, it had a hole." "The carrot had a hole" has a label of 1, as it was, in fact, the carrot that had a hole (i.e., not I).
Diagnostics Main	Multi-class classification	Similar to what we discussed earlier, this is a textual entailment task.

13.3.2 Processing data

This data set has several integrity issues that need to be taken care of. We will fix those issues and then create a tf.data pipeline to pump the data. The first issues that need to be fixed are alignment issues between the given answer_start and the actual answer_start. Some examples tend to have an offset of around two characters between the given and the actual answer_start positions. We will write a function to correct for this offset, as well as add the end index. The next listing outlines the code to perform this operation.

Listing 13.5 Fixing the unwanted offsets in the answer start/end indices

```
def correct_indices_add_end_idx(answers, contexts):
    """ Correct the answer index of the samples (if wrong) """

    n_correct, n_fix = 0, 0                    Track how many were
    fixed_answers = []                         correct and fixed.
    for answer, context in zip(answers, contexts):    Iterate through each
                                                      answer context pair.
        gold_text = answer['text'][0]          Convert the answer from a
        answer['text'] = gold_text             list of strings to a string.
        start_idx = answer['answer_start'][0]
        answer['answer_start'] = start_idx     Convert the start of the
        if start_idx <0 or len(gold_text.strip())==0:   answer from a list of
            print(answer)                               integers to an integer.
        end_idx = start_idx + len(gold_text)

        # sometimes squad answers are off by a character or two - fix this
        if context[start_idx:end_idx] == gold_text:
            answer['answer_end'] = end_idx
            n_correct += 1
        elif context[start_idx-1:end_idx-1] == gold_text:
            answer['answer_start'] = start_idx - 1
            answer['answer_end'] = end_idx - 1
            n_fix += 1
        elif context[start_idx-2:end_idx-2] == gold_text:
            answer['answer_start'] = start_idx - 2
            answer['answer_end'] = end_idx - 2
            n_fix +=1

        fixed_answers.append(answer)

    print(
        "\t{}/{} examples had the correct answer indices".format(
            n_correct, len(answers)
        )
    )
    print(
        "\t{}/{} examples had the wrong answer indices".format(
            n_fix, len(answers)
        )
    )
    return fixed_answers, contexts
```

New fixed answers will be held in this variable.

Compute the end index by adding the answer's length to the start_idx.

If the slice from start_idx to end_idx needs to be offset by 1 to match the answer, offset accordingly.

If the slice from start_idx to end_idx exactly matches the answer text, no changes are required.

If the slice from start_idx to end_idx needs to be offset by 2 to match the answer, offset accordingly.

Print the number of correct answers (requires no change).

Print the number of answers that required fixing.

Now we can call this function on the two subsets (train and validation) of the data set. We will use the validation subset as our testing set (unseen examples). A proportion of the training examples will be set aside as validation samples:

```
train_questions = dataset["train"]["question"]
train_answers, train_contexts = correct_indices_add_end_idx(
    dataset["train"]["answers"], dataset["train"]["context"]
)

test_questions = dataset["validation"]["question"]
test_answers, test_contexts = correct_indices_add_end_idx(
    dataset["validation"]["answers"], dataset["validation"]["context"]
)
```

When you run this code, you will see the following statistics:

- Training data corrections
  - 87,341/87,599 examples had the correct answer indices.
  - 258/87,599 examples had the wrong answer indices.
- Validation data correction
  - 10,565/10,570 examples had the correct answer indices.
  - 5/10,570 examples had the wrong answer indices.

We have to make sure that the required number of corrections is not drastically high. If the number of corrections is significantly high, typically it could mean a bug in the code or problems with the data-loading logic. Here, we can clearly see that the number of examples that required corrections is low.

DEFINING AND USING THE TOKENIZER

All the data we need to solve the problem is available to us. Now it's time to tokenize the data like we did before. Remember that these pretrained NLP models come in two parts: the tokenizer and the model itself. The tokenizer tokenizes the text into smaller parts (e.g., sub-words) and presents those to the model in the form of a sequence of IDs. Then the model takes in those IDs and performs embedding lookups on them, as well as various computations, to come up with the final token representation that will be used as inputs to the downstream classification model (i.e., the question-answering classification layer). In a similar fashion, in the transformers library, you have the tokenizer object and the model object:

```
from transformers import DistilBertTokenizerFast
tokenizer = DistilBertTokenizerFast.from_pretrained('distilbert-base-uncased')
```

You can see that we are using a tokenizer called DistilBertTokenizerFast. This tokenizer comes from a model known as the DistilBERT. DistilBERT is a smaller version of BERT that shows similar performance as BERT but smaller in size. It has been trained using a transfer learning technique known as *knowledge distillation* (https://devopedia.org/knowledge-distillation). To get the tokenizer, all we need to do is call the DistilBertTokenizerFast.from_pretrained() function with the model tag (i.e., `distilbert-base-uncased`). This tag says the model is a DistilBERT-type model with `base` size (there are different-sized models available) and ignores the case of the characters (denoted by `uncased`). The model tag points to a model available in Hugging Face's model repository (https://huggingface.co/models) and downloads it for us. It will be stored on your computer.

Hugging Face provides two different variants of tokenizers: standard tokenizers (`PreTrainedTokenizer` objects; http://mng.bz/95d7) and fast tokenizers (`PreTrained-TokenizerFast` objects; http://mng.bz/j2Xr). You can read about their differences on http://mng.bz/WxEa). They are significantly faster when encoding (i.e., converting strings to token sequences) in a batch-wise fashion. Furthermore, fast tokenizers have additional methods that will help us to process inputs easily for the question-answering model.

What is DistilBERT?

Following BERT, DistilBERT is a model introduced by Hugging Face in the paper "Distil-BERT, a distilled version of BERT: smaller, faster, cheaper and lighter" by Sanh et al. (https://arxiv.org/pdf/1910.01108v4.pdf) in 2019. It is trained using a transfer learning technique known as knowledge distillation. The idea is to have a teacher model (i.e., BERT), where a smaller model (i.e., DistilBERT) is trying to mimic the teacher's output, which becomes the learning objective for DistilBERT. DistilBERT is smaller compared to BERT and has only six layers, as opposed to BERT's 12. Another key difference of DistilBERT is that it is only trained on the masked language modeling task and not on the next-sentence prediction task. This decision is backed up by several studies that question the contribution made by next-sentence prediction tasks (compared to the masked language modeling task) toward natural language understanding.

With the tokenizer downloaded, let's examine the tokenizer and how it transforms the inputs by providing some sample text:

```
context = "This is the context"
question = "This is the question"

token_ids = tokenizer(context, question, return_tensors='tf')
print(token_ids)
```

This returns

```
{'input_ids': <tf.Tensor: shape=(1, 11), dtype=int32, numpy=
array([[ 101, 2023, 2003, 1996, 6123,  102, 2023, 2003, 1996, 3160,  102]],
     dtype=int32)>,
 'attention_mask': <tf.Tensor: shape=(1, 11), dtype=int32, numpy=array([[1,
     1, 1, 1, 1, 1, 1, 1, 1, 1, 1]], dtype=int32)>
}
```

Next, print the tokens corresponding to the IDs with

```
print(tokenizer.convert_ids_to_tokens(token_ids['input_ids'].numpy()[0]))
```

This will give

```
['[CLS]', 'this', 'is', 'the', 'context', '[SEP]', 'this', 'is', 'the',
'question', '[SEP]']
```

We can now encode all the training and test data we have with the code in the next listing.

Listing 13.6   Encoding training and test data

```
train_encodings = tokenizer(          ◁─┐ Encode train data.
    train_contexts, train_questions, truncation=True, padding=True,
➥  return_tensors='tf'
)
print(
    "train_encodings.shape: {}".format(train_encodings["input_ids"].shape)
)

test_encodings = tokenizer(
    test_contexts, test_questions, truncation=True, padding=True,
➥  return_tensors='tf'
)
print("test_encodings.shape: {}".format(test_encodings["input_ids"].shape))
```

Encode test data. ┐ (points to test_encodings)

Note that we are using several arguments when calling the tokenizer. When truncation and padding are enabled (i.e., set to `True`), the tokenizer will pad/truncate input sequences as necessary. You can pass an argument to the tokenizer (`model_max_length`) during the creation to pad or truncate text to a certain length. If this argument is not given, it will use the default length available to the tokenizer as one of the configurations set when it was pretrained. When padding/truncation is enabled, your inputs will go through one of the following changes:

- If the sequence is shorter than the length, add the special token [PAD] to the end of the sequence until it reaches the length.
- If the sequence is longer than the length, it will be truncated.
- If the sequence has exactly the same length, no change will be introduced.

When you run the code in listing 13.6, it prints

```
train_encodings.shape: (87599, 512)
test_encodings.shape: (10570, 512)
```

We can see that all sequences are either padded or truncated until they reach a length of 512, the sequence length set during the model pretraining. Let's look at some of the important arguments you need to be aware of when defining a tokenizer with the `transformers` library:

- `model_max_length` (int, *optional*)—The maximum length (in number of tokens) for the inputs to be padded to.

- padding_side (str, *optional*)—To which side the model should apply padding. Can be ['right', 'left']. The default value is picked from the class attribute of the same name.
- model_input_names (List[string], *optional*)—The list of inputs accepted by the forward pass of the model (e.g., "token_type_ids" or "attention_mask"). The default value is picked from the class attribute of the same name.
- bos_token (str or tokenizers.AddedToken, *optional*)—A special token representing the beginning of a sentence.
- eos_token (str or tokenizers.AddedToken, *optional*)—A special token representing the end of a sentence.
- unk_token (str or tokenizers.AddedToken, *optional*)—A special token representing an out-of-vocabulary token. Out-of-vocabulary tokens are important if the model encounters words it has not seen before.

Most of these arguments can be safely ignored as we are using a pretrained tokenizer model, which already had these attributes set before the training.

Unfortunately for us, we still have to do a few more things. One important transformation we have to do is to how we represent the start and end of the answer to the model. As I said earlier, we are given the starting and ending character positions of the answer. But our model understands only token-level decomposition, not character-level decomposition. Therefore, we have to find the token positions from the given character positions. Fortunately, the fast tokenizers provide a convenient function: char_to_token(). Note that this function is only available for fast tokenizers (i.e., PreTrainedTokenizerFast objects), not the standard tokenizers (i.e., PreTrained-Tokenizer objects). The char_to_token() function takes in the following arguments:

- batch_or_char_index (int)—The example index in the batch. If the batch has one example, it will be used as the character index we're interested in converting to a token index.
- char_index (int, optional—If the batch index is provided, this will denote the character index we want to convert to a token index.
- sequence_index (int, optional—If the input has multiple sequences, this denotes which sequence the character/token belongs to.

Using this function, we will write the update_char_to_token_positions_inplace() function to convert the char-based indices to token-based indices (see the next listing)..

> **Listing 13.7 Converting the char indices to token-based indices**

```
def update_char_to_token_positions_inplace(encodings, answers):
    start_positions = []
    end_positions = []
    n_updates = 0

    for i in range(len(answers)):          ⊲──┐ Go through all
                                               the answers.
```

Get the token position for both start and end char positions.

```
start_positions.append(
    encodings.char_to_token(i, answers[i]['answer_start'])
)
end_positions.append(
    encodings.char_to_token(i, answers[i]['answer_end'] - 1)
)
```

Keep track of how many samples were missing answers.

```
if start_positions[-1] is None or end_positions[-1] is None:
    n_updates += 1

# if start position is None, the answer passage has been truncated
# In the guide,
https://huggingface.co/transformers/custom_datasets.html#qa-squad
    # they set it to model_max_length, but this will result in NaN
losses as the last
    # available label is model_max_length-1 (zero-indexed)
```

If a starting position was not found, set it to the last available index.

```
    if start_positions[-1] is None:
        start_positions[-1] = tokenizer.model_max_length -1

    if end_positions[-1] is None:
        end_positions[-1] = tokenizer.model_max_length -1
```

If an ending position was not found, set it to the last available index.

Update the encodings in place.

```
print("{}/{} had answers truncated".format(n_updates, len(answers)))
encodings.update({
    'start_positions': start_positions, 'end_positions': end_positions
})
```

```
update_char_to_token_positions_inplace(train_encodings, train_answers)
update_char_to_token_positions_inplace(test_encodings, test_answers)
```

This will print

```
10/87599 had answers truncated
8/10570 had answers truncated
```

In the code in listing 13.7, we go through every answer in the data set and call the char_to_token() method on every answer_start and answer_end element that marks the start and end (char index) of answers, respectively. The new starting and ending token indices of the answers are assigned to new keys, start_positions and end_positions. Furthermore, you can see that there is a validation step that checks if the starting or ending indices are None (i.e., a suitable token ID was not found). This can happen if the answer has been truncated from the context when preprocessing. If that's the case, we assign the very last index of the sequence as the positions.

How many rotten eggs?

You can see that we are printing the number of examples that needed modifications (e.g., needed correction) or were corrupted (truncated answers). This is an important sanity check, as a very high number can indicate problems with data quality or a bug in your data processing workflow. Therefore, always print these numbers and make sure they are low enough to be safely ignored.

We will now see how we can define a `tf.data` pipeline.

FROM TOKENS TO THE TF.DATA PIPELINE

After all the cleaning and required transformations, our data set is as good as new. All that's left for us is to create a `tf.data.Dataset` from the data. Our data pipeline will be very simple. It will create a training data set, which will be broken into two subsets, training and validation, and batch the data set. Then the test data set will be created and batched. First let's import TensorFlow:

```
import tensorflow as tf
```

Then we will define a generator that will produce the inputs and outputs necessary for our model to be trained. As you can see, our input is a tuple of two items. It has

- The padded input token IDs (having the shape [<dataset size>, 512])
- The attention mask (having the shape [<dataset size>, 512])

The outputs will be comprised of

- The starting token positions (having the shape [<dataset size>])
- The ending token positions (having the shape [<dataset size>]

```
def data_gen(input_ids, attention_mask, start_positions, end_positions):
    for inps, attn, start_pos, end_pos in zip(
        input_ids, attention_mask, start_positions, end_positions
    ):

        yield (inps, attn), (start_pos, end_pos)
```

Our data generator returns data in a very specific format. It returns an input tuple and an output tuple. The input tuple has the token IDs (`input_ids`) returned by the tokenizer and the attention mask (`attention_mask`), in that order. The output tuple has the answer's start positions (`start_positions`) and end positions (`end_positions`) of all the inputs.

We must define our data generator as a callable (i.e., it returns a function, not the generator object). This is a requirement for the `tf.data.Dataset` we will be defining. To get a callable function from the generator we defined earlier, let's use the `partial()` function,. `partial()` function takes in a callable, optional keyword argument of the callable and returns a partially populated callable, to which you only need to provide the missing arguments (i.e., arguments not specified during the partial call):

```
from functools import partial

train_data_gen = partial(
    data_gen,
    input_ids=train_encodings['input_ids'],
    attention_mask=train_encodings['attention_mask'],
    start_positions=train_encodings['start_positions'],
    end_positions=train_encodings['end_positions']
)
```

`train_data_gen` can be treated as a function that has no arguments, as we have already provided all arguments in the partial call. As we have defined our data in the form of a generator, we can use the `tf.data.Dataset.from_generator()` function to generate the data. Remember that we have to pass the `output_types` argument when defining the data through a generator. All our outputs are `int32` type. But they come as a pair of tuples:

```
train_dataset = tf.data.Dataset.from_generator(
    train_data_gen, output_types=(('int32', 'int32'), ('int32', 'int32'))
)
```

Next, we shuffle the data to make sure there's no order. Make sure you pass the `buffer_size` argument that specifies how many samples are brought into memory for the shuffle. We will set the `buffer_size` to 20,000 as we plan to use 10,000 samples from that as validation samples:

```
train_dataset = train_dataset.shuffle(20000)
```

It's time to split the `train_dataset` into training and validation data, as we will be using the original validation data subset as the testing data. To split the `train_dataset` into training and validation subsets, we will take the following approach. After the shuffle, define the first 10,000 samples as the valid data set. We will be batching the data using the `tf.data.Dataset.batch()` function with a batch size of 8:

```
valid_dataset = train_dataset.take(10000)
valid_dataset = valid_dataset.batch(8)
```

Skip the first 10,000 datapoints, as they belong to the validation set, and have the rest as the `train_dataset`. We will be batching the data using the `tf.data.Dataset.batch()` function with a batch size of 8:

```
train_dataset = train_dataset.skip(10000)
train_dataset = train_dataset.batch(8)
```

Finally, the test data is defined using the same data generator:

```
test_data_gen = partial(data_gen,
    input_ids=test_encodings['input_ids'],
    attention_mask=test_encodings['attention_mask'],
    start_positions=test_encodings['start_positions'],
    end_positions=test_encodings['end_positions']
)
test_dataset = tf.data.Dataset.from_generator(
    test_data_gen, output_types=(('int32', 'int32'), ('int32', 'int32'))
)
test_dataset = test_dataset.batch(8)
```

Next we will work through defining the model.

13.3.3 *Defining the DistilBERT model*

We have looked closely at the data, cleaned and processed it using a tokenizer, and defined a `tf.data.Dataset` to quickly retrieve batches of examples in the format our model will accept. It's time to define the model. To define the model, we will import the following module:

```
from transformers import TFDistilBertForQuestionAnswering
```

The `transformers` library provides you with a remarkable selection of ready-made model templates that you can download and train on the task. In other words, you don't have to fiddle around with the library to find out how to plug downstream models on top of the pretrained transformers. For example, we are solving a question-answering problem and we want to use the DistilBERT model for that. The `transformers` library has the built-in question-answering adaptation of the DistilBERT model. All you need to do is import the module and call the `from_pretrained()` function with the model tag to download it:

```
model = TFDistilBertForQuestionAnswering.from_pretrained("distilbert-base-uncased")
```

This will download the model and save it on your local computer.

> ### What other ready-to-use models does the Transformers library provide?
>
> You can a look at http://mng.bz/8Mwz to get an idea about what you can and cannot easily do with the DistilBERT model. `transformers` is a fully fledged library that you can use to solve almost all the common NLP tasks with Transformer models. Here we will look at the options for the DistilBERT model.
>
> #### TFDistilBertForMaskedLM
>
> This allows you to pretrain the DistilBERT model using the masked language modeling task. In the masked language modeling task, in a given corpus of text, words are masked at random and the model is asked to predict the masked words.
>
> #### TFDistilBertForSequenceClassification
>
> If your problem has a single input sequence and you want to predict a label for the input (e.g., spam classification, sentiment analysis, etc.), you can use this model to train the model end to end.
>
> #### TFDistilBertForMultipleChoice
>
> DistilBERT can be used to solve multiple-choice problems with this variant. The input consists of a question and several answers. These are typically combined into a single sequence (i.e., [CLS] [Question] [SEP] [Answer 1] [SEP] [Answer 2] [SEP], etc.), and the model is asked to predict the best answer to the question, which is typically done by feeding the representation for the [CLS] token to a classification layer that will predict the index of the correct answer (e.g., first answer, second answer, etc.).

TFDistilBertForTokenClassification

Tasks like named-entity recognition or part-of-speech tagging require the model to predict a label (e.g., person, organization, etc.) for every token in the input sequence. For such tasks, this type of model can be used simply.

TFDistilBertForQuestionAnswering

This is the model we will use in our scenario. We have a question and a context, and the model needs to predict the answer (or the starting/ending positions of the answer in the context). Such problems can be solved using this module.

Table 13.1 is a summary of the models in this sidebar and their usage.

Table 13.1   Different models in Hugging Face's `transformers` library and their usage

Model	Description	Task
TFDistilBertForMaskedLM	Masks tokens randomly in the input sequence, and the model predicts the missing tokens.	Language modeling
TFDistilBertForSequenceClassification	The model takes in a token sequence and produces a single output (e.g., a class) for the input sequence.	Sentiment analysis
TFDistilBertForMultipleChoice	The model takes in several components in the input and produces a single output (e.g., a class) for the input sequence.	Multiple-choice question answering
TFDistilBertForTokenClassification	The model takes in an input sequence and predicts an output (e.g., a class) for each token in the sequence.	Named entity recognition
TFDistilBertForQuestionAnswering	The model takes in a context and a question as the input sequence and predicts the position of the answer in the context as the output.	Question answering

The blog http://jalammar.github.io/illustrated-bert/ provides a very informative diagram of how BERT-like models can be used for different tasks (as outlined under the "Task-specific models" section).

(continued)

The training and evaluation of these models will be very similar to how you would use them if they were Keras models. You can call `model.fit()`, `model.predict()` or `model.evaluate()` on these models given that the data is in the correct format the model expects.

To train these models, you also have the ability to use an advanced Trainer (http://mng.bz/EWZd). We will discuss the Trainer object in more detail later.

The next part of this came from a wakeup call that I had while using the library. Typically, once the model is defined, you can use it just like a Keras model. This means you can call `model.fit()` with a `tf.data.Dataset` and train the model. TensorFlow and Keras, when training models, expect the model output to be a tensor or a tuple of tensors. However, Transformer models' outputs are specific objects (a descendant of the `transformers.file_utils.ModelOutput` object), as outlined in http://mng.bz/N6Rn. This will throw an error like

```
TypeError: The two structures don't have the same sequence type.
Input structure has type <class 'tuple'>, while shallow structure has type
<class 'transformers.modeling_tf_outputs.TFQuestionAnsweringModelOutput'>.
```

To fix this, the `transformers` library allows you to set a certain configuration called `return_dict` and make sure the model returns a tuple, not an object. Then we define a `Config` object that has `return_dict=False` and override the default config of the model with the new config object. For example, for the DistilBERT model, this can be done with

```
from transformers import DistilBertConfig, TFDistilBertForQuestionAnswering

config = DistilBertConfig.from_pretrained(
    "distilbert-base-uncased", return_dict=False
)
model = TFDistilBertForQuestionAnswering.from_pretrained(
    "distilbert-base-uncased", config=config
)
```

Unfortunately, I was not able to get the model to behave in the way I expected it to by using this configuration. This goes to show that when writing code, you need to anticipate things that can go wrong even when using top-notch libraries. The easiest fix would be to let the `transformers` library output an `ModelOutput` object and write a wrapper function that will extract the required outputs of that object and create a `tf.keras.Model` from those outputs. The function in the following listing does that for us.

Listing 13.8   Wrapping the model in a `tf.keras.models.Model` object to prevent errors

```
def tf_wrap_model(model):
    """ Wraps the huggingface's model with in the Keras Functional API """

    # Define inputs
    input_ids = tf.keras.layers.Input(
        [None,], dtype=tf.int32, name="input_ids"
    )
    attention_mask = tf.keras.layers.Input(
        [None,], dtype=tf.int32, name="attention_mask"
    )

    out = model([input_ids, attention_mask])

    wrap_model = tf.keras.models.Model(
        [input_ids, attention_mask],
        outputs=(out.start_logits, out.end_logits)
    )

    return wrap_model
```

Define an input for the attention mask returned when encoding with the tokenizer.

Get the model output given the input_ids and the attention_mask.

Define a wrapper model that takes the defined inputs as the inputs and output logits of the start and end indices' prediction layers.

Define an input layer that will take a batch of a token sequence.

You can generate the model that generates the corrected outputs by calling the function in listing 13.8:

```
model_v2 = tf_wrap_model(model)
```

Finally, compile the model with a loss function (sparse categorical cross-entropy, as we are using integer labels), metric(s) (sparse accuracy), and an optimizer (Adam optimizer):

```
loss = tf.keras.losses.SparseCategoricalCrossentropy(from_logits=True)
acc = tf.keras.metrics.SparseCategoricalAccuracy()
optimizer = tf.keras.optimizers.Adam(learning_rate=1e-5)

model_v2.compile(optimizer=optimizer, loss=loss, metrics=[acc])
```

Transformers in vision

Transformer models typically thrive in the NLP domain. Until recently, little effort was put into understanding their place in the computer vision domain. Then came several notable papers from Google and Facebook AI that investigated how Transformer models could be used in the computer vision domain.

(continued)

Vision Transformer (ViT)

First, the paper "An Image Is Worth 16X16 Words: Transformers for Image Recognition at Scale" by Dosovitskiy et al. was published in October 2020 (https://arxiv .org/pdf/2010.11929.pdf). This can be considered the first substantial step toward vision transformers. In this paper, the authors adapt the original Transformer model proposed for the NLP domain to a computer vision with minimal changes to the architecture. This model is called the Vision Transformer (ViT).

The idea is to decompose an image to small patches of 16 × 16 and consider each as a separate token. Each image path is flattened to a 1D vector, and its position is encoded by a positional-encoding mechanism similar to the original Transformer. It is important to note that the positional encoding in the original Transformer is 1D. However, images are 2D. The authors argue that a 1D positional encoding was adequate and there was no major performance difference between 1D and 2D positional encoding. Once the image is broken into patches of 16 × 16 and flattened, each image can be presented as a sequence of tokens, just like a textual input sequence.

Then the model is pretrained in a self-supervised fashion, using a vision data set called JFT-300M (https://paperswithcode.com/dataset/jft-300m). It is not trivial to formulate a self-supervised task in vision as it is in NLP. In NLP, you can form an objective simply to predict masked tokens in a text sequence. However, in the context of computer vision, a token is a sequence of continuous values (normalized pixel values). Therefore, ViT is pretrained to predict the mean three-bit RGB color of a given image patch. Each channel (i.e., red, green, and blue) is represented with three bits (i.e., each bit having the value of 0 or 1), which gives 512 possibilities or classes. In other words, for a given image, patches are masked randomly (using the same approach as BERT), and the model is asked to predict the mean three-bit RGB color of that image patch.

After pretraining, the model can be fine-tuned for a task-specific problem by fitting a classification or a regression head on top of ViT, just like BERT. ViT also has the [CLS] token at the beginning of the sequence, which will be used as the input representation for downstream vision models that are plugged on top of ViT. The following figure illustrates the mechanics of ViT.

The original code for ViT is written with a framework known as Jax (https://github .com/google-research/vision_transformer). However, there are several third-party TensorFlow wrappers for the model (e.g., https://github.com/emla2805/vision-transformer). If using a third-party version, make sure you read the code and verify the correctness as the third party is not affiliated with the original research team.

(continued)

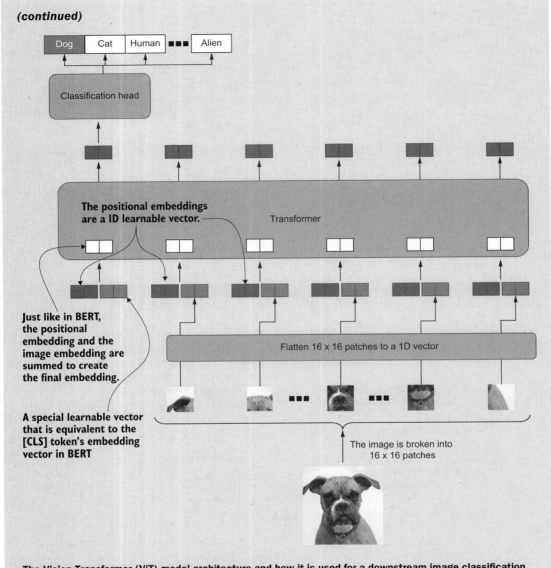

The positional embeddings are a 1D learnable vector.

Just like in BERT, the positional embedding and the image embedding are summed to create the final embedding.

A special learnable vector that is equivalent to the [CLS] token's embedding vector in BERT

Flatten 16 x 16 patches to a 1D vector

The image is broken into 16 x 16 patches

The Vision Transformer (ViT) model architecture and how it is used for a downstream image classification task

(continued)

Unified Transformer (UniT)

Then came an even more groundbreaking paper from Facebook AI called "Transformer Is All You Need: Multimodal Multitask Learning with a Unified Transformer" by Hu et al. (https://arxiv.org/pdf/2102.10772.pdf). The model is called the Unified Transformer (UniT). UniT can perform a plethora of tasks in both computer vision and NLP domains, just by changing the classification head.

The model, even though it is complex, is straightforward. There are three Transformer models. One Transformer encodes the image input (if present) to generate an encoded representation of an image. The next Transformer encodes the text input (if present). Finally, another Transformer takes a task index as the input, gets the embedding, and passes it to a cross self-attention layer that takes the concatenated image and text encoding as the query and key and the task embedding (after passing through a self-attention layer) as the value. This is similar to how the Transformer decoder, in its encoder-decoder attention layer, uses the last encoder output to generate the query and key and uses the decoder's input as the value. This model is depicted in the figure on the next page.

UniT is evaluated on seven tasks involving eight data sets. These tasks include object detection, visual question answering, object annotation, and four language-only tasks. The four language-only tasks are from the GLUE benchmarking data sets, which include the following:

Tasks

Object detection—The model predicts the rectangular coordinates of objects present in images (data sets COCO and Visual Genome Detection [VGD]).

Visual question answering (VQAv2)—An image and a question is given, and then the model predicts the answer to the question, which can be found in the image (data set: VQAv2).

Visual entailment task—A visual entailment task where an image and a text sequence are given and the model predicts whether the sentence semantically entails the image (SNLI-VE).

Question Natural Language Inference (QNLI)—Question answering by extracting the answer from a given context.

Quora Question Pairs (QQP)—Identify duplicate questions from a given pair of questions.

Textual entailment—Textual entailment focuses on predicting if sentence A entails/contradicts/is neutral to sentence B. (data set MNLI).

Sentiment analysis—Predicts a sentiment (positive/negative/is neutral) for a given review/text (data set Stanford Sentiment Treebank [SST-2]).

(continued)

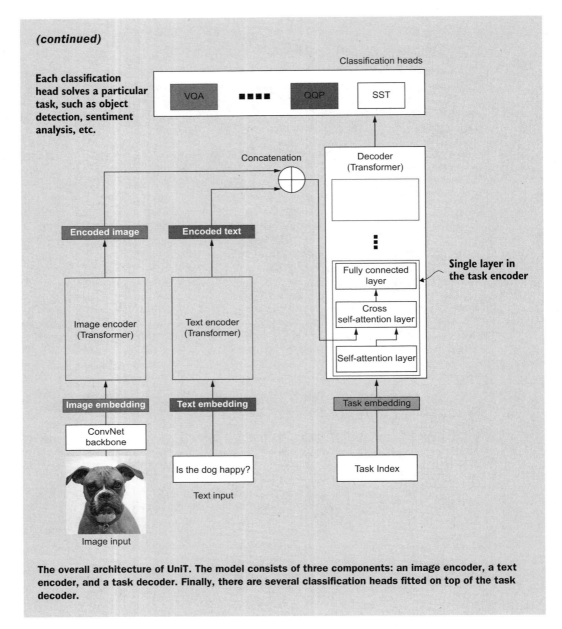

Classification heads

Each classification head solves a particular task, such as object detection, sentiment analysis, etc.

The overall architecture of UniT. The model consists of three components: an image encoder, a text encoder, and a task decoder. Finally, there are several classification heads fitted on top of the task decoder.

Next we will train the model we just defined.

13.3.4 *Training the model*

We have been patiently chipping away at this problem to arrive at this moment. Finally, we can train the model we just defined with the `train_dataset` data set we created earlier and use the `valid_dataset` to monitor the accuracy of the model:

```
model_v2.fit(
    train_dataset,
    validation_data=valid_dataset,
    epochs=3
)
```

This will print the following output:

```
Epoch 1/3
WARNING:tensorflow:The parameters `output_attentions`,
➥ `output_hidden_states` and `use_cache` cannot be updated when calling a
➥ model.They have to be set to True/False in the config object (i.e.:
➥ `config=XConfig.from_pretrained('name', output_attentions=True)`).

WARNING:tensorflow:The parameter `return_dict` cannot be set in graph mode
➥ and will always be set to `True`.

9700/9700 [==============================] - 3308s 340ms/step - loss:
➥ 4.3138 - tf_distil_bert_for_question_answering_loss: 2.2146 -
➥ tf_distil_bert_for_question_answering_1_loss: 2.0992 -
➥ tf_distil_bert_for_question_answering_sparse_categorical_accuracy:
➥ 0.4180 -
➥ tf_distil_bert_for_question_answering_1_sparse_categorical_accuracy:
➥ 0.4487 - val_loss: 2.3849 -
➥ val_tf_distil_bert_for_question_answering_loss: 1.2053 -
➥ val_tf_distil_bert_for_question_answering_1_loss: 1.1796 -
➥ val_tf_distil_bert_for_question_answering_sparse_categorical_accuracy:
➥ 0.6681 -
➥ val_tf_distil_bert_for_question_answering_1_sparse_categorical_accuracy
➥ : 0.6909

...

Epoch 3/3
9700/9700 [==============================] - 3293s 339ms/step - loss:
➥ 1.6349 - tf_distil_bert_for_question_answering_loss: 0.8647 -
➥ tf_distil_bert_for_question_answering_1_loss: 0.7703 -
➥ tf_distil_bert_for_question_answering_sparse_categorical_accuracy:
➥ 0.7294 -
➥ tf_distil_bert_for_question_answering_1_sparse_categorical_accuracy:
➥ 0.7672 - val_loss: 2.4049 -
➥ val_tf_distil_bert_for_question_answering_loss: 1.2048 -
➥ val_tf_distil_bert_for_question_answering_1_loss: 1.2001 -
➥ val_tf_distil_bert_for_question_answering_sparse_categorical_accuracy:
➥ 0.6975 -
➥ val_tf_distil_bert_for_question_answering_1_sparse_categorical_accuracy
➥ : 0.7200
```

The training updates are quite long, so let's break them down a bit. There are two losses:

- `tf_distil_bert_for_question_answering_loss`—Measures the loss on the starting index prediction head
- `tf_distil_bert_for_question_answering_1_loss`—Measures the loss on the ending index prediction head

As mentioned earlier, for question answering, we have two classification heads: one to predict the starting index and one to predict the ending index. We have something similar for the accuracy. There are two accuracies to measure the performance of individual heads:

- `tf_distil_bert_for_question_answering_sparse_categorical_accuracy`— Measures the accuracy of the classification head predicting the starting index
- `tf_distil_bert_for_question_answering_1_sparse_categorical_accuracy` —Measures the accuracy of the classification head predicting the ending index

We can see that the model has achieved a training accuracy of around 77% for both starting and ending index prediction, where the validation accuracy is around 70% and 72% for starting/ending index prediction, respectively. These are good accuracies given that we only trained the model for three epochs.

NOTE On an Intel Core i5 machine with an NVIDIA GeForce RTX 2070 8 GB, the training took approximately 2 hours and 45 minutes to run three epochs.

You can see that there are several warnings produced during the model training. Since this is a new library, it is extremely important to pay attention to these warnings to make sure they make sense in the context we're using these models. You don't need to worry about these as you would if you saw an error, as warnings do not always indicate a problem. Depending on the problem we're solving, some warnings are not applicable and can be safely ignored. The first warning says that the parameters `output_attentions`, `output_hidden_states` and `use_cache` cannot be updated when calling the model but need to be passed in as config objects. We are not worried about this as we are not interested in introducing any custom modifications to the model, and we are using one that is already designed for question answering.

The second warning says that `return_dict` will always be set to `TRUE`. Setting `return_dict=True` means that the Transformer model will return a `ModelOutput` object that is not understood by TensorFlow or Keras. This creates problems down the road when we want to use the model with a Keras API. This is one of the reasons we create the `tf_wrap_model()` function: to make sure we get a `tf.keras.Model` that always outputs a tuple and not a `ModelOutput` object.

Finally, we will save the model:

```
import os

# Create folders
if not os.path.exists('models'):
    os.makedirs('models')
if not os.path.exists('tokenizers'):
    os.makedirs('tokenizers')

tokenizer.save_pretrained(os.path.join('tokenizers', 'distilbert_qa'))
```

```
model_v2.get_layer(
    "tf_distil_bert_for_question_answering").save_pretrained(
        os.path.join('models', 'distilbert_qa')
    )
)
```

Make sure to save both the tokenizer and the model. To save the tokenizer, you can simply call the save_pretrained() function and provide it a folder path. The tokenizer will be saved in that directory. Saving the model requires a bit more work. We will not be able to save the model (model_v2) as is, because when your model has a custom layer, to be saved correctly, the layer needs to implement the get_config() function and specify all the attributes of that layer. However, doing this for the Transformer model, which is there as a custom layer, would be extremely difficult. Therefore, we will only save the Transformer model by calling the model_v2.get_layer() function with the layer name (i.e., tf_distil_bert_for_question_answering) and then calling the save_pretrained() method with a folder path. Any time we have to build the full model, we can simply call the tf_wrap_model() function on that saved model.

13.3.5 *Ask BERT a question*

Evaluating the model is also a matter of calling the model_v2.evaluate() function with the test_dataset we created earlier:

```
model_v2.evaluate(test_dataset)
```

This will print

```
1322/1322 [==============================] - 166s 126ms/step - loss: 2.4756
 - tf_distil_bert_for_question_answering_loss: 1.2702 -
 tf_distil_bert_for_question_answering_1_loss: 1.2054 -
 tf_distil_bert_for_question_answering_sparse_categorical_accuracy:
 0.6577 -
 tf_distil_bert_for_question_answering_1_sparse_categorical_accuracy:
 0.6942
```

This is wonderful news! We have achieved around 65.7% accuracy on predicting the start index of the answer, where the model can predict the end index with approximately 69.4% accuracy. Two things to observe are that both starting and ending accuracies are similar, meaning that the model gets the answer correct (start to end) around that accuracy. Finally, this accuracy falls close to the validation accuracy, meaning that we don't have unusual overfitting occurring.

As I have alluded to numerous times, it is usually not enough to look at a number alone to judge a model on its performance. Visual inspection has always been a natural tendency for humans when evaluating an object. Therefore, as a scrupulous data scientist or a machine learning engineer, it should be a part of the machine learning workflow whenever possible. In the next listing, we will provide our model a question from the test set and see what the model produces.

Listing 13.9   Inferring the textual answer from the model for a given question

```
i = 5

sample_q = test_questions[i]          Define a sample
sample_c = test_contexts[i]           question, context,
sample_a = test_answers[i]            and answer.
sample_input = (
    test_encodings["input_ids"][i:i+1],
    test_encodings["attention_mask"][i:i+1]
)

def ask_bert(sample_input, tokenizer):

    out = model_v2.predict(sample_input)
    pred_ans_start = tf.argmax(out[0][0])
    pred_ans_end = tf.argmax(out[1][0])
    print(
        "{}-{} token ids contain the answer".format(
            pred_ans_start, pred_ans_end
        )
    )
    ans_tokens = sample_input[0][0][pred_ans_start:pred_ans_end+1]

    return " ".join(tokenizer.convert_ids_to_tokens(ans_tokens))

print("Question")
print("\t", sample_q, "\n")
print("Context")
print("\t", sample_c, "\n")
print("Answer (char indexed)")
print("\t", sample_a, "\n")
print('='*50,'\n')

sample_pred_ans = ask_bert(sample_input, tokenizer)

print("Answer (predicted)")
print(sample_pred_ans)
print('='*50,'\n')
```

Predict with the model for the sample input. This returns the starting and ending index probability vectors.

Get the predicted starting index by getting the maximum index from the starting index probability vector.

Get the predicted ending index by getting the maximum index from the ending index probability vector.

Get the string answer tokens by getting the text between the starting/ending indices.

Return the list of tokens as a single string.

Print the inputs to the model.

Call the ask_bert function on the defined input.

Print the answer.

Let's flesh out the details of the code in listing 13.9. First, we define an index i. This index will be used to retrieve a sample from the test set. sample_q, sample_c, and sample_a represent the question, context, and answer of the sample we have selected. With these, we can define the sample_input, which will contain the encoded representation of the input understood by the model. The function ask_bert() takes in an input prepared for the model with the tokenizer (denoted by the sample_input) to convert token IDs of the answer back to readable tokens. The function first predicts the output for the input and gets the starting and ending token IDs of the answer.

Finally, the function converts these IDs along with the words in between into a single comprehensible answer and returns the text. If you print the output of this process, you will get the following:

```
Question
    What was the theme of Super Bowl 50?

Context
    Super Bowl 50 was an American football game to determine the
champion of the National Football League (NFL) for the 2015 season. The
American Football Conference (AFC) champion Denver Broncos defeated the
National Football Conference (NFC) champion Carolina Panthers 24-10 to
earn their third Super Bowl title. The game was played on February 7,
2016, at Levi's Stadium in the San Francisco Bay Area at Santa Clara,
California. As this was the 50th Super Bowl, the league emphasized the
"golden anniversary" with various gold-themed initiatives, as well as
temporarily suspending the tradition of naming each Super Bowl game
with Roman numerals (under which the game would have been known as
"Super Bowl L"), so that the logo could prominently feature the Arabic
numerals 50.

Answer (char indexed)
    {'answer_start': 487, 'text': '"golden anniversary"',
'answer_end': 507}


==================================================

98-99 token ids contain the answer
Answer (predicted)
golden anniversary
==================================================
```

This ends our conversation about using Hugging Face's Transformer library to implement Transformer models. We have gone through all the steps you are likely to come across while solving any NLP task with a Transformer model. And Hugging Face's transformers library still enjoys its reputation as one of the best libraries for implementing Transformer models in TensorFlow or PyTorch.

Visualizing attention heads

Whenever there's a chance for us to interpret deep learning models and understand why a model made a certain decision, it is important to make the most of it. Having the ability to dissect and interpret models helps to build trust among users. Interpreting Transformer models is made very easy due to the presence of the self-attention layers. Using the self-attention layer, we can find out which words the model paid attention to while coming up with a hidden representation of a token.

We can use the bert_viz library (https://github.com/jessevig/bertviz) to visualize the attention patterns in any attention head found in any layer. It is important to note that bert_viz does not support TensorFlow but uses the PyTorch library. Despite this small technical difference, using bert_viz is easy and straightforward.

First, import the required libraries:

```
import torch
from bertviz import head_view
```

Next, define a BERT model. Make sure to pass the `output_attentions=True` config to output attention outputs, as it is turned off by default:

```
config = BertConfig.from_pretrained(
    'bert-base-uncased', output_attentions=True
)
bert = TFBertModel.from_pretrained(
    "bert-base-uncased", config=config
)
```

Encode the input text and then get the output of the model:

```
encoded_input = tokenizer(text, return_tensors='tf')
output = model(encoded_input)
```

Finally call the `head_view()` function. You can get the attention outputs by simply calling `output.attentions`, which will return a tuple of 12 tensors. Each tensor corresponds to a separate layer in BERT. Also, make sure you convert them to `torch` tensors. Otherwise, this function errors out. The output is visualized in figure 13.10.

```
head_view(
    [torch.from_numpy(layer_attn.numpy()) for layer_attn in
            output.attentions],
    encoded_tokens
)
```

This ends our discussion about Transformer models. However, it's important to keep in mind that Transformer models are evolving and becoming better even as we speak. In the next chapter, we will discuss an important visualization tool, called Tensor-Board, that is shipped with TensorFlow.

EXERCISE 3

You are asked to implement a named-entity recognition model. Named-entity recognition is a token classification task, where each token is assigned a label (e.g., person, organization, geographical, other, etc.). There are seven different labels. If you want to use the `distilbert-base-uncased` model for this, how would you define the model? Remember that in the `transformers` library, you can pass the `num_labels` as a keyword to define the number of output classes. For example, if you have a config "a" that you would like to set to "abc", you can do

```
<model>.from_pretrained(<model_tag>, "a"= "abc")
```

Layer: [0 ⌄]

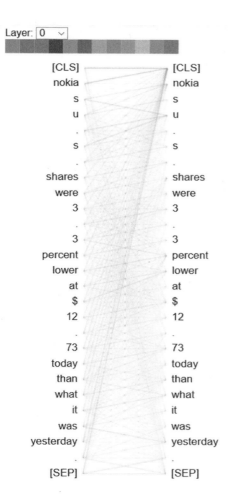

Figure 13.10 The attention output of the `bert_viz` **library. You can select different layers from the dropdown menu. The different shades represent different attention heads in that layer, which can be switched on or off. The lines between the two columns represent which words the model paid attention to when generating the hidden representation of a given token.**

Summary

- The main subcomponents of a Transformer model are embeddings (token and positional), a self-attention sublayer, a fully connected sublayer, residual connections, and layer normalization sublayers.
- BERT is a Transformer encoder model that produces a hidden (attended) representation for each token passed in the input.
- BERT uses special tokens like [CLS] (denotes the beginning and is used to generate the output for classification heads), [SEP] (to mark the separation between two subsequences; e.g., question and the context in question answering), [PAD] (to denote padded tokens to bring all sequences to a fixed length), and [MASK] (to mask out tokens in the input sequence; e.g., padded tokens).
- BERT can be used for downstream, task-specific classification tasks by fitting a classification head (e.g., a logistic regression layer) on top of the final output of

BERT. Depending on the type of task, multiple classification heads might be required, and the utilization of the classification head might differ.

- Hugging Face's `transformers` library provides implementations of all the NLP-related Transformer models and can be easily downloaded and used in the workflow. The pretrained models available for download have two main components: the tokenizer that will tokenize a provided string to a sequence of tokens and the model that takes in the sequence of tokens to generate the final hidden output.

Answers to exercises

Exercise 1

$$PE(pos, 2i) = \sin\left(pos/10000^{21/d_{model}}\right)$$

```
import tensorflow as tf

# Defining some hyperparameters
n_steps = 25 # Sequence length
n_en_vocab = 300 # Encoder's vocabulary size
n_heads = 8 # Number of attention heads
d = 512 # The feature dimensionality of each layer

# Encoder input layer
en_inp = tf.keras.layers.Input(shape=(n_steps,))
# Encoder input embedddings
en_emb = tf.keras.layers.Embedding(
    n_en_vocab, 512, input_length=n_steps
)(en_inp)

pos_inp = tf.constant(
    [[p/(10000**(2*i/d)) for p in range(d)] for i in range(n_steps)]
)
pos_inp = tf.expand_dims(pos_inp, axis=0)
en_pos_emb = tf.math.sin(pos_inp)

en_final_emb = en_emb + en_pos_emb

# Two encoder layers
en_out1 = EncoderLayer(d, n_heads)(en_emb)
en_out2 = EncoderLayer(d, n_heads)(en_out1)

model = tf.keras.models.Model(inputs=en_inp, output=en_out2)
```

Exercise 2

```
hub_classifier, hub_encoder = bert.bert_models.classifier_model(
    bert_config=bert_config, hub_module_url=bert_url, num_labels=5
)
```

Exercise 3

```
from transformers import TFDistilBertForTokenClassification

model = TFDistilBertForTokenClassification.from_pretrained(
    "distilbert-base-uncased", num_labels=7
)
```

14

TensorBoard:
Big brother of TensorFlow

This chapter covers

- Running and visualizing image data in TensorBoard
- Monitoring model performance and behaviors in real time
- Performance profiling models using TensorBoard
- Using `tf.summary` to log custom metrics during customized model training
- Visualizing and analyzing word vectors on TensorBoard

Thus far we have focused on various models. We have talked about fully connected models (e.g., autoencoders), convolutional neural networks, and recurrent neural networks (e.g., LSTMs, GRUs). In chapter 13, we talked about Transformers, a powerful family of deep learning models that have paved the way to a new state-of-the-art performance in language understanding. Furthermore, inspired by the achievements in the field of natural language processing, Transformers are making waves in the computer vision field. We are past the modeling step, but we still have to plough through several more steps to reap the final harvest. One such step is making sure the data/features to the model are correct and the models are working as expected.

In this chapter, we will explore a new facet of machine learning: leveraging a visualization tool kit to visualize high-dimensional data (e.g., images, word vectors, etc.) as well as track and monitor model performance. Let's understand why this is a crucial need. Due to the success demonstrated by using machine learning in many different fields, machine learning has become deeply rooted in many industries and fields of research. Consequently, this means that we need more rapid cycles in training new models and less friction when performing various steps in the data science workflow (e.g., understanding data, model training, model evaluation, etc.). TensorBoard is a step in that direction. It allows you to easily track and visualize data, model performance, and even profile models to understand where data spends the most time.

You typically write data and model metrics or other things you want to visualize to a logging directory. What is written to the logging directory is typically organized into subfolders, which are named to have information like the date, time, and a brief description of the experiment. This will help to identify an experiment quickly in Tensor-Board. TensorBoard will constantly search the designated logging directory for changes and visualize them on the dashboard. You will learn the specifics of these steps in the coming sections.

14.1 *Visualize data with TensorBoard*

Imagine you are working for a fashion company as a data scientist. They have asked you to assess the feasibility of building a model that can identify clothing items in a given photo. For this, you pick the Fashion-MNIST data set, which has images of clothes in black and white belonging to one of 10 categories. Some categories are T-shirt, trouser, and dress. You will first load the data and analyze it through Tensor-Board, a visualization tool for visualizing data and models. Here, you will visualize a few images and make sure they have the correct class label assigned after loading to memory.

The first thing we will do is download the Fashion-MNIST data set. Fashion-MNIST is a labeled data set that contains images of various garments and corresponding labels/categories. Fashion-MNIST is primarily inspired by the MNIST data set. To refresh our memories, the MNIST data set consists of 28×28–sized images of digits 0–9, and the corresponding digit is the label. Fashion-MNIST emerged as a solution as many were recommending moving away from MNIST as a performance benchmarking data set due to the easiness of the task. Fashion-MNIST is considered a more challenging task compared to MNIST.

Downloading the Fashion-MNIST data set is a very easy step, as it is available through the `tensorflow_datasets` library:

```
import tensorflow_datasets as tfds

# Construct a tf.data.Dataset
fashion_ds = tfds.load('fashion_mnist')
```

Now, let's print to see the format of the data:

```
print(fashion_ds)
```

This will return

```
{'test': <PrefetchDataset shapes: {image: (28, 28, 1), label: ()}, types:
    {image: tf.uint8, label: tf.int64}>, 'train': <PrefetchDataset shapes:
    {image: (28, 28, 1), label: ()}, types: {image: tf.uint8, label:
    tf.int64}>}
```

The data set has two components, a training data set and a testing data set. The training set has two items: images, each of which is $28 \times 28 \times 1$, and an integer label. The same items are available for the test set. Next, we are going to create three tf.data data sets: training, validation, and testing. We will split the original training data set into two, a training and a validation set, and then keep the test set as it is (see the next listing).

Listing 14.1 Generating training, validation, and test data sets

```
def get_train_valid_test_datasets(fashion_ds, batch_size,
    flatten_images=False):

    train_ds = fashion_ds["train"].shuffle(batch_size*20).map(
        lambda xy: (xy["image"], tf.reshape(xy["label"], [-1]))
    )
    test_ds = fashion_ds["test"].map(
        lambda xy: (xy["image"], tf.reshape(xy["label"], [-1]))
    )

    if flatten_images:
        train_ds = train_ds.map(lambda x,y: (tf.reshape(x, [-1]), y))
        test_ds = test_ds.map(lambda x,y: (tf.reshape(x, [-1]), y))

    valid_ds = train_ds.take(10000).batch(batch_size)

    train_ds = train_ds.skip(10000).batch(batch_size)

    return train_ds, valid_ds, test_ds
```

Get the training data set, shuffle it, and output a tuple of (image, label).

Get the testing data set and output a tuple of (image, label).

Flatten the images to a ID vector for fully connected networks.

Make the validation data set the first 10,000 data points.

Make training data set the rest.

This is a simple data pipeline. Each record in the original data set is provided as a dictionary with two keys: image and label. First, we convert dictionary-based records to a tuple of (<image>, <label>) using the tf.data.Dataset.map() function. Then, we have an optional step of flattening the 2D images to a 1D vector if the data set is to be used for fully connected networks. In other words, the 28×28 image will become a 784-sized vector. Finally, we create the valid set as the first 10,000 data points in the train_ds (after shuffling) and keep the rest as the training set.

The way to visualize data on TensorBoard is by logging information to a predefined log directory through a tf.summary.SummaryWriter(). This writer will write the data we're interested in, in a special format the TensorBoard understands. Next, you spin up an instance of TensorBoard, pointing it to the log directory. Using this approach, let's visualize some of the training data using the TensorBoard. First, we define a mapping from the label ID to the string label:

```
id2label_map = {
    0: "T-shirt/top",
    1: "Trouser",
    2:"Pullover",
    3: "Dress",
    4: "Coat",
    5: "Sandal",
    6: "Shirt",
    7: "Sneaker",
    8: "Bag",
    9: "Ankle boot"
}
```

These mappings are obtained from http://mng.bz/DgdR. Then we will define the logging directory. We are going to use date-timestamps to generate a unique identifier for different runs, as shown:

```
log_datetimestamp_format = "%Y%m%d%H%M%S"

log_datetimestamp = datetime.strftime(datetime.now(),
    log_datetimestamp_format)
image_logdir = "./logs/data_{}/train".format(log_datetimestamp)
```

If you're wondering about the strange-looking format found in the `log_datetime-stamp_format` variable, it is a standard format used by Python's `datetime` library to define the format of dates and times (http://mng.bz/lxM2), should you use them in your code. Specifically, we are going to the time of running (given by `datetime.now()`) as a string of digits with no separators in between. We will get the year (`%Y`), month (`%m`), day (`%d`), hour in 24-hour format (`%H`), minutes (`%M`), and seconds (`%S`) of a given time of the day. Then we append the string of digits to the logging directory to create a unique identifier based on the time of running. Next, we define a `tf.summary.SummaryWriter()` by calling the following function, with the logging directory as an argument. With that, any write we do with this summary writer will be logged in the defined directory:

```
image_writer = tf.summary.create_file_writer(image_logdir)
```

Next, we open the defined summary writer as the default writer, using a with clause. Once the summary writer is open, any `tf.summary.<data type>` object will log that information to the log directory. Here, we use a `tf.summary.image` object. There are several different objects you can use to log (https://www.tensorflow.org/api_docs/python/tf/summary):

- tf.summary.audio—A type of object used to log audio files and listen to them on TensorBoard
- tf.summary.histogram—A type of object used to log histograms and view them on TensorBoard
- tf.summary.image—A type of object used to log images and view them on TensorBoard
- tf.summary.scalar—A type of object used to log scalar values (e.g., model losses computed over several epochs) and show them on TensorBoard
- tf.summary.text—A type of object used to log raw textual data and show it on TensorBoard

Here, we will use tf.summary.image() to write and display images on TensorBoard. tf.summary.image() takes in several arguments:

- name—A description of the summary. This will be used as a tag when displaying images on TensorBoard.
- data—A batch of images of size [b, h, w, c], where b is the batch size, h is the image height, w is the image width, and c is the number of channels (e.g., RGB).
- step—An integer that can be used to show images belonging to different batches/iterations (defaults to None).
- max_outputs—The maximum number of outputs to display at a given time. If there are more images than max_outputs in the data, the first max_outputs images will be shown, and the rest will be silently discarded (defaults to three).
- description—A detailed description of the summary (defaults to None)

We will write two sets of image data in two ways:

- First, we will take 10 images, one by one, from the training data set and write them with their class label tagged. Then, images with the same class label (i.e., category) are nested under the same section on TensorBoard.
- Finally, we will write a batch of 20 images at once.

```
with image_writer.as_default():
    for data in fashion_ds["train"].batch(1).take(10):
        tf.summary.image(
            id2label_map[int(data["label"].numpy())],
            data["image"],
            max_outputs=10,
            step=0
        )

# Write a batch of 20 images at once
with image_writer.as_default():
    for data in fashion_ds["train"].batch(20).take(1):
        pass
    tf.summary.image("A training data batch", data["image"],
max_outputs=20, step=0)
```

Then we are all set to visualize the TensorBoard. Initializing and loading the Tensor-Board can be done simply by running the following commands in a Jupyter notebook code cell. As you know by now, a Jupyter notebook is made of cells, where you can enter text/code. Cells can be code cells, Markdown cells, and so on:

```
%load_ext tensorboard
%tensorboard --logdir ./logs --port 6006
```

Figure 14.1 shows how the code will look in a notebook cell.

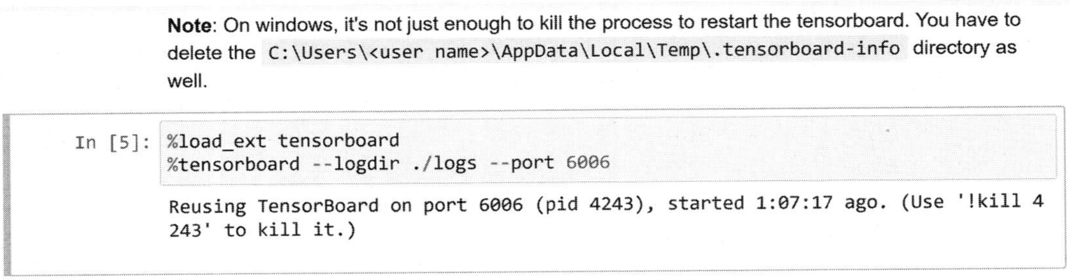

> **Note**: On windows, it's not just enough to kill the process to restart the tensorboard. You have to delete the `C:\Users\<user name>\AppData\Local\Temp\.tensorboard-info` directory as well.

```
In [5]:  %load_ext tensorboard
         %tensorboard --logdir ./logs --port 6006

         Reusing TensorBoard on port 6006 (pid 4243), started 1:07:17 ago. (Use '!kill 4
         243' to kill it.)
```

Figure 14.1   Jupyter magic commands in a notebook cell

You might notice that this is not typical Python syntax. Commands such as these that start with a % sign are known as Jupyter magic commands. Remember that Jupyter is the name of the Python library that is producing notebooks that we have our code in. You can see a list of such commands at http://mng.bz/BMd1. The first command loads the TensorBoard Jupyter notebook extension. The second command instanti-ates a TensorBoard with the provided logging directory (`--logdir`) argument and a port (`--port`) argument. If you don't specify a port, TensorBoard will run on 6006 (or the first unused port greater than 6006) by default. Figure 14.2 shows how the Tensor-Board looks with visualized images.

Alternatively, you can also visualize the TensorBoard on a browser tab independent of the Jupyter notebook. After you run the two commands in your browser, open http://localhost:6006, which will display the TensorBoard as shown in figure 14.2. In the next section, we will see how TensorBoard can be used to track and monitor model performance as models are trained.

EXERCISE 1

You have a list of five batches of images in a variable called `step_image_batches`. Each item in the list corresponds to the first five steps of the training. You want to have these batches shown in the TensorBoard, each with the correct step value. You can name each batch as batch_0, batch_1, and so on. How would you do this?

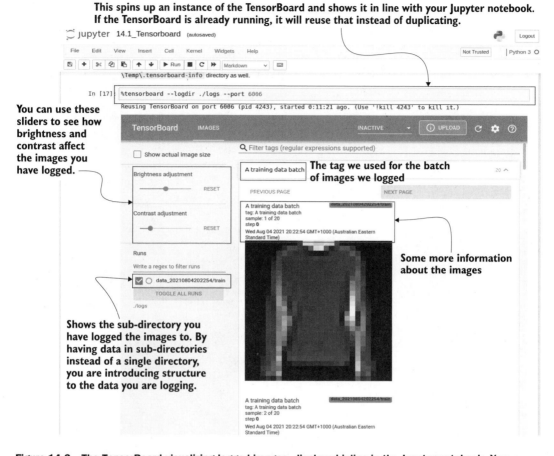

Figure 14.2   The TensorBoard visualizing logged images, displayed inline in the Jupyter notebook. You can perform various operations on images, such as adjusting brightness or contrast. Furthermore, the subdirectories to which the data is logged are shown on the left-hand panel, allowing you to easily show/ hide different subdirectories for easier comparison.

14.2   Tracking and monitoring models with TensorBoard

With a good understanding of the data in the Fashion-MNIST data set, you will use a neural network to train a model on this data to gauge how accurately you can classify different types of apparel. You are planning to use a dense network and a convolutional neural network. You will train both these models under the same conditions (e.g., data sets) and visualize the model's accuracy and loss on the TensorBoard.

The primary purpose served by the TensorBoard is the ability to visualize a model's performance as it is trained. Deep neural networks are notoriously known for their long training times. There is no doubt that identifying problems with a model as early as possible pays off well. The TensorBoard plays a vital role in that. You can pipe model performance (through evaluation metrics) to be displayed in real time on Tensor-Board. Therefore, you can spot any abnormal behaviors in the model before spending too much time and take necessary actions quickly.

In this section, we will compare the performance of a fully connected network and a convolutional neural network on the Fashion-MNIST data set. Let's define a small fully connected model as the first model we want to test with this data set. It will have three layers:

- A layer with 512 neurons and ReLU activation that takes a flattened image from the Fashion-MNIST data set
- A layer with 256 neurons and ReLU activation that takes the previous layer's output
- A layer with 10 outputs (representing the categories) that has a softmax activation

The model is compiled with sparse categorical cross-entropy loss and the Adam optimizer. Since we're interested in the model accuracy, we add that to the list of metrics that are tracked:

```
from tensorflow.keras import layers, models


dense_model = models.Sequential([
    layers.Dense(512, activation='relu', input_shape=(784,)),
    layers.Dense(256, activation='relu'),
    layers.Dense(10, activation='softmax')
])

dense_model.compile(loss="sparse_categorical_crossentropy", optimizer='adam',
    metrics=['accuracy'])
```

With the model fully defined, we train it on the training data and evaluate it on the validation data set. First, let's define the logging directory for the fully connected model:

```
log_datetimestamp_format = "%Y%m%d%H%M%S"
log_datetimestamp = datetime.strftime(
    datetime.now(), log_datetimestamp_format
)

dense_log_dir = os.path.join("logs","dense_{}".format(log_datetimestamp))
```

As before, you can see that we are not only writing to subdirectories instead of the plain flat directory, but we are also using a unique identifier that is based on the time of running. Each of these subdirectories represents what is called a *run* in Tensor-Board terminology.

> ## Organizing runs in TensorBoard
>
> Typically, users leverage some kind of run organization when visualizing them via the TensorBoard. Other than having multiple runs for multiple algorithms, a standard thing to do is add a date-time stamp to the runs to discriminate between different runs of the same algorithm running at different occasions.
>
> For example, you might test the same algorithm with different hyperparameters (e.g., number of layers, learning rate, optimizer, etc.) and may want to see them all in one place. Let's say you want to test a fully connected layer with different learning rates (0.01, 0.001, and 0.0005). You would have the following directory structure in your main logging directory:
>
> ```
> ./logs/dense/run_2021-05-27-03-14-21_lr=0.01
> ./logs/dense/run_2021-05-27-09-02-52_lr=0.001
> ./logs/dense/run_2021-05-27-10-12-09_lr=0.001
> ./logs/dense/run_2021-05-27-14-43-12_lr=0.0005
> ```
>
> Or you could even use a more nested directory structure:
>
> ```
> ./logs/dense/lr=0.01/2021-05-27-03-14-21
> ./logs/dense/lr=0.001/2021-05-27-09-02-52
> ./logs/dense/lr=0.001/2021-05-27-10-12-09
> ./logs/dense/lr=0.0005/2021-05-27-14-43-12
> ```

I would like to stress that it is important to time stamp your runs, as explained in the sidebar. This way you will have a unique folder for each run and can always go back to previous runs to compare if needed. Next, let's generate training/validation/testing data sets using the `get_train_valid_test()` function. Make sure to set the `flatten_images=True`:

```
batch_size = 64
tr_ds, v_ds, ts_ds = get_train_valid_test_datasets(
    fashion_ds, batch_size=batch_size, flatten_images=True
)
```

Modeling metrics to the TensorBoard is very easy. There is a special callback for the TensorBoard that you can pass during the model training/evaluation:

```
tb_callback = tf.keras.callbacks.TensorBoard(
    log_dir=dense_log_dir, profile_batch=0
)
```

Let's discuss some of the key arguments you can pass to the TensorBoard callback. The default TensorBoard callback looks as follows:

```
tf.keras.callbacks.TensorBoard(
    log_dir='logs', histogram_freq=0, write_graph=True,
    write_images=False, write_steps_per_second=False, update_freq='epoch',
    profile_batch=2, embeddings_freq=0, embeddings_metadata=None,
)
```

Now we will look at the arguments provided:

- `log_dir`—The directory to log information to. Once the TensorBoard is spun up using the `log dir` as this (or a parent of this) directory, the information can be visualized on the TensorBoard (defaults to `'logs'`).
- `histogram_freq`—Creates histograms of activation distribution in layers (discussed in detail later). This specifies how frequently (in epochs) these histograms need to be recorded (defaults to `0`, meaning it's disabled).
- `write_graph`—Determines whether to write the model as a graph to visualize on the TensorBoard (defaults to `True`).
- `write_image`—Determines whether to write model weights as an image (i.e., a heat map) to visualize the weights on the TensorBoard (defaults to `False`).
- `write_steps_per_second`—Determines whether to write the number of steps performed in a second to the TensorBoard (defaults to `False`).
- `update_freq` (`'batch'`, `'epoch'` or an integer)—Determines whether to write updates to the TensorBoard every batch (if the value is set to `batch`) or epoch (if value is set to `epoch`). Passing an integer, TensorFlow will interpret it as "write to the TensorBoard every x batches." By default, updates will be written every epoch. Writing to the disk is expensive; therefore, writing too frequently will slow your training down.
- `profile_batch` (an integer or a list of two numbers)—Determines which batches to use for profiling the model. Profiling computes computational and memory profiles of the model (discussed in detail later). If an integer is passed, it will profile a single batch. If a range (i.e., a list of two numbers) is passed, it will profile batches in that range. If set to zero, profiling will not happen (defaults to `2`).
- `embedding_freq`—If the model has an embedding layer, this parameter specifies the interval (in epochs) to visualize the embedding layer. If set to zero, this is disabled (defaults to `0`).
- `embedding_metadata`—A dictionary that maps the embedding layer name to a file name. The file should consist of the tokens corresponding to each row in the embedding matrix (in that order; defaults to `None`).

Finally, we will train the model as we have done before. The only difference is that we pass `tb_callback` as a callback to the model:

```
dense_model.fit(tr_ds, validation_data=v_ds, epochs=10, callbacks=[tb_callback])
```

The model should reach a validation accuracy of around 85%. Now open the TensorBoard by visiting http://localhost:6006. It will display a dashboard similar to figure 14.3. The dashboard will be refreshed automatically as new data appears in the log directory.

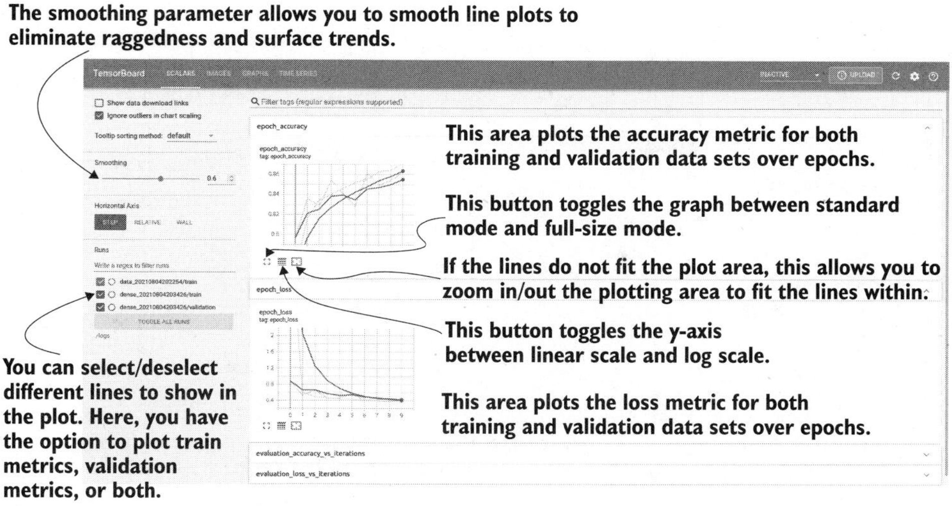

The smoothing parameter allows you to smooth line plots to eliminate raggedness and surface trends.

This area plots the accuracy metric for both training and validation data sets over epochs.

This button toggles the graph between standard mode and full-size mode.

If the lines do not fit the plot area, this allows you to zoom in/out the plotting area to fit the lines within.

This button toggles the y-axis between linear scale and log scale.

This area plots the loss metric for both training and validation data sets over epochs.

You can select/deselect different lines to show in the plot. Here, you have the option to plot train metrics, validation metrics, or both.

Figure 14.3 How tracked metrics are displayed on the TensorBoard. You can see the training and validation accuracy and the loss are plotted as line graphs. Furthermore, you have various controls, such as maximizing the graph, switching to a log-scale y-axis, and so on.

The TensorBoard dashboard has many controls that help users understand their models in great depth with the help of logged metrics. You can turn different runs on or off depending on what you want to analyze. For example, if you only want to look at validation metrics, you can switch off dense/train run, and vice versa. Data/train run does not affect this panel as it contains images we logged from the training data. To view them, you can click on the IMAGES panel.

Next, you can change the smoothing parameter to control the smoothness of the line. It helps to remove localized small changes in metrics and focus on global trends by having a smoother version of the line. Figure 14.4 depicts the effect of the smoothing parameter on line plots.

Additionally, you have other controls such as switching to a log-scale y-axis instead of a linear one. This is useful if metrics observe large changes over time. In log scale, such large changes will become smaller. You can also toggle between standard-sized plots and full-sized plots if you need to examine the graphs in more detail. Figure 14.3 highlights these controls.

After that, we will define a simple convolutional neural network and do the same. That is, we will define the network first, and then train the model while using a callback to the TensorBoard.

How the line plot changes with the smoothing parameter

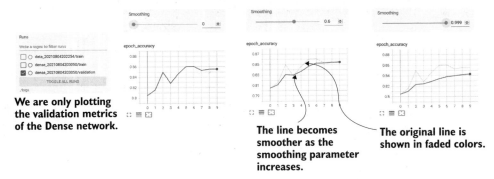

We are only plotting the validation metrics of the Dense network.

The line becomes smoother as the smoothing parameter increases.

The original line is shown in faded colors.

Figure 14.4   How the smoothing parameter changes the line plot. Here, we are showing the same line plot under different smoothing parameters. You can see how the line gets smoother as the smoothing parameter increases. The original line is shown in faded colors.

Let's define the next model we will compare our fully connected network to: a convolutional neural network (CNN). Again, we are defining a very simple CNN that encompasses

- A 2D convolution layer with 32 filters with a 5 × 5 kernel, 2 × 2 strides, and ReLU activation that takes a 2D 28 × 28–sized image from the Fashion-MNIST data set
- A 2D convolution layer with 16 filters with a 3 × 3 kernel, 1 × 1 strides, and ReLU activation that takes the previous layer's output
- A `Flatten` layer that will flatten the convolutional output to a 1D vector suitable for a `Dense` layer
- A layer with 10 outputs (representing the categories) that has a softmax activation

```
conv_model = models.Sequential([
    layers.Conv2D(
        filters=32,
        kernel_size=(5,5),
        strides=(2,2),
        padding='same',
        activation='relu',
        input_shape=(28,28,1)
    ),
    layers.Conv2D(
        filters=16,
        kernel_size=(3,3),
        strides=(1,1),
        padding='same',
        activation='relu'
    ),
```

```
        layers.Flatten(),
        layers.Dense(10, activation='softmax')
    ])

    conv_model.compile(
        loss="sparse_categorical_crossentropy", optimizer='adam',
➥   metrics=['accuracy']
    )
    conv_model.summary()
```

Moving onto the model training, we will log the CNN-related metrics to a separate directory called `./logs/conv_{datetimestamp}`. This way, we can plot the evaluation metrics of the fully connected network and the CNN under two separate runs. We will generate training and validation data sets and a TensorBoard callback, as we did earlier. These are then passed to the model when calling the `fit()` method to train the model:

```
log_datetimestamp_format = "%Y%m%d%H%M%S"
log_datetimestamp = datetime.strftime(
    datetime.now(), log_datetimestamp_format
)

conv_log_dir = os.path.join("logs","conv_{}".format(log_datetimestamp))

batch_size = 64
tr_ds, v_ds, ts_ds = get_train_valid_test_datasets(
    fashion_ds, batch_size=batch_size, flatten_images=False
)

tb_callback = tf.keras.callbacks.TensorBoard(
    log_dir=conv_log_dir, histogram_freq=2, profile_batch=0
)

conv_model.fit(
    tr_ds, validation_data=v_ds, epochs=10, callbacks=[tb_callback]
)
```

Notice the changes we have made when training the CNN. First, we do not flatten the images like we did when training the fully connected network (i.e., we set `flatten_images=False` in the `get_train_valid_test_datasets()` function). Next, we introduce a new argument to the TensorBoard callback. We will use the `histogram_freq` argument to log layer activation histograms of the model during the training process. We will discuss layer activation histograms in more depth shortly. This will display the accuracy and loss metrics of both models (i.e., dense model and convolutional model) in the same graph, so they can be easily compared (figure 14.5).

Let's come back to activation histograms again. Activation histograms let us visualize the neuron activation distribution of different layers as the training progresses. This is an important check that allows you to see whether or not the model

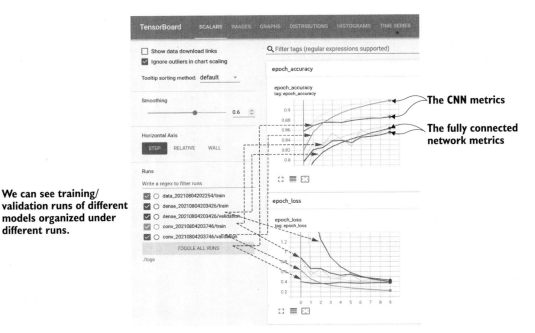

Figure 14.5   Viewing metrics of both the dense model and the convolutional model. You can switch different runs off/on depending on what you want to compare.

is converging during the optimization, giving insights into problems in model training or data quality.

Let's look at what these histograms show in more depth. Figure 14.6 illustrates the histograms generated for the CNN we have trained. We have plotted histograms every two epochs. Weights represented as histograms are stacked behind each other so we can easily understand how they evolved over time. Each slice in the histogram shows the weight distribution in a given layer and a given epoch. In other words, it will provide information such as "there were x number of outputs, having a value of y, approximately."

Typically, if you have a vector of values, it is quite straightforward to create the histogram. For example, assume the values are [0.1, 0.3, 0.35, 0.5, 0.6, 0.61, 0.63], and say that you have four bins: [0.0, 0.2), [0.2, 0.4), [0.4, 0.6), and [0.6, 0.8). You'd get the histogram shown in figure 14.7. If you look at the line connecting the midpoints of the bars, it's similar to what you see in the dashboard.

However, computing histograms involves more complex data manipulations when data is large and sparse, like in a weight matrix. For example, computing histograms in TensorBoard involves using exponential bin sizes (as opposed to uniform bin sizes, as in the example), which gives more fine-grained bins near zero and wider bins as you move away from zero. Then it resamples these uneven-sized bins to uniformly

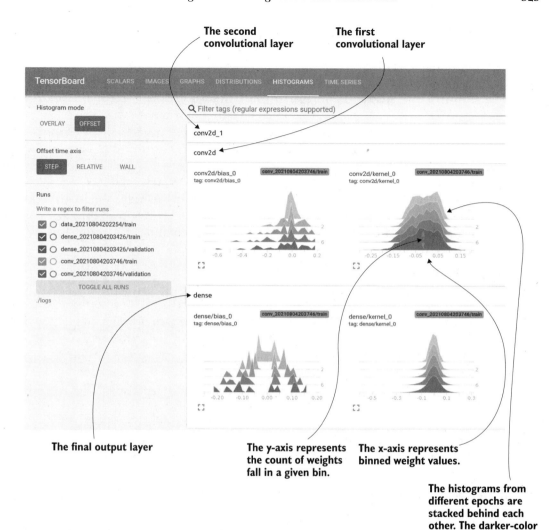

The second convolutional layer

The first convolutional layer

The final output layer

The y-axis represents the count of weights fall in a given bin.

The x-axis represents binned weight values.

The histograms from different epochs are stacked behind each other. The darker-color histograms represent more recent epochs.

Figure 14.6   Activation histograms displayed by the TensorBoard. These graphs indicate how the distribution of activations in a given layer changed over time (lighter ones represent more recent epochs).

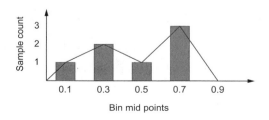

Figure 14.7   A histogram generated for the sequence [0.1, 0.3, 0.35, 0.5, 0.6, 0.61, 0.63]

sized bins for easier and more meaningful visualizations. The specific details of these computations are beyond the scope of this book. If you want more details, refer to http://mng.bz/d26o.

We can see in the graphs that the weights are converging to an approximate normal distribution as the training progresses. But the bias converges to a multi-modal distribution, with spikes appearing in many different places.

This section elucidated how you can use the TensorBoard for some of the primary data visualization and model performance tracking. These are vital parts of the core checkpoints you have to set up in your data science project. Visualizing data needs to be done early in your project to help you understand the data and its structure. Model performance tracking is important as deep learning models take longer to train, and you need to complete that training within a limited budget (of both time and cost). In the next section, we will discuss how we can log custom metrics to the TensorBoard and visualize them.

EXERCISE 2

You have a binary classification model represented by `classif_model`. You'd like to track precision and recall for this model in the TensorBoard. Furthermore, you'd like to visualize the activation histograms every epoch. How would you compile the model and fit it with data using the TensorBoard callback to achieve this? TensorFlow provides `tf.keras.metrics.Precision()` and `tf.keras.metrics.Recall()` to compute precision and recall, respectively. You can assume that you are logging directly to the `./logs` directory. Assume that you have been provided training data (`tr_ds`) and validation data (`v_ds`) as `tf.data.Dataset` objects.

14.3 *Using tf.summary to write custom metrics during model training*

Imagine you are a PhD student researching the effects of batch normalization. Particularly, you need to analyze how the weights' mean and standard deviation in a given layer change over time, with and without batch normalization. For this, you will use a fully connected network and log the weights' mean and standard deviation at every step on the TensorBoard. As this is not a typical metric that you can produce using the Keras model, you will log it (for every step) during model training in a custom training loop.

In order to compare the effects of batch normalization, we need to define two different models: one without batch normalization and one with batch normalization. Both these models will have the same specifications, apart from using batch normalization. First, let's define a model without batch normalization:

```
from tensorflow.keras import layers, models
import tensorflow.keras.backend as K

K.clear_session()
```

```
dense_model = models.Sequential([
    layers.Dense(512, activation='relu', input_shape=(784,)),
    layers.Dense(256, activation='relu', name='log_layer'),
    layers.Dense(10, activation='softmax')
])

dense_model.compile(loss="sparse_categorical_crossentropy", optimizer='adam',
    metrics=['accuracy'])
```

The model is quite straightforward and identical to the fully connected model we defined earlier. It has three layers, with 512, 256, and 10 nodes, respectively. The first two layers use ReLU activation, whereas the last layer uses softmax activation. Note that we name the second Dense layer log_layer. We will use this layer to compute the metrics we're interested in. Finally, the model is compiled with sparse categorical cross-entropy loss, the Adam optimizer, and accuracy as metrics. Next, we define the same model with batch normalization:

```
dense_model_bn = models.Sequential([
    layers.Dense(512, activation='relu', input_shape=(784,)),
    layers.BatchNormalization(),
    layers.Dense(256, activation='relu', name='log_layer_bn'),
    layers.BatchNormalization(),
    layers.Dense(10, activation='softmax')
])

dense_model_bn.compile(
    loss="sparse_categorical_crossentropy", optimizer='adam',
    metrics=['accuracy']
)
```

Introducing batch normalization means adding tf.keras.layers.BatchNormalization() layers between the Dense layers. We name the layer of interest in the second model as log_layer_bn, as we cannot have two layers with the same name at once.

With the models defined, our task is to compute the mean and standard deviation of weights at every step. To do that, we will observe the mean and standard deviation of the weights in the second layer of both networks (log_layer and log_layer_bn). As we have already discussed, we cannot simply pass a TensorBoard callback and expect these metrics to be available. Since the metrics we're interested in are not commonly used, we have to do the heavy lifting and make sure the metrics are logged every step.

We will define a train_model() function, to which we can pass the defined model and train it on the data. While training, we will compute the mean and the standard deviation of the weights in every step and log that to the TensorBoard (see the next listing).

> **Listing 14.2 Writing a `tf.summary` object while training the model in a custom loop**

```
def train_model(model, dataset, log_dir, log_layer_name, epochs):

    writer = tf.summary.create_file_writer(log_dir)        ⟵┘ Define the writer.
```

```
        step = 0

        with writer.as_default():       ◁─┘  Open the writer.

            for e in range(epochs):
                print("Training epoch {}".format(e+1))
                for batch in tr_ds:

                    model.train_on_batch(*batch)

                    weights = model.get_layer(log_layer_name).get_weights()[0]  ◁─┐

                    tf.summary.scalar("mean_weights",np.mean(np.abs(weights)),
          step=step)
                    tf.summary.scalar("std_weights", np.std(np.abs(weights)),
          step=step)

                    writer.flush()

                    step += 1
                print('\tDone')

        print("Training completed\n")
```

Open the writer.

Get the weights of the layer. It's a list of arrays [weights, bias] in that order. Therefore, we're only taking the weights (index 0).

Train with one batch.

Log mean and std of absolute weights (which are two scalars for a given epoch).

Flush to the disk from the buffer.

Note how we open a `tf.summary.writer()` and then log the metrics in every step using the `tf.summary.scalar()` call. We are giving the metrics meaningful names to make sure we know which is which when visualizing them on the TensorBoard. With the function defined, we call it for the two different models we have compiled:

```
batch_size = 64
tr_ds, _, _ = get_train_valid_test_datasets(
    fashion_ds, batch_size=batch_size, flatten_images=True
)
train_model(dense_model, tr_ds, exp_log_dir + '/standard', "log_layer", 5)

tr_ds, _, _ = get_train_valid_test_datasets(
    fashion_ds, batch_size=batch_size, flatten_images=True
)
train_model(dense_model_bn, tr_ds, exp_log_dir + '/bn', "log_layer_bn", 5)
```

Note that we are specifying different logging subdirectories to make sure the two models that appear are different runs. After running this, you will see two new additional sections called mean_weights and std_weights (figure 14.8). It seems that the mean and variance of weights change more drastically when batch normalization is used. This could be because, as batch normalization introduces explicit normalization between layers, weights of layers have more freedom to move around.

The next section expands on how the TensorBoard can be used to profile models and provides in-depth analysis of how time spent and memory are consumed when models are executed.

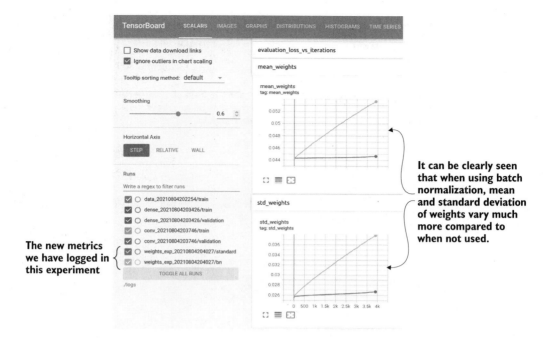

Figure 14.8   The mean and standard deviation of weights plotted in the TensorBoard

EXERCISE 3

You are planning to compute Fibonacci numbers (i.e., 0, 1, 1, 2, 3, 5, 8, 13, 21, 34, 55, etc.), where the nth number x_n is given by x_n = x_{n − 1} + x_{n − 2}. Write a code to compute the Fibonacci series for 100 steps and plot it as a line graph in TensorBoard. You can use the name "fibonacci" as the name for the metric.

14.4   Profiling models to detect performance bottlenecks

You are starting off as a data scientist at a bio-tech company that is identifying endangered flower species. One of the previous data scientists developed a model, and you are continuing that work. First, you want to determine if there are any performance bottlenecks. To analyze such issues, you plan to use the TensorBoard profiler. You will be using a smaller flower data set for the purpose of training the model so that the profiler can capture various computational profiles.

We start with the model in listing 14.3. It is a CNN model that has four convolutional layers, with pooling layers in between and three fully connected layers, including a final softmax layer with 17 output classes.

Listing 14.3   The CNN model available to you

```
def get_cnn_model():

    conv_model = models.Sequential([          ←   Define a Keras
        layers.Conv2D(              ←                 model using the
            filters=64,                               sequential API.
            kernel_size=(5,5),            Define the first convolutional
            strides=(1,1),                layer that takes a 64 × 64 × 3–
            padding='same',               sized input.
            activation='relu',
            input_shape=(64,64,3)          A batch
        ),                                 normalization layer      A max
        layers.BatchNormalization(),    ←                          pooling
        layers.MaxPooling2D(pool_size=(3,3), strides=(2,2)),  ←    layer
        layers.Conv2D(
            filters=128,
            kernel_size=(3,3),
            strides=(1,1),
            padding='same',
            activation='relu'
        ),
        layers.BatchNormalization(),
        layers.Conv2D(
            filters=256,
            kernel_size=(3,3),            A series of alternating
            strides=(1,1),                convolution and
            padding='same',              batch normalization
            activation='relu'           layers
        ),
        layers.BatchNormalization(),
        layers.Conv2D(
            filters=512,
            kernel_size=(3,3),
            strides=(1,1),                           An average pooling
            padding='same',                          layer that marks the end
            activation='relu'                        of convolutional/pooling
        ),                                           layers
        layers.BatchNormalization(),
        layers.AveragePooling2D(pool_size=(2,2), strides=(2,2)),  ←
        layers.Flatten(),
        layers.Dense(512),
        layers.LeakyReLU(),                          A set of Dense
        layers.LayerNormalization(),                 layers (with leaky
        layers.Dense(256),                           ReLU activation),
        layers.LeakyReLU(),                          followed by a layer
        layers.LayerNormalization(),                 with softmax
        layers.Dense(17),                            activation
        layers.Activation('softmax', dtype='float32')
    ])
    return conv_model
```

Flatten the output of the last pooling layer.

The data set we're going to use is a flower data set found at https://www.robots.ox
.ac.uk/~vgg/data/flowers, specifically, the 17-category data set. It has a single folder

with images of flowers, and each image filename has a number. The images are numbered in such a way that, when sorted by the filename, the first 80 images belong to class 0, the next 80 images belong to class 1, and so on. You have been provided the code to download the data set in the notebook Ch14/14.1_Tensorboard.ipynb, which we will not discuss here. Next, we will write a simple tf.data pipeline to create batches of data by reading these images in:

```python
def get_flower_datasets(image_dir, batch_size, flatten_images=False):

    # Get the training dataset, shuffle it, and output a tuple of (image,
    label)
    dataset = tf.data.Dataset.list_files(
        os.path.join(image_dir,'*.jpg'), shuffle=False
    )


    def get_image_and_label(file_path):

        tokens = tf.strings.split(file_path, os.path.sep)
        label = (
            tf.strings.to_number(
                tf.strings.split(
                    tf.strings.split(tokens[-1],'.')[0], '_'
                )[-1]
            ) -1
        )//80

        # load the raw data from the file as a string
        img = tf.io.read_file(file_path)
        img = tf.image.decode_jpeg(img, channels=3)

        return tf.image.resize(img, [64, 64]), label

    dataset = dataset.map(get_image_and_label).shuffle(400)

    # Make the validation dataset the first 10000 data
    valid_ds = dataset.take(250).batch(batch_size)
    # Make training dataset the rest
    train_ds = dataset.skip(250).batch(batch_size)
    )

    return train_ds, valid_ds
```

Let's analyze what we're doing here. First, we read the files which have a .jpg extension from a given folder. Then we have a nested function called get_image_and_label(), which takes a file path of an image and produces the image by reading it from the disk and the label. The label can be computed by

- Extracting the image ID
- Subtracting 1 (i.e., to make IDs zero-based indices) and dividing by 80

After that, we shuffle the data and take the first 250 as validation data and the rest as training data. Next, we use these functions defined and train the CNN model while creating various computational profiles of the model. In order for the profiling to work, you need two main prerequisites:

- Install the Python package `tensorboard_plugin_profile`.
- Install `libcupti`, the CUDA Profiling Toolkit Interface.

Installing the CUDA Profiling Toolkit Interface (libcupti)

TensorBoard requires the `libcupti` CUDA library in order for model profiling to work. Installing this library requires different steps depending on which operating system is used. This assumes that your computer is equipped with an NVIDIA GPU. Unfortunately, you will not be able to perform this on a Mac, as the profiling API for data collection is not available on Mac. (Look at the Requirements section in https://developer.nvidia .com/cupti-ctk10_1u1.)

Installing `libcupti` on Ubuntu

To install `libcupti` on Linux, simply run `sudo apt-get install libcupti-dev`.

Installing `libcupti` on Windows

Installing `libcupti` on Windows requires more work:

- Make sure you have installed the recommended CUDA installation (e.g., CUDA 11 [>= TensorFlow 2.4.0]). For more information on the CUDA version, visit https://www.tensorflow.org/install/source#gpu.
- Next, open the NVIDIA control panel (by right-clicking on the desktop and selecting the menu item) to make several changes (http://mng.bz/rJVJ):
  - Make sure you set the developer mode by clicking Desktop > Set Developer Mode.
  - Make sure you enabled GRU profiling to all users and not just the administrator (figure 14.9).
  - For more errors that you might face, refer to http://mng.bz/VMxy from the official NVIDIA website.
- To install `libcupti` (http://mng.bz/xn2d)
  - Copy `libcupti_<version>.dll`, `nvperf_host.dll`, and `nvperf_target .dll` from extras\CUPTI\lib64 to the bin folder. Make sure the libcupti file has the name libcupti_110.dll.
  - Copy all files in extras\CUPTI\lib64 to lib\x64
  - Copy all files in extras\CUPTI\include to include.

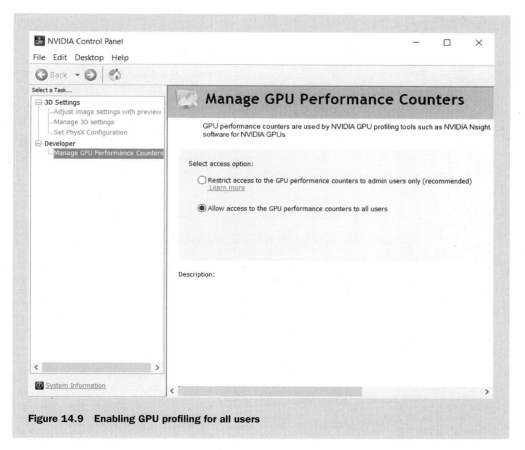

Figure 14.9   Enabling GPU profiling for all users

Make sure you have `libcupti` installed properly in the environment you are using (e.g., Ubuntu or Windows). Otherwise, you will not see the expected results. Then, to enable profiling, all you need to do is pass the argument `profile_batch` to the TensorBoard callback. The value is a list of two numbers: the starting step and the ending step. Profiling is typically done across a span of several batches and therefore requires a range as the value. However, profiling can be done for a single batch too:

```
batch_size = 32
tr_ds, v_ds = get_flower_datasets(
    os.path.join(
        'data', '17flowers','jpg'), batch_size=batch_size,
➥ flatten_images=False
)

tb_callback = tf.keras.callbacks.TensorBoard(
    log_dir=profile_log_dir, profile_batch=[10, 20]
)
```

```
conv_model.fit(
    tr_ds, validation_data=v_ds, epochs=2, callbacks=[tb_callback]
)
```

Once the training finishes, you can view the results on the TensorBoard. TensorBoard provides a large collection of valuable information and insights on model performance. It breaks down the computation into smaller subtasks and provides fine-grained computational time decomposition based on those subtasks. Furthermore, TensorBoard provides recommendations on where there is room for improvement (figure 14.10). Let's now delve into more details about the information provided on this page.

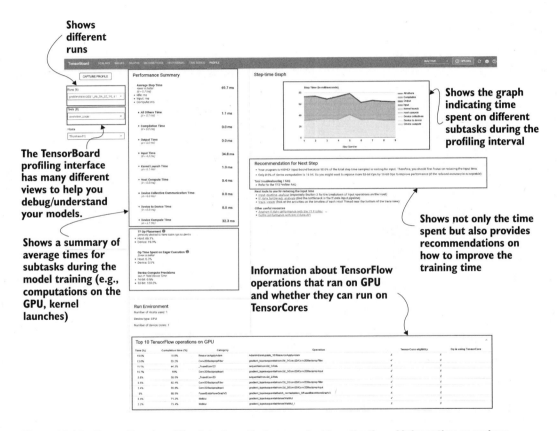

Figure 14.10   TensorBoard profiling interface. It gives a valuable collection of information on various subtasks involved in running models on the GPU. In addition, it provides recommendations on how to improve the performance of the models.

The average step time is a summation of several smaller tasks:

- *Input time*—Time spent on reading data-related operations (e.g., tf.data.Dataset operations).

- *Host compute time*—Model-related computations done on the host (e.g., CPU).
- *Device-to-device time*—To run things on the GPU, data first needs to be transferred to the GPU. This subtask measures the time taken for such transfers.
- *Kernel launch time*—For the GPU to execute operations on the transferred data, the CPU needs to launch the kernels for the GPU. A kernel encapsulates a primitive computation performed on data (e.g., matrix multiplication). This measures the time taken for launching kernels.
- *Device compute time*—Model-related computations that happen on the device (e.g., GPU).
- *Device collective communication time*—Relates to time spent on communicating in multi-device (e.g., multiple GPUs) or multi-node environments.
- All the other times (e.g., compilation time, output time, all other remaining time).

Here we can see that the most time is spent on device computations. This is, in a way, good, as it means that most computations happen on the GPU. The next-biggest time consumer is the input time. This makes sense as we are not using any optimizations for our `tf.data` pipeline and it is a highly disk-bound pipeline as images are read from the disk.

Then, right below that, you can see some more information. Close to 80% of the TensorFlow ops were placed on this host, whereas only 20% ran on the GPU. Furthermore, all the operations were 32-bit operations, and none were 16-bit; 16-bit (half-precision floating point) operations run faster and save a lot of memory compared to 32-bit (single-precision floating point) data types. GPUs and Tensor Processing Units (TPUs) are optimized hardware that can run 16-bit operations much faster than 32-bit operations. Therefore, they must be incorporated whenever possible. Having said that, we must be careful how we use 16-bit operations, as incorrect usage can hurt model performance (e.g., model accuracy) significantly. Incorporating 16-bit operations along with 32-bit operations to train the model is known as *mixed precision training*.

If you look at the recommendation section, you can see two main recommendations:

- Optimize the input data pipeline.
- Utilize more 16-bit operations in model training.

> **Brain Floating Point data type (bfloat16)**
>
> Brain Floating Point values, or bfloat16 values, are a data type proposed by Google. It has the same number of bits as float16 (i.e., 16 bits) but is able to represent the dynamic range of float32 values with some loss in precision. This change is implemented by having more exponent bits (left side of the decimal point) and less fraction bits (right side of the decimal point). This data type can give significant advantages on optimized hardware like TPUs and GPUs (given they have Tensor Cores; https://developer.nvidia.com/tensor-cores).

Let's see how we can use these recommendations to reduce model training time.

14.4.1 Optimizing the input pipeline

To optimize the data pipeline, we will introduce two changes to our get_flower_
datasets() function:

- Use data prefetching to avoid the model having to wait for the data to become
  available.
- Use the parallelized map function when calling the get_image_and_label()
  function.

In terms of how these changes are reflected in the code, they are minor changes. In
the following listing, the changes are in bold.

> **Listing 14.4   The function generating training/validation data sets from flower data set**

```
def get_flower_datasets(image_dir, batch_size, flatten_images=False):

    dataset = tf.data.Dataset.list_files(          Get the training
        os.path.join(image_dir,'*.jpg'), shuffle=False      data set, shuffle it,
    )                                              and output a tuple
                                                   of (image, label).

    def get_image_and_label(file_path):

        tokens = tf.strings.split(file_path, os.path.sep)      Get the tokens
        label = (tf.strings.to_number(                         in the file path
            tf.strings.split(                                  and compute
                tf.strings.split(tokens[-1],'.')[0], '_')[-1]  the label from
            ) - 1                                              the image ID.
        )//80

        img = tf.io.read_file(file_path)           Read the image and
        img = tf.image.decode_jpeg(img, channels=3)   convert to a tensor.

        return tf.image.resize(img, [64, 64]), label

    dataset = dataset.map(                Parallelize
        get_image_and_label,             the map
        num_parallel_calls=tf.data.AUTOTUNE      function.
    ).shuffle(400)

    # Make the validation dataset the first 10000 data
    valid_ds = dataset.take(250).batch(batch_size)
    # Make training dataset the rest
    train_ds = dataset.skip(250).batch(batch_size).prefetch(
        tf.data.experimental.AUTOTUNE
    )                                    Incorporate
                                         prefetching.
    return train_ds, valid_ds
```

Define a function to get the image and the label given a file name.

To parallelize the dataset.map() function, we add the num_parallel_calls=tf.data
.AUTOTUNE argument, which will cause TensorFlow to execute the map function in
parallel, where the number of threads will be determined by the workload carried out

by the host at the time. Next, we invoke the `prefetch()` function on the data after batching to make sure the model training is not hindered by waiting for the data to become available.

Next, we will set a special environment variable called `TF_GPU_THREAD_MODE`. To understand the effects of this variable, you first need to grok how GPUs execute instructions at a high level. When you run deep learning models on a machine with a GPU, most of the data-parallel operations (i.e., operations that can be parallelly executed on data) get executed on the GPU. But how do data and instructions get to the GPU? Assume use of a GPU to execute an element-wise multiplication between two matrices. Since individual elements can be multiplied in parallel, this is a data-parallel operation. To execute this operation (defined as a set of instructions and referred to as a *kernel*) on the GPU, the host (CPU) first needs to launch the kernel in order for the GPU to use that function on data. Particularly, a thread in the CPU (a modern Intel CPU has around two threads per core) will need to trigger this. Think about what will happen if all the threads in the CPU are very busy. In other words, if there are a lot of CPU-bound operations happening (e.g., doing lot of reads from the disk), it can create CPU contention, causing these GPU kernel launches to be delayed. This, in turn, delays code getting executed on the GPU. With the `TF_GPU_THREAD_MODE` variable, you can alleviate the delays on the GPU caused by CPU contention. More concretely, this variable controls how CPU threads are allocated to launch kernels on the GPU. It can take three different values:

- `Global`—There is no special preference as to how threads are allocated for the different processes (default).
- `gpu_private`—A number of dedicated threads are allocated to launch kernels for the GPU. This way, kernel launch will not be delayed, even when a CPU is executing a significant load. If there are multiple GPUs, they will have their own private threads. The number of threads defaults to two and can be changed by setting the `TF_GPU_THREAD_COUNT` variable.
- `shared`—Same as `gpu_private`, except in multi-GPU environments, a pool of threads will be shared between the GPUs.

We will set this variable to `gpu_private`. We will keep the number of dedicate threads to two, so it will not create the `TF_GPU_THREAD_COUNT` variable.

Setting environment variables

To set the TF_GPU_THREAD_MODE environment variable, you can do the following:

Linux operating systems (e.g., Ubuntu)

To set the environment variable

- Open a terminal.
- Run export `TF_GPU_THREAD_MODE=gpu_private`.

(continued)

- Verify the environment variable is set by calling `echo $TF_GPU_THREAD_MODE`.
- Open a new shell and start the Jupyter notebook server.

Windows operating system

To the environment variable

- From the start menu, select Edit the system environment variables.
- Click the button called environment variables.
- Add a new environment variable, `TF_GPU_THREAD_MODE=gpu_private`, in the opened dialog.
- Open a new command prompt and start the Jupyter notebook server.

conda environment (Anaconda)

To set environment variables in a conda environment

- Activate the conda environment with `conda activate manning.tf2`.
- Run `conda env config vars set TF_GPU_THREAD_MODE=gpu_private`.
- Deactivate and reactivate the environment for the variable to take effect.
- Start the Jupyter notebook server.

It is important to restart the notebook server after changing environment variables in your operating system or the conda environment. Refer to the following sidebar for more details.

Important: Restart the notebook server after setting the environment variable

When you create the notebook server from a shell (e.g., Command prompt on Windows or Terminal on Linux), the notebook server is created as a child process of the shell. The changes you do to the environment (e.g., adding an environment variable) after starting the notebook server will not be reflected in that child process. Therefore, you have to kill any existing notebook servers, change the environment variables, and then restart the notebook server to see the effects.

We introduced three optimizations to our `tf.data` pipeline:

- Prefetching batches of data
- Using the parallelized `map()` function instead of the standard `map()` function
- Using dedicated kernel launch threads by setting `TF_GPU_THREAD_MODE=gpu_private`

14.4.2 *Mixed precision training*

As explained earlier, mixed precision training refers to employing a combination of 16-bit and 32-bit operations in model training. For example, the trainable parameters (i.e., variables) are kept as 32-bit floating point values and operations (e.g., matrix multiplication) and produce 16-bit floating point outputs.

In Keras, it's very easy to enable mixed precision training. You simply import the `mixed_precision` namespace from Keras and create a policy that uses mixed precision data types by passing `mixed_float16`. Finally, you set it as a global policy. Then, whenever you define a new model, it will use this policy to determine the data types for the model:

```
from tensorflow.keras import mixed_precision
policy = mixed_precision.Policy('mixed_float16')
mixed_precision.set_global_policy(policy)
```

Let's redefine the CNN model we defined and do a quick check on data types to understand how this new policy has changed the model data types:

```
conv_model = get_cnn_model()
```

Now we will pick a layer and check the data types of the inputs/internal parameters (e.g., trainable weights) and outputs:

```
print("Input to the layers have the data type: {}".format(
    conv_model.get_layer("conv2d_1").input.dtype)
)
print("Variables in the layers have the data type: {}".format(
    conv_model.get_layer("conv2d_1").trainable_variables[0].dtype)
)
print("Output of the layers have the data type: {}".format(
    conv_model.get_layer("conv2d_1").output.dtype)
)
```

This will print

```
Input to the layers have the data type: <dtype: 'float16'>
Variables in the layers have the data type: <dtype: 'float32'>
Output of the layers have the data type: <dtype: 'float16'>
```

As you can see, the inputs and outputs have the `float16` data type, whereas the variables have the `float32` type. This is a design principle incorporated by mixed precision training. The variables are kept as type `float32` to make sure the precision is preserved as the weights are updated.

> ### Loss scaling to avoid numerical underflow
>
> When mixed precision training is used, the loss needs to be treated with care. Half precision floating point (float16) values have a smaller dynamic range than single precision floating point values (float32). Dynamic range refers to the range of values each data type can represent. For example, the maximum value that can be represented by float16 is 65,504 (minimum positive 0.000000059604645), whereas float32 can go up to 3.4 × 10^38 (minimum positive 1.4012984643 × 10 · 45). Due to this small dynamic range of the float16 data type, the loss value can easily underflow (or overflow), causing numerical issues during back propagation. To avoid this, the loss needs to be scaled by an appropriate value, such that the gradients stay within the dynamic range of float16 values. Fortunately, Keras automatically takes care of this.
>
> When the policy is set to `mixed_float16` and you call `model.compile()`, the optimizer is automatically wrapped in a `tf.keras.mixed_precision.LossScale-Optimizer()` (http://mng.bz/Aydo). The `LossScaleOptimizer()` will automatically scale the loss dynamically during model optimization to avoid numerical issues. If you did not using Keras to build the model, then you have to manually take care of this.

With that, rerun the model training:

```
batch_size = 32
tr_ds, v_ds = get_flower_datasets(
    os.path.join('data', '17flowers','jpg'), batch_size=batch_size,
    flatten_images=False
)

# This tensorboard call back does the following
# 1. Log loss and accuracy
# 2. Profile the model memory/time for 10  batches
tb_callback = tf.keras.callbacks.TensorBoard(
    log_dir=profile_log_dir, profile_batch=[10, 20]
)

conv_model.fit(
    tr_ds, validation_data=v_ds, epochs=2, callbacks=[tb_callback]
)
```

After running the model training with the various optimization steps that we introduced, we can compare the results by changing the run on the TensorBoard. For example, we show a side-by-side comparison of the elements on the overview page with and without optimizations. We can see that the time has reduced significantly after introducing the `tf.data` pipeline–related optimizations (figure 14.11).

You might be thinking that the device compute time has not gone down much after incorporating the 16-bit operations. The largest benefit of using 16-bit operations is in the memory consumption of the GPU. The TensorBoard provides a separate view called

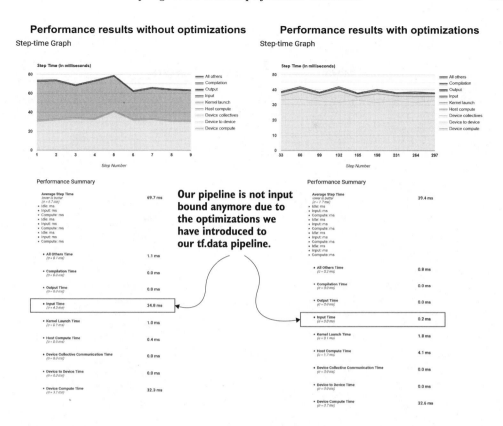

Figure 14.11   Side-by-side comparison of the profiling overview with and without data- and model-related optimizations. We can see a significant reduction of the input time after introducing the optimizations.

the *memory profile* to analyze the memory profile of the model (figure 14.12). You can use this view to analyze memory bottlenecks or memory leaks of the model.

You can clearly see how the memory requirements have taken a plunge after incorporating mixed precision training. The model's appetite for memory has gone down by approximately 76% when mixed precision training is used (from 5.48 GB to 1.25 GB).

The graph specifically refers to two types of memory: *heap* and *stack*. These are fundamental memory spaces used by programs to keep track of variables a function calls when a program is executed. From these, the heap will help us to learn about memory usage patterns or memory-related issues, as that's where various objects and variables created during program execution are kept. For example, if memory leaks are present, you will see an increasing amount of memory used by the heap. Here, we can see that the memory usage is quite linear and can assume that there are no significant memory leaks. You can read more about heaps and stacks in the sidebar on the next page.

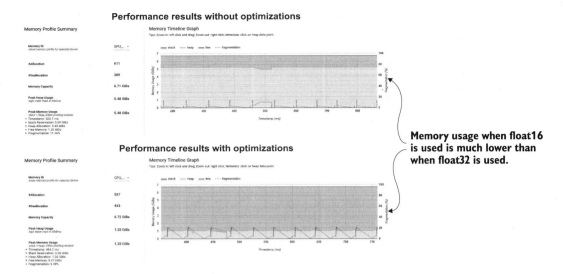

Figure 14.12   Memory profile with and without the optimizations. The difference from using 16-bit operations is very clear, as it has reduced the memory consumption of the model significantly.

Stack vs. heap

Memory of a running program is kept either in the stack or in the heap. For example, function calls are kept in a stack, where the last call is on top of the stack and the oldest is at the bottom. When these function calls create objects, for example, they are written to the heap (the term "heap" comes from a collection of objects that has nothing to do with the heap data structure). You can imagine that the heap contains many objects and attributes, without a particular order (thus the term "heap"). Items are automatically popped out from the stack as function calls end. But it is up to the programmer to free up the heap when objects are no longer used, as they persist even after the function call has ended. However, in modern programming languages, the garbage collector automatically takes care of this. (See http://mng.bz/VMZ5 and http://mng.bz/ZAER.)

You probably have heard the term "stack overflow," which happens when recursive function calls in the code do not meet termination conditions in a reasonable manner, leading the large number of function calls to spill the stack. On a different note, we cannot ignore how the name of a popular website among developers came to be (stackoverflow.com). I can't think of a better resource than Stack Overflow itself to explain this: http://mng.bz/R4ZZ.

We also can see fine-grained details about which operations used how much memory. For example, we know that the main bottleneck of a CNN is the first `Dense` layer after a series of convolutional/pooling layers. Table 14.1 confirms that. That is, it shows that the Dense layer, with a shape of [115200, 512] (i.e., first Dense layer), uses the most memory.

Table 14.1 Memory breakdown table. The table shows the memory usage of various TensorFlow operations along with their data shape.

Op name	Allocation size (GiBs)	Requested size (GiBs)	Occurrences	Region type	Data type	Shape
preallocated/unknown	0.743	0.743	1	persist/ dynamic	INVALID	unknown
gradient_tape/sequential/ dense/MatMul/Cast/Cast	0.220	0.220	1	output	float	[115200,512]
gradient_tape/sequential/ batch_normalisation_3/ FusedBatchNormGradV3	0.051	0.029	1	temp	half	[32,512,31,31]
gradient_tape/sequen- tial/average_pooling2d/ AvgPool/AvgPoolGrad	0.036	0.029	1	output	half	[32,31,31,512]
gradient_tape/sequential/ batch_normalisation_3/ FusedBatchNormGradV3	0.029	0.029	1	output	half	[32,31,31,512]
gradient_tape/sequential/ batch_normalisation_3/ FusedBatchNormGradV3	0.029	0.029	2	temp	half	[32,512,31,31]

Finally, you have the *trace viewer*. This gives a longitudinal view of how various operations were executed on the CPU or GPU and how much time it took. This gives a very detailed view of when and how various operations were scheduled and executed.

On your left, you can see what was executed on your CPU versus on the GPU. For example, you can see that most model-related operations (e.g., convolution) were executed on the GPU, whereas tf.data operations (e.g., decoding images) were executed on the GPU. You can also note that the trace viewer shows GPU private threads separately.

TensorBoard has far more uses than what we have listed here. To know more about these, please refer the following sidebar.

Other views on the TensorBoard

There are many different views available for the TensorBoard. We have discussed the most used view, and I will leave it to the readers to explore the views we haven't discussed. However, out of the ones left out, there are views that are worth noting:

(continued)

Debugger v2

Debugger v2 is a tool introduced since TensorFlow 2.3. The primary purpose of it is to debug numerical issues in models. For example, NaN values creeping in during model training are a very common issue for deep networks. Debugger v2 will provide a comprehensive step-by-step breakdown of various elements in your model (e.g. ,input and output tensors) and which ones produced numerical errors. For more information, visit https://www.tensorflow.org/tensorboard/debugger_v2.

HParams

Hparams is a view that helps hyperparameter optimization and allows you to dive into individual runs to understand which parameters help improve model performance. The `tensorboard.plugins.hparams.api` provides various useful functions and callbacks to hyperparameter-optimize Keras models easily. Then, the trials that happened during the hyperparameter optimization can be viewed in the HParams view. For more information, visit http://mng.bz/2nKg.

What-If Tool

What-If is a tool that can give valuable insights into black-box models, helping with the interpretability of such models. For example, you can run a model inference with some data. Then you can modify the data and see how the output changes through the What-If tool. Furthermore, it provides various tools for analyzing the performance and fairness of models. For more information, visit http://mng.bz/AyjW.

In the next section, we will discuss how we can visualize and interact with word vectors on the TensorBoard.

EXERCISE 4

You have a model that you have already profiled. You have seen the following overview of times:

- Input time: 1.5 ms
- Device compute time: 6.7 ms
- Kernel launch time: 9.8 ms
- Output time: 10.1 ms
- Host compute time: 21.2 ms

For this scenario, assume a time recorded more than 5 ms is an opportunity for improvement. List three code/environment change recommendations to improve the model performance.

14.5 *Visualizing word vectors with the TensorBoard*

You are working as an NLP engineer for a movie recommendation company and have been tasked with developing a movie recommendation model that can be trained on small devices. To reduce the training overhead, one of the techniques used is using pretrained word vectors and freezing them (i.e., not training them). You think GloVe word vectors will give a good initial point and plan to use them. But before that, you have to make sure the vectors capture the semantics/relationships in the movie-specific terminology/words adequately. For that, you need to visualize word vectors for these words on TensorBoard and analyze whether GloVe vectors represent sensible relationships between words.

The first thing we need to do is download the GloVe word vectors. You have been provided the code to download GloVe vectors in the notebook, and it is very similar to how we have downloaded datasets in the past. Therefore, we will not discuss the download in detail. The GloVe word vectors are obtained from https://nlp.stanford.edu/projects/glove/. There are several different versions of GloVe vectors; they have different dimensionalities and vocabulary sizes:

- Trained on Wikipedia 2014 + Gigaword 5 data sets with 6 billion tokens; 400,000 vocabulary; uncased tokens; and 50D, 100D, 200D, and 300D vectors
- Trained on the Common Crawl data set with 42 billion tokens, 1,900,000 vocabulary, uncased tokens, and 300D vectors
- Trained on the Common Crawl data set with 840 billion tokens, 2,200,000 vocabulary, cased tokens, and 300D vectors
- Trained on the Twitter data set with 2 billion tweets; 27 billion tokens; 1,200,000 vocabulary; uncased tokens; and 25D, 50D, 100D, and 200D vectors

---

GloVe word vectors

GloVe (standing for *Global Vectors*) is a word vector algorithm that generates word vectors by looking at both global and local statistics of a corpus. For example, word vector algorithms such as Skip-gram or Continuous Bag-of-Words rely only on the local context of a given word to learn the word vector for that word. The lack of attention to global information about how the word is used in a larger corpus leads to suboptimal word vectors. GloVe incorporates the global statistics by computing a large co-occurrence matrix to indicate the co-occurrence frequency (i.e., if a given word appears in the context of another word) between all words. For more information about GloVe vectors, see http://mng.bz/1oGX.

We will use the 50-dimensional word vectors from the first category (which is the smallest). A 50-dimensional word vector will have 50 values in each word vector designated for each token in the corpus. Once the data is extracted by running the code in the notebook, you will see a file with the name `glove.6B.50d.txt` in the `data` folder. Let's load that as a pandas DataFrame using the `pd.read_csv()` function:

```
df = pd.read_csv(
    os.path.join('data', 'glove.6B.50d.txt'),
    header=None,
    index_col=0,
```

```
        sep=None,
        error_bad_lines=False,
        encoding='utf-8'
)
df.head()
```

This will return table 14.2. Now we will download the IMDB movie reviews data set (https://ai.stanford.edu/~amaas/data/sentiment/). Since this data set is readily available as a TensorFlow data set (through the `tensorflow_datasets` library), we can use that:

```
review_ds = tfds.load('imdb_reviews')
train_review_ds = review_ds["train"]
```

Once we download the data, we will create a corpus that contains all the reviews (text) in the training set as a list of strings:

```
corpus = []
for data in train_review_ds:
    txt = str(np.char.decode(data["text"].numpy(), encoding='utf-8')).lower()
    corpus.append(str(txt))
```

Next, we want to get the most common 5,000 words in this corpus so that we can compare the GloVe vectors of these common words to see if they contain sensible relationships. To get the most common words, we will use the built-in `Counter` object. The `Counter` object counts the frequencies of the words in the vocabulary:

```
from collections import Counter

corpus = " ".join(corpus)

cnt = Counter(corpus.split())
most_common_words = [w for w,_ in cnt.most_common(5000)]
print(cnt.most_common(100))
```

This will print

```
[('the', 322198), ('a', 159953), ('and', 158572), ('of', 144462), ('to',
 133967), ('is', 104171), ('in', 90527), ('i', 70480), ('this', 69714),
 ('that', 66292), ('it', 65505), ('/><br', 50935), ('was', 47024),
 ('as', 45102), ('for', 42843), ('with', 42729), ('but', 39764), ('on',
 31619), ('movie', 30887), ('his', 29059),
 ... ,
 ('other', 8229), ('also', 8007), ('first', 7985), ('its', 7963),
 ('time', 7945), ('do', 7904), ("don't", 7879), ('me', 7722), ('great',
 7714), ('people', 7676), ('could', 7594), ('make', 7590), ('any',
 7507), ('/>the', 7409), ('after', 7118), ('made', 7041), ('then',
 6945), ('bad', 6816), ('think', 6773), ('being', 6390), ('many', 6388),
 ('him', 6385)]
```

Table 14.2 A sample of word vectors for several words

0	1	2	3	4	5	6	7	8	9	10	...	41	42	43	44	45
the	0.418000	0.249680	-0.41242	0.12170	0.34527	-0.044457	-0.49688	-0.17862	-0.00066	-0.656600	⋮	-0.298710	-0.157490	-0.347580	-0.045637	-0.44251
,	0.013441	0.236820	-0.16899	0.40951	0.63812	0.477090	-0.42852	-0.55641	-0.55641	-0.239380	⋮	-0.080262	0.630030	0.321110	-0.467650	0.22786
.	0.151640	0.301770	-0.16763	0.17684	0.31719	0.339730	-0.43478	-0.31086	-0.31086	-0.294860	⋮	-0.000064	0.068987	0.087939	-0.102850	-0.13931
of	0.708530	0.570880	-0.47160	0.18048	0.54449	0.726030	0.18157	-0.52393	-0.52393	-0.175660	⋮	-0.347270	0.284830	0.075693	-0.062178	-0.38988
to	0.680470	-0.039263	0.30186	-0.17792	0.42962	0.032246	-0.41376	-0.13228	0.13228	-0.085253	⋮	-0.094324	0.018324	0.210480	-0.030880	-0.19722

With both the GloVe vectors and the corpus containing the most common 5,000 words in the IMDB movie reviews data set, we find the common tokens between the two sets for visualization:

```
df_common = df.loc[df.index.isin(most_common_words)]
```

This will give a list of roughly 3,600 tokens that appear in both sets.

Next, we can visualize these vectors on the TensorBoard. To reiterate, word vectors are numerical representations of tokens in a given corpus. The specialty of these word vectors (as opposed to one-hot encoding words) is that they capture the semantics of words. For example, if you compute the distance between the word vector of "cat" and "dog," they will be a lot closer than "cat" and "volcano." But when analyzing relationships between a larger set of tokens, we prefer a visual aid. It would be great if there was a way to visualize these word vectors on a 2D or 3D plane, which is much easier to visualize and understand. There are dimensionality-reduction algorithms such as Principal Component Analysis (PCA) (http://mng.bz/PnZw) or t-SNE (https://distill.pub/2016/misread-tsne/) that can achieve this. The specific algorithms used for this are out of scope for this book. The good news is that with TensorBoard, you can do this. TensorBoard can map these high-dimensional vectors to a smaller projection space. To do that, we have to first load these weights as a TensorFlow variable and then save it to the disk as a TensorFlow checkpoint. Then we also save the words or tokens as a new file, with one token per line, corresponding to each vector in the set of word vectors we just saved. With that, you can visualize the word vectors on the TensorBoard (see the next listing).

Listing 14.5   Visualizing word vectors on TensorBoard

```
from tensorboard.plugins import projector

log_dir=os.path.join('logs', 'embeddings')          ⊲─┐ Create a tf.Variable
weights = tf.Variable(df_common.values)              ⊲─┘ with the embeddings
                                                          we captured.

checkpoint = tf.train.Checkpoint(embedding=weights)    │ Save the embeddings as a
checkpoint.save(os.path.join(log_dir, "embedding.ckpt"))│ TensorFlow checkpoint.

with open(os.path.join(log_dir, 'metadata.tsv'), 'w') as f:   ⊲─┐
    for w in df_common.index:                                    │ Save the metadata (a TSV file), where each
        f.write(w+'\n')                                          │ word corresponding to the embeddings is
                                                                   appended as a new line.

config = projector.ProjectorConfig()              ⊲─┐ Create a configuration
embedding = config.embeddings.add()                  │ specific to the projector
embedding.metadata_path = 'metadata.tsv'             │ and embeddings (details
projector.visualize_embeddings(log_dir, config)      │ are discussed in the text).
```

Set the metadata path so that
TensorBoard can incorporate
that in the visualization.

To visualize the word vectors from the saved TensorFlow checkpoint and the metadata (i.e., tokens corresponding to the word vectors saved), we use the `tensorboard.plugins` `.projector` object. We then define a `ProjectorConfig` object and an embedding config. We will keep them with the default configurations, which suit our problem. When `config.embeddings.add()` is invoked, it will generate an embedding config (of type `EmbeddingInfo` object) with default configuration. The `ProjectorConfig` contains information such as the following:

- `model_checkpoint_directory`—The directory to which the checkpoint containing embeddings was saved

The `EmbeddingInfo` contains

- `tensor_name`—If a special tensor name was used for embeddings
- `metadata_path`—The path to a TSV file that contains the labels of the embeddings

To see a full list of available configurations, refer to the file at http://mng.bz/J2Zo. In its current state, the projector's config does not support a lot of customizations. For this reason, we will keep them as default. One config we will set in the `EmbeddingInfo` config is the `metadata_path`. We will set the `metadata_path` to the file containing the tokens and finally pass it to the `projecter.visualize_embeddings()` function. We give it a logging directory, and the projector will automatically detect the TensorFlow checkpoint and load it.

We're all good to go. On your notebook, execute the following line to bring up the TensorBoard:

```
%tensorboard --logdir logs/embeddings/ --port 6007
```

To visualize word vectors, they need to be in the exact directory the `--logdir` is pointing to (i.e., not in a nested folder). Therefore, we need a new TensorBoard server. This line will open a new TensorBoard server on port 6007. Figure 14.13 depicts what is displayed in the TensorBoard.

> **Interesting facts about the %tensorboard magic command**
>
> The `%tensorboard` magic command is smart enough to know when to open a new TensorBoard server and when not to. If you are executing the same command over and over again, it will reuse the existing TensorBoard. However, if you execute a command with a different `--logdir` or a `--port`, it will open a new TensorBoard server.

You can hover over the dots shown in the visualization, and they will show which word in the corpus they represent. You have the ability to visualize the word vectors in a 2D or a 3D space by toggling the dimensionality controller. You might be wondering about the word vectors that we chose. They initially had 50 dimensions—how can we visualize such high-dimensional data in a 2D or 3D space? There's a suite of dimensionality-reduction algorithms that can do this for us. A few examples are t-SNE (http://mng.bz/woxO), PCA (principal component analysis; http://mng.bz/ZAmZ), and UMAP (Uniform Manifold Approximation and Projection; https://arxiv.org/pdf/1802.03426.pdf). Refer to the accompanied links to learn more about these algorithms.

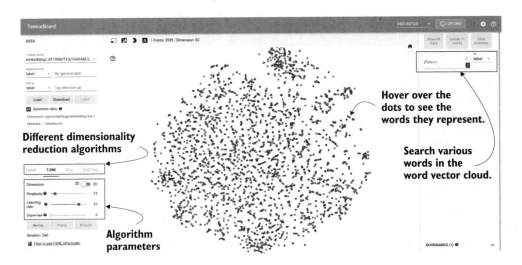

Figure 14.13 The word vector view on the TensorBoard. You have the ability to pick which dimensionality-reduction algorithm (along with parameters) to use in order to get a 2D or 3D representation of the word vectors. Hovering over the dots in the visualization will show the word represented by the dot.

You can do more than a plain visualization of word vectors on the TensorBoard. You can do more detailed analysis by highlighting specific words in the visualization. For that, you can employ regular expressions. For example, the visualization shown in figure 14.14 is generated using the regular expression (?:fred|larry|mrs\.|mr\.|michelle|sea|denzel|beach|comedy|theater|idiotic|sadistic|marvelous|loving|gorg|bus|truck|lugosi).

This concludes our discussion about the TensorBoard. In the next chapter, we will discuss how TensorFlow can help us to create machine learning pipelines and deploy models with ease.

EXERCISE 5

Instead of just the word, say you want to include a unique ID when displaying word vectors in the TensorBoard. For example, instead of the word "loving" you want to see "loving; 218," where 218 is the unique ID given to the word. To do this, you need to change what's written to the metadata.tsv file. Instead of just the word, write an incrementing ID separated by a semicolon on each line. For example, if the words are ["a", "b", "c"], in that order, then the new lines should be ["a;1", "b;2", "c;3"]. How would you make changes?

You can use regex (i.e., regular expressions) to search for words in the cloud.

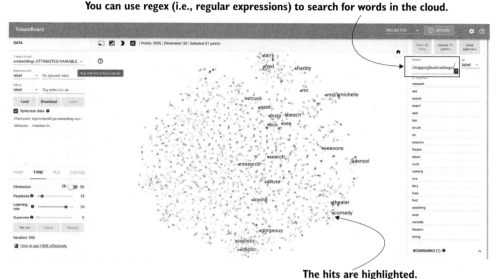

The hits are highlighted.

Figure 14.14 Searching words in the visualizations. You can use regular expressions to search combinations of words.

Summary

- TensorBoard is a great visualization aid for visualizing data (e.g., images) and tracking model performance in real time.
- When building models with Keras, you can use the convenient `tf.keras.call-backs.TensorBoard()` callback to log model performance, layer activation histograms, and much more.
- If you have custom metrics that you want to log to the TensorBoard, you can use the corresponding data type in the `tf.summary` namespace (e.g., use `tf.summary.scalar()` if you want to log a scalar value, like model accuracy over time).
- Each session where you log information to the TensorBoard is called a run. You should incorporate a readable and robust naming convention for the different runs. A good naming convention should capture major changes you did and the date/time the run was executed.
- TensorBoard Profile provides a diverse collection of profiling (using `libcupti` library by NVIDIA) results such as time taken by various subtasks during model training (e.g., device compute time, host compute time, input time, etc.), memory used by the model, and a sequential view of when and how various operations are carried out.
- TensorBoard is a great tool for visualizing high-dimensional data like images and word vectors.

Answers to exercises

Exercise 1

```
image_writer = tf.summary.create_file_writer(image_logdir)

with image_writer.as_default():
    for bi, batch in enumerate(steps_image_batches):
        tf.summary.image(
            "batch_{}".format(bi),
            batch,
            max_outputs=10,
            step=bi
        )
```

Exercise 2

```
log_dir = "./logs "

classif_model.compile(
    loss='binary_crossentropy',
    optimizer='adam',
    metrics=[tf.keras.metrics.Precision(), tf.keras.metrics.Recall()]
)

tb_callback = tf.keras.callbacks.TensorBoard(
    log_dir=log_dir, histogram_freq=1, profile_batch=0
)

classif_model.fit(tr_ds, validation_data=v_ds, epochs=10,
    callbacks=[tb_callback])
```

Exercise 3

```
writer = tf.summary.create_file_writer(log_dir)

x_n_minus_1 = 1
x_n_minus_2 = 0

with writer.as_default():
    for i in range(100):
        x_n = x_n_minus_1 + x_n_minus_2
        x_n_minus_1 = x_n
    x_n_minus_2 = x_n_minus_1

        tf.summary.scalar("fibonacci", x_n, step=i)

        writer.flush()
```

Exercise 4

1 There are a lot of computations happening on the host. This could be because the device (e.g., GPU) does not have enough memory. Using mixed precision training will help to alleviate the issue. Furthermore, there might be too much

non-TensorFlow code that cannot run on the GPU. For that, using more Tensor-Flow operations and converting such code to TensorFlow will gain speed-ups.

2 The Kernel launch time has increased. This could be because the workload is heavily CPU-bound. In this case, we can incorporate the TF_GPU_THREAD_MODE environment variable and set it to gpu_private. This will make sure there will be several dedicated threads to launch kernels for the GPU.

3 Output time is significantly high. This could be because of writing too many outputs too frequently to the disk. To solve that, we can incorporate keeping data in memory for longer and flushing it to the disk only a few times.

Exercise 5

```
log_dir=os.path.join('logs', 'embeddings')

weights = tf.Variable(df_common.values)
    checkpoint = tf.train.Checkpoint(embedding=weights)
checkpoint.save(os.path.join(log_dir, "embedding.ckpt"))

with open(os.path.join(log_dir, 'metadata.tsv'), 'w') as f:
    for i, w in enumerate(df_common.index):
        f.write(w+'; '+str(i)+'\n')
```

15

TFX: MLOps and deploying models with TensorFlow

This chapter covers

- Writing an end-to-end data pipeline using TFX (TensorFlow-Extended)
- Training a simple neural network through the TFX Trainer API
- Using Docker to containerize model serving (inference) and present it as a service
- Deploying the model on your local machine so it can be used through an API

In chapter 14, we looked at a very versatile tool that comes with TensorFlow: the TensorBoard. TensorBoard is a visualization tool that helps you understand data and models better. Among other things, it facilitates

- Monitoring and tracking model performance
- Visualizing data inputs to models (e.g., images, audio)
- Profiling models to understand their performance or memory bottlenecks

We learned how we can use the TensorBoard to visualize high-dimensional data like images and word vectors. We looked at how we can incorporate Keras callbacks to send information to the TensorBoard to visualize model performance (accuracy and loss) and custom metrics. We then analyzed the execution of the model using the CUDA profiling tool kit to understand execution patterns and memory bottlenecks.

In this chapter, we will explore a new domain of machine learning that has gained an enormous amount of attention in the recent past: MLOps. MLOps is derived from the terms ML and DevOps (derived from development and operations). According to Amazon Web Services, "DevOps is the combination of cultural philosophies, practices, and tools that increases an organization's ability to deliver applications and services at high velocity: evolving and improving products at a faster pace than organizations using traditional software development and infrastructure management processes." There is another term that goes hand in hand with MLOps, which is productionization of models. It is somewhat difficult to discriminate between the two terms as they overlap and occasionally are used interchangeably, but I like to think of these two things as follows: MLOps defines a workflow that will automate most of the steps, from collecting data to delivering a model trained on that data, with very little human intervention. Productionization is deploying a trained model (on a private server or cloud), enabling customers to use the model for its designed purpose in a robust fashion. It can include tasks such as designing scalable APIs that can scale to serve thousands of requests per second. In other words, MLOps is the journey that gets you to the destination, which is the productionization of a model.

Let's discuss why it is important to have a (mostly) automated pipeline to develop machine learning models. To realize the value of it, you have to think in scale. For companies like Google, Facebook, and Amazon, machine learning is deeply rooted in the products they offer. This means hundreds if not thousands of models produce predictions every second. Moreover, with a few billion users, they can't afford their models to go stale, which means continuously training/fine-tuning the existing models as new data is collected. MLOps can take care of this problem. MLOps can be used to ingest the collected data, train models, automatically evaluate models, and push them to the production environment if they pass a predefined validation check. A validation check is important to ensure models meet expected performance standards and to safeguard against rogue underperforming models (e.g., a rogue model can be generated due to large changes in new incoming training data, a new untested hyperparameter change that is pushed, etc.). Finally, the model is pushed to a production environment, which is accessed through a Web API to retrieve predictions for an input. Specifically, the API will provide certain endpoints (in the form of URLs) to the user that the user can visit (optionally with parameters needed to complete the request). Having said that, even for a smaller company that is relying on machine learning models, MLOps can greatly standardize and speed up the workflows of data scientists and machine learning engineers. This will greatly reduce the time data scientists and machine learning engineers spend creating such workflows from the ground up every time they work on a new project. Read more about MLOps at http://mng.bz/Pnd9.

How can we do MLOps in TensorFlow? Look no further than TFX (TensorFlow Extended). TFX is a library that gives you all the bells and whistles needed to implement a machine learning pipeline that will ingest data, transform data into features, train a model, and push the model to a designated production environment. This is done by defining a series of components that perform very specific tasks. In the coming sections, we will look at how to use TFX to achieve this.

15.1   *Writing a data pipeline with TFX*

Imagine you are developing a system to predict the severity of a forest fire given the weather conditions. You have been given a data set from past observed forest fires and asked to make a model. To make sure you can provide the model as a service, you decide to create a workflow to ingest data and train a model using TFX. The first step in this is to create a data pipeline that can read the data (in CSV format) and convert it to features. As part of this pipeline, you will have a data reader (that generates examples from CSV), show summary statistics of the fields, learn the schema of the data, and convert it to a proper format the model understands.

Important information about the environment

To run the code for this chapter, we highly recommend using a Linux environment (e.g., Ubuntu), and the instructions will be provided for that environment. TFX is not tested against a Windows environment (http://mng.bz/J2Y0). Another important thing to note is that we will be using a slightly older version of TFX (1.6.0). At the time of writing, the latest version is 1.9.0. This is because a crucial component necessary to run TFX in interactive environments such as notebooks is broken in versions after 1.6.0. Additionally, later on in the chapter we will use a technology called Docker. It can be quite difficult to get Docker to behave in the way we need on Windows due to the highly restricted access to resources. Additionally, for this chapter, we will define a new Anaconda environment. To do that follow the following instructions:

- Open a terminal window and move `cd` into the `Ch15-TFX-for-MLOps-in-TF2` directory in the code repository.
- If you have an already activated Anaconda virtual environment (e.g., manning.tf2), deactivate it by running `conda deactivate manning.tf2`.
- Run `conda create -n manning.tf2.tfx python=3.6` to create a new virtual Anaconda environment.
- Run `conda activate manning.tf2.tfx` to activate the new environment.
- Run `pip install --use-deprecated=legacy-resolver -r requirements.txt`.
- Run `jupyter notebook`.
- Open the `tfx/15.1_MLOps_with_tensorflow.ipynb` notebook.

The first thing to do is download the data sets (listing 15.1). We will use a data set that has recorded historical forest fires in the Montesinho park in Portugal. The data set is freely available at http://archive.ics.uci.edu/ml/datasets/Forest+Fires. It is is a CSV file with the following features:

- *X*—x-axis spatial coordinate within the Montesinho park map
- *Y*—y-axis spatial coordinate within the Montesinho park map
- *month*—Month of the year
- *day*—Day of the week
- *Fine Fuel Moisture Code* (FFMC)—Represents fuel moisture of forest litter fuels under the shade of a forest canopy
- *DMC*—A numerical rating of the average moisture content of soil
- *Drought Code* (DC)—Represents the depth of dryness in the soil
- *Initial Spread Index* (ISI)—An expected rate of fire spread
- *temp*—Temperature in Celsius degrees
- *RH*—Relative humidity in %
- *wind*—Wind speed in km/h
- *rain*—Outside rain in mm/m2
- *area*—The burnt area of the forest (in hectares)

> ### Selecting features for a machine learning model
> Feature selection for a machine learning model is not a trivial task. Often you have to understand features, inter-feature correlation, feature-target correlation, and so on before making a good judgment call on whether a feature should be used. Therefore, one should not use all the given features of a model blindly. In this case, however, as the focus is more on MLOps and less on data-science decisions, we will use all features. Using all of these features will later lend itself to explaining various options that are available when defining an MLOps pipeline.

Our task will be to predict the burnt area, given all the other features. Note that predicting a continuous value such as the area warrants a regression model. Therefore, this is a regression problem, not a classification problem.

Listing 15.1 Downloading the data set

```
import os
import requests
import tarfile                                          If the data file is
                                                        not downloaded,
import shutil                                           download the file.

if not os.path.exists(os.path.join('data', 'csv', 'forestfires.csv')):    ◁
    url = "http://archive.ics.uci.edu/ml/machine-learning-databases/forest-
    fires/forestfires.csv"
    r = requests.get(url)        ◁──│ This line downloads a
                                     │ file given by a URL.

    if not os.path.exists(os.path.join('data', 'csv')):
        os.makedirs(os.path.join('data', 'csv'))

    with open(os.path.join('data', 'csv', 'forestfires.csv'), 'wb') as f:
        f.write(r.content)
```

Create the necessary folders and write the downloaded data into it.

```
    else:
        print("The forestfires.csv file already exists.")
```

If the file containing the data set description is not downloaded, download it.

```
if not os.path.exists(os.path.join('data', 'forestfires.names')):

    url = "http://archive.ics.uci.edu/ml/machine-learning-databases/forest-
fires/forestfires.names"
    r = requests.get(url)

    if not os.path.exists('data'):
        os.makedirs('data')

    with open(os.path.join('data', 'forestfires.names'), 'wb') as f:
        f.write(r.content)

else:
    print("The forestfires.names file already exists.")
```

Create the necessary directories and write the data into them.

Here, we download two files: forestfires.csv and forestfires.names. forestfires.csv contains the data in a comma-separated format, where the first line is the header followed by data in the rest of the file. forestfires.names contains more information about the data, in case you want to understand more about it. Next, we will separate a small test data set to do manual testing on later. Having a dedicated test set that is not seen by the model at any stage will tell us how well the model has generalized. This will be 5% of the original data set. The other 95% will be left for training and validation data:

```
import pandas as pd

df = pd.read_csv(
    os.path.join('data', 'csv', 'forestfires.csv'), index_col=None,
    header=0
)
train_df = df.sample(frac=0.95, random_state=random_seed)
test_df = df.loc[~df.index.isin(train_df.index), :]

train_path = os.path.join('data','csv','train')
os.makedirs(train_path, exist_ok=True)
test_path = os.path.join('data','csv','test')
os.makedirs(test_path, exist_ok=True)

train_df.to_csv(
    os.path.join(train_path, 'forestfires.csv'), index=False, header=True
)
test_df.to_csv(
    os.path.join(test_path, 'forestfires.csv'), index=False, header=True
)
```

We will now start with the TFX pipeline. The first step is to define a root directory for storing pipeline artifacts. What are pipeline artifacts, you might ask? When running the TFX pipeline, it stores interim results of various stages in a directory (under a certain subdirectory structure). One example of this is that when you read the data from the CSV file, the TFX pipeline will split the data into train and validation subsets, convert those examples to TFRecord objects (i.e., an object type used by TensorFlow internally for data), and store the data as compressed files:

```
_pipeline_root = os.path.join(
    os.getcwd(), 'pipeline', 'examples', 'forest_fires_pipeline'
)
```

TFX uses Abseil for logging purposes. Abseil is an open-source collection of C++ libraries drawn from Google's internal codebase. It provides facilities for logging, command-line argument parsing, and so forth. If you are interested, read more about the library at https://abseil.io/docs/python/. We will set the logging level to INFO so that we will see logging statements at the INFO level or higher. Logging is an important functionality to have, as we can glean lots of insights, including what steps ran successfully and what errors were thrown:

```
absl.logging.set_verbosity(absl.logging.INFO)
```

After the initial housekeeping, we will define an InteractiveContext:

```
from tfx.orchestration.experimental.interactive.interactive_context import
    InteractiveContext

context = InteractiveContext(
    pipeline_name = "forest_fires", pipeline_root=_pipeline_root
)
```

TFX runs pipelines in a context. The context is used to run various steps you define in the pipeline. It also serves a very important purpose, which is to manage states between different steps as we are progressing through the pipeline. In order to manage transitions between states and make sure the pipeline operates as expected, it also maintains a metadata store (a small-scale database). The metadata store contains various information, such as an execution order, the final state of the components, and resulting errors. You can read about metadata in the following sidebar.

What's in the metadata?

As soon as you create your InteractiveContext, you will see a database called metadata.sqlite in the pipeline root. This is an SQLite database (https://www .sqlite.org/index.html), a lightweight, fast SQL database designed for small amounts of data and incoming requests. This database will log important information about inputs, outputs, and execution-related outputs (the component's run identifier, errors). This information can be used to debug your TFX pipeline. Metadata can be thought of as data that is not a direct input or an output but is still necessary to execute components correctly with greater transparency. Metadata can be immensely helpful for

> **(continued)**
> debugging complex TFX pipelines with many components interconnected in many different ways. You can read more about this at https://www.tensorflow.org/tfx/guide/mlmd.

We're off to defining the pipeline. The primary purpose of the pipeline in this section is to

- Load the data from a CSV file and split to training and validation data
- Learn the schema of the data (e.g., various columns, data types, min/max bounds, etc.)
- Display summary statistics and graphs about the distribution of various features
- Transform the raw columns to features, which may require special intermediate processing steps

These steps are a lead-up to model training and deployment. Each of these tasks will be a single component in the pipeline, and we will discuss these in more detail when the time comes.

15.1.1   Loading data from CSV files

The first step is to define a component to read examples from the CSV file and split the data to train and eval. For that, you can use the `tfx.components.CsvExampleGen` object. All we need to do is provide the directory containing the data to the `input_base` argument:

```
from tfx.components import CsvExampleGen

example_gen = CsvExampleGen(input_base=os.path.join('data', 'csv', 'train'))
```

Then we use the previously defined `InteractiveContext` to run the example generator:

```
context.run(example_gen)
```

Let's look at what this step produces. To see the data, let's go to the `_pipeline_root` directory (e.g., Ch15-TFX-for-MLOps-in-TF2/tfx/pipeline). It should have a directory/file structure similar to what's shown in figure 15.1.

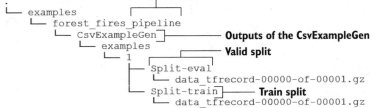

Figure 15.1 The directory/file structure after running the CsvExampleGen

You will see two GZip files (i.e., with a .gz extension) created within the pipeline. You will notice that there are two sub-directories in the CsvExampleGen folder: Split-train and Split-eval, which contain training and validation data, respectively. When you run the notebook cell containing the previous code, you will also see an output HTML table displaying the inputs and outputs of the TFX component (figure 15.2).

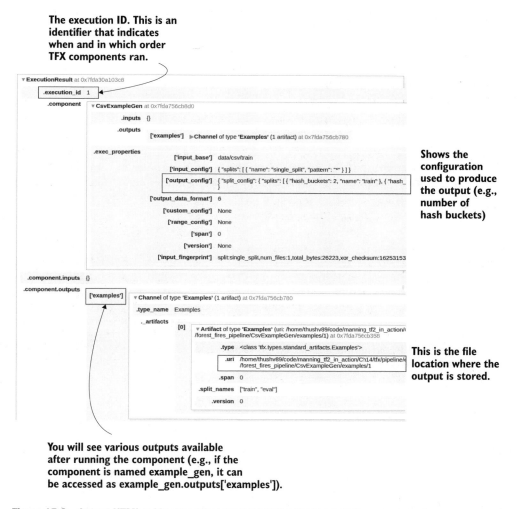

Figure 15.2 Output HTML table generated by running the CsvExampleGen component

There are a few things worth noting. To start, you will see the execution_id, which is the value produced by a counter that keeps track of the number of times you run TFX components. In other words, every time you run a TFX component (like CsvExample-Gen), the counter goes up by 1. If you go down further, you can see some important information about how the CsvExampleGen has split your data. If you look under component > CsvExampleGen > exec_properties > output_config, you will see something like

```
"split_config": {
    "splits": [
        { "hash_buckets": 2, "name": "train" },
        { "hash_buckets": 1, "name": "eval" }
    ]
}
```

This says that the data set has been split into two sets: train and eval. The train set is roughly two-thirds of the original data, and the eval set is around one-third of the original data. This information is inferred by looking at the hash_buckets property. TFX uses hashing to split the data into train and eval. By default, it will define three hash buckets. Then TFX uses the values in each record to generate a hash for that record. The values in the record are passed to a hashing function to generate a hash. The generated hash is then used to assign that example to a bucket. For example, if the hash is 7, then TFX can easily find the bucket with 7%, 3 = 1, meaning it will be assigned to the second bucket (as buckets are zero indexed). You can access the elements in CsvExampleGen as follows.

> **More on hashing**
> There are many hashing functions, such as MD5, SHA1, and so forth. You can read more about hashing functions at https://blog.jscrambler.com/hashing-algorithms/. In TensorFlow, there are two different functions that can be used to generate hashes: tf.strings.to_hash_bucket_fast (http://mng.bz/woJq) and tf.strings.to_hash_bucket_strong (). The strong hash function is slower but is more robust against malicious attacks that may manipulate inputs in order to control the generated hash value.

```
artifact = example_gen.outputs['examples'].get()[0]

print("Artifact split names: {}".format(artifact.split_names))
print("Artifact URI: {}".format(artifact.uri))
```

This will print the following output:

```
Artifact split names: ["train", "eval"]
Artifact URI: <path to project>/Ch15-TFX-for-MLOps-in-
➥ TF2/tfx/pipeline/examples/forest_fires_pipeline/CsvExampleGen/examples/1
```

Earlier we said that TFX stores the interim outputs as we progress through the pipeline. We saw that the CsvExampleGen component has stored the data as .gz files. It in fact stores the examples found in the CSV file as TFRecord objects. A TFRecord is used to store data as byte streams. As TFRecord is a common method for storing data when working with TensorFlow; these records can be retrieved easily as a `tf.data.Dataset`, and the data can be inspected. The next listing shows how this can be done.

Listing 15.2 Printing the data stored by the CsvExampleGen

Create a TFRecordDataset to read these files. The GZip (extension .gz) has a set of TFRecord objects.

Get the URL of the output artifact representing the training examples, which is a directory.

```
train_uri = os.path.join(
    example_gen.outputs['examples'].get()[0].uri, 'Split-train'
)

tfrecord_filenames = [
    os.path.join(train_uri, name) for name in os.listdir(train_uri)
]

dataset = tf.data.TFRecordDataset(
    tfrecord_filenames, compression_type="GZIP"
)

for tfrecord in dataset.take(2):
    serialized_example = tfrecord.numpy()
    example = tf.train.Example()
    example.ParseFromString(serialized_example)
    print(example)
```

Get the list of files in this directory (all compressed TFRecord files).

Iterate over the first two records (can be any number less than or equal to the size of the data set).

Define a tf.train.Example object that knows how to parse the byte stream.

Get the byte stream from the TFRecord (containing one example).

Print the data.

Parse the byte stream to a proper readable example.

If you run this code, you will see the following:

```
features {
  feature {
    key: "DC"
    value {
      float_list {
        value: 605.7999877929688
      }
    }
  }
  ...
  feature {
    key: "RH"
    value {
      int64_list {
        value: 43
      }
    }
  }
  feature {
    key: "X"
    value {
      int64_list {
        value: 5
      }
```

```
        }
      }
      ...
    feature {
      key: "area"
      value {
        float_list {
          value: 2.0
        }
      }
    }
    feature {
      key: "day"
      value {
        bytes_list {
          value: "tue"
        }
      }
    }
    ...
  }

  ...
```

`tf.train.Example` keeps the data as a collection of features, where each feature has a key (column descriptor) and a value. You will see all of the features for a given example. For example, the `DC` feature has a floating value of 605.799, feature `RH` has an int value of 43, feature `area` has a floating value of 2.0, and feature `day` has a `bytes_list` (used to store strings) value of `"tue"` (i.e., Tuesday).

Before moving to the next section, let's remind ourselves what our objective is: to develop a model that can predict the fire spread (in hectares) given all the other features in the data set. This problem is framed as a regression problem.

15.1.2 *Generating basic statistics from the data*

As the next step, we will understand the data better. This is known as exploratory data analysis (EDA). EDA is not typically well defined and very much depends on the problem you are solving and the data. And you have to factor in the limited time you usually have until the delivery of a project. In other words, you cannot test everything and have to prioritize what you want to test and what you want to assume. For the structured data we are tackling here, a great place to start is understanding type (numerical versus categorical) and the distribution of values of the various columns present. TFX provides you a component just for that. `StatisticsGen` will automatically generate those statistics for you. We will soon see in more detail what sort of insights this module provides:

```
from tfx.components import StatisticsGen

statistics_gen = StatisticsGen(
    examples=example_gen.outputs['examples'])

context.run(statistics_gen)
```

This will produce an HTML table similar to what you saw after running CsvExample-Gen (figure 15.3).

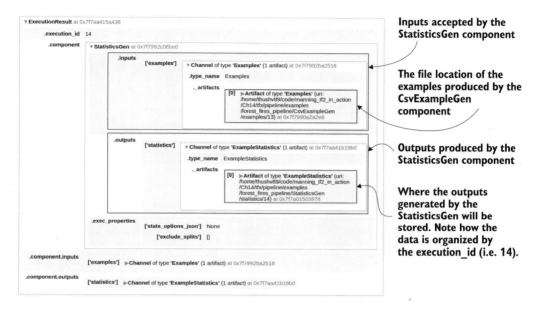

Figure 15.3   The output provided by the `StatisticsGen` **component**

However, to retrieve the most valuable output of this step, you have to run the following line:

```
context.show(statistics_gen.outputs['statistics'])
```

This will create the following files in the pipeline root (figure 15.4).

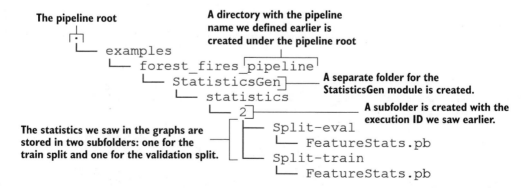

Figure 15.4   The directory/file structure after running `StatisticsGen`

Figure 15.5 shows the valuable collection of information about data provided by TFX. The output graph shown in figure 15.5 is a goldmine containing rich information about the data we're dealing with. It provides you a basic yet holistic suite of graphs that provides lots of information about the columns present in the data. Let's go from top to bottom. At the top, you have options to sort and filter the outputs shown in figure 15.5. For example, you can change the order of the graphs, select graphs based on data types, or filter them by a regular expression.

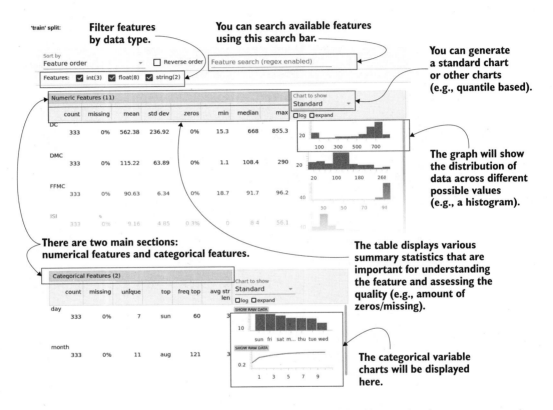

Figure 15.5   The summary statistics graphs generated for the data by the `StatisticsGen` component

By default, `StatisticsGen` will generate graphs for both `train` and `eval` data sets. Then each `train` and `eval` section will have several subsections; in this case, we have a section for numerical columns and categorical columns.

On the left, you can see some numerical statistics and assessments of a feature, whereas on the right side, you can see a visual representation of how a feature is distributed. For example, take the FFMC feature in the training set. We can see that it has 333 examples and 0% have missing values for that feature. It has a mean of ~90 and a standard deviation of 6.34. In the graph, you can see that the distribution is quite skewed. Almost all values are concentrated around the 80–90 range. You will see later how this might create problems for us and how we will solve them.

In the categorical section, you can see the values of the day and month features. For example, the day feature has seven unique values and 0% missing. The most frequent value (i.e., mode) of the day feature appears 60 times. Note that the day is represented as a bar graph and the month is represented as a line graph because for features with unique values above a threshold, a line graph is used to make the graph clear and less cluttered.

15.1.3 Inferring the schema from data

Thus far, we have loaded the data from a CSV file and explored the basic statistics of the data set. The next big step is to infer the schema of the data. TFX can automatically derive the schema of the data once the data is provided. If you have worked with databases, the schema derived is the same as a database schema. It can be thought of as a blueprint for the data, expressing the structure and important attributes of data. It can also be thought of as a set of rules that dictate what the data should look like. For example, if you have the schema, you can classify whether a given record is valid by referring to the schema.

Without further ado, let's create a SchemaGen object. The SchemaGen requires the output of the previous step (i.e., output of the StatisticsGen) and a Boolean argument named infer_feature_shape:

```
from tfx.components import SchemaGen

schema_gen = SchemaGen(
    statistics=statistics_gen.outputs['statistics'],
    infer_feature_shape=False)

context.run(schema_gen)
```

Here, we set the infer_feature_shape to False, as we will do some transformations to the features down the road. Therefore, we will have the flexibility to manipulate the feature shapes more freely. However, setting this argument (infer_feature_shape) means an important change for a downstream step (called the transform step). When infer_feature_shape is set to False, the tensors passed to the transform step are represented as tf.SparseTensor objects, not tf.Tensor objects. If set to True, it will need to be a tf.Tensor object with a known shape. Next, to see the output of the SchemaGen, you can do

```
context.show(schema_gen.outputs['schema'])
```

which will produce the output shown in table 15.1.

Table 15.1 The schema output generated by TFX

Feature name	Type	Presence	Valency	Domain
'day'	STRING	required	single	'day'
'month'	STRING	required	single	'month'
'DC'	FLOAT	required	single	–
'DMC'	FLOAT	required	single	–
'FFMC'	FLOAT	required	single	–
'ISI'	FLOAT	required	single	–
'RH'	INT	required	single	–
'X'	INT	required	single	–
'Y'	INT	required	single	–
'area'	FLOAT	required	single	–
'rain'	FLOAT	required	single	–
'temp'	FLOAT	required	single	–
'wind'	FLOAT	required	single	

Domain	Values												
'day'						'fri'	'mon'	'sat'	'sun'	'thu'	'tue'	'wed'	
'month'	'apr'	'aug'	'dec'	'feb'	'jan'	'jul'	'jun'	'mar'	'may'	'oct'	'sep'	'nov'	

`Domain` defines the constraints of a given feature. We list some of the most popular domains defined in TFX:

- *Integer domain values* (e.g., defines minimum/maximum of an integer feature)
- *Float domain values* (e.g., defines minimum/maximum of a floating-value feature)
- *String domain value* (e.g., defines allowed values/tokens for a string features)
- *Boolean domain values* (e.g., can be used to define custom values for true/false states)
- *Struct domain values* (e.g., can be used to define recursive domains [a domain within a domain] or domains with multiple features)
- *Natural language domain values* (e.g., defines a vocabulary [allowed collection of tokens] for a related language feature)
- *Image domain values* (e.g., can be used to restrict the maximum byte size of images)
- *Time domain values* (e.g., can be used to define data/time features)
- *Time of day domain values* (e.g., can be used to define a time without a date)

The list of domains is available in a file called schema.proto. schema.proto is defined at http://mng.bz/7yp9. These files are defined using a library called `Protobuf`. `Protobuf` is a library designed for object serialization. You can read the following sidebar to learn more about the `Protobuf` library.

Protobuf library

`Protobuf` is an object serialization/deserialization library developed by Google. The object that needs to be serialized is defined as a `Protobuf` message. The template of a message is defined with a .proto file. Then, to deserialize, `Protobuf` provides functions such as `ParseFromString()`. To read more about the library, refer to http://mng.bz/R45P.

Next, we will see how we can convert data to features.

15.1.4 *Converting data to features*

We have reached the final stage of our data-processing pipeline. The final step is to convert the columns we have extracted to features that are meaningful to our model. We are going to create three types of features:

- *Dense floating-point features*—Values are presented as floating-point numbers (e.g., temperature). This means the value is passed as it is (with an optional normalizing step; e.g., Z-score normalization) to create a feature.
- *Bucketized features*—Numerical values that are binned according to predefined binning intervals. This means the value will be converted to a bin index, depending on which bin the value falls into (e.g., we can bucketize relative humidity to three values: low [-inf, 33), medium [33, 66), and high [66, inf)).
- *Categorical features* (integer-based or string-based)—Value is chosen from a predefined set of values (e.g., day or month). If the value is not already an integer index (e.g., day as a string), it will be converted to an integer index using a vocabulary that maps each word to an index (e.g., `"mon"` is mapped to 0, `"tue"` is mapped to 1, etc.).

We will introduce one of these feature transformations to each of the fields in the data set:

- *X* (spatial coordinate)—Presented as a floating-point value
- *Y* (spatial coordinate)—Presented as a floating-point value
- *wind* (wind speed)—Presented as a floating-point value
- *rain* (outside rain)—Presented as a floating-point value
- *FFMC* (fuel moisture)—Presented as a floating-point value
- *DMC* (average moisture content)—Presented as a floating-point value
- *DC* (depth of dryness in the soil)—Presented as a floating-point value
- *ISI* (expected rate of fire spread)—Presented as a floating-point value

- *temp* (temperature)—Presented as a floating-point value
- *RH* (relative humidity)—Presented as a bucketized value
- *month*—Presented as a categorical feature
- *day*—Presented as a categorical feature
- *area* (the burned area)—The label feature kept as a numerical value

We are first going to define some constants, which will help us to keep track of which feature is assigned to which category. Additionally, we will keep variable specific properties (e.g., maximum number of classes for categorical features; see the next listing).

Listing 15.3   Defining feature-related constants for the feature transformation step

This command will write the content of this cell to a file (read the sidebar for more information).

Vocabulary-based (or string-based) categorical features.

```
%%writefile forest_fires_constants.py

VOCAB_FEATURE_KEYS = ['day','month']

MAX_CATEGORICAL_FEATURE_VALUES = [7, 12]

DENSE_FLOAT_FEATURE_KEYS = [
    'DC', 'DMC', 'FFMC', 'ISI', 'rain', 'temp', 'wind', 'X', 'Y'
]

BUCKET_FEATURE_KEYS = ['RH']

BUCKET_FEATURE_BOUNDARIES = [(33, 66)]

LABEL_KEY = 'area'

def transformed_name(key):

    return key + '_xf'
```

Categorical features are assumed to each have a maximum value in the data set.

Dense features (these will go to the model as they are, or normalized)

Bucketized features

The bucket boundaries for bucketized features (e.g., the feature RH will be bucketed to three bins: [0, 33), [33, 66), [66, inf)).

Label features will be kept as numerical features as we are solving a regression problem.

Define a function that will add a suffix to the feature name. This will help us to distinguish the generated features from original data columns.

The reason we are writing these notebook cells as Python scripts (or Python modules) is because TFX expects some parts of the code it needs to run as a Python module.

%%writefile magic command

`%%writefile` is a Jupyter magic command (similar to `%%tensorboard`). It will cause the Jupyter notebook to write the content in a cell to a new file (e.g., a Python module/script). This is a great way to create isolated Python modules from notebook cells. Notebooks are great for experimenting, but for production-level code, Python scripts are better. For example, our TFX pipeline expects certain functions (e.g., how to preprocess raw columns to features) to be independent Python modules. We can conveniently use the `%%writefile` command to achieve that.

This command must be specified as the very top command in the cell you want to be written out to a file.

Next, we will write another module called forest_fires_transform.py, which will have a preprocessing function (called `preprocessing_fn`) that defines how each data column should be treated in order to become a feature (see the next listing).

Listing 15.4 Defining a Python module to convert raw data to features

```python
%%writefile forest_fires_transform.py

import tensorflow as tf
import tensorflow_transform as tft

import forest_fires_constants

_DENSE_FLOAT_FEATURE_KEYS = forest_fires_constants.DENSE_FLOAT_FEATURE_KEYS
_VOCAB_FEATURE_KEYS = forest_fires_constants.VOCAB_FEATURE_KEYS
_BUCKET_FEATURE_KEYS = forest_fires_constants.BUCKET_FEATURE_KEYS
_BUCKET_FEATURE_BOUNDARIES =
  forest_fires_constants.BUCKET_FEATURE_BOUNDARIES
_LABEL_KEY = forest_fires_constants.LABEL_KEY
_transformed_name = forest_fires_constants.transformed_name


def preprocessing_fn(inputs):

    outputs = {}

    for key in _DENSE_FLOAT_FEATURE_KEYS:
        outputs[_transformed_name(key)] = tft.scale_to_z_score(
            sparse_to_dense(inputs[key])
        )
    for key in _VOCAB_FEATURE_KEYS:
        outputs[_transformed_name(key)] = tft.compute_and_apply_vocabulary(
            sparse_to_dense(inputs[key]),
            num_oov_buckets=1)

    for key, boundary in zip(_BUCKET_FEATURE_KEYS,
      _BUCKET_FEATURE_BOUNDARIES):
        outputs[_transformed_name(key)] = tft.apply_buckets(
            sparse_to_dense(inputs[key]), bucket_boundaries=[boundary]
        )

    outputs[_transformed_name(_LABEL_KEY)] =
      sparse_to_dense(inputs[_LABEL_KEY])

    return outputs

def sparse_to_dense(x):
```

The content in this code listing will be written to a separate Python module.

Imports the feature constants defined previously

Imports all the constants defined in the forest_fires_constants module

This is a must-have callback function for the tf.transform library to convert raw columns to features.

Treats all the dense features

Perform Z-score-based scaling (or normalization) on dense features

For the vocabulary-based features, build the vocabulary and convert each token to an integer ID.

For the to-be-bucketized features, using the bucket boundaries defined, bucketize the features.

The label feature is simply converted to dense without any other feature transformations.

A utility function for converting sparse tensors to dense tensors

Because infer_feature_shape is set to False in the SchemaGen step, we have sparse tensors as inputs. They need to be converted to dense tensors.

```
return tf.squeeze(
    tf.sparse.to_dense(
        tf.SparseTensor(x.indices, x.values, [x.dense_shape[0], 1])
    ),
    axis=1
)
```

You can see that this file is written as forest_fires_transform.py. It defines a pre-processing_fn(), which takes an argument called inputs. inputs is a dictionary mapping from feature keys to columns of data found in the CSV, flowing from the example_gen output. Finally, it returns a dictionary with feature keys mapped to transformed features using the tensorflow_transform library. In the middle of the method, you can see the preprocessing function doing three important jobs.

First, it reads all dense features (whose names are stored in _DENSE_FLOAT_FEATURE_KEYS) and normalizes the values using z-score. The z-score normalizes a column *x* as

$$\frac{x - \mu(x)}{\sigma(x)},$$

where $\mu(x)$ is mean value of the column and $\sigma(x)$ is the standard deviation of the column. To normalize data, you can call the function scale_to_z_score() in the tensorflow_transform library. You can read the sidebar on tensorflow_transform to understand more about what the library offers. Then the function stores each feature in the outputs under a new key (via the _transformed_name function) derived from the original feature name (the new key is generated by appending _xf to the end of the original feature name).

Next, it treats the vocabulary-based categorical features (where names are stored in _VOCAB_FEATURE_KEYS) by converting each string to an index using a dictionary. The dictionary maps each string to an index and is learned from the provided training data automatically. This is similar to how we used the Keras Tokenizer object to learn a dictionary that we used to convert words to word IDs. In the tensorflow_transform library you have the handy compute_and_apply_vocabulary() function. To the compute_and_apply_vocabulary() function, we can pass num_oov_buckets=1 in order to assign any unseen strings to a special category (apart from the ones already assigned to known categories).

Afterward, the function tackles the to-be-bucketized features. Bucketization is the process of applying a continuous value to a bucket, where a bucket is defined by a set of boundaries. Bucketizing features can be achieved effortlessly with the apply_buckets() function, which takes the feature (provided in the inputs dictionary) and bucket boundaries as the input arguments.

Finally, we keep the column containing the label as it is. With that, we define the Transform component (http://mng.bz/mOGr).

tensorflow_transform: Converting raw data to features

`tensorflow_transform` is a sub-library in TensorFlow primarily focused on feature transformations. It offers a variety of functions to compute things:

- Bucketizing features (e.g., binning a range of values to a predefined set of bins)
- Bag-of-words features from a string column
- Covariance matrices of a data set
- Mean, standard deviation, min, max, count, and so forth of columns

You can read more about the functions this library offers at http://mng.bz/5QgB.

```
from tfx.components import Transform

transform = Transform(
    examples=example_gen.outputs['examples'],
    schema=schema_gen.outputs['schema'],
    module_file=os.path.abspath('forest_fires_transform.py'),
)

context.run(transform)
```

The `Transform` component takes three inputs:

- Output examples of the `CsvExampleGen` component
- Schema from the `SchemaGen`
- The Python module that defines the `preprocessing_fn()` function for transforming data to features

One thing we must do when it comes to multi-component pipelines, like a TFX pipeline, is check every interim output whenever we can. It's a much better choice than leaving things to chance and praying things work out fine (which is normally never the case). So, let's inspect the output by printing some of the data saved to the disk after running the `Transform` step (see the next listing). The code for printing the data will be similar to when we printed the data when using the CsvExampleGen component.

Listing 15.5 Inspecting the outputs produced by the TFX `Transform` step

```
import forest_fires_constants

_DENSE_FLOAT_FEATURE_KEYS = forest_fires_constants.DENSE_FLOAT_FEATURE_KEYS
_VOCAB_FEATURE_KEYS = forest_fires_constants.VOCAB_FEATURE_KEYS
_BUCKET_FEATURE_KEYS = forest_fires_constants.BUCKET_FEATURE_KEYS
_LABEL_KEY = forest_fires_constants.LABEL_KEY

# Get the URI of the output artifact representing the training examples,
    which is a directory
train_uri = os.path.join(
    transform.outputs['transformed_examples'].get()[0].uri, 'Split-train'
)
```

```
tfrecord_filenames = [
    os.path.join(train_uri, name) for name in os.listdir(train_uri)
]

dataset = tf.data.TFRecordDataset(
    tfrecord_filenames, compression_type="GZIP"
)

example_records = []
float_features = [
    _transformed_name(f) for f in _DENSE_FLOAT_FEATURE_KEYS + [_LABEL_KEY]
]
int_features = [
    _transformed_name(f) for f in _BUCKET_FEATURE_KEYS +
    _VOCAB_FEATURE_KEYS
]
for tfrecord in dataset.take(5):
    serialized_example = tfrecord.numpy()
    example = tf.train.Example()
    example.ParseFromString(serialized_example)
    record = [
        example.features.feature[f].int64_list.value for f in int_features
    ] + [
        example.features.feature[f].float_list.value for f in float_features
    ]
    example_records.append(record)
    print(example)
    print("="*50)
```

Get the list of files in this directory (all compressed TFRecord files).

Create a TFRecordDataset to read these files.

Used to store the retrieved feature values (for later inspection)

Dense (i.e., float) and integer (i.e., vocab-based and bucketized) features

Get the first five examples in the data set.

Get a tf record and convert that to a readable tf.train.Example.

We will extract the values of the features from the tf.train.Example object for subsequent inspections.

Append the extracted values as a record (i.e., tuple of values) to example_records.

The code explained will print the data after feature transformation. Each example stores integer values in the attribute path, example.features.feature[<feature name>] .int64_list.value, whereas the floating values are stored at example.features.feature [<feature name>].float_list.value. This will print examples such as

```
features {
  feature {
    key: "DC_xf"
    value {
      float_list {
        value: 0.4196213185787201
      }
    }
  }

  ...

  feature {
    key: "RH_xf"
    value {
      int64_list {
        value: 0
```

```
        }
      }
    }

    . . .

    feature {
      key: "area_xf"
      value {
        float_list {
          value: 2.7699999809265137
        }
      }
    }

    . . .

}
```

Note that we are using the _transformed_name() function to obtain the transformed feature names. We can see that the floating-point values (DC_xf) are normalized using z-score normalization, vocabulary-based features (day_xf) are converted to an integer, and bucketized features (RH_xf) are presented as integers.

> ### Rule of thumb: Check your pipeline whenever possible
>
> When using components offered by third-party libraries like TFX, there is very low visibility into what is actually taking place under the hood. This is exacerbated by the fact that TFX is not a highly matured tool and is in the process of development. Therefore, we always try to incorporate pieces of code that probe into these components, which will help us to sanity-check inputs and outputs of these components.

In the next section, we will train a simple regression model as a part of the pipeline we've been creating.

EXERCISE 1

Let's say that, instead of the previously defined feature transformations, you want to do the following:

- *DC*—Scale data to a range of [0, 1]
- *temp*—Bucketize with the boundaries (-inf, 20], (20, 30] and (30, inf)

Once the features are transformed, add them to a dictionary named outputs, where each feature is keyed by the transformed feature name. Assume you can obtain the transformed feature name for temp by calling, _transformed_name('temp'). How would you use the tensorflow_transform library to achieve this? You can use the scale_to_0_1() and apply_buckets() functions to achieve this.

15.2   *Training a simple regression neural network: TFX Trainer API*

You have defined a TFX data pipeline that can convert examples in a CSV file to model-ready features. Now you will train a model on this data. You will use TFX to define a model trainer, which will take a simple two-layer fully connected regression model and train that on the data flowing from the data pipeline. Finally, you will predict using the model on some sample evaluation data.

With a well-defined data pipeline defined using TFX, we're at the cusp of training a model with the data flowing from that pipeline. Training a model with TFX can be slightly demanding at first sight due to the rigid structure of functions and data it expects. However, once you are familiar with the format you need to adhere to, it gets easier.

We will go through this section in three stages. First, let's examine how we can define a Keras model to suit the output features we have defined in the TFX `Transform` component. Ultimately, the model will receive the output of the `Transform` component. Next, we will look at how we can write a function that encapsulates model training. This function will use the model defined and, along with several user-defined arguments, train the model and save it to a desired path. The saved model cannot be just any model; it has to have what are known as *signatures* in TensorFlow. These signatures dictate what the inputs to the model and outputs of the model look like when it's finally used via an API. The API is served via a server that exposes a network port for the client to communicate with the API. Figure 15.6 depicts how the API ties in with the model.

Let's understand what is taking place in figure 15.6. First, an HTTP client sends a request to the server. The server (i.e., a TensorFlow serving server) that is listening for any incoming requests will read the request and direct that to the required model signature. Once the data is received by the model signature, it will perform necessary processing on the data, run it through the model, and produce the output (e.g., predictions). Once the predictions are available, they will be returned by the server to the client. We will discuss the API and the server side in detail in a separate section. In this section, our focus is on the model.

What is a signature in TensorFlow serving?

In real life, the purpose of a signature is to uniquely identify a person. Similarly, TensorFlow uses signatures to uniquely determine how a model should behave when an input is passed to the model via a HTTP request. A signature has a key and a value. The key is a unique identifier that defines to which exact URL that signature will be activated. The value is defined as a TensorFlow function (i.e., a function decorated with `@tf.function`). This function will define how an input is handled and passed to the model to obtain the final desired result. You don't need to worry about the details at this point. We have a separate section dedicated to learning about signatures.

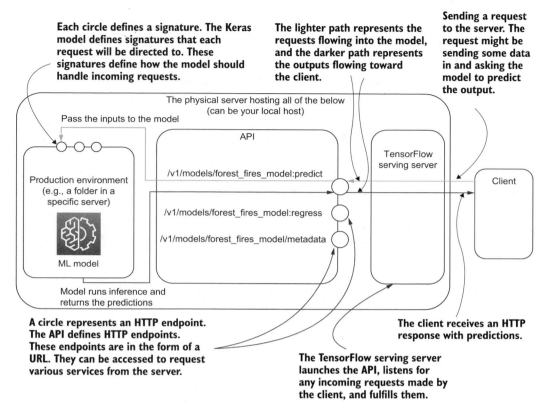

Figure 15.6   How the model interacts with the API, the TensorFlow server, and the client

We will circle back to signatures in a separate subsection to understand them in more detail. Finally, we will visually inspect model predictions by loading the model and feeding some data into it.

15.2.1   Defining a Keras model

The cornerstone for training the model with TFX is defining a model. There are two ways to define models for TFX: using the Estimator API or using the Keras API. We are going to go with the Keras API, as the Estimator API is not recommended for TensorFlow 2 (see the following sidebar for more details).

> **Estimator API vs. Keras API**
>
> My view is that going forward, Keras is probably going to be the go-to API for building models, and the Estimator API could perhaps be deprecated. The TensorFlow website says the following:

(continued)

Estimators are not recommended for new code. Estimators run v1.Session-style code which is more difficult to write correctly, and can behave unexpectedly, especially when combined with TF 2 code. Estimators do fall under our compatibility guarantees but will receive no fixes other than security vulnerabilities. See the migration guide for details.

Source: https://www.tensorflow.org/tfx/tutorials/tfx/components

We are first going to create a function called `_build_keras_model()`, which will do two things. First, it will create `tf.feature_column`-type objects for all the features we have defined in our `Transform` step. `tf.feature_column` is a feature representation standard and is accepted by models defined in TensorFlow. It is a handy tool for defining data in a column-oriented fashion (i.e., each feature represented as a column). Columnar representation is very suitable for structured data, where each column typically is an independent predictor for the target variable. Let's examine a few specific `tf.feature_column` types that are found in TensorFlow:

- `tf.feature_column.numeric_column`—Used to represent dense floating-point fields like temperature.
- `tf.feature_column.categorical_column_with_identity`—Used to represent categorical fields or bucketized fields where the value is an integer index pointing to a category or a bucket, such as day or month. Because the value passed to the column itself is the category ID, the term "identity" is used.
- `tf.feature_column.indicator_column`—Converts a `tf.feature_column.categorical_column_with_identity` to a one-hot encoded representation.
- `tf.feature_column.embedding_column`—Can be used to generate an embedding from an integer-based column like `tf.feature_column.categorical_column_with_identity`. It maintains an embedding layer internally and will return the corresponding embedding, given an integer ID.

To see the full list, refer to http://mng.bz/6Xeo. Here, we will use the top three types of `tf.feature_columns` as inputs to our to-be defined model. The following listing outlines how `tf.feature_columns` are used as inputs.

Listing 15.6   Building the Keras model using feature columns

```
def _build_keras_model() -> tf.keras.Model:

    real_valued_columns = [
        tf.feature_column.numeric_column(key=key, shape=(1,))
        for key in _transformed_names(_DENSE_FLOAT_FEATURE_KEYS)
    ]
```

Create tf.feature_column objects for dense features.

Define the function signature. It returns a Keras model as the output.

```
categorical_columns = [                                    ◄─────────────┐
    tf.feature_column.indicator_column(                                  │
        tf.feature_column.categorical_column_with_identity(              │
            key,                                       Create tf.feature_column
            num_buckets=len(boundaries)+1              objects for the bucketized
        )                                                           features.
    ) for key, boundaries in zip(
        _transformed_names(_BUCKET_FEATURE_KEYS),
        _BUCKET_FEATURE_BOUNDARIES
    )
]                                              Create tf.feature_column
                                               objects for the categorical
categorical_columns += [               ◄────   features.
    tf.feature_column.indicator_column(
        tf.feature_column.categorical_column_with_identity(
            key,
            num_buckets=num_buckets,
            default_value=num_buckets-1
        )
    ) for key, num_buckets in zip(
        _transformed_names(_VOCAB_FEATURE_KEYS),
        _MAX_CATEGORICAL_FEATURE_VALUES
    )
]                                     Define a deep
                                      regressor model
                                      using the function.          Uses the columns
model = _dnn_regressor(        ◄───                                defined above
    columns=real_valued_columns+categorical_columns,    ◄──┘
    dnn_hidden_units=[128, 64]    ◄───
)                                         It will have two intermediate
                                          layers: 128 nodes and 64
return model                              nodes.
```

Let's look at the first set of feature columns stored in real_valued_columns. We take transformed names of the original keys of dense floating-point valued columns, and for each column, we create a tf.feature_column.numeric_column. You can see that we are passing

- *A key* (string)—Name of the feature
- *A shape* (a list/tuple)—Full shape will be derived as [batch size] + shape

For example, the column temp will have the key as temp_xf and shape as (1,), meaning that the full shape is [batch size, 1]. This shape of [batch size, 1] makes sense since each dense feature has a single value per record (meaning that we don't need a feature dimensionality in the shape). Let's go through a toy example to see a tf.feature_column.numeric_column in action:

```
a = tf.feature_column.numeric_column("a")
x = tf.keras.layers.DenseFeatures(a)({'a': [0.5, 0.6]})
print(x)
```

This will output

```
tf.Tensor(
[[0.5]
 [0.6]], shape=(2, 1), dtype=float32)
```

When defining `tf.feature_column.categorical_column_with_identity` for the bucketized features, you need to pass

- A key (string)—Name of the feature
- num_buckets (int)—Number of buckets in the bucketized feature

For instance, the RH feature that was bucketized will have the key RH_xf and num_buckets = 3, where the buckets are [[-inf, 33), [33, 66), [66, inf]]. Since we defined the bucket boundary for RH as (33, 66), num_buckets is defined as `len(boundaries)` +1 = 3. Finally, each categorical feature is wrapped in a `tf.feature_column.indicator_` column to convert each feature to one-hot encoded representation. Again, we can do a quick experiment to see the effects of these feature columns as follows:

```
b = tf.feature_column.indicator_column(
    tf.feature_column.categorical_column_with_identity('b', num_buckets=10)
)
y = tf.keras.layers.DenseFeatures(b)({'b': [5, 2]})
print(y)
```

This will produce

```
tf.Tensor(
[[0. 0. 0. 0. 0. 1. 0. 0. 0. 0.]
 [0. 0. 1. 0. 0. 0. 0. 0. 0. 0.]], shape=(2, 10), dtype=float32)
```

Finally, the vocabulary-based categorical features are treated similarly to the bucketized features. For each feature, we get the feature name and the maximum number of categories and define a `tf.feature_column.categorical_column_with_identity` column with

- key (string)—Name of the feature.
- num_buckets (int)—Number of categories.
- default_value (int)—If a previously unseen category is encountered, it will be assigned this value.

Here, default_value is an important part. It will dictate what happens to any unseen categories that might appear in the testing data and that weren't a part of the training data. The vocabulary-based categorical features in our problem were day and month, which can only have 7 and 12 distinct values. But there could be situations where the training set only has 11 months and the test set has 12 months. To tackle this, we will assign any unseen category to the last category ID (i.e., num_buckets - 1) available to us.

We now have a collection of well-defined data columns that are wrapped in `tf.feature_column` objects ready to be fed to a model. Finally, we see a function called `_dnn_regressor()` that will create a Keras model, which is shown in the next listing, and pass the columns we create and some other hyperparameters. Let's now discuss the specifics of this function.

Listing 15.7   Defining the regression neural network

Inputs to the model: an input dictionary where the key is the feature name and the value is a Keras Input layer

```
def _dnn_regressor(columns, dnn_hidden_units):
```
← **Define a function that takes a bunch of columns and a list of hidden dimensions as the input.**

```
    input_layers = {
        colname: tf.keras.layers.Input(
            name=colname, shape=(), dtype=tf.float32
        )
        for colname in _transformed_names(_DENSE_FLOAT_FEATURE_KEYS)
    }
    input_layers.update({
        colname: tf.keras.layers.Input(
            name=colname, shape=(), dtype='int32'
        )
        for colname in _transformed_names(_VOCAB_FEATURE_KEYS)
    })
```
← **Update the dictionary by creating Input layers for vocabulary-based categorical features.**

```
    input_layers.update({
        colname: tf.keras.layers.Input(
            name=colname, shape=(), dtype='int32'
        )
        for colname in _transformed_names(_BUCKET_FEATURE_KEYS)
    })
```
← **Update the dictionary by creating Input layers for bucketized features.**

```
    output = tf.keras.layers.DenseFeatures(columns)(input_layers)
    for numnodes in dnn_hidden_units:
        output = tf.keras.layers.Dense(numnodes, activation='tanh')(output)

    output = tf.keras.layers.Dense(1)(output)
```
← **Create a final regression layer that has one output node and a linear activation.**

```
    model = tf.keras.Model(input_layers, output)
    model.compile(
        loss='mean_squared_error',
        optimizer=tf.keras.optimizers.Adam(lr=0.001)
    )
    model.summary(print_fn=absl.logging.info)

    return model
```
← **Define the model using inputs and outputs.**

← **Compile the model. Note how it uses the mean squared error as the loss function.**

← **Print a summary of the model through the absl logger we defined at the beginning.**

We recursively compute the output by creating a sequence of Dense layers.

As input layers are defined as a dictionary, we use the DenseFeatures layer to generate a single tensor output.

We have defined the data in a columnar fashion, where each column is a TensorFlow feature column. Once the data defined in this way, we use a special layer called `tf.keras.layers.DenseFeatures` to process this data. The DenseFeatures layer accepts

- A list of feature columns
- A dictionary of `tf.keras.layers.Input` layers, where each Input layer is keyed with a column name found in the list of feature columns

With this data, the DenseFeatures layer can map each Input layer to the corresponding feature column and produce a single tensor output at the end (stored in the variable `output`) (figure 15.7).

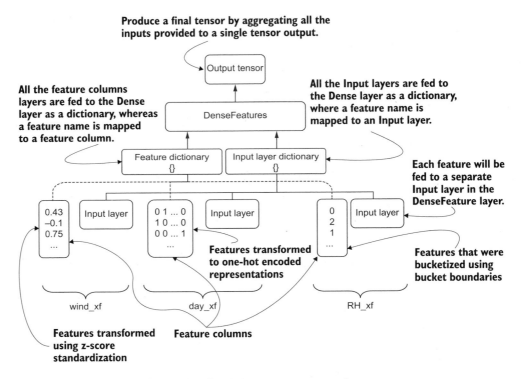

Figure 15.7   Overview of the functionality of the `DenseFeatures` layer

Then we recursively compute the output by flowing the data through several hidden layers. The sizes of these hidden layers (a list of integers) are passed in as an argument to the function. We will use tanh nonlinear activation for the hidden layers. The final hidden output goes to a single node regression layer that has a linear activation.

Finally, we compile the model with the Adam optimizer and mean-squared loss as the loss function. It is important to note that we have to use a regression-compatible loss function for the model. The mean-squared error is a very common loss function chosen for regression problems.

Type hinting in Python

You will see some functions defined differently than we have done in the past. For example, functions are defined as

```
def _build_keras_model() -> tf.keras.Model:
```

or

```
def run_fn(fn_args: tfx.components.FnArgs):
```

This is visual type-hinting and is available in Python. This means that the types are not enforced by the Python interpreter in any way; rather, they are a visual cue to make sure the developer uses the correct types of inputs and outputs. When defining arguments in a function, you can define the type of the data expected for that argument using the syntax `def <function>(<argument>: <type>):`. For example, in the function `run_fn()`, the first argument `fn_args` must be of type `tfx.components .FnArgs`.

Then you can also define the output returned by the function as `def <function> (<argument>: <type>) -> <return type>:`. For example, the returned object by `_build_keras_model()` function must be a `tf.keras.Model` object.

Some objects require complex data types that need to be created using multiple data types or custom data types (e.g., a list of strings). For this, you can use a built-in Python library called `typing`. `typing` allows you to define data types conveniently. For more information, refer to https://docs.python.org/3/library/typing.html.

In listing 15.8, we define a function that, given a set of training data filenames and evaluation data filenames, generates `tf.data.Dataset` objects for training and evaluation data. We define this special function as `_input_fn()`. `_input_fn()` takes in three things:

- `file_pattern`—A set of file paths, where files contain data
- `data_accessor`—A special object in TFX that creates a `tf.data.Dataset` by taking in a list of filenames and other configuration
- `batch_size`—An integer specifying the size of a batch of data

Listing 15.8   A function to generate a `tf.data.Dataset` using the input files

List of paths or patterns of input tfrecord files. It is a list of objects of type Text (i.e., strings).

The typing library defines the type of inputs to the function.

DataAccessor for converting input to RecordBatch

```
from typing import List, Text

def _input_fn(file_pattern: List[Text],
              data_accessor: tfx.components.DataAccessor,
```

A TFTransformOutput ┌──▷ `tf_transform_output: tft.TFTransformOutput,`
`                            batch_size: int = 200) -> tf.data.Dataset:` ◁──┤ **Represents the number of consecutive elements of the returned data set to combine in a single batch**

```
    return data_accessor.tf_dataset_factory(
        file_pattern,
        tfxio.TensorFlowDatasetOptions(
            batch_size=batch_size, label_key=_transformed_name(_LABEL_KEY)),
        tf_transform_output.transformed_metadata.schema)
```

You can see how we are using type hints for the arguments as well as the return object. The function returns a `tf.data.Dataset` obtained by calling the `tf_dataset_factory()` function with a list of file paths and data set options like batch size and label key. The label key is important for the `data_accessor` to determine input fields and the target. You can see that the data accessor takes in the schema from the `Transform` step as well. This helps the `data_accessor` to transform the raw examples to features and then separate the inputs and the label. With all the key functions explained, we now move on to see how all of these will be orchestrated in order to do the model training.

15.2.2 *Defining the model training*

The main task that's standing between us and a train model is the actual training of the model. The TFX component responsible for training the model (known as `Trainer`) expects a special function named `run_fn()` that will tell how the model should be trained and eventually saved (listing 15.9). This function takes in a special type of object called `FnArgs`, a utility object in TensorFlow that can be used to declare model training–related user-defined arguments that need to be passed to a model training function.

Listing 15.9   Running the Keras model training with the data

---

Define a function called run_fn that takes a tfx.components.FnArgs object as the input.

```
┌──▷ def run_fn(fn_args: tfx.components.FnArgs):                    Log the values in
                                                                   the fn_args object.
        absl.logging.info("="*50)
        absl.logging.info("Printing the tfx.components.FnArgs object")
        absl.logging.info(fn_args)
        absl.logging.info("="*50)

        tf_transform_output = tft.TFTransformOutput(               Convert the data in the
          fn_args.transform_graph_path                            CSV files to tf.data.Dataset
        )                                  ◁─── Load the tensorflow_   objects using the function
                                                transform graph.       _input_fn (discussed
        train_dataset = _input_fn(                                          soon).
          fn_args.train_files, fn_args.data_accessor, tf_transform_output,
   ⟿ 40                                                      ◁─────────────────────────┤
        )
        eval_dataset = _input_fn(
          fn_args.eval_files, fn_args.data_accessor, tf_transform_output,
   ⟿ 40                                                      ◁─────────────────────────┘
        )
```

```
                    model = _build_keras_model()                  ◄─────────────┐   Build the Keras model
                                                                                     using the previously
                    csv_write_dir = os.path.join(                                     defined function.
                      fn_args.model_run_dir,'model_performance'
                    )                                             ◄─────────────┐   Define a directory to store
                    os.makedirs(csv_write_dir, exist_ok=True)                        CSV logs produced by the
                                                                                     Keras callback CSVLogger.
   Define the      csv_callback = tf.keras.callbacks.CSVLogger(
   CSVLogger         os.path.join(csv_write_dir, 'performance.csv'), append=False
   callback.   └─▷ )
```

```
                                                           ┌── Fit the model using the data sets
                    model.fit(                     ◄───────┤   created and the hyperparameters
                        train_dataset,                     └── present in the fn_args object.
                        steps_per_epoch=fn_args.train_steps,
                        validation_data=eval_dataset,
                        validation_steps=fn_args.eval_steps,
                        epochs=10,
                        callbacks=[csv_callback]
                    )                                   ┌── Define signatures for the model. Signatures
                                                        │   tell the model what to do when data is sent
                    signatures = {               ◄──────┤   via an API call when the model is deployed.
                        'serving_default':
                            _get_serve_tf_examples_fn(
                                model, tf_transform_output
                            ).get_concrete_function(
                                tf.TensorSpec(
                                    shape=[None],
                                    dtype=tf.string,
                                    name='examples'
                                )
                            ),
```

```
   Save the         }
   model to         model.save(fn_args.serving_model_dir, save_format='tf',
   the disk.  └─▷       signatures=signatures)
```

Let's first check the method signature of the run_fn(). run_fn() takes in a single argument of type FnArgs as the input. As mentioned earlier, FnArgs is a utility object that stores a collection of key-value pairs that are useful for model training. Most of the elements in this object are populated by the TFX component itself. However, you also have the flexibility to pass some of the values. We will define some of the most important attributes in this object. But we will learn more about the full list of attributes once we see the full output produced by the TFX Trainer component. Table 15.2 provides you a taste of what is stored in this object. Don't worry if you don't fully understand the purpose of these elements. It will be clearer as we go through the chapter. Once we run the Trainer component, it will display the values used for every one of these attributes, as we have included logging statements to log the fn_args object. This will help us to contextualize these properties with the example we're running and understand them more clearly.

Table 15.2   An overview of the attributes stored in the `fn_args`-type object

Attribute	Description	Example
`train_files`	A list of train filenames	`['.../Transform/transformed_examples/16/Split-train/*'],`
`eval_files`	A list of evaluation/validation filenames	`['.../Transform/transformed_examples/16/Split-eval/*']`
`train_steps`	Number of training steps	100
`eval_steps`	Number of evaluation/validation steps	100
`schema_path`	Path to the schema generated by the TFX component `SchemaGen`	`'.../SchemaGen/schema/15/schema.pbtxt'`
`transform_graph_path`	Path to the transform graph generated by the TFX component `Transform`	`'.../SchemaGen/schema/15/schema.pbtxt'`
`serve_model_dir`	Output directory where the serve-able model will be saved	`'.../Trainer/model/17/Format-Serving'`
`model_run_dir`	Output directory where the model is saved	`'.../Trainer/model_run/17'`

The first important task done by this function is generating `tf.data.Dataset` objects for training and evaluation data. We have defined a special function called `_input_fn()` that achieves this (listing 15.8).

Once the data sets are defined, we define the Keras model using the `_build_keras_model()` function we discussed earlier. Then we define a `CSVLogger` callback to log the performance metrics over epochs, as we did earlier. As a brief review, the `tf.keras.callbacks.CSVLogger` creates a CSV file with all the losses and metrics defined during model compilation, logged every epoch. We will use the `fn_arg` object's `model_run_dir` attribute to create a path for the CSV file inside the model creation directory. This will make sure that if we run multiple training trials, each will have its own CSV file saved along with the model. After that, we call the `model.fit()` function as we have done countless times. The arguments we have used are straightforward, so we will not discuss them in detail and lengthen this discussion unnecessarily.

15.2.3   SignatureDefs: Defining how models are used outside TensorFlow

Once the model is trained, we have to store the model on disk so that it can be reused later. The objective of storing this model is to use this via a web-based API (i.e., a REST API) to query the model using inputs and get predictions out. This is typically how machine learning models are used to serve customers in an online environment. For

models to understand web-based requests, we need to define things called `Signature-`
`Defs`. A signature defines things like what an input or target to the model looks like
(e.g., data type). You can see that we have defined a dictionary called `signatures` and
passed it as an argument to `model.save()` (listing 15.9).

The `signatures` dictionary should have key-value pairs, where key is a signature
name and value is a function decorated with the `@tf.function` decorator. If you want
a quick refresher on what this decorator does, read the following sidebar.

The @tf.function decorator

The `@tf.function` decorator takes in a function that performs various TensorFlow
operations with TensorFlow operands, and then traces all the steps and turns that
into a data-flow graph. In most cases, TensorFlow requires a data-flow graph showing how inputs and outputs are connected between operations. Though in Tensor-
Flow 1.x you had to explicitly build this graph, TensorFlow 2.x onward doesn't
encumber the developer with this responsibility. Whenever a function is decorated
with the `@tf.function` decorator, it builds the data-flow graph for us.

It is also important to note that you cannot use arbitrary names as signature names.
TensorFlow has a set of defined signature names, depending on your needs. These are
defined in a special constant module in TensorFlow (http://mng.bz/o2Kd). There
are four signatures to choose from:

- `PREDICT_METHOD_NAME` (value: `'tensorflow/serving/predict'`)—This signature is used to predict the target for incoming inputs. This does not expect the
  target to be present.
- `REGRESS_METHOD_NAME` (value: `'tensorflow/serving/regress'`)—This signature can be used to regress from an example. It expects both an input and an
  output (i.e., target value) to be present in the HTTP request body.
- `CLASSIFY_METHOD_NAME` (value: `'tensorflow/serving/classify'`)—This is similar to `REGRESS_METHOD_NAME`, except for classification. This signature can be
  used to classify an example. It expects both an input and an output (i.e., target
  value) to be present in the HTTP.
- `DEFAULT_SERVING_SIGNATURE_DEF_KEY` (value: `'serving_default'`)—This is
  the default signature name. A model should at least have the default serving signature in order to be used via an API. If none of the other signatures are
  defined, requests will go through this signature.

We will only define the default signature here. Signatures take a TensorFlow function
(i.e., a function decorated with `@tf.function`) as a value. Therefore, we need to
define a function (which we will call `_get_serve_tf_examples_fn()`) that will tell
TensorFlow what to do with an input (see the next listing).

Listing 15.10   Parsing examples sent through API requests and predicting from them

Returns a function that parses a serialized
tf.Example and applies feature transformations

Get the feature transformations to
be performed as a Keras layer.

```
def _get_serve_tf_examples_fn(model, tf_transform_output):

    model.tft_layer = tf_transform_output.transform_features_layer()

    @tf.function
    def serve_tf_examples_fn(serialized_tf_examples):
        """Returns the output to be used in the serving signature."""
        feature_spec = tf_transform_output.raw_feature_spec()
        feature_spec.pop(_LABEL_KEY)
        parsed_features = tf.io.parse_example(serialized_tf_examples,
    feature_spec)
        transformed_features = model.tft_layer(parsed_features)
        return model(transformed_features)

    return serve_tf_examples_fn
```

The function decorated with
@tf.function to be returned

Get the
raw column
specifications.

Parse the
serialized example
using the feature
specifications.

Convert raw columns
to features using the
layer defined.

Return the output
of the model after
feeding the
transformed
features.

Remove the feature spec for
the label as we do not want
that during predictions.

Return the
TensorFlow
function.

The first important thing to note is that _get_serve_tf_examples_fn() returns a function (i.e., serve_tf_examples_fn), which is a TensorFlow function. The _get_serve_tf_examples_fn() accepts two inputs:

- Model—The Keras model we built during training time
- tf_transform_output—The transformation graph to convert raw data to features

This returned function should instruct TensorFlow on what to do with the data that came in through an API request once the model is deployed. The returned function takes serialized examples as inputs, parses them to be in the correct format as per the model input specifications, generates the output, and returns it. We will not dive too deeply into what the inputs and outputs are of this function, as we will not call it directly, but rather access TFX, which will access it when an API call is made.

In this process, the function first gets a raw feature specifications map, which is a dictionary of column names mapped to a Feature type. The Feature type describes the type of data that goes in a feature. For instance, for our data, the feature spec will look like this:

```
{
  'DC': VarLenFeature(dtype=tf.float32),
  'DMC': VarLenFeature(dtype=tf.float32),
  'RH': VarLenFeature(dtype=tf.int64),
  ...
  'X': VarLenFeature(dtype=tf.int64),
  'area': VarLenFeature(dtype=tf.float32),
```

```
        'day': VarLenFeature(dtype=tf.string),
        'month': VarLenFeature(dtype=tf.string)
}
```

It can be observed that different data types are used (e.g., float, int, string) depending on the data found in that column. You can see a list of feature types at https://www.tensorflow.org/api_docs/python/tf/io/. Next, we remove the feature having the _LABEL_KEY as it should not be a part of the input. We then use the tf.io.parse_example() function to parse the serialized examples by passing the feature specification map. The results are passed to a TransformFeaturesLayer (http://mng.bz/nNRa) that knows how to convert a set of parsed examples to a batch of inputs, where each input has multiple features. Finally, the transformed features are passed to the model, which returns the final output (i.e., predicted forest burnt area). Let's revisit the signature definition from listing 15.9:

```
signatures = {
    'serving_default':
        _get_serve_tf_examples_fn(
            model, tf_transform_output
        ).get_concrete_function(
            tf.TensorSpec(
                shape=[None],
                dtype=tf.string,
                name='examples'
            )
        ),
}
```

You can see that we are not simply passing the returning TensorFlow function of _get_serve_tf_examples_fn(). Instead, we call the get_concrete_function() on the return function (i.e., TensorFlow function). If you remember from our previous discussions, when you execute a function decorated with @tf.function, it does two things:

- Traces the function and creates the data-flow graph to perform the work of the function
- Executes the graph to return outputs

get_concrete_function() does the first task only. In other words, it returns the traced function. You can read more about this at http://mng.bz/v6K7.

15.2.4 *Training the Keras model with TFX Trainer*

We now have all the bells and whistles to train the model. To reiterate, we first defined a Keras model, defined a function to run the model training, and finally defined signatures that instruct the model how to behave when an HTTP request is sent via the API. Now we will train the model as a part of the TFX pipeline. To train the model, we are going to use the TFX Trainer component:

```
from tfx.components import Trainer
from tfx.proto import trainer_pb2
import tensorflow.keras.backend as K

K.clear_session()

n_dataset_size = df.shape[0]
batch_size = 40

n_train_steps_mod = 2*n_dataset_size % (3*batch_size)
n_train_steps = int(2*n_dataset_size/(3*batch_size))
if n_train_steps_mod != 0:
    n_train_steps += 1

n_eval_steps_mod = n_dataset_size % (3*batch_size)
n_eval_steps = int(n_dataset_size/(3*batch_size))
if n_eval_steps != 0:
    n_eval_steps += 1

trainer = Trainer(
    module_file=os.path.abspath("forest_fires_trainer.py"),
    transformed_examples=transform.outputs['transformed_examples'],
    schema=schema_gen.outputs['schema'],
    transform_graph=transform.outputs['transform_graph'],
    train_args=trainer_pb2.TrainArgs(num_steps=n_train_steps),
    eval_args=trainer_pb2.EvalArgs(num_steps=n_eval_steps))

context.run(trainer)
```

The code leading up to the `Trainer` component simply computes the correct number of iterations required in an epoch. To calculate that, we first get the total size of the data (remember that we stored our data set in the DataFrame df). We then used two hash buckets for training and one for evaluation. Therefore, we would have roughly two-thirds training data and one-third evaluation data. Finally, if the value is not fully divisible, we add +1 to incorporate the remainder of the data.

Let's investigate the instantiation of the `Trainer` component in more detail. There are several important arguments to pass to the constructor:

- `module_file`—Path to the Python module containing the `run_fn()`.
- `transformed_examples`—Output of the TFX `Transform` step, particularly the transformed examples.
- `schema`—Output of the TFX `SchemaGen` step.
- `train_args`—A `TrainArgs` object specifying training-related arguments. (To see the proto message defined for this object, see http://mng.bz/44aw.)
- `eval_args`—An `EvalArgs` object specifying evaluation-related arguments. (To see the proto message defined for this object, see http://mng.bz/44aw.)

This will output the following log. Due to the length of the log output, we have truncated certain parts of the log messages:

```
INFO:absl:Generating ephemeral wheel package for
⮕ '/home/thushv89/code/manning_tf2_in_action/Ch15-TFX-for-MLOps-in-
⮕ TF2/tfx/forest_fires_trainer.py' (including modules:
⮕ ['forest_fires_constants', 'forest_fires_transform',
⮕ 'forest_fires_trainer']).

...

INFO:absl:Training model.

...

43840.0703WARNING:tensorflow:11 out of the last 11 calls to <function
⮕ recreate_function.<locals>.restored_function_body at 0x7f53c000ea60>
⮕ triggered tf.function retracing. Tracing is expensive and the excessive
⮕ number of tracings could be due to (1) creating @tf.function repeatedly
⮕ in a loop, (2) passing tensors with different shapes, (3) passing
⮕ Python objects instead of tensors.

INFO:absl:_____
    _____
INFO:absl:Layer (type)                    Output Shape          Param #
⮕ Connected to
INFO:absl:=====================================================================
⮕ ===========

...

INFO:absl:dense_features (DenseFeatures)  (None, 31)                    0
⮕ DC_xf[0][0]
INFO:absl:
⮕ DMC_xf[0][0]
INFO:absl:
⮕ FFMC_xf[0][0]
...
INFO:absl:
⮕ temp_xf[0][0]
INFO:absl:
⮕ wind_xf[0][0]
INFO:absl:_____
⮕ _____

...

INFO:absl:Total params: 12,417

...

Epoch 1/10
9/9 [==============================] - ETA: 3s - loss: 43840.070 - 1s
⮕ 32ms/step - loss: 13635.6658 - val_loss: 574.2498
Epoch 2/10
9/9 [==============================] - ETA: 0s - loss: 240.241 - 0s
⮕ 10ms/step - loss: 3909.4543 - val_loss: 495.7877
...
```

```
Epoch 9/10
9/9 [==============================] - ETA: 0s - loss: 42774.250 - 0s
⮩ 8ms/step - loss: 15405.1482 - val_loss: 481.4183
Epoch 10/10
9/9 [==============================] - 1s 104ms/step - loss: 1104.7073 -
⮩ val_loss: 456.1211
...

INFO:tensorflow:Assets written to:
⮩ /home/thushv89/code/manning_tf2_in_action/Ch15-TFX-for-MLOps-in-
⮩ TF2/tfx/pipeline/examples/forest_fires_pipeline/Trainer/model/5/Format-
⮩ Serving/assets
INFO:absl:Training complete. Model written to
⮩ /home/thushv89/code/manning_tf2_in_action/Ch15-TFX-for-MLOps-in-
⮩ TF2/tfx/pipeline/examples/forest_fires_pipeline/Trainer/model/5/Format-
⮩ Serving. ModelRun written to
⮩ /home/thushv89/code/manning_tf2_in_action/Ch15-TFX-for-MLOps-in-
⮩ TF2/tfx/pipeline/examples/forest_fires_pipeline/Trainer/model_run/5
INFO:absl:Running publisher for Trainer
INFO:absl:MetadataStore with DB connection initialized
```

In the log message, we can see that the Trainer does a lot of heavy lifting. First, it creates a wheel package using the model training code defined in the forest_fires_trainer.py. wheel (extension `.whl`) is how Python would package a library. For instance, when you do `pip install tensorflow`, it will first download the wheel package with the latest version and install it locally. If you have a locally downloaded wheel package, you can use `pip install <path to wheel>`. You can find the resulting wheel package at the <path to pipeline root>/examples/forest_fires_pipeline/_wheels directory. Then it prints the model summary. It has an `Input` layer for every feature passed to the model. You can see that the `DenseFeatures` layer aggregates all these `Input` layers to produce a [None, 31]–sized tensor. As the final output, the model produces a [None, 1]–sized tensor. Then the model training takes place. You will see warnings such as

```
out of the last x calls to <function
⮩ recreate_function.<locals>.restored_function_body at 0x7f53c000ea60>
⮩ triggered tf.function retracing. Tracing is expensive and the excessive
⮩ number of tracings could be due to
```

This warning comes up when TensorFlow function tracing happens too many times. It can be a sign of poorly written code (e.g., the model getting recreated many times within a loop) and is sometimes unavoidable. In our case, it's the latter. The behavior of the Trainer module is causing this behavior, and there's not much we can do about that. Finally, the component writes the model as well as some utilities to a folder in the pipeline root. Here's what our pipeline root directory looks like so far (figure 15.8).

A major issue we can note in the Trainer's output log is the training and validation losses. For this problem, they are quite large. We are using the mean-squared error that is computed as

$$\frac{1}{N}\sum_{i=0}^{N}(y_1 - \hat{y}_1)^2$$

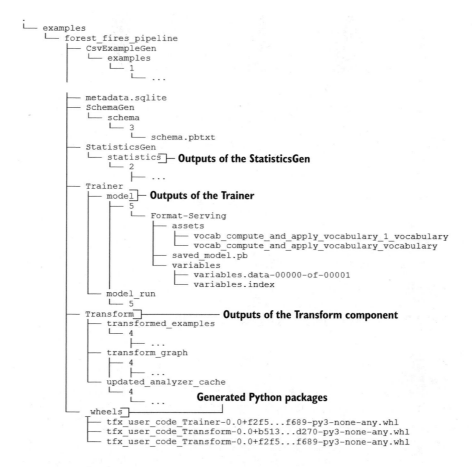

```
i
└── examples
    └── forest_fires_pipeline
        ├── CsvExampleGen
        │   └── examples
        │       └── 1
        │           └── ...
        │
        ├── metadata.sqlite
        ├── SchemaGen
        │   └── schema
        │       └── 3
        │           └── schema.pbtxt
        ├── StatisticsGen
        │   └── statistics ── Outputs of the StatisticsGen
        │       └── 2
        │           ├── ...
        ├── Trainer
        │   ├── model ── Outputs of the Trainer
        │   │   └── 5
        │   │       └── Format-Serving
        │   │           ├── assets
        │   │           │   ├── vocab_compute_and_apply_vocabulary_1_vocabulary
        │   │           │   └── vocab_compute_and_apply_vocabulary_vocabulary
        │   │           ├── saved_model.pb
        │   │           └── variables
        │   │               ├── variables.data-00000-of-00001
        │   │               └── variables.index
        │   └── model_run
        │       └── 5
        ├── Transform ──────────── Outputs of the Transform component
        │   ├── transformed_examples
        │   │   └── 4
        │   │       ├── ...
        │   ├── transform_graph
        │   │   ├── 4
        │   │   ├── ...
        │   └── updated_analyzer_cache
        │       └── 4
        │           └── ...        Generated Python packages
        └── wheels
            ├── tfx_user_code_Trainer-0.0+f2f5...f689-py3-none-any.whl
            ├── tfx_user_code_Transform-0.0+b513...d270-py3-none-any.whl
            └── tfx_user_code_Transform-0.0+f2f5...f689-py3-none-any.whl
```

Figure 15.8   The complete directory/file structure after running the Trainer

where N is the number of examples, y_i is the ith example, and $\hat{y}_1$ is the predicted value for i^{th} example. At the end of the training, we have a squared loss of around 481, meaning an error of around 22 hectares (i.e., 0.22 km^2) per example. This is not a small error. If you investigate this matter, you will realize this is largely caused by anomalies present in the data. Some anomalies are so large that they can skew the model heavily in the wrong direction. We will address this in an upcoming section in the chapter. You will be able to see the values in the FnArgs object passed to the run_fn():

```
INFO:absl:====================================================
INFO:absl:Printing the tfx.components.FnArgs object
INFO:absl:FnArgs(
    working_dir=None,
    train_files=['.../Transform/transformed_examples/16/Split-train/*'],
    eval_files=['.../Transform/transformed_examples/16/Split-eval/*'],
    train_steps=100,
```

```
        eval_steps=100,
        schema_path='.../SchemaGen/schema/15/schema.pbtxt',
        schema_file='.../SchemaGen/schema/15/schema.pbtxt',
        transform_graph_path='.../Transform/transform_graph/16',
        transform_output='.../Transform/transform_graph/16',
        data_accessor=DataAccessor(
            tf_dataset_factory=<function
    get_tf_dataset_factory_from_artifact.<locals>.dataset_factory at
    0x7f7a56329a60>,
            record_batch_factory=<function
    get_record_batch_factory_from_artifact.<locals>.record_batch_factory at
    0x7f7a563297b8>,
            data_view_decode_fn=None
        ),
        serving_model_dir='.../Trainer/model/17/Format-Serving',
        eval_model_dir='.../Trainer/model/17/Format-TFMA',
        model_run_dir='.../Trainer/model_run/17',
        base_model=None,
        hyperparameters=None,
        custom_config=None
    )
INFO:absl:==================================================
```

The following sidebar discusses how we can evaluate the model at this point in our discussion.

Evaluating the saved model

In the pipeline, our model will be served via an HTTP interface in the form of URLs. But rather than waiting to do that, let's load the model manually and use it to predict data. Doing so will provide us with two advantages:

- Verifying the model is working as intended
- Providing a deeper understanding of the format of the inputs and outputs of the model

We will not go into details about this in the book to keep our discussion focused on the pipeline. However, the code has been provided in the tfx/15.1_MLOps_with_tensorflow.ipynb notebook so you can experiment with it.

Next, we will discuss how we can detect anomalies present in the data and remove them to create a clean data set to train our model.

Detecting and removing anomalies

Our model is currently showing a validation loss of around 568. The loss used here is the mean-squared error. We have already seen that this means every prediction is 24 hectares (i.e., 0.24 km^2) off. This is no negligible matter. There are lots of outliers in our data, which could be a key reason we're seeing such large error margins. The following figure shows the statistics graph we created earlier.

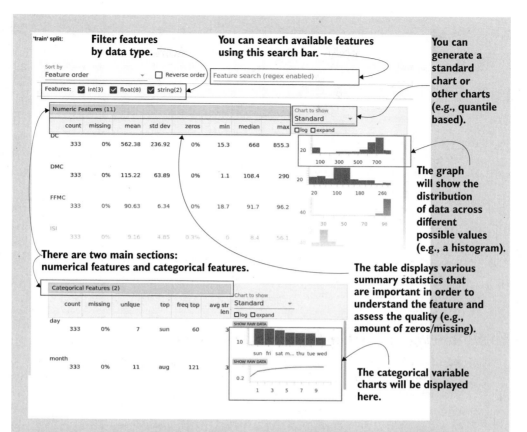

The summary statistics graphs generated for the data by the `StatisticsGen` **component**

You can see that some columns are heavily skewed. For example, the feature FFMC has the highest density, around 80–90, but has a range of 18.7–96.2.

To tackle this issue, we will use the `tensorflow_data_validation` (abbreviated as `tfdv`) library. It provides valuable functions like `tfdv.validate_statistics()`, which can be used to validate data against the data schema we generated earlier, as well as the `tfdv.display_anomalies()` function to list the anomalous samples. Furthermore, we can edit the schema in order to modify the criteria for outliers. For example, to change the maximum value allowed for the ISI feature, you can do the following:

```
isi_feature = tfdv.get_feature(schema, 'ISI')
isi_feature.float_domain.max = 30.0
```

Finally, you can visualize original data versus cleaned data using the `tfdv.visualize_statistics()` function. Finally, you can use the `ExampleValidator` object (http://mng.bz/XZxv) from the TFX pipeline to make sure there are no anomalies in your data set.

(continued)

Once you run this, you should get a smaller loss than previously. For example, in this experiment, a loss of ~150 on average was observed. This is a 75% reduction of the previous error. You can find the code for this in the tfx/15.1_MLOps_ with_tensor-flow.ipynb notebook.

Next, we'll look at a technology called Docker that is used for deploying models in isolated and portable environments. We will see how we can deploy our model in what is known as a Docker container.

EXERCISE 2

Instead of using one-hot encoding for day and month features and appending them to the categorical_columns variable, let's imagine you want to use embeddings to represent these features. You can use the feature column tf.feature_column.embedding_ column for this. Assume an embedding dimensionality of 32. You have the feature names of day and month columns stored in _VOCAB_FEATURE_KEYS (contains ['day', 'month']) and their dimensionality in _MAX_CATEGORICAL_FEATURE_VALUES (contains [7, 12]).

15.3   *Setting up Docker to serve a trained model*

You have developed a data pipeline and a robust model that can be used to predict the severity of forest fires based on the weather data. Now you want to go a step further and offer this as a more accessible service by deploying the model on a machine and enabling access through a REST API. This process is also known as productionizing a machine learning model. To do that, you are first going to create an isolated environment dedicated to model serving. The technology you will use is Docker.

> **CAUTION**   It is vitally important that you have Docker installed on your machine before proceeding further. To install Docker, follow the guide: https://docs .docker.com/engine/install/ubuntu/.

In TFX, you can deploy your model as a container, where the container is provisioned by Docker. According to the official Docker website, a Docker container is

> *a standard unit of software that packages up code and all its dependencies so the application runs quickly and reliably from one computing environment to another.*

> Source: https://www.docker.com/resources/what-container

Docker is a containerization technology that helps you run a software (or a microservice) isolated from the host. In Docker, you can create an image, which will instruct Docker with various specifications (e.g., OS, libraries, dependencies) that you need in the container for it to run the software correctly. Then a container is simply a run time instance of that image. This means you enjoy a higher portability as you can create a container on one computer and run it on another computer easily (as long as Docker is installed on two computers). Virtual machines (VMs) also try to achieve a similar goal. There are many resources out there comparing and contrasting Docker containers and VMs (e.g., http://mng.bz/yvNB).

As we have said, to run a Docker container, you first need a Docker image. Docker has a public image registry (known as Docker Hub) available at https://hub.docker .com/. The Docker image we are looking for is the TensorFlow serving image. This image has everything installed to serve a TensorFlow model, using the TensorFlow serving (https://github.com/tensorflow/serving), a sub-library in TensorFlow that can create a REST API around a given model so that you can send HTTP requests to use the model. You can download this image simply by running the following command:

```
docker pull tensorflow/serving:2.6.3-gpu
```

Let's break down the anatomy of this command. `docker pull` is the command for downloading an image. `tensorflow/serving` is the image name. Docker images are version controlled, meaning every Docker image has a version tag (it defaults to the latest if you don't provide one). `2.6.3-gpu` is the image's version. This image is quite large because it supports GPU execution. If you don't have a GPU, you can use `docker pull tensorflow/serving:2.6.3`, which is more lightweight. Once the command successfully executes, you can run

```
docker images
```

to list all the images you have downloaded. With the image downloaded, you can use the `docker run <options> <Image>` command to stand up a container using a given image. The command `docker run` is a very flexible command and comes with lots of parameters that you can set and change. We are using several of those:

```
docker run \
  --rm \
  -it \
  --gpus all \
  -p 8501:8501 \
  --user $(id -u):$(id -g) \
  -v ${PWD}/tfx/forest-fires-pushed:/models/forest_fires_model \
  -e MODEL_NAME=forest_fires_model \
  tensorflow/serving:2.6.3-gpu
```

It's important to understand the arguments provided here. Typically, when defining arguments in a shell environment, a single-dash prefix is used for single character–based arguments (e.g., -p) and a double-dash prefix is used for more verbose arguments (e.g., `--gpus`):

- `--rm`—Containers are temporary runtimes that can be removed after the service has run. `--rm` implies that the container will be removed after exiting it.
- `-it` (short for `-i` and `-t`)—This means that you can go into the container and interactively run commands in a shell within the container.

- `--gpus all`—This tells the container to ensure that GPU devices (if they exist) are visible inside the container.
- `-p`—This maps a network port in the container to the host. This is important if you want to expose some service (e.g., the API that will be up to serve the model) to the outside. For instance, TensorFlow serving runs on 8501 by default. Therefore, we are mapping the container's 8501 port to the host's 8501 port.
- `--user $(id -u):$(id -g)`—This means the commands will be run as the same user you're logged in as on the host. Each user is identified by a user ID and is assigned to one or more groups (identified by the group ID). You can pass the user and the group following the syntax `--user <user ID>:<group ID>`. For example, your current user ID is given by the command `id -u`, and the group is given by `id -g`. By default, containers run commands as `root` user (i.e., running via `sudo`), which can make your services more vulnerable to outside attacks. So, we use a less-privileged user to execute commands in the container.
- `-v`—This mounts a directory on the host to a location inside the container. By default, things you store within a container are not visible to the outside. This is because the container has its own storage space/volume. If you need to make the container see something on the host or vice versa, you need to mount a directory on the host to a path inside the container. This is known as *bind mounting*. For instance, here we expose our pushed model (which will be at `./tfx/forest-fires-pushed`) to the path `/models/forest_fires_model` inside the container.
- `-e`—This option can be used to pass special environment variables to the container. For example, the TensorFlow serving service expects a model name (which will be a part of the URL you need to hit in order to get results from the model).

This command is provided to you in the `tfx/run_server.sh` script in the Ch15-TFX-for-MLOps-in-TF2 directory. Let's run the `run_server.sh` script to see what we will get. To run the script

1 Open a terminal.
2 Move cd into the Ch15-TFX-for-MLOps-in-TF2/tfx directory.
3 Run `./run_server.sh`.

It will show an output similar to the following:

```
2.6.3-gpu: Pulling from tensorflow/serving
Digest:
➥ sha256:e55c44c088f6b3896a8f66d8736f38b56a8c5687c105af65a58f2bfb0bf90812
Status: Image is up to date for tensorflow/serving:2.6.3-gpu
docker.io/tensorflow/serving:2.6.3-gpu
2021-07-16 05:59:37.786770: I
tensorflow_serving/model_servers/server.cc:88] Building single TensorFlow
➥ model file config: model_name: forest_fires_model model_base_path:
➥ /models/forest_fires_model
```

```
2021-07-16 05:59:37.786895: I
tensorflow_serving/model_servers/server_core.cc:464] Adding/updating
➡ models.
2021-07-16 05:59:37.786915: I
tensorflow_serving/model_servers/server_core.cc:587]  (Re-)adding model:
➡ forest_fires_model
2021-07-16 05:59:37.787498: W
tensorflow_serving/sources/storage_path/file_system_storage_path_source.cc:
➡ 267] No versions of servable forest_fires_model found under base path
➡ /models/forest_fires_model. Did you forget to name your leaf directory
➡ as a number (eg. '/1/')?
...
```

Of course, it will not work fully, as the directory we provided as model's location is not populated. We still need to do a few things to have the final model in the right location.

In the next section, we will complete the rest of our pipeline. We will see how we can automatically evaluate as new models are trained in the pipeline, deploy the model if the performance is good, and enable prediction from the model using a REST API (i.e., a web-based API).

EXERCISE 3
Say you want to download the TensorFlow Docker image (it has the name `tensorflow/tensorflow`) with version 2.5.0 and stand up a container that mounts the /tmp/inputs directory on your computer to /data volume within the container. Additionally, you would like to map the 5000 port in the container to 5000 on your computer. How would you do this using Docker commands? You can assume you're running the commands as the root within the container.

15.4   *Deploying the model and serving it through an API*

You now have a data pipeline, a trained model, and a shell script that can run a Docker container with everything needed to run the model and the API to access the model. Now, using some services provided in TFX, you will deploy the model within a Docker container and make it available to be used through an API. In this process, you will run steps to validate the infrastructure (e.g., the container can be run and is healthy) and the model (i.e., when a new version of the model comes out, check if it is better than the last one), and finally, if everything is good, deploy the model on the infrastructure.

It has been a long journey. Let's look back and see what we've accomplished so far. We have used the following TFX components:

- `CsvExampleGen`—Load data as `TFRecord` objects from CSV files.
- `StatisticsGen`—Basic statistics and visualizations about the distribution of various columns in the CSV data.
- `SchemaGen`—Generate the schema/template of the data (e.g., data types, domains, minimum/maximum values allowed, etc.).

- `Transform`—Transform the raw columns to features using the operations available in the `tensorflow_transform` library (e.g., one-hot encoding, bucketizing).
- `Trainer`—Define a Keras model, train it using the transformed data, and save to the disk. This model has a signature called serving default, which instructs the model what to do for an incoming request.
- `ExampleValidator`—This is used to validate that training and evaluation examples used adhere to the defined schema and can be used to detect anomalies.

15.4.1 *Validating the infrastructure*

Using TFX, you can ensure almost everything works well when you have a fully automated pipeline. We will discuss one such step here: the infrastructure validation step. In this, `tfx.components.InfraValidator` will automatically

- Create a container using a specific version of the TensorFlow serving image provided
- Load and run the model in it
- Send several requests to make sure the model responds
- Stand down the container

Let's look at how we can use this component to validate the local Docker configuration we set up in the previous section (see the next listing).

Listing 15.11   Defining the `InfraValidator`

Holds a collection of model serving–related specifications

InfraValidator needs the location of the model it's going to validate.

Source for the data that will be used to build API calls to the model

Defines the version/tag of the TensorFlow serving Docker Image to be used

Defines which model signature to use

Defines how many requests to make to the model

Holds a collection of specifications related to the specific call made to the model

Says to the InfraValidator that we are going to use the local Docker service to test

```
from tfx.components import InfraValidator
from tfx.proto import infra_validator_pb2

infra_validator = InfraValidator(
    model=trainer.outputs['model'],

    examples=example_gen.outputs['examples'],
    serving_spec=infra_validator_pb2.ServingSpec(
        tensorflow_serving=infra_validator_pb2.TensorFlowServing(
            tags=['2.6.3-gpu']
        ),
        local_docker=infra_validator_pb2.LocalDockerConfig(),
    ),
    request_spec=infra_validator_pb2.RequestSpec(
        tensorflow_serving=infra_validator_pb2.TensorFlowServingRequestSpec(
            signature_names=['serving_default']
        ),
        num_examples=5
    )
)

context.run(infra_validator)
```

The `InfraValidator`, just like any other TFX component, expects several arguments to run accurately:

- `model`—The Keras model returned by the `Trainer` component.
- `examples`—Loaded raw examples given by the `CSVExampleGen`.
- `serving_spec`—Expects a `ServingSpec` protobuf message. It will specify the version of the TensorFlow serving Docker image and whether to use local Docker installation (which is done here).
- `request_spec`—A `RequestSpec` protobuf message that will specify the signature that needs to be reached to verify the model is working.

If this step completes error-free, you will see the files shown in figure 15.9 in the pipeline root.

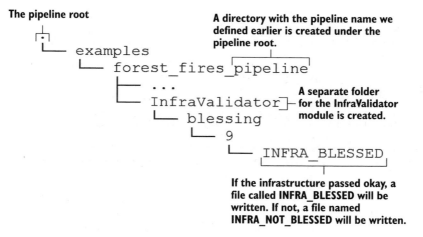

Figure 15.9   The directory/file structure after running the `InfraValidator`

You can see a file called INFRA_BLESSED appearing in the `InfraValidator` subdirectory. This brings us to the concept of *blessing*. TFX will bless certain elements in the pipeline when they run successfully. Once blessed, it will create a file with the suffix BLESSED. If the step fails, then a file with the suffix NOT_BLESSED will be created. Blessing helps to discriminate between things that ran fine and things that failed. For examples, once blessed, we can be sure that the infrastructure is working as expected. This means that things like

- Standing up a container
- Loading the model
- Reaching a defined API endpoint

can be performed without issues.

15.4.2 *Resolving the correct model*

Moving forward, we will define a resolver. The purpose of the resolver is to resolve a special artifact (like a model) that can evolve over time using a well-defined strategy (e.g., the model with the lowest validation error). Then the resolver informs subsequent components (e.g., the model Evaluator component we will be defining next) which artifact version to use. As you might have guessed, we will use the resolver to resolve the trained Keras model in the pipeline. So, if you run the pipeline multiple times, the resolver will make sure the latest and greatest model is used in the downstream components:

```
from tfx import v1 as tfx

model_resolver = tfx.dsl.Resolver(
    strategy_class=tfx.dsl.experimental.LatestBlessedModelStrategy,
    model=tfx.dsl.Channel(type=tfx.types.standard_artifacts.Model),
    model_blessing=tfx.dsl.Channel(
        type=tfx.types.standard_artifacts.ModelBlessing
    )
).with_id('latest_blessed_model_resolver')

context.run(model_resolver)
```

When defining the resolver to validate a model, we will define three things:

- `strategy_class` (a class from the `tfx.dsl.components.common.resolver` `.ResolverStrategy` namespace)—Defines the resolution strategy. There are two strategies supported currently: the latest blessed model (i.e., the model that has passed a set of defined evaluation checks) and the latest model.
- `model` (`tfx.dsl.Channel`)—Wraps a TFX artifact-type model in a `tfx.dsl` `.Channel` object. A `tfx.dsl.Channel` is an TFX-specific abstract concept that connects data consumers and data producers. For example, a channel is required to choose the correct model from a pool of models available in the pipeline.
- `model_blessing` (`tfx.dsl.Channel`)—Wraps a TFX artifact of type `Model-` `Blessing` in a `tfx.dsl.Channel` object.

You can look at various artifacts that you can wrap in a `tfx.dsl.Channel` object at http://mng.bz/2nQX.

15.4.3 *Evaluating the model*

We will evaluate the model as the last step before pushing it to a designated production environment. Essentially, we will define several evaluation checks that the model needs to pass. When a model is passed, TFX will bless the model. Otherwise, TFX will leave the model unblessed. We will learn later how to check if the model was blessed. To define the evaluation checks, we are going to use the `tensorflow_model_analysis` library. The first step is to define an evaluation configuration that specifies the checks:

```
import tensorflow_model_analysis as tfma

eval_config = tfma.EvalConfig(
    model_specs=[
        tfma.ModelSpec(label_key='area')
    ],
    metrics_specs=[
        tfma.MetricsSpec(
            metrics=[
                tfma.MetricConfig(class_name='ExampleCount'),
                tfma.MetricConfig(
                    class_name='MeanSquaredError',
                    threshold=tfma.MetricThreshold(
                        value_threshold=tfma.GenericValueThreshold(
                            upper_bound={'value': 200.0}
                        ),
                        change_threshold=tfma.GenericChangeThreshold(
                            direction=tfma.MetricDirection.LOWER_IS_BETTER,
                            absolute={'value': 1e-10}
                        )
                    )
                )
            ]
        )
    ],
    slicing_specs=[
        tfma.SlicingSpec(),
        tfma.SlicingSpec(feature_keys=['month'])
    ])
```

Define a model spec containing the label feature name.

Define a list of metric specifications.

Get the number of examples evaluated on.

Define the mean-squared error as a metric.

Define a threshold upper bound as a check.

Slicing specs define how data needs to be partitioned when evaluating.

Define Change in error (compared to previous models) as a check (i.e., the lower the error the better).

Evaluate on the whole data set without slicing (i.e., an empty slice).

Evaluate on partitioned data, where data is partitioned based on the month field.

The `EvalConfig` is quite a mouthful. Let's go through it slowly. We have to define three things: model specifications (as a `ModelSpec` object), metric specifications (as a list of `MetricsSpec` objects), and slicing specifications (as a list of `SlicingSpec` objects). The `ModelSpec` object can be used to define the following:

- `name`—An alias model name that can be used to identify the model in this step.
- `model_type`—A string identifying the type of model. Allowed values include `tf_keras`, `tf_estimator`, `tf_lite`, and `tf_js`, `tf_generic`. For Keras models like ours, type is automatically derived.
- `signature_name`—The model signature to be used for inference. By default, `serving_default` is used.
- `label_key`—The name of the label feature in the examples.
- `label_keys`—For multi-output models, a list of label keys is used.
- `example_weight_key`—An optional key (or feature name) to retrieve example weights if present.

For more information about the `ModelSpec` object, refer to http://mng.bz/M5wW. In a `MetricsSpec` object, the following attributes can be set:

- metrics—A list of MetricConfig objects. Each MetricConfig object takes a class_name as an input. You can choose any class defined in tfma.metrics.Metric (http://mng.bz/aJ97) or tf.keras.metrics.Metric (http://mng.bz/gwmV) namespaces.

The SlicingSpec defines how the data needs to be partitioned during evaluation. For example, for time series problems, you will need to see how the model performs across different months or days. For that, SlicingSpec is a handy config. SlicingSpec has the following arguments:

- feature_keys—Can be used to define a feature key on which you can partition the data. For example, for feature key month, it will create a partition of data for each month by selecting data having a specific month. If not passed, it will return the whole data set.

Note that TFX uses the evaluation split you defined at the very beginning of the pipeline (i.e., when implementing the CsvExampleGen component) if not provided. In other words, all the metrics are evaluated on the evaluation split of the data set. Next, it defines two criteria for the evaluation to pass:

- The mean squared error is smaller than 200.
- The mean squared loss has improved by 1e - 10.

A model will be blessed (i.e., marked as passed) if these two conditions are satisfied for a newly trained model. Remember that we have seen a loss of around 150 in our better model, so let's set the threshold to 200. The metrics added here are in addition to those saved when using the model.compile() step. For example, since the mean-squared error is used as the loss, it will already be a part of the metrics (even without defining it in eval_config).

Finally, we define the Evaluator (http://mng.bz/e7BQ) that will take in a model and run the evaluation checks defined in eval_config. You can define a TFX Evaluator as follows by passing in values for examples, model, baseline_model, and eval_config arguments. baseline_model is resolved by the Resolver:

```
from tfx.components import Evaluator

evaluator = Evaluator(
    examples=example_gen.outputs['examples'],
    model=trainer.outputs['model'],
    baseline_model=model_resolver.outputs['model'],
    eval_config=eval_config)
context.run(evaluator)
```

Unfortunately, running the Evaluator will not provide the results you need. It will, in fact, fail the evaluation. At the bottom of the log, you will see an output like this

```
INFO:absl:Evaluation complete. Results written to
 ➡ .../pipeline/examples/forest_fires_pipeline/Evaluator/evaluation/14.
INFO:absl:Checking validation results.
```

```
INFO:absl:Blessing result False written to
➥ .../pipeline/examples/forest_fires_pipeline/Evaluator/blessing/14.
```

which says `Blessing` resulted `False`. It's still a mystery why the model failed, given it showed only a loss of around 150 and we set the threshold to 200. To understand what happened, we need to look at the results written to the disk. If you look inside the `<pipeline root>/ examples\forest_fires_pipeline\Evaluator\<execution ID>` directory, you will see files like validation, metrics, and so forth. Along with the `tensorflow_model_analysis` library, these can provide invaluable insights to understand what when wrong. The `tensorflow_model_analysis` library provides several convenient functions to load the results stored in these files:

```
import tensorflow_model_analysis as tfma

validation_path = os.path.join(
    evaluator.outputs['evaluation']._artifacts[0].uri, "validations"
)
validation_res = tfma.load_validation_result(validation_path)

print('='*20, " Output stored in validations file ", '='*20)
print(validation_res)
print("="*75)
```

This will print out

```
metric_validations_per_slice {
  slice_key {
    single_slice_keys {
      column: "month"
      bytes_value: "sep"
    }
  }
  failures {
    metric_key {
      name: "mean_squared_error"
    }
    metric_threshold {
      value_threshold {
        upper_bound {
          value: 200.0
        }
      }
    }
    metric_value {
      double_value {
        value: 269.11712646484375
      }
    }
  }
}
validation_details {
  slicing_details {
```

```
    slicing_spec {
    }
    num_matching_slices: 12
  }
}
```

You can clearly see what happened. It says that the slice created for the month `"sep"` resulted in an error of `269`, which is why our evaluation failed. If you want details about all of the slices used and their results, you can inspect the metrics file:

```
metrics_path = os.path.join(
    evaluator.outputs['evaluation']._artifacts[0].uri, "metrics"
)
metrics_res = tfma.load_metrics(metrics_path)

print('='*20, " Output stored in metrics file ", '='*20)
for r in metrics_res:
    print(r)
    print('-'*75)
print("="*75)
```

This would output the following. You will only see a small snippet of the full output here to save space:

```
slice_key {
  single_slice_keys {
    column: "month"
    bytes_value: "sep"
  }
}
metric_keys_and_values {
  key {
    name: "loss"
  }
  value {
    double_value {
      value: 269.11712646484375
    }
  }
}
metric_keys_and_values {
  key {
    name: "mean_squared_error"
  }
  value {
    double_value {
      value: 269.11712646484375
    }
  }
}
metric_keys_and_values {
  key {
    name: "example_count"
  }
}
```

```
value {
  double_value {
    value: 52.0
  }
}
}
}


--------------------------------------------------------------------
slice_key {
}
metric_keys_and_values {
  key {
    name: "loss"
  }
  value {
    double_value {
      value: 160.19691467285156
    }
  }
}
metric_keys_and_values {
  key {
    name: "mean_squared_error"
  }
  value {
    double_value {
      value: 160.19691467285156
    }
  }
}
metric_keys_and_values {
  key {
    name: "example_count"
  }
  value {
    double_value {
      value: 153.0
    }
  }
}
}
...
```

This output sheds more light on what happened. Since we used the example count as one of the metrics, we can see the number of examples in each slice. For example, in month May, there's only one example present in the evaluation split, which is most probably an outlier. To fix this, we will bump up the threshold to 300. Once you do that, you need to rerun the Evaluator, and you will see from the Evaluator's logs that our model passes the checks:

```
INFO:absl:Evaluation complete. Results written to
➥ .../pipeline/examples/forest_fires_pipeline/Evaluator/evaluation/15.
INFO:absl:Checking validation results.
INFO:absl:Blessing result True written to
➥ .../pipeline/examples/forest_fires_pipeline/Evaluator/blessing/15.
```

The best way to address this is to identify why the month of `"sep"` is giving such a large value while other months are on par with or below the overall loss value. After identifying the issue, we should identify remediation steps to correct this (e.g., reconsidering outlier definitions). On that note, we will move on to the next part of our pipeline.

15.4.4   *Pushing the final model*

We have reached the last steps in our pipeline. We need to define a Pusher. The Pusher (http://mng .bz/pOZz) is responsible for pushing a blessed model (i.e., a model that passes the evaluation checks) to a defined production environment. The production environment can simply be a local location in your file system:

```
from tfx.components import Pusher
from tfx.proto import pusher_pb2

pusher = Pusher(
  model=trainer.outputs['model'],
  model_blessing=evaluator.outputs['blessing'],
  infra_blessing=infra_validator.outputs['blessing'],
  push_destination=pusher_pb2.PushDestination(
    filesystem=pusher_pb2.PushDestination.Filesystem(
        base_directory=os.path.join('forestfires-model-pushed'))
  )
)
context.run(pusher)
```

The Pusher takes the following elements as arguments:

- `model`—The Keras model returned by the Trainer component
- `model_blessing`—Evaluator component's blessed state
- `infra_blessing`—InfraValidator's blessed state
- `push_destination`—A destination to be pushed to as a `PushDestination` protobuf message

If the step runs successfully, you will have a model saved in a directory called forestfires-model-pushed in our pipeline root.

15.4.5   *Predicting with the TensorFlow serving API*

The very last step is to retrieve the model from the pushed destination and start a Docker container based on the TensorFlow serving image we downloaded. The Docker container will provide an API that we can ping with various requests.

Let's look at how the API fits into the big picture in more detail (figure 15.10). The machine learning model sits behind an API. The API defines various HTTP endpoints you can ping (through Python or a package like curl). These endpoints will be in the form of a URL and can expect parameters in the URL or data embedded in the request body. The API is served via a server. The server exposes a network port in

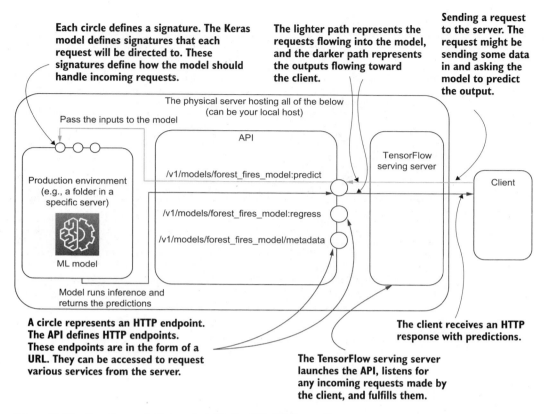

Figure 15.10   How the model interacts with the API, the TensorFlow server, and the client

which clients can communicate with the server. The client can send requests to the server using the format <host name>:<port>/<end point>. We will discuss what the request actually looks like in more detail.

To start the container, simply

1   Open a terminal
2   Move the cd into the Ch15-TFX-for-MLOps-in-TF2/tfx directory
3   Run ./run_server.sh

Next, in the Jupyter notebook, we will send a HTTP POST request. There are two main types of HTTP requests: GET and POST. Refer the sidebar if you're interested in the differences. An HTTP POST request is a request that not only contains a URL to reach and header information, but also contains a payload, which is necessary for the API to complete the request. For example, if we are hitting the API endpoint corresponding to the serving_default signature, we have to send an input to predict with.

GET vs. POST requests

GET and POST are HTTP methods. HTTP is a protocol that defines how a client and a server should communicate. A client will send requests, and the server will listen for requests on a specific network port. The client and the server don't necessarily need to be two separate machines. In our case, the client and the server are both on the same machine.

Every time you visit a website by typing a URL, you are making a request to that specific website. A request has the following anatomy (http://mng.bz/OowE):

- *A method type*—GET or POST
- *A path*—The URL to reach the endpoint of the server you want to reach
- *A body*—Any large payload that needs the client to complete the request (e.g., the input for a machine learning prediction service)
- *A header*—Additional information needed for the server (e.g., the type of data sent in the body)

The main difference is that GET is used to request data, as opposed to a POST request, which is used to post or send data to the server (which can optionally return something). A GET request will not have a request body, whereas a POST request will have a request body. Another difference is that GET requests can be cached, whereas POST requests will not be cached, making them more secure for sensitive data. You can read more about this at http://mng.bz/YGZA.

We will define a request body, which contains the signature name we want to hit and the input we want to predict for. Next, we will use the `requests` library in Python to send a request to our TensorFlow model server (i.e., Docker container). In this request, we will define the URL to reach (automatically generated by the TensorFlow model server) and the payload to carry. If the request is successful, we should get a valid prediction as the output:

```
import base64
import json
import requests

req_body = {
  "signature_name": "serving_default",

  "instances":
    [
          str(base64.b64encode(
              b"{\"X\": 7,\"Y\":
 4,\"month\":\"oct\",\"day\":\"fri\",\"FFMC\":60,\"DMC\":30,\"DC\":200,\
 "ISI\":9,\"temp\":30,\"RH\":50,\"wind\":10,\"rain\":0}]")
              )
    ]

}
```

```
data = json.dumps(req_body)

json_response = requests.post(
    'http://localhost:8501/v1/models/forest_fires_model:predict',
    data=data,
    headers={"content-type": "application/json"}
)
predictions = json.loads(json_response.text)
```

The first thing we do is define a request with a specific request body. The requirements for the request body are defined at https://www.tensorflow.org/tfx/serving/api_rest. It is a dictionary of key-value pairs that should have two keys: `signature_name` and `instances`. `signature_name` defines which signature to invoke in the model, and `instances` will contain the input data. Note that we're not passing input data in its raw form. Rather, we use base64 encoding. It encodes a byte stream (i.e., a binary input) to an ASCII text string. You can read more about this at http://mng .bz/1o4g. You can see that we are first converting our dictionary to a byte-stream (i.e., with a `b"<data>"` format) and then using base64 encoding on that. If you remember from our previous discussion on writing the model serve function (which had the signature `def serve_tf_examples_fn(serialized_tf_examples):`), it expects a serialized set of examples. Serialization is done by converting the data to a byte stream.

When the data is ready, we use the `requests` library to create a POST request for the API. First, we define a header to say that the content or payload we're passing is JSON. Next, we send a POST request via `requests.post()` giving the URL, which is in http://<server's hostname>:<port>/v1/models/<model name>:predict format, data (i.e., the JSON payload), and the header. This is not the only API endpoint available to us. There are other endpoints as well (https://www.tensorflow.org/tfx/serving/api_rest). There are four main endpoints that are available:

- *http://<server's hostname>:<port>/v1/models/<model name>:predict*—Predicts the output value using the model and the data passed in the request. Does not require a target to be available for the provided input.
- *http:// <server's hostname>:<port>/v1/models/<model name>:regress*—Used in regression problems. Used when both inputs and target are available (i.e., an error can be calculated).
- *http:// <server's hostname>:<port>/v1/models/<model name>:classify*—Used in classification problems. Used when both inputs and target are available (i.e., an error can be calculated).
- *http:// <server's hostname>:<port>/v1/models/<model name>/metadata*—Provides metadata about available endpoints/model signatures.

This will return some response. If the request was successful, it will have the response; otherwise, it will contain an HTTP error. You can see various HTTP status/error codes at http://mng.bz/Pn2P. In our case, we should get something like

```
{'predictions': [[2.77522683]]}
```

This means our model has successfully processed the input and produced a valid prediction. We can see that the model has returned a prediction that is well within the possible range of values we saw during our data exploration. This concludes our discussion of TensorFlow Extended (TFX).

EXERCISE 4

How would you send multiple inputs in your HTTP request to the model? Assume you have the following two inputs that you want to predict for using the model.

	Example 1	Example 2
X	9	7
Y	6	4
month	aug	aug
day	fri	fri
FFMC	91	91
DMC	248	248
DC	553	553
ISI	6	6
temp	20.5	20.5
RH	58	20
wind	3	0
rain	0	0

To pass multiple values for that input in an HTTP request, you can append more examples to the instances list in the JSON data.

Summary

- MLOps defines a workflow that will automate most of the steps, from collecting data to delivering a model trained on that data.
- Productionization involves deploying a trained model with a robust API to access the model, enabling customers to use the model for its designed purpose. The API provides several HTTP endpoints, which are in the form of URLs, which clients can use to communicate with the server.
- In TFX, you define a MLOps pipeline as a series of TFX components.
- TFX has components to load data (CsvExampleGen), generate basic statistics and visualizations (StatisticsGen), infer the schema (SchemaGen), and convert raw columns to features (Transform).

- For a Keras model to be served via HTTP requests, signatures are required.
  - Signatures define the data format of inputs and outputs as well as the steps that need to happen in order to produce the output via a TensorFlow function (e.g., a function decorated with `@tf.function`).
- Docker is a containerization technology that can be used to encapsulate a unit of software as a single container and can be ported easily between different environments (or computers).
- Docker runs a unit of software in a container.
- TFX provides validation components for validating infrastructure and the model. TFX can stand up a container and make sure it's running as expected, as well as make sure the model passes various evaluation criteria (e.g., loss being smaller than a threshold), ensuring a high-quality model.
- Once the model is pushed to a production environment, we start a Docker container (based on the TensorFlow serving image) that will mount the model into the container and serve it via an API. We can make HTTP requests (with the inputs embedded) to generate predictions.

Answers to exercises

Exercise 1

```
outputs = {}

# Treating dense features
outputs[_transformed_name('DC')] = tft.scale_to_0_1(
    sparse_to_dense(inputs['DC'])
)


# Treating bucketized features
outputs[_transformed_name('temp')] = tft.apply_buckets(
    sparse_to_dense(inputs['temp']), bucket_boundaries=[(20, 30)])
```

Exercise 2

```
categorical_columns = [
    tf.feature_column.embedding_column(
        tf.feature_column.categorical_column_with_identity(
            key,
            num_buckets=num_buckets,
            default_value=0
        ),
        dimension=32
    ) for key, num_buckets in zip(
        _transformed_names(_VOCAB_FEATURE_KEYS),
        _MAX_CATEGORICAL_FEATURE_VALUES
    )
```

Exercise 3

```
docker run -v /tmp/inputs:/data -p 5000:5000 tensorflow/tensorflow:2.5.0
```

Exercise 4

```python
req_body = {
  "signature_name": "serving_default",

  "instances":
    [
        str(base64.b64encode(
            b"{\"X\": 9,\"Y\":
6,\"month\":\"aug\",\"day\":\"fri\",\"FFMC\":91,\"DMC\":248,\"DC\":553,
\"ISI\":6,\"temp\":20.5,\"RH\":58,\"wind\":3,\"rain\":0}]")
        ),
        str(base64.b64encode(
            b"{\"X\": 7,\"Y\":
4,\"month\":\"aug\",\"day\":\"fri\",\"FFMC\":91,\"DMC\":248,\"DC\":553,
\"ISI\":6,\"temp\":20.5,\"RH\":20,\"wind\":0,\"rain\":0}]")
        ),

    ]

}
```

appendix A
Setting up the environment

In this appendix, you will configure the development and runtime environments on your computer. Two installation procedures are given: one for the Unix-based environments and one for Windows environments. Note that we will keep our Unix environment discussion focused mostly on Ubuntu and not MacOS. This is because, for machine learning and deep learning, Ubuntu is more popular and better supported than MacOS. However, we will list the resources you need to run this on MacOS.

A.1 In a Unix-based environment

Our discussion will be split into three sections. In the first section, we will discuss setting up a virtual Python environment to install the required libraries to run the code. Next, we will discuss things needed for GPU support. Finally, we will discuss doing the same on MacOS.

A.1.1 Creating a virtual Python environment with Anaconda distribution (Ubuntu)

In this section, we will discuss the steps for setting up a conda environment (a term used to describe virtual Python environments created via the Anaconda software package) in Ubuntu:

1 Install Anaconda on your Linux system (https://docs.anaconda.com/anaconda/install/linux/).
2 Open a terminal and open the ~/.bashrc file with your favourite text editor (e.g., for vim, type vim ~/.bashrc).
3 Add the following lines to the end of the file (with the placeholder filled with your path):

```
if ! [[ "$PATH" == *"anaconda3"* ]]; then
  export PATH=${PATH}:<your anaconda3 installation path>/bin
fi
```

4 Save and close the editor.

5 Open a new command line terminal.

6 Set up a new conda virtual environment by running `conda create -n manning .tf2 python=3.9`.

7 (Recommended) Create a folder named code in your home folder, where you will store code locally, and go into the folder using `cd ~/code`.

8 Clone the code repository hosted on Github using `git clone https://github .com/thushv89/manning_tf2_in_action.git`. Make sure you have Git installed on your operating system.

9 Move `cd` into the cloned code repository with `cd manning_tf2_in_action`.

10 Activate the environment with

    a Anaconda < 4.4: `source activate manning.tf2`

    b Anaconda >= 4.4: `conda activate manning.tf2`

11 Install the required libraries using `pip install -r requirements.txt`.

A.1.2 *Prerequisites for GPU support (Ubuntu)*

INSTALLING THE NVIDIA DRIVER

Make sure you have installed the latest NVIDIA graphics driver for your GPU. You can find the driver installers at http://mng.bz/xnKe. You may run into problems with the subsequent steps of getting GPU support for TensorFlow if you don't install the latest drivers.

INSTALLING CUDA

In this section, we will install CUDA 11.2, as we are using a TensorFlow version higher than 2.5.0. However, you need to pick the right CUDA version suitable for your TensorFlow version, as specified at https://www.tensorflow.org/install/source#gpu. The CUDA versions for the most recent TensorFlow versions are listed in table A.1.

Table A.1   CUDA versions supported by latest TensorFlow versions

TensorFlow version	CUDA version
2.4.x	11.0
2.8.x	11.2
2.9.x	11.2

To install the desired CUDA version, complete the following steps:

1 Go to the https://developer.nvidia.com/cuda-toolkit-archive page. This will show you all the available versions of CUDA that you can download.

2 Go to the desired CUDA version by clicking on it, and you will be shown a page like the one in figure A.1. For example, figure A.1 depicts the options for downloading CUDA version 11.7 for the Ubuntu distribution.

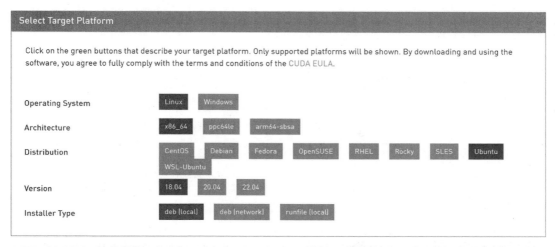

Figure A.1 CUDA download page (Ubuntu installation)

3 Make sure you have execution rights for the downloaded file (e.g., on Ubuntu, you can run chmod a+x <path to the downloaded file> through the terminal to provide execution privileges).

4 Install the downloaded package by opening it through the command line terminal (e.g., on Ubuntu, simply go to the download directory and run the installation with ./<file name>).

Once the installation is complete, the installation path needs to be added to a special environment variable:

1 Open a terminal, and open the ~/.bashrc file with your favorite text editor (e.g., for vim, type vim ~/.bashrc).

2 Add the following lines to the end of the file. For example, the path might look like /usr/local/cuda-11.0:

```
if ! [[ "$PATH" == *"cuda"* ]]; then
  export PATH=${PATH}:<path to CUDA>/bin
fi

export LD_LIBRARY_PATH=<path to CUDA>/lib64
```

3 Save and close the editor.

INSTALLING CuDNN

Similar to CUDA, the cuDNN version needs to be picked carefully. Table A.2 lists the cuDNN versions supported by the latest TensorFlow versions. To get the full list, visit https://www.tensorflow.org/install/source#gpu.

Table A.2 cuDNN versions supported by the latest TensorFlow versions

TensorFlow version	cuDNN version
2.4.x	8.0
2.6.x	8.1
2.9.x	8.1

First, download the preferred cuDNN package by following the instructions and prompts at https://developer.nvidia.com/cudnn. To install cuDNN, follow the instructions provided at http://mng.bz/AyQK.

A.1.3 Notes on MacOS

Unfortunately, CUDA is no longer actively supported by NVIDIA, as it is not recognized as a dominant development environment for CUDA-related development work (http://mng.bz/ZAlO). You can still install Anaconda, create a virtual environment, and install TensorFlow to carry development work. However, you might not be able to run any TensorFlow computations (that execute CUDA implementations underneath) on your NVIDIA GPU (if one exists).

To install Anaconda on MacOS, follow the guide provided at https://docs.anaconda.com/anaconda/install/mac-os/. The guide for managing conda environments is provided at http://mng.bz/R4V0.

A.2 In Windows Environments

In this section, we will discuss how to install a virtual environment with Windows and ensure GPU support.

A.2.1 Creating a Virtual Python Environment (Anaconda)

This section discusses the steps to create a conda environment on a Windows host:

1 Install Anaconda on your Windows system (https://docs.anaconda.com/anaconda/install/linux/), which will also install a CLI (command line interface) for executing Anaconda-specific commands.
2 Open the Anaconda Prompt by typing Anaconda Prompt in the search bar of the start menu (figure A.2).

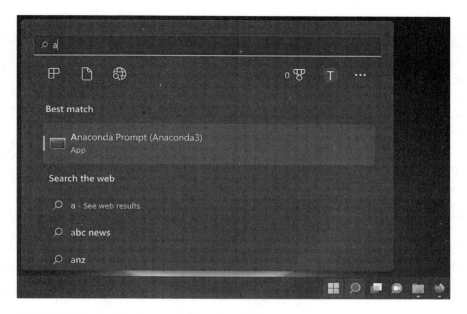

Figure A.2   Opening the Anaconda Prompt on Windows

3 In the terminal, run `conda create -n manning.tf2 python=3.9` to set up a conda virtual environment.
4 (Recommended) Create a folder named code in your home folder (e.g., `C:\Users\<username>\Documents`), where we will store code locally and go into the folder using `cd C:\Users\<username>\Documents`.
5 If not already installed, install Git for Windows (e.g., https://git-scm.com/download/win).
6 Clone the code repository hosted on Github using `git clone https://github.com/thushv89/manning_tf2_in_action.git`.
7 Move `cd` into the cloned code repository with `cd manning_tf2_in_action`.
8 Activate the environment with `conda activate manning.tf2`.
9 Install the required libraries using `pip install -r requirements.txt`.

A.2.2   *Prerequisites for GPU support*

In this section, we will discuss several prerequisites to make sure the GPU is recognized and working as expected.

INSTALLING THE NVIDIA DRIVER

Make sure you have installed the latest NVIDIA graphics driver for your GPU. You can find the driver installers at http://mng.bz/xnKe. If you don't install the latest drivers, you could run into problems with the subsequent steps of getting GPU support for TensorFlow.

INSTALLING CUDA

In this section, we will install CUDA 11.2, as we are using a TensorFlow version higher than 2.5.0. However, you need to pick the right CUDA version suitable for your TensorFlow version, as specified at https://www.tensorflow.org/install/source#gpu.

To install the desired CUDA version, complete the following steps:

1 Go to the https://developer.nvidia.com/cuda-toolkit-archive page. This will show you all the available versions of CUDA that you can download.

2 Go to the desired CUDA version by clicking on it, and you will be shown a page like figure A.3. For example, figure A.3 depicts the options that would be chosen to fetch CUDA 11.7 for the Windows operating system.

3 Run the downloaded .exe as the administrator and follow the prompts.

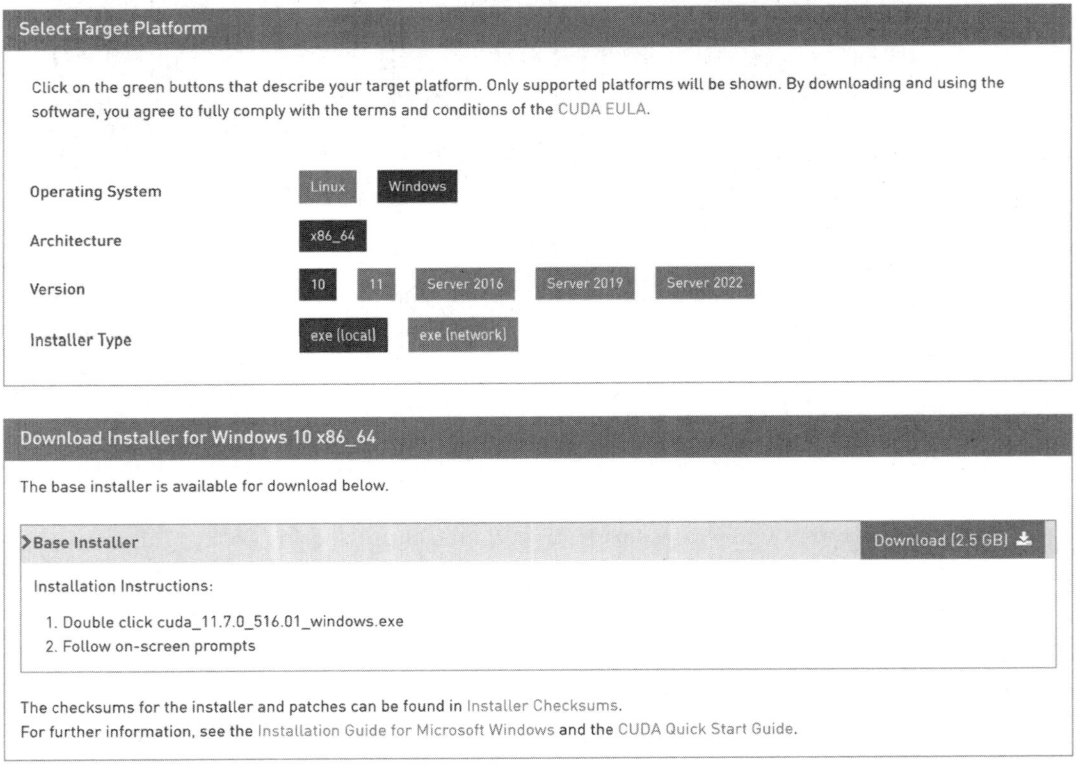

Select Target Platform

Click on the green buttons that describe your target platform. Only supported platforms will be shown. By downloading and using the software, you agree to fully comply with the terms and conditions of the CUDA EULA.

Operating System	Linux	Windows
Architecture	x86_64
Version	10	11	Server 2016	Server 2019	Server 2022
Installer Type	exe (local)	exe (network)

Download Installer for Windows 10 x86_64

The base installer is available for download below.

> Base Installer   Download (2.5 GB) ⬇

Installation Instructions:

1. Double click cuda_11.7.0_516.01_windows.exe
2. Follow on-screen prompts

The checksums for the installer and patches can be found in Installer Checksums.
For further information, see the Installation Guide for Microsoft Windows and the CUDA Quick Start Guide.

Figure A.3   CUDA download page (Windows installation)

Once the installation is complete, the installation path needs to be added to a special environment variable:

1 Open the Environment variables window by selecting "Edit the system environment variable" from the start menu (figure A.4).

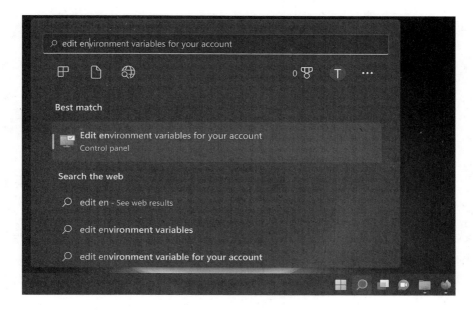

Figure A.4 Opening the system properties window

2 Add the following paths to the path variables, as outlined in table A.3. Figure A.5 shows how environment variables can be added/modified on Windows.

Table A.3 The path variables that need to be added and modified

PATH	\<path to your CUDA installation\>\bin
CUDA_PATH	\<path to your CUDA installation\>

To add a new path, click New and add the path.

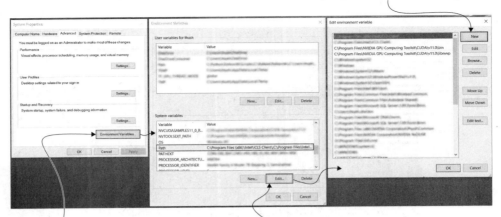

Click the Environment Variables button to open the window to the right.

Select the variable you want to edit and select Edit, which will open the window to the right.

Figure A.5   Steps to follow in order to add/modify a path variable

INSTALLING CuDNN

Similar to CUDA, the cuDNN version needs to be picked carefully. Table A.4 lists the cuDNN versions supported by the latest TensorFlow versions. To get the full list, visit https://www.tensorflow.org/install/source#gpu.

Table A.4   cuDNN versions supported by the latest TensorFlow versions

TensorFlow version	cuDNN version
2.4.x	8.1
2.5.x	8.1
2.6.x	8.0

First, download the preferred cuDNN package following the instructions and prompts at https://developer.nvidia.com/cudnn. To install cuDNN, follow the instructions provided at http://mng.bz/AyQK.

A.3   *Activating and deactivating the conda environment*

Once the conda environment is created, complete the following steps to activate or deactivate the environment.

On Windows (through the Anaconda Prompt) (figure A.6)

1 Run `conda activate <environment name>` to activate the environment.
2 Run `conda deactivate` to deactivate the currently active environment.

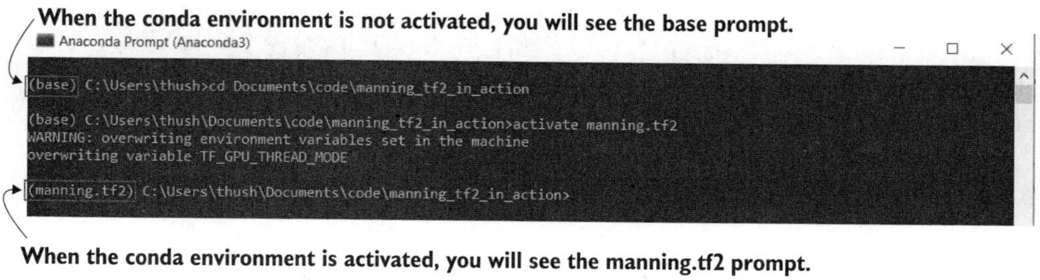

When the conda environment is not activated, you will see the base prompt.

When the conda environment is activated, you will see the manning.tf2 prompt.

Figure A.6   Activating a conda environment

On Ubuntu (through the terminal)

1 Run `source activate <environment name>` (Anaconda < 4.4) or `conda activate <environment name>` (Anaconda >= 4.4) to activate the environment.
2 Run `conda deactivate` to deactivate the currently active environment.

A.4 Running the Jupyter Notebook server and creating notebooks

We will be writing code and executing it using a Jupyter Notebook server. Specifically, we will start the Jupyter Notebook server, which will provide you a dashboard (a webpage) to create Jupyter Notebooks. The Jupyter Notebook is an interactive Python runtime environment. This means you can write code in the Jupyter Notebooks and run different code snippets on demand. This is because code can be separated into what are known as *notebook cells*. Let's see how we can start a Jupyter Notebook server and start coding:

1 Open the command line terminal (e.g., Ubuntu terminal or the Windows Anaconda Prompt), and activate the virtual environment `manning.tf2` if you haven't already.
2 Go into the directory you downloaded code to using `cd` in the CLI (e.g., `cd C:\Users\<user>\Documents\code\manning_tf2_in_action`).
3 Run the command `jupyter notebook` in the CLI.
4 This should open the Jupyter Notebook server's landing page on your default browser.
5 Now you can navigate the folder structure within that directory, open any notebook, and run it (figure A.7).
6 Once a notebook is opened, you have the ability to do various things, such as creating code cells, running code cells, and so on (figure A.8).

A.5 Miscellaneous notes

To make the plotting capability provided in TensorFlow/Keras work, you installed a Python package called `graphviz`. You might need to append the path to this library (e.g., `<path to Anaconda>\envs\manning.tf2\Library\bin\graphviz` if you used Anaconda installation) to the PATH variable of your operating system.

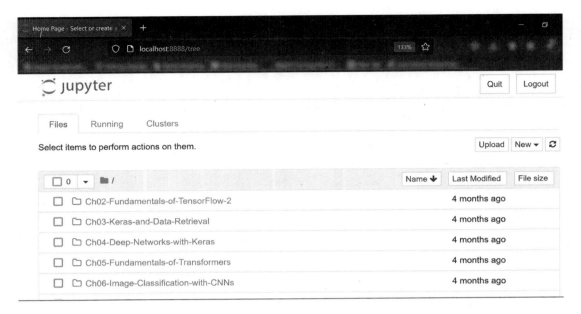

Figure A.7   The landing page created by the Jupyter Notebook server

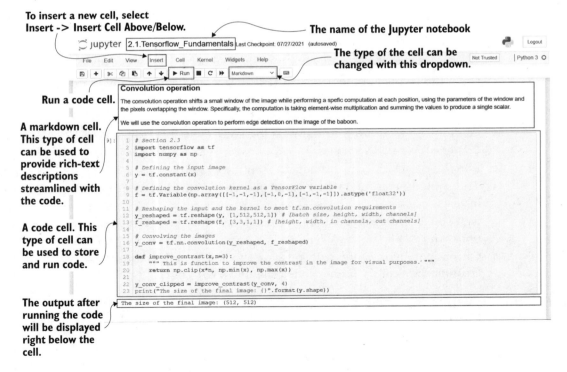

Figure A.8   An overview of a Jupyter Notebook

appendix B
Computer vision

B.1 Grad-CAM: Interpreting computer vision models

Grad-CAM (which stands for gradient class activation map) was introduced in chapter 7 and is a model interpretation technique introduced for deep neural networks by Ramprasaath R. Selvaraju et al. in "Grad-CAM: Visual Explanations from Deep Networks via Gradient-based Localization" (https://arxiv.org/pdf/1610.02391.pdf). Deep networks are notorious for their inexplicable nature and are thus termed *black boxes*. Therefore, we must do some analysis and ensure that the model is working as intended.

Let's refresh our memory on the model we implemented in chapter 7: a pretrained Inception-based model called InceptionResNet v2, topped with a softmax classifier that has 200 nodes (i.e., the same as the number of classes in our image classification data set, TinyImageNet; see the following listing).

Listing B.1 The InceptionResNet v2 model we defined in chapter 7

```
import tensorflow as tf
import tensorflow.keras.backend as K
from tensorflow.keras.applications import InceptionResNetV2
from tensorflow.keras.models import Sequential
from tensorflow.keras.layers import Input, Dense, Dropout

K.clear_session()

def get_inception_resnet_v2_pretrained():
    model = Sequential([
        Input(shape=(224,224,3)),
        InceptionResNetV2(include_top=False, pooling='avg'),
        Dropout(0.4),
        Dense(200, activation='softmax')
    ])
```

- **Add a dropout layer.**
- **Define a model using the Sequential API.**
- **Define an input layer to take in a 224 × 224 × 3–sized batch of images.**
- **Download and use the pretrained InceptionResNetV2 model (without the built-in classifier).**
- **Add a new classifier layer that has 200 nodes.**

```
    loss = tf.keras.losses.CategoricalCrossentropy()
    adam = tf.keras.optimizers.Adam(learning_rate=0.0001)
    model.compile(loss=loss, optimizer=adam, metrics=['accuracy'])
    return model

model = get_inception_resnet_v2_pretrained()
model.summary()
```

If you print the summary of this model, you will get the following output:

```
Model: "sequential"

Layer (type)                    Output Shape           Param #
================================================================
inception_resnet_v2 (Model)     (None, 1536)           54336736
_____
dropout (Dropout)               (None, 1536)           0
_____
dense (Dense)                   (None, 200)            307400
================================================================
Total params: 54,644,136
Trainable params: 54,583,592
Non-trainable params: 60,544
```

As you can see, the InceptionResNet v2 model is considered a single layer in our model. In other words, it's a nested model, where the outer model (sequential) has an inner model (inception_resnet_v2). But we need more transparency, as we are going to access a particular layer inside the inception_resnet_v2 model in order to implement Grad-CAM. Therefore, we are going to "unwrap" or remove this nesting and have the model described by layers only. We can achieve this using the following code:

```
K.clear_session()

model = load_model(os.path.join('models','inception_resnet_v2.h5'))

def unwrap_model(model):
    inception = model.get_layer('inception_resnet_v2')
    inp = inception.input
    out = model.get_layer('dropout')(inception.output)
    out = model.get_layer('dense')(out)
    return Model(inp, out)

unwrapped_model = unwrap_model(model)

unwrapped_model.summary()
```

Essentially what we are doing is taking the existing model and changing the input of it slightly. After taking the existing model, we change the input to the input layer of the inception_resnet_v2 model. With that, we define a new model (which essentially uses the same parameters as the old model). Then you will see the following output. There are no more models within models:

```
Model: "model"

_____
Layer (type)                    Output Shape            Param #     Connected
to
================================================================================
================
input_2 (InputLayer)          [(None, None, None,  0

_____
conv2d (Conv2D)                 (None, None, None, 3 864
    input_2[0][0]

_____
batch_normalization (BatchNorma (None, None, None, 3 96
    conv2d[0][0]

_____
activation (Activation)         (None, None, None, 3 0
    batch_normalization[0][0]

_____


...

_____
conv_7b (Conv2D)                (None, None, None, 1 3194880
    block8_10[0][0]

_____
conv_7b_bn (BatchNormalization) (None, None, None, 1 4608
    conv_7b[0][0]

_____
conv_7b_ac (Activation)         (None, None, None, 1 0
    conv_7b_bn[0][0]

_____
global_average_pooling2d (Globa (None, 1536)             0
    conv_7b_ac[0][0]

_____
dropout (Dropout)               (None, 1536)             0
    global_average_pooling2d[0][0]

_____
dense (Dense)                   (None, 200)              307400
    dropout[1][0]
================================================================================
================
Total params: 54,644,136
```

```
Trainable params: 54,583,592
Non-trainable params: 60,544
```

Next, we are going to make one more change: introduce a new output to our model. Remember that we used the functional API to define our model. This means we can define multiple outputs in our model. The output we need is the feature maps produced by the last convolutional layer in the inception_resnet_v2 model. This is a core part of the Grad-CAM computations. You can get the layer name of the last convolutional layer by looking at the model summary of the unwrapped model:

```
last_conv_layer = 'conv_7b' # This is the name of the last conv layer of the
    model

grad_model = Model(
    inputs=unwrapped_model.inputs,
    outputs=[
        unwrapped_model.get_layer(last_conv_layer).output,
        unwrapped_model.output
    ]
)
```

With our model ready, let's move on to the data. We will use the validation data set to inspect our model. Particularly, we will write a function (listing B.2) that takes in the following:

- image_path (str)—Path to an image in the data set.
- val_df (pd.DataFrame)—A pandas DataFrame that contains a mapping from an image name to wnid (i.e., a WordNet ID). Remember that a wnid is a special coding used to identify a specific class of objects.
- class_indices (dict)—A wnid (string) to class (integer between 0-199) mapping. This keeps information about which wnid is represented by which index in the final output layer of the model.
- words (pd.DataFrame)—A pandas DataFrame that contains a mapping from a wnid to a human-readable description of the class.

Listing B.2 Retrieving the transformed image, class index, and human-readable label

**Reads in the val_annotations.txt. This will create a data frame that
has a mapping from an image filename to a wnid (i.e., WordNet ID).**

```
img_path = 'data/tiny-imagenet-200/val/images/val_434.JPEG'

val_df = pd.read_csv(
    os.path.join('data','tiny-imagenet-200', 'val', 'val_annotations.txt'),
    sep='\t', index_col=0, header=None
)

with open(os.path.join('data','class_indices'),'rb') as f:
    class_indices = pickle.load(f)
```

Load the class indices that map a wnid to a class index (integer).

```
words = pd.read_csv(
    os.path.join('data','tiny-imagenet-200', 'words.txt'),
    sep='\t', index_col=0, header=None
)
```

This will create a data frame that has a mapping from a wnid to a class description.

```
def get_image_class_label(img_path, val_df, class_indices, words):
    """ Returns the normalized input, class (int) and the label name for a
    given image"""

    img = np.expand_dims(
        np.asarray(
            Image.open(img_path).resize((224,224)
        ), dtype='float32'), axis=0
    )
```

Loads the image given by the filepath. First, we add an extra dimension to represent the batch dimension.

Resize the image to a 224 × 224–sized image.

```
    img /= 127.5
    img -= 1
```

Bring image pixels to a range of [-1, 1].

If the image is grayscale, repeat the image three times across the channel dimension to have the same format as an RGB image.

```
    if img.ndim == 3:
        img = np.repeat(np.expand_dims(img, axis=-1), 3, axis=-1)

    _, img_name = os.path.split(img_path)
```

Get the wnid of the image.

```
    wnid = val_df.loc[img_name,1]
    cls = class_indices[wnid]
    label = words.loc[wnid, 1]
    return img, cls, label
```

Get the class index of the image.

Get the string label of the class.

```
# Test the function with a test image
img, cls, label = get_image_class_label(img_path, val_df, class_indices, words)
```

Run the function for an example image.

The get_image_class_label() function takes the arguments specified and loads the image given by the image_path. First, we resize the image to a 224 × 224–sized image. We also add an extra dimension at the beginning to represent the image as a batch of one image. Then it performs a specific numerical transformation (i.e., divide element-wise by 127.5 and subtract 1). This is a special transformation that is used to train the InceptionResNet v2 model. Afterward, we get the class index (i.e., an integer) and the human-readable label of that class using the data frames and class_indices we passed into the function. Finally, it returns the transformed image, the class index, and the label of the class the image belongs to.

The next listing shows how the Grad-CAMs are computed for images. We will use 10 images to compute Grad-CAMs for each individually.

Listing B.3 Computing Grad-CAM for 10 images

```
# Define a sample probe set to get Grad-CAM
image_fnames = [
    os.path.join('data','tiny-imagenet-200', 'val','images',f) \
    for f in [
        'val_9917.JPEG', 'val_9816.JPEG', 'val_9800.JPEG', 'val_9673.JPEG',
        'val_9470.JPEG',
```

```
        'val_4.JPEG', 'val_127.JPEG', 'val_120.JPEG', 'val_256.JPEG',
    'val_692.JPEG'
    ]
]

grad_info = {}
for fname in image_fnames:
    img, cls, label = get_image_class_label(fname, val_df, class_indices, words)

    with tf.GradientTape() as tape:
        conv_output, preds = grad_model(img)
        loss = preds[:, cls]

    grads = tape.gradient(loss, conv_output)

    weights = tf.reduce_mean(grads, axis=(1, 2), keepdims=True)
    grads *= weights

    grads = tf.reduce_sum(grads, axis=(0,3))
    grads = tf.nn.relu(grads)

    grads /= tf.reduce_max(grads)
    grads = tf.cast(grads*255.0, 'uint8')

    grad_info[fname] = {'image': img, 'class': cls, 'label':label, 'gradcam':
    grads}
```

Get the normalized input, class(int), and label (string) for each image.

We compute the output of the model in the GradientTape context.

We only take the loss corresponding to the class index of the input image.

This will enable us to later access the gradients that appeared during the computation.

Get the gradients of the loss with respect to the last convolutional feature map.

Compute and apply weights.

Collapse the feature maps to a single channel to get the final heatmap.

Normalize the values to be in the range of 0–255.

Store the computed GradCAMs in a dictionary to visualize later.

To compute the Grad-CAM for one image, we follow the following procedure. First, we get the transformed image, class index, and label for a given image path.

Next is the most important step of this computation! You know that, given an image and a label, the final loss is computed as the sum of class-specific losses for all the available classes. That is, if you imagine a one-hot encoded label and a probability vector output by the model, we compute element-wise loss between each output node. Here each node represents a single class. To compute the gradient map, we first compute the gradients of the class-specific loss only for the true label of that image, with respect to the output of the last convolutional layer. This gives a tensor the same size as the output of the last convolutional layer. It is important to note the difference between the typical loss we use and the loss used here. Typically, we sum the loss across all classes, whereas in Grad-CAM, we only consider the loss of the specific node that corresponds to the true class of the input.

Note how we are computing the gradients. We use something called the Gradient-Tape (http://mng.bz/wo1Q). It's an innovative piece of technology from TensorFlow. Whenever you compute something in the context of a GradientTape, it will record the gradients of all those computations. This means that when we compute the output in the context of a GradientTape, we can access the gradients of that computation later.

Then we do a few more transformations. First, we compute weights for each channel of the output feature map. The weights are simply the mean value of that feature map. The feature map values are multiplied by those weights. We then sum the output across all the channels. This means we will get an output with a width and height that have a single channel. This is essentially a heatmap, where a high value indicates more importance at a given pixel. To clip negative values to 0, we then apply ReLU activation on the output. As the final normalization step, we bring all the values to a range of 0–255 so that we can superimpose this on the actual image as a heatmap. Then it's a simple matter of using the `matplotlib` library to plot the images and overlap the Grad-CAM outputs we generated on top of the images. If you want to see the code for this, please refer to the Ch07-Improving-CNNs-and-Explaining/7.3.Interpreting_CNNs_Grad-CAM.ipynb notebook. The final output will look like figure B.1.

Figure B.1   Visualization of the Grad-CAM output for several probe images. The redder an area in the image, the more the model focuses on that part of the image. You can see that our model has learned to understand some complex scenes and separate the model that it needs to focus on.

B.2   *Image segmentation: U-Net model*

In chapter 8, we discussed the DeepLab v3: an image segmentation model. In this section we will discuss a different image segmentation model known as U-Net. It has a different architecture compared to a DeepLab model and is quite commonly used in the rea world. Therefore, it's a model worth learning about.

B.2.1   *Understanding and defining the U-Net model*

The U-Net model is essentially two mirrored fully convolutional networks that act as the encoder and the decoder, with some additional connections that connect parts of the encoder to parts of the decoder.

> **Background of U-Net**
>
> U-Net was introduced in the paper "U-Net: Convolution Networks for Biomedical Image Segmentation" (https://arxiv.org/pdf/1505.04597.pdf) and has its origins in biomedical image segmentation. The name U-net is derived from what the network looks like. It is still a popular pick for segmentation tasks in biology/medicine domains and has been shown to work well for more general-purpose tasks as well.

First, we will look at the original U-Net model introduced in the paper. Later, we will slightly change the direction of our discussion to make it more suited to the problem at hand. The original model consumed a $572 \times 572 \times 1$–sized image (i.e., a grayscale image) and outputted a $392 \times 392 \times 2$–sized image. The network was trained to identify/segment cell boundaries from bodies. Therefore, the two channels in the output represent a binary output of whether the pixel belongs to a cell boundary.

The encoder consists of several downsampling modules, which gradually downsample the input. A downsampling module consists of two convolution layers and one max pooling layer. Specifically, a downsampling module comprises

- A 3×3 convolution layer (with valid padding) $\times 2$
- A 2×2 max-pooling layer (except in the last downsampling module)

A series of such downsampling layers brings the $572 \times 572 \times 1$–sized input to a $28 \times 28 \times 1024$–sized output.

Next, the decoder consists of several upsampling layers. Specifically, each decoder upsampling module consists of

- A 2×2 transpose convolution layer
- A 3×3 convolution layer (with valid padding) $\times 2$

You might already be wondering, what is a transpose convolution layer? Transpose convolution is what you get if you reverse the computations happening in a convolution layer. Instead of the convolution operation reducing the size of the output (i.e., using strides), transpose convolution *increases* the size of the output (i.e., upsamples the input). This is also known as *fractional striding*, as increasing the stride leads to larger outputs when using transpose convolution. This is illustrated in figure B.2.

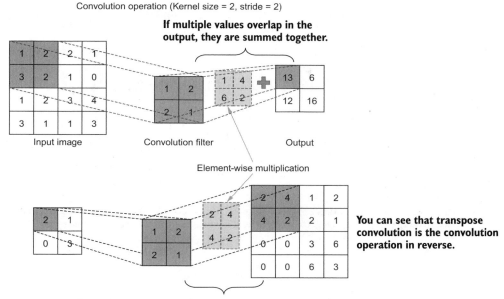

Figure B.2 Standard convolution versus transpose convolution. A positive stride on standard convolution leads to a smaller output, whereas a positive stride on transpose convolution leads to a bigger image.

Finally, there are skip connections that connect interim layers of the encoder to interim layers of the decoder. This is an important architectural design, as this provides the much needed spatial/contextual information to the decoder that otherwise would have been lost. Particularly, the output of the encoder's i^{th} level output is concatenated to the output of the decoder's n-i^{th} level input (e.g., the output of the first level [of size $568 \times 568 \times 64$] is concatenated to the input of the last level of the decoder [of size $392 \times 392 \times 64$]; figure B.3). In order to do so, the encoder's output first needs to be cropped slightly to match the corresponding decoder layer's output.

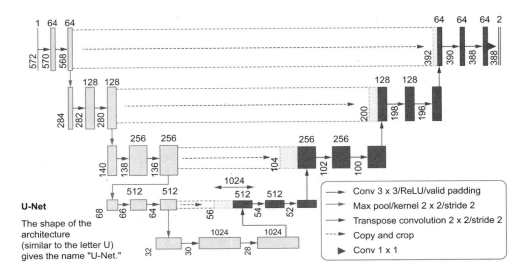

Figure B.3   The original U-Net model proposed. The light blocks represent the encoder, and the dark blocks represent the decoder. The vertical numbers represent the size of the output (height and width) at a given position, and the number on top represents the number of filters.

B.2.2   *What's better than an encoder? A pretrained encoder*

If you use the original network as is for the Pascal VOC data set, you will likely be very disappointed with its performance. There could be several reasons behind this behavior:

- The data in the Pascal VOC is much more complex than what the original U-Net was designed for. For example, as opposed to the images containing simple cell structures in black and white, we have RGB images containing complex scenes in the real world.
- As a fully convolution network, U-Net is highly regularized (due to the small number of parameters). This number of parameters is not enough to solve the complex task we have with adequate accuracy.
- As a network that started with a random initialization, it needs to learn to solve the task without the pretrained knowledge from a pretrained model.

In line with this reasoning, let's discuss a few changes that we will make to the original U-Net architecture. We will be implementing a U-Net network that has

- A pretrained encoder
- A larger number of filters in each decoder module

The pretrained encoder we will use is a ResNet-50 model (https://arxiv.org/pdf/1512.03385.pdf). It is one of the pioneering residual networks that made waves in the computer vision community a few years ago. We will look at ResNet-50 on the surface only, as we will discuss this model in detail in our section on the DeepLab v3 model. The ResNet-50 model consists of several convolution blocks, followed by a global average pooling layer and a fully connected final prediction layer with softmax activation. The convolution block is the innovative part of the model (denoted by B in figure B.4). The original model has 16 convolution blocks organized into 5 groups. We will only use the first 13 blocks (i.e., first 4 groups). A single block consists of three convolution layers (1×1 convolution layer with stride 2, 3×3 convolution layer, and 1×1 convolution layer), batch normalization, and residual connections, as shown in figure B.4. We discussed residual connections in depth in chapter 7.

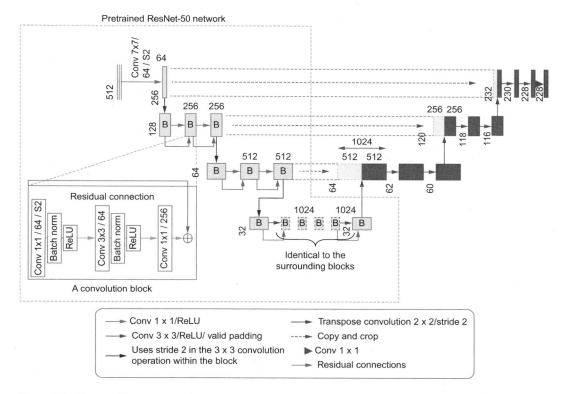

Figure B.4   The modified U-Net architecture (best viewed in color). This version of U-Net has the first four blocks of the ResNet-50 model as the encoder, and the decoder specifications (e.g., number of filters) are increased to match the specifications of the matching encoder layers.

IMPLEMENTING THE MODIFIED U-NET

With a sound conceptual understanding of the model and its different components, it's time to implement it in Keras. We will use the Keras functional API. First, we define the encoder part of the network:

```
inp = layers.Input(shape=(512, 512, 3))
# Defining the pretrained resnet 50 as the encoder
encoder = tf.keras.applications.ResNet50 (
    include_top=False, input_tensor=inp,pooling=None
)
```

Next, we discuss the bells and whistles of the decoder. The decoder consists of several upsampling layers, which serve two important functions:

- Upsampling the input to the layer to a larger output
- Copying, cropping, and concatenating the matched encoder input

The function shown in the following listing encapsulates the computations we outlined.

Listing B.4   The upsampling layer of the modified UNet's decoder

```python
def upsample_conv(inp, copy_and_crop, filters):
    """ Up sampling layer of the U-net """

    # 2x2 transpose convolution layer
    conv1_out = layers.Conv2DTranspose(
        filters, (2,2), (2,2), activation='relu'
    )(inp)
    # Size of the crop length for one side
    crop_side = int((copy_and_crop.shape[1]-conv1_out.shape[1])/2)

    # Crop if crop side is > 0
    if crop_side > 0:
        cropped_copy = layers.Cropping2D(crop_side)(copy_and_crop)
    else:
        cropped_copy = copy_and_crop

    # Concat the cropped encoder output and the decoder output
    concat_out = layers.Concatenate(axis=-1)([conv1_out, cropped_copy])

    # 3x3 convolution layer
    conv2_out = layers.Conv2D(
        filters, (3,3), activation='relu', padding='valid'
    )(concat_out)

    # 3x3 Convolution layer
    out = layers.Conv2D(
        filters, (3,3), activation='relu', padding='valid'
    )(conv2_out)

    return out
```

Let's analyze the function we wrote. It takes the following arguments:

- `input`—The input to the layer
- `copy_and_crop`—The input that is copied across from the encoder
- `filters`—The number of output filters after performing transpose convolution

First, we perform transpose convolution as

```python
conv1_out = layers.Conv2DTranspose(
                filters=filters, kernel_size=(2,2),
                strides=(2,2), activation='relu'
    )(inp)
```

The `Conv2DTranspose` has identical syntax to the `Conv2D` we have used many times. It has a number of filters, a kernel size (height and width), strides (height and width), activation, and padding (defaults to valid). We will compute the crop parameters depending on the size of the transpose convolution output and the encoder's input. Then we perform cropping using the Keras layer `Cropping2D` as required:

```
crop_side = int((copy_and_crop.shape[1]-conv1_out.shape[1])/2)
if crop_side > 0:
        cropped_copy = layers.Cropping2D(crop_side)(copy_and_crop)
    else:
        cropped_copy = copy_and_crop
```

Here, we first compute how much to crop from one side by subtracting the encoder's size from the upsampled output `conv1_out`. Then, if the size is greater than zero, `cropped_copy` is computed by passing the `crop_side` as a parameter to a `Cropping2D` Keras layer. The cropped encoder's output and the upsampled `conv1_out` is then concatenated to produce a single tensor. This goes through two 3×3 convolution layers with ReLU activation and valid padding to produce the final output. We now define the decoder fully (see the next listing). The decoder consists of three upsampling layers, which consume the output of the previous layer, as well as an encoder output that is copied across.

Listing B.5 The decoder of the modified U-Net model

```
def decoder(inp, encoder):
    """ Define the decoder of the U-net model """

    up_1 = upsample_conv(inp, encoder.get_layer("conv3_block4_out").output,
➡ 512) # 32x32

    up_2 = upsample_conv(up_1,
➡ encoder.get_layer("conv2_block3_out").output, 256) # 64x64

    up_3 = upsample_conv(up_2, encoder.get_layer("conv1_relu").output, 64)
➡ # 128 x 128

    return up_3
```

Copying an interim output of a predefined model across is not something we have done previously. Therefore, it is worth investigating further. We don't have the luxury of resorting to previously defined variables that represent the encoders' outputs because this is a predefined model we downloaded through Keras, without the references to actual variables that were used in creating the model.

But accessing intermediate outputs and using them to create new connections is not that difficult. All you need to know is the name of the layer that you want to access. This can be done by looking at the output of `encoder.summary()`. For example, here (according to figure B.4) we get the last outputs of the conv3, conv2, and conv1 modules. To get the output of conv3_block4_out, all you need to do is

```
encoder.get_layer("conv3_block4_out").output
```

and pass that to the upsample_conv layer we just defined. The ability to perform such complex manipulations is a testament to how flexible the Keras functional API is. Finally, you can define the holistic modified U-Net model in the function unet_pretrained_encoder(), as shown in the next listing.

Listing B.6   Full modified U-Net model

```
def unet_pretrained_encoder():
    """ Define a pretrained encoder based on the Resnet50 model """

    # Defining an input layer of size 384x384x3
    inp = layers.Input(shape=(512, 512, 3))
    # Defining the pretrained resnet 50 as the encoder
    encoder = tf.keras.applications.ResNet50 (
        include_top=False, input_tensor=inp,pooling=None
    )

    # Encoder output # 8x8
    decoder_out = decoder(encoder.get_layer("conv4_block6_out").output, encoder)

    # Final output of the model (note no activation)
    final_out = layers.Conv2D(num_classes, (1,1))(decoder_out)
    # Final model
    model = models.Model(encoder.input, final_out)
    return model
```

What's happening here is quite clear. We first define a $512 \times 512 \times 3$–sized input that is passed to the encoder. Our encoder is a ResNet-50 model without the top prediction layer or global pooling. Next, we define the decoder, which takes the conv4_block6_out layer's output as the input (i.e., final output of the conv4 block of the ResNet-50 model) and then upsamples it gradually using transpose convolution operations. Moreover, the decoder copies, crops, and concatenates matching encoder layers. We also define a 1×1 convolution layer that produces the final output. Finally, we define an end-to-end model using the Keras functional API.

appendix C
Natural language
processing

C.1 Touring around the zoo: Meeting other Transformer models

In chapter 13, we discussed a powerful Transformer-based model known as BERT (bidirectional encoder representations from Transformers). But BERT was just the beginning of a wave of Transformer models. These models grew stronger and better, either by solving theoretical issues with BERT or re-engineering various aspects of the model to perform faster and better. Let's understand some of these popular models to learn what sets them apart from BERT.

C.1.1 Generative pre-training (GPT) model (2018)

The story actually starts even before BERT. OpenAI introduced a model called GPT in the paper "Improving Language Understanding by Generative Pre-Training" by Radford et al. (http://mng.bz/1oXV). It is trained in a similar fashion to BERT, pretraining on a large corpus of text followed by fine-tuning on a discriminative task. The GPT model is a *Transformer decoder* compared to BERT, which is a *Transformer encoder*. The difference is that the GPT model has left-to-right (or causal) attention, whereas BERT has bidirectional (i.e., left-to-right and right-to-left) attention used when computing self-attention outputs. In other words, the GPU model pays attention only to the words to the left of it as it computes the self-attention output of a given word. This is the same as the masked attention component we discussed in chapter 5. Due to this, GPT is also called an *autoregressive model*, whereas BERT is called an *autoencoder*. In addition, unlike BERT, adapting GPT to different tasks like sequence classification, token classification, or question answering requires slight architectural changes, which is cumbersome. GPT has three versions (GPT-1, GPT-2, and GPT-3); each model became bigger while introducing slight changes to improve performance.

> **NOTE**   OpenAI, TensorFlow: https://github.com/openai/gpt-2.

C.1.2   *DistilBERT (2019)*

Following BERT, DistilBERT is a model introduced by Hugging Face in the paper "Distil-BERT, a distilled version of BERT: Smaller, faster, cheaper and lighter" by Sanh et al. (https://arxiv.org/pdf/1910.01108v4.pdf) in 2019. The primary focus of DistilBERT is to compress BERT while keeping the performance similar. It is trained using a transfer learning technique known as *knowledge distillation* (http://mng.bz/qYV2). The idea is to have a teacher model (i.e., BERT), and a smaller model (i.e., DistilBERT) that tries to mimic the teacher's output. The DistilBERT model is smaller compared to BERT and only has 6 layers, as opposed to BERT, which has 12 layers. The DistilBERT model is initialized with the initialization of every other layer of BERT (because Distil-BERT has exactly half the layers of BERT). Another key difference of DistilBERT is that it is only trained on the masked language modeling task and not on the next-sentence prediction task.

> **NOTE**   Hugging Face's Transformers: https://huggingface.co/transformers/model_doc/distilbert.html.

C.1.3   *RoBERT/ToBERT (2019)*

RoBERT (recurrence over BERT) and ToBERT (Transformer over BERT) are two models introduced in the paper "Hierarchical Transformer Models for Long Document Classification" by Pappagari et al. (https://arxiv.org/pdf/1910.10781.pdf). The main problem addressed by this paper is the inability or the performance degradation experienced for long text sequences (e.g., call transcripts) in BERT. This is because the self-attention layer has a computational complexity of $O(n^2)$ for a sequence of length n. The solution proposed in these models is to factorize long sequences to smaller segments of length k (with overlap) and feed each segment to BERT to generate the pooled output (i.e., the output of the [CLS] token) or the posterior probabilities (from a task-specific classification layer). Next, stack the outputs returned by BERT for each segment and pass them on to a recurrent model like LSTM (RoBERT) or a smaller Transformer (ToBERT).

> **NOTE**   Hugging Face's Transformers: https://huggingface.co/transformers/model_doc/roberta.html.

C.1.4   *BART (2019)*

BART (bidirectional and auto-regressive Transformers), proposed in "BART: Denoising Sequence-to-Sequence Pre-training for Natural Language Generation, Translation, and Comprehension" by Lewis et al. (https://arxiv.org/pdf/1910.13461.pdf) is a sequence-to-sequence model. We discussed sequence-to-sequence models in chapters 11 and 12, and BART draws on the same concepts. BART has an encoder and a decoder. If you remember from chapter 5, the Transformer model also has an encoder and a decoder and can be thought of as a sequence-to-sequence model. The encoder of a Transformer has bidirectional attention, whereas the decoder of a Transformer has left-to-right attention (i.e., is autoregressive).

Unlike the vanilla Transformer model, BART uses several innovative pre-training techniques (document reconstruction) to pretrain the model. Particularly, BART is trained as a denoising autoencoder, where a noisy input is provided and the model needs to reconstruct the true input. In this case, the input is a document (a collection of sentences). The documents are corrupted using the methods listed in table C.1.

Table C.1 Various methods employed in corrupting documents. The true document is "I was hungry. I went to the café." The "_" character denotes the mask token.

Method	Description	Example
Token masking	Tokens in the sentences are randomly masked.	I was _ . I _ to the cafe
Token deletion	Tokens are randomly deleted.	I hungry . I went to café
Sentence permutation	Change the order of the sentences.	I went to the café . I was hungry
Document rotation	Rotate the document so that the starting and ending of the document changes.	Café . I was hungry . I went to the
Text infilling	Instead of a single token, mask spans tokens with a single mask token. A 0 length span would insert the mask token.	I was _ hungry . I _ the café

With the corruption logic, we generate inputs to BART, and the target will be the true document without corruptions. Initially, the corrupted document is input to the encoder, and then the decoder is asked to recursively predict the true sequence while using the previously predicted output(s) as the next input. This is similar to how we predicted translations using a machine translation model in chapter 11.

Once the model is pretrained, you can use BART for any of the NLP tasks that Transformer models are typically used for. For example, BART can be used for sequence classification tasks (e.g., sentiment analysis) in the following way:

1 Input the token sequence (e.g., movie review) to both the encoder and the decoder.
2 Add a special token (e.g., [CLS]) to the end of the sequence when feeding the decoder input. We added the special token to the beginning of the sequence when working with BERT.
3 Get the hidden representation output for the special token by the decoder and feed that to a downstream classifier that will predict the final output (e.g., positive/negative prediction).

To use BART for sequence-to-sequence problems (e.g., machine translation), follow these steps:

1 Input the source sequence to the encoder.
2 Add a starting (e.g., [SOS]) and ending (e.g., [EOS]) special token to the start and end of the target sequence, respectively.
3 During training, train the decoder with all tokens in the target sequence except the last as the input and all tokens but the first as the target (i.e., teacher forcing).
4 During inference, provide the starting token as the first input to the decoder and recursively predict the next output while using the previous output(s) as the input (i.e., autoregressive),

NOTE Hugging Face's Transformers: http://mng.bz/7ygy.

C.1.5 *XLNet (2020)*

XLNet was introduced in the paper "XLNet: Generalized Autoregressive Pretraining for Language Understanding" by Yang et al. (https://arxiv.org/pdf/1906.08237.pdf) in early 2020. Its primary focus was to capture the best of both worlds in autoencoder-based models (e.g., BERT) and autoregressive models (e.g., GPT). For this discourse, it is important to understand the advantages and drawbacks of the two approaches.

A key advantage that BERT has as an autoencoder model is that the task-specific classification head has hidden representations of tokens that are enriched by bidirectional context, as it can pay attention to both sides of a given token. And as you can imagine, knowing what comes before as well as after for a given token yield results in better downstream tasks. Conversely, GPT pays attention to only the left side of a given word to generate the representation. Therefore, GPT's token representations are suboptimal in the sense that they only pay unidirectional attention (left side) to the token.

On the other hand, the pretraining methodology of BERT involves introducing the special token [MASK]. Though this token appears in the pretraining context, it never appears in the fine-tuning context, creating a pretraining fine-tuning discrepancy.

There's a more critical issue that is lurking in BERT. BERT formulates the language modeling under the assumption that masked tokens are separately constructed (i.e., independence assumption). In other words, if you have the sentence "I love [MASK]$_1$ [MASK]$_2$ city," the second mask token is generated with no attention to what was chosen for the [MASK]$_1$ token. This is wrong because to generate a valid city name, you must know the value of [MASK]$_1$ before generating [MASK]$_2$. However, the autoregressive nature of GPT allows the model to first predict the value for [MASK]$_1$ and then use that along with other words to its left to generate the value for [MASK]$_2$ about the first word in the city before generating the second word (i.e., context aware).

XLNet blends these two language modeling approaches into one so that you have the bidirectional context coming from the approach used in BERT and the context awareness from GPT's approach. The new approach is called *permutation language modeling*. The idea is as follows. Consider a T elements-long sequence of words. There are T! permutations for that sequence. For example, the sentence "Bob loves cats" will have 3! = 3 × 2 × 1 = 6 permutations:

```
Bob loves cats
Bob cats loves
loves Bob cats
loves cats Bob
cats Bob loves
cats loves Bob
```

If the parameters of the language model used to learn this are shared across all the permutations, not only can we use an autoregressive approach to learn it, but we can also capture information from both sides of the text for a given word. This is the main idea explored in the paper.

NOTE Hugging Face's Transformers: http://mng.bz/mOl2.

C.1.6   *Albert (2020)*

Albert is a variant BERT model that delivers competitive performance to BERT with fewer parameters. Albert makes two important contributions: reducing the model size and introducing a new self-supervised loss that helps the model capture language better.

FACTORIZATION OF THE EMBEDDING LAYER

First, Albert factorizes the embedding matrix used in BERT. In BERT the embeddings are metrics of size $V \times H$, where V is the vocabulary size and H is the hidden state size. In other words, there is a tight coupling between the embedding size (i.e., length of an embedding vector) and the final hidden representation size. However, the embeddings (e.g., WordPiece embeddings in BERT) are not designed to capture context, whereas hidden states are computed taking both the token and its context into account. Therefore, it makes sense to have a large hidden state size H, as the hidden state captures a more informative representation of a token than embeddings. But doing so increases the size of the embedding matrix due to the tight coupling present. Therefore, Albert suggests factorizing the embedding matrix to two matrices, $V \times E$ and $E \times H$, decoupling the embedding size and the hidden state size. With this design, one can increase the hidden state size while keeping the embedding size small.

CROSS-LAYER PARAMETER SHARING

Cross-layer parameter sharing is another technique introduced in Albert to reduce the parameter space. Since all layers in BERT (as well the Transformer model in general) have uniform layers from top to bottom, parameter sharing is trivial. Parameter sharing can happen in one of the following three ways:

- Across all self-attention sublayers
- Across all the fully connected sublayers
- Across self-attention and fully connected sublayers (separately)

Albert uses sharing all parameters across layers as the default strategy. By using this strategy, Albert achieves a 71%–86% parameter reduction without compromising the performance of the model significantly.

SENTENCE-ORDER PREDICTION INSTEAD OF NEXT SENTENCE PREDICTION

Finally, the authors of the paper argue that the value added by the next-sentence prediction pretraining task in BERT is doubtful, which is supported by several previous studies. Therefore, they introduce a new, more challenging model that focuses primarily on language coherence: sentence-order prediction. In this, the model is trained with a binary classification head to predict whether a given pair of sentences are in the correct order. The data can be easily generated, where positive samples are taken as sentences next to each other in that order, and negative samples are generated by swapping two adjacent sentences. The authors argue that this is more challenging than next-sentence prediction, leading to a more informed model than BERT.

> **NOTE** TFHub: (https://tfhub.dev/google/albert_base/3). Hugging Face's Transformers: (http://mng.bz/5QM1).

C.1.7   *Reformer (2020)*

The Reformer was one of the latest to join the family of Transformers. The main idea behind the Reformer is its ability to scale to sequences that are several tens of thousands of tokens long. The Reformer was introduced in the paper "Reformer: The Efficient Transformer" by Kitaev et al. (https://arxiv.org/pdf/2001.04451.pdf) in early 2020.

The main limitation of the vanilla Transformers that prevents them from being used for long sequences is the computational complexity of the self-attention layer. It needs to look at every other word for every word to generate the final representation, which has a $O(L^2)$ complexity for a sequence that has L tokens. The reformer uses locality-sensitive hashing (LSH) to reduce this complexity to O(L logL). The idea of LSH is to assign every input a hash; the inputs having the same hash are considered similar and assigned to the same bucket. With that, similar inputs are placed in one bucket. To do that, we have to introduce several modifications to the self-attention sublayer.

LOCALITY-SENSITIVE HASHING IN THE SELF-ATTENTION LAYER

First, we need to make sure the Q and K matrices are identical. This is a necessity as the idea is to compute similarity between queries and keys. This is easily done by sharing the weights between Q and K weight matrices. Next, a hashing function needs to be developed, which can generate a hash for a given query/key so that similar queries/keys (shared-qk) get similar hashes. Also remember that this must be done in a differentiable way to ensure end-to-end training of the model. The following hashing function is used

```
h(x) = argmax([xR; - xR])
```

where R is a random matrix of size [d_model, b/2] for a user-defined b (i.e., number of buckets) and x is the input of shape [b, L, d_model]. By using this hashing function, you get a bucket ID for each input token in a batch in a given position. To learn more about this technique, refer to the original paper "Practical and Optimal LSH for Angular Distance" by Andoni et al. (https://arxiv.org/pdf/1509.02897.pdf). According to the bucket ID, the shared-qk items are sorted.

Then the sorted shared-qk items are chunked using a fixed chunk size. A larger chunk size means more computations (i.e., more words are considered for a given token), whereas a smaller chunk size can mean underperformance (i.e., not enough tokens to look at).

Finally, the self-attention is computed as follows. For a given token, look in the same chunk that it's in as well as the previous chunk and attend to the words with the same bucket ID in both of those chunks. This will produce the self-attention output for all the tokens provided in the input. This way, the model does not have to look at every other word for every token and can focus on a subset of words or tokens for a given token. This makes the model scalable to sequences several tens of thousands of tokens long.

NOTE Hugging Face's Transformers: http://mng.bz/6XaD.

index